The Economics of the European Community

Edited by

Ali M. El-Agraa

THIRD EDITION

Philip Allan
New York London Toronto Sydney Tokyo Singapore

First published 1990 by
Philip Allan
Second edition 1983
Third edition 1990
66 Wood Lane End, Hemel Hempstead
Hertfordshire, HP2 4RG
A division of
Simon & Schuster International Group

Typeset in 10 point Plantin
Typeset by Excel Typesetters Company

Printed and bound in Great Britain at
the University Press, Cambridge

British Library Cataloguing in Publication Data

The Economics of the European Community.
  1. European Community countries. Economic integration
  I. El-Agraa, A. M. (Ali Mohammed) *1941*–
  337.142

  ISBN 0-86003-079-2
  ISBN 0-86003-188-8 pbk

1 2 3 4 5   94 93 92 91 90

To Diana

"Lest it be forgotten, the European Community stands for the harmonised integration of some of the oldest countries in the world with very diverse cultures and extremely complicated economic systems." P285

Contents

Part III Microeconomic policies

List of figures

List of tables

List of contributors

Professor Michael J. Artis, Department of Economics, University of Manchester, UK.

Professor Brian T. Bayliss, Director, Centre for European Industrial Studies, Bath University.

Dr C. Doreen E. Collins was Senior Lecturer in Social Policy and Administration, University of Leeds, UK, before taking early retirement in 1985.

Professor Ali M. El-Agraa, Faculty of Commerce, Fukuoka University, Japan. He is also Senior Lecturer in Economics, School of Business and Economic Studies, University of Leeds, UK.

Professor Kenneth M. Gwilliam, Director, Centre for Transport Studies and Logistics, Erasmus University, the Netherlands.

Mr Alan Marin, Lecturer in Economics, London School of Economics and Political Science, University of London, UK.

Dr David G. Mayes, Senior Research Fellow, National Institute for Economic and Social Research, London, UK.

Professor Dermot McAleese, Head, Department of Economics, Trinity College, University of Dublin, Eire.

Mr Francis McGowan, Fellow, Science Policy Research Unit, University of Sussex, UK.

Professor Edwin T. Nevin, Head, Department of Economics, University College of Swansea, University of Wales, UK.

Professor Victoria Curzon Price, Institut Universitaire D'Études Européennes, Geneva, Switzerland.

Preface to first edition

This book is in three parts. The first gives general background information about the historical development of the EEC, its institutions, and basic statistics of member nations; also included are their potential partners in the near future and, for comparative purposes, Canada, Japan, the United States and the USSR. The second discusses the theory of customs unions and the measurement of the effects of the formation of the EEC on both the participating nations and the rest of the world. The third deals with the problems of hidden barriers to trade and of policy coordination and harmonisation in the specific context of the Community.

The book is aimed at students of international economics in general and at those interested in international economic integration with specific reference to Western Europe in particular. Hopefully, however, the policy chapters will appeal also to general economists interested in the implications of EEC membership.

A number of contributors have written chapters specially for the book. In such a venture, one can never achieve total harmonisation(!) but, as author and editor, I have endeavoured to ensure reasonable continuity.

The idea of a book on the economics of the European Community has been with me for some time. In this I have been influenced by three factors. Firstly, I specialise in international economics and am particularly interested in the field of international economic integration with specific reference to Western Europe. Secondly, there is no single book which gives adequate coverage of the impact and consequences of the EEC on both partner and non-participating countries; there are several books on the subject, but these are either outdated (on both the theoretical and policy aspects) or deal only with specialised areas of interest such as the historical, institutional, fiscal or empirical aspects. Thirdly, since 1972 Mr A. J. Jones and I have been running an undergraduate third year course at Leeds entitled 'Britain in the Common Market', which has proved not only the popularity of the topic, but also further underlined the lack of a comprehensive guide to the subject matter. All these considerations finally convinced me of the great need for a book which gives an up-to-date and comprehensive account of the European Community.

Acknowledgements

The book could not have taken its present form or structure without the help and contributions of colleagues both at the University of Leeds and elsewhere. Mr A. J. Jones, a specialist in international trade theory, has written the chapter on the theory of customs unions. Professor A. J. Brown, who was a member of the McDougall Committee which reported to the EEC Commission on the role of public finance in the Community, has contributed the chapter on the EEC budget. Professor K. M. Gwilliam, a specialist in transport economics, a member of several EEC committees on Community transport policy and currently in receipt of a grant for research in this field, has written the chapter on EEC transport policy. Dr C. D. E. Collins, who specialises in social policy and administration, has written the chapters on the history and institutions of the EEC and on social policy. Dr P. S. Goodrich, a political scientist turned accountant in the area of management studies, has written, with me, the chapter on factor mobility.

I have also drawn on the expertise of colleagues from other universities and research institutions. Professor B. T. Bayliss of Bath University, who is Director of the Institute of European Industrial Studies, has contributed the chapter on Community competition and industrial policies. Professor E. T. Nevin of the University College of Swansea, a specialist in regional policy (among other areas), has contributed the chapter on regional policy. Dr Y. S. Hu of Chatham House, who researches into EEC problems on behalf of the Federal Trust, has written the chapter on energy policy. I wish to express my gratitude to all the above.

Other Leeds colleagues have contributed to this book in an indirect way through their help in the teaching of the course 'Britain in the Common Market'. These are: Professor J. R. Crossley, a specialist in industrial relations and an EEC consultant on employment policies; Mr G. F. Rainnie, an industrial economist who takes special interest in EEC competition and industrial policies; and Mr P. J. Mackie who is a specialist in transport economics. I am very grateful to them all for their help in running the course and for their indirect inspiration in the writing of this book.

Mr Geoffrey Denton, Reader in Economics at the University of Reading, who has been Director of the Federal Trust since 1976 and is Specialist Adviser to the House of Lords European Communities Committee, has read most of the chapters of the book and made important suggests with regard to both its content and presentation. I owe him a special debt of gratitude.

Finally, I would like to thank all those in the office of the School of Economic Studies at the University of Leeds, and the Chairman's secretary, Mrs T. E. Brier, for their typing assistance.

University of Leeds   A. M. El-Agraa
January, 1980

Preface to second edition

This edition is more than simply an up-dated version of the first edition: the chapters have been rearranged in a more logical sequence suggested by Professor E. T. Nevin; there are new chapters on the Common Fisheries Policy, the costs of the Common Agricultural Policy, and the European Monetary System; and the chapters on factor mobility and energy have been virtually rewritten.

Of course, the Preface to the first edition does not acknowledge my new contributors. Therefore, this is an appropriate place to thank: Dr David G. Mayes, Chief Statistician at NEDO, for contributing the chapter on factor mobility; Dr Allan E. Buckwell of the Department of Agricultural Economics, University of Newcastle, presently holding a Visiting Chair at Cornell University, New York, for the chapter on the costs of the Common Agricultural Policy; and Dr Geoffrey E. J. Dennis of the Bank for International Settlements for the chapter on the European Monetary System.

Also, I would like to take this opportunity to repeat my gratitude to the other contributors and to express my thanks for all the generous reviews that the book has received.

University of Leeds   A. M. El-Agraa
November, 1983

Preface to third edition

The EC Commission's far-reaching White Paper of 1985 did not appear until after the second edition of this book was actually in print. Thus the whole new image of the EC, created through the Single European Act, and the drive to accomplish the internal market by 1992, was completely missing. This edition is intended not only to rectify this serious deficiency but also to update previous material and to add new areas of EC policy.

The approach in this book continues to be one of perceiving the EC as an evolving and dynamic integration group with its ultimate objective being the one clearly defined by the founding fathers: the creation of a United Stated of Western Europe. This edition treats these new developments within precisely this context. The book retains its original title, and the economics of 1992, as a distinct area of study, is confined to one chapter only since its various manifestations and implications are tackled in virtually every chapter of the book.

A glance at the contents of the book will show that there are two major changes from the previous two editions. Firstly, there are both new chapters and contributors. The new chapters are on EC environmental policy, the Lomé Agreement, the economics of 1992 and the development of the EC. The new contributors are Professors Michael J. Artis (Manchester University, UK), Dermot McAleese (Dublin University, Eire) and Victoria Curzon Price (Institute of European Studies, Switzerland); Mr Alan Marin (London School of Economics) and Mr Francis McGowan (Sussex University, UK). Some contributors to the second edition are, for various reasons, no longer with us: Professors Arthur J. Brown (Leeds University, UK; emeritus), and Allan E. Buckwell (Wye College, UK); Dr Geoffrey J. E. Dennis (James Capel and Co., UK) and Mr Anthony J. Jones (Leeds University, UK). I would like to take this opportunity to welcome the former group and to bid farewell to the latter group.

Secondly, the chapter sequence has been slightly altered to one that is, I hope, more logical. I say I hope, because although the decision to move the chapter on factor mobility away from the section on theory and measurement is a logical one, the idea of placing it within the group on macroeconomic policies – the movement of labour has regional effects and that of capital has balance of payments repercussions – is, perhaps, arguable since the movement of labour and capital may, in some respects, be considered a microeconomic phenomenon. Some other chapters are subject to this reservation, too: for example the chapter on tax harmonisation.

Finally, I would like to extend my special gratitude to those contributors who are still with me and to express my thanks to all the institutions which continue to use this book as their main guide to the economics of the EC. I really appreciate all the encouraging letters I receive from those who use the book and all the generous reviews that the book continues to receive.

Universities of Leeds (UK) and   Ali M. El-Agraa
Fukuoka (Japan)
November, 1989

List of abbreviations

AAMS	Association of African and Malagasy States
AAU	Arab African Union
ACC	Arab Cooperation Council
ACM	Arab Common Market
ACP	African, Caribbean and Pacific countries party to the Lomé Convention
AEC	Arab Economic Council
AIM	Advanced informatics in medicine
AL	Arab League
ALADI	Association for Latin American Integration
AMU	Arab Maghreb Union
ANZCERTA	Australia and New Zealand Closer Economic Relations and Trade Agreement
ASEAN	Association of South-East Asian Nations
BAP	Biotechnology action programme
BC-NET	Business Cooperation Network
BCR	Community Bureau of References
BEP	Biomolecular engineering programme
BRAIN	Basic research in adaptive intelligence and neurocomputing
BRITE/EURAM	Basic research in industrial technologies for Europe/raw materials and advanced materials
BU	Benin Union
CAA	Civil Aviation Authority
CACM	Central American Common Market
CADDIA	Cooperation in automation of data and documentation for imports/exports and agriculture
CAEU	Council for Arab Economic Unity
CARICOM	Caribbean Community
CARIFTA	Caribbean Free Trade Association

CCP	Common Commercial Policy
CCT	Common Customs Tariff
CEAO	Communauté Economique de l'Afrique de l'Ouest
CEDB	Component event data bank
CEDEFOP	European Centre for Development of Vocational Training
CEN	European Committee for Standardization
CENELEC	European Committee for Electrotechnical Standardization
CEP	Common Energy Policy
CEPGL	Economic Community of the Countries of the Great Lakes
CET	Common external tariff
CFP	Common Fisheries Policy
CM	Common Market
CMEA	Council for Mutual Economic Assistance
CN	Combined Nomenclature
CODEST	Committee for the European Development of Science and Technology
COMECON	see CMEA
COMETT	Community programme in education and training for technology
CORDIS	Community research and development information service
COREPER	Committee of permanent representatives
CORINE	Coordination of information on the environment in Europe
COSINE	Cooperation for open systems interconnection networking in Europe
COST	European cooperation on scientific and technical research
CREST	Scientific and Technical Research Committee
CSCE	Conference on Security and Cooperation in Europe
CSTID	Committee for Scientific and Technical Information and Documentation
CTP	Common Transport Policy
CTS	Conformance testing services
CU	Customs union
DAC	Development Assistance Committee (OECD)
DELTA	Developing European learning through technological advance
DI	Divergence indicator
DRIVE	Dedicated road infrastructure for vehicle safety in Europe
EAC	East African Community
EAGGF	European Agricultural Guidance and Guarantee Fund
ECLAIR	European collaborative linkage of agriculture and industry through research
ECOFIN	European Council of Ministers for Financial Affairs
ECOWAS	Economic Community of West African States
ECSC	European Coal and Steel Community
ECU	European currency unit
EDC	European Defence community

EDF	European Development Fund
EDIFACT	Electronic data interchange for administration, commerce and transport
EFTA	European Free Trade Association
EIB	European Investment Bank
EMS	European Monetary System
EMCF	European Monetary Cooperation Fund
EMF	European Monetary Fund
EMU	European monetary union
EPOCH	European programme on climatology and natural hazards
EQS	Environmental quality standard
ERASMUS	European Community action scheme for the mobility of university students
ERDF	European Regional Development Fund
ERM	Exchange rate mechanism
ESCB	European System of Central Banks
ESF	European Social Fund
ESI	Electricity supply industry
ESPRIT	European strategic programme for research and development in information technology
EU	Economic union
EUA	European unit of account
EURATOM	European Atomic Energy Commission
EUREKA	European Research Cooperation Agency
EURONET-DIANE	Direct information access network for Europe
EVCA	European Venture Capital Association
FADN	EEC farm accountancy data network
FAO	Food and Agriculture Organization of the United Nations
FAST	Forecasting and assessment in the field of science and technology
FEOGA	Fonds Européen d'Orientation et de Garantie Agricole
FLAIR	Food-linked agro-industrial research
FTA	Free trade area
GATT	General Agreement on Tariffs and Trade (UN)
GCC	Gulf Cooperation Council
GSP	Generalised system of preferences
HDTV	High-definition television
HELIOS	Action programme to promote social and economic integration and an independent way of life for disabled people
HS	Harmonized Commodity Description and Coding System
IAEA	International Atomic Energy Agency (UN)
IATA	International Air Transport Association
IBRD	International Bank for Reconstruction and Development (World Bank) (UN)

ICONE	Comparative index of national and European standards
IDA	International Development Association (UN)
IDB	Inter-American Development Bank
IDO	Integrated development operation
IEA	International Energy Agency (OECD)
IEM	Internal energy market
IMF	International Monetary Fund (UN)
IMP	Integrated Mediterranean programme
IMPACT	Information market policy actions
INSIS	Interinstitutional system of integrated services
IRCC	International Radio Consultative Committee
IRIS	Network of demonstration projects on vocational training for women
IRTE	Integrated road transport environment
ISIS	Integrated standards information system
ITER	International thermonuclear experimental reactor
JET	Joint European Torus
JOULE	Joint opportunities for unconventional or long-term energy supply
JRC	Joint Research Centre
LDC	Less developed country
LEDA	Local employment development action programme
LLDC	Least developed country
MAST	Marine science and technology
MCA	Monetary compensatory amount
MEDIA	Measures to encourage the development of the audio-visual industry
MERM	Multi-lateral exchange rate model
MFA	Multifibre Arrangement (Arrangement regarding International Trade in Textiles)
MISEP	Mutual information system on employment policies
MONITOR	Research programme on strategic analysis, forecasting and assessment in research and technology
MRU	Mano River Union
NCI	New Community Instrument
NEAFC	North-East Atlantic Fisheries Commission
NET	Next European Torus
NETT	Network for environmental technology transfer
NIC	Newly industrialising country
NIE	Newly industrialising economy
NIEO	New International Economic Order
NGO	Non-governmental organisation
NPCI	National programme of Community interest
NTB	Non-tariff barrier

NUTS	Nomenclature of Territorial Units for Statistics
OAPEC	Organisation of Arab petroleum exporting countries
OAU	Organisation for African Unity
OCTs	Overseas countries and territories
OECD	Organisation for Economic Cooperation and Development
OEEC	Organisation for European Economic Cooperation
OPEC	Organisation of Petroleum Exporting Countries
OSI	Open systems interconnection
PAFTAD	Pacific Trade and Development Conference
PBEC	Pacific Basin Economic Council
PECC	Pacific Economic Cooperation Conference
PEDIP	Programme to modernise Portuguese industry
PETRA	Action programme for the vocational training of young people and their preparation for adult and working life
POSEIDOM	Programme of options specific to the remote and insular nature of the overseas departments
PPP	Polluter pays principle
PTA	Preferential trade area
PTC	Pacific Telecommunications Conference
PTT	Posts, Telegraphs and Telecommunications
RACE	Research and development in advanced communication technologies for Europe
R&TD	Research and technological development
RARE	Réseaux associés pour la recherche européenne
RCD	Regional Cooperation for Development
REIMEP	Regular European interlaboratory measurements evaluation programme
RENAVAL	Programme to assist the conversion of shipbuilding areas
RESIDER	Programme to assist the conversion of steel areas
SACU	Southern African Customs Union
SAP	Social Action Programme
SAST	Strategic analysis in the field of science and technology
SCENT	System for a customs enforcement network
SCIENCE	Plan to stimulate the international cooperation and interchange necessary for European researchers
SEA	Single European Act
SEDOC	Inter-state notification of job vacancies
SEM	Single European market
SPEAR	Support programme for a European assessment of research
SPES	Stimulation plan for economic science
SPRINT	Strategic programme for innovation and technology transfer
STABEX	System for the stabilization of ACP and OCT export earnings
STAR	Community programme for the development of certain less-favoured regions of the Community by improving access to

	advanced telecommunications services
STEP	Science and technology for environmental protection
SYSMIN	Special financing facility for ACP and OCT mining products
TAC	Total allowable catch
TARIC	Integrated Community tariff
TEDIS	Trade electronic data interchange systems
TELEMAN	Research and training programme on remote handling in nuclear hazardous and disordered environments
UDEAC	Union Douanière et Economique de l'Afrique Centrale
UES	Uniform Emission Standards
UN	United Nations
UNCLOS	United Nations Conference on the Law of the Sea
UNCTAD	United Nations Conference on Trade and Development
UNECA	United Nations Economic Commission for Africa
UNEP	United Nations Environment Programme
UNESCO	United Nations Educational, Scientific and Cultural Organization
UNHCR	United Nations High Commissioner for Refugees
UNIDO	United Nations Industrial Development Organization
UNRWA	United Nations Relief and Works Agency for Palestine Refugees in the Near East
VALOREN	Community programme for the development of certain less-favoured regions of the Community by exploiting endogenous energy potential
VALUE	Programme for the dissemination and utilization of research results
VER	Voluntary export restraint
VSTF	Very short-term financing facility
WFC	World Food Council (UN)
WFP	World Food Programme (UN)
WIPO	World Intellectual Property Organization (UN)
YES	'Youth for Europe' programme (youth exchange scheme)

General introduction

A. M. El-Agraa

'International economic integration' is one aspect of 'international economics' which has been growing in importance in the past three decades or so. The term itself has a rather short history; indeed, Machlup (1977a) was unable to find a single instance of its use prior to 1942. Since then the term has been used at various times to refer to virtually any area of international economic relations. By 1950, however, the term had been given a specific definition by economists specialising in international trade to denote a state of affairs or a process which involves the amalgamation of separate economies into larger regions, and it is in this more limited sense that the term is used today. More specifically, international economic integration is concerned with the discriminatory removal of all trade impediments between the participating nations and with the establishment of certain elements of cooperation and coordination between them. The latter depends entirely on the actual form that integration takes. Different forms of international integration can be envisaged and some have actually been implemented:

1. *Free trade areas* where the member nations remove all trade impediments among themselves but retain their freedom with regard to the determination of their policies *vis-à-vis* the outside world (the non-participants); the European Free Trade Association (EFTA) and the Latin American Free Trade Area (LAFTA) are examples.
2. *Customs unions*, which are very similar to free trade areas except that member nations must conduct and pursue common external commercial relations; for instance, they must adopt common external tariffs (CETs) on imports from the non-participants as is the case in the European Community (EC). The EC is in this particular sense a customs union, but it is also more than that.
3. *Common markets*, which are customs unions that also allow for free factor mobility across national member frontiers, i.e. capital, labour, enterprise should move unhindered between the participating countries; examples are the East African Community (EAC), and the EC (but again the latter is more complex).

1

4. *Complete economic unions*, which are common markets that ask for complete unification of monetary and fiscal policies, i.e. a central authority is introduced to exercise control over these matters so that existing member nations effectively become regions of one nation.
5. *Complete political integration* where the participants become literally one nation, i.e. the central authority needed in (4) not only controls monetary and fiscal policies but is also responsible to a central parliament with the sovereignty of a nation's government.

It should be stressed that each of these forms of economic integration can be introduced in its own right: they should not be confused with *stages* in a *process* which eventually leads to complete political integration. It should also be noted that within each scheme there may be *sectoral* integration in particular areas of the economy, for example the Common Agricultural Policy (CAP) of the EC. Of course, sectoral integration can be introduced as an aim in itself, as was the case in the European Coal and Steel Community (ECSC); but sectoral integration is a form of 'cooperation' since it is not consistent with the accepted definition of international economic integration.

It should also be pointed out that international economic integration can be *positive* or *negative*. The term 'negative integration' was coined by Tinbergen (1954) to refer to the removal of impediments on trade between the participating nations or to the elimination of any restrictions on the process of trade liberalisation. The term 'positive integration' relates to the modification of existing instruments and institutions and, more importantly, to the creation of new ones so as to enable the market of the integrated area to function properly and effectively and also to promote other broader policy aims of the union. At the risk of oversimplification it can be stated that sectoral integration and free trade areas are forms of international economic integration which require only 'negative integration', while the remaining types require 'positive integration' since they all require the positive act of adopting common external relations, or, as a minimum, a CET. In reality, however, this distinction is unfair since virtually all existing types of international economic integration have found it necessary to introduce some elements of 'positive integration'. On the relevance of this to the particular case of the EC, see below.

1.1 Economic integration and GATT rules

The rules of GATT allow the formation of regional groupings on the understanding that, although customs unions, free trade areas, etc., are discriminatory associations, they may not pursue policies which increase the level of their discrimination beyond that which existed prior to their formation, and that tariffs and other trade restrictions (with some exceptions) are removed on substantially all the trade among the participants. Once allowance was made for the proviso regarding the external trade relations of the regional grouping (the CET level, or common level of discrimination against extra-area trade, in a customs union, and the average tariff or trade discrimination level in a free trade area), it seemed to the drafters of Article XXIV (see appendix to this chapter) that regional groupings did not contradict the basic principles of GATT – liberalism, stability and transparency – or more generally the principles of non-discrimination and reciprocity.

There are various arguments that Article XXIV is in direct contradiction to the spirit of GATT – see, for instance, Dam (1970). However, Wolf (1983, p. 156) argues that if nations decide to treat one another as if they are part of a single economy, nothing can be done to prevent them, and that regional groupings, particularly those like the EC, have a strong impulse towards liberalisation; in the case of the EC, the setting of the CET happened to coincide with the Kennedy Round of tariff reductions.

Of course, these considerations are more complicated than is suggested here, particularly since there are those who would argue that nothing could be more discriminatory than for a group of countries to removal all tariffs and trade impediments on their mutual trade while at the same time maintaining the initial levels against outsiders. Moreover, as we shall see in Chapter 4, regional groupings may lead to resource reallocation effects which are economically undesirable. However, to have denied nations the right to form such associations, particularly when the main driving force may be political rather than economic, would have been a major setback for the world community. All that needs to be stated here is that as much as GATT's Article XXIV raises problems, it also reflects its drafters' deep understanding of the future development of the world economy.

1.2 The global experience

Although this book is concerned with the EC alone, it is important to view the EC within the context of the global experience of international economic integration. This section provides a brief summary of this experience.

Since the end of the Second World War various forms of international economic integration have been proposed and numerous schemes have actually been implemented. Even though some of those introduced were later discontinued or completely reformulated, the number adopted during the decade commencing in 1957 was so impressive as to prompt Haberler (1964) to describe that period as 'the age of integration'.

The EC is the most significant and influential of these arrangements since it comprises some of the most advanced nations of Western Europe: Belgium, Denmark, France, West Germany, Greece, Ireland, Italy, Luxemburg, the Netherlands, Portugal, Spain and the United Kingdom. The EC was founded by six of these nations (usually referred to as the original six) under the Treaty of Rome in 1957, with three of the remaining six (Denmark, Ireland and the United Kingdom) joining later in 1973. Greece became a full member in January 1981, and Portugal and Spain joined in January 1986 after a lengthy period of negotiation. Turkey has submitted an application for membership. Although the Treaty of Rome relates simply to the formation of a customs union and provides the basis for a common market in terms of factor mobility, many of the originators of the EC saw it as a phase in a process culminating in complete economic and political integration. Thus the present efforts to achieve harmonisation in member countries' monetary, fiscal and social policies, to accomplish a monetary union and to revive the concept of European union, and to amend the treaties in a way which will promote a democratic decision-making process (some of this has already been achieved in terms of the so-called Single European Act) can be seen as positive steps towards the attainment of the desired goals. (A full discussion of this is given in Chapter 2.)

EFTA is the other major scheme of international economic integration in Western Europe. To understand its membership one has to learn something about its history. In the mid-1950s, when a European Community comprising the whole of Western Europe was being contemplated, the United Kingdom was unprepared to commit itself to some of the economic and political aims envisaged for that Community. For example, the adoption of a common policy for agriculture and the eventual political unity of Western Europe were seen as aims which were in direct conflict with the United Kingdom's interests in the Commonwealth, particularly with regard to Commonwealth preference, which granted preferential access to the markets of member nations of the Commonwealth. The United Kingdom therefore favoured the idea of a Western Europe which adopted free trade in industrial products only, thus securing the advantages of Commonwealth preference as well as opening up Western Europe as a free market for its industrial goods. In short, the United Kingdom sought to achieve the best of both worlds for itself, which is of course quite understandable. However, it is equally understandable that such an arrangement was not acceptable to those seriously contemplating the formation of the EC. As a result the United Kingdom approached those Western European nations which had similar interests with the purpose of forming an alternative scheme of international economic integration to counteract any possible damage arising from the formation of the EC.

The outcome was EFTA, which was established in 1960 by the Stockholm Convention with the object of creating a free market for industrial products only; there were some arrangements on non-manufactures but these were relatively unimportant. The membership consisted of Austria, Denmark, Norway, Portugal, Sweden, Switzerland (and Liechtenstein) and the United Kingdom. Finland became an associate member in 1961; Iceland joined in 1970 as a full member. But, as already stated, Denmark and the United Kingdom, together with Ireland, joined the EC in 1973. This left EFTA with a membership consisting mainly of the relatively smaller nations of Western Europe. However, in 1972, owing to the insistance of the United Kingdom prior to joining the EC, the EC and EFTA entered into a series of free trade agreements which have in effect resulted in virtual free trade in industrial products in a market which includes their joint membership. This outcome has provided the cynical observer of British attitudes towards Western Europe with a great deal to reflect upon!

International economic integration is not confined to the so-called free nations of the world. The socialist planned economies of Eastern Europe have their own arrangement which operates under the Council for Mutual Economic Assistance (CMEA), or

COMECON, as it is generally known in the West. The CMEA was formed in 1949 by Bulgaria, Czechoslovakia, the German Democratic Republic, Hungary, Poland, Romania and the USSR; they were later joined by three non-European countries, Mongolia (1962), Cuba (1972) and Vietnam (1978). In its earlier days, before the death of Stalin, the activities of the CMEA were confined to the collation of the plans of the member states, the development of a uniform system of reporting statistical data and the recording of foreign trade statistics. However, during the 1970s a series of measures were adopted by the CMEA to implement the Comprehensive Programme of Socialist Integration, thereby indicating that the organisation is moving towards a form of integration based principally on methods of plan coordination and joint planning activity, rather than on market levers (Smith, 1977). Finally, attention should be drawn to the fact that the CMEA comprises a group of relatively small countries and one 'super power' and that the long-term aim of the organisation is to achieve a highly organised and integrated economic bloc, without any agreement having yet been made on how and when this will be accomplished.

Before leaving Europe it should be stated that another scheme exists in the form of regional cooperation between the five Nordic countries (the Nordic Community): Denmark, Finland, Iceland, Norway and Sweden. However, in spite of claims to the contrary (Sundelius and Wiklund, 1979), the Nordic scheme is one of cooperation rather than international economic integration since Denmark is a full member of the EC while the other countries are full members of EFTA; a substantial group of economists would argue that the Nordic Community has little practical relevance.

In Africa, there are several schemes of international economic integration (Robson, 1987; Inukai, 1987). The *Union Douanière et Economique de l'Afrique Centrale* (UDEAC) comprises the People's Republic of the Congo, Gabon, Cameroon and the Central African Republic. Member nations of UDEAC plus Chad, a former member, constitute a monetary union. The *Communauté Economique de l'Afrique de l'Ouest* (CEAO), which was formed under the Treaty of Abidjan in 1973, consists of the Ivory Coast, Mali, Mauritania, Niger, Senegal and Upper Volta (renamed Burkina Faso); Benin joined in 1984. Member countries of CEAO, except for Mauritania plus Benin and Togo, are participants in a monetary union. In 1973 the Mano River Union (MRU) was established between Liberia and Sierra Leone. The MRU is a customs union which involves a certain degree of cooperation, particularly in the industrial sector. The Economic Community of West African States (ECOWAS) was formed in 1975 with fifteen signatories: its membership consists of all those countries who participate in UDEAC, CEAO, MRU plus some other West African States. In 1969 the Southern African Customs Union (SACU) was established between Botswana, Lesotho, Swaziland and the Republic of South Africa. The Economic Community of the Countries of the Great Lakes (CEPGL) was created in 1976 by Rwanda, Burundi and Zaire. Until its collapse in 1977, there was the East African Community (EAC) between Kenya, Tanzania and Uganda. In 1981 fifteen states from the eastern and southern African region adopted a draft treaty for a Preferential Trade Area (PTA): Angola, Botswana, the Comoros, Djibouti, Ethiopia, Kenya, Lesotho, Malawi, Mauritius, Mozambique, Swaziland, Tanzania, Uganda, Zambia and Zimbabwe. In

August 1984 a treaty was signed by Libya and Morocco to establish the Arab–African Union, the main aim of which is to tackle their political conflicts in the Sahara Desert. Several other schemes were in existence in the past but have been discontinued, while others never got off the ground. A unique characteristic of economic integration in eastern, southern and western Africa is the multiplicity and overlapping of the schemes. For example, in West Africa alone, there is a total of 32 schemes, which is why a Benin Union (BU) consisting of Benin, Ghana, Nigeria and Togo has been recommended recently (UNECA, 1984) in an attempt to rationalise economic cooperation arrangements in West Africa.

There are four schemes of international economic integration in Latin America and the Caribbean. Under the 1960 Treaty of Montevideo, the Latin American Free Trade Association (LAFTA) was formed between Mexico and all the countries of South America except for Guyana and Surinam. LAFTA came to an end in the late 1970s but was promptly succeeded by the Association for Latin American Integration (ALADI) in 1980. The Managua Treaty of 1960 established the Central American Common Market (CACM) between Costa Rica, El Salvador, Guatemala, Honduras and Nicaragua. In 1969 the Andean Group was established under the Cartagena Agreement between Bolivia, Chile, Colombia, Ecuador, Peru and Venezuela; the Andean Group forms a closer link between some of the least developed nations of ALADI. In 1973 the Caribbean Community (CARICOM) was formed between Antigua, Barbados, Belize, Dominica, Grenada, Guyana, Jamaica, Montserrat, St Kitts–Nevis–Anguilla, St Lucia, St Vincent, Trinidad and Tobago – CARICOM replaced the Caribbean Free Trade Association (CARIFTA).

Asia does not figure very prominently in the league of international economic integration; but this is not surprising given the existence of such large (either in population or GNP terms) countries as China, India and Japan. The Regional Cooperation for Development (RCD) is a very limited arrangement for sectoral integration between Iran, Pakistan and Turkey. The Association of South-East Asian Nations (ASEAN) comprises six nations: Brunei, Indonesia, Malaysia, the Philippines, Singapore and Thailand. ASEAN was founded in 1967 in the shadow of the Vietnam War. After almost a decade of inactivity 'it was galvanized into renewed vigour in 1976 by the security problems which the reunification of Vietnam seemed to present to its membership' (Arndt and Garnaut, 1979). The drive for the establishment of ASEAN and for its vigorous reactivation in 1976 was both political and strategic. However, right from the start economic cooperation was one of the most important aims of ASEAN; indeed most of the vigorous activities of the group between 1976 and 1978 were predominantly in the economic field (Arndt and Garnaut, 1979).

A scheme of integration-cum-cooperation that is presently being hotly discussed is that of Pacific Basin Integration/Cooperation. Given the diversity of countries within the Pacific region, it seems highly unlikely that a very involved scheme of integration will evolve over the next decade or so. This is in spite of the fact that the following organisations already exist:

1.   The PECC (Pacific Economic Cooperation Conference), which is a tripartite structured organisation with representatives from governments, businesses and

academic circles and with the secretariat work being handled between general meetings by the country next hosting a meeting.

2. The PAFTAD (Pacific Trade and Development Conference) which is an academically oriented organisation.
3. The PBEC (Pacific Basin Economic Council) which is a private-sector business organisation for regional cooperation.
4. The PTC (Pacific Telecommunications Conference) which is a specialised organisation for regional cooperation in this particular field.

The reason for the pessimism is that the region under consideration covers the whole of North America and South-east Asia, with Pacific South America, the People's Republic of China and the USSR all claiming an interest since they are all on the Pacific. Even if one were to exclude this latter group, there still remains the cultural diversity of such countries as Australia, Canada, Japan, New Zealand and the United States, plus the diversity that already exists within ASEAN. It would therefore seem that unless the group of participants is severely limited, Pacific Basin *cooperation* will be the logical outcome.

While discussing the Pacific area, it should be added that a decade ago Australia and New Zealand entered into a free trade area arrangement (the New Zealand Australia Free Trade Area – NAFTA). NAFTA was later replaced by the more important Australia New Zealand Closer Economic Relations and Trade Agreement (ANZCERTA): not only have major trade barriers been removed, but the Treaty has had significant effects on the New Zealand economy – see Mayes (1988). Also, 'Canadians are actively engaged in debating the merits of further trade liberalisation through commercial integration with the [United States]' (Sarna, 1985, p. 299), with the Canadian Senate Committee taking 'pains to design carefully the contours of a Canada–US free trade regime' (Sarna, 1985, p. 301); the free trade area was ratified by both nations in 1988.

A scheme which covers more than one continent is the Arab League (AL), which consists of 21 independent nations, extending from the Gulf in the east to Mauritania and Morocco in the west. The geographical area covered by the group thus includes the whole of North Africa, a large part of the Middle East, plus Somalia and Djibouti. The purpose of the organisation is to strengthen the close ties linking Arab states, to coordinate their policies and activities and direct them to their common good and to mediate in disputes between them. These may seem like vague terms of reference; but the Arab Economic Council, whose membership consists of all Arab ministers of economic affairs, was entrusted with 'suggesting ways for economic development, cooperation, and organisation and coordination' (Sayigh, 1982, p. 123). The Council for Arab Economic Unity (CAEU), which was formed in 1957, had the aim of establishing an integrated economy of all member states of the AL. In 1964 the Arab Common Market was formed between Egypt, Iraq, Jordan and Syria, and the Gulf Cooperation Council (GCC) was established between Bahrain, Kuwait, Oman, Qatar, Saudi Arabia and the United Arab Emirates to bring together the Gulf states and to prepare the ground for them to join forces in the economic, political and military spheres. Two new schemes were formed in 1989: the Arab Cooperation Council

(ACC) and the Arab Maghreb Union (AMU); the ACC comprises Egypt, Iraq, Jordan and the Yemen Arab Republic, while the AMU consists of Algeria, Libya, Mauritania, Morocco and Tunisia. However, so far nothing concrete has emerged from these efforts.

There are two schemes of sectoral international economic integration. The first is the Organisation of Petroleum Exporting Countries (OPEC), founded in 1960 with a truly international membership. Its aim was to protect the main interest of its member nations: petroleum. The second is the Organisation of Arab Petroleum Exporting Countries (OAPEC), established in January 1968 by Kuwait, Libya and Saudi Arabia. These were joined in May 1970 by Algeria and the four Arab Gulf Emirates (Qatar, Abu Dhabi, Bahrain and Dubai). In March 1972 Egypt, Iraq and Syria became members. OAPEC was temporarily liquidated in June 1971 and Dubai is no longer a member. The agreement establishing the organisation states that the principal objectives of OAPEC are the cooperation of the member nations in various forms of economic activity; the realisation of the closest ties among them; the determination of ways and means of securing their legitimate interests; the use of joint efforts to ensure the flow of petroleum to its consumers; and the creation of an appropriate atmosphere for the capital and expertise invested in the petroleum industry in the member nations (*Middle East Economic Survey*, 1968). OAPEC was originally conceived as an example of sectoral integration with the political objective of using petroleum as a weapon for international bargaining against the Israeli occupation of certain Arab areas. Recently, however, the organisation has undertaken a number of projects both internally and externally – see Mingst (1977–8).

Finally, there are also the North Atlantic Treaty Organisation (NATO), the Organisation for Economic Cooperation and Development (OECD) and the Organisation for African Unity (OAU); but these and the AL are strictly speaking for political and economic cooperation only.

1.3 The EC

Since this book is devoted to the EC, it is important to establish the nature of the EC in the context of the different types of international integration discussed earlier – readers interested in the other schemes will find adequate discussion of them in El-Agraa (1988b). Article 3 of the treaty establishing the EC (known as the Treaty of Rome)[1] states that for the purposes set out in Article 2:[2]

> The activities of the Community shall include, on the conditions and in accordance with the time-table provided in this Treaty:
>
> (a) the elimination, as between Member States, of customs duties and of quantitative restrictions in regard to the import and export of goods, as well as of all other measures having equivalent effect;
>
> (b) the establishment of a common customs tariff and of a common commercial policy towards third countries;

(c) the abolition, as between Member States, of obstacles to freedom of movement for persons, services and capital;

(d) the establishment of a common policy in the sphere of agriculture;

(e) the adoption of a common policy in the sphere of transport;

(f) the establishment of a system ensuring that competition in the common market is not distorted;

(g) the application of procedures by which the economic policies of Member States can be co-ordinated and disequilibria in their balances of payments can be remedied;

(h) the approximation of the laws of Member States to the extent required for proper functioning of the common market;

(i) the creation of a European Social Fund in order to improve the possibilities of employment for workers and to contribute to the raising of their standard of living;

(j) the establishment of a European Investment Bank to facilitate the economic expansion of the Community by opening up fresh resources; and

(k) the association of overseas countries and territories with a view to increasing trade and to promoting jointly economic and social development. (*Treaty of Rome*, pp. 3–4)

These elements are stated more elaborately in later articles. For instance, Article 9(1) states:

The Community shall be based upon a customs union which shall cover all trade in goods and which shall involve the prohibition between Member States of customs duties on imports and exports and of all charges having equivalent effect, and the adoption of a common customs tariff in their relations with third countries. (*Treaty of Rome*, p. 6)

Articles 35–7 elaborate on the CAP; Articles 48–73 on the conditions for freedom of movement for factors of production; Articles 74–84 on the Community Transport Policy; and Articles 99 and 100 on the harmonisation of certain taxes.

The Treaty of Rome provisions should, however, be considered in conjunction with later developments. These have been incorporated into the Single European Act (SEA) which includes the European Monetary System and the creation of a true single market by 1992 – these are fully discussed in Chapter 2. Here, it can be categorically stated that *the EC is a common market aspiring to become a complete economic and political union.*

It also needs to be mentioned that the European Community is in fact an amalgamation of three Communities: the European Coal and Steel Community; the European Atomic Energy Commission (Euratom); and the European Economic Community. (This point is explained and discussed in Chapter 2.)

1.4 The meaning of economic union

The above discussion amounts to an abstract statement of the nature of the EC as a form of economic integration. In this introductory chapter there is some need to supplement this discussion with practical or operational definitions of economic union and economic integration.

The reader may be surprised to learn that there are difficulties regarding operational definitions of these terms, but Pinder (1969), using the *Concise Oxford English Dictionary* as a reference, asserts that 'integration is the combination of parts into a whole, and union is a whole resulting from the combination of parts or members'. Hence 'integration is the process of reaching a state of union'. Pinder argues that it is better to make this distinction between union and integration, 'rather than to sow a seed of confusion in the discussion by defining integration as meaning both the process and the state', as Balassa (1961, pp. 1–2) does.

This distinction provides a significant choice regarding the definition of union in terms of when the combination of the parts (nations) is to be seen as a whole. According to Balassa a state of economic union is reached not only when two or more countries allow for the free movement of factors and commodities between them, but also when 'some degree of harmonisation of national economic policies' is made regarding the removal of any hidden discrimination that could exist because of them. He also distinguishes between union and complete economic integration in that the latter 'presupposes the unification of monetary, fiscal, social and counter-cyclical policies and requires the setting-up of a supra-national authority whose decisions are binding for the member states' (Balassa, 1961, p. 2).

Pinder has two objections to Balassa's definitions. First, since economic union is the term generally used to describe the ultimate goal of the EC, the act of abolishing discrimination could be seen as the limit of the EC integration process. Secondly, the term 'complete economic integration' implies that the EC will become a 'replica of an existing national economy' which is tightly centralised, and this will preclude any discussion of what form the EC could take.

Because of these objections, Pinder (p. 45) then defines economic integration as 'both the removal of discrimination as between the economic agents of the member countries, and the formation and application of co-ordinated and common policies on a sufficient scale to ensure that major economic and welfare objectives are fulfilled'. Hence 'economic union is a state in which discrimination has been largely removed, and co-ordination and common policies have been and are being applied on a sufficient scale'.

In order to promote meaningful discussion about the EC, Pinder suggests that it is necessary to distinguish the abolition of discrimination by itself from the other ingredients of economic integration. For this purpose he uses his own versions of 'negative integration' and 'positive integration' – see above. For Pinder, negative integration consists only of the removal of discrimination, while positive integration consists of the establishment and adoption of coordinated and common policies with the object of fulfilling economic and welfare aims other than negative integration. Hence the combination of both negative and positive integration comprises economic integration, whose ultimate aim is economic union. One can therefore conceive of various forms of economic integration: those which constitute negative integration, those which constitute both negative and positive integration, those which constitute less than complete negative integration plus positive integration, etc. The EC is an example of the third form since, in practice, member countries pursue their own regional policies (see Chapter 16). Pinder therefore concludes that a common market falls short of an economic union and 'without economic union will prove to be unviable' (p. 146). For technical problems related to this topic, but in a limited way, the reader is advised to consult El-Agraa (1979a), El-Agraa and Jones (1981, Chapter 3) and El-Agraa (1989a).

The discussion of an operational definition of economic union and economic integration was pursued further by the Federal Trust Group.[3] The outcome of the Group's deliberations was published in a short report with the title *Economic Union in the EEC* (Federal Trust, 1974) and a book on a similar theme was edited by a member of the Group (Denton, 1974).

The Group stressed the point that for certain members of a society the primary objective of economic union may be to facilitate or to promote the evolution of a political union (a point discussed in Chapter 2). The political union itself may be desired for intra-union or extra-union aims which may be political, strategic or both: a political union of Western Europe may be desired in order to avoid the long-sustained conflict among the participating nations or to strengthen Western Europe's bargaining position *vis-à-vis* the outside world, i.e. the United States and the USSR. However, the Group shied away from this question and devoted its attention to the problem of assessing the costs and benefits of economic union.

As the discussion regarding the United Kingdom membership of the EC has clearly shown (particularly at the time of the referendum), an economic union may be assessed in terms of whether or not it can result in an improvement in the economic welfare of those concerned. This welfare criterion can be expressed in terms of the usual national economic objectives of the growth in per capita output, the efficiency of reallocation and utilisation of factors of production, the stabilisation of levels of economic activity, employment and income, the equitable distribution of income, balanced regional growth and the provision of a healthy physical and social environment. The Group rightly emphasised that some of these aims may be controversial; for example, not everyone would describe the phenomenon of regional imbalance as a problem, since there may be certain societies whose development positively requires some regional imbalance (a point which is lucidly expressed by Professor Nevin in Chapter 16 on the EC regional policy). Listing aims does not, therefore, serve a useful purpose; it is more meaningful to establish an order of priorities regarding such aims and to define the trade-offs which are likely to be acceptable when the aims are in conflict. Since these are points of much political debate in the individual member nations, they are very likely to be even more so in the wider context of the EC as a whole. The Group also emphasised the point that a ranked set of economic objectives for any society needs an adequate provision of the necessary political institutions for determining them. Since these institutions are not yet adequately established at EC level (see Chapter 2), it follows that there is a great deal of 'difficulty in arriving at a set of aims of a European economic union' (Denton, 1974, p. 2).

It is therefore not surprising that the Group should conclude that the definition of economic union in the context of the EC is an extremely difficult one. In the light of this conclusion the Group decided to 'let the definition emerge from the detailed accounts of problems and policies in specific areas' of enquiry. This is more or less the essence of the approach adopted in this book.

The Group then went on to discuss the relation between economic union and monetary union. In the earlier years of the development of the EC, some took the position that economic union (in the form of coordination of economic policies) was a necessary prerequisite for a successful monetary union – the so-called economists, of which the Dutch and the Germans were the main protagonists. There were also those who believed that monetary integration (in the form of permanently and irrevocably fixed rates of exchange) was essential for a properly functioning economic union – the so-called monetarists of whom the Belgians, French and Luxemburgers were the main advocates. The Group concluded that if the position held by the 'economists' were accepted, this would amount to being content to let the 'monetary tail wag the economic dog with vengeance. Economic union as a requirement of monetary union can only be accepted if the case for monetary union can itself be firmly based on theory and empirical evidence' (see Denton, 1974, p. 3). However, this is not the place to discuss this point, since a detailed analysis is given in the chapters on European monetary integration and the European Monetary System.

It is no doubt evident that the problems of defining economic unions, political unions and monetary unions can be fascinating. Some of these problems are tackled in the specific chapters where they arise and some are not the concern of this book. The interested reader is therefore advised to consult Pinder (1969), Denton (1974), Hodges (1972), Tsoukalis (1982) and references given there.

1.5 The possible economic gains from integration

In reality, almost all existing cases of economic integration were either proposed or formed for political reasons even though the arguments popularly put forward in their favour were expressed in terms of possible economic gains. However, no matter what the motives for economic integration are, it is still necessary to analyse the economic implications of such geographically discriminatory groupings.

At the customs union (CU) and free trade area (FTA) level, the possible sources of economic gain can be attributed to:

1. Enhanced efficiency in production made possible by increased specialisation in accordance with the law of comparative advantage.
2. Increased production levels arising from better exploitation of economies of scale made possible by the increased size of the market.
3. An improved international bargaining position, made possible by larger size, leading to better terms of trade.
4. Enforced changes in economic efficiency brought about by enhanced competition.

5. Changes affecting both the amount and quality of the factors of production, brought about by technological advances.

If the level of economic integration proceeds beyond the CU level, to the common market (CM) or economic union (EU) level, as is the case in the EC, then further sources of gain become possible because of:

6. Factor mobility across the borders of member nations.
7. The coordination of monetary and fiscal policies.
8. The goals of near full employment, higher rates of economic growth and better income distribution becoming unified targets.

It should be apparent that some of these considerations relate to the static resource reallocation effects while the rest relate to the long-term or dynamic effects. The possible attainment of the benefits of these effects must be considered with great caution.

Membership of an economic grouping cannot of itself guarantee to a member state or the group a satisfactory economic performance, or even a better performance than in the past. The static gains from integration, although significant, can be – and often are – swamped by the influence of factors of domestic or international origin that have nothing to do with integration. The more fundamental factors influencing a country's economic performance (the dynamic factors) are unlikely to be affected by integration except in the long run. It is clearly not a necessary condition for economic success that a country should be a member of an economic community, as the experience of several small countries confirms, although such countries might have done even better as members of a suitable group. Equally, a large integrated market is in itself no guarantee of performance, as the experience of India suggests. However, although integration is clearly no panacea for all economic ills, nor indispensable to success, there are many convincing reasons for supposing that significant economic benefits may be derived from properly conceived arrangements for economic integration (Robson, 1980).

However, in the context of the EC, one should always keep in mind that the 'founding fathers' had the formation of a United States of Western Europe as the ultimate goal and that economic integration became the immediate objective so as to facilitate the attainment of political unity via the back door (see Chapter 2). Those who fail to appreciate this will always undermine the EC's serious attempts at the achievement of economic and monetary union – see Chapter 5.

1.6 Areas of economic enquiry

The necessary areas of economic enquiry are quite apparent now that we have established the nature of the EC. It is necessary to analyse the effect and consequences of the removal of trade impediments between the participating nations and to make an equivalent study of the establishment of the common external relations. These aspects are tackled in Chapters 4 and 6. It is also extremely important to discuss the role of competition and industrial policies and the presence of multinational firms. These aspects are discussed in Chapter 19. Moreover, it is necessary to analyse the implications and consequences of a special provision for the CAP (Chapter 9), the fisheries policy (Chapter 10), transport policy (Chapter 11), European monetary integration (Chapters 5 and 15), the fiscal policy (Chapters 13 and 14), the regional policy (Chapter 16), the energy policy (Chapter 12), the social policy (Chapter 17), factor mobility (Chapter 19), environmental concerns (Chapter 18) and external trade relations (Chapters 20 and 21). The book also contains two chapters on the development of the EC (Chapter 22) and the future of the Community (Chapter 24) as well as a chapter on the 'economics of 1992' (Chapter 23).

1.7 About this book

This book offers, more or less, a comprehensive but brief coverage of the theoretical issues: trade creation, trade diversion and the Cooper–Massell criticism; the domestic distortions argument; the terms of trade effects; and the scale economies argument. It also offers a fresh look at the different attempts at economic justification for customs union formation. A chapter is included on the methodology and results of the measurements of the effects of the EC formation on member nations. These are discussed briefly since a comprehensive book on them is now available – see El-Agraa (1989a). There is a comprehensive treatment of most of the policy considerations.

Although chapters on EC political cooperation, distribution problems and political considerations may appear to be absent, these aspects have not been omitted: some elements of political cooperation are discussed in Chapters 2 and 22, while some of the most significant elements of the distribution problem are discussed in the chapters on the role of the Community budget, fiscal harmonisation and social policy. This is not meant to imply that these aspects are not worthy of more comprehensive consideration, as one could in fact argue that these are the most important issues in the EC. The treatment given to them in this book is such that the significant aspects of these policies are tackled where they are particularly relevant. Moreover, with regard to some of these policies, the EC is not yet very certain in which direction it is going to proceed in the future, and this is in spite of the SEA and the recent commitment to EMU in three stages. The wider political considerations lie outside our scope.

Notes

1. *Treaty setting up the European Economic Community*, Rome, 25 March 1957, HMSO, 1967.
2. 'The Community shall have as its task, by setting up a common market and progressively approximating the economic policies of Member States, to promote throughout the Community an harmonious development of economic activities, a continuous and balanced

expansion, an increase in stability, an accelerated raising of the standard of living and closer relations between the Member States belonging to it.' (Article 2, p. 3)

3. The Group was established in November 1972 to study the implications of the creation of a monetary union by the members of the EC.

Appendix: GATT's Article XXIV

Territorial application – frontier traffic – customs unions and free trade areas

1. The provisions of this Agreement shall apply to the metropolitan customs territories of the contracting parties and to any other customs territories in respect of which this Agreement has been accepted under Article XXVI or is being applied under Article XXXIII or pursuant to the Protocol of Provisional Application. Each such customs territory shall, exclusively for the purposes of the territorial application of this Agreement, be treated as though it were a contracting party; *Provided* that the provisions of this paragraph shall not be construed to create any rights or obligations as between two or more customs territories in respect of which this Agreement has been accepted under Article XXVI or is being applied under Article XXXIII or pursuant to the Protocol of Provisional Application by a single contracting party.

2. For the purposes of this Agreement a customs territory shall be understood to mean any territory with respect to which separate tariffs or other regulations of commerce are maintained for a substantial part of the trade to such territory with other territories.

3. The provisions of this Agreement shall not be construed to prevent:

(*a*) Advantages accorded by any contracting party to adjacent countries in order to facilitate frontier traffic;
(*b*) Advantages accorded to the trade with the Free Territory of Trieste by countries contiguous to that territory, provided that such advantages are not in conflict with the Treaties of Peace arising out of the Second World War.

4. The contracting parties recognize the desirability of increasing freedom of trade by the development, through voluntary agreements, of closer integration between the economies of the countries parties to such agreements. They also recognize that the purpose of a customs union or of a free-trade area should be to facilitate trade between the constituent territories and not to raise barriers to the trade of other contracting parties with such territories.

5. Accordingly, the provisions of this Agreement shall not prevent, as between the territories of contracting parties, the formation of a customs union or of a free-trade area or the adoption of an interim agreement necessary for the formation of a customs union or of a free-trade area; *Provided* that:

(*a*) with respect to a customs union, or an interim agreement leading to the formation of a customs union, the duties and other regulations of commerce imposed at the institution of any such union or interim agreement with respect to trade with contracting parties not parties to such union or agreement shall not on the whole be higher or more restrictive than the general incidence of the duties and regulations of commerce applicable in the constituent territories prior to the formation of such union or the adoption of such interim agreement, as the case may be;
(*b*) with respect to a free-trade area, or an interim agreement leading to the

formation of a free-trade area, the duties and other regulations of commerce maintained in each of the constituent territories and applicable at the formation of such free-trade area or the adoption of such interim agreement to the trade of contracting parties not included in such area or not parties to such agreement shall not be higher or more restrictive than the corresponding duties and other regulations of commerce existing in the same constituent territories prior to the formation of the free-trade area, or interim agreement, as the case may be; and

(c) any interim agreement referred to in sub-paragraphs (a) and (b) shall include a plan and schedule for the formation of such a customs union or of such free-trade area within a reasonable length of time.

6. If, in fulfilling the requirements of sub-paragraph 5(a), a contracting party proposes to increase any rate of duty inconsistently with the provisions of Article II, the procedure set forth in Article XXVIII shall apply. In providing for compensatory adjustment, due account shall be taken of the compensation already afforded by the reductions brought about in the corresponding duty of the other constituents of the union.

7.

(a) Any contracting party deciding to enter into a customs union or a free-trade area, or an interim agreement leading to the formation of such a union or area, shall promptly notify the CONTRACTING PARTIES and shall make available to them such information regarding the proposed union or area as will enable them to make such reports and recommendations to contracting parties as they may deem appropriate.

(b) If, after having studied the plan and schedule included in an interim agreement referred to in paragraph 5 in consultation with the parties to that agreement and taking due account of the information made available in accordance with the provisions of sub-paragraph (a), the CONTRACTING PARTIES find that such agreement is not likely to result in the formation of a customs union or a free-trade area within the period contemplated by the parties to the agreement or such a period is not a reasonable one, the CONTRACTING PARTIES shall make recommendations to the parties to the agreement. The parties shall not maintain or put into force, as the case may be, such agreement if they are not prepared to modify it in accordance with these recommendations.

(c) Any substantial change in the plan or schedule referred to in paragraph 5(c) shall be communicated to the CONTRACTING PARTIES, which may request the contracting parties concerned to consult with them if the change seems likely to jeopardize or delay unduly the formation of the customs union or of the free-trade area.

8. For the purposes of this Agreement:

(a) A customs union shall be understood to mean the substitution of a single customs territory for two or more customs territories, so that

    (i) duties and other restrictive regulations of commerce (except, where necessary, those permitted under Articles XI, XII, XIII, XIV, XV, and XX) are eliminated with respect to substantially all the trade between the constituent territories and the union or at least with respect to substantially all the trade in products originating in such territories, and,

    (ii) subject to the provisions of paragraph 9, substantially the same duties and other regulations of commerce are applied by each of the members of the union to the trade of territories not included in the union;

(*b*) A free-trade area shall be understood to mean a group of two or more customs territories in which the duties and other restrictive regulations of commerce (except, where necessary, those permitted under Articles XI, XII, XIII, XIV, XV and XX) are eliminated on substantially all the trade between the constituent territories in products originating in such territories.

9. The preferences referred to in paragraph 2 of Article I shall not be affected by the formation of a customs union or of a free-trade area but may be eliminated or adjusted by means of negotiations with contracting parties affected. This procedure of negotiations with affected parties shall, in particular, apply to the elimination of preferences required to conform with the provisions of paragraph 8(*a*)(i) and paragraph 8(*b*).

10. The CONTRACTING PARTIES may by a two-thirds majority approve proposals which do not fully comply with the requirements of paragraphs 5 to 9 inclusive, provided that such proposals lead to the formation of a customs union or a free-trade area in the sense of this Article.

11. Taking into account the exceptional circumstances arising out of the establishment of India and Pakistan as independent States and recognizing the fact that they have long constituted an economic unit, the contracting parties agree that the provisions of this Agreement shall not prevent the two countries from entering into special arrangements with respect to the trade between them, pending the establishment of their mutual trade relations on a definitive basis.

12. Each contracting party shall take such reasonable measures as may be available to it to ensure observance of the provisions of this Agreement by the regional and local governments and authorities within its territory.

Part I

Historical, institutional and statistical background

The aim of this section is to provide the reader with a general background to the EC. Chapter 2 gives a short account of the historical development of the EC and describes its institutions and their functioning. Chapter 3 is a general statistical survey of the major economic indicators for members of the EC, but it also provides relevant information concerning the potential members of the EC and compares the state of the twelve nations plus the potential members with that of Canada, Japan and the United States.

2 | History and institutions of the EC

C. D. E. Collins

2.1 The creation of the Community

The EC is a unique political institution. Thus political analysis based on the behaviour of nation states, whether unitary or federal, or upon long-standing international organisations, is of only limited application. Nor has the EC yet reached its final form, so judgements about it must be tentative. It is helpful to look behind the formal working of the institutions to the broader political environment in which the EC operates, and this chapter accordingly begins by looking at the circumstances in which the EC was created before considering its structure. Although the emphasis in this book is on economic policies, in the last analysis the objectives of the Community go beyond economic ones, which were conceived as a means rather than as an end. In the words of the preamble of the Treaty of Rome, the EC is to 'lay the foundations of an ever closer union among the people of Europe and by pooling resources is to preserve and strengthen peace and liberty'.[1]

The idea of creating a political unit in Europe is a very old one and the classic argument for it rested on the need to preserve peace in a traditionally bellicose part of the world. At both the intellectual and emotional levels there has been a constant interplay between the opposing forces of nationalism, on the one hand, and, on the other, the desire to create an organisation which would express the enduring sense of common history, culture, ideas and experience in Europe. During the twentieth century, and particularly since 1945, this task has seemed more urgent.[2]

It is hardly surprising that the need to find a new way of conducting affairs should have been acutely felt as the Second World War finally came to an end. The exhaustion of Europe was a fact visible to all in the form of physical devastation, a poor standard of living and immense human loss; its weakness was demonstrated by its inability to restore its economy without aid from the United States and its vulnerability was soon exposed by a growing mistrust of the Soviet Union's policy in Europe. Under such circumstances, the psychological barrier which had hitherto prevented effective steps towards integration in Western Europe was breached.

There remained, however, divergent views about how to proceed and the organisations created in the early post-war years reflected several different ideas. It was in 1947 that General Marshall launched the plan of aid from the United States to revitalise the European economy, provided assistance programmes were organised on a continental and not a state basis. The following years saw the creation of the Organisation for European Economic Cooperation (OEEC) to control a joint recovery programme and to work for the establishment of freer trade, although this was to be limited to Western Europe only. The organisation was given substantial powers to consider and comment upon the activities of the members and has continued to be a body whose views on the handling of national economies have considerable influence and prestige. By doing a great deal to ensure European recovery and to re-create a West European trading area it helped to provide the context within which a more tightly organised grouping could flourish. Its later expansion into the Organisation for Economic Cooperation and Development (OECD) brought worldwide membership and thus gave expression to the world liberal trading area which forms part of the environment within which the EC has taken root.[3]

Defence considerations demanded special arrangements. The Brussels Treaty of 1948 was a pact of mutual assistance between the United Kingdom, France and the Benelux countries and was neatly balanced in aim between the perpetuation of the wartime alliance against Germany and the realisation of a newer threat from the USSR. The realisation of the interdependence of the defence of Western Europe with wider defence concerns was marked by the signature of the North Atlantic Treaty in 1949 by the Brussels Treaty powers in association not only with the United States and Canada, but also Denmark, Iceland, Italy, Norway and Portugal. This brought a new dimension to the integrative process by recognising that Western Europe was part of a larger military grouping, but in a way which ensured that defence arrangements were handled separately from subsequent political and economic developments.

The same period saw yet another attempt to express the unity of Europe through the creation of the Council of Europe in 1949. This body has very broad political and cultural objectives, including the notable contribution of protecting the individual through the Convention on Human Rights and Fundamental Freedoms. Its statute expresses a belief in a common political heritage based on accepted spiritual and moral values, political liberty, the rule of law and the maintenance of democratic forms of government. The Council of Europe was able to obtain wide support in Western Europe but it contained no real drive towards European unification. It was impatience with this omission that led activists to try a new approach which was to result in the setting up of the three European Communities.

It was not long before a means was found of offering a possible solution to certain pressing questions. A working relationship between the Western Alliance and West Germany had still not been established. The old Germany was, in practice, now divided but the western half was not yet fully accepted as an independent state. However, West Germany's economic recovery had begun and with the onset of the cold war it was needed as a contributor to the prosperity and defence of the West. A way, therefore, had to be found of re-establishing Germany without arousing the historic fears of its recent enemies. In short, a means of reconciliation acceptable to France was required.

The beauty of the proposal for the European Coal and Steel Community (ECSC) was its ability to appeal to so many interests. To the argument that it was no more than rational to treat the coal and steel industries of the area as a single whole, and thus reap the benefits of a unified market operating with greater efficiency, could be added the political argument that it was a means of integrating, and supervising, the essentials of war-making capacity. It would thus make it physically impossible for the members to go to war with each other again. It was to be the first stone in the sound and practical foundation of a united Europe creating a base for economic unity under the guidance of a strong executive. These ideas were contained in a speech delivered by Robert Schuman, the French Foreign Minister, on 9 May 1950. It marked the formal launching of the Community idea.[4]

The sectoral approach to integration, based upon a pooling system, was familiar to many of those who had experienced the cooperative efforts of the wartime alliance. It was based upon a concept of functional integration which allowed for common action in performing common tasks, and the creation of the ECSC was firmly based upon the belief that it was essential to find solutions to common problems. This approach, so different from classical diplomacy, formed the basis of what was to become known as the Community method.[5] Although operative in a limited field, its method of promoting integration found favour as a model in the ensuing years. It was rapidly launched and initially worked relatively smoothly thus establishing its credentials; it was not long, therefore, before a new project was launched.

The outbreak of the Korean war in June 1950 resulted in US pressure on the West Europeans to do more for themselves to defend Western Europe against possible Soviet attack. This raised the issue of a military contribution from West Germany. Since the situation bore at least a superficial resemblance to that which had made possible the launching of the ECSC, a similar attempt was made again. A proposal was launched for a European Defence Community (EDC) and the six members of the ECSC initialled a treaty in 1952. As before, the EDC was intended to kill several birds with one stone. Since it required the military rearmament of West Germany, a number of conditions were necessary to make this acceptable to its neighbours. An organisation promoting West European unity would be a further move to attach Germany and the Germans to the West, both in a political and a psychological sense. Thus institutional controls were thought to be equally as necessary as the novel feature of a European army, in which small national units would be merged into an integrated force which would in turn be subordinated to the NATO command.[6] The parallel with the method of achieving control of the coal and steel industries is striking.

The new proposal, however, did not stand alone, and for good reasons. The idea of a unified army was hardly practical while member states still went their own ways in foreign policy or controlled their own defence efforts. A method of democratic control over such an army would need to be found. Almost inevitably, therefore, the project had to be enlarged with the proposal for a parallel European political authority whose institutions would ultimately absorb those of the ECSC and EDC and which would push forward towards more general economic integration.

The total project was, therefore, larger and more sensitive than the launching of the ECSC and in the event it failed to receive French approval. A solution was found to the immediate problem of West German rearmament through merging the Brussels Treaty Organisation into a new body, the Western European Union, in which West Germany could make its defence contribution. Italy, too, became a member. At the same time, it was agreed that West Germany should enter NATO, that the occupation of West Germany should be finally ended, that UK forces should remain on the continent as a counterbalance to rearmament and that West Germany should accept certain restrictions on its military production. A Franco-German agreement foreshadowed a solution to the question of the status of the Saar. Thus, although formally the integration of Western Europe had received a set back, an essential foundation had been laid. A means had been found whereby West Germany could become a full member of the Western community of states. Although the German question was not dead, the states of Western Europe were increasingly able to put the past behind them and concentrate upon the future.

A new attempt at integration was soon made and in June 1955 the foreign ministers of the six ECSC countries met at Messina. They discussed the possibility of pursuing further integration on a more general basis as well as the creation of organisations for transport and the peaceful development of atomic energy. While the first aim was conceived as the means towards political unity this was not a goal which was unduly stressed for fear of reviving the old arguments for and against political union. The conference established an intergovernmental committee under the chairmanship of Paul-Henri Spaak, then Foreign Minister of Belgium. Its task was to examine the suggestions in further detail and to prepare the ground for action. It is in the report of this committee that the ideas which lay behind the Treaty of Rome are most clearly stated.

The vision of the Spaak Report (Comité intergouvernemental créé par la conference de Messina, 1956) is of a Western Europe which can win for itself a place in the world comparable with that of the super powers and which would once again have the capacity to influence world events. It was thus searching for a way of liberating the abilities of the European people and of improving the foundations of European society. The chosen method was to be the creation of a common market to provide the necessary productive base; this would require certain collective measures, the establishment of a broadly common economic policy to ensure economic expansion and higher living standards, and measures to develop and utilise European resources, including labour reserves. The resulting Treaty of Rome thus contained the detailed means of working towards these goals with a heavy emphasis upon the measures immediately necessary to create the common market. In many respects the report was content to ensure that the new organisation would be able to take powers in the future by giving it a general capacity to act. Indeed, it would have been quite impractical to lay down detailed policies for an unknown future ten or twenty years ahead. The treaty also established the necessary institutions but it is noticeable that the sections dealing with these were cautious in political tone. Far from developing beyond the ECSC towards political unification, the new treaty was generally held to be less supranational in character than the ECSC. Here it reflected a change of mood in Western Europe and an unwillingness to plunge into renewed political debate. It must be remembered, too, that an organisation charged with integrating the whole economy rather than one sector was faced with larger, more difficult, and often unknown, tasks so that states were likely to be more hesitant about transferring large powers to it. The price paid for the new venture was therefore caution in the political sphere, and the institutions of the European Economic Community (EEC) left a great deal of power in the hands of the member states. Thus the clash of national interests between the member nations continued, albeit within a unique cooperative framework.

The past makes it plain that the EC does not exist in a vacuum. The major elements on the political stage, which were important at the time of its creation, are still enduring policy issues in the EC. The states which formed the EC were part of a wider grouping, anxious to ensure economic recovery after depression and war and committed to the re-creation of a liberal, trading world economy. The efforts of the six countries to go further along the road to economic integration were potentially discriminatory with regard to other trading states with whom the six had close trading ties. These included the United Kingdom, the United States, the Scandinavian states and other European nations. Thus the pursuit of the economic goal of the Treaty of Rome has always had to be balanced against the need to consider relations with outside states, with whose well-being the EC's welfare is interdependent. The interest of the EC, as a major trading unit, is also in a peaceful world, including a peaceful Europe; but members have relied primarily on their own foreign policies, defence efforts and American defence protection. There have been many conflicting views in Western Europe about defence issues but, while it has often resented reliance upon America, it has also found it extremely convenient to be relieved of so much defence expenditure. This is a field which is riddled with anomalies. It contributes to the close, but often abrasive, relationship with the United States which the EC is ill equipped to handle since it has no competence in defence matters.

It must also be remembered that the members of the EC are part of a broader European movement which recognises the need to identify and promote the political and cultural values common to the area. This aim is expressed through the Council of Europe. In sum, the EC can be seen as a specialised unit which forms part of several wider groupings. These constrain its overall freedom of action but at the same time they allow states to pursue some interests but not others.

Despite developments in foreign policy cooperation, the EC lacks two essential attributes of a state. These are responsibility for external affairs and for defence. It thus has a great gap in its competences; but its weight makes it highly significant in world economics and thus in world politics. Its attraction has been demonstrated by the first round of enlargement, which included Denmark, Ireland and the United Kingdom, by the second which brought in Greece and, thirdly, the entry of Spain and Portugal on 1 January 1986. So far, there has been one withdrawal. The position of

Greenland was renegotiated in 1984 but it remains associated under the rules for overseas countries and territories. A special agreement regulates mutual fishing interests.

2.2 Political developments

The EC created a special set of institutions to handle its affairs. These centre on a Council of Ministers and a Commission, backed up by a Parliament and Court of Justice (see next section). By the 1970s, however, it was clear that the EC was entering a period of political change for which these institutions were less suitable than they had been and for which they lacked adequate strength. Major internal objectives had to be formulated and a way found of acting more effectively on the world stage. Rather than see a strengthening of the existing institutions, a method was found of bringing national political leaders more closely into EC affairs by the introduction of summit meetings. These were formalised under the name of the European Council in 1974. The first major summit was held in The Hague in December 1969. Here the member nations effectively recognised that they were so closely interdependent that they had no choice but to continue with the EC and were thus compelled to reach agreement on such matters as the Common Agricultural Policy (CAP) and budgetary changes. A vital point was the recognition that the EC possessed the political will to work for enlargement and thus to stabilise the vexing question of relations with the United Kingdom.

The Hague summit also recognised that the international status of the EC needed further consideration. Its formal responsibilities neither matched its economic weight nor allowed effective consideration of the political aspects of its external economic relations. Individual members still conducted external affairs themselves and could thus cut across EC interests. The attraction of bringing foreign policy into the EC orbit was the greater effectiveness this might bring in world affairs; but the idea raised issues of great sensitivity, notably concerning relations with the United States and the Soviet Union, as well as defence matters. In fact, by a somewhat different route and with a different emphasis, the question of the future political objectives of Western Europe had again been reached. The Hague conference requested the foreign ministers to study the best way of achieving further political integration, on the assumption of enlargement, and to present a report. Subsequent moves to achieve political cooperation, which still emphasise foreign affairs, have been important in helping the EC to identify its common aims and thus to articulate the nature of the group. Political cooperation has itself led to institutional innovation. This has occurred alongside the original institutions of the EC and not as part of them, although new and old are now coming closer together.

In 1972 an important summit meeting was held in Paris and attended by the three new members, Denmark, Ireland and the United Kingdom. It devoted considerable attention to the need to strengthen the social and regional aims of the EC. The deterioration in the international climate and the preoccupation of member governments with economic matters at home seemed to require frequent meetings of heads of government to ensure that the EC remained an effective economic unit. Differences of policy between governments as they reacted to new problems made summit meetings essential to establish the extent of common ground and ensure that this was used as the basis for action by member nations. At first sight this seemed to strengthen the intergovernmental structure of the EC at the expense of the supranational element; but it was also recognition by the member states that their fortunes were inextricably intertwined and required the formulation of joint goals and policies over a wide field. Informal discussion of general issues, whether economic or political, domestic or worldwide, was a necessary preliminary to further, formal integration and through the summit meetings and the political cooperation procedure the scope of the subject matter of the EC was steadily enlarged. By the time of the Paris summit meeting in 1972, member states had laid down for themselves an ambitious programme of activity designed to lead to a European Union. Much remained to be defined but a number of external issues were pinpointed. These included the need to maintain a constructive dialogue with the United States, Canada and Japan, to act jointly in matters of external trade policy and for member nations to make a concerted contribution to the Conference on Security and Cooperation in Europe. Foreign ministers were to meet more frequently to discuss this last issue.

The worldwide economic difficulties of the 1970s created a harsh environment within which the EC had to strive to establish its identity, its future goals and executive responsibilities. Progress was extremely slow. The Paris summit of 1974 formally agreed that the distinction between EC affairs and political cooperation was untenable, while in 1981 the foreign ministers agreed that political cooperation between member nations had become central to their foreign policies (EC Commission, 1983d, p. 3). Proceedings became formalised and relations established with the Commission. The same summit asked Leo Tindemans (then Prime Minister of Belgium) to tour the EC capitals and write a report on the concept of European union. This brought out into the open the long-standing question of whether the member nations of the EC did, or could, constitute an effective economic whole or whether progress as a two-tier Community might be preferable. So far this has been avoided by the adoption of special measures within the EC to help the weaker member nations. A further suggestion was that the EC should take steps towards making itself more of a citizens' Europe by including action on matters such as consumer rights, environmental protection and the safeguarding of fundamental rights. A common stand in foreign policy, which could then be applied by the member states, and a tentative start on defence issues were further ideas which were aired. Institutional reform would be required in several directions.

The twin issues of constitutional development and institutional reform continued to exercise EC circles, but for a number of years little progress was made. The EC appeared to be in danger of running out of steam. The deepening of the integrative process required action which the member states found controversial, new member nations introduced their own problems and perspectives, while the recession meant that the attitudes of the member nations hardened towards the necessary give and take that would be required if cooperative solutions to problems were to be found. A particular constraint was presented by the limits on EC finance which prevented the development of EC policies and led to bitter arguments about the resources devoted to the CAP. Internal divisions were compounded by fears of a lack of dynamism in the EC economy which threatened a relative decline in world terms. Such worries suggested that a significant leap forward was needed to ensure a real common market and to encourage new growth. To move the EC in this direction, however, and to modernise its institutions so that they worked more efficiently proved a laborious process. While member nations could agree upon the aim, in practice each one fought hard to ensure that the reforms incorporated measures favourable to its national interests.

As the debate progressed, a major division emerged between those who were primarily interested in the political ideal of European union and who wished to see institutional reform which would strengthen the EC's capacity to act, and those who had a more pragmatic approach which stressed the need for new policies, especially those directed to the stimulation of the economy. The idea of European union was built on, notably by an Italo–German proposal for a European Act (the Genscher–Colombo plan) and by the European Parliament, which adopted a draft treaty on European union in 1984. Meanwhile, a series of summit meetings was keeping the momentum going at the level of heads of state or government. The Stuttgart summit meeting of 1983 agreed on an impressive work programme of issues which needed solution and produced a 'Solemn Declaration on European Union'.[7] The vehement discussions of the following two years, often complicated by the need to solve more immediate problems, meant that it was not until the Luxemburg meeting in December 1985 that the lines of agreement could be settled. These were brought together in the Single European Act (SEA) which became operative on 1 July 1987.[8] Policy development is based upon the intention of having a true, single market in place by the end of 1992 with free movement of capital, labour, services and goods replacing the patchy arrangements of the past. The SEA also introduces, or strengthens, other policy fields. These include responsibilities towards the environment, the encouragement of further action to promote health and safety at work, technological research and development, work to strengthen economic and social cohesion so that weaker members may participate fully in the freer market, and cooperation in economic and monetary policy. In addition, the SEA brings foreign policy cooperation under its umbrella and provides it with a more effective support structure than it has had hitherto, including its own secretariat housed in the Council building in Brussels. Institutionally, it was agreed that the Council would take decisions on qualified majority vote in relation to the internal market, research, cohesion and improved working conditions and that, in such cases, Parliament should share in decision making (EC Commission, 1986c, pp. 29–31).

The work needed to achieve the single market in 1992 meant that Community institutions became more involved in matters upon which member states felt sensitive. At the same time, tumultuous changes in Eastern Europe altered the political environment for the EC. Both factors combined in the late 1980s to sharpen the debate about the future of the EC.

2.3 Community institutions

The EC in reality consists of three separate entities, each one created by its own treaty: the ECSC set up by the Treaty of Paris in 1951, valid for fifty years; the EEC by the Treaty of Rome in 1957, of unlimited duration; and the European Atomic Energy Community (Euratom) by a second, unlimited Treaty of Rome signed in 1957. Other texts have subsequently added to, or amended, these basic documents and the more important changes are incorporated in treaties which must be ratified by each member nation in accordance with its own legal processes. Thus changes in the budget procedures, agreements to admit new members and the changes to the SEA all form the subjects of special treaty instruments and the totality of these documents, together with the legislative acts to which they give rise and the rulings of the Court of Justice, can be considered as the constitution of the Community. EC legislation takes precedence over national decisions and a moment's reflection will show that this is a necessary precondition for the EC to work at all; it would be impossible otherwise to create the single economic unit, to establish the necessary confidence between the members or to handle external economic relations. The EC can be considered as a special form of international organisation, given the importance, complexity and far-reaching nature of the matters with which it deals, the integrative elements in its objectives and the close, intensive nature of its working methods. The fact that it does not always demonstrate a capacity to work well as a unit, together with the difficulty which arises because it is not fully competent in all respects, suggests that it is still in a transitional stage. Some authorities consider that it is, at present, best considered as a union of states (Brewin, 1987).

With the setting up of the EEC and Euratom by the same six countries that were already operating the ECSC, there was clearly a problem in the duplication of institutions. From the start all three had a single Assembly and Court of Justice and the two later Communities were provided with the same Economic and Social Committee. In 1965, in a document usually referred to as the Merger Treaty, a single Council and a single Commission were established for all three organisations and, from that time on, it has seemed more logical to refer to the whole structure as the European Community. However, the original treaties are still valid so that the responsibilities of the institutions vary according to the treaty under which they are operating. Significant differences relate to the responsibilities of the Commission which are more direct and decisive in relation to coal and steel than for the economy as a whole. If the executive (originally called the High Authority) was the centre of activity for the regulation of the coal and steel industries, the focal point for the EEC was rather the dual responsibility of the Council and Commission. The following discussion relates to the powers deriving from the Treaty of Rome setting up the EEC and from subsequent legislation, including the SEA.

All formal institutions created by the treaties have their part to play in the functioning of the EC. It is the totality of these activities which constitutes the EC method in decision taking which thus depends upon a *modus vivendi* existing between the units to allow the processes to operate. In practice, tensions exist between them and a traditional struggle for power is exhibited internally within the EC, as well as between the EC and the member states. The most critical struggle to date is probably still that between the Council and the Commission. This was an element in the political stagnation affecting the EC during 1965 and 1966 from which the Commission emerged chastened; but the budget arguments from the late 1970s onwards demonstrate the reality of the power struggle between Parliament and Council.

A Community decision normally arises as a result of a formal proposal from the Commission to the Council, which must itself decide whether to accept or reject the proposal in accordance with the agreed procedure. The Council can amend a proposal only on a unanimous vote; this is in order to prevent the emasculation of general propositions in the interest of individual member nations. If action is then required, the proposal will take one of two forms. It may become a *regulation*, which is directly applicable in its precise form to all members. Alternatively, it may emerge as a *directive* which is binding in its objective but allows states to achieve it in their own way. It is also possible to take a *decision* which is binding on those, whether states or firms, to whom it is addressed, while *recommendations* and *opinions*, which can also be made, have no binding force.[9] These formal acts, more particularly the regulations and directives, are constantly adding to EC law.

Behind this legal structure lies a very complex process which involves a great many people and much political machinery. However, there is little doubt that, in relation to the formulation of policy and its translation into the necessary decisions, the two key units are still the Council and the Commission. It is convenient, therefore, to begin with them.

The Council consists of representatives of member governments and meetings are therefore attended by governmental ministers. Its decisions are taken by unanimous, simple or qualified majority voting and, when the last method is used, the system is weighted both in favour of the larger members and by the necessity of carrying at least one of the smaller ones along with the decision. In this way it is hoped to arrive at decisions supported by a wide spectrum of opinion. It was originally intended that, as the EC became established and confidence grew, the Council would increasingly move towards the use of majority voting; but states have proved extremely reluctant to allow this to happen. By 1966, a formal agreement recognised that unanimity would continue to be used whenever a member considered the matter under discussion to be of vital national importance. The Council has subsequently used unanimous voting as its general rule, with the understanding that a state can abstain from voting on a matter which is not of vital interest to it, but which it would rather not support, without preventing agreement among the rest. Swifter methods of decision making in the Council became urgently necessary and were debated at the highest level until the agreement, already mentioned, in the SEA. This extends the use of qualified majority voting to a wide range of decisions concerning the completion of the EC internal market, research and development and the improvement of the working environment. However, even here there are certain matters, for example taxation, where the new voting rule does not apply or where derogations can be permitted (Article 100A). Unanimity is also required for setting up the broad, framework programmes for technological research and development.

Representatives of the Commission also attend Council meetings and play an active part in helping to reach a decision, although the Commission has no voting rights. It is here, however, that it can perform an important mediatory function between national viewpoints and its own, which is intended to represent the general EC interest.

The presidency of the Council is held by each member state in turn for a six-month period and the chairmanship of many EC committees alters correspondingly. It has become the practice for each member state to try to establish a particular style of working and to single out certain matters to which it wishes to give priority. Since any chairman can influence business significantly, the president of the Council may occupy an important, albeit temporary, role. The president will also fulfil certain representational functions both towards other EC institutions, notably the European Parliament, and in external negotiations where the presidents of the Council and the Commission may act in association.

Membership of the Council varies according to the subject matter under review. Although the Council of Foreign Ministers is still thought of as the most senior, an increasingly wide range of national ministers is called upon to attend as the scope of the EC develops. This growth has brought its own problems for national governments. As EC issues are handled by various ministers briefed by their own departments it becomes less likely that any government can see its EC policy as a coherent whole. In turn, coordination methods at home become important. For the EC, too, the greater specialisation of the Council creates difficulties. The ensuing compartmentalisation of business means it is more difficult to negotiate EC policy. One issue can no longer be so readily considered in relation to others so that the famous 'package deals' which enabled the EC to arrive at new positions are harder to achieve. The Council of Agricultural Ministers, in particular, has developed a life and status of its own (Edwards and Wallace, 1977, p. 6).

The Council is served by its own secretariat which is separate from the Commission and it is also supported by a most important body, the *Committee of Permanent Representatives* (Coreper). The member states gave formal recognition to this group in 1965, but the need for an organisation of senior officials to prepare meetings and to handle business between meetings of the Council had been felt for a long time. Members of this committee are of ambassadorial rank and are supported by a web of specialist and subordinate committees, often including members of home departments who travel to Brussels when they are required.

Coreper also prepares the work of the Council which can, in turn, assign work to it. In 1966, it was agreed that it would be desirable for the Commission to contact national governments, via Coreper, before deciding on the form of an intended proposal. As a result of its links with both Council and Commission, Coreper is involved in all major stages of EC policy making, ranging from early discussions to final Council decision taking and it forms an essential link between the Community and national governments. Many matters of policy are, in fact, agreed by Coreper and reach the Council only in a formal sense.

While this was one way of keeping EC business, which was growing rapidly, under control, it meant that the Council itself became concerned only with important matters or those which, of no great substance in themselves, were still politically sensitive. Even though they might be of only sectional interest it became easy for the domestic media to present Council meetings as national battles in which victory or defeat was the key issue. Politicians, too, became more adept at using publicity in order to rally support for the national view. This result is the opposite of what was originally intended when it was thought that the experience of working together would make it progressively easier to reach agreement expressive of the general good for which majority voting would be a suitable tool. The conflict between national interests is now openly expressed at the European Council as well.

Practical problems are also encountered by the Council. The great press of business, the fact that ministers can attend to Council affairs only part-time, the highly sensitive nature of their activities and the larger number of members all contribute to a grave timelag in reaching policy decisions. The reforms of the SEA are designed to improve Council working and prevent it being the bottleneck it has been in the past (Edwards and Wallace, 1977, p. 103). Efficiency depends upon maintaining the political impetus towards achieving the internal market by the agreed date and only the future can show if the balance between EC unity, on the one hand, and the protection of national interests, on the other, has in fact nudged towards the former.

The second essential element in the making of EC policy is the *Commission*. This now consists of seventeen members, all nationals of the twelve member states and chosen on grounds of competence and capacity to act independently in the interest of the EC itself. They are thus charged not to take instructions from governments and accept the responsibility and limitations on action involved in this position. France, West Germany, Italy, Spain and the United Kingdom have two members each and Belgium, Denmark, Greece, Ireland, Luxemburg, the Netherlands and Portugal have one each. Commissioners are chosen by common agreement of governments for a period of four years with renewable appointments. Both the president and vice-presidents are chosen from the seventeen by governments for a two-year renewable period. In practice, an individual can expect at least two terms of presidential office, although not all presidents have remained for so long. Many of them, however, have been men significant in national politics, thus able to meet ministers of the Council on equal terms and familiar with the political pressures with which the EC must grapple. This experience should enable the Commission to retain both the political stature and sense of touch which are essential attributes for its effective functioning. The Commission that was appointed in 1989 contained two women members for the first time.

Each commissioner has responsibility for one or more major EC policies and, although in form the Commission is a collegiate body accepting responsibility for action as a group, in practice policy rests mainly with the responsible commissioner, often in association with two or more colleagues. Many observers believe that there are now too many commissioners for the work available, but national pride has prevented any reform. Adoption by the Commission as a body is often formal but, unlike the Council, it has always used majority voting in its meetings. No other arrangement would permit the Commission to deal with the large volume of work now involved.

The commissioners are supported in two ways. The Continental practice of a private office has been followed and each commissioner has his own *chef de cabinet*, normally of the same nationality as him or herself, who is not a career diplomat. These assistants take many decisions on behalf of their chiefs. Secondly, there is the Commission staff itself. This is organised into *general directorates* corresponding to the main areas of EC policy. In total, there are about eleven thousand civil servants, including a large number of translators and interpreters. Often the work of the Commission seems rather slow; but integrating the detail of national economies and using nine official languages makes for great complexity. The general directorates are composed of staff of various nationalities and it is, of course, important to try to ensure that no one national viewpoint becomes predominant, especially among the more senior staff. Over time some directorates have won a higher prestige than others, while the development of EC policies brings the possibility of conflict between one directorate and another. For example, a stronger regional policy can cut across the competition policy, or special access for Third World goods can conflict with some agricultural interests. In the resolution of policy conflicts the relative strength and competence of the directorates is likely to be one factor determining the result if not, as yet, the major one. Directorates also alter to meet the changing pattern of work. Thus the introduction of the internal market and the impact of information technology are two subjects currently involving great Commission activity.

The directorates are not only responsible for the initiation of proposals which will become the basis of a Commission proposal and, if accepted, of an EC decision; they are also involved in the administration of policy once it is agreed. The extent of their involvement varies and a great deal of EC policy is not executed by the Commission at all, but by national administrations. One area in which the Commission is closely involved is agriculture because of the daily management of markets which the CAP involves. Here a structure of management committees brings both the Commission and the national administrations into a joint system. Even so the day-to-day execution of the CAP, as well as the application and collection of the important levies and duties on imports, is handled by national ministries on behalf of the EC. A second area of work in which the Commission is administratively concerned is competition policy, which requires the Commission to register and investigate certain agreements between firms to ensure they conform to EC rules. Here it is in direct contact with individual firms and this is also the case in the execution of certain functions relating to the coal and steel industries.

Of rather different character is the work of the Commission in administering the various funds of the EC. Although the governing rules reflect EC policy, there is a degree of discretion in the allocation of monies to particular schemes and it is usual for the Commission to be assisted by an advisory committee in the administration of the social (ESF), regional (ERDF) and agricultural guidance (EAGGF) funds. Since the grants, in turn, are disbursed to projects by national administrations, there is again close contact between home civil services and the Commission.

It was recognised by the SEA (Article 10) that the implementation of Council acts would have to be done by the Commission but this sparked off a bitter dispute about the proper extent of the Commission's powers and the need for an associated committee structure. It also presented a further challenge to the Commission to act effectively. The development of the internal market requires a vast array of harmonising directives and other legislation which it will be important to monitor closely. Progress will be needed in other policies, too, if the EC is not to develop lopsidedly. These tasks require internal adaptation by the Commission and require it to be increasingly active. However, if it becomes more powerful, the question of its accountability will become more important. The collective responsibility of the Commission at present is to Parliament, which alone has the power to dismiss it as a body, although it cannot dismiss individual commissioners. It is Parliament, too, which debates the annual report which the Commission is obliged to issue and which receives a verbal statement of the Commission's intentions for the year ahead. As detailed executive responsibilities grow, the case for individual commissioners to be more openly responsible for their decisions and those of their staffs will become stronger.

An important function of the Commission is to ensure that the members abide by their obligations or, as it is normally described, to act as the guardian of the treaties. It is essential that the rules are actively applied in each member state and that states retain confidence in the arrangements and each other. In many cases, keeping states and firms up to the mark results simply from day-to-day business and through normal liaison between them and the Commission but, in more important cases, or if there should be a deliberate evasion of the rules, other steps become necessary. The Commission can investigate a suspected breach of obligation and issue a *reasoned opinion*. If matters are not set right, the Commission is entitled to refer the matter to the Court of Justice. Although the Commission has few direct sanctions it has the power to fine firms which breach certain operational rules, while member states have, so far, generally accepted their obligations to abide by EC decisions. Recent evidence suggests that member states are becoming more reluctant to implement agreed decisions and if this trend is confirmed it will have a serious effect on development (Butt Philip, 1988).

Considerable interest attaches to the functions of the Commission as initiator of policy and exponent of the EC interest. These arise in a formal sense from the fact that the Council waits upon the Commission to send it proposals upon which it must take its decisions. Thus the working of the EC depends upon the activity of the Commission and the quality of its work. With the need to develop a range of policies and to implement them through legislation in order to fulfil the provisions of the SEA, the Commission's role is crucial. In working out its proposals, however, the Commission is subject to a number of influences. It must take account of the views of Parliament if the cooperation procedure is to work well (see below), while the regular meetings of the European Council provide broad directional guidelines for policy. In order to formulate a policy proposal, the appropriate directorate will undertake extensive discussions with both government departments and representatives of interested firms and other groups. It may carry out, or commission, initial studies. All this knowledge will contribute to a Commission proposal. Once a matter has reached this stage, it can then be discussed with Coreper and by Parliament and the Economic and Social Committee before finally reaching the Council itself. These extensive and lengthy discussions are undertaken to try to obtain an agreed position which will prove to be acceptable to member states and, at the same time, enhance the process of European integration.

Thus the responsibilities of the Commission fall under several headings. Some are executive in nature; but its functions extend to the initiation of policy, the protection of EC interests, the mediation between national interests and the protection of the treaty structure and subsequent rules. It also has the power to raise loans for agreed purposes. Thus the Commission is a body not paralleled by any national equivalent. At one time it was thought that the Commission might become a neutral body for the implementation of Council decisions; but the structure of the treaties prevents this. The link with Parliament, and its own treaty powers, mean that the Commission is not just the creature of the Council, although the balance tipped towards the Council after the middle of the 1960s. With the rise of the Council, the introduction of the European Council and the build up of political cooperation the Commission can pursue its integrative tasks only in ways which are broadly acceptable to the member nations and other European institutions.

The *Court of Justice* is an integral part of the institutional structure. The EC is a highly complex body, created by treaties which lay down the operating rules for the various institutions and the basic rules for economic integration. They constantly give rise to new legal obligations in the form of regulations and directives. A court is necessary for several reasons. It must ensure that the institutions act in a constitutional manner, fulfilling the obligations laid on them by the treaties; but it must also ensure the observance of an ever growing volume of EC rules by member states, firms and individuals. This is not just a question of pronouncing upon any possible infringements of the EC legal system, although these may include matters ranging from a refusal to implement an EC rule to slow application due to lax national administration. It includes the need to guide national courts in their interpretation of EC law. A uniform application of the law, although necessary for the EC to function properly, is a slow business and difficult to achieve since it has to be incorporated into twelve legal systems, each with their own norms and methods of work. The difficulty is compounded since in many areas EC rules continue to operate alongside national ones, for the treaty is not fully comprehensive and the problems presented by overlapping systems may prove complicated. It is not surprising that a great deal of work for the Court arises from policies for agriculture, competition and social security for migrants where states have their own pre-existing policies, where both national and EC rules are complex and where interests overlap.

The Court consists of thirteen judges and six advocates-general, the latter being responsible for preliminary investigation of a matter and for submitting a reasoned opinion to the judges to help them come to a decision. In its method of working the Court is heavily influenced by the legal systems of the members, particularly of the original six member states. It will hear cases brought by the Commission against member states or against the Council, cases brought by member states against each other or against the Council or Commission or by a natural or legal person against an EC decision which affects him or her. The Council and Commission can also be charged with failure to act. The Court may impose penalties for the infringement of regulations. It is also responsible for the interpretation of the treaties and their secondary legislation at the request of a national court or tribunal which has to apply the rules. States agreed from the start that they would abide by the judgements of the Court and the fact that, in practice, they mainly do so is an important factor in maintaining the validity of the EC system.

In recent years the Court of Justice has become increasingly worried about the build up of work. It is important that there should be no serious delay since large business and commercial decisions may be affected and the whole basis of the single market could be jeopardised if firms have to wait too long before knowing where they stand. Similarly, if the Court cannot pronounce with reasonable despatch, national courts will become reluctant to refer for preliminary rulings and the application of a uniform EC law will falter. A provision was, therefore, inserted into the SEA to allow the Council to establish a *Court of First Instance*. This will handle issues on the business side, such as cases involving competition policy, together with staff cases. It will not, at present, be able to hear cases brought by states or EC institutions or handle requests for preliminary rulings and there will be a right of appeal on points of law from the cases that it does hear. The future will show if the reform has been enough to keep the flow of cases moving.

A relatively young institution is the *Court of Auditors*, which began work in 1977 in response to growing demands, especially from Parliament, for a closer audit and clarification of the EC general budget. This is now a complicated affair, made up in a tortuous way and, since it grows by accretion, is likely to become more, rather than less, difficult to understand. It is the job of the Court of Auditors to monitor income and expenditure much more thoroughly than in the past, by checking on the use made of EC monies by the member states and on their procedures for the collection of duties and levies as well as on the administrative procedures of the institutions, particularly of the Commission.

It is now time to turn to the place of the *European Parliament*. This depends not just on treaty provision but upon Parliament's own ability to exploit its position to its own advantage. In recent years it has become more adroit at this. It has a major, formal control mechanism in its ability to dismiss the Commission. This is usually considered to be a power of little value for, by exercising it, Parliament would bring the EC to a halt and it has no responsibility for appointing a new Commission. It could, however, continue to dismiss the Commission until it was satisfied with the result. A vote of censure on the Commission has been used occasionally and this can be a way of expressing a strongly held view, carrying the possibility of a change of heart by the Commission or, indirectly, the Council; Parliament has experimented with this tactic. Parliament may use it as a form of protest when, for example, it considers that intended policy reflects national interests too much and EC interest too little. Here it is not so much legal form that is important as the political weight carried by Parliament, which can make Council and Commission unwilling to flout its views.

Parliament has also become more effective in the use of its powers to ask questions, both verbally and in writing, as a means of keeping both Council and Commission up to the mark, and it receives, and comments on, reports from these two bodies. Since 1974, the foreign ministers have been meeting four times a year with the Political Committee of the European Parliament for discussions on foreign policy issues and, two years later, this work was brought into question time.

The original treaties laid down occasions upon which Parliament must be consulted before a final decision is taken by the Council and, in practice, it has been consulted on all significant issues. This is done by Parliament formulating views on Commission proposals which are studied and reported on by the appropriate parliamentary committee. The main parliamentary session then discusses the report and passes a resolution on it, in this way coming to a formal view. The committees meet between sessions and are in close contact with the Commission while working on their reports; committee members may therefore develop considerable expertise in particular problems.

Until recently it was possible for Parliament's views to be legally disregarded, although they had to be received by the Council. There is no doubt that members felt considerable frustration as a result. However, the SEA gave Parliament a limited, but real, place in the legislative process which may ultimately lead to a more even balance between Council, Commission and Parliament. It did this by introducing a new stage so that a second reading is taken, although only on certain matters. Under the 'cooperation procedure' (SEA Article 6), the Council must act in cooperation with Parliament in policy concerning the internal market and related affairs, the ERDF and the detailed application of research and development programmes. Here the Council, which will have previously received Parliament's opinion, must adopt a common position. Parliament can accept, reject or amend Council policy within three months. If it rejects the policy, then the Council can still go ahead but only on a unanimous view. If the proposal is amended then a complex re-examination procedure by both Council and Commission begins which may result in the acceptance of Parliament's amendments, possibly in a modified form.

Parliament thus has a toe in the legislative process. It is more than ever to its advantage to work closly with the Commission at all stages in order to ensure that its views find their way into the proposals formally submitted to the Council in the first place. The changes also require more efficient working procedures for Parliament so that decisions are taken within the time limit and any amendments are clear and precise. Parliament has had to devise new working methods which are a good deal sharper than those used in the past. It is necessary, too, for it to ensure a majority vote in favour of its amendments. Since Parliament contains views which cross the political spectrum it now has to engage in more political bargaining among its political parties than hitherto.

One important development of Parliament's powers came when it was given a degree of control over the budget. This followed the Council agreement of 1970 that the EC should become autonomous in financial matters over a phased period through allowing the proceeds of the agricultural levies and customs duties to accrue to the EC as a unit. Since it was known that this money would not be enough for EC activities, it was further agreed that, after a temporary period when member nations would fill the gap by direct contributions, it should acquire a proportion of VAT levied in all member countries. This, in its turn, became inadequate and in February 1988 a summit meeting agreed a new basis for additional contribution, based on GNP (see Chapter 14). There have been, and remain, grave administrative problems associated with the arrangements and the budget has, at least in the past, given rise to serious political difficulties. Nevertheless, once the principle that the EC should become responsible for its own monies had been accepted, it was agreed that some form of parliamentary control had to be established and a treaty to give effect to such streng-thened powers was signed in 1970, with amendments in 1971 and 1975. The actual stages for the establishment and adoption of the Community's budget have become extremely complex and Parliament has fought hard to see its powers extended as a way of obtaining a more important position in the EC structure.

A draft budget is made up by the Commission, normally by September, for expenditure for the following year. This is then adopted by the Council acting on a qualified majority vote. This draft budget is then sent to Parliament for discussion. The key to understanding Parliament's budgetary control lies in the distinction between 'compulsory' and 'non-compulsory' expenditure, the former deriving from the treaty and largely consisting of the costs of the CAP – see Chapters 9 and 14. Compulsory expenditure has formed about 70 per cent of the total budget although, consequent upon the 1988 budget agreement, it is planned that the budget share taken by agriculture should fall. Compulsory expenditure may be modified in the first instance by a majority of parliamentary votes cast, but these changes must subse-quently be agreed, or rejected, by the Council. Non-compulsory expenditure may be modified by a parliamentary majority of all members, but there is a given limit beyond which Parliament cannot make increases in non-compulsory expenditure. Although the Council may subsequently amend the decision, Parliament must receive the total draft budget back for a second reading and at this point it may reject the Council's changes in the non-compulsory category. Finally, Parliament is entitled to reject the draft budget entirely and demand a new one or, alternatively, it must formally approve the final form. Parliament has made full use of the procedural powers thus given to it to try to force changes in budget expenditure.

Once both Council and Parliament had been given budgetary powers, it was necessary to strengthen procedures for consultation between them. Procedural matters are dealt with through the concertation procedure and policy issues through the conciliation procedure. These methods are intended to resolve disagreements through mutual concession and compromise and to allow for early discussion of proposals likely to give rise to future expenditure (Secretariat of the European Parlia-ment, 1983, p. 12). Council, Commission and Parliament now all realise that they must try to resolve their budgetary aims so that EC activity will not be held up because the budget has not been passed and in 1982 the three institutions issued a declaration on this point.[10]

Parliament has two important practical problems to resolve. It does not yet have a single, uniform voting procedure in use throughout the EC for the election of its members, and there are severe imbalances of size and population between the constituencies. A major question relates to the site of Parliament. Nowadays it normally meets in Strasbourg, while most committee work is carried out in Brussels with a large part of the secretariat based in Luxemburg. So far, agreement on a more viable plan has proved elusive. A more rational arrangement would not only ease many practical difficulties but help Parliament to become a more coherent and effective organisation.

The European Parliament is remarkable for having achieved the first international election in June 1979 and members (MEPs) are elected every five years. Once elected, MEPs are organised in political rather than in national groups although, in some cases, national identity remains very strong. Before the 1989 elections, there were 165 Socialists, 115 European People's Party (including Christian Democrats, Fine Gael), 66 European Democrats (including British Conservatives), 48 Communist and Allies, 44 Liberal and Democratic Reformist group, 29 European Democratic Alliance (including Gaullists, Fianna Fail, Scottish Nationalists), 20 Rainbow group (including Greens), 16 European Right group, 15 Independent, although there is some movement between the parties. There are 518 members in all; 81 from West Germany, France, Italy and the United Kingdom, 60 from Spain, 25 from the Netherlands, 24 from Belgium, Greece and Portugal, 16 from Denmark, 15 from Ireland and 6 from Luxemburg.

The 1989 elections saw a general swing away from support for the parties holding national power and a rise in support for fringe parties. The immediate results made the Socialists into the largest single party with 180 seats followed by the European People's Party with 123 (Christian Democrats and Spanish People's Party). The Liberals won 44 seats, the Communists 41, the Rainbow group (including Greens) 39, the European Democratic Group 34, European Right 21, European Democratic Alliance 20 and Independents 16. The greatest uncertainty at the moment relates to the European Democratic group, which consists of a diminished British Conservative group and two Conservative Danes who are expected to look for a base elsewhere. The British Conservatives thus find themselves in an unloved position and their final home is uncertain. They may draw some comfort from the fact that there is more interest at Westminster in strengthening links with the British MEPs now that the European Parliament has greater power and as the internal market approaches.

Parliament is still in an evolutionary stage and a belief that it will develop into an institution akin to a national parliament is not necessarily correct. Apart from the fact that it now has twelve national models to follow, it operates in a different environment from any of them. Fears that it will become locked in a struggle with national parliaments have not materialised, for its attention is primarily fixed on its relations with the Council and Commission and the need to formulate views on matters which are EC-wide in scope.

Apart from its specific functions, Parliament plays an important role of a general consultative and informative nature, helping to make public opinion more aware of EC activity. It is an important channel through which information and knowledge are transmitted back to member states. This task is not, however, exclusive to Parliament and a vast battery of machinery exists to act as another link in the communications chain and which plays its part in shaping EC decisions. One of the formal mechanisms is the *Economic and Social Committee* which was given advisory status by the Treaty of Rome and designed to represent the various categories of economic and social activity such as employers, unions, farmers and the self-employed together with representatives from community and social organisations. It has 189 members, appointed by the Council on the basis of national lists, each member appointed for four years and acting in a personal capacity. For practical purposes members are considered as coming from three main groups, namely employers, unions and representatives of the general interests. Each national delegation reflects this tripartite composition. It is usual to seek the opinion of the committee on all major policy proposals and the committee will also formulate its own opinions on subjects it considers important.

The committee has found it difficult to establish an effective voice in EC affairs and there are several reasons for this. Not only did the treaty give it a purely consultative role, but its heterogeneous composition suggests that it is unlikely to be able to produce a single point of view except of a general nature. Thus the choice before the committee is either to produce an agreed, but bland, report or to recognise the diverse interests of its members by producing a set of reports on each significant issue. Either way, the committee findings are likely to be of limited effectiveness and the search for agreement which it often undertakes means that the reports frequently appear too late to be useful. Thus the utility of the committee must be looked for elsewhere. It is helpful to the Council and, more particularly, the Commission that the views of these groups throughout the EC should be available before policy has hardened and the discussions in the committee provide this information. Meetings also enable like-minded people throughout the EC to meet and discuss and help to build up a core of people knowledgeable about EC affairs. It seems logical, too, that Parliament should find a way of making use of the specialised knowledge of committee members.

The committee, which is paralleled by a *Consultative Committee* confined to the coal and steel industry, by no means exhausts the EC committee structure. The Commission is supported by a set of advisory committees in its fund-giving operations and by a range of working parties and committees for particular industries and problems. During the 1970s, a *Standing Committee on Employment* was reactivated and strengthened. This represents national employment ministers, employers and unions as well as the Commission and is a reflection of the current concern with the economy, the effect of inflation and structural change on employment levels and the particular difficulties experienced by workers in declining industries. To some extent this group overlaps in interest with the Economic and Social Committee and there may be room for rationalisation, leaving the former to industrial interests and the latter to develop a stronger citizen voice.

In some ways, for both interest groups and for the man or woman in the street who wishes to make the effort, the EC, and particularly the Commission, is more accessible than a national administration. This is in part because of the consultation procedures which, although clumsy, do bring a wide range of people into contact with EC affairs. It is also the result of a well-established Commission policy of informing and educating the public in order to mobilise public opinion behind the integration process. So far, the EC has been more successful in creating this awareness among opinion formers and those whose work brings them into direct contact with the EC than it has with the general public. Its purpose and intentions have been better understood by bankers, industrialists and union and organisational representatives than by the ordinary citizen, thus giving an elitist impression. Many of the proposals of the drive to achieve a 'People's Europe' (see Chapter 17) are designed to counter this image.

Standing apart from these institutions is the *European Investment Bank* (EIB) which was given the task of contributing to the balanced and steady development of the common market in the interest of the EC. It has three main fields of operation: to aid regional development, to help with projects made necessary by the establishment of the common market for which normal financial means are lacking and to assist projects of common interest to members which need extra finance. Thus the EIB is an additional source of finance in many different circumstances, designed to assist in the development of the EC. It is not, however, a grant-aiding fund but a bank operating normal banking criteria whose capital is contributed by the member nations and by its own ability to raise money on normal markets. In recent years its fields of interest have included the reduction of dependence on imported energy supplies, the modernisation of communications, the development of advanced technology and environmental protection; it is particularly concerned with regional disparities. It is also used as the channel for loans guaranteed by the EC budget and this is especially important for loans made to Third World and Mediterranean countries.

It can therefore be seen that the formal structure of the institutions presents a deceptively simple picture of the working of the EC and perhaps particularly so in the area of decision making. There is a constant hum of discussion and negotiation with both formal and informal institutions as well as with interested individuals and this is often duplicated in the national capitals. The problem is not so much one of lack of consultation as of the lack of decisiveness which results from the accommodation of many interests and the alignment of national policies in which agreement may have to take precedence over the soundness of policy. To this we may add the lack of consideration of points of view which are not effectively organised and the slowness of action to which the procedures contribute.

2.4 The future

The EC recently took a step towards internal consolidation and accepted the need for consequential institutional reform by passing the SEA. Discussions on the internal market revealed a range of issues for which the EC has to find a solution. For example, full and easy movement for EC citizens implies a loosening of national border controls and this in turn requires stronger, and agreed, checks on the external frontiers. The ramifications of the internal market are very wide and its implementation will extend the scope of EC interest as gaps in policy are revealed. A second group of problems relates to the economic development of the EC. This runs a risk of becoming seriously ill balanced under the pressure of the single-market drive. A strong political will is necessary to establish countervailing policies whose costs are likely to be heavy. A third question is that of EC accountability to a democratic electorate. The SEA has not solved this problem but the issue must become of greater importance as EC policies develop. Existing scrutiny arrangements have developed nationally and they are known to vary considerably in their effectiveness. It is believed they will become harder to operate as the single market matures (House of Lords, 1985–6).

The EC also faces a new political situation to set alongside its economic future. The recent admission of Portugal and Spain means that the balance of interest of the members has shifted towards the geographical south and to problems of regional backwardness. This is a counterweight to the drive to a single internal market from which the sophisticated, industrial members hope to benefit, and it gives point to the policy of economic and social cohesion. Much time is likely to be spent on the problems of the Mediterranean area, not just because of the last enlargement but because the non-members in North Africa are keenly interested in, and affected by, the changing internal emphasis. Turkey is actively canvassing for membership although it is generally accepted that this will not occur for many years. Other non-members, such as the EFTA states, may seek membership or close association as the attractions of the internal market are felt. It seems likely that the EC will have to go further in establishing its international identity. Political cooperation is a necessity if the EC is to 'speak with one voice' abroad and it may not be able to avoid the defence implications of foreign policy indefinitely. At present, there are great differences of view on these matters. A noticeable development of recent years has been the growth of European cooperative ventures outside the framework of the EC but within the broad grouping of the Western European nations: the European Space Agency and Eureka are two examples. The EC may have to adjust to finding a place in a wider spectrum rather than simply confining itself to its own affairs. The issue raised at the outset, namely the relationship between the EC and the rest of Western Europe, may be about to return to the political agenda.

In the recent past, the EC dissipated much energy on its internal problems, often centring them around finance and the share of resources devoted to agriculture. These issues have stood in the way of the rational consideration of other questions. It is probably overoptimistic to suppose that these arguments have been finally laid to rest. The hope has to be that the visible benefits of the internal market outweigh the disadvantages and imperfections that the political compromises on these matters will, no doubt, bring. There is a great contrast between the success of the EC in its early years and its stagnation in the 1970s. This was not due solely to its internal inadequacies but was, in part, the result of the unfavourable international economic environment of the later period. This made members acutely conscious of the price they would pay for necessary reforms and fearful in case compensating benefits did not materialise. This attitude can still be detected in the SEA in the areas reserved for unanimous decision, the possibility of derogations from the rules and in the reservations which members have attached to the treaty. The EC has to take on board the fact that it is vulnerable to the outside world. A major task for the immediate future is to find the means of exerting the influence its weight demands in order to maintain the buoyant liberal trading community it requires in order to flourish and ensure the achievement of its own internal goals. For all these reasons, it seems that the EC will have to devote increasing attention to external relations. All these changing policy requirements are bound to place great weight on the institutional structure, querying its adequacy and keeping alive the issue of the need to strengthen it further.

Notes

1. Sweet & Maxwell, *European Community Treaties*, is regularly updated.
2. There is a considerable literature on the post-1945 attempts to give Europe new political institutions. See, e.g., Camps (1964), Haas (1967), Lindberg (1963), Mayne (1970), Palmer and Lambert (1968). Pryce (1973) provides a later account, while for recent developments see Pryce (1987), Wallace and Ridley (1985).
3. On OEEC and the various moves to create European organisations see Palmer and Lambert (1968).
4. The Schuman Plan of 9 May 1950 is printed in Royal Institute of International Affairs (1953) *Documents on International Affairs, 1949–50*, pp. 315–17.
5. This is very clearly explained by Max Kohnstamm in his essay *The European Tide*; see Graubard (1964), especially pp. 151–2. The author was part of the Dutch delegation for the ECSC talks and subsequently had a distinguished career in EC institutions.
6. There were several versions of the plan during the negotiations but it is unnecessary to consider the details here.
7. *Bulletin of the European Communities*, 1983, no. 6; 'Work programme', 1.5.2 *et seq.*; 'Solemn declaration', 1.6.1 *et seq.*
8. *Bulletin of the European Communities*, Supplement 2/1986; text of the SEA.
9. Terminology under the Treaty of Paris is confusingly different. *Decisions* are binding in entirety, *recommendations* binding as to ends but not means, and *opinions* have no binding force.
10. Joint Tripartite Declaration, *OJC*, 194, 28 July 1982.

3 The basic statistics of the EC

A. M. El-Agraa

The purpose of this chapter is to provide the reader with a brief summary of the basic economic statistics of the EC which are used in the analytical chapters. For comparative purposes and in order to preserve a general sense of perspective, similar information is given for Canada, Japan, the United States, the USSR (where available) and for the potential EC member countries: Turkey (because it has already applied for membership) and all the member nations of EFTA.

The main purpose of this chapter is to provide information; the analysis of most of these statistics and the economic forces that determine them is one of the main tasks of the rest of this book. For example, the analysis of the composition and pattern of trade prior to the inception of the EC and subsequent to its formation is the basic aim of the theoretical and empirical section of the book. Moreover, the policy chapters are concerned with the analysis of particular areas of interest: the CAP, the role of the EC general budget, competition and industrial policies, the EC regional policy, etc., and these specialist chapters contain further relevant and more detailed information.

The statistical data given in this chapter are not intended to provide a comprehensive coverage of all the comparative information needed for a proper understanding of each nation's economic situation in isolation, nor in relation to the EC as a whole, but rather to give some notion of the general economic structure of the individual countries. Hence the choice of the sample years (for most tables) between 1965 and 1986 as the reference years is, for the purposes of this chapter, somewhat arbitrary: 1986 is the latest year for which data are available at the time of writing. Finally, since most of the data are self-explanatory, the description in this chapter is confined to just some of the tables.

3.1 The basic statistics

3.1.1 Area, population, life and death

Table A3.1a (the tables may be found in the appendix at the end of the chapter) gives information about area, population, crude birth and death rates and life expectancy at birth. The data are more or less self-explanatory but a few points warrant particular attention.

The Community of twelve has a larger population (about 323 million) than any country in the advanced Western world. This population exceeds that of the USSR (about 281 million) and of the United States (about 242 million) and is more than two and a half times that of Japan. It exceeds the combined population of the United States and Canada (which have agreed to form a free trade area) by more than 50 million and is only about 40 million less than the combined population of Japan and the United States.

A quick comparison of the first two columns of Table A3.1a reveals that the member nations of the EC have higher population densities than Canada and the United States. However, the population densities within the EC exhibit great diversity with the Netherlands and Belgium at the top of the league and Spain, Greece and Ireland at the bottom. It should be stressed that population density has important implications for the potential growth and the future of the social policies of the EC.

The average rate of increase of population between 1965 and 1980 was quite variable for the member nations of the EC. It was low in the United Kingdom (0.2 per cent), Belgium (0.3 per cent) and West Germany (0.3 per cent), but high in the Netherlands (0.9 per cent), Spain (1.0 per cent) and Ireland (1.2 per cent). The remaining EC nations occupied the middle ground. For the same period, among the member countries of EFTA, Austria and Finland had the same rate as West Germany with the remaining countries experiencing a rate of about 0.5 per cent, which is near the average for the EC as a whole. All the other countries shown in the table had high rates, with Turkey being completely out of line with a rate of 2.4 per cent. For the period 1980–6, the rates declined for all the countries except for Finland, Turkey and the USSR, where it increased by about one percentage point, and the United States where it remained at the 1.0 per cent rate. Thus Turkey continued to be the only country completely out of line within this group of nations.

The crude birth rate for Ireland (1.2 per cent) is distinctly different from that of the remaining member nations of the EC, although the Netherlands (0.9 per cent) and Spain (1.0 per cent) are not, in this respect, far behind. The rates for the potential member countries are about the average for the EC as whole, except for Turkey which has a rate exceeding that of Ireland by just under two-thirds. It is interesting to note that the rates for the 'other' countries are similar to those of Ireland and Spain. The crude death rate is also high for Ireland (0.8 per cent) and Spain (0.6 per cent), and is even higher for the 'other' countries, with Turkey (2.5 per cent) again being the real exception. There is no contradiction between these rates and those for the annual average rates of growth of population; indeed, the two seem to reinforce each other. If there are any discrepancies at all, differences in infant mortality rates, death rates, population composition, migration, etc., would readily explain these. The figures of particular importance are the annual average rates of growth and life expectancy at birth (which is not appreciably different for all the countries in the table except for Turkey – the low provision of doctors and nurses given in Table A3.20 for Turkey may provide a partial explanation).

However, one should be careful not to read too much into such comparisons – there is always the danger that they may distract the reader from some obvious and basic realities of life: the cultural diversity of the member nations of the EC relative to the almost common historical evolution and economic development of the United States, the contrasting political systems of the countries compared, etc.

3.1.2 GNP and inflation

Table A3.1b gives GNP per capita (total GDP is provided in Table A3.2) and its average annual rate of growth between 1965 and 1986. The table also provides the annual inflation rates for the period 1980–6. One of the salient features of this table is the disparity between the member nations of the EC in terms of per capita GNP: Portugal, Greece, Spain and Ireland lag far behind (in the order given) the rest. Most of the member countries of EFTA have per capita incomes exceeding the highest within the EC. Turkey's is just less than half that of the poorest nation within the EC. Note also that Denmark and West Germany are on equal terms with Japan, but lag behind Switzerland, the United States, Norway and Canada (which rank in that order).

The reader should also note that the 'net material product' of the USSR for 1971 was $288 billion and the per capita 'net material product' for the same year was $1,175 (Cairncross, 1974, p. 20), which is equivalent to a per capita income of $1,645 (the discrepancy arises from a difference in definition: the USSR does not include 'services' in its net material product). In 1974 the per capita income (using GDP equivalent terminology) was $2,964 according to the 1974 edition of the *National Economy of the USSR*. By 1979, per capita income had risen to $4,110, but this is the latest information available at the time of writing.

For the period 1958–64, the United Kingdom showed the slowest rate of growth of GDP in comparison with the original six member nations of the EC. Indeed, if a longer period is considered (1953–64), the average exponential growth rate of the United Kingdom is only 2.7 per cent, with the United States next in the league with 3.1 per cent (Kaldor, 1966, p. 5). On the other hand, Japan shows exceptionally high growth rates – for the period 1953–64 the average exponential growth rate is 9.6 per cent. This picture remains essentially valid for the rate of growth of GNP per capita for the period 1965–86, except for the fact that the rates have declined overall and that the United Kingdom's position has been taken over by Switzerland and the United States (in that order); the United Kingdom now occupies the third lowest position: see Table A3.1b.

A word of caution is necessary here. One should not be tempted to conclude from these data that the performance of the United Kingdom can be attributed to its failure to join the EC at an earlier date. There are more fundamental causes than that. For instance, Kaldor (1966, p. 3) suggests that the basic problem with the UK economy is that it suffers from 'premature maturity':

> fast rates of economic growth are associated with the fast rate of growth of the 'secondary' sector of the economy – mainly the manufacturing sector – and this

is an attribute of an intermediate stage of economic development: it is the characteristic of the transition from 'immaturity' to 'maturity'; and ... the trouble with the British economy is that it has reached a high stage of 'maturity' *earlier* than others, with the result that it had exhausted the potential for fast growth before it had attained particularly high levels of productivity or real income per head.

Brown (1977, p. 30), referring to the United Kingdom, suggests that there:

certainly remains strong evidence that the inferior rate of growth of our capital stock is the biggest factor in our slow growth of output, though ... other factors ... – notably the much slower 'moving-up' of labour from low-productivity to higher-productivity employments, and what we may politely call our 'more sensible' working pace – no doubt assist it.

The reader who is interested in pursuing this subject should consult El-Agraa (1983a).

Table A3.1b also provides information on the annual inflation rates during 1980–6. During this period Greece and Portugal had exceptionally high rates, Italy, Spain and Ireland had two-digit rates while the rest had one-digit rates, with Germany and the Netherlands on the reasonable rate of 3 per cent – only Japan seems to have done better than these two countries. Thus the data clearly demonstrate the disparity in performance by the member nations of the EC in this respect.

3.1.3 Work

Table A3.1c provides data on the percentage of population of working age (between 16 and 64 years), the unemployment rates and the sectoral distribution of the labour force in terms of the broad categories of agriculture, industry and services. Of course, from this information and the total population figures given in Table A3.1a, one can easily arrive at the absolute total for the labour force.

With regard to the percentage of population of working age, there is no striking difference between the member nations of the EC, except that Germany ranks at the top with 70 per cent and Portugal at the bottom with 64 per cent. Of all the nations in the table, Turkey again stands out with a figure of 57 per cent; it is the only country with a figure below 60 per cent.

The unemployment rates are high for all the member countries of the EC except for Luxemburg. However, Luxemburg is so small and so dominated by EC bureaucrats and parliamentarians that it should be discounted in any serious comparison. Portugal has the exceptionally high rate of about 21 per cent, but Ireland with about 18 per cent is not far behind. The rest fall into two groups of about 8 per cent and 12 per cent with Denmark, Germany, Greece and Spain having the lower unemployment rates. It is interesting to note that all the member nations of the EFTA except Finland experienced rates of less than 5 per cent with Norway and Sweden having lower rates than Japan's. Of the 'other' countries, Canada and the United States have rates just below the average for the EC, while Turkey has a rate closer to Ireland's.

Of particular interest is the relative size of the services sector. This is mainly the tertiary sector (it comprises such divergent items as banking, distribution, insurance, transport, catering and hotels, laundries and hairdressers, professional services of a more varied kind, publicly and privately provided, etc.) and is, for all the countries under consideration except for Turkey, the largest. For instance, the size of this sector in Belgium, Denmark and the Netherlands in 1980 exceeded 60 per cent, with the United Kingdom just behind on 59 per cent. The equivalent figures for Canada and the United States were about 65 per cent and for Japan 55 per cent. Member countries of EFTA are also in a similar position with Norway and Sweden exceeding 60 per cent and the rest on 50 per cent or more. This is a significant point, particularly since it has frequently been alleged in the not so distant past that the size of this sector is the cause of the slow rate of growth of the UK economy; there is nothing in the data to suggest that the United Kingdom is unique in this respect.

As one would expect, all the countries considered show a decline in the percentage of the labour force engaged in agriculture, except for the United Kingdom whose percentage has remained consistently at 3 per cent (which is understandable since this percentage has been very low for a long time). However, Ireland, Portugal and Spain still have about a third of their total labour force engaged in agriculture and Greece has about half its total employment in the same sector.

3.1.4 Employment and unemployment

Although some aspects of EC employment and unemployment are tackled in various chapters of the book, especially those on the social and competition and industrial policies, this may be the appropriate point to consider briefly certain aspects of this topic which are not tackled in those chapters. Employment is a political and socio-economic issue which needs to be tackled in all its aspects. It is quite obvious that the solution to the unemployment problem necessitates a close integration of economic policies and social and manpower policies. The unemployment problem has two basic features. First, there is the transitional problem: given existing levels of unemployment and possible rates of growth of population, the achievement of acceptable levels of manpower utilisation will inevitably be slow, and in some countries may take many years. In addition, there is the longer-term problem: the effect of evolving structures of the labour force, attitudes to work and changing social objectives which may affect employment in a fundamental sense.

Table A3.1d gives a longer-term perspective for manpower utilisation and unemployment rates. One should note that between 1973 and 1975 unemployment either grew more slowly than in the boom years of the 1960s or fell and that the maximum declines in the 1973–5 recession were much greater than any that had occurred in the 1960s (the reader should note that the absolute levels of unemployment of these countries are not strictly comparable because of differences in measurement techniques).

A great deal of the slack in manpower utilisation which developed during the period 1973–5 was absorbed by various measures which diverted the growth of overt unemployment. Working hours fell in a number of countries, jobs were preserved by subsidies to employers, by restrictions on dismissals or deterrents such as redundancy payments which make employers reluctant to dismiss labour. As a result, output per employee fell in many cases.

The table also gives some indication of the change in working hours in the major countries. Many of the figures refer only to manufacturing and may therefore be more sensitive to a recession than those for the economy as a whole; but they do indicate that working hours dropped more than the 1960–70 trend would have suggested. The biggest fall was in Japan. This explains some of the fall in output per employee; but the reduction in working hours does not by any means explain the whole of this decline.

The bottom half of the table gives recorded unemployment for the EC nine projected to 1985. It should be apparant that West Germany remained the country with the lowest unemployment rate, albeit the rate is higher than previously.

3.1.5 Demand

Table A3.4 gives information on the structure of demand, i.e. on the distribution of GDP between private consumption, collective consumption of the general government, investment expenditure, savings, the export of goods and non-factor services and resource balance. With regard to private consumption, the lowest percentage within the EC belongs to Denmark (55 per cent) and the highest is that of Greece and Portugal (66 per cent). As to gross domestic investment, the lowest percentages belongs to Belgium (16 per cent) and the highest is that of Greece (23 per cent). The percentages for savings show a larger divergence between the lowest (14 per cent for Greece) and the highest (25 per cent for the Netherlands). Denmark (22 per cent) and the United Kingdom (18 per cent) are the only two EC nations to have an equality between the percentages devoted to savings and investment and, except for Greece and Portugal, all the remaining EC countries spend a lower percentage on investment relative to the percentage they save. Exports of goods and non-factor services loom large in the case of Belgium (69 per cent), Ireland (57 per cent) and the Netherlands (54 per cent) but vary between 20 per cent and 34 per cent for the rest. The general pattern for the EFTA countries is similar to that of the EC nations, and, except for Turkey, so is that for the 'other' nations.

3.1.6 Government sector

Tables A3.6, A3.7, A3.16 and A3.17 provide data on what can loosely be referred to as the 'government sector'. They give information about current government revenue and expenditure as a percentage of GDP, net official development assistance to developing countries and multilateral agents, total official reserves, etc.

There is a dissimilarity between the member nations of the EC with respect to both their current government expenditure and revenue as a percentage of their GDPs. In terms of expenditure, five nations (Belgium, Greece, Ireland, Italy and the Netherlands) spend in the range of 50–7 per cent, three nations (Denmark, France and the United Kingdom) in the 40–4 per cent range and two (Germany and Spain) spend about 29 per cent. Turkey's percentage (21.8 per cent) is lower than that of any EC member nation, three of the EFTA nations (Austria, Norway and Sweden) are in the France/United Kingdom category while Finland (31.1 per cent) is closer to Germany, and Switzerland (18.6 per cent) comes below Turkey. Canada and the United States are similar with about a quarter of GDP; thus they spend less than any current member nation of the EC. Japan is at the bottom of the whole league with about 17 per cent.

A particularly interesting feature is the percentage of GDP spent on net official assistance to developing countries and multilateral agents. Norway (1.2 per cent) and the Netherlands (1.01 per cent) come at the top of the league while Austria (0.21 per cent), the United States (0.23 per cent) and Japan (0.29 per cent) come at the bottom of the league if one rightly excludes Ireland (0.28 per cent) from this comparison since its level of development does not match that of these three countries. One does not want to dwell too much on this matter, but the information suggests that the advanced world, in resisting the demands made by the developing world, is more interested in absolute figures than in percentages. The latter clearly indicate the significant implications for development assistance of the developing countries' plea (through UNCTAD) that this figure should be raised to 1 per cent of donor countries' GDP, particularly since such a request weighs heavily against Germany, Japan, the United Kingdom and the United States. Therefore, as far as developing countries are concerned, only Norway and the Netherlands will be applauded while Belgium, France and Sweden may come close to being so treated.

For a proper and detailed discussion of the role played by the governments' budgets, the reader is advised to turn to the chapters on the role of the EC general budget and on fiscal harmonisation.

3.1.7 Exports, imports and balance of payments

Tables A3.8–A3.16 give information on the structure of manufacturing and merchandise exports and imports; the growth of merchandise trade; the destination of merchandise and manufactured exports; imports from and exports to the EC; and the balance of payments and reserves.

All these tables are more or less self-explanatory, but Tables A3.14 and A3.15 warrant particular attention. They should be considered together since they give the percentages for the share of imports of the importing country coming from the EC and the share of exports of the exporting country to the EC. The reader should be warned that these percentages are not strictly comparable, because for the years 1957–64 the EC refers to the original six, while for the years 1974–6 it refers to the nine and in

1981 and 1986 it refers, respectively, to the ten and twelve. For an analysis of the proper trends, the reader should consult Chapter 6, and for a full analysis should consult El-Agraa (1989b).

The tables show that the member nations of the EC purchase more than 50 per cent of their imports from each other, with the lowest percentage (50.4 per cent) relating to the United Kingdom and the highest ((73 per cent) to Ireland. The percentages for exports are slightly different in that Denmark (46.8 per cent) and the United Kingdom (47.9 per cent) sell less than half their exports to the EC, while three countries (Belgium, Ireland and the Netherlands) sell more than 70 per cent of their exports to the EC. Thus Ireland conducts a high percentage of its trade with the EC (which is not surprising, given the close ties between Ireland and the United Kingdom) while the United Kingdom is coming close to conducting about half of its trade with the EC. Of the potential EC partners, all member nations of EFTA, except Finland (38.3 per cent and 43.1 per cent for exports and imports respectively), conduct more than half of their trade with the EC, with Turkey being closer to Finland in this respect.

3.1.8 Education

Table A3.21 gives the enrolment rates at the primary, secondary and tertiary levels of education. The table shows that there are no drastic differences between the countries compared with regard to the primary levels, but that major deviations are noticeable at the secondary and tertiary levels. At the secondary level, Portugal stands out with an enrolment rate of less than 50 per cent while all the others, except for Germany (74 per cent) and Ireland (75 per cent) are in the 90 per cent region. In EFTA, Finland and Norway match the high rates for, respectively, the Netherlands and France, while Austria (79 per cent) and Sweden (83 per cent) are on the lower side. All the 'other' nations are close to 100 per cent, except for Turkey which records the lowest rate of all (42 per cent).

At the tertiary level, Belgium, Denmark, France, Germany and the Netherlands have a 30 per cent enrolment rate, and all the other member nations of the EC are in the 21–7 per cent range, except for Portugal with 13 per cent. Three of the EFTA countries are in the 30 per cent zone, with Sweden at the high rate of 38 per cent, but Austria (27 per cent) and Switzerland (22 per cent) compare with, respectively, Spain and the United Kingdom. Of the 'other' countries, Canada and the United States stand out with rates of 55 per cent and 57 per cent, with Japan matching France and Germany, but with Turkey right at the bottom with 9 per cent. These rates suggest that a general positive relationship does exist between economic development and higher rates of enrolment at the tertiary level, but they do not suggest such a relationship if one concentrates on the most developed of the nations in the table; for example, Switzerland has the highest per capita income within this group yet its enrolment rate is one of the lowest.

3.1.9 Income distribution

Table A3.19 gives some information on income distribution. The table shows that in Portugal and Turkey 10 per cent of the households receive more than one-third of the total household income, and, except for France (26.4 per cent), Ireland (25.1 per cent), Italy (28.1 per cent) and Sweden (28.1 per cent), in all the remaining countries they receive about one-fifth.

3.1.10 Tariffs

Table A3.22 provides information on the average tariff levels in the original six as well as in Denmark, the United Kingdom, Canada and the United States. To see how these compare with the tariff levels that are presently in existence, one should turn to the chapter on the EC common commercial policy.

3.2 Conclusion

As stated at the beginning of this chapter, there are no conclusions to be drawn from this general statistical survey; the information is provided only for the purpose of giving a general sense of perspective. The reader who is seeking conclusions should turn to the relevant specialist chapter/chapters.

Appendix: the statistical tables

In all tables, na means not available. Most Luxemburg data is either insignificant or reported with Belgian data.

The sources for all tables (except A3.1d and A3.22) are the World Bank's *World Development Report*, Eurostat's *Basic Statistics of the EC* and *Statistical Review*, and OECD publications, all for various years.

The data are subject to technical explanations as well as to some critical qualifications. The reader is strongly advised to turn to the original sources for these.

Table A3.1a Area and population

	Area (000 km²)	Population (millions) mid-1986	Average annual growth of population (%) 1965–80	1980–6	Crude birth rate (per 000 population) 1986	Crude death rate (per 000 population) 1986	Life expectancy at birth (years) 1986
Belgium	31	9.9	12	12	0.3	0.0	75
Denmark	43	5.1	11	11	0.5	0.0	75
France	549	55.4	14	10	0.7	0.5	77
W. Germany	249	60.9	10	12	0.3	−0.2	75
Greece	132	10.0	11	9	0.7	0.5	76
Ireland	70	3.6	18	9	1.2	0.8	74
Italy	301	57.2	10	10	0.6	0.3	77
Luxemburg	3	0.4	—	—	—	—	—
Netherlands	42	14.6	13	9	0.9	0.5	77
Portugal	92	10.2	13	10	0.6	0.5	73
Spain	505	38.5	13	9	1.0	0.6	76
United Kingdom	244	56.7	13	12	0.2	0.1	75
EC (12)	2,261	322.5					
EFTA countries							
Austria	84	7.6	11	11	0.3	0.0	74
Finland	337	4.9	12	10	0.3	0.5	75
Iceland	103	0.2	na	na	na	na	77
Norway	324	4.2	13	11	0.6	0.3	77
Sweden	450	8.4	12	11	0.5	0.1	77
Switzerland	41	6.5	12	9	0.5	0.3	77
Other countries							
Canada	9,976	25.6	15	7	1.3	1.1	76
Japan	372	121.5	12	7	1.2	0.7	78
Turkey	781	51.5	29	8	2.4	2.5	65
United States	9,373	241.6	19	9	1.0	1.0	75
USSR	22,402	281.1	19	10	0.9	1.0	70

Table A3.1b GNP per capita and inflation rates

	GNP per capita		Annual
	US$ 1986	Average annual growth rate (%) 1965–86	inflation rate (%) 1980–6
EC countries			
Belgium	9,230	2.7	5.7
Denmark	12,600	1.9	7.3
France	10,720	2.8	8.8
W. Germany	12,080	2.5	3.0
Greece	3,680	3.3	20.3
Ireland	5,070	1.7	10.7
Italy	8,550	2.6	13.2
Luxemburg	—	—	—
Netherlands	10,020	1.9	3.1
Portugal	2,250	3.2	22.0
Spain	4,860	2.9	11.3
United Kingdom	8,870	1.7	6.0
EFTA countries			
Austria	9,990	3.3	4.5
Finland	12,160	3.2	8.1
Iceland	13,410	3.1	46.7
Norway	15,400	3.4	7.0
Sweden	13,160	1.6	8.2
Switzerland	17,680	1.4	4.2
Other countries			
Canada	14,120	2.6	5.5
Japan	12,840	4.3	1.6
Turkey	1,110	2.7	37.3
United States	17,480	1.6	4.4

Table A3.1c Labour force and unemployment rates

	% of population of working age (16–64 years)		Agriculture		Industry		Services		Unemployment rates (% of civilian workers)
				% of labour force in					
	1965	1985	1965	1980	1965	1980	1965	1980	1986
EC countries									
Belgium	63	68	6	3	46	36	48	61	12.5
Denmark	65	66	14	7	37	32	49	61	7.4
France	62	66	18	9	39	35	43	56	10.7
W. Germany	65	70	11	6	48	44	41	50	8.1
Greece	65	65	47	31	24	29	29	40	7.4
Ireland	57	60	31	19	28	34	41	48	18.3
Italy	66	67	25	12	42	41	34	48	13.7
Luxemburg	—	—	—	—	—	—	—	—	1.5
Netherlands	62	69	9	6	41	32	51	63	12.4
Portugal	62	64	38	26	30	37	32	38	21.2
Spain	64	65	34	17	35	37	32	46	8.8
United Kingdom	65	65	3	3	47	38	50	59	12.0
EFTA countries									
Austria	63	67	19	9	45	41	36	50	3.6[a]
Finland	65	67	24	12	35	35	41	53	5.3
Iceland	na	na	na	na	na	na	na	na	na
Norway	63	64	16	8	37	29	48	62	2.0
Sweden	66	65	11	6	43	33	46	62	2.7
Switzerland	65	67	9	6	49	39	41	55	1.0[a]
Other countries									
Canada	59	68	10	5	33	29	57	65	9.5
Japan	67	68	26	11	32	34	42	55	2.8
Turkey	53	57	75	58	11	17	14	25	15.7[b]
United States	60	66	5	4	35	31	60	66	6.9
USSR	62	66	34	20	33	39	33	41	na

Notes
[a] 1985.
[b] 1984.

Table A3.1d Manpower utilisation and unemployment rates

	Employment		Hours worked per person		Output per man hour		Unemployment % of labour	
	1960–73	1973–5	1960–73	1973–5	1960–73	1973–5	1960–73	1974
EC countries[a]								
Belgium/								
Luxemburg	0.7	na	−1.2	na	5.4	na	2.2	2.6
Denmark	1.3	na	−1.5	na	5.0	na	1.1	2.1
France	0.7	−0.5	−0.5	−2.1	5.5	3.6	1.6	2.3
W. Germany	0.1	−2.8	−0.9	−2.7	5.5	4.0	0.8	2.2
Italy	−0.7	1.2	1.9	na	7.8	na	3.3	2.9
Netherlands	0.9	na	na	na	na	na	1.3	3.0
United Kingdom	0.1	0.0	−0.5	−0.8	3.4	0.1	1.9	2.1
Other countries								
Canada	2.9	3.1	−0.3	−1.4	2.8	−0.8	5.3	5.4
Japan	1.2	−0.8	−1.0	−5.3	10.1	6.2	1.3	1.4
United States	1.9	0.1	0.1	−0.2	2.3	−2.4	4.8	5.4

Recorded unemployment in the EC[a] (% of labour force)

	1973	1979	1981	1985
Belgium/Luxemburg	3	8	11	14 (0.62)[b]
Denmark	1	5	9	12 (0.32)
France	2	6	8	12 (2.29)
W. Germany	1	3	5	7 (1.78)
Ireland	6	8	11	15 (0.18)
Italy	5	7	8	12 (2.88)
Netherlands	2	4	8	12 (0.64)
United Kingdom	2	5	10	16 (4.09)
EC (9)	2	5	8	12

Notes
[a] Ireland (top half of the table) and Greece, Portugal and Spain (bottom half) are missing due to lack of appropriate data.
[b] Figures in brackets are millions.

Source: *Cambridge Economic Policy Review*, vol. 7, no. 2, December 1981.

Table A3.2 Structure of production

	GDP (million US$) 1986	Distribution of gross domestic product (%)			
		Agriculture 1986	Industry 1986	(of which manufacturing) 1986	Services, etc. 1986
Belgium[a]	112,180	2	33	23[b]	64
Denmark	68,820	6	28	20	66
France[a]	727,200	4	34	na	63
W. Germany[a]	891,990	2	40	32[b]	58
Greece	35,210	17	29	18	54
Ireland	21,910	14	45	na	41
Italy[a]	599,920	5	39	22[b]	56
Luxemburg	—	—	—	—	—
Netherlands[a]	175,330	4	34	18[b]	62
Portugal	27,480	10	40	na	51[b]
Spain	229,100	6	37	27[b]	56
United Kingdom	468,290	2	43	26[b]	55
EC (12)	3,357,430				
EFTA countries					
Austria[a]	93,830	3	38	28[b]	59
Finland	62,370	8	37	25[b]	55
Iceland	na	na	na	na	na
Norway[a]	69,780	4	41	14[b]	56
Sweden	114,470	3	35	24[b]	62
Switzerland[a]	135,050	na	na	na	na
Total	475,500				
Other countries					
Canada	323,790	3	36	na	61
Japan[a]	1,955,650	3	41	30[b]	56
Turkey	52,620	18	36	25	46
United States[a]	4,185,490	2	31	20	67

Notes
[a] GDP and its components are given at purchaser values.
[b] Figures are for years other than 1986.

Table A3.3 Growth of production

	Average annual growth rate (%)									
	GDP		Agriculture		Industry		(of which manufacturing)		Services, etc.	
	1965–80	1980–6	1965–80	1980–6	1965–80	1980–6	1965–80	1980–6	1965–80	1980–6
EC countries										
Belgium[a]	3.9	0.9	0.5	3.1	4.4	0.5	4.8	1.6[b]	3.8	1.1
Denmark	2.7	2.8	0.9[b]	4.6	1.9[b]	2.6	3.2[b]	2.9[b]	3.1[b]	2.4
France[a]	4.4	1.3	0.8	2.8	4.6	0.6	5.3	na	4.6	1.6
W. Germany[a]	3.3	1.5	1.4	3.1	2.9	0.7	3.3	0.8[b]	3.7	2.1
Greece	5.6	1.5	2.3	0.3	7.1	0.4	8.4	0.2	6.2	2.5
Ireland	5.1	0.7	na	−6.2	na	na	na	na	na	3.8
Italy	3.9	1.3	0.8	0.5	4.2	0.2	5.1	−0.2	4.1	2.1
Luxemburg	–	–	–	–	–	–	–	–	–	–
Netherlands	3.7	1.0	4.3[b]	4.5	3.6[b]	0.5	4.3[b]	na	4.0[b]	1.9
Portugal	5.5	1.4	na	0.1	na	1.4	na	na	na	1.7
Spain[a]	5.2	1.8	3.0	2.8	5.8	0.8	6.7	0.3[b]	4.6	2.3
United Kingdom	2.2	2.3	1.7	4.1	1.2	2.0	1.1	1.2[b]	2.9	2.6
EFTA countries										
Austria[a]	4.3	1.8	2.2	1.2	4.5	1.6	4.7	2.1[b]	4.4	1.9[b]
Finland	4.1	2.7	0.1	0.2	4.4	2.8	5.0	3.0[b]	4.8	2.2
Iceland	na	na	na	na	na	na	na	na	na	na
Norway	4.4	3.5	−0.4	3.0	5.6	3.8	2.6	0.3[b]	4.2	3.4
Sweden	2.8	2.0[b]	−0.2	2.5	2.2	2.5	2.3	2.3[b]	3.3	0.5
Switzerland	2.0	1.5	na	na	na	na	na	na	na	na
Other countries										
Canada	4.4	2.9	0.7	2.8	3.4	2.9	3.8	3.6	5.5	2.9
Japan	6.3	3.7	0.8	1.0	8.5	5.0	9.4	7.8[b]	5.2	2.9
Turkey	6.3	4.9	3.2	3.1	7.2	6.4	7.5	8.0	7.6	4.7
United States	2.8	3.1	1.1	3.1	1.9	3.2	2.7	4.0	3.4	3.0[b]

Notes
[a] GDP and its components are given at purchaser values.
[b] World Bank estimate.

Table A3.4 Structure of demand

| | Distribution of gross domestic product (%) | | | | | |
	General government consumption 1986	Private consumption, etc. 1986	Gross domestic investment 1986	Gross domestic savings 1986	Exports of goods and non-factor services 1986	Resource balance 1986
EC countries						
Belgium	17	64	16	20	69	4
Denmark	24	55	22	22	32	0
France	19	61	19	20	22	1
W. Germany	20	56	19	24	30	5
Greece	19	66	23	14	22	−8
Ireland	19	58	19	23	57	3
Italy	16	61	21	23	20	2
Luxemburg	—	—	—	—	—	—
Netherlands	16	59	21	25	54	4
Portugal	14	66	22	20	34	−2
Spain	14	63	21	23	20	2
United Kingdom	21	62	18	18	26	−1
EFTA countries						
Austria	19	56	24	25	37	1
Finland	21	55	23	24	27	1
Iceland	na	na	na	na	na	na
Norway	20	54	29	26	38	−3
Sweden	27	52	18	21	33	3
Switzerland	13	60	26	27	37	1
Other countries						
Canada	20	58	21	22	27	1
Japan	10	58	28	32	12	4
Turkey	9	69	25	22	18	−3
United States	19	66	18	15	7	−3

Table A3.5 Growth of consumption and investment

| | Average annual growth rate (%) | | | | | |
| | General government consumption | | Private consumption, etc. | | Gross domestic investment | |
	1965−80	1980−6	1965−80	1980−6	1965−80	1980−6
EC countries						
Belgium	4.6	0.3	4.3	0.6	2.9	−2.2
Denmark	4.8	0.9	2.3	2.5	1.2	7.1
France	3.5	1.8	4.9	2.0	3.8	−0.2
W. Germany	3.5	1.3	4.0	1.1	1.7	−0.1
Greece	6.6	2.9	5.2	3.1	4.5	−2.4
Ireland	6.1	1.2	3.8	−2.4	6.8	−1.6
Italy	3.3	2.6	4.6	1.9	2.5	−1.1

Table A3.5 (Con't)

	Average annual growth rate (%)					
	General government consumption		Private consumption, etc.		Gross domestic investment	
	1965–80	1980–6	1965–80	1980–6	1965–80	1980–6
Luxemburg	—	—	—	—	—	—
Netherlands	3.1	0.8	4.3	0.2	1.6	2.4
Portugal	8.1	3.0	7.2	−0.2	4.5	−6.2
Spain	5.0	3.9	5.4	0.7	4.0	−0.2
United Kingdom	2.3	1.0	2.2	2.7	1.2	4.7
EFTA countries						
Austria	3.7	1.9	4.4	1.9	4.5	1.4
Finland	5.3	3.7	3.9	3.1	2.7	1.0
Iceland	na	na	na	na	na	na
Norway	5.5	3.7	3.8	3.4	4.4	2.9
Sweden	4.0	1.5	2.4	1.1	0.9	1.2
Switzerland	2.7	2.2	2.5	1.3	0.8	2.6
Other countries						
Canada	4.8	1.8	5.0	2.6	4.7	1.6
Japan	5.1	3.1	6.2	2.9	6.7	3.2
Turkey	6.1	2.9	5.7	4.9	8.9	5.1
United States	1.4	4.5	3.4	3.5	2.1	5.6

Table A3.6 Central government expenditure

| | Total expenditure (% of GDP) 1986[a] | % of total expenditure | | | | | | Overall surplus or deficit (% of GDP) 1986[a] |
		Defence 1986[a]	Education 1986[a]	Health 1986[a]	Housing, amenities, social services and welfare 1986[a]	Economic services 1986[a]	Other[b] 1986	
EC countries								
Belgium	56.7	5.3	13.0	1.7	41.5	11.9	26.5	−10.6
Denmark	39.5	5.2	9.2	1.0	40.0	6.8	37.8	−3.8
France	44.1	na	na	na	na	na	na	−2.8
W. Germany	29.9	8.8	0.6	17.9	50.5	6.8	15.4	−0.7
Greece	50.9	14.9	9.1	7.4	30.6	26.4	11.7	−14.4
Ireland	54.7	3.1	11.7	13.2	30.1	15.0	26.9	−11.6
Italy	50.2	3.2	7.2	9.9	30.0	13.2	36.5	−14.1
Luxembourg	–	–	–	–	–	–	–	–
Netherlands	56.6	5.2	11.1	10.8	39.8	10.7	22.5	−1.7
Portugal	na	na	na	na	na	na	na	na
Spain	29.1	4.4	6.2	13.1	48.5	11.7	16.3	−7.7
United Kingdom	40.6	13.3	2.1	12.6	30.2	8.9	33.0	−3.4
EFTA countries								
Austria	40.5	3.1	9.7	12.0	42.6	13.8	18.8	−5.9
Finland	31.1	5.2	13.7	10.6	35.7	21.0	13.7	−0.5
Iceland	na	na	na	na	na	na	na	na
Norway	40.6	8.3	8.7	10.5	35.0	19.5	17.9	3.9
Sweden	44.1	6.6	8.9	1.1	51.8	6.8	24.8	−2.6
Switzerland	18.6	10.3	3.1	13.1	50.6	12.2	10.8	−0.1
Other countries								
Canada	25.4	7.6	3.4	6.1	35.0	14.9	33.1	−6.2
Japan	17.4	na	na	na	na	na	na	4.9
Turkey	21.8	13.5	11.9	2.2	2.8	24.3	45.3	−3.3
United States	24.5	25.8	1.7	11.6	31.0	8.8	21.1	−5.0

Notes
[a] Except for those of Italy, the Netherlands, Austria, Sweden and the United States, these data belong to dates other than 1986.
[b] The data in this column are budgetary data.

Table A3.7 Central government current revenue

	Tax revenue (% of total current revenue) (1986)[a]					
	Taxes on income, profit and capital gains	Social security contributions	Domestic taxes on goods and services	Taxes on international trade and transactions	Other taxes	Non-tax revenue
EC countries						
Belgium	37.9	34.0	21.4	0.0	2.1	4.5
Denmark	37.2	3.7	41.7	0.1	3.8	13.5
France	17.5	43.8	29.9	0.1	4.0	4.7
W. Germany	17.5	53.3	21.8	0.0	0.2	7.3
Greece	17.9	34.9	36.3	0.5	0.2	10.2
Ireland	33.6	14.4	32.1	7.2	1.2	11.5
Italy	38.5	28.7	23.5	0.0	9.3	3.1
Luxemburg	—	—	—	—	—	—
Netherlands	24.3	37.9	20.6	0.0	2.3	14.8
Portugal	0.0	0.0	63.1	35.6	0.0	1.3
Spain	22.9	45.2	15.8	4.1	2.2	9.8
United Kingdom	38.9	17.5	30.4	0.0	1.9	11.4
EFTA countries						
Austria	19.4	36.7	26.6	1.4	7.3	8.6
Finland	31.5	9.6	45.7	0.8	4.4	7.9
Iceland	na	na	na	na	na	na
Norway	20.2	21.8	39.7	0.5	1.0	16.7
Sweden	16.0	29.8	29.6	0.5	8.3	15.8
Switzerland	14.8	52.7	20.5	7.8	−1.3	5.5
Other countries						
Canada	49.3	14.5	18.5	4.7	0.0	13.0
Japan	67.4	0.0	18.9	1.7	7.5	4.6
Turkey	43.5	na	31.0	6.6	4.3	14.6
United States	50.1	33.9	3.9	1.7	0.8	9.5

Note
[a] The data for Belgium, Greece, Spain, United Kingdom, Finland, Switzerland, Canada and Japan are for years other than 1986.

Table A3.8 Structure of manufacturing

	Value-added in manufacturing (US$m) 1985	Distribution of manufacturing value-added (%, current prices)				
		Fuel and agriculture 1985	Textiles and clothing 1985	Machinery and transport equipment 1985	Chemicals 1985	Other[a] 1985
Belgium[a]	18,570	20	8	23	14	36
Denmark	9,729	22	6	24	10	38
France[a]	124,436[c]	18	7	33	9	34
W. Germany[a]	201,640	12	5	38	10	36

Table A3.8 (Con't)

	Value-added in manufacturing (US$m) 1985	Distribution of manufacturing value-added (%, current prices)				
		Fuel and agriculture 1985	Textiles and clothing 1985	Machinery and transport equipment 1985	Chemicals 1985	Other[a] 1985
Greece	5,448	20	22	14	7	38
Ireland	696[c]	28	7	20	15	28
Italy[a]	93,973	7	13	32	11	37
Luxemburg	—	—	—	—	—	—
Netherlands[a]	23,063	19	4	28	11	38
Portugal	na	17	22	16	8	38
Spain[a]	44,891	17	10	22	9	43
United Kingdom	101,470	15	6	32	11	37
EC (12)	623,916					
EFTA countries						
Austria[a]	18,570	20	8	23	14	36
Finland	12,199	13	7	24	7	50
Iceland	na	na	na	na	na	na
Norway[a]	7,939	20	3	26	7	44
Sweden	20,878	10	2	35	8	45
Switzerland[a]	na	na	na	na	na	na
Other countries						
Canada[a]	58,862[c]	15	7	25	9	44
Japan[a]	395,148	10	6	37	9	38
Turkey	12,277	20	14	15	8	43
United States[a]	803,391	12	5	36	10	38

Notes
[a] Includes unallocable data.
[b] Value-added in manufacturing data is at purchaser values.
[c] Figures are for years other than 1985.

Table A3.9 Structure of merchandise exports

	% share of merchandise exports									
	Fuels, minerals and metals		Other primary commodities		Machinery and transport equipment		Other manu-factures		Textiles and clothing[a]	
	1965	1986	1965	1986	1965	1986	1965	1986	1965	1986
EC countries										
Belgium	13	9	11	12	20	26	55	54	12	7
Denmark	2	4	55	36	22	25	21	35	4	5
France	8	5	21	19	26	35	45	41	10	5
W. Germany	7	4	5	6	46	48	42	41	5	5
Greece	8	14	78	35	2	3	11	48	3	29
Ireland	3	2	63	28	5	31	29	39	7	5

Table A3.9 (Con't)

| | % share of merchandise exports | | | | | | | | | |
| | Fuels, minerals and metals | | Other primary commodities | | Machinery and transport equipment | | Other manu-factures | | Textiles and clothing[a] | |
	1965	1986	1965	1986	1965	1986	1965	1986	1965	1986
Italy	8	4	14	8	30	34	47	54	15	14
Luxemburg	—	—	—	—	—	—	—	—	—	—
Netherlands	12	18	32	25	21	19	35	38	9	4
Portugal	4	5	34	16	3	16	58	64	24	31
Spain	9	9	51	19	10	31	29	42	6	4
United Kingdom	7	15	10	9	41	36	41	40	7	4
EFTA countries										
Austria	8	5	16	8	20	32	55	55	12	9
Finland	3	5	40	14	12	28	45	53	2	5
Iceland	na	na	na	na	na	na	na	na	na	na
Norway	21	53	28	10	17	18	34	20	2	1
Sweden	9	6	23	10	35	44	33	40	2	2
Switzerland	3	3	7	4	30	35	60	59	10	6
Other countries										
Canada	28	18	35	18	15	42	22	22	1	1
Japan	2	1	7	1	31	64	60	34	17	3
Turkey	9	11	89	33	0	5	2	51	1	29
United States	8	7	27	17	37	48	28	28	3	2

Note
[a] Textiles and clothing is a subgroup of manufactures.

Table A3.10 Structure of merchandise imports

| | % share of merchandise imports | | | | | | | | | |
| | Food | | Fuels | | Other primary commodities | | Machinery and transport equipment | | Other manu-factures | |
	1965	1986	1965	1986	1965	1986	1965	1986	1965	1986
EC countries										
Belgium	14	11	9	11	21	9	24	28	32	41
Denmark	14	11	11	9	11	6	25	31	39	42
France	19	11	15	13	18	7	20	29	27	40
W. Germany	22	12	8	12	21	9	13	26	35	41
Greece	15	16	8	17	11	8	35	25	30	34
Ireland	18	13	8	8	10	5	25	31	39	43
Italy	24	14	16	17	24	11	15	25	21	32
Luxemburg	—	—	—	—	—	—	—	—	—	—
Netherlands	15	14	10	12	13	6	25	28	37	40
Portugal	16	13	8	15	19	9	27	29	30	33

Table A3.10 (Con't)

| | % share of merchandise imports | | | | | | | | | |
| | Food | | Fuels | | Other primary commodities | | Machinery and transport equipment | | Other manu-factures | |
	1965	1986	1965	1986	1965	1986	1965	1986	1965	1986
Spain	19	12	10	19	16	11	27	29	28	29
United Kingdom	30	12	11	7	25	8	11	33	23	39
EFTA countries										
Austria	14	11	9	11	21	9	24	28	32	41
Finland	10	6	10	15	12	7	35	36	34	36
Iceland	na	na	na	na	na	na	na	na	na	na
Norway	10	6	7	6	12	6	38	40	32	42
Sweden	12	7	11	11	12	7	30	36	36	39
Switzerland	16	7	6	6	11	6	24	30	43	51
Other countries										
Canada	10	6	7	5	9	5	40	56	34	29
Japan	22	17	20	31	38	17	9	11	11	24
Turkey	6	4	10	18	10	8	37	34	37	35
United States	19	7	10	10	20	5	14	42	36	36

Table A3.11 Growth of merchandise trade

| | Merchandise trade (US$m) | | Average annual growth rate (%) | | Terms of trade (1980 = 100) |
	Exports 1986	Imports 1986	Exports 1980–6	Imports 1980–6	1986
Belgium	68,892	68,656	3.8	6.9	102
Denmark	21,293	22,878	4.5	3.9	106
France	124,948	129,402	2.1	2.1	114
W. Germany	243,327	191,084	4.3	3.0	115
Greece	5,648	11,350	4.6	4.1	99
Ireland	12,657	11,619	9.3	3.4	109
Italy	97,811	99,452	4.3	2.6	108
Luxemburg	—	—	—	—	—
Netherlands	79,436	75,292	3.4	2.8	107
Portugal	7,242	9,650	11.0	0.8	104
Spain	27,187	35,055	6.4	2.6	120
United Kingdom	106,929	126,330	4.0	5.6	97
EC (12)	795,370	780,768			
EFTA countries					
Austria	22,622	26,104	5.3	3.8	108
Finland	16,356	15,339	2.8	1.9	114
Iceland	na	na	na	na	na

Table A3.11 (Con't)

	Merchandise trade (US$m)		Average annual growth rate (%)		Terms of trade (1980 = 100)
	Exports 1986	Imports 1986	Exports 1980–6	Imports 1980–6	1986
Norway	18,230	20,300	5.1	5.8	87
Sweden	37,263	32,693	5.7	4.0	110
Switzerland	37,471	41,039	3.7	4.2	117
Other countries					
Canada	90,193	85,068	7.2	5.2	89
Japan	210,757	127,553	6.4	3.5	156
Turkey	7,985	11,027	19.9	9.9	102
United States	217,307	387,081	−2.7	9.0	119

Table A3.12 Origin and destination of merchandise exports

	Merchandise exports (US$m) 1985	Destination of merchandise exports (%)							
		Industrial market economies		Non-reporting non-members		High income oil exporters		Developing economies[a]	
		1965	1985	1965[b]	1985[b]	1965[b]	1985[b]	1965	1985
Belgium	56,147	86	84	1	2	#	2	12	13
Denmark	18,246	85	81	3	1	#	2	12	16
France	107,588	68	71	2	3	#	2	29	24
W. Germany	25,268	77	78	2	3	1	2	21	18
Greece	4,539	64	68	16	6	2	6	19	20
Ireland	10,049	91	89	1	#	#	1	8	9
Italy	91,123	71	70	3	3	2	5	25	22
Luxemburg	—	—	—	—	—	—	—	—	—
Netherlands	65,212	83	85	1	1	1	1	15	12
Portugal	7,652	65	85	15	4	#	#	20	11
Spain	30,066	73	66	5	4	#	3	21	26
United Kingdom	109,110	63	77	2	1	1	4	33	18
EC (12)	525,000								
EFTA countries									
Austria	20,803	71	73	9	7	#	2	19	18
Finland	13,226	71	65	17	23	#	1	12	12
Iceland	na	na	na	na	na	na	na	na	na
Norway	15,556	82	88	3	1	#	#	14	11
Sweden	28,538	85	83	3	2	#	2	12	13
Switzerland	30,626	76	75	2	2	1	4	21	20
Other countries									
Canada	81,477	87	89	4	2	#	#	10	9
Japan	130,488	49	58	3	2	2	4	47	36
Turkey	11,035	71	51	10	3	#	9	19	37
United States	361,627	61	60	#	1	1	3	38	36

Notes
[a] Includes unallocable data.
[b] # = below 0.5 percentage point.

Table A3.13 Origin and destination of manufactured exports

| | Manufactured exports (US$m) 1986 | Destination of manufactured exports (%) | | | | | | | |
| | | Industrial market economies | | Non-reporting non-members | | High income oil exporters | | Developing economies[a] | |
		1965	1986	1965	1986	1965	1986	1965	1986
Belgium	54,342	86	85	1	1	0	1	13	12
Denmark	12,334	79	80	3	2	0	1	17	17
France	90,495	64	72	2	2	1	2	33	24
W. Germany	217,471	76	78	2	3	1	1	22	17
Greece	3,048	56	75	6	2	9	5	29	18
Ireland	8,773	82	94	0	0	0	1	17	5
Italy	85,724	68	75	3	3	2	3	27	19
Luxemburg	—	—	—	—	—	—	—	—	—
Netherlands	46,197	81	85	2	1	1	1	17	12
Portugal	5,707	59	91	18	2	0	0	23	7
Spain	19,742	57	71	9	3	0	2	34	24
United Kingdom	80,544	61	72	2	1	1	5	36	22
EC (12)	624,377								
EFTA countries									
Austria	19,622	67	77	12	6	0	1	21	15
Finland	13,188	63	66	23	24	0	1	14	10
Iceland	na	na	na	na	na	na	na	na	na
Norway	6,825	78	69	2	1	0	1	20	30
Sweden	31,196	82	85	3	2	0	1	15	12
Switzerland	34,997	75	75	2	2	1	2	22	20
Other countries									
Canada	53,509	88	94	0	0	0	0	12	6
Japan	203,896	47	62	3	2	2	3	49	33
Turkey	4,352	83	57	1	2	0	5	15	35
United States	162,838	58	63	0	0	1	2	40	35

Note
[a] Includes unallocable data.

Table A3.14 Exports to EC member countries

| | % share of total exports of exporting country | | | |
Exporting country	1957	1974	1981	1986
EC countries				
Belgium	46.1	69.9	70.0	72.9
Denmark	31.2	43.1	46.7	46.8
France	25.1	53.2	48.2	57.8
W. Germany	29.2	53.2	46.9	50.8
Greece	52.5	50.1	43.3	63.5
Ireland	na	74.1	69.9	71.9
Italy	24.9	45.4	43.2	53.5
Luxemburg	—	—	—	—

Table A3.14 (Con't)

Exporting country	% share of total exports of exporting country			
	1957	1974	1981	1986
Netherlands	41.6	70.8	71.2	75.7
Portugal	22.2	48.2	53.7	68.0
Spain	29.8	47.4	43.0	60.9
United Kingdom	14.6	33.4	41.2	47.9
EFTA countries				
Austria	na	na	na	60.1
Finland	na	na	na	38.3
Iceland	na	na	na	na
Norway	na	na	na	65.1
Sweden	na	na	na	50.0
Switzerland	na	na	na	54.9
Other countries				
Canada	8.3	12.6	10.7	6.8
Japan	na	10.7	12.4	14.8
Turkey	na	na	na	44.0
United States	15.3	21.9	22.4	24.5
USSR	na	na	na	12.9

Table A3.15 Imports from EC member countries

Importing country	% share of total imports of importing country			
	1957	1974	1981	1986
EC countries				
Belgium	43.5	66.1	59.3	69.9
Denmark	31.2	45.5	47.9	53.2
France	21.4	47.6	48.2	64.4
W. Germany	23.5	48.1	48.2	54.2
Greece	40.8	43.3	50.0	58.3
Ireland	na	68.3	74.7	73.0
Italy	21.4	42.4	40.7	55.4
Luxemburg	—	—	—	—
Netherlands	41.1	57.4	52.4	61.0
Portugal	37.1	43.5	38.0	58.8
Spain	21.3	35.8	29.0	51.3
United Kingdom	12.1	30.0	39.4	50.4
EFTA countries				
Austria	na	na	na	66.9
Finland	na	na	na	43.1
Iceland	na	na	na	na
Norway	na	na	na	50.1
Sweden	na	na	na	57.2
Switzerland	na	na	na	73.0

Table A3.15 (Con't)

Importing country	% share of total imports of importing country			
	1957	1974	1981	1986
Other countries				
Canada	4.2	6.9	8.0	11.3
Japan	na	6.4	6.0	11.1
Turkey	na	na	na	41.0
United States	11.7	9.0	16.0	20.5
USSR	na	na	na	11.2

Table A3.16 Balance of payments and reserves (US$ million)

	Current account balance 1986	External financial requirement 1986	Receipts of workers' remittances 1986	Net direct private investment 1986	Gross international reserves 1986	in months of import coverage 1986
EC countries						
Belgium	3,586	4,363	479	−990	18,900	2.3
Denmark	−4,313	−4,146	na	na	5,601	2.0
France	2,922	5,768	320	−2,116	63,450	4.2
W. Germany	37,357	45,551	na	−8,121	88,941	4.3
Greece	−1,676	−3,068	942	471	2,812	2.8
Ireland	−450	−1,859	na	161	3,377	2.4
Italy	3,961	6,948	1,205	−2,917	46,049	4.5
Luxemburg	—	—	—	—	—	—
Netherlands	4,686	5,665	na	−2,198	28,368	3.6
Portugal	1,121	929	2,529	239	9,336	9.6
Spain	4,102	4,500	1,180	3,057	20,548	5.7
United Kingdom	−1,392	1,825	na	−8,378	25,853	1.5
EFTA countries						
Austria	133	178	267	−41	14,427	4.5
Finland	−887	−660	na	−419	2,535	1.5
Iceland	na	na	na	na	na	na
Norway	−4,440	−3,777	12	−107	12,987	4.8
Sweden	3,795	4,651	na	−2,300	8,923	2.6
Switzerland	4,525	4,427	93	383	54,339	9.5
Other countries						
Canada	−6,723	−6,854	na	−1,824	10,961	1.2
Japan	85,831	87,301	na	−14,250	51,727	3.6
Turkey	−1,528	−1,774	1,634	125	2,966	2.5
United States	−141,460	−127,450	na	−3,000	139,884	3.4

Table A3.17 Official development assistance

	Amount in US$m[a]				% of donor country GNP			
	1965	1975	1985	1986	1965	1975	1985	1986
EC countries								
Belgium	102	378	440	549	0.60	0.59	0.55	0.49
Denmark	13	205	440	695	0.13	0.58	0.80	0.89
France	752	2,093	3,995	5,105	0.76	0.62	0.78	0.72
W. Germany	456	1,689	2,942	3,832	0.40	0.40	0.47	0.43
Greece			−11	−19				0.00
Ireland	0	8	39	62	0.00	0.09	0.24	0.28
Italy	60	182	1,098	2,404	0.10	0.11	0.26	0.40
Luxemburg	—	—	—	—	—	—	—	—
Netherlands	70	608	1,136	1,740	0.36	0.75	0.91	1.01
Portugal			−101	−139				0.50
Spain			0	0			0.00	0.00
United Kingdom	472	904	1,530	1,750	0.47	0.39	0.33	0.32
EFTA countries								
Austria	10	79	248	198	0.11	0.21	0.38	0.21
Finland	2	48	211	313	0.02	0.18	0.40	0.45
Iceland	na	na	na	na	na	na	na	na
Norway	11	184	574	798	0.16	0.66	1.01	1.20
Sweden	38	566	840	1,090	0.19	0.82	0.86	0.85
Switzerland	12	104	302	422	0.09	0.19	0.31	0.30
Other countries								
Canada	96	880	1,631	1,695	0.19	0.54	0.49	0.48
Japan	244	1,148	3,797	5,634	0.27	0.23	0.29	0.29
Turkey			−175	−346				0.60
United States	4,023	4,161	9,403	9,564	0.58	0.27	0.24	0.23

Note
[a] Negative figures indicate receipt of assistance.

Table A3.18 Money and interest rates

	Money holdings (broadly defined)				Nominal interest rates of banks (average annual %)	
	Average nominal rate	Annual growth (%)	Average outstanding (% of GDP)		Deposit rate	Lending rate
	1980−6		1965	1986	1986	1986
EC countries						
Belgium	6.5		59.2	56.2	5.33	10.44
Denmark	16.9		45.8	57.5	6.58	12.98
France	10.0		53.5	68.9	5.32	16.38
W. Germany	5.7		46.1	63.7	3.71	8.75
Greece	25.7		35.0	75.8	15.50	20.50
Ireland	6.5		na	47.6	6.50	12.23
Italy	12.2		60.0	66.5	8.97	14.18
Luxemburg	—		—	—	—	—

Table A3.18 (Con't)

| | Money holdings (broadly defined) | | | | Nominal interest rates of banks (average annual %) | |
| | Average nominal rate 1980–6 | Annual growth (%) | Average outstanding (% of GDP) | | Deposit rate 1986 | Lending rate 1986 |
			1965	1986		
Netherlands	5.8		54.5	87.7	3.93	8.63
Portugal	na		77.7	na	26.80	25.59
Spain	8.7		60.3	63.7	9.05	12.19
United Kingdom	13.3		48.6	63.5	6.89	10.83
EFTA countries						
Austria	7.5		49.0	80.8	3.50	na
Finland	14.3		39.1	48.2	7.33	9.08
Iceland	na		na	na	na	na
Norway	12.9		51.9	59.9	5.35[a]	13.46[a]
Sweden	na		39.3	na	9.58	14.18
Switzerland	8.8		101.1	119.4	3.63	5.46
Other countries						
Canada	6.7		40.5	62.8	8.25	9.75
Japan	8.6		106.9	163.5	2.32	5.91
Turkey	51.0		23.0	25.4	49.20[a]	na
United States	10.5		63.8	68.4	6.52	8.35

Note
[a] Data is for years other than 1986.

Table A3.19 Income distribution

| | | % share of household income (by percentile group of households) | | | | | |
	Year	Lowest 20%	Second	Third Quantile	Fourth	Highest 20%	Highest 10%
EC countries							
Belgium	1978–9	7.9	13.7	18.6	23.8	36.0	21.5
Denmark	1981	5.4	12.0	18.4	25.6	38.6	22.3
France	1975	5.5	11.5	17.1	23.7	42.2	26.4
W. Germany	1978	7.9	12.5	17.0	23.1	39.5	24.0
Greece		na	na	na	na	na	na
Ireland	1973	7.2	13.1	16.6	23.7	39.4	25.1
Italy	1977	6.2	11.3	15.9	22.7	43.9	28.1
Luxemburg		—	—	—	—	—	—
Netherlands	1981	8.3	14.1	18.2	23.2	36.2	21.5
Portugal	1973–4	5.2	10.0	14.4	21.3	49.1	33.4
Spain	1980–1	6.9	12.5	17.3	23.2	40.0	24.0
United Kingdom	1979	7.0	11.5	17.0	24.8	39.7	23.4

Table A3.19 (Con't)

	Year	Lowest 20%	Second	Third Quantile	Fourth	Highest 20%	Highest 10%
				% share of household income (by percentile group of households)			
EFTA countries							
Austria		na	na	na	na	na	na
Finland	1981	6.3	12.1	18.4	25.5	37.6	21.7
Iceland		na	na	na	na	na	na
Norway	1982	6.0	12.9	18.3	24.6	38.2	22.8
Sweden	1981	7.4	13.1	16.8	21.0	41.7	28.1
Switzerland	1978	6.6	13.5	18.5	23.4	38.0	23.7
Other countries							
Canada	1981	5.3	11.8	18.0	24.9	40.0	23.8
Japan	1979	8.7	13.2	17.5	23.1	37.5	22.4
Turkey	1973	3.5	8.0	12.5	19.5	56.5	40.7
United States	1980	5.3	11.9	17.9	25.0	39.9	23.3

Table A3.20 Health and nutrition

	Population per				Daily calorie supply (per capita)		Babies with low weights (%)
	Physician		Nursing person				
	1965	1981	1965	1981	1985	1981	1984
EC countries							
Belgium	700	370	590	130	na	3,679	5
Denmark	740	420	190	140	3,417	3,489	6
France	830	460	380	110	3,303	3,358	5
W. Germany	640	420	500	170	3,143	3,519	6
Greece	710	390	600	370	3,086	3,637	6
Ireland	950	770	170	140	3,530	3,736	4
Italy	1,850	750	790	250	3,113	3,493	7
Luxemburg	—	—	—	—	—	—	—
Netherlands	860	480	270	170	3,149	3,348	4
Portugal	1,240	500	1,160	na	2,531	3,122	8
Spain	800	360	1,220	280	2,844	3,303	1
United Kingdom	870	680	200	120	3,346	3,148	7
EFTA countries							
Austria	720	440	350	170	3,303	3,440	6
Finland	1,300	460	180	100	3,119	2,961	4
Iceland	na	na	na	na	na	na	na
Norway	790	460	340	70	3,047	3,171	4
Sweden	910	410	310	100	2,922	3,007	4
Switzerland	710	390	270	130	3,413	3,406	5
Other countries							
Canada	770	550	190	120	3,289	3,443	6
Japan	970	740	410	210	2,669	2,695	5
Turkey	2,900	1,530	2,290	1,240	2,636	3,218	8
United States	670	500	310	180	3,292	3,682	7
USSR	480	270	280	na	3,231	3,332	6

Table A3.21 Education (enrolment ratios)

	Primary[b] Total		Total		Secondary Male		Female		Tertiary[c] Total	
	1965	1985	1965	1985	1965	1985	1965	1985	1965	1985
EC countries										
Belgium	106	95	75	96	77	94	72	97	15	31
Denmark	98	98	83	103[a]	98	104[a]	67	103[a]	14	29[a]
France	134	114	56	96	53	88[a]	59	95[a]	18	30
W. Germany	na	96	na	74	na	73	na	75	9	30
Greece	110	106[a]	49	86[a]	57	87[a]	41	84[a]	10	21[a]
Ireland	108	100	51	96[a]	53	91[a]	50	101[a]	12	22[a]
Italy	112	98	47	75	53	74[a]	41	73[a]	11	26[a]
Luxemburg	—	—	—	—	—	—	—	—	—	—
Netherlands	104	95[a]	61	102[a]	64	103[a]	57	100[a]	17	31[a]
Portugal	84	112	42	47[a]	49	43[a]	34	51[a]	5	13[a]
Spain	115	104	38	91	46	88[a]	29	91[a]	6	27[a]
United Kingdom	92	101	66	89	67	83[a]	66	87[a]	12	22[a]
EFTA countries										
Austria	106	99	52	79	52	77	52	81	9	27
Finland	92	104	76	102	72	95	80	110	11	33
Iceland	na	na	na	na	na	na	na	na	na	na
Norway	97	97	64	97[a]	97	66[a]	95	100[a]	11	31
Sweden	95	98	62	83	63	79[a]	60	88[a]	13	38[a]
Switzerland	87	na	37	na	38	na	35	na	8	22
Other countries										
Canada	105	105	56	103	57	103	55	103	26	55
Japan	100	102	82	96	82	95	81	97	13	30[a]
Turkey	101	116	16	42	22	47	9	28	4	9
United States	na	101	na	99	na	99	na	98	40	57
USSR	103	106	72	99	65	na	79	na	na	21

Notes
[a] The data refer to years other than those specified.
[b] The male/female ratios at the primary level of education have been omitted due to the insignificant differences between them in all countries except for Finland and Turkey where the female ratios were lower than their male equivalent in 1965.
[c] The male/female ratios at the tertiary level of education are not available because not many countries choose to have them.

Table A3.22 Average tariffs (per cent) 1958[a]

	Benelux	France	W. Germany	Italy	EC (6)	Denmark	United Kingdom	Canada	United States
Instruments (86)	13	22	8	17	16	3	27	19	29
Footwear (851)	20	21	10	21	19	19	25	24	19
Clothing (84)	20	26	13	25	21	19	26	25	32½
Furniture (821)	13	23	8	21	17	11	20	25	24
Building parts and fittings (81)	15	19	8	25	17	8	15	16	20
Transport equipment (73)	17	29	12	34	22	8	25	17	13
Electric machinery, etc. (72)	11	19	6	21	15	8	23	18	20
Machinery other than electric (71)	8	18	5	20	13	6	17	9	12
Manufactures of metal (699)	11	20	10	23	16	6	21	18	23
Ordnance (691)	9	14	7	17	11	1	22	13	26
Iron and steel (681)	5	13	7	17	10	1	14	12	13
Silver, platinum, gems, jewellery (67)	5	13	3	7	6	5	11	13	29
Non-metallic mineral manufactures (66)	12	16	6	21	13	5	17	21	13
Textiles, etc., except clothing (65)	14	19	11	20	16	9	23	21	26
Paper, paperboard, etc. (64)	14	16	8	18	15	6	13	17	10½
Wood manufactures, etc., except furniture (63)	11	19	7	22	16	4	15	12	18
Rubber manufactures (62)	17	19	10	19	18	8	21	18	18
Leather, etc. (61)	11	17	12	18	12	11	16	17	17
Chemicals (5)	7	16	8	17	12	4	15	11	24

Note

[a] The figures are subject to the reservations stated in the source. The figures in brackets refer to SITC classification.

Source: PEP, *Atlantic Tariffs and Trade,* Allen and Unwin, 1962.

Part II

Theory and measurement

This section of the book is devoted to the discussion of the theoretical aspects of the EC and to the measurement of the impact of the formation of the EC on trade, production and factor mobility.

The whole section is basically concerned with two concepts: 'trade creation' and 'trade diversion'. These can be illustrated rather simplistically as follows. In Table II.1 the cost of beef per lb is given in new pence for the United Kingdom, France and New Zealand. With a 50 per cent non-discriminatory tariff rate the cheapest source of supply of beef for the United Kingdom is the home producer. When the United Kingdom and France form a customs union, the cheapest source of supply becomes France. Hence the United Kingdom saves 10p per lb of beef making a total saving of £1 million for ten million lb. This is '*trade creation*': *the replacement of expensive domestic production by cheaper imports from the partner.*

In Table II.2 the situation is different as a result of a lower initial non-discriminatory tariff rate (25 per cent) by the United Kingdom. Before the

Table II.1 Beef

	UK	France	New Zealand
The cost per unit (p)	90	80	70
UK domestic price with a 50% tariff rate (p)	90	120	105
UK domestic price when the UK and France form a customs union (p)	90	80	105

Total cost before the customs union = 90p × 10 million lb = £9 million
Total cost after the customs union = 80p × 10 million lb = £8 million
Total savings for the UK consumer = £1 million

Table II.2 Beef

	UK	France	New Zealand
The cost per unit (p)	90	80	70
UK domestic price with a 25% tariff rate (p)	90	100	87½
UK domestic price when the UK and France form a customs union (p)	90	80	87½

Total cost to the UK government before the customs union = 70p × 10 million lb = £7 million
Total cost to the UK after the customs union = 80p × 10 million lb = £8 million
Total loss to the UK government = £1 million

Table II.3a Beef

	UK	France	New Zealand
The cost per unit (p)	90	80	70
UK domestic price with a 50% tariff rate (p)	90	120	105
UK domestic price with a non-discriminatory tariff reduction of 80% (i.e. tariff rate becomes 10%) (p)	90	88	77

Total cost to the UK before the tariff reduction = 90p × 10 million lb = £9 million
Total cost to the UK after the tariff reduction = 70p × 10 million lb = £7 million
Total savings for the UK = £2 million

Table II.3b Butter

	UK	France	New Zealand
The cost per unit (p)	90	80	70
UK domestic price with a 25% tariff rate (p)	90	100	87½
UK domestic price with a non-discriminatory tariff reduction of 80% (i.e. tariff rate becomes 5%) (p)	90	84	73½

Total cost to the UK before the tariff reduction = 70p × 10 million lb = £7 million
Total cost to the UK after the tariff reduction = 70p × 10 million lb = £7 million
Total savings for the UK = nil

customs union, New Zealand is the cheapest source of supply. After the customs union, France becomes the cheapest source. There is a total loss to the United Kingdom of £1 million, since the tax revenue is claimed by the government. This is '*trade diversion*': *the replacement of cheaper initial imports from the outside world by expensive imports from the partner.*

In Tables II.3a and II.3b there are two commodities: beef and butter. The cost of beef per lb is the same as in the previous examples and so is the cost of butter per lb. Note that Table II.3a starts from the same position as Table II.1 and Table II.3b from the same position as Table II.2. Here the United Kingdom does not form a customs union with France, rather it reduces its tariff rate by 80 per cent on a non-discriminatory basis. This gives a saving of £2 million in comparison with the customs union situation. Therefore, *a non-discriminatory tariff reduction is superior to customs union formation.*

Now consider Tables II.3a and II.3b in comparison with Tables II.1 and II.2. The total cost for tables II.1, II.2 and II.3 before the customs union is £9 million + £7 million = £16 million.

The total cost for Tables II.1 and II.2 after the customs union = £8 million + £8 million = £16 million.

The total cost for Table II.3 after the customs union = £7 million + £7 million = £14 million.

Hence, a non-discriminatory tariff reduction is more economical for the United Kingdom than the formation of a customs union with France.

This dangerously (?) simple analysis has been the inspiration of a massive literature on customs union theory. Admittedly, some of the contributions are misguided in that they concentrate on a non-problem.

Chapter 4 tackles the basic concepts of trade creation and trade diversion, considers the implications of domestic distortions and scale economies for the basic analysis and discusses the terms of trade effects. Chapter 5 contains an analysis of the vital issue of monetary integration. Chapters 6 and 7 discuss the measurement of the theoretical concepts discussed in Chapter 4.

4 The theory of economic integration

A. M. El-Agraa

In reality, almost all existing cases of economic integration were either proposed or formed for political reasons even though the arguments popularly put forward in their favour were expressed in terms of possible economic gains. However, no matter what the motives for economic integration are, it is still necessary to analyse the economic implications of such geographically discriminatory groupings.

As mentioned in the introduction, at the customs union (and free trade area) level, the possible sources of economic gain can be attributed to the following:

1. Enhanced efficiency in production made possible by increased specialisation in accordance with the law of comparative advantage.
2. Increased production level due to better exploitation of economies of scale made possible by the increased size of the market.
3. An improved international bargaining position, made possible by the larger size, leading to better terms of trade.
4. Enforced changes in economic efficiency brought about by enhanced competition.
5. Changes affecting both the amount and quality of the factors of production arising from technological advances.

If the level of economic integration is to proceed beyond the customs union (CU) level, to the economic union level, then further sources of gain become possible as a result of:

6. Factor mobility across the borders of member nations.
7. The coordination of monetary and fiscal policies.
8. The goals of near full employment, higher rates of economic growth and better income distribution becoming unified targets.

I shall now discuss these considerations in some detail.

4.1 The customs union aspects

4.1.1 The basic concepts

Before the theory of second best was introduced, it used to be the accepted tradition that CU formation should be encouraged. The rationale for this was that since free trade maximised world welfare and since CU formation was a move towards free trade, CUs increased welfare even though they did not maximise it. This rationale certainly lies behind the guidelines of the GATT Article XXIV (see appendix to Chapter 1) which permits the formation of CUs and free trade areas as the special exceptions to the rules against international discrimination.

Viner (1950) and Byé (1950) challenged this proposition by stressing the point that CU formation is by no means equivalent to a move to free trade since it amounts to free trade *between* the members and *protection vis-à-vis* the outside world. This combination of free trade and protectionism could result in trade creation and/or trade diversion. Trade creation is the replacement of expensive domestic production by cheaper imports from a partner and trade diversion is the replacement of cheaper initial imports from the outside world by more expensive imports from a partner. Viner and Byé stressed the point that trade creation is beneficial since it does not affect the rest of the world, while trade diversion is harmful; it is the relative strength of these two effects which determines whether or not CU formation should be advocated. It is therefore important to understand the implications of these concepts.

Assuming perfect competition in both the commodity and factor markets, automatic full employment of all resources, costless adjustment procedures, perfect factor mobility nationally but perfect immobility across national boundaries, prices determined by cost, three countries H (the home country), P (the potential customs union partner) and W (the outside world), plus all the traditional assumptions employed in tariff theory, we can use a simple diagram to illustrate these two concepts.

In Figure 4.1 I am using partial-equilibrium diagrams because it has been demonstrated that partial- and general-equilibrium analyses are, under certain circumstances, equivalent – see El-Agraa and Jones (1981). S_W is W's perfectly elastic tariff-free supply curve for this commodity; S_H is H's supply curve while S_{H+P} is the joint H and P tariff-free supply curve. With a non-discriminatory tariff imposition by H of $AD(t_H)$, the effective supply curve facing H is $BREFQT$, i.e. its own supply curve up to E and W's, subject to the tariff $[S_W(1 + t_H)]$ after that. The domestic price is therefore OD, which gives domestic production of Oq_2, domestic consumption of Oq_3 and imports of q_2q_3. H pays q_2LMq_3 for these imports while the domestic consumer pays q_2EFq_3 with the difference ($LEFM$) being the tariff revenue which accrues to the H government. This government revenue can be viewed as a transfer from the consumers to the government with the implication that when the government spends it, the marginal valuation of that expenditure should be exactly equal to its valuation by the private consumers so that no distortions should occur.

If H and W form a CU, the free trade position will be restored so that Oq_5 will be consumed in H and this amount will be imported from W. Hence free trade is

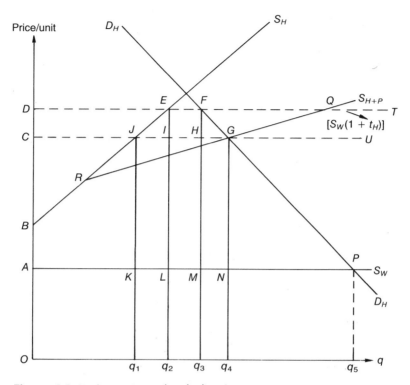

Figure 4.1 Trade creation and trade diversion

obviously the ideal situation. But if H and P form a CU, the tariff imposition will still apply to W while it is removed from P. The effective supply curve in this case is $BRGQT$. The union price falls to OC resulting in a fall in domestic production to Oq_1, an increase in consumption to Oq_4 and an increase in imports to q_1q_4. These imports now come from P.

The welfare implications of these changes can be examined by employing the concepts of consumers' and producers' surpluses. As a result of increased consumption, consumers' surplus rises by $CDFG$. Part of this ($CDEJ$) is a fall in producers' surplus due to the decline in domestic production and another part ($IEFH$) is a portion of the tariff revenue now transferred back to the consumer subject to the same condition of equal marginal valuation. This leaves the triangles JEI and HFG as gains from CU formation. However, before we conclude whether or not these triangles represent *net* gains we need to consider the overall effects more carefully.

The fall in domestic production from Oq_2 to Oq_1 leads to increased imports of q_1q_2. These cost q_1JIq_2 to import from P while they originally cost q_1JEq_2 to produce domestically. (Note that these resources are assumed to be employed elsewhere in the economy without any adjustment costs or redundancies.) There is therefore a saving of $\mathcal{J}EI$. The increase in consumption from Oq_3 to Oq_4 leads to new imports of q_3q_4 which cost q_3HGq_4 to import from P. These give a welfare satisfaction to the consumer equal to q_3FGq_4. There is therefore an increase in satisfaction of HFG. However, the *initial* imports of q_2q_3 cost the country q_2LMq_3 but these imports now come from P costing q_2IHq_3. Therefore these imports lead to a loss equal to the loss in government revenue of $LIHM$ ($IEFH$ being a retransfer). It follows that the triangle gains ($\mathcal{J}EI + HFG$) have to be compared with the loss of tariff revenue ($LIHM$) before a definite conclusion can be made regarding whether or not the net effect of CU formation has been one of gain or loss.

It should be apparent that q_2q_3 represents, in terms of our definition, trade diversion, and $q_1q_2 + q_3q_4$ represents trade creation, or alternatively that areas $\mathcal{J}EI$ plus HFG are trade creation (benefits) while area $LIHM$ is trade diversion (loss). (The reader should note that I am using Johnson's 1974 definition so as to avoid the unnecessary literature relating to a trade-diverting welfare-improving CU promoted by Lipsey (1960), Gehrels (1956–7) and Bhagwati (1971).) It is, then, obvious that trade creation is economically desirable while trade diversion is undesirable. Hence Viner and Byé's conclusion that it is the relative strength of these two effects which should determine whether or not CU formation is beneficial or harmful.

The reader should note that if the initial price is that given by the intersection of D_H and S_H (due to a higher tariff rate), the CU would result in pure trade creation since the tariff rate is prohibitive. If the price is initially OC (due to a lower tariff rate), then CU formation would result in pure trade diversion. It should also be apparent that the size of the gains and losses depends on the price elasticities of S_H, and S_{H+P} and D_H and on the divergence between S_W and S_{H+P}, i.e. cost differences.

4.1.2 The Cooper–Massell criticism

Viner and Byé's conclusion was challenged by Cooper and Massell (1965a). They suggested that the reduction in price from OD to OC should be considered in two stages: firstly, reduce the tariff level indiscriminately (i.e. for both W and P) to AC which gives the same union price and production, consumption and import changes; secondly, introduce the CU starting from the new price OC. The effect of these two steps is that the gains from trade creation ($\mathcal{J}EI + HFG$) still accrue while the losses from trade diversion ($LIHM$) no longer apply since the new effective supply curve facing H is $B\mathcal{J}GU$ which ensures that imports continue to come from W at the cost of q_2LMq_3. In addition, the new imports due to trade creation ($q_1q_2 + q_3q_4$) now cost less, leading to a further gain of $K\mathcal{J}IL$ plus $MHGN$. Cooper and Massell then conclude that *a policy of unilateral tariff reduction is superior to customs union formation*.

4.1.3 Further contributions

Following the Cooper–Massell criticism have come two independent but somewhat similar contributions to the theory of CUs. The first development is by Cooper and

Massell (1965b) themselves, the essence of which is that two countries acting together can do better than each acting in isolation. The second is by Johnson (1965b) which is a private plus social costs and benefits analysis expressed in political economy terms. Both contributions utilise a 'public good' argument, with Cooper and Massell's expressed in practical terms and Johnson's in theoretical terms. However, since the Johnson approach is expressed in familiar terms this section is devoted to it – space limitations do not permit a consideration of both.

Johnson's method is based on four major assumptions:

1. Governments use tariffs to achieve certain non-economic (political, etc.) objectives.
2. Actions taken by governments are aimed at offsetting differences between private and social costs. They are, therefore, rational efforts.
3. Government policy is a rational response to the demands of the electorate.
4. Countries have a preference for industrial production.

In addition to these assumptions, Johnson makes a distinction between private and public consumption goods, real income (utility enjoyed from both private and public consumption, where consumption is the sum of planned consumption expenditure and planned investment expenditure) and real product (defined as total production of privately appropriable goods and services).

These assumptions have important implications. Firstly, competition among political parties will make the government adopt policies that will tend to maximise consumer satisfaction from both 'private' and 'collective' consumption goods. Satisfaction is obviously maximised when the *rate of satisfaction per unit of resources is the same in both types of consumption goods*. Secondly, 'collective preference' for industrial production implies that consumers are willing to expand industrial production (and industrial employment) beyond what it would be under free international trade.

Tariffs are the main source of financing this policy simply because GATT regulations rule out the use of export subsidies, and domestic political considerations make tariffs, rather than the more efficient production subsidies, the usual instruments of protection.

Protection will be carried to the point where *the value of the marginal utility derived from collective consumption of domestic and industrial activity is just equal to the marginal excess private cost of protected industrial production*.

The marginal excess cost of protected industrial production consists of two parts: the marginal production cost and the marginal private consumption cost. The marginal production cost is equal to the proportion by which domestic cost exceeds world market cost. In a very simple model this is equal to the tariff rate. The marginal private consumption cost is equal to the loss of consumer surplus due to the fall in consumption brought about by the tariff rate which is necessary to induce the marginal unit of domestic production. This depends on the tariff rate and the price elasticities of supply and demand.

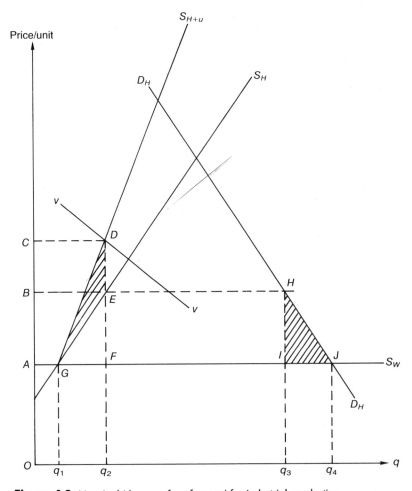

Figure 4.2 Marginal 'degree of preference' for industrial production

In equilibrium, the proportional marginal excess private cost of protected production measures the marginal 'degree of preference' for industrial production. This is illustrated in Figure 4.2 where S_W is the world supply curve at world market prices; D_H is the constant-utility demand curve (at free trade private utility level); S_H is the domestic supply curve; S_{H+u} is the marginal private cost curve of protected industrial production, including the excess private consumption cost (FE is the first component of marginal excess cost – determined by the excess marginal cost of domestic production in relation to the free trade situation due to the tariff imposition (AB) – and the area GED (= IHJ) is the second component which is the dead loss in consumer surplus due to the tariff imposition); the height of vv above S_W represents the marginal value of industrial production in collective consumption and vv represents the preference for industrial production which is assumed to yield a diminishing marginal rate of satisfaction.

The maximisation of *real* income is achieved at the intersection of vv with S_{H+u} requiring the use of tariff rate AB/OA to increase industrial production from Oq_1 to Oq_2 and involving the marginal degree of preference for industrial production v.

Note that the higher the value of v, the higher the tariff rate, and that the degree of protection will tend to vary inversely with the ability to compete with foreign industrial producers.

It is also important to note that, in equilibrium, the government is maximising real income, not real product: maximisation of real income makes it necessary to sacrifice real product in order to gratify the preference for collective consumption of industrial production.

It is also important to note that this analysis is not confined to net importing countries. It is equally applicable to net exporters, but lack of space prevents such elaboration – see El-Agraa (1984a) for a detailed explanation.

The above model helps to explain the significance of Johnson's assumptions. It does not, however, throw any light on the CU issue. To make the model useful for this purpose it is necessary to alter some of the assumptions. Let us assume that industrial production is not one aggregate but a variety of products in which countries have varying degrees of comparative advantage; that countries differ in their overall comparative advantage in industry as compared with non-industrial production; that no country has monopoly/monopsony power (conditions for optimum tariffs do not exist); and that no export subsidies are allowed (GATT).

The variety of industrial production allows countries to be both importers and exporters of industrial products. This, in combination with the 'preference for industrial production', will motivate each country to practise some degree of protection.

Given the third assumption, a country can gratify its preference for industrial production only by protecting the domestic producers of the commodities it imports (import-competing industries). Hence the condition for equilibrium remains the same: $vv = S_{H+u}$. The condition must now be reckoned differently, however: S_{H+u} is slightly different because, firstly, the protection of import-competing industries will reduce exports of both industrial and non-industrial products (for balance of payments purposes). Hence, in order to increase total industrial production by one unit it will be necessary to increase protected industrial production by more than one unit so as to compensate for the induced loss of industrial exports. Secondly, the protection of import-competing industries reduces industrial exports by raising their production costs (because of perfect factor mobility). The stronger this effect, *ceteris paribus*, the higher the marginal excess cost of industrial production. This will be greater the larger the industrial sector compared with the non-industrial sector and the larger the protected industrial sector relative to the exporting industrial sector.

If the world consists of two countries, one must be a net exporter and the other necessarily a net importer of industrial products and the balance of payments is settled in terms of the non-industrial sector. Hence both countries can expand industrial production at the expense of the non-industrial sector. Therefore for each country the prospective gain from reciprocal tariff reduction must lie in the expansion of exports of industrial products. The reduction of a country's own tariff rate is therefore a source of loss which can be compensated for only by a reduction of the other country's tariff rate (for an alternative, orthodox, explanation see El-Agraa, 1979b).

What if there are more than two countries? If reciprocal tariff reductions are arrived at on a 'most-favoured nation' basis, then the reduction of a country's tariff rate will increase imports from *all* the other countries. If the tariff rate reduction is, however, discriminatory (starting from a position of non-discrimination), then there are two advantages: firstly, a country can offer its partner an increase in exports of industrial products without any loss of its own industrial production by diverting imports from third countries (trade diversion); secondly, when trade diversion is exhausted any increase in partner industrial exports to this country is exactly equal to the reduction in industrial production in the same country (trade creation), hence eliminating the gain to third countries.

Therefore, discriminatory reciprocal tariff reduction costs each partner country less, in terms of the reduction in domestic industrial production (if any) incurred per unit increase in partner industrial production, than does non-discriminatory reciprocal tariff reduction. On the other hand, preferential tariff reduction imposes an additional cost on the tariff-reducing country: the excess of the costs of imports from the partner country over their cost in the world market.

The implications of this analysis are as follows:

1. Both trade creation and trade diversion yield a gain to the CU partners.
2. Trade diversion is preferable to trade creation for the preference-granting country since a sacrifice of domestic industrial production is not required.
3. Both trade creation and trade diversion may lead to increased efficiency due to economies of scale.

Johnson's contribution has not achieved the popularity it deserves because of the alleged nature of his assumptions. However, a careful consideration of these assumptions indicates that they are neither extreme nor unique: they are the kind of assumptions that are adopted in any analysis dealing with differences between social and private costs and benefits. It can, of course, be claimed that an

> economic rationale for customs unions on public goods grounds can only be established if for political or some such reasons governments are denied the use of direct production subsidies – and while this may be the case in certain countries at certain periods in their economic evolution, there would appear to be no acceptable reason why this should generally be true. Johnson's analysis demonstrates that customs union and other acts of commercial policy may make economic sense under certain restricted conditions, but in no way does it establish or seek to establish a general argument for these acts. (Krauss, 1972)

While this is a legitimate criticism it is of no relevance to the world we live in: subsidies are superior to tariffs, yet all countries prefer the use of tariffs to subsidies!

It is a criticism related to a first best view of the world. It therefore seems unfair to criticise an analysis on grounds which do not portray what actually exists; it is what prevails in practice that matters. That is what Johnson's approach is all about and that is what the theory of second best tries to tackle. In short, the lack of belief in this approach is tantamount to a lack of belief in the validity of the distinction between social and private costs and benefits.

4.1.4 Dynamic effects

The so-called dynamic effects (Balassa, 1961) relate to the numerous means by which economic integration may influence the rate of growth of GNP of the participating nations. These ways include the following:

1. Scale economies made possible by the increased size of the market for both firms and industries operating below optimum capacity before integration occurs.
2. Economies external to the firm and industry which may have a downward influence on both specific and general cost structures.
3. The polarisation effect, by which is meant the cumulative decline either in relative or absolute terms of the economic situation of a particular participating nation or of a specific region within it due either to the benefits of trade creation becoming concentrated in one region or to the fact that an area may develop a tendency to attract factors of production.
4. The influence on the location and volume of real investment.
5. The effect on economic efficiency and the smoothness with which trade transactions are carried out due to enhanced competition and changes in uncertainty.

Hence these dynamic effects include various and completely different phenomena. Apart from economies of scale, the possible gains are extremely long term and cannot be tackled in orthodox economic terms: for example, intensified competition leading to the adoption of best business practices and to an American type of attitude, etc. (Scitovsky, 1958), seems like a naive socio-psychological abstraction that has no solid foundation with regard to either the aspirations of those countries contemplating economic integration or to its actually materialising.

Economies of scale can, however, be analysed in orthodox economic terms. In a highly simplistic model, like that depicted in Figure 4.3 where scale economies are internal to the industry, their effects can easily be demonstrated – a mathematical discussion can be found in, *inter alia*, Choi and Yu (1984), but the reader must be warned that the assumptions made about the nature of the economies concerned are extremely limited, e.g. H and P are 'similar'. $D_{H,P}$ is the identical demand curve for this commodity in both H and P and D_{H+P} is their joint demand curve; S_W is the world supply curve; AC_P and AC_H are the average cost curves for this commodity in P and H respectively. Note that the diagram is drawn in such a manner that W has constant average costs and is the most efficient supplier of this commodity. Hence free

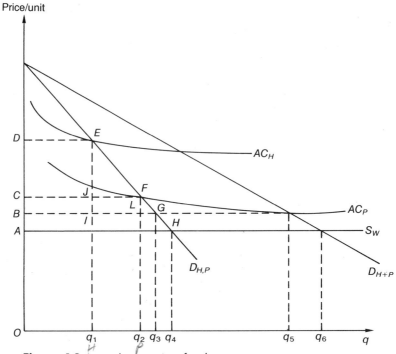

Figure 4.3 Internal economies of scale

trade is the best policy resulting in price OA with consumption which is satisfied entirely by imports of Oq_4 in each of H and P giving a total of Oq_6.

If H and P impose tariffs, the only justification for this is that uncorrected distortions exist between the privately and socially valued costs in these countries – see Jones (1979) and El-Agraa and Jones (1981). The best tariff rates to impose are Corden's (1972a) made to measure tariffs which can be defined as those which encourage domestic production to a level that just satisfies domestic consumption without giving rise to monopoly profits. These tariffs are equal to AD and AC for H and P respectively, resulting in Oq_1 and Oq_2 production in H and P respectively.

When H and P enter into a CU, P, being the cheaper producer, will produce the entire union output – Oq_5 – at a price OB. This gives rise to consumption in each of H and P of Oq_3 with gains of $BDEG$ and $BCFG$ for H and P respectively. Parts of these gains, $BDEI$ for H and $BCFL$ for P, are 'cost-reduction' effects. There also results a production gain for P and a production loss in H due to abandoning production altogether.

Whether or not CU formation can be justified in terms of the existence of economies of scale will depend on whether or not the net effect is a gain or a loss, since in this example P gains and H loses, as the loss from abandoning production in H must outweigh the consumption gain in order for the tariff to have been imposed in the first

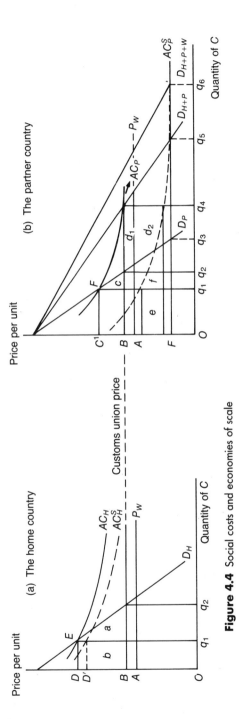

Figure 4.4 Social costs and economies of scale

place. If the overall result is net gain, then the distribution of these gains becomes an important consideration. Alternatively, if economies of scale accrue to an integrated industry, then the locational distribution of the production units becomes an essential issue.

4.1.5 Domestic distortions

A substantial literature has tried to tackle the important question of whether or not the formation of a CU may be economically desirable when there are domestic distortions. Such distortions could be attributed to the presence of trade unions which negotiate wage rates in excess of the equilibrium rates or to governments introducing minimum wage legislation – both of which are widespread activities in most countries. It is usually assumed that the domestic distortion results in a *social* average cost curve which lies below the private one. Hence, in Figure 4.4, which is adapted from Figure 4.3, I have incorporated AC_H^s and AC_P^s as the *social* curves in the context of economies of scale and a separate representation of countries H and P.

Note that AC_H^s is drawn to be consistently above AP_W, while AC_P^s is below it for higher levels of output. Before the formation of a CU, H may have been adopting a made to measure tariff to protect its industry, but the first best policy would have been one of free trade, as argued in the previous section. The formation of the CU will therefore lead to the same effects as in the previous section, with the exception that the cost-reduction effect (Figure 4.4b) will be less by DD' times Oq_1. For P, the effects will be as follows:

1. As before, a consumption gain of area c.
2. A cost-reduction effect of area e due to calculations relating to social rather than private costs.
3. Gains from sales to H of areas d_1 and d_2, with d_1 being an income transfer from H to P, and d_2 the difference between domestic social costs in P and P_W – the world price.
4. The social benefits accruing from extra production made possible by the CU – area f – which is measured by the extra consumption multiplied by the difference between P_W and the domestic social costs.

However, this analysis does not lead to an economic rationale for the formation of CUs, since P could have used first best policy instruments to eliminate the divergence between private and social cost. This would have made AC_P^s the operative cost curve, and assuming that D_{H+P+W} is the world demand curve, this would have led to a world price of OF and exports of q_3q_5 and q_5q_6 to H and W respectively, with obviously greater benefits than those offered by the CU. Hence the economic rationale for the CU will have to depend on factors that can explain why first best instruments could not have been employed in the first instance (Jones, 1980). In short, this is not an absolute argument for CU formation.

4.1.6 Terms of trade effects

So far the analysis has been conducted on the assumption that CU formation has no effect on the terms of trade. This implies that the countries concerned are too insignificant to have any appreciable influence on the international economy. Particularly in the context of the EC and groupings of a similar size, this is a very unrealistic assumption.

The analysis of the effects of CU formation on the terms of trade is extremely complicated – see Mundell (1964), Arndt (1968) and El-Agraa (1989a). At this level of generality, however, it suffices to state that nations acting in consort or in unison are more likely to exert an influence than each acting alone. It could also be argued that the bigger the group the stronger its bargaining position *vis-à-vis* the outside world. Indeed, Petith (1977) found evidence of improved terms of trade for the EC.

It should be stressed, however, that possible gains from improved terms of trade can be achieved only if the outside world does not retaliate. Indeed, the gains found by Petith for the EC could be attributed entirely to this factor. Hence, larger groupings do not necessarily automatically guarantee favourable changes in the terms of trade since such groupings may also encourage joint action by those nations excluded from them.

4.2 Customs unions versus free trade areas

The analysis so far has been conducted on the premise that differences between CUs and free trade areas can be ignored. However, the ability of the member nations of free trade areas to decide their own commercial policies *vis-à-vis* the outside world raises certain issues. Balassa (1962) pointed out that free trade areas may result in deflection of trade, production and investment. Deflection of trade occurs when imports from W (the cheapest source of supply) come via the member country with the lower tariff rate, assuming that transport and administrative costs do not outweigh the tariff differential. Deflection of production and investment occur in commodities whose production requires a substantial quantity of raw materials imported from W – the tariff differential regarding these materials might distort the true comparative advantage in domestic materials therefore resulting in resource allocations according to overall comparative disadvantage.

If deflection of trade does occur, then the free trade area effectively becomes a CU with a CET equal to the lowest tariff rate which is obviously beneficial for the world – see Curzon Price (1974). However, most free trade areas seem to adopt 'rules of origin' so that only those commodities which originate in a member state are exempt from tariff imposition. If deflection of production and investment does take place, we have the case of the so-called 'tariff factories'; but the necessary conditions for this to occur are extremely limited – see El-Agraa in El-Agraa and Jones (1981, Chapter 3), El-Agraa (1984b) and El-Agraa (1989a).

4.3 Economic unions

The analysis of CUs needs drastic extension when applied to economic unions (EUs). Firstly, the introduction of free factor mobility may enhance efficiency through a more rational reallocation of resources but it may also result in depressed areas therefore creating or aggravating regional problems and imbalances – see Mayes (1983a) and Robson (1984). Secondly, fiscal harmonisation may also improve efficiency by eliminating non-tariff barriers (NTBs) and distortions and by equalising their effective protective rates – see Chapter 13. Thirdly, the coordination of monetary and fiscal policies which is implied by monetary integration may ease unnecessarily severe imbalances, hence resulting in the promotion of the right atmosphere for stability in the economies of the member nations.

These EU elements must be tackled *simultaneously* with trade creation and diversion as well as economies of scale and market distortions. However, such interactions are too complicated to consider here: the interested reader should consult El-Agraa (1983a; 1983b; 1984a; 1985a; 1989a). This section will be devoted to a brief discussion of factor mobility. Since monetary integration is probably the most crucial of commitments for a regional grouping and because it is one of the immediate aspirations of the EC, the following chapter is devoted to it.

With regard to *factor mobility*, it should be apparent that the removal (or harmonisation) of all barriers to labour (L) and capital (K) will encourage both L and K to move. L will move to those areas where it can fetch the highest possible reward, i.e. 'net advantage'. This encouragement need not necessarily lead to an increase in actual mobility since there are socio-political factors which normally result in people remaining near their birthplace – social proximity is a dominant consideration, which is why the average person does not move. If the reward to K is not equalised, i.e. differences in marginal productivities (mps) exist before the formation of an EU, K will move until the mps are equalised. This will result in benefits which can be clearly described in terms of Figure 4.5, which depicts the production characteristics in H and P. M_H and M_P are the schedules which relate the K stocks to their mps in H and P respectively, given the quantity of L in each country (assuming two factors of production only).

Prior to EU formation, the K stock (which is assumed to remain constant throughout the analysis) is Oq_2 in H and Oq_1^* in P. Assuming that K is immobile internationally, all K stocks must be nationally owned and, ignoring taxation, profit per unit of K will be equal to its mp, given conditions of perfect competition. Hence the total profit in H is equal to $b + e$ and $i + k$ in P. Total output is, of course, the whole area below the M_P curve but within Oq_2 in H and Oq_1^* in P, i.e. areas $a + b + c + d + e$ in H and $j + i + k$ in P. Therefore, L's share is $a + c + d$ in H and j in P.

Since the mp in P exceeds that in H, the removal of barriers to K mobility or the harmonisation of such barriers will induce K to move away from H and into P. This is because nothing has happened to affect K in W. Such movement will continue until the mp of K is the same in both H and P. This results in q_1q_2 ($= q_1^*q_2^*$) of K moving

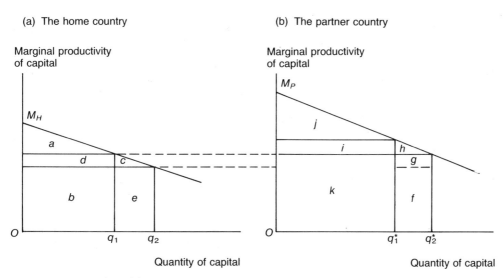

Figure 4.5 Capital mobility

from H to P. Hence the output of H falls to $a + b + c$ while its *national* product including the return of the profit earned on K in P ($= g + f$) increases by ($g - c$). In P, *domestic* product rises by ($f + g + h$) while *national* product (excluding the remittance of profits to H) increases by area h only. Both H and P experience a change in the relative share of L and K in national product, with K owners being favourably disposed in H and unfavourably disposed in P.

Of course, this analysis is too simplistic since, apart from the fact that K and L are never perfectly immobile at the international level and multinational corporations have their own ways of transferring K (see McManus, 1972; Buckley and Casson, 1976; Dunning, 1977), the analysis does not take into account the fact that K may actually move to areas with low wages after the formation of an EU. Moreover, if K moves predominantly in only one direction, one country may become a depressed area; hence the 'social' costs and benefits of such an occurrence need to be taken into consideration, particularly if the EU deems it important that the economies of both H and P should be balanced. Therefore, the above gains have to be discounted or supplemented by such costs and benefits.

4.4 Macroeconomics of integration

We have seen that trade creation and trade diversion are the two concepts most widely used in international economic integration. We have also seen that their economic implications for resource reallocation are usually tackled in terms of particular commodities under conditions of global full employment. However, the economic consequences for the outside world and their repercussions on the integrated area are usually left to intuition. Moreover, their implications for employment are usually ruled out by assumption.

In an effort to rectify these serious shortcomings, I have used a macroeconomic model (see Chapters 6–8 of El-Agraa and Jones, 1981 and El-Agraa, 1989a) with the purpose of investigating these aspects. The model is still in its infancy and a sophisticated model is now being constructed (see Jones, 1983). However, even the crude model so far published indicates that the advantages of using a macro model are that it clearly demonstrates the once and for all nature of trade creation and trade diversion. It also shows the insignificance of their overall impact given realistic values of the relevant coefficients: marginal propensities to import; marginal propensities to consume); tariff rates, etc. The model also demonstrates that trade creation is beneficial for the partner gaining the new output and exports but is detrimental to the other partner and the outside world; and that trade diversion is beneficial for the partner now exporting the commodity but is detrimental for the other partner and the outside world. The author feels that a more sophisticated model will corroborate these conclusions.

4.5 Economic integration in developing countries

It has been claimed that the body of economic integration theory as so far developed has no relevance for the Third World. This is because the theory suggests that there would be more scope for trade creation if the countries concerned were initially very competitive in production but potentially very complementary and that a CU would be more likely to be trade creating if the partners conducted most of their foreign trade among themselves – see Lipsey (1960) and Meade (1955). These conditions are unlikely to be satisfied in the majority of the developing nations. Moreover, most of the effects of integration are initially bound to be trade diverting, particularly since most of the Third World seeks to industrialise.

On the other hand, it was also realised that an important obstacle to the development of industry in these countries is the inadequate size of their individual markets – see Brown (1961), Hazlewood (1967, 1975) and Robson (1980; 1983; 1984). It is therefore necessary to increase the market size so as to encourage optimum plant installations: hence the need for economic integration. This would, however, result in industries clustering together in the relatively more advanced of these nations – those that have already commenced the process of industrialisation.

I have demonstrated elsewhere (El-Agraa, 1979a) that there is essentially *no theoretical difference* between economic integration in the advanced world and the Third World but that there is a major difference in terms of the *type* of economic integration that suits the particular *circumstances* of developing countries and that is politically feasible: the need for an equitable distribution of the gains from industrialisation and the location of industries is an important issue (see above). This suggests that any type of economic integration that is being contemplated must incorporate as an essential element a common fiscal authority and some coordination of economic policies. But then one could equally well argue that *some degree* of these elements is necessary in *any* type of integration – see the Raisman Committee recommendations for the EAC (1961).

4.6 Economic integration among communist countries

The only example up to now of economic integration among communist countries is the CMEA. However, here the economic system perpetuates a fundamental lack of interest of domestic producers in becoming integrated with both consumers and producers in other member countries. As Marer and Montias (1988) emphasise, the integration policies of member nations must focus on the mechanism of state to state relations rather than on domestic economic policies which would make CMEA integration more attractive to producers and consumers alike. That is, integration must be planned by the state at the highest possible level and imposed on ministries, trusts and enterprises. It should also be stated that the CMEA operates different pricing mechanisms for intra- and extra-area trade. Moreover, the attitude of the USSR is extremely important since the policies of the East European members of the CMEA are somewhat constrained by the policies adopted by the organisation's most powerful member, for economic as well as political reasons. CMEA integration, therefore, has to be approached within an entirely different framework but this is not the appropriate place for discussing it – the interested reader can consult El-Agraa (1989a).

4.7 Conclusions

The conclusions reached here are consistent with my 1979 and 1989a conclusions and with those of Jones in El-Agraa and Jones (1981). They are as follows:

Firstly, that the rationale for regional economic integration rests upon the existence of constraints on the use of first best policy instruments. Economic analysis has had little to say about the nature of these constraints, and presumably the evaluation of any regional scheme of economic integration should incorporate a consideration of the validity of the view that such constraints do exist to justify the pursuit of second rather than first best solutions.

Secondly, that even when the existence of constraints on superior policy instruments is acknowledged, it is misleading to identify the results of regional economic integration by comparing an arbitrarily chosen common policy with an arbitrarily chosen national policy. Of course, ignorance and inertia provide sufficient reasons why existing policies may be non-optimal; but it is clearly wrong to attribute gains which would have been achieved by appropriate unilateral action to a policy of regional integration. Equally, although it is appropriate to use the optimal common policy as a point of reference, it must be recognised that this may overstate the gains to be achieved if, as seems highly likely, constraints and inefficiencies in the political processes by which policies are agreed prove to be greater among a group of countries than within any individual country.

Although the first two conclusions raise doubts about the case for regional economic integration, in principle at least, a strong general case for economic integration does exist. In unions where economies of scale may be in part external to national industries, the rationale for unions rests essentially upon the recognition of the externalities and market imperfections which extend beyond the boundaries of national states. In such circumstances, unilateral national action will not be optimal while integrated action offers the scope for potential gain.

As with the solution to most problems of externalities and market imperfections, however, customs union theory frequently illustrates the proposition that a major stumbling block to obtaining the gains from joint optimal action lies in agreeing an acceptable distribution of such gains. Thus the fourth conclusion is that the achievement of the potential gains from economic integration will be limited to countries able and willing to cooperate to distribute the gains from integration so that all partners may benefit compared to the results achieved by independent action. It is easy to argue from this that regional economic integration may be more readily achieved than global solutions but, as the debate about monetary integration in the EC illustrates (see Chapter 5), the chances of obtaining potential mutual gain may well founder in the presence of disparate views about the distribution of such gains and weak arrangements for redistribution.

5 European monetary integration

A. M. El-Agraa

The previous chapter was devoted to a discussion of the economic consequences of tariff removal and the establishment of the common external tariff (CET), i.e. the chapter was concerned mainly with the customs union (CU) and some of the economic union (EU) aspects of the EC. It is now well established that monetary integration is by far the most important feature of economic integration. The purpose of this chapter is to discuss the theoretical aspects of monetary integration, with the practical considerations to be tackled in Chapter 14.

Although the Treaty of Rome does not specifically state that a European monetary union (EMU) should be established, its architects foresaw the EC evolving into a fully-fledged common market with complete monetary and economic integration of its member states. The serious monetary upheavals of 1970, which culminated in the devaluation of the French franc and in speculation in favour of the German mark leading to its eventual revaluation, prompted the ministers at The Hague to agree in principle to the establishment of an EMU. The Community later agreed to introduce a complete EMU by 1980, in stages, with the first phase to begin on 1 January 1971. Later, when the six became nine and the world monetary system was in complete disarray, it was inevitable that the 1980 date should be waived. In 1978, the Bremen Conference affirmed its commitment to achieving the objective in the near future by adopting the European Monetary System (EMS) which was incorporated into the Single European Act (SEA) that came into effect on 1 July 1987 – see Chapter 14. This commitment came closer to becoming a reality when the leaders of the twelve member nations agreed to establish an economic and monetary union in three stages, with the first to commence on 1 July 1990 (see below).

In spite of this progress, some influential economists have expressed great doubts as to whether there will be any gains from monetary integration and have emphasised the (so-called) costs to members of such a union. The purpose of this chapter is to reappraise the whole issue with the object of finding out whether or not there is a case against complete monetary integration.

5.1 What is monetary integration?

Full monetary integration is required only in very involved schemes of economic integration, such as EUs. Monetary integration has two essential components: an exchange-rate union and capital (K) market integration. An exchange-rate union is established when member countries have what is in effect one currency. The actual existence of one currency is not necessary, however, because if member countries have *permanently* and *irrevocably* fixed exchange rates among themselves, the result is effectively the same. Of course, one could argue that the adoption of a single currency would guarantee the irreversibility of undertaking membership of a monetary union, which would have vast repercussions for the discussion in terms of actual unions; but one could equally well argue that if a member nation decided to opt out of a monetary union, it would do so irrespective of whether or not the union entailed the use of a single currency.

Convertibility refers to the *permanent* absence of all exchange controls for both current and K transactions, including interest and dividend payments (and the harmonisation of relevant taxes and measures affecting the K market) within the union. It is, of course, absolutely necessary to have complete convertibility for trade transactions, otherwise an important requirement of CU formation is threatened, namely the promotion of free trade among members of the CU, which is an integral part of an EU. That is why this aspect of monetary integration does not need any discussion; it applies even in the case of a free trade area (FTA). Convertibility for K transactions is related to free factor mobility and is therefore an important aspect of K market integration which is necessary in common markets (CMs), not in CUs or FTAs.

In practice, this definition of monetary integration should specifically include the following:

1. An explicit harmonisation of monetary policies.
2. A common pool of foreign exchange reserves.
3. A single central bank.

There are important reasons for including these elements. Suppose union members decide either that one of their currencies will be a reference currency, or that a new unit of account will be established. Also assume that each member country has its own foreign exchange reserves and conducts its own monetary and fiscal policies. If a member finds itself running out of reserves, it will have to engage in a monetary and fiscal contraction sufficient to restore the reserve position. This will necessitate the fairly frequent meeting of the finance ministers or central bank governors, to consider whether or not to change the parity of the reference currency. If they do decide to change it, then all the member currencies will have to move with it. Such a situation could create the sorts of difficulty which plagued the Bretton Woods System:

1. Each finance minister might fight for the rate of exchange that was most suitable for his/her country. This might make bargaining hard; agreement might become difficult to reach and the whole system might be subject to continuous strain.
2. Each meeting might be accompanied by speculation about its outcome. This might result in undesirable speculative private K movements into or out of the union.
3. The difficulties that might be created by (1) and (2) might result in the reference currency being permanently fixed relative to outside currencies, e.g. the US dollar.
4. However, the system does allow for the possibility of the reference currency floating relative to non-member currencies, or floating within a band. If the reference currency does float, it might do so in response to conditions in its own market. This would be the case, however, only if the union required the monetary authorities in the partner countries to vary their exchange rates so as to maintain constant parities relative to the reference currency. They would then have to buy and sell the reserve currency so as to maintain or bring about the necessary exchange-rate alteration. Therefore, the monetary authorities of the reference currency would, in fact, be able to determine the exchange rate for the whole union.
5. Such a system does not guarantee the permanence of the parities between the union currencies that is required by the appropriate specification of monetary integration. There is the possibility that the delegates will not reach agreement, or that one of the partners might finally choose not to deflate to the extent necessary to maintain its rate at the required parity or that a partner in surplus might choose neither to build up its reserves nor to inflate as required and so might allow its rate to rise above the agreed level.

In order to avoid such difficulties, it is necessary to include in the definition of monetary integration the three elements specified. The central bank would operate in the market so as to permanently maintain the exchange parities among the union currencies and, at the same time, it would allow the rate of the reference currency to fluctuate, or to alter intermittently, relative to the outside reserve currency. For instance, if the foreign exchange reserves in the common pool were running down, the common central bank would allow the reference currency, and with it all the partner currencies, to depreciate. This would have the advantage of economising in the use of foreign exchange reserves, since all partners would not tend to be in deficit or surplus at the same time. Also surplus countries would automatically be helping deficit countries.

However, without explicit policy coordination, a monetary union would not be effective. If each country conducted its own monetary policy, and hence could engage in as much domestic credit creation as it wished, surplus countries would be financing deficit nations without any incentives for the deficit countries to restore equilibrium. If one country ran a large deficit, the union exchange rate would depreciate, but this might put some partner countries into surplus. If wage rates were rising in the member countries at different rates, while productivity growth did not differ in such a way as to offset the effects on relative prices, those partners with the lower inflation rates would be permanently financing the other partners.

In short,

> Monetary integration, in the sense defined, requires the unification and joint management both of monetary policy and of the external exchange-rate policy of the union. This in turn entails further consequences. First, in the monetary field the rate of increase of the money supply must be decided jointly. Beyond an agreed amount of credit expansion, which is allocated to each member state's central bank, a member state would have to finance any budget deficit in the union's capital market at the ruling rate of interest. A unified monetary policy would remove one of the main reasons for disparate movements in members' price levels, and thus one of the main reasons for the existence of intra-union payment imbalances prior to monetary union. Secondly, the balance of payments of the entire union with the rest of the world must be regulated at union level. For this purpose the monetary authority must dispose of a common pool of exchange reserves, and the union exchange rates with other currencies must be regulated at the union level. (Robson, 1980)

Monetary integration which explicitly includes the three requirements specified will therefore enable the partners to do away with all these problems right from the start. Incidentally, this also suggests the advantages of having a single currency.

5.2 The gains and losses

The gains due to membership of a monetary union could be both economic and non-economic, i.e. political, sociological, etc. The non-economic benefits are too obvious to warrant space; for example it is difficult to imagine that a complete political union could become a reality without the establishment of a monetary union. The discussion will therefore be confined to the economic benefits, which can be briefly summarised as follows:

1. The common pool of foreign exchange reserves already discussed has the incidental advantage of economising in the use of foreign exchange reserves both in terms of the fact that member nations will not go into deficit *simultaneously* and that intra-union trade transactions will no longer be financed by foreign exchange. In the context of the EC this will reduce the role of the US dollar or reduce the EC's dependence on the dollar.
2. In the case of forms of economic integration like the EC, the adoption of the common unit of account (say, the *European Currency Unit*, ECU) as a common currency would transform it into a major world currency able to compete with the

US dollar or Japanese yen on equal terms. The advantages of such a currency are too well established to discuss here. However, the use of an integrated area's currency as a major reserve currency doubtless imposes certain burdens on the area; but in the particular case of the EC, it would create an oligopolistic market situation which could either lead to collusion, resulting in a permanent sensible reform of the international monetary system, or intensify the reserve currency crisis and lead to a complete collapse of the international monetary order. The latter possibility is, of course, extremely likely to result in the former outcome; it is difficult to imagine that the leading nations in the world economy would allow monetary chaos to be the order of the day.

3. Another source of gain could be a reduction in the cost of financial management. Monetary integration should enable the spreading of overhead costs of financial transactions more widely. Also, some of the activities of the institutions dealing in foreign exchanges might be discontinued, leading to a saving in the use of resources.

4. There also exist the classical advantages of having permanently fixed exchange rates (or one currency) among members of a monetary union for free trade and factor movements. Stability of exchange rates enhances trade, encourages K to move to where it is most productively rewarded and ensures that labour (L) will move to where the highest rewards prevail. It seems unnecessary to emphasise that this does not mean that *all L* and *all K* should be mobile, but simply enough of each to generate the necessary adjustment to any situation. Nor is it necessary to stress that hedging can tackle the problem of exchange-rate fluctuations only at a cost, no matter how low that cost may be.

5. The integration of the K market has a further advantage. If a member country of a monetary union is in deficit (assuming that countries can be recognised within such a union), it can borrow directly on the union market, or raise its rate of interest to attract K inflow and therefore ease the situation. However, the integration of economic policies within the union ensures that this help will occur automatically under the auspices of the common central bank. Since no single area is likely to be in deficit permanently, such help can be envisaged for all the members. Hence there is no basis for the assertion that one country can borrow indefinitely to sustain real wages and consumption levels that are out of line with that nation's productivity and the demand for its products (Corden, 1972a).

6. When a monetary union establishes a central fiscal authority with its own budget, then the larger the size of this budget, the higher the degree of fiscal harmonisation (the *MacDougall Report*, 1977). This has some advantages: regional deviations from internal balance can be financed from the centre; and the centralisation of social security payments financed by contributions or taxes on a progressive basis would have some stabilising and compensating effects, modifying the harmful effects of monetary integration (Corden, 1972a).

7. There are negative advantages in the case of the EC in the sense that monetary integration is necessary for maintaining the EC as it exists; for example, the *Common Agricultural Policy* (CAP – see Chapter 9) would be undermined if

exchange rates were to be flexible (Ingram, 1973), i.e. an EMU would enable the EC to rid itself of its troublesome *monetary compensatory amounts* (MCAs).

These benefits of monetary integration are clear and there are few economists who would question them. However, there is no consensus of opinion with regard to its costs.

The losses from membership of a monetary union are emphasised by Fleming (1971) and Corden (1972a). Assume that the world consists of three countries: the home country (H), the potential partner country (P) and the rest of the world (W). Also assume that, in order to maintain both internal and external equilibrium, one country (H) needs to devalue its currency relative to W, while P needs to revalue *vis-à-vis* W. Moreover, assume that H and P use fiscal and monetary policies for achieving internal equilibrium. If H and P were partners in an exchange-rate union, they would devalue together – which is consistent with H's policy requirements in isolation – or revalue together – which is consistent with P's requirements in isolation – but they would not be able to alter the rate of exchange in a way that was consistent with both. Under such circumstances, the alteration in the exchange rate could leave H with an external deficit, forcing it to deflate its economy and increase/create unemployment, or it could leave it with a surplus, forcing it into accumulating foreign reserves or allowing its prices and wages to rise. If countries deprive themselves of rates of exchange (or trade impediments) as policy instruments, they impose on themselves losses that are essentially the losses emanating from *enforced departure from internal balance* (Corden, 1972a).

In short, the rationale for retaining flexibility in the rates of exchange rests on the assumption that governments aim to achieve both internal and external balance, and as Tinbergen (1952) has shown, to achieve these *simultaneously* at least an equal number of instruments is needed. This can be explained in the following manner. Orthodoxy has it that there are two macroeconomic policy targets and two policy instruments. Internal equilibrium is tackled via financial instruments, which have their greatest impact on the level of aggregate demand, and the exchange rate is used to achieve external equilibrium. Of course, financial instruments can be activated via both monetary and fiscal policies and may have a varied impact on both internal and external equilibria. Given this understanding, the case for maintaining flexibility in exchange rates depends entirely on the presumption that the loss of one of the two policy instruments will conflict with the achievement of both internal and external equilibria.

With this background in mind, it is vital to follow the Corden–Fleming explanation of the enforced departure from internal equilibrium. Suppose a country is initially in internal equilibrium but has a deficit in its external account. If the country were free to vary its rate of exchange, the appropriate policy for it to adopt to achieve overall balance would be a combination of devaluation and expenditure reduction. When the rate of exchange is not available as a policy instrument, it is necessary to reduce expenditure by more than is required in the optimal situation, with the result of extra unemployment. The *excess* unemployment, which can be valued in terms of output or whatever, is the cost to that country of depriving itself of the exchange rate as a policy instrument. The extent of this loss is determined, *ceteris paribus*, by the marginal propensity to import and to consume exportables, or, more generally, by the marginal propensity to consume tradables relative to non-tradables.

The expenditure reduction which is required for eliminating the initial external account deficit will be smaller the higher the marginal propensity to import. Moreover, the higher the marginal propensity to import, the less the effect of that reduction in expenditure on demand for domestically produced commodities. For both reasons, therefore, the higher the marginal propensity to import, the less domestic unemployment will result from abandoning the devaluation of the rate of exchange as a policy instrument. If the logic of this explanation is correct, it follows that as long as the marginal propensity to consume domestic goods is greater than zero, there will be some cost due to fixing the rate of exchange. A similar argument applies to a country which cannot use the exchange-rate instrument when it has a surplus in its external account and internal equilibrium: the required excess expenditure will have little effect on demand for domestically produced goods and will therefore exert little inflationary pressure if the country's marginal propensity to import is high.

This analysis is based on the assumption that there exists a trade-off between rates of change in costs and levels of unemployment – the Phillips curve. Assuming that there is a Phillips (1958) curve relationship (a negative response of rates of change in

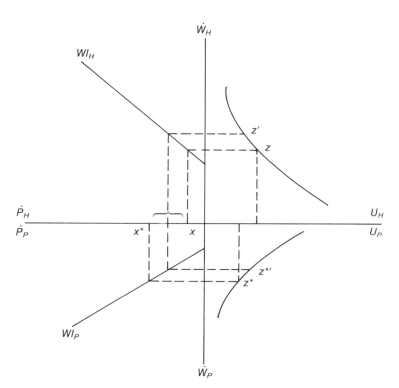

Figure 5.1 The Fleming–Corden analysis of monetary integration

money wages – $\dot{W}$ – and the level of unemployment – U), Fleming's (1971) and Corden's (1972a) analysis can be explained by using a simple diagram devised by de Grauwe (1978). Hence, in Figure 5.1, the top half depicts the position of H while the lower half depicts that of P. The top right and the lower right corners represent the two countries' Phillips curves while the remaining quadrants show their inflation rates corresponding to the rates of change in wages – $\dot{P}$. WI (which stands for *wage-rate change* and corresponding *inflation*) and WI_P are, of course, determined by the share of L in total GNP, the rate of change in the productivity of L and the degree of competition in both the factor and commodity markets, with perfect competition resulting in the WIs being straight lines. Note that the intersection of the WIs with the vertical axes will be determined by the rates of change of L's share in GNP and its rate of productivity change. The diagram has been drawn on the presumption that the L productivity changes are positive.

The diagram is drawn in such a way that countries H and P differ in all respects: the positions of their Phillips curves; their preferred trade-offs between $\dot{W}$ and $\dot{P}$; and their rates of productivity growth. H has a lower rate of inflation, x, than P, $x^\star$ (equilibria being at z and $z^\star$); hence, without monetary integration, P's currency should depreciate relative to H's; note that it is only a chance in a million that the two countries' inflation rates would coincide. Altering the exchange rates would then enable each country to maintain its preferred internal equilibrium: z and $z^\star$ for respectively countries H and P.

When H and P enter into an exchange-rate union, i.e. have irrevocably fixed exchange rates *vis-à-vis* each other, their inflation rates cannot differ from each other, given a model without traded goods. Each country will therefore have to settle for a combination of U and $\dot{P}$ which is different from what it would have liked. The Fleming–Corden conclusion is thus vindicated.

However, this analysis rests entirely on the acceptance of the Phillips curve. The on-going controversy between Keynesians and monetarists, although still far from being resolved, has at least led to the consensus that the form of the Phillips curve just presented is too crude. This is because many economists no longer believe that there is a trade-off between unemployment and inflation; if there is any relationship at all, it must be a short-term one such that the rate of unemployment is in the long term independent of the rate of inflation: there is a 'natural rate' of unemployment which is determined by rigidities in the market for L. The crude version of the Phillips curve has been replaced by an expectations-adjusted one along the lines suggested by Phelps (1968) and Friedman (1975), i.e. the Phillips curves become vertical in the long run. This position can be explained with reference to Figure 5.2 which depicts three Phillips curves for one of the two countries. Assume that unemployment is initially at point U_2, i.e. the rate of inflation is equal to zero, given the short-term Phillips curve indicated by ST_1. The expectations-augmented Phillips curve suggests that if the government tries to lower unemployment by the use of monetary policy, the short-term effect would be to move to point a, with positive inflation and lower unemployment. However, in the long term, people would adjust their expectations, causing an upward shift of the Phillips curve to ST_2 which leads to equilibrium at point b. The

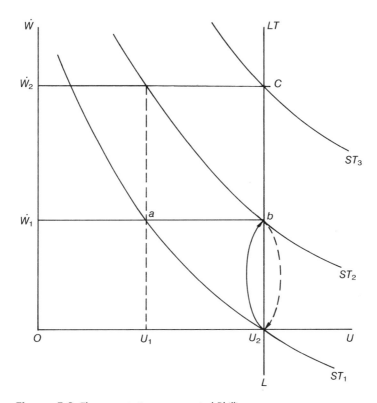

Figure 5.2 The expectations-augmented Phillips curve

initial level of unemployment is thus restored but with a positive rate of inflation. A repetition of this process gives the vertical long-term curve labelled LT.

If both partners H and P have vertical LT curves, Figure 5.1 will have to be adjusted to give Figure 5.3. The implications of this are that:

1. Monetary integration will have no long-term effect on either partner's rate of unemployment since this will be fixed at the appropriate 'natural rate' for each country – U_H, U_P.
2. If monetary integration is adopted to bring about balanced growth as well as equal 'natural rates' of unemployment, this can be achieved only if other policy instruments are introduced to bring about uniformity in the two L markets.

Therefore, this alternative interpretation of the Phillips curve renders the Fleming–Corden conclusion invalid.

Be that as it may, it should be noted that Allen and Kenen (1980) and Allen (1983) have demonstrated, using a sophisticated and elaborate model with financial assets, that, although monetary policy has severe drawbacks as an instrument for

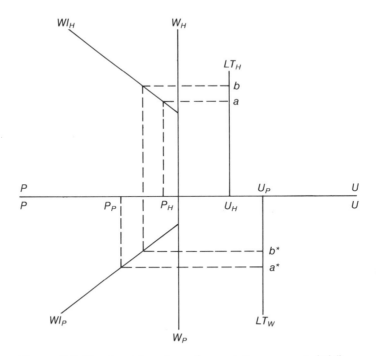

Figure 5.3 Monetary integration with expectations-augmented Phillips curves

adjusting cyclical imbalances within a monetary union, it may be able to influence the demand for the goods produced by member countries in a differential manner within the short term, provided the markets of the member nations are not too closely integrated. Their model indicates that economic integration, in this sense, can come about as a consequence of the substitutability between nations' commodities, especially their financial assets, and of country biases in the purchase of commodities and financial assets. The moral of this is that the central bank of a monetary union can operate disparate monetary policies in the different partner countries without compromising their internal and external equilibria – a severe blow to those who stress the costs from monetary integration.

Moreover, once non-traded goods are incorporated into the model and/or K and L mobility are allowed for, it follows that the losses due to deviating from internal equilibrium vanish into oblivion, a point which Corden (1972a; 1977) readily accedes to. Finally, this model does not allow for the fact that monetary integration involves at least three countries; hence W has to be explicitly included in the model. Allen and Kenen (1980) tried to develop a model along these lines, but their model is not a straightforward extension of that depicted in Figure 5.1.

In concluding this section, it may be appropriate to highlight the limitations in the argument put forward by Fleming and Corden.

1. It is clearly stated in the definition of monetary integration that the fixity of exchange rate parities within a monetary union (or the adoption of one currency) does not mean that the different member currencies cannot vary in unison relative to extra-union currencies. Hence the monetary union is not forgoing the availability of exchange rate variations relative to the outside world.

2. In a proper monetary union, an extra deficit for one region can come about only as a result of a revaluation of the union currency – the union as a whole has an external surplus *vis-à-vis* the outside world. Such an act would increase the foreign exchange earnings of the surplus region, and therefore of the union as a whole, provided the conditions for a successful revaluation exist. The common central bank and the integration of monetary policies will ensure that the extra burden on the first region is alleviated: the overall extra earnings will be used to help the region with the extra deficit. Needless to say, such a situation does not lead to surplus regions financing deficit regions indefinitely because no single region is likely to be in deficit or surplus permanently and because the policy coordination will not allow one region to behave in such a manner unless there are reasons of a different nature which permit such a situation to be sustained.

3. Even if one accepts the Fleming–Corden argument at its face value, the assumptions are extremely controversial. For instance, devaluation can work effectively only when there is 'monetary illusion'; otherwise it would be pointless since it would not work. Is it really permissible to assume that trade unionists, wherever they may be, suffer from money illusion? Johnson, Ingram and others (in Krause and Salant, 1973b, pp. 184–202) have all pointed to the fallacious nature of such an assumption in the context of the EC – see Sumner and Zis (1982) for a full discussion of this issue. Corden's response has been to suggest that exchange-rate alterations may work if money wages are forced up because the catching-up process is never complete. Such an argument is far from convincing simply because the catching-up process has no validity as a true adjustment; it cannot be maintained indefinitely because, sooner or later, trade unionists will allow for it when negotiating money wage increases.

4. One must remember that in practice there would never be a separation between the exchange-rate union and K market integration. Once one allows for the role of convertibility for K transactions, K will always come to the rescue. Corden has reservations about this too since he argues that K integration can help in the short run, but, in the long term, while it has its own advantages, it cannot solve the problem. The rationale for this is that no region can borrow indefinitely on a private market, no matter how efficient and open the market is, to sustain levels of real wages, and hence real consumption levels, which are too high, given the productivity level in the region. Clearly, this is a switching of grounds: devaluation is nothing but a temporary adjustment device as the discussion of the monetary approach to the balance of payments has shown. Why then should devaluation be more desirable than short-term K adjustment? Moreover, for a region that is permanently in deficit, all economists would agree that devaluation is no panacea.

5.   We have seen that monetary integration can be contemplated only when the countries concerned have an EU in mind. In such conditions, the mobility of L will also help in the adjustment process. This point is conceded by Corden, but he believes that L mobility may help only marginally since it would take prolonged unemployment to induce people to emigrate, and, if monetary integration proceeded far in advance of 'psychological integration' (defined as the suppression of existing nationalisms and a sense of attachment to place in favour of an integrated community nationalism and an American-style geographic rooted-ness), nationalistic reactions to any nation's depopulation may become very intense. This reasoning is similar to that in the previous case since it presupposes that the problem region is a *permanently* depressed area. Since no region in the union is ever likely to experience chronic maladjustments, L mobility needs only to be marginal and national depopulation is far from the truth.

6.   Finally, and more fundamentally, a very crucial element is missing from the Fleming–Corden argument. Their analysis relates to a country in internal equilibrium and external deficit. If such a country were outside a monetary union, it could devalue its currency. Assuming that the necessary conditions for effective devaluation prevailed, then devaluation would increase the national income of the country, increase its price level, or result in some combination of the two. Hence a deflationary policy would be required to restore the internal balance. However, if the country were to lose its freedom to alter its exchange rate, it would have to deflate in order to depress its imports and restore external balance. According to the Fleming–Corden analysis, this alternative would entail unemployment in excess of that prevailing in the initial situation. The missing element in this argument can be found by specifying how devaluation actually works. Devaluation of a country's currency results in changes in relative price levels and is price inflationary for, at least, both exportables and importables. These relative price changes, given the necessary stability conditions, will depress imports and (perhaps) increase exports. The deflationary policy which is required (to accompany devaluation) in order to restore internal balance should therefore eliminate the *newly injected* inflation as well as the *extra* national income. By disregarding the 'inflationary' implications of devaluation, Fleming and Corden reach the unjustifiable *a priori* conclusion that membership of a monetary union would necessitate extra sacrifice of employment in order to achieve the same target. Any serious comparison of the two situations would indicate that no such *a priori* conclusion can be reached – one must compare like with like.

In addition to the above limitations, one should point out a fundamental contradiction in the analysis of those who exaggerate the costs. If a nation decides to become a member of a monetary union, this implies that it accedes to the notion that the benefits of such a union must outweigh any possible losses and/or that it feels that a monetary union is essential for maintaining a rational EU. It will want to do so because its economy is more interdependent with its partners than with W. Why then would such a country prize the availability of the exchange rate as a policy instrument for its own domestic purposes? The answer is that there is no conceivable rational reason for its doing so: it will want to have an inflation rate, monetary growth target and unemployment rate which are consistent with those of its partners. Also, the use of an EU's rate of exchange *vis-à-vis* W, plus the rational operations of the common central bank and its general activities, should ensure that any worries on the part of the home country are alleviated. For such a country to feel that there is something intrinsically good about having such a policy instrument at its own disposal is tantamount to its not having any faith in or a true commitment to the EU to which it has voluntarily decided to belong.

Expressed in terms of Tinbergen's criterion of an equal number of policy instruments and objectives, it should be remembered that the formation of a *complete* EU is effectively just a step short of complete political union. However, given that the necessary conditions for an effective EU require a great deal of political unification, EU and complete political integration are hardly distinguishable in a realistic situation. In forming an EU, the countries concerned will actually be acquiring a free policy instrument: they will have two instruments for internal policy adjustments and one for external (joint) adjustment when all they effectively need is only one of the former instruments. Therefore, an analysis which does not explicitly incorporate this dimension can hardly claim to have any relevance to the situation under consideration.

5.3 European monetary integration

For the purposes of this chapter, it is of the utmost importance to establish the nature of the envisaged EMU in the light of the agreed definition of monetary integration.

According to the EC 1972 document on 'Economic and monetary union', usually referred to as the Werner Report,

> The Community would, according to the Council resolution:
> 1. Constitute a zone where persons, goods, services and capital would move freely – but without distorting competition, or creating structural and regional imbalances – and where economic undertakings could develop their activities on a Community scale;
> 2. Form a single monetary entity within the international monetary system, characterised by the total and irreversible convertibility of currencies; the elimination of fluctuation margins of exchange rates between the [members]; the irrevocable fixing of their parity relationships. These steps would be essential for the creation of a single currency, and they would involve a Community-level organisation of central banks;
> 3. Hold the powers and responsibilities in the economic and monetary field that would enable its institutions to ensure the administration of the economic union. To this end, the necessary economic policy decisions would be taken at Community level and the necessary powers would be attributed to Community institutions.
>
> The Community organisation of central banks would assist, in the framework of its own responsibilities, in achieving the objectives of stability and growth in the Community.

These three principles would apply to:
(a) The internal monetary and credit policies of the union;
(b) Monetary policy *vis-à-vis* the rest of the world;
(c) Policy on a unified capital market and capital movements to and from non-member countries;
(d) Budgetary and taxation policies, as related to the policy for stability and growth...
(e) Structural and regional action needed to contribute to the balanced development of the Community.

As progress was made in moving closer to the final objectives, Community instruments would be created whenever they seemed necessary to replace or complement the action of national instruments. All actions would be interdependent; in particular, the development of monetary unification would be backed by parallel progress in the convergence, and then the unification of economic policies.

It is clear that the EMU envisaged in the Werner Report is consistent with, and satisfies all the requirements of, the accepted definition of monetary integration. However, one needs to ask if both the EMS and the EMU envisaged in the Delors Report satisfy the requirements of complete monetary integration. With respect to the EMS the answer is given at the end of this chapter and in Chapter 14. The answer concerning the Delors Report cannot be contemplated without a brief summary of both its contents and the background to its creation.

5.4 The Delors Report

The EC summit which was held in Hanover on 27 and 28 June 1988 decided that in adopting the Single Act, the EC member states had confirmed the objective of 'progressive realisation of economic and monetary union'. The heads of state agreed to discuss the means of achieving this in their meeting in Madrid in June of the following year, and to help them in their deliberations then they entrusted to a committee of central bankers and others, chaired by Mr Jacques Delors, President of the EC Commission, the 'task of studying and proposing concrete stages leading towards this union'. The committee reported just before the Madrid summit and its report is referred to as the Delors Report on EMU.

The committee was of the opinion that the creation of the EMU must be seen as a single process, but that this process should be in stages which progressively led to the ultimate goal; thus the decision to enter upon the first stage should commit a member state to the entire process. Emphasising that the creation of the EMU would necessitate a common monetary policy and require a high degree of compatibility of economic policies and consistency in a number of other policy areas, particularly in the fiscal field, the Report pointed out that the realisation of the EMU would require new arrangements which could be established only on the basis of a change in the relevant Treaty of Rome and consequent changes in national legislation.

The first stage should be concerned with the initiation of the process of creating the EMU. During this stage there would be a greater convergence of economic performance through the strengthening of economic and monetary policy coordination within the existing institutional framework. The economic measures would be concerned with the completion of the internal market and the reduction of existing disparities through programmes of budgetary consolidation in the member states involved and more effective structural and regional policies. In the monetary field the emphasis would be on the removal of all obstacles to financial integration and on the intensification of cooperation and coordination of monetary policies. Realignment of exchange rates was seen to be possible, but efforts would be made by every member state to make the functioning of other adjustment mechanisms more effective. The committee was of the opinion that it would be important to include all EC currencies in the exchange-rate mechanism of the EMS during this stage. The 1974 Council decision defining the mandate of central bank governors would be replaced by a new decision indicating that the committee itself should formulate opinions on the overall orientation of monetary and exchange-rate policy.

In the second stage, which would commence only when the Treaty had been amended, the basic organs and structure of the EMU would be set up. The committee stressed that this stage should be seen as a transition period leading to the final stage; thus it should constitute a 'training process leading to collective decision-making', but the ultimate responsibility for policy decisions would remain with national authorities during this stage. The procedure established during the first stage would be further strengthened and extended on the basis of the amended Treaty, and policy guidelines would be adopted on a majority basis. Given this understanding, the EC would:

1. Establish 'a medium-term framework for key economic objectives aimed at achieving stable growth, with a follow-up procedure for monitoring performances and intervening when significant deviations occurred'.
2. 'Set precise, although not yet binding, rules relating to the size of annual budget deficits and their financing'.
3. 'Assume a more active role as a single entity in the discussions of questions arising in the economic and exchange rate field'.

In the monetary field, the most significant feature of this stage would be the establishment of the European System of Central Banks (ESCB) to absorb the previous institutional monetary arrangements. The ESCB would start the transition with a first stage in which the coordination of independent monetary policies would be carried out by the Committee of Central Bank Governors. It was envisaged that the formulation and implementation of a common monetary policy would take place in the final stage; during this stage exchange-rate realignments would not be allowed except in exceptional circumstances.

The Report stresses that the nature of the second stage would require a number of actions, e.g.:

1. National monetary policy would be executed in accordance with the general monetary orientations set up for the EC as a whole.
2. A certain amount of foreign exchange reserves would be pooled and used to conduct interventions in accordance with the guidelines established by the ESCB.
3. The ESCB would have to regulate the monetary and banking system to achieve a minimum harmonisation of provisions (such as reserve requirements or payment arrangements) necessary for the future conduct of a common monetary policy.

The final stage would begin with the irrevocable fixing of member states' exchange rates and the attribution to the EC institutions of the full monetary and economic consequences. It is envisaged that during this stage the national currencies would eventually be replaced by a single EC currency. In the economic field, the transition to this stage is seen to be marked by three developments:

1. EC structural and regional policies may have to be further strengthened.
2. EC macroeconomic and budgetary rules and procedures would have to become binding.
3. The EC role in the process of international policy cooperation would have to become fuller and more positive.

In the monetary field, the irrevocable fixing of exchange rates would come into effect and the transition to a single monetary policy and a single currency would be made. The ESCB would assume full responsibilities, especially in four specific areas:

1. The formulation and implementation of monetary policy.
2. Exchange-market interventions in third currencies.
3. The pooling and management of all foreign exchange reserves.
4. Technical and regulatory preparations necessary for the transition to a single EC currency.

As agreed, the Report was the main item for discussion in the EC summit which opened in Madrid on 24 June 1989. In that meeting EC member nations agreed to call a conference which would decide the route to be taken to EMU. This agreement was facilitated by a surprisingly conciliatory Mrs Thatcher on the opening day of the summit. Instead of insisting (as was expected) that the United Kingdom would join the exchange-rate mechanism of the EC 'when the time is ripe', she set out five conditions for joining:

1. A lower inflation rate in the United Kingdom, and in the EC as a whole.
2. Abolition of all exchange controls (at the time of writing, Italy, France and Spain have them).
3. Progress towards the single EC market.
4. Liberalisation of financial services.
5. Agreement on competition policy.

Since these were minor conditions relative to the demands for creating the EMU, all member nations endorsed the Report and agreed on 1 July 1990 as the deadline for the commencement of the first stage. Indeed, the economic and finance ministers of the EC at a meeting on 10 July agreed to complete the preparatory work for the first stage by December, thus giving themselves six months to accommodate the adjustments that would be needed before the beginning of the first stage.

It should be clear that the EMU envisaged in the Delors Report is consistent with and satisfies all the requirements of a true economic and monetary union. Needless to add, sceptics will insist that this does not mean that the EMU will actually materialise since there is always the possibility of a loss of momentum (Delors has been both vigorous and successful), more British stalling and German vacillation, and that the process itself may take more than two decades to complete.

5.5 The transition to monetary integration

It was pointed out earlier that the most pessimistic conclusion that an economist can reach is that the gains from European monetary integration must exceed any possible losses from its formulation. If that is the case, why is that the Corden–Fleming argument used to be so dominant in this field?

The answer is twofold. Firstly, it is because economists had failed to point out the fallacy in their argument. Secondly, it is due to Corden's distinction between a *complete* and a *pseudo* exchange-rate union and to his equating the latter with the EMU envisaged in the Werner Report. This last point should be discussed in some detail.

The *pseudo* union, unlike the *complete* union, does not allow for economic policy coordination, a pool of foreign exchange reserves and a common central bank. It therefore creates the problems discussed in the definitional section. This raises the practical question: is the EMU envisaged in the Werner Report equivalent to a *pseudo* union?

The Werner Report (which was endorsed by the Community Council of Ministers in February 1971, but the implementation of which was later halted for reasons discussed below and in the Marjolin Report 1975) recommended the following (the emphasis is not in the original text):

(a) An economic and monetary union could be attained during this decade, if the plan had the permanent political support of the member governments;

(b) The first phase should begin on January 1, 1971, and could technically be completed within three years. This phase would be used to make the Community instruments more operational and to mark the beginnings of the Community's individuality within the international monetary system;

(c) *The first phase should not be considered as an objective in itself; it should be associated with the complete process of economic and monetary integration.* It should therefore be launched with the determination to arrive at the final goal;

(d) *In the first phase consultation procedures should be strengthened; the budgetary policies of the member states should accord with Community objectives; some taxes should be harmonised; monetary and credit policies should be coordinated; and integration of financial markets should be intensified.*

There are therefore two points to emphasise about the first stage of the EMU envisaged in the Werner Report. Firstly, it is more than a pseudo exchange-rate union – the underlined points, particularly (d), clearly indicate this. Secondly, it is only the *first stage* in a *process* leading to complete monetary integration. Even Corden admits that this first stage, even though it might take a long time to achieve, cannot be the permanent reality.

Given the stated objectives of the Delors Report mentioned in the previous section and the mechanism set out for attaining them it should be clear that the EMU envisaged is even more consistent with economic and monetary integration as rigorously defined. Hence, the same conclusion applies here: the problem of transition does not arise.

The confusion between the ultimate objective (complete monetary integration) and the first stage as a step in that direction is clearly demonstrated by the discussion relating to whether or not the EC (or some members of it) is a feasible or optimum currency area. Such a discussion, useful as it may be, has no relevance here: the fact that the members of the Community *are committed* to monetary integration has been substantiated by the declaration of the summit meeting of July 1978 and by the endorsement of the Delors Report. (One way of exposing the fallacious nature of this argument is to ask whether, if it could be conclusively proved that the United States was more than a feasible currency area, economists should advise its disintegration.) There are, of course, great *difficulties* in the *transition* to complete monetary integration, but no economist is able, or should even attempt, to predict that these difficulties would be permanent ones. In the words of Ingram,

> Perhaps the modes of thought used by economists cause them to neglect important economic aspects of the changing institutional structure of Europe. We should not forget that economists were also skeptical about the European Common Market. (Ingram, 1973)

(Readers interested in a critical evaluation of the approach to the theory of economic integration are advised to consult El-Agraa (1978), or refer to El-Agraa and Jones (1981) and El-Agraa (1989a).)

5.6 Tackling the transition problem

It is necessary for the purposes of this chapter to recall the brief reference made in Chapter 1 of this book to the positions of the 'monetarists' and the 'economists' regarding European monetary integration as envisaged in the Werner Report. The 'monetarists', whose leading protagonist was France, insisted on the immediate implementation of *irrevocably fixed rates of exchange* within the EC, accompanied by the imposition of very strict controls over capital mobility; the coordination and harmonisation of economic policies should be introduced as a later date. The 'economists', on the other hand, whose main leader was West Germany, proposed the more or less immediate introduction of the coordination and harmonisation of economic policies, to be followed almost immediately by complete freedom of capital mobility; only then should the irrevocable fixing of exchange rates be implemented. The 'monetarists' were mainly influenced by their interest in achieving a successful CAP; the adoption of permanently fixed rates of exchange would have, for example, eliminated the problems which led to the MCA system of border taxes and subsidies discussed in Chapter 8. The 'economists' were influenced by the fact that the members of the EC were at different stages in their economic development and they were particularly worried that the permanent fixing of exchange rates would force the 'weaker' members to manage their economies by interest-rate policies, with the result of increasing their unemployment levels. However, the point was a general one in that the fixing of exchange rates could have led to heavy inflation in West Germany, resulting in an underpricing of its industrial commodities. For France, which needed to restructure its agricultural sector, and the United Kingdom, which needed to restructure its industrial sector, the fixing of exchange rates could have resulted in balance of payments deficits which would have forced them to adopt deflationary policies, with resulting high levels of unemployment.

The Werner Report was essentially a compromise between the positions of the 'monetarists' and the 'economists'. The Report, however, remained essentially a background document in that it became a blueprint for European monetary integration, without becoming embodied in a Council resolution until it emerged anew, disguised as the Delors Report. It recommended the establishment of the EMU by *stages*, with the achievement of complete monetary integration by 1980. The monetary upheavals of the 1970s, the oil crisis and the entry negotiations of the new members made that target impossible; hence the Marjolin Report recommended the postponement of that date. Thus, despite the endorsement of the Delors Report, it is necessary to reflect on the nature of the transition to monetary integration.

It was pointed out earlier that the recommendations of the Werner Report are consistent with *complete* monetary integration, in that the stages *taken together* do lead to the attainment of the ultimate goal. Hence the problems associated with Corden's pseudo exchange-rate union cannot be envisaged in the context of the Werner Report, unless one is convinced that the EC was never likely to proceed beyond the first stage, i.e. the first stage would have become the permanent reality. I shall return to this point shortly, but it ought to be mentioned that the Werner Report was not the only set of recommendations available to the EC; a number of proposals were made and are still being made regarding the minimisation of the costs of transition – see Meade (1973), Johnson (1973), Johnson and Krauss (1973), Coffey and Presley (1971), Magnifico and Williamson (1972), Cairncross *et al.* (1974), Giersch *et al.* (1975), Tindemans (1976) and Sumner and Zis (1982). Since the literature on this subject is extensive, brief reference to it would not do it justice. I shall therefore give only a summary of the main categories of ideas. For a more detailed discussion, the reader is advised to consult Coffey and Presley (1971), Cairncross *et al.* (1974), Coffey (1977), Corden (1977), Sumner and Zis (1982), Coffey (1987) and Giavazzi *et al.* (1988).

There are four basic groups of recommendations on ways of tackling the problems of the transition to European monetary integration.

5.6.1 Monetary integration all at once

This amounts to introducing *all* the necessary ingredients of complete monetary integration *together* as soon as a commitment has been made to launch the EMU. An EC central bank is created and is vested with the powers of controlling the pool of all members' foreign exchange reserves, of conducting the Community monetary and economic policies and of producing the legal tender and therefore the money base. Such a step has to be decisive, definitive and irrevocable, so that all possible expectations are immediately adjusted once and for all. This proposal gives all the advantages and none of the disadvantages of complete monetary integration. The essence of it is to tackle the problems of transition through the simple act of eliminating the process of transition itself.

Since this is the best method, why was it not adopted by the EC in the past? According to Cairncross *et al.* (1974, p. 31):

> to abandon exchange-rate changes completely and finally without indicating how imbalances will be dealt with in future . . . would be to run serious risks in relation to both economic stability and to that political will without which economic union will not hold.

However, if these serious risks are to disappear, the EC central bank has to be responsible for tackling the regional problems that are likely to arise as a result of the EMU – those problems that worry the 'economists'. The regional problem has to become part and parcel of the management of the EC economic and monetary policies conducted by the central bank. It is therefore evident that an 'all at once' implementation of the EMU cannot be envisaged without a properly functioning EC central bank; the prior commitment of the member countries to a political union therefore becomes an absolute necessity. The Delors Report is thus perfectly justified in emphasising both points.

5.6.2 The step-by-step approach

This approach is in effect that of a considerable number of the proposals and certainly forms the essence of both the Werner and Delors Reports. There are two sets of recommendations within this approach broadly consistent with the two sides of the 'monetarists' and 'economists' dichotomy, but they can be treated together – for a detailed description the reader should consult Cairncross *et al.* (1974).

The step-by-step approach means that exchange-rate margins are narrowed over a period of time and that the narrowing of the margins is very gradual. Some collaboration between the members is envisaged, such that those with balance of payments surpluses come to the rescue of those with deficits. At a later stage, the pooling of all foreign exchange reserves is introduced and the complete and irrevocable elimination of all exchange-rate margins then follows. Finally, when the member nations declare their solemn commitment to monetary integration, an EC central bank with the necessary powers is created.

It should be emphasised that this approach is, strictly speaking, not very different from the 'all at once' approach, provided those participating make the political commitment that is necessary for the effective support of *all the stages* leading to the implementation of complete monetary integration, i.e. members must not only declare themselves to act, but must also be seen to act in the spirit of the final goal. Otherwise, the national versus Community interests discussed earlier become the order of the day and therefore reduce the whole exercise to a pseudo exchange-rate union. Hence this approach cannot be envisaged without the political commitment of the participants *from the start*.

5.6.3 Approaching the EMU via the snake

In this set of proposals, members of the EC approach monetary integration via the snake; they join the snake when they feel ready to do so. Those who are either ready for or keen on achieving monetary integration go ahead, while those who are either not yet ready or not so eager join when they are. From there on the process is similar to the step-by-step approach. Hence, the most vital moment comes when those members who are in the snake take a solemn vow to go the whole way to monetary integration. Such a step, as already indicated, is not feasible without the prior political commitment of the members.

This approach is similar to that advocated by the Tindemans Report (1976) and is different from both the Werner and Delors Reports in that the various stages do not have to be coordinated. It could be argued, however, that a lack of coordination is necessary if member countries are to be free to join if and when they are ready or feel so inclined. As Corden (1977) has pointed out, this amounts to there being a 'two-tier' EC, consisting of those moving towards monetary integration via the snake, and the others. For a general background discussion, the reader should consult Cairncross *et al.* (1974), Coffey (1977), Sumner and Zis (1982) and Chapter 2.

5.6.4 Parallel-currency proposals

The fourth set of proposals is for achieving monetary integration through the creation of a parallel currency called the *Europa* or the *Monnet*. One version of this proposal calls for the creation of a *Europa* supported by US dollars, gold and SDRs, as well as by the domestic currencies of members of the EC. The *Europa* is held by the EC central banks alone, or by them and by members of the general public. The implication of this is that countries of the EC have the freedom of altering their own rates of exchange relative to the *Europa* and that the *Europa* itself can be devalued or revalued relative to the US dollar. The object of the exercise is for member nations to narrow the margins between their domestic currencies and the *Europa* with the eventual permanent and irrevocable fixing of their parities.

The second version of this approach was suggested by Giersch *et al.* (1976). This is different from the first in that the *Europa* has a *constant purchasing power* and is therefore inflation proof. The *Europa* is held simultaneously with local currencies and it is hoped that the competition between the *Europa* and the local currencies proves favourable to the former. When the *Europa* becomes dominant, it establishes itself as the EC currency.

It is obvious that if such a parallel currency is introduced and proves to be more attractive than local currencies, a mechanism of controlling its supply must be created. This must be an EC central bank which must have the power to conduct its financial operations anywhere within the EC. Such an EC central bank cannot be established and cannot function properly without the necessary backing of the EC nations. There is therefore a need for the prior political commitment to support it and to guide it in the direction of the ultimate objective of monetary integration. Needless to add, the Delors Report, and the Werner Report before it, satisfy this point.

It is therefore evident that none of these four sets of proposals can be achieved without a firm commitment by the participating nations to a United States of the EC countries.

5.7 The Bremen Declaration

At this juncture it is appropriate to ask: how do the Bremen Declaration (6 and 7 July 1978), its Bonn affirmation (16 and 17 July 1978) and its adoption by the Council in the form of a resolution 'on the establishment of the European Monetary System (EMS) and related matters' on 5 December of the same year fare in the context of the proposals considered in the previous section? To answer this question meaningfully, it is necessary to explain the aims of the EMS.

The EMS was introduced with the immediate support of six of the EC nations. Ireland, Italy and the United Kingdom adopted a wait-and-see attitude; 'time for reflection' was needed by Ireland and Italy and a definite reservation was expressed by the United Kingdom. Later, Ireland and Italy joined the system, while the United Kingdom expressed a 'spirit of sympathetic cooperation'. The EMS was to start operating on 1 January 1979, but France, who wanted assurances regarding the MCA system (see Chapter 8), delayed that start.

The main features of the EMS are given in the annex to the conclusions of the EC presidency (*Bulletin of the European Communities*, no. 6, 1978, pp. 20–1):

>   1. In terms of exchange rate management, the European Monetary System (EMS) will be at least as strict as the 'snake'. In the initial stages of its operation and for a limited period of time, member countries currently not participating in the 'snake' may opt for somewhat wider margins around central rates. In principle, intervention will be in the currencies of participating countries. Changes in central rates will be subject to mutual consent. Non-member countries with

particularly strong economic and financial ties with the Community may become associate members of the system. The European Currency Unit (ECU) will be at the centre of the system; in particular, it will be used as a means of settlement between EEC monetary authorities.

2. An initial supply of ECUs (for use among Community central banks) will be created against deposit of US dollars and gold on the one hand (e.g. 20% of the stock currently held by member central banks) and member currencies on the other hand in an amount of a comparable order of magnitude.

   The use of ECUs created against member currencies will be subject to conditions varying with the amount and the maturity; due account will be given to the need for substantial short-term facilities (up to 1 year).

3. Participating countries will coordinate their exchange rate policies *vis-à-vis* third countries. To this end, they will intensify the consultations in the appropriate bodies and between central banks participating in the scheme. Ways to coordinate dollar interventions should be sought which avoid simultaneous reserve interventions. Central banks buying dollars will deposit a fraction (say 20%) and receive ECUs in return; likewise, central banks selling dollars will receive a fraction (say 20%) against ECUs.

4. Not later than two years after the start of the scheme, the existing arrangements and institutions will be consolidated in a European Monetary Fund.

5. A system of closer monetary cooperation will only be successful if participating countries pursue policies conducive to greater stability at home and abroad; this applies to deficit and surplus countries alike.

Thus, in essence, the EMS is concerned with the creation of an EC currency zone within which there is discipline for managing exchange rates. This discipline is similar to that practised within the 'snake' arrangements. This however does not apply to all the member nations of the EC, since wider margins of fluctuation for those not participating in the snake were allowed for. The ECU, which is similar to the European Unit of Account in that it is a basket of all EC currencies, lies at the heart of the system; it is the means of settlement between the EC central banks. The EMS is supported by a European Monetary Fund (EMF) which (supposedly within two years) will absorb the short-term financing arrangement operating within the snake, the short-term monetary support agreement which is managed by the European Monetary Cooperation Fund and the medium-term loan facilities for balance of payments assistance (*Bulletin of the European Communities*, no. 12, 1978). The EMF will be backed by approximately 20 per cent of national gold and US dollar reserves and by a similar percentage in national currencies. The EMF will issue ECUs which will be used as new reserve assets. An Exchange-Stabilisation Fund (which is scarcely different from the Cairncross *et al.* (1974) proposal for an exchange-equalisation account) able to issue about 50 billion US dollars will be created (*Bulletin of the European Communities*, no. 12, 1978).

Since the ECU is only an official EC reserve asset, necessary interventions in the markets for foreign exchange will be conducted with national currencies and for this purpose only EC currencies are allowed. It is also envisaged that the use of ECUs credited against reserves will be unconditional, but the use of ECUs credited against national currencies will be subject to provisos more or less equivalent to those in the 'conditional drawings' from the IMF – see De Grauwe and Peeters (1978). There is provision for substantial short-term borrowing for day-to-day intervention. The repayment period will be 45 days, with the possibility of a further three months for specified amounts. It is intended that adjustments in rates of exchange will be based on mutual consent.

Section 4 of the annex stresses the point that the status of associate membership will be conferred on those countries with close economic and financial ties with the EC, for example, Austria, Norway, etc. As far as other currencies are concerned, and particularly against the US dollar, there will be close coordination of exchange-rate policies.

Finally, and more importantly, the annex stresses the point that the success of closer monetary cooperation will depend largely on closer policy coordination in both the domestic and international fields.

As De Grauwe and Peeters (1978) have indicated, the EMS differs from previous attempts in at least two important respects. The first difference is that an exchange-rate management mechanism will be introduced and that the ECU will play a central role in it. The second difference is that the EC currency zone will be backed by a considerable pool of foreign exchange reserves which could provide confidence in the system and therefore enhance its stability.

However, apart from the technical problems regarding its actual operation (these are rigorously analysed in Chapter 17), the EMS cannot work without the coordination of monetary policies (De Grauwe and Peeters, 1978, p. 22) and cannot cope with the problems of the weaker areas without a deliberate policy regarding the redistribution of the gains and losses. Finally, the EMS does not envisage a *particular* future date for fixing exchange rates completely – 'margins should be gradually reduced as soon as economic conditions permit to do so' (*Bulletin of the European Communities*, no. 12, 1978, pp. 10–11), but this point is not significant now that the twelve EC member nations have accepted the Delors Report.

In spite of its superiority over previous proposals, the EMS *is not complete monetary integration*. It lacks the EC central bank (vested with the appropriate powers) which is necessary for coordinating monetary and economic policies. Hence, the endorsement of the Delors Report.

5.8 Conclusion

The conclusion of this chapter is that the alleged disadvantages of monetary integration apply only to the so-called pseudo exchange-rate union. Such a union is neither consistent with the first stage of the EMU envisaged in both the Werner and Delors Reports nor with their nature as processes leading to complete EMU. All economists would concede the difficulties associated with a transitional phase, but none of them, in their strict area of competence, should pass political judgements regarding the reality of attaining the ultimate objective. The EC is here to stay and, as the endorsement of the Delors Report by all twelve EC member nations clearly indicates, the EC is committed to the achievement of a full economic and monetary union. Indeed, Mr Roy Jenkins, who was President of the EC Commission at the time, emphasised in his 1977 speech (delivered in Florence) that EMU was to remain a clear EC objective; thus even during the interval between the Werner and Delors Reports there was never any doubt regarding the ultimate goal for the EC.

6 Measuring the impact of economic integration

A. M. El-Agraa

A growing area of research in the field of international economic integration is concerned with the measurement of the impact of the formation of the EC, EFTA and similar associations on the economies of member states and on the outside world. The purpose of this chapter is to explain the nature of the problem, to evaluate the attempts at measurement that have so far been made and to suggest an alternative approach. The reader who is interested in a comprehenive survey and assessment of the actual estimates that have been carried out is advised to read El-Agraa (1989a).

6.1 Nature of the problem

It is extremely important to comprehend the nature of the methodology of measuring the impact of international economic integration in order to appreciate the difficulties associated with such measurements.

Assume that the world is constituted of three mutually exclusive and collectively exhaustive areas: the EC, EFTA and the rest of the world (W). The object of the exercise is to contrast the world trade matrix[1] Y as it appears in year t (indicated by a subscript), with the situation that would have materialised in year t if the EC and EFTA had not been formed. The latter is referred to as the 'anti-monde' – alternative world in which all events except one are identical – or non-integration position. The differences between this hypothetical position and the actual position can then be attributed to the following:

1. Trade creation: the substitution of cheaper imports from the partner country for expensive domestic production.
2. Trade diversion: the replacement of cheap *initial* imports from non-partners by expensive imports from a partner country.
3. External trade creation: the replacement of expensive domestic production by cheaper imports from a non-partner country due to a reduction in the common

external tariff rate which is necessary in a customs union but not in a free trade area.

4. 'Supply-side diversion; i.e. the replacement of exports to non-partners by exports to partners'.[2]

5. Balance of payments induced adjustments due to (1)–(4) which are made necessary for equilibrating purposes.

Let us adopt the notation used by Williamson and Bottrill (1971) where:

c_{ii} = intra-ith area trade creation

d_{ij} = diversion of the ith area's imports from area j

$d_{ii} = \sum_{j \neq i} d_{ij}$ = diversion of ith area's imports (to area i)

e_{ij} = increase in i's imports from j caused by external trade creation

$e_i = \sum_j e_{ij}$ = total external trade creation of area i

r_{ij} = increase in i's imports from j caused by balance of payments reactions

s_{ij} = reduction in j's exports to i caused by supply-side constraints

x_{ij} = (hypothetical) imports of area i from area j in the non-integration position

$x_i = \sum_j x_{ij}$ = (hypothetical) imports of area i in the non-integration position

$y_i = \sum_j y_{ij}$ = actual imports of area i

The world trade matrix Y is:

			Exports by		
		EC	EFTA	W	Total
Imports of	EC	y_{11}	y_{12}	y_{13}	y_1
	EFTA	y_{21}	y_{22}	y_{23}	y_2
	W	y_{31}	y_{32}	y_{33}	y_3

The world trade matrix can be disaggregated to show the various effects that followed the formation of the EC and EFTA. Both these areas could have led to internal trade creation and/or could have diverted imports from W. The EC may have been responsible for external trade creation (in the partner countries that levelled down their external tariff rates) and external trade destruction (in the low tariff partner countries which raised their external tariff rates to the level of the common external tariff rates).

> The attractions of partners' markets may have directed some EC and EFTA exports away from non-partners' markets, but this effect may have been partially, wholly, or more than fully offset by the greater competitiveness of exports from those blocs resulting from the advantages of a larger 'home' market. (Williamson and Bottrill, 1971, pp. 324–5).

Also, every trade flow in the matrix may have been affected by reactions made necessary in order to re-equilibrate payments positions.

The Y matrix can be disaggregated to show all these changes:

$$\begin{bmatrix} y_{11}\, y_{12}\, y_{13} \\ y_{21}\, y_{22}\, y_{23} \\ y_{31}\, y_{32}\, y_{33} \end{bmatrix} =$$

$$\begin{bmatrix} x_{11} + c_{11} + d_{11} + r_{11} & x_{12} - d_{12} + e_{12} - s_{12} + r_{12} & x_{13} - d_{13} + e_{13} + r_{13} \\ x_{21} - d_{21} - s_{21} + r_{21} & x_{22} + c_{22} + d_{22} + r_{22} & x_{23} - d_{23} + r_{23} \\ x_{31} - s_{31} + r_{31} & x_{32} - s_{32} + r_{32} & x_{33} + r_{33} \end{bmatrix} \quad (1)$$

Most of the studies in this field have disregarded some of these effects, particularly the supply-side constraints and the balance of payments re-equilibrating reactions. This amounts to assuming that s_{ij} and v_{ij} are equal to zero. This leads to the much simpler framework:

$$\begin{bmatrix} y_{11}\, y_{12}\, y_{13} \\ y_{21}\, y_{22}\, y_{23} \\ y_{31}\, y_{32}\, y_{33} \end{bmatrix} = \begin{bmatrix} x_{11} + c_{11} + d_{11} & x_{12} - d_{12} + e_{12} & x_{13} - d_{13} + e_{13} \\ x_{21} - d_{21} & x_{22} + c_{22} + d_{22} & x_{23} - d_{23} \\ x_{31} & x_{32} & x_{33} \end{bmatrix} \quad (2)$$

This implies that:

$$y_i = x_i + c_{ii} + e_i \quad (3)$$

Even though this methodology is very useful for analysing the *overall* effects of the formation of the EC and EFTA, it is inadequate for analysing the effects on particular countries. For example, the method cannot provide information about the consequences for the United Kingdom of membership of the EC. In order to deal with this problem, it is necessary to alter the matrix so as to allow for at least two areas for each of the EC and EFTA. This would provide the freedom to investigate the impact of the formation of EFTA and the EC on one member of the EC (United Kingdom), on that country's relationship with EFTA, with a particular member of EFTA (Norway) and with the rest of the world. Hence, the matrix should look like this:

			Exports by					
			EC		EFTA		*W*	Total
			(1) UK	(2) Rest of EC	(3) Norway	(4) Rest of EFTA		
Imports of	EC	(1)	y_{11}	y_{12}	y_{13}	y_{14}	y_{15}	y_1
		(2)	y_{21}	y_{22}	y_{23}	y_{24}	y_{25}	y_2
	EFTA	(3)	y_{31}	y_{32}	y_{33}	y_{34}	y_{35}	y_3
		(4)	y_{41}	y_{42}	y_{43}	y_{44}	y_{45}	y_4
	W	(5)	y_{51}	y_{52}	y_{53}	y_{54}	y_{55}	y_5

Disaggregating in terms of trade creation, trade diversion and external trade creation (assuming $s_{ij} = 0$ and $r_{ij} = 0$) gives:

$$
\begin{bmatrix}
y_{11} & y_{12} & y_{13} & y_{14} & y_{15} \\
y_{21} & y_{22} & y_{23} & y_{24} & y_{25} \\
y_{31} & y_{32} & y_{33} & y_{34} & y_{35} \\
y_{41} & y_{42} & y_{43} & y_{44} & y_{45} \\
y_{51} & y_{52} & y_{53} & y_{54} & y_{55}
\end{bmatrix}
=
$$

$$
\begin{bmatrix}
\text{\textemdash} & x_{12}+c_{12}+d_{12} & x_{13}-d_{13}+e_{13} & x_{14}-d_{14}+e_{14} & x_{15}-d_{15}+e_{15} \\
x_{21}+c_{21}+d_{21} & \text{\textemdash} & x_{23}-d_{23}+e_{23} & x_{24}-d_{24}+e_{24} & x_{25}-d_{25}+e_{25} \\
x_{31}-d_{31} & x_{32}-d_{22} & \text{\textemdash} & x_{34}+c_{34}+d_{34} & x_{35}-d_{35} \\
x_{41}-d_{41} & x_{42}-d_{42} & x_{43}+c_{43}+d_{43} & \text{\textemdash} & x_{45}-d_{45} \\
x_{51} & x_{52} & x_{53} & x_{54} & x_{55}
\end{bmatrix}
\quad (4)
$$

The matrix could, of course, be made more suitable for studying the impact of the formation of the EC and EFTA on particular areas of the rest of the world, e.g. the impact of UK membership of the EC on imports from New Zealand. This can easily be done by an appropriate breakdown of W. The most significant consideration that remains is the effect of the formation of the EC and EFTA on their economies and on the outside world.

Thus the problem of measuring the impact of economic integration relates to the empirical calculation of the indicated changes in the world trade matrix. However, it seems evident that any sensible approach to the analysis of these changes should have the following characteristics:

1. It should be capable of being carried out at the appropriate level of dis-aggregation.
2. It should be able to distinguish between trade creation, trade diversion and external trade creation.
3. It should be capable of discerning the effects of economic growth on trade that would have taken place in the absence of economic integration.
4. It should be 'analytic': it should be capable of providing an economic explanation of the actual post-integration situation.
5. It should be a general-equilibrium approach capable of allowing for the effects of economic integration on an interdependent world.

6.2 The effects on trade

The general trend of the empirical work on economic integration has been to examine various specific aspects of integration (mainly the effects on trading patterns) and to analyse them separately. The most important practical distinction made is between 'price' and 'income' effects. This is largely because the main initial instruments in economic integration are tariffs and quotas and other trade impediments which act mainly on relative prices in the first instance. However, all sources of possible economic gain (see Chapter 4) incorporate income as well as price effects.

The removal of quotas and other trade impediments is usually subsumed within the tariff changes for estimation purposes. These tariff changes are thought to result in a series of relative price changes: the price of imports from the partner countries falls, for commodities where the tariff is removed, relative to the price of the same commodity produced in the domestic country. In third countries which are excluded from the union relative prices may change for more than one reason. They will change differently if the tariff with respect to third countries is shifted from its pre-integration level or they may change if producers in third countries have different pricing reactions to the change in price competition. Some third country producers may decide to absorb rather more of the potential change by reducing profits rather than by increasing prices relative to domestic producers. Relative prices are also likely to change with respect to different commodities and hence there is a complex set of interrelated income and substitution effects to be explained.

The immediate difficulty is thus the translation of tariff changes and other agreed measures in the customs union treaty into changes in prices and other variables which are known to have an impact on economic behaviour. Such evidence as there is suggests that there are wide discrepancies among the reactions of importers benefiting from tariff cuts and also among competitors adversely affected by them (EFTA, 1968) and that reactions of trade to tariff changes are different from those to price changes (Kreinin, 1961). Two routes would appear to be open: one is to estimate the effect of tariff changes on prices and then estimate the effects of these derived price changes on trade patterns; the other is to operate directly with observed relative price movements. This latter course exemplifies a problem which runs right through the estimation of the effects of economic integration and makes the obtaining of generally satisfactory results almost impossible. It is that to measure the effect of integration one must decide what would have happened if integration had not occurred (see the previous section). Thus, if in the present instance any observed change in relative prices were assumed to be the result of the adjustment to tariff changes, all other sources of variation in prices would be ignored, which is clearly an exaggeration and could be subject to important biases if other factors were affecting trade at the same time.

6.3 The dynamic effects

While in the discussion of the exploitation of comparative advantage, the gains from a favourable movement in the terms of trade and often those from economies of scale are expressed in terms of comparative statics, it is difficult to disentangle them from feedback on to incomes and activity. The essence of the gains from increased efficiency and technological change is that the economy should reap dynamic gains. In other words integration should enhance the rate of growth of GDP rather than just giving a step-up in welfare. Again it is necessary to explain how this might come about explicitly.

There are two generalised ways in which this can take place, first through increased productivity growth at a given investment ratio or secondly through increased investment itself. This is true whether the increased sales are generated internally or through the pressures of demand for exports from abroad through integration. Growth gains can, of course, occur temporarily in so far as there are slack resources in the economy. Again it is possible to observe whether the rate of growth has changed; but it is much more difficult to decide whether that is attributable to integration.

Krause (1968) attempted to apply a version of Denison's (1967) method of identifying the causes of economic growth but suggested that *all* changes in the rate of business investment were due to the formation of the EC (or EFTA in the case of those countries). Mayes (1978) showed that if the same contrast between business investment before and after the formation of the EC (EFTA) were applied to Japan a bigger effect would be observed than in any of the integrating countries. Clearly changes in the rate of business investment can occur for reasons other than integration.

6.4 Previous studies

As stated in the introduction to this chapter, a comprehensive survey of previous studies is now available in El-Agraa (1989a). There is therefore no need to go through these studies here. However, a few general comments may be in order.

Most of the measurements can be broadly classified as *ex ante* or *ex post*. The *ex ante* estimates are based on *a priori* knowledge of the pre-integration period (i.e. structural models), while the *ex post* studies are based on assumptions about the actual experience of economic integration (i.e. residual-imputation models). However, recall that either type can be analytic or otherwise.

There are two types of *ex ante* studies: those undertaken before the EC and EFTA were actually operative and those undertaken after they became operative.[3] The most influential studies to use this approach are those of Krause (1968), who predicted the trade diversion that would be brought about by the EC and EFTA on the basis of assumptions about demand elasticities, and Han and Leisner (1970), who predicted the effect on the United Kingdom by identifying those industries that had a comparative cost advantage/disadvantage *vis-à-vis* the EC and finding out how they were likely to be affected by membership, on the assumption that the pattern of trade prior to UK membership provided an indication of the underlying cost conditions and that this would be one of the determinants of the pattern of trade and domestic production after membership. This approach is of very limited value, however, for the simple reason that 'it does not provide a method of enabling one to improve previous estimates on the basis of new historical experience' (Williamson and Bottrill, 1971, p. 326).

The most significant studies to use the *ex post* approach are those of Lamfalussy (1964) and Verdoorn and Meyer zu Schlochtern (1964), who all use a relative shares method; Balassa (1967 and 1975), who uses an income elasticity of import demand method;[4] the EFTA Secretariat, which uses a share of imports in apparent consumption method;[5] Williamson and Bottrill, who use a more sophisticated share analysis;[6] Prewo, who uses an input–output method;[7] and Barten *et al.*, who use a medium-term macroeconomic method.[8] The advantage of the *ex post* method is that it can be constructed in such a way as to benefit from historical experience and hence to provide a basis for continuous research. However, the major obstacle in this approach concerns the difficulty regarding the construction of an adequate hypothetical post-integration picture of the economies concerned.

6.5 A critique of previous studies

There are some general and some specific points of criticism to be made against these studies:

1. All the studies, excepting the Brada and Méndez (1985), Truman (1975) and Williamson and Bottrill (1971) studies, and to a certain extent the Aitken (1973) and Mayes (1978) estimates, assume that the formation of the EC (or EFTA) has been the sole factor to influence the pattern of trade. Since the EC and EFTA were established more or less simultaneously (there is a year's difference between them), it is not justifiable to attribute changes in the pattern of trade to either alone. After all, EFTA was established in order to counteract the possible damaging effects of the EC. Moreover, a few years after the establishment of these two blocs, a number of schemes were formed all over the world – see El-Agraa (1982c; 1988b) and Chapter 1 of this book for a detailed specification and discussion of these. The impact of these latter groupings should not have been ignored by studies conducted in the late 1960s and thereafter.
2. Most of the recent studies ignore the fact that Britain used to be a member of EFTA before joining the EC. Since the United Kingdom is a substantial force as a member of either scheme, it seems misleading to attempt estimates which do not take into consideration this switch by the United Kingdom. A similar argument applies to Denmark. This point of course lends force to the previous one.
3. In the period prior to the formation of the EC and EFTA, certain significant changes were happening on the international scene. The most important of these was that the discrimination against the United States was greatly reduced. Is it at all possible that such developments had no effect whatsoever on the trade pattern of the EC and EFTA? It seems unrealistic to assume that this should have been the case.
4. All the studies, except for Truman's (1975) and to some extent Winters' (1984a), dealt with trade data in spite of the fact that a proper evaluation of the effects of economic integration requires analysis of *both* trade *and* production data. Trade creation indicates a reduction in domestic production combined with new imports of the same quantity from the partner, while trade diversion indicates new

imports from the partner combined with less imports from the rest of the world (W) and a reduction in production in the W.

5. Tariffs are universally recognised as only one of many trade impediments, yet all the studies, except Krause's (1968) and Prewo's (1974), were based on the assumption that the only effect of economic integration in Western Europe was on discriminatory tariff removal. This is a very unsatisfactory premise, particularly if one recalls that the EC had to resort to explicit legislation against cheaper imports of textiles from India, Japan and Pakistan in the 1960s and early 1970s. The EC later forced Japan to adopt voluntary export restraints (VERs) with regard to cars, and some unusual practices were adopted, like France's diverting of Japanese video recorders to the relatively small town of Poitiers to slow down their penetration of the French market – see El-Agraa (1988a) for a detailed specification of these issues. Moreover, the level of tariffs and their effective protection is very difficult to measure:

> Tariff schedules are public, but their interpretation is often made difficult by peculiar institutional clauses. Furthermore, it is difficult to obtain a good measure of the restrictive impact of tariffs. Average tariff rates will not do, for, if the rate is zero on one good and prohibitive on another, the average tariff is zero. It is necessary to use *a priori* weights, which inevitably is arbitrary . . . [Others] raised a more subtle issue by proposing to use input–output analysis to measure the effective *rates of protection* achieved by tariffs on value added. This approach raises a host of problems. The assumptions of fixed technical coefficients and of perfectly competitive price adjustments are both debatable. It is clear that the concept of effective protection . . . relies on oversimplified assumptions. (Waelbroeck, 1977, p. 89)

6. The Dillon and Kennedy Rounds of tariff negotiations resulted in global tariff reductions which coincided with the first stage of the removal of tariffs by the EC. Does this not mean that any evidence of external trade creation should be devalued, and any evidence of trade diversion is an underestimate?

More specifically, however:

> In all these studies, the integration effect, whether trade creation or trade diversion, is estimated by the difference between actual and extrapolated imports for a post-integration year. The extrapolation of imports is done by a time trend of imports or by relating imports with income or consumption in the importing country. The difference between the actual and estimated imports would be due to (i) autonomous changes in prices in the supplying and importing countries, (ii) changes in income, consumption or some other variable representing macroeconomic activity, (iii) changes in variables other than income/consumption and autonomous price movements, (iv) revisions of tariffs and/or other barriers as a result of integration, (v) residual errors due to the random error term in the estimating equation, misspecification of the form of the equation, errors in the data, omission or misrepresentation of certain variables, etc. The studies . . . try to segregate the effect of (ii) only. The remaining difference between the actual and estimated imports would be due to (i), (iii), (iv) and (v), but it is ascribed only to (iv), i.e. the effect of revision of tariff and/or other barriers to trade as a result of integration. Clearly, it

is a totally unreliable way of estimating the integration effect on trade creation
or trade diversion. Even if prices are included as an additional variable in the
estimating equation, it would amount to segregating the effect of (i) and (ii), so that
the difference between the actual and estimated imports would be due to (iii), (iv)
and (v). It would still be wrong to ascribe it to (iv) only. The error term at (v) is
often responsible for a divergence of ±10% between the actual and estimated
imports, which might often overshadow the effect of integration. For this reason,
the 'residual method' used by Balassa, the EFTA Secretariat and many others, is
highly unreliable for estimating the trade creation and trade diversion effects of
integration. (Dayal, R. and N., 1977, pp. 136–7)

Moreover, the effects of economic integration, be they trade creation or trade
diversion, occur in two stages: the effects of changes in tariffs on prices and the effect
of price changes on trade. These two effects have to be separately calculated before the
trade creation and trade diversion effects of economic integration can be estimated.
This procedure is not followed.

In addition, the accuracy of the *ex ante* forecasts of the impact of economic
integration on the level and direction of trade rests on the reliability of the price
elasticities utilised. Furthermore, apart from this general problem, a critical issue is
whether the effect of a tariff is the same as that of an equivalent price change; tariff
elasticities substantially exceed the usual import demand elasticities, and the
elimination of a tariff is perceived by the business world as irreversible.

It therefore seems inevitable to conclude that:

> All estimates of trade creation and diversion by the [EC] which have been pre-
> sented in the empirical literature are so much affected by *ceteris paribus* assump-
> tions, by the choice of the length of the pre- and post-integration periods, by
> the choice of benchmark year (or years), by the methods to compute income
> elasticities, changes in trade matrices and in relative shares and by structural
> changes not attributable to the [EC] but which occurred during the pre- and post-
> integration periods (such as the trade liberalisation amongst industrial countries
> and autonomous changes in relative prices) that the magnitude of no . . . estimate
> should be taken too seriously. (Sellekaerts, 1973, p. 548)

Moreover, given the validity of these criticisms, one should not take seriously
such statements as:

> There are a number of studies that have reported on attempts to construct . . .
> estimates. Individually the various methods must be judged unreliable. . . . But
> collectively the available evidence is capable of indicating conclusions of about the
> same degree of reliability as is customary in applied economics. That is to say,
> there is a wide margin of uncertainty about the correct figure, but the order of
> magnitude can be established with reasonable confidence. (Williamson and Bottrill,
> 1971, p. 323)

Since no single study can be justified in its own right and the fact that the degree of
reliability in applied economics leaves a lot to be desired, it is difficult to see the collective virtue in individual misgivings.

6.6 The alternative

It seems evident that there is nothing wrong with the methodology for the empirical testing of integration effects, but that the problems of actual measurement are insurmountable. However, these difficulties are due to some basic misconceptions regarding the welfare implications of trade creation and trade diversion: trade creation is good while trade diversion is bad – using the Johnson (1974) definition.

In an interdependent macroeconomic world, trade creation is inferior to trade diversion for the country concerned – see Chapter 6 of El-Agraa (1989a) – and both are certainly detrimental to the outside world. This conclusion is also substantiated by Johnson's work which incorporates the collective consumption of a public good – see Chapter 4 of this book and Johnson (1965a). It therefore seems rather futile, for estimation purposes, to attach too much significance to the welfare implications of trade creation versus trade diversion in this respect. Lest it be misunderstood, I should hasten to add that this is not a criticism of the trade creation–trade diversion theoretical dichotomy, rather the futility/impossibility of its empirical estimation. Moreover:

> trade creation and trade diversion . . . are static concepts. Their effects are once-for-all changes in the allocation of resources. At any date in the future their effects must be measured against what *would otherwise have been*, not by what is happening to trade at that time. In the economic theorist's model without adjustment lags, the introduction of a scheme for regional integration causes a once-for-all shift to more intra-integrated area trade and less trade with the outside world, and the forces that *subsequently* influence the allocation of resources become once again cost changes due to technological advance, and demand changes due to differing income elasticities of demand as real income rises as a result of growth [,] . . . call the first set of forces affecting the allocation of resources *integration induced* and the second set *growth induced*. . . . The two sets of forces . . . are intermixed (the problem becomes even more complex conceptually if integration itself affects the growth rate). The more sudden the integration, the more likely it is that integration induced effects will dominate, at least for the first few years; but the longer the time lapse the more would normal growth-induced effects dominate. The morals are: (1) the longer the time since a relatively sudden move towards integration, the harder it is to discern the effects by studying changes in the pattern of trade; and (2) the more gradually the integration measures are introduced, the more will the effects be mixed up, even in the short term, with growth-induced effects. (Lipsey, 1977, pp. 37–8)

For all these reasons I have suggested (see the first edition of this book) that the measurement of the impact of economic integration should be confined to estimating its effect on intra-union trade and, if at all possible, to finding out whether or not any changes have been at the expense of the outside world. The statistical procedure for such estimates should be straightforward if one uses the El-Agraa/Jones interdependent global macro model (see Chapter 6 of El-Agraa 1989a) and incorporates into it the import demand functions suggested by the Dayals (1977). One can then utilise the concepts of income and substitution effects (suggested by the Dayals and spelt out in the macroeconomic model) without some of the unnecessary details created by using simple marginal utility functions. Although the macroeconomic framework is subject to some serious limitations, it provides, at the very least, a genuine alternative against which one can judge the quality of the estimates obtained from the previous models.

Notes

1. An equivalent world production matrix is also necessary, see (1)–(3).
2.   It is possible that the fast growth of EEC and EFTA intra-trade in the years immediately following their formation (and also of EC intra-trade in 1969) was particularly at the expense of slower growth in exports to ... [W]. There is no conclusive evidence as to whether this was an important factor. In the long run, however, one would expect supply bottlenecks to be overcome, and one might also expect their effect to be counteracted by the greater competitive strength resulting from a larger 'home market'. We therefore follow a well-established precedent in assuming $s_{ij} = 0$ (no supply-side diversion exists). (Williamson and Bottrill, 1971, p. 325)
3. See for instance, Verdoorn, 1954; Janssen, 1961; and Krause and Salant, 1973a.
4.   Ex-post income elasticities of import demand were defined as the ratio of the average annual rate of change of imports to that of GNP, both expressed in constant prices. Under the assumption that income elasticities of import demand would have remained unchanged in the absence of integration, a rise in the income elasticity of demand for intra-area imports would indicate gross trade creation – increases in intra-area trade – irrespective of whether this resulted from substitution for domestic or for foreign sources of supply. In turn, a rise in the income elasticity of demand for imports from all sources taken together would give expression of trade creation proper, i.e. a shift from domestic to partner-country sources. Finally, trade diversion, a shift from foreign to partner-country producers, would be indicated by a decline in the income elasticity of demand for extra-area imports. (Balassa, 1975, p. 80)
5. The EFTA Secretariat's study is based on the assumption that had EFTA not been established, the import shares in the apparent consumption of a particular commodity in any of the EFTA countries would have developed in the post-integration period in precisely the same fashion as they had during the pre-integration period 1954–9. (See EFTA Secretariat 1969 and 1972.)
6.   We believe that the most promising hypothesis is that originally introduced by Lamfalussy. According to this, the share performance of the jth supplier in markets where he neither gains nor loses preferential advantages gives a good indication of his hypothetical performance in markets which were in fact being affected by integration. In terms of the present analysis, the rest of the world provides a control which indicates what share performance would have been in EEC and EFTA markets if these two organisations had not been formed. (Williamson and Bottrill 1971, p. 333)
The methods selected are:
1. Using an *a priori* formula which ensures that the predicted gain in market shares will be small if the previous market share was either very small or very large.
2. Extrapolating from a regression of data on relative export shares.
3. Assuming that market shares would have remained constant in the absence of economic integration.

7. Prewo (1974) uses a gravitational model which links the national input–output tables of the EC countries by a system of trade equations. In this model, trade between members of the EC is assumed to be proportional to demand in the importing, and supply in the exporting, country and inversely proportional to trade impediments, whereas extra-area imports are assumed to be related to demand in the EC countries. In this model, changes in final demand have a direct effect on imports of final goods, as well as an indirect effect through their impact on the imports of inputs for domestic production.

The basis of the analysis is that the 'difference between the actual trade flows of the customs union and the hypothetical trade flows of the customs union's antimonde is taken to be indicative of the integration effects.' (Prewo, 1974, p. 380)

8. 'It basically consists of eight similarly specified country models which are linked by *bilateral trade equations* and equations specifying the formation on import and export prices.' (Barten *et al.*, 1976, p. 63)

Part III

Microecon

The previous section of this book was devoted to the theo
empirical aspects of common market elements of the EC and t
of European monetary integration. This section provides an ext
discussion of virtually all the microeconomic policies of the EC.

omic policies

retical and
o an analysis
ensive

7 Competition and industrial policies with emphasis on competition policy

B. T. Bayliss and A. M. El-Agraa

Industrial policy embraces all acts and policies of the state in relation to industry. Such policy can be either positive or negative, i.e. positive in relation to the state's participation in, or control of, industry; or negative, to the extent that it might be the industrial policy of the state to minimise intervention in industry.

The increasing influence of the state in industry has been a feature of post-war European development. This 'positive' industrial policy covers such areas as the distribution of resources between industries (including such areas as energy, pricing, monopolies and restrictive practices); the structure of industry (including such areas as the degree of concentration, its location, state aid towards declining and expanding industries, the public sector); industry and the environment; conditions of employment; and fiscal and monetary policy. In other words, industrial policy embraces all aspects of state attitudes towards industry in its economic, social and environmental setting.

The Treaty of Rome covers certain aspects of industrial policy. In particular these deal with such factors as state aid, dominant firms, cartels, the right of establishment, the free movement of capital and labour, dumping, and the creation of the common market itself. The Treaty is, however, not comprehensive in the areas covered, nor does it specify the interrelationship between areas of policy where they are covered by the Treaty.

It appears that the founding fathers of the Treaty of Rome considered that once a common market was established this would of its own volition result in industrial policies and change related to a new situation, i.e. the birth of a common market.

The Commission, in its first major statement on industrial policy, also stressed the 'Community aspects' of such a policy.

> The new framework for industrial activity is that of the Community: it is therefore for the Community to review its industrial structures and to co-ordinate the operations of Member States or even to adopt the measures required itself. (EC Commission, 1967)

During the 1960s the Commission saw the creation of a single market and moves to achieve 'European firms' through legal and fiscal harmonisation as the major emphasis of its policy; industrial structure as such received major consideration. By the end of the decade, however, two aspects of industrial policy had become very marked.

Firstly, not only was there no spontaneous move towards the creation of an industrial policy catalysed through the creation of a common market, but there was a real indifference to its existence. Secondly, the decline of industries in prosperous areas (as opposed to development areas) highlighted the structural aspects of industry alongside the regional aspects.

Thus in March 1970 the Commission presented a 'Memorandum on industrial policy in the Community' in an attempt both to galvanise action in this area and to argue the importance of the structural aspects of industrial policy. The 1970 Memorandum developed six principal themes:

1. The removal of remaining barriers to the creation of a single market.
2. The harmonisation of company law and taxation, and the creation of a Community capital market.
3. The reorganisation of industry to adapt it to the needs of the Common Market.
4. The promotion of technology.
5. The social and regional aspects of industrial development.
6. Relations with third countries.

Following lack of progress in relation to this Memorandum the Commission attempted, three years later, to focus attention on a particular aspect of industrial policy, rather than remaining with a broad strategy, in an attempt to instigate some activity in this policy area. In May 1973, following a request from the Paris summit the previous year, the Commission submitted to Council an 'Action programme in the field of technological and industrial policy'. The Programme centred on nine areas of action:[1]

1. Abolition of technical barriers to trade.
2. Liberalisation of public contracts.
3. Abolition of fiscal barriers to cooperation between firms.
4. Abolition of legal barriers to cooperation between firms.
5. Community promotion of advanced technology undertakings.
6. Restructuring and modernisation of certain industrial sectors.
7. Concentration and competition.
8. Exports and credit insurance.
9. Raw material supplies – particularly non-ferrous.

However, like the Memorandum three years earlier, little ensued from it.

Essentially, a broad strategy of industrial policy prior to the Single European Act (SEA) had failed on account of both lack of interested parties in the member states and differences in the economic philosophies of member governments. In other words, neither inside nor outside government was there any strong body of feeling that such a policy would bring benefits which would otherwise not be forthcoming. An analysis of the reasons for the failure of a broad-based industrial policy before the adoption of the SEA is the domain of the political commentator,[2] but in one wide area of industrial policy, namely competition, there have been some notable achievements, and the remainder of this chapter is devoted to that aspect of industrial policy. The emergence of a coherent industrial policy since the SEA is of enough significance to warrant separate treatment – see Chapter 8.

Competition policy within the EC covers a wide range of industrial activities including, alongside the more conventional aspects of price setting and monopoly control, such activities as public sector industries, state aid, multinationals and restrictions on imports and exports.

In a resolution of 7 June 1971 the European Parliament requested the Commission to prepare an annual report on the development of competition policy. In its first such report (EC Commission, 1972a, p. 11) the Commission spelt out its philosophy of competition:

> Competition is the best stimulant of economic activity since it guarantees the widest possible freedom of action to all. An active competition policy pursued in accordance with the provisions of the Treaties establishing the Communities makes it easier for the supply and demand structures continually to adjust to technological development. Through the interplay of decentralised decision-making machinery, competition enables enterprises continuously to improve their efficiency, which is the *sine qua non* for a steady improvement in living standards and employment prospects within the countries of the Community. From this point of view, competition policy is an essential means for satisfying to a great extent the individual and collective needs of our society.

With respect to the rules of competition applicable to enterprises, the Commission has commented (EC Commission, 1972a, p. 13):

> The Community's policy must, in the first place, prevent governmental restrictions and barriers – which have been abolished – from being replaced by similar measures of a private nature. Agreements on quotas as well as agreements for the purpose of dividing the Common Market into regions, or of dividing up or fragmenting markets by other means are in flagrant contradiction to the provisions of the Treaties.

The basic market economic argument relates to the role of competition, in the absence of externalities, in the optimum allocation of resources. But neither this nor indeed the dynamic and pragmatic arguments espoused by the Commission provide an adequate explanation of the competition rules contained in the Treaties of Paris and Rome.

The driving force behind the ECSC was political. In the Schuman Communiqué of 9 May 1950, which formalised the original idea of the ECSC, the view was expressed that 'the solidarity in production thus established will make it plain that any war between France and Germany is not merely unthinkable but materially impossible'. The Allied Powers in Germany under the leadership of the United States had split up the major industrial and commercial concerns into separate organisations with operations regionally constrained, and France was keen to exercise a continuing control over a re-emerging German industry.

The French were thus prepared to surrender some control over their own industry in order to exercise some control over the future form of German industry. The Germans, for their part, were keen to participate in a European Community as this proffered a far preferable situation to one where their coal and steel industries were under the control of the Allies.

Although the wishes of the United States had to be taken into account in the formulation of the Paris Treaty, it was the hand of the French which was overriding: a fact clearly underlined by the appearance of a Treaty in which the only official and authentic text was in the French language, and where the single original was deposited in the archives of the French government.

The desire of the French to prevent a renewed concentration of the German coal and steel industries found expression in Articles 65 and 66 of Chapter VI of the Treaty of Paris. Basically, under Article 65,

> all agreements . . . tending, directly or indirectly, to prevent, restrict or distort the normal operation of competition within the common market are forbidden [and under Article 66] any course of action shall require the prior authorisation of the High Authority . . . if it has in itself the direct or indirect effect of bringing about . . . a concentration between undertakings.

In the six years (1951–7) between the signing of the Paris and Rome Treaties substantial changes took place in the relative political and negotiating strengths of the member countries of the ECSC. The Rome Treaty was drawn up, signed and ratified in four official languages (Dutch, French, German and Italian) instead of solely in French, and this time it was the Germans who were both to determine and to dictate the pertinent competition clauses in the Treaty.

The change of emphasis between the two Treaties is nowhere more marked than in the preamble. Of the five points covered by the preamble to the Paris Treaty, four are devoted to 'peace' and 'bloody conflict', whereas in the Rome Treaty only one of eight preamble points is so devoted.

A substantial change in the powers of the two executives (the High Authority of the ECSC and the Commission of the EC) accompanied the change in political emphasis and the inclusion of all sectors rather than just two. Under Article 8 of the Paris Treaty, 'it shall be the duty of the High Authority to ensure the attainment of the objects set out in the Treaty', whereas under Article 145 of the Rome Treaty, 'with a view to ensuring the achievement of the objectives laid down in this Treaty, and under the conditions provided for therein, the Council shall ensure the co-ordination of the general economic policies of the Member States; and dispose of a power of decision'.

Thus, in general, power for ensuring compliance with the objectives of the Treaties was removed from the executive and given to the Council, with the resulting increased opportunity for individual countries to determine the course of policies.

This change in emphasis in the two Treaties in so far as the political aspects are concerned can be summarised as follows: the force behind the ECSC was the desire to so integrate the member countries' economies that war was 'materially impossible', and simultaneously to control the re-formation of German industry. The corollary of this was a powerful executive able both to determine and enforce policy. With this intention the High Authority was given power to raise its own budget (up to 1 per cent of the coal and steel production of the member states – Article 50 of the Treaty of Paris) and power to impose fines (in the case of prices, fines could be twice the value of the offending sales and double that in the case of repetition – Article 64 of the Treaty of Paris).

By contrast, by the time of the Treaty of Rome negotiations, Europe had recovered from the worst of the war devastation and was beginning to enjoy what was to be an unparalleled growth in production and standards of living. There was much greater emphasis in the Rome Treaty on social questions, and politicians no longer saw the need to hand over large responsibilities to a powerful executive in order to ensure a speedy implementation of Treaty provisions. The Council – a body which did not even appear in the original Schuman proposals – thus assumed much more real power under the Rome Treaty.

The extension of the Common Market to include all sectors also necessitated a weakening of the power of the executive. The Paris Treaty dealt with two sectors and their specific problems; thus solutions to those problems were sought within the Treaty articles themselves. In the Rome Treaty only broad outlines of policy could be included, detailed policies for individual sectors being impossible within the framework of a Treaty. The development of such policies *ex post* the Treaty could not be left entirely to the Commission; hence the need to give the Council a much more prominent role. In summary, the articles of the Paris Treaty are much more akin to resolutions in the EC than the articles of the Rome Treaty.

An exception to this change in the relative powers of the executives under the Paris and Rome Treaties is witnessed in relation to competition policy. It is thus of interest to consider the pre-Treaty negotiations and the determination of the competition clauses in the Treaty of Rome.

It has frequently been argued that the hopes and demands of German industrialists and French agriculturalists during the negotiations were the overriding factors in determining the competition and agricultural policies, i.e. the competition policy which the Germans wanted was the *quid pro quo* for the agricultural policy which the French wanted. Although there is some truth in this supposition, it is not a fair reflection of the trade-offs made during the negotiations.

Agriculture, like transport, has a separate chapter in the Rome Treaty, and although the outlines of a common agricultural policy are defined in the Treaty, the policy itself was established in negotiations between the six only following the signing of the Treaty. It was in these post-Treaty negotiations that the Germans found themselves in strongest opposition to the French proposals. In the pre-Treaty negotiations the Germans insisted on a rigorous competition policy as the *quid pro quo* for agreeing to the French demands in relation to Euratom and the association of overseas territories (mainly the French West African territories).

It is of interest to reflect upon the overseas territories question briefly. At the time of Treaty negotiations the African countries were seeking independence and the French saw their inclusion in the Rome Treaty as a means of retaining their own influence in these countries while at the same time sharing the cost of maintaining such influence, in terms of aid, with the other five and Germany in particular. The French were very concerned about the ability of their industry to stand up to competition, but they needed German aid for their former colonies and were thus prepared to concede to German demands in relation to competition.

Thus, in the few years between the signing of the Paris and Rome Treaties, it was German industry that had not only become the most competitive industrial force in Europe but was also required to finance French ambitions in relation to its African territories.

The basic German philosophy towards the economy is that of the free market and there has been little change in the Federal government's attitudes during the last quarter of a century: total state expenditure as a percentage of GNP, for example, has hardly changed, with such expenditure equivalent to an average of 30 per cent of GNP in the 1970s and 1960s, and 29 per cent in the 1950s.

In order to safeguard this basic philosophy and to ensure that new restrictive practices did not handicap German industrial exports to other EC countries, the Germans insisted in the post-Treaty negotiations on the implementation of competition policy that the Commission be given strong executive powers in relation to competition. It was during this post-Treaty phase that the Germans found themselves in strongest conflict with the French in relation to agriculture; and the Community agreement to the control of competition policy demanded by the Federal Republic in this post-Treaty phase was the *quid pro quo* for French demands in relation to agriculture.[3]

The German competition views towards control found expression in Regulation No. 17 of the council of February 1962 relating to the Competition Articles 85 and 86 of the Treaty of Rome which deal with restrictive practices and dominant positions. Under Article 9 of that regulation the Commission was granted powers to apply Articles 85 and 86 of the Treaty, and in the exercise of such powers was accorded both substantial investigatory rights (Article 14) and extensive pecuniary enforcement rights (Article 15).

The Commission is empowered to:

1. Examine the books and other business records.
2. Take copies of extracts from the books and business records.
3. Ask for oral explanations on the spot.
4. Enter any premises, land and means of transport of undertakings.

If the Commission is supplied with incorrect or misleading information it may levy substantial fines and, in the case of infringement, the regulation allowed fines of up to one million units of account, or in excess of this if they did not exceed 10 per cent of the previous year's turnover of an undertaking.

Decisions of the Commission can all be the subject of appeal to the Court of Justice. These extensive powers of the executive, which far exceed anything, for instance, in the United Kingdom, with appeal only to the Court of Justice, have taken the development of this part of competition policy out of the political arena.

Similar powers of jurisdiction and enforcement of penalties were granted to the High Authority under the Treaty of Paris (Articles 65 and 66) but, as is discussed below, the terms of reference of the High Authority were much narrower than those granted to the Commission under the Treaty of Rome.

7.1 Scope of competition policy

The Treaty of Rome encompasses many aspects of competition which include:

1. Patents, licensing agreements and trade marks.
2. Price discrimination and fixing.
3. Resale price maintenance.
4. State aid.
5. Abuse of dominant market positions.
6. Dumping.
7. Quantitative restrictions on imports and exports.
8. Mergers and concentrations.
9. State undertakings.

Its range is thus much wider than the competition policy envisaged by the Treaty of Paris, and indeed the main emphasis of the Paris Treaty (mergers and concentrations) is not specifically covered by the Rome Treaty. Merger policy has, in fact, to be dealt with under the dominant position clauses (Article 86) or under the 'catch-all' article, Article 235.[4]

Many of the EC policies have their origins in both national policies of member states and compromise. The competition policy is an exception to this in that the policy has developed as a result of case law promulgated by the Commission and the Court of Justice. It has thus been specifically developed for a particular purpose and it is to be assumed that it should be free of many of the problems that have arisen through attempting to modify national policies to deal with Community problems. Modification has often had to be achieved through substantial compromise as, for instance, in the Common Agricultural Policy and transport policies.

The law embodied in the Treaties of Paris and Rome and the clarification of th law by Community institutions constitutes a body of law which is quite separate from both the municipal law of member states and international law. Not only is this body of law separate from the national laws of member states, it is also independent of them in that it can be enforced upon the government, institutions and individuals of member states without reference to or action on the part of such states.

The independence of Community law is made quite explicit in section 2(1) of the European Communities Act which requires that the Act's provisions 'are without further enactment to be given legal effect or used in the United Kingdom'.

Not only is Community law both separate and independent of national law, it takes precedence over it in cases of conflict between the two. Mr Rippon, chief UK negotiator for the entry of Britain into the EC, speaking in the House of Commons in February 1972 with respect to the European Communities Bill, commented:

> Clause 3 subsection (1) provides for the acceptance of the jurisprudence of the European Court. As the 1967 White Paper (Cmnd. 3301) recognises, the directly applicable provisions of the Community are designed to take precedence over the domestic law of Member States, in the sense that they prevail in the case of a conflict. By accepting the directly applicable law in clause 2(1) and accepting the jurisprudence of the European Court in clause 3(1), the Bill provides the necessary precedence. In relation to statute law, this means that the directly applicable provisions ought to prevail over future Acts of Parliament in so far as they might be inconsistent with them. In practice this means that it would be implicit in our acceptance of the Treaties that the United Kingdom would, in future, refrain from enacting legislation inconsistent with Community law.[5]

Although the Community institutions have the power to impose pecuniary obligations on institutions and individuals of member states, they do not have power of enforcement. Under Article 192 of the Treaty of Rome member states are required to enforce any pecuniary obligations on persons other than states under their jurisdiction. To refuse to do so would place them in breach of their Treaty obligations.[6]

Competition policy is restricted to inter-member state trade and relations. Thus, for example, Article 85 on restrictive practices refers to 'practices which are likely to affect trade between Member States', and Article 92 on state aid refers to aid which 'adversely affects trade between Member States'.

Such a constraint covers both direct and indirect effects. If, for example, aid is granted to a non-exporting UK firm, the activities of that firm may reduce exports of other EC firms to the United Kingdom, or they may influence the operating base of a competing UK firm to the extent that its exports are affected. Thus, although the influence on trade may be indirect, as opposed to direct, this would still be covered by the Treaty obligations and the competition regulations ensuing from them.

Moreover, the competition policy encompasses firms in third countries and legally independent firms in member states in a manner which is not found in the national legislation of any member state and which has important implications in international law.

As has been pointed out above, EC competition regulations only apply to those situations where trade *between* Community countries is affected. Thus, actions having a purely domestic effect in a member state, or having effect outside the EC, are excluded. On the other hand, actions occurring outside the EC, but having effects within it, are included. This latter interpretation has consequently had important implications for multinational companies.

Companies incorporated outside the Community but having trading relations with it can, for the purposes of competition law, be grouped into three categories. Firstly, there are those who have a corporate presence in the Community through, for example, a branch; secondly, those who have a subsidiary in the Community; and thirdly, those with no presence of any type in the Community.

The case of the formal corporate presence falls quite clearly under the Treaty provisions. In the case of subsidiaries (even not entirely owned) of firms incorporated outside the Community, the Commission and the Court of Justice have ruled that in the case of 'restrictive practices' parent companies are responsible for the actions of their legally independent subsidiaries, and that in the case of 'dominant market positions' the world position of the parent company is to be taken into account.

Both the Commission and the Court of Justice have relied upon an analysis of economic cause and effect to interpret the legal implications of the Rome Treaty. Thus it is not a case of legal nicety but of economic fact which has determined decisions. In law, parent and subsidiary are separate legal entities, but the European Court of Justice has ruled:

> The fact that the subsidiary has its own legal personality does not serve to rule out the possibility that its conduct is attributable to the parent company. This could be the case where the subsidiary, even though it has its own legal personality, does not independently determine its own market behaviour but essentially follows the instructions given to it by the parent company. (The Dyestuffs Case, 1972)

Thus where, for example, two parent companies outside the EC agree to fix prices and their subsidiaries pursue such a policy, an offence has been committed even though the subsidiaries have not individually come to any price-fixing agreement with each other.

In relation to the 'abuse of a dominant position', the Court has held that the position of a non-EC parent in the world market, not just in the EC market, is relevant (Commercial Solvents Case, 1974). Also, if an external parent acquires control of a number of companies in the EC, with each of the acquired companies having legally independent subsidiary status, all the companies including parent and subsidiaries can be treated as one company for the purpose of deciding whether such mergers are desirable in the public interest (Continental Can Case, 1971).

It follows, therefore, that if companies wholly outside the EC and without affiliates, branches or subsidiaries there pursued a common policy which had detrimental effects upon the EC, action could theoretically be taken against them under the Community competition law. Such action might imply the use of commercial power, e.g. the banning or limiting of imports into the EC from these companies.

7.2 Development of competition policy

Three distinct elements can be isolated in the development of competition policy. Initially, as already noted, the principal aim of policy was to prevent private barriers to trade building up in place of governmental ones which were being dismantled between member states of the Community. With the end of the transitional period another aspect of policy became increasingly important, namely, the desire to foster competition as an allocations- and efficiency-stimulating instrument. In this respect, account had to be taken of the changing structure of industry and particularly the cross-frontier development within the Community. In the two decades since the establishment of the EC, industry has changed its structure and practices in order to take advantage of the enlarged markets. Competition policy has thus increasingly had to take account of those changes, structures and practices which result in constraints on competition. Finally, states have increasingly sought to aid certain depressed sectors and regions since the establishment of the EC, and this has been particularly noticeable since the onset of the world depression which has existed since 1974. As a result, a policy towards state aid has had to be developed within the framework of competition policy in order to prevent state practices from militating against the twin aims of competition policy – the development of a single market and the propagation of efficiency.

Reference has already been made to the wide scope of competition policy, and coverage of this must of necessity be restricted. In the following paragraphs some of the more important aspects of that policy are dealt with under the three headings of restrictive practices, dominant positions, and state aid and state-owned undertakings. Policies relating specifically to the ECSC have had to be excluded – see Chapter 12.

7.2.1 Restrictive practices

Under Article 85 of the Rome Treaty any agreements, decisions or concerted practices between enterprises which affect intra-Community trade and prevent, restrict or distort competition are as a general rule prohibited. An exception to this general rule is made where such practices 'contribute to the improvement of the production or distribution of goods or to the promotion of technical or economic progress while reserving to users an equitable share in the profit resulting therefrom', providing that the restrictions are indispensable to the objects quoted above and competition is not eliminated in respect of a substantial proportion of the goods involved.

Article 85 is of great interest in that at the time of the signing of the Rome Treaty only Germany had legislated to any general degree in relation to restrictive practices; and even in the case of that country the legislation had been passed only in July 1957. Since then, with the exception of Belgium,[7] all the original six member states have introduced legislation curbing restrictive practices.

During the 1970s the twin pressures of inflation and consumer protection left their mark on restrictive legislation, and it is interesting to note that it was only in the late 1970s that France and Italy introduced comprehensive legislation in this area. Previously, a very limited constraint existed under the provision of Article 1379 of the Civil Code in Italy; and under Ordinance 45 – 1483 of June 1945 in France certain controls over prices could be exercised.

Common pressures have led to similarities in national legislation in Europe, but both Community and national policies differ markedly from legislation in the United States in that, in contrast to US anti-trust legislation, they differentiate between 'good' and 'bad' cartels. Thus, under Article 85, if benefits accrue from restrictive practices this is not contrary to the Treaty, whereas cartels in the United States are held to be detrimental and *per se* illegal.

Reference has already been made to the powers accorded the Commission under Regulation 17, and two procedural points should be mentioned here. Firstly, under Articles 4 and 5 of that regulation, both existing (i.e. at the time of entry into force of the regulation) and new agreements had to be ratified, and under Article 2 the Commission was empowered to grant 'negative clearance', i.e. to rule that there were no grounds for action on its part under Article 85.

The inapplicability of the prohibition of restrictive practices provided for under paragraph 3 of Article 85 (see above) can apply to specific agreements or to groups of agreements. In relation to group negative clearance, the Council adopted a regulation in 1965 empowering the Commission to exclude by regulation from the prohibition certain agreements relating to:

1. Only two undertakings.
2. Industrial property rights – in particular of patents, utility models, designs or trade marks.
3. Rights to use a method of manufacture or knowledge relating to the use, or to the application, of industrial processes.

The Commission was empowered under this Council regulation to specify the exact details of the exemptions, and this it did initially in a regulation in 1967. That regulation has now been replaced by two further regulations: Regulation 1983/83, dealing with exclusive distribution agreements, and Regulation 1984/83, dealing with exclusive purchasing agreements. Under Article 1 of the former, it is

> declared that Article 85(1) of the Treaty shall not apply to agreements to which only two undertakings are party and whereby one party agrees with the others to supply certain goods for resale within the whole or a defined area of the common market only to that other.

However, this exemption does not apply where the two parties are manufacturers of identical goods, or where there is no alternative source of supply outside the contract territory. Under Article 1 of Regulation 1984/83, it is

> declared that Article 85(1) of the Treaty shall not apply to agreements to which only two undertakings are party and whereby one party, the reseller, agrees with

the other, the supplier, to purchase certain goods specified in the agreement for resale only from the supplier or from a connected undertaking or from another undertaking which the supplier has entrusted with the sale of his goods.

Again, the exemption does not apply in the case of manufacturers of identical goods; or when 'the exclusive purchasing obligation is agreed for more than one type of goods where these are neither by their nature nor according to commercial usage connected to each other' (Article 3(c)); or when the agreement is for an unspecified period, or for a period of more than five years.

A regulation passed by Council in 1971 empowered the Commission to declare the following categories of agreements free of the Article 85 prohibition:

1. The application of standards or types.
2. The research and development of products or processes up to the stage of industrial application, and exploitation of the results, including provisions regarding industrial property rights and confidential technical knowledge.
3. Specialisation, including agreements necessary for achieving it.

The Commission issued a number of notices in relation to these regulations, dealing with exclusive contracts with commercial agents (1962); patent licensing agreements (1962); cooperation between enterprises (1968); and agreements of minor importance (1970, amended 1977). But with the exception of the 1966 notice on cooperation, these are in the light of the development of case law no longer of importance.

In the development of case law dealing with patent licensing agreements it has been held that, even where these comprise a restraint on trade exemption can be granted if the restriction is not appreciable, because of the small share of the market held by the licensee (Burroughs–Delplanque, 1971 and Burroughs/Geha-Werke, 1971). Exemption may, however, also be granted even where a major share of the market is concerned. Thus, even where the licensing arrangements covered the whole of the Community, and one licensee held 20 per cent of its national market and another 40 per cent with its licenses, exemption was granted (Davidson Rubber Co., 1972). In this instance it was held that the patent promoted economic progress through allowing mass production at low cost. Thus the advantages were held to outweigh the disadvantages in that the consumers derived a fair share of the increased profit resulting from the lower production costs.

By contrast, industrial property rights (trade marks) have been suppressed in relation to intra-Community trade. Industrial property rights are national rights and confined to a national territory, and in cases where a manufacturer desires rights in several countries, application must be made in each individual country, and rights granted are specific to that country and the regulations in it.

In cases where such agreements have led to territorial constraints of trade, such as when the import of goods by a trader in member state A from member state B constitutes a trade mark infringement of another firm in A, such infringement is not upheld under Community competition law as it comprises a restrictive practice under the terms of Article 85.[8]

In cases where Article 85 cannot be applied to prevent territorial restraints to trade through industrial property rights because no 'agreement' in the terms of Article 85 exists, the Court has acted through Articles 30 and 34 of Chapter 1 on the elimination of quantitative restrictions. Thus, for example, where entirely independent firms have the same trade mark in different countries, the Court has ruled that no trade mark infringement exists where the owner of the trade mark in one member state exports to the other member state ('Hag' Case, 1974). Also, where trade marks are owned by parent and subsidiary in different countries (Centrafarm Case, 1974), imports between these two countries, by other firms, of goods covered by the trade mark cannot be prevented on account of any trade mark infringement.

Exclusive territorial rights will, however, be allowed where the consumer is seen to benefit from them. In the Omega case (1970), for example, which dealt with the question of exclusive retail outlets, the Commission ruled that Omega watches were highly technical and relatively expensive and

> any approval as authorized Omega dealers of all the retailers in the Common Market who have the necessary professional qualifications ... would reduce the sales possibilities of each to a few units each year. The result would be a deterioration rather than an improvement of the services expected of them by the manufacturer as well as by the consumers.

An extremely firm position has been taken by the Commission and the Court in relation to price-fixing cartels as evidenced in the Dyestuffs case quoted above, where substantial fines were levied.

7.2.2 Dominant positions

Under the terms of Article 86 of the Treaty of Rome, any actions which 'take improper advantage of a dominant position' and which affect trade between member states is prohibited.

Some of the most important (and controversial in respect to international law) developments in Community law have taken place with respect to Article 86. Of primary importance has been the development of the concept that it is economic control and not legal control that is of relevance here. Thus, a parent company can be held responsible for the actions of a legally independent subsidiary, and the combined trade of parent and subsidiary is the relevant measure in assessing whether a dominant position exists.[9] These principles apply even in those cases where the parent is incorporated outside the Community.

In the late 1970s, the definition of dominance was extended to apply to situations other than those where the undertaking dominated through sheer size (United Brands Case, 1978). Dominance can derive from a combination of several factors which, taken separately, would not necessarily be determinate. Thus, dominance occurs where an undertaking has 'the power to behave to an appreciable extent independently of its competitors, customers and alternatively of its consumers' (judgement in United Brands Case, 1978).

Following a ruling of the Court (ABG Case, 1978) it appeared that a dominant position could arise in a situation of shortage (such as the mid-1970s oil crisis) where traditional customers become dependent upon their suppliers and competition between suppliers no longer exists. In such a case it appeared that any discrimination between traditional customers in the allocation of the available supplies would constitute an abuse of a dominant position.[10] It was subsequently held, in a decision of the following year (Hoffmann-La Roche, 1979), that a Swiss company was in a dominant position in operating a system of fidelity rebates for its customers for various vitamins.

However, despite the legal history created in the area of dominant positions, it is also in this area that the Community has been least successful in the formulation of policy – namely, in relation to mergers. Mergers can be dealt with under Article 86 only if an abuse of the dominant positions results from the act of merger itself. It is highly unlikely that the mere act of merging can of itself result in an abuse, and any subsequent abuse is irrelevant to the merger *per se*, as the Community certainly has no powers to order a company to divest itself of any part of its assets.

At the Paris summit of October 1972 it was held that merger regulation was required, and that the use of all dispositions of the Treaty, including the 'catch-all' Article 235, should be made.[11] Following this declaration, the Commission prepared a proposal for a regulation on the control of mergers. Basically, the proposal was aimed at those mergers 'whereby the undertakings involved acquire the power or enhance their power to hinder effective competition' (EC Commission 1974b, p. 33). It proposed excluding from the regulation mergers where the turnover involved was low or where the share of the total market involved was small. The regulation has, however, still failed to pass the proposal stage.

Interestingly, research coordinated by the Berlin-based International Institute for Management, covering a period of ten years and 765 merger cases in Belgium, France, the Netherlands, the United Kingdom, Germany, Sweden and the United States, suggested that mergers do not result in improved efficiency, lower prices, expanded sales and increased benefits for the consumer. It is suggested that current mergers often seem akin to empire building, with no demonstrable social benefit to compensate for the inherent reduction in competition.

Such findings underline the importance of making progress in this area of competition policy.

7.2.3 State aid and state-owned undertakings

As a general rule, state aid which favours certain enterprises or products[12] and which distorts trade between member states is, under the terms of Article 92, 'incompatible with the Common Market'. However, as with Article 85, this incompatibility is not absolute. Thus, three types of aid are specifically deemed to be compatible and other types of aid *may* be deemed to be compatible. The three *de jure* exceptions relate to:

1. Aid of a social character to individuals where no discrimination on basis of origin exists.
2. Aid related to national calamities.
3. Aid to assist regions of the Federal Republic affected by the division of Germany.

Over and above these three categories, aid may be deemed compatible if it is intended to aid:

1. Development of underdeveloped regions.
2. Promotion of important projects with a European interest.
3. Development of certain activities or certain economic regions.
4. Any situation specified by the Council.

As a rule, it is for the Commission to decide whether aid is compatible with the aims of the Common Market, with leave for appeal to the Court, but in 'exceptional circumstances' any type of aid may be approved by the Council.

No aid may be modified or introduced without the member state in question informing the Commission in due time in order to enable it to submit its comments. If states act precipitately, any interested party can have the aid declared illegal,[13] and if the Commission subsequently deems the aid incompatible, it can order repayment of the aid.[14]

Of prime importance in the development of competition policy have been exceptions (1) and (3) in the second group of exceptions mentioned above, namely, aid to underdeveloped regions and aid to certain activities or economic regions.

In the early stages of the Community, the main emphasis was on aid to underdeveloped regions. It was a basic aim of the Treaty to help regions of 'serious' unemployment and 'abnormally low' living standards, and there was thus both a common interest and obligation upon signatories of the Rome Treaty towards aiding these areas. As this was a Community obligation, 'serious' and 'abnormally low' must be interpreted in relation to the Community as a whole and not in relation to an individual country. There have thus been differences of opinion between individual states, which have viewed the situation from a national viewpoint, and the Commission, which has viewed the situation from a Community viewpoint.

By the mid-1960s, however, the problems of declining regions and declining industries had become increasingly more important and took precedence over the development of underdeveloped regions. Unlike aid to underdeveloped regions which is, as an aim of the Community, by definition of common interest, the only question open to debate is what constitutes an underdeveloped region. Sectoral or regional aid for declining industries and areas is only compatible within the Treaty in so far as it 'does not change trading conditions to such a degree as would be contrary to the common interest'.

Massive aid has been granted by states to these declining industries and regions, and the Commission, both on account of the level of aid and the difficulty of assessing its effect on the Community, found itself unable to keep abreast of the problem. A major problem faced by the Commission in this connection was the competition between member states to woo foreign investors to these areas by all manner of incentives. It was thus a major achievement of the Commission in 1973 to instigate a resolution in the Council detailing eight principles for such sectoral and regional aid. These principles aimed both at regulating competition between states for foreign investment and at assisting the Commission in its task of evaluation.

In relation to state enterprises, a differentiation must be made between state monopolies and public sector companies. Chapter 2 of Title I of the Rome Treaty deals with the 'Elimination of quantitative restrictions as between Member States', and basically the Treaty requires that all quantitative restrictions on imports and all measures with equivalent effect shall be terminated in trade between member states. Article 37 of that chapter relates to state monopolies of a commercial character, including any body 'by means of which a Member State shall *de jure* or *de facto* either directly or indirectly control . . .', and requires that policies of such monopolies or bodies be adjusted so as to ensure the exclusion 'of all discrimination between the nationals of Member States in regard to conditions of supply or marketing of goods'.

In interpreting this article, the Commission has maintained that its objective is the same as that for other products, as covered by Articles 30 to 34 of Chapter 2: that is, the free movement of goods must not be hindered. In order to ensure this free movement, the Commission has argued not only that the removal of discrimination is required, but that Article 37 also aims at excluding the 'possibility' of discrimination – such a possibility resulting from powers concerning import, export, or distribution of products. The Commission thus concluded that the most effective course of action was the elimination of the exclusive rights of the state monopolies, and it has been successful in a number of areas in obtaining agreement to such a policy from member states.

Public sector companies are required to observe the rules of the Treaty in exactly the same manner as private enterprises. It seems clear that they are only specifically picked out in the Treaty on account of the ability of member states to use such enterprises to influence trade between member states, a classic example being the manipulation of railway tariffs so as to assist exports and handicap imports (for a fuller discussion, see Bayliss, 1979).

The only difference between private and state-owned or controlled companies[15] is in relation to the enforcement of the Treaty provisions. Private undertakings can be fined, but in the case of public sector companies the Commission has only the options of issuing directives or decisions to the member states (Article 90(3)) or commencing proceedings in accordance with Article 169.

7.3 A significant development

Recent developments in EC competition policy are quite extensive, and, as already indicated, depend largely on EC case law which is determined by the rulings of the EC

Court of Justice. Therefore, legal expertise is required if one is to be able to select the most salient features within these developments. However, the careful reader should be able to follow these developments by sifting through the *Reports on Competition Policy* published annually by the EC Commission. Here, it suffices to discuss those cases which particularly relate to the SEA and the achievement of the single market at the end of 1992, especially one significant ruling which has enabled the EC to develop its strategy for the 'internal market'.

The case law that is relevant to this area is that dealing with the five 'freedoms' provided for in the Treaty of Rome: the free movement of goods, persons, services, capital and payments. Since these freedoms are discussed in detail elsewhere in this book, this section will concentrate on one case law which relates to the free movement of goods. Before doing so, however, one should note that Article 13 of the SEA defines, in a new Article 8A of the Treaty of Rome, the internal market as 'an area without internal frontiers in which the free movement of goods, persons, services and capital is ensured in accordance with the provisions of this Treaty'. The first paragraph of Article 8A suggests that the internal market is a rather narrow concept since it indicates that the accomplishment of the internal market by the beginning of 1993 requires not only the provisions in this article, but also those in Articles 8B, 8C, 28, 57(2), 59, 70(1), 84, 99, 100A and 100B, without prejudice to the other articles of the Treaty of Rome. Except for Articles 84 and 99, these deal exclusively with the specified four freedoms.

With regard to the free movement of goods, the area rated by businesses as the most important single category of trade barrier is that of technical regulations. These are in great detail and are rather complex. It was once estimated that the EC had over one hundred thousand different technical regulations and standards. Indeed, the number is on the increase owing to technological developments and growing concern for such issues as health, safety and consumer protection.

Note that the distinction between technical regulations and standards is a legal one. Technical regulations are legal and are written by national standardisation bodies. Standards are voluntarily agreed codifications regarding products and production methods. They are not legally binding and arise from the self-interests of the producers and consumers concerned.

The EC now possesses a number of instruments for dealing with the market segmentation effects of technical barriers. The most significant of these is the 'principle of mutual recognition' which states that products lawfully produced or marketed in one member nation can have access to all member countries. This was the essence of the ruling of the EC Court of Justice in 1978 in the Cassis de Dijon case which was followed by a whole line of further judgements.

A quotation from the London *Economist* (9 July 1988) may help explain the importance of this case:

> Until the end of the 1970s the route to a common market was thought to lie through 'harmonisation'. Frontiers would wither as the pasta, taxes, company laws and anti-terrorist policies on either side of them were forced by the Eurocracy to conform to Euro-norms that would make the Community a seamless continuum. It

was a hopeless prospect wherever countries were to take unanimous decisions over national quirks that were dear to them.

But in 1978 along came a West German company called Rewe Zentral AG, an unsung European hero, whose contribution to the great market should be toasted regularly in kir. This firm wanted to import Crème de Cassis, a liqueur otherwise known as Cassis de Dijon, into West Germany. It found it could not, because the elixir did not contain enough alcohol to be deemed a liqueur by West German standards. Rewe started legal proceedings which led to the European Court of Justice in Luxemburg, a body that will loom larger and larger as the 1992 story unfolds. The court looked at West Germany's claim that its liqueur norms did not discriminate between West Germans and foreigners, and ruled that it would not wash. West Germany had no right to block the import of a drink that was on sale in France, unless it could show that it was blocked for reasons of health, fiscal supervision, fair trading or consumer protection. West Germany could not.

This ruling helped the EC develop a whole new way for tackling technical barriers. This is enshrined in the SEA: 'the Council may decide that provisions in force in a member-state must be recognised as being equivalent to those applied by another'. Thus a new approach to industrial standards has evolved from this case: banks in one EC member nation will be able to establish themselves in all the other member states; insurance can be sold across the borders of the member nations, etc.

Indeed, this case has proved quite effective. In a recent case, the EC Court of Justice asked West Germany to admit beer from the other member countries, not brewed in accordance with West German purity laws, to be freely imported. However, it should be stressed that while the mutual recognition principle reduces the need for harmonisation, it does not solve the whole problem. In the absence of specific EC legislation, the member nations may still invoke certain provisions in the Treaty (notably Article 36) to restrict the free circulation of goods on grounds of certain public policies or interests. Hence, other policy instruments are also needed.

7.4 Conclusion

In conclusion, it can be stated that in the area of competition policy some notable successes have been achieved. In particular, success has been achieved in relation to restrictive practices, but mergers and state aid continue to present major problems. Also, that the EC Court of Justice has enhanced competition rules greatly via its ruling on the Cassis de Dijon case.

Notes

1. For a summary of each of these nine action areas see Eeckhout (1975).
2. For an interesting analysis of the reasons for failure see Hodges (1977).
3. In the event, the Germans were to do extremely well out of the Common Agricultural Policy, but no one seemed aware of that possibility at this early stage.
4. Article 235 of the Treaty of Rome reads: 'If any action by the Community appears neces-

Competition and industrial poli... with emphas... industrial ...

V. Curzon P...

This chapter will be divide...
tional problems. The se...
policy. The third will...
Community, from...
this historical a...
'theory' of in...

8.1

terms of the Treaty.
13. Lorenz v. Federal Republic of Germany (1973).
14. Commission v. Germany (1973).
15. Enterprises which are accorded 'special or exclusive rights' by the state are included alongside public sector companies even if not wholly owned by the state.

...cies
...sis on
...policy

...rice

...ed into four main sections. The first will address defini-
...cond will discuss the intellectual foundations for industrial
... review the development of industrial policy in the European
... the early 1970s to this day. The fourth will attempt to evaluate
...nd current experience in the light of what might be termed the
...dustrial policy presented in the second section.

What is industrial policy?

Professors Bayliss and El-Agraa, authors of the previous chapter, on 'Competition and industrial policy', define industrial policy thus: 'Industrial policy embraces all acts and policies of the state in relation to industry', adding that it can be either positive (to the extent that the state wishes to influence industry) or negative (to the extent that it might be the industrial policy of the state to *minimise* intervention in industry) – see Chapter 7.

This, it seems to me, is an excellent starting point for our discussion. It shows, for instance, what a very broad spectrum of state acts (or non-acts) can be covered by the term 'industrial policy'. Indeed, the ground covered implicitly by such a definition is so extensive that a whole book would be insufficient to do it justice, let alone a mere chapter. Our immediate task, therefore, is to reduce 'industrial policy' to manageable proportions.

As much of what follows will be concerned with state intervention in industry, and indeed that is what is usually understood by industrial policy, we shall reserve the terms 'positive' and 'negative' for (infrequently) qualifying such interventions, and use words like 'market-oriented' or 'non-interventionist' to describe the policy of minimising attempts by the state to affect industry. Thus, while conceding the point made by Bayliss and El-Agraa, we shall in this chapter narrow the sense of the term 'industrial policy' to cover only proactive state policies.

Another way to reduce the field to manageable proportions is to look at the level of generality of the policy under discussion. Thus, while it is true that the rate of interest affects investment, hence industry, few people would hold that monetary policy is a subset of industrial policy. The same would hold for social policy, or environmental policy, or even regional policy (in its purest form). These broad, general policies, as long as they do not discriminate explicitly between industries, do not affect the allocation of resources between industries *as their primary purpose*. That they may well affect inter-industrial allocation as a secondary result is obvious: thus capital-intensive operations will be more penalised by a tight monetary policy than labour-intensive ones; or polluting industries will be more affected by stiff anti-pollution norms than 'clean' business activities. But the general legal or policy framework is established to fulfil a particular purpose, and the pattern of industrial allocation falls into place behind it – in principle without the need for central direction.

We therefore propose to limit the term 'industrial policy' to mean any state measure designed primarily to affect the allocation of resources *between* economic activities, in other words, to impose a new direction on pure market structures. For instance, any public policy to support the steel or clothing industry, whatever the form of the support, would qualify as 'industrial policy' under this definition, since resources would be encouraged to stay on in these sectors despite market signals to the contrary. Similarly, any public policy to support, say, aeronautics, telecommunications, electronics and so forth (usually known as 'high-tech' activities) would also qualify as 'industrial policy' since, by implication, more resources would be drawn into these sectors than would be the case without the policy – and, indeed, that would be its exact purpose. One might wish to use terms such as 'forward looking' and 'backward looking', or 'positive' or 'negative' (or, if one were writing for the press, 'sunrise' and 'sunset') policies to qualify these two examples; but the main point to remember is that both of them aim to affect the allocation of resources between sectors, whether broadly or narrowly defined.

It is also worth noting that in both the examples just given, the aim of the policy is to *encourage* the 'target' activity – whatever one might think about its future prospects. In fact, there are very few examples of state intervention to explicitly penalise or run down an industry, although of course, any action to promote a particular economic activity implicitly discourages all other non-aided activities. This is no accident. The Prince, after all, wants to be loved and is most unlikely to want to make enemies by obviously selecting the victims of his policies. He will far prefer to make friends by selecting the beneficiaries. But, in principle, the term 'industrial policy', to be logically consistent, would have to cover any action by the state to help *or penalise* any particular economic activity relative to any other.

In addition, although this widens our field of investigation, I would argue that agricultural policy is a subset of industrial policy because it affects the allocation of resources between identifiable categories of business activities. The term 'industrial' is in fact retained only because it has entered into common usage: it would be much clearer if one called what we are talking about 'resource allocation policy' – a precise but unlovely term. But it goes without saying that a policy to help or hinder certain service activities, for instance, would also qualify as an 'industrial policy'. In fact, the conventional threefold division of the economy into agricultural, industrial and service activities is a statistical artefact, with no satisfactory *economic* definition of any of these three types of economic activity.

There are some borderline cases in deciding on what to include, or not, in our definition of industrial policy. For instance, competition policy (known in the United States as anti-trust policy) – see Chapter 7 – could perhaps be included. It attempts to affect the internal structure of industries by controlling mergers, joint ventures and minority acquisitions and by attempting to prevent cartels. In principle, since its main purpose is to promote competition rather than to affect the intersectoral allocation of resources, it falls outside our definition. However, to the extent that the authorities wielding the weapon of competition policy possess a certain amount of discretion, they may well practise an implicit industrial policy. For instance, they may close their eyes to a 'restructuring' cartel in the chemical industry, or, alternatively, pick on a large foreign multinational for close investigation. Either of these options would affect the allocation of national resources between sectors. Similarly, anti-dumping regulations would not normally fit our definition of industrial policy, because their main purpose is to promote 'fair' competition in *all* sectors exposed to the dangers of international competition. Since there is no reason to believe that dumping would affect some industries more than others, the sectors coming under anti-dumping investigation would tend to be purely random. If, however, there is an abnormal concentration of anti-dumping cases in, say, the textile or electronic sectors, one might begin to wonder whether an implicit industrial policy is not at work.

Another form of borderline case exists at the level of generality of the policy. Earlier, I suggested that agricultural policy was a form of industrial policy, which implies that some very general policies might qualify. Although this is purely a matter of taste, I would argue in favour of reserving for 'industrial policy' only truly microeconomic policies. And there is, incidentally, no problem when it comes to agricultural policy because if one looks carefully at what it actually does, one sees clearly that different segments are treated very differently – see Chapter 9.

It is clear that industrial policy also includes state action to discriminate between economic actors *within* a given sector (micro-microeconomic policy), as for instance happens when one motor car manufacturer gets a huge subsidy in the form of a write-off of accumulated debt, while competitors get nothing. This kind of favouritism, however, is hard to justify on any grounds save those of straightforward political expediency, which may make it hard for it to qualify for the term 'policy'. Other policies, such as regional policy, employment policy or social policy may have to be called in to help.

A brief word is needed on the *instruments* of industrial policy. The favoured instruments of state intervention, whether forward or backward looking, are subsidies and protection from foreign competition. Both instruments are easy to aim at the desired target – the sector selected for preferential treatment. There is much overlap between these two, and it is not even very clear whether the distinction can be maintained at all. For instance, a public procurement policy to 'buy national' at twice the price and half the quality of a foreign competitor is *both* a form of hidden subsidy *and* a clear non-tariff barrier against foreign competition. Also, any protective barrier, whether tariff or non-tariff in nature, against foreign competition permits local firms to raise their prices, which means that they enjoy a hidden subsidy which does not even transit through government coffers, but is transferred directly to producers from consumers. This makes the point that both protection and subsidisation can take many forms: what one is looking for is evidence that the policy instrument, explicitly or implicitly, discriminates between sectors, or between firms within a sector.

On the question of whether direct or indirect (i.e. tariff) subsidisation is to be preferred, trade theorists of the 1960s and 1970s came out clearly in favour of direct subsidies, arguing that tariffs caused distortions on the consumer side of the equation, which direct subsidies avoided. After practical experience of widespread subsidisation of industry from the mid-1970s to the mid-1980s in Western Europe, and observing the sheer ingenuity of governments in covering their tracks, the advantages of subsidies over tariffs are today much less obvious.

It is worth noting that both the policy instruments just described are *indirect*. They are aimed by the state at private industry in order to modify the market's allocation of resources. But of course there is a continuum here too, running from the most 'market-friendly' instruments (those operating through the price mechanism) to the most heavy-handed (operating through the use of permits, licences and open state pressure to do this or that). At the end of this spectrum lies outright nationalisation and/or state planning of the economy. In this chapter we shall be limiting ourselves to industrial policy in a market economy.

8.2 Industrial policy: for and against

Historically speaking, economists have devoted a great deal of thought to the theme of international trade and were inevitably led to ask why nations practised discriminatory protection, thus favouring some industries and penalising others. Most if not all the work to date on why governments practise industrial policy has therefore in fact already been done by the trade theorists. It just needs transposing to the slightly broader framework implied by 'industrial policy' as opposed to 'trade policy' (for instance by including non-traded goods and services in the analysis), and shedding some (but not all) of its expressly mercantilist overtones.

Since this is a very well-charted area, I shall do no more than list the traditional reasons advanced for protection which are relevant to the industrial policy debate, referring the reader to any number of excellent texts or more detailed analyses of the pros and cons – see *inter alia*, Corden (1965; 1974), Hindley (1974), Johnson (1971), Kreinin (1979) and *Oxford Review of Economic Policy* (1987); a comprehensive review is provided in El-Agraa (1989b). This will allow us to concentrate on two new theoretical developments of greater relevance to the contemporary discussion on industrial policy: the 'new trade theory' on the one hand, and the theory of rent seeking and public choice on the other.

Traditional arguments for state intervention in industry can be divided into three broad categories: there are respectable economic arguments (1–5); false economic arguments (6 and 7); and non-economic arguments (8 and 9).

8.2.1 Market failure

A case for government action can be made whenever an instance of market failure can be spotted. Two problems nevertheless remain. First, instances of market failure can usually be traced to some kind of previous public policy (a wage rigidity here, a capital market imperfection there), in which case one is not confronted with a genuine *market* failure, but rather a policy-induced *domestic distortion* (see next point); secondly, government action is not costless (see below), which implies that it may be better to live with market imperfections than to attempt to circumvent them with government intervention.

8.2.2 Domestic distortions

In a second best world of political and social constraints, with numerous public policies affecting every aspect of economic life, we are certainly far removed from the welfare optimum described by Pareto. In these circumstances reducing or eliminating government intervention in one segment of the economy might increase the total quantum of distortion in the entire economy and thus reduce welfare. Take, for instance, a reasonably uniform VAT system, covering all goods and services. This is in itself a source of inefficiency, since it places a barrier between producers and consumers. We then decide to eliminate this barrier for one set of goods – say children's clothes. This brings about a distortion in resource allocation which could well be worse than the initial distortion caused by the uniform VAT system. One cannot tell in advance and must let common sense (illuminated by standard economic theory) guide us. Applied to the question of industrial policy, one could, for example, argue that domestic distortions arising from tax and institutional structures are such that industry, collectively, fails to invest enough in research and development. Rather than unravel the whole complex of measures causing this failure, it might be more practical simply to find ways of subsidising extra investment of R&D (always remembering, however, that every government policy has its cost).

8.2.3 Infant industries

This is by far the oldest and most popular of the (economic) arguments for sub-sidisation and/or protection. Even in its traditional formulation, it appeals to such concepts as economies of scale and positive externalities. Thus, it asserts that an industry below optimum size will not generate around itself the necessary physical infrastructure, intellectual and managerial resources, network of suppliers and sub-contractors, financing capabilities, etc., and will therefore operate indefinitely above its potential long-run average cost curve. An initial subsidy, on the other hand, could allow it to achieve the 'critical' size and thus bridge the gap with its world-scale competitors, after which subsidies would no longer be needed.

Essentially, this is an argument about obtuse capital markets, which cannot see the potential for such a profitable business, refuse to lend the money to achieve the optimum scale and make it necessary for the government to step in (i.e. it is a particular instance of the market-failure/domestic distortion argument above – see El-Agraa (1983b; 1984b; 1989b).

That this notion has validity may be inferred from the example of Japan and other East Asian countries, which have succeeded in creating efficient world-scale industries with the help of protection, government guidance and various forms of subsidisation – in other words, industrial policy. One should, however, resist jumping to the conclusion that the Japanese example 'proves' that industrial policy works: it is impossible to say how the Japanese economy would have evolved without state intervention – it might, after all, have grown even quicker. More tellingly, even if industrial policies *have* helped Japan, South Korea and Taiwan to grow more quickly than market forces alone would have achieved, it is still not clear that industrial policies will always help a country to develop. In fact, the risk of failure is at least as high as in any normal business venture, and probably much higher.

The pitfalls are all too easy to spot. How does one select the industries to be promoted (the so-called 'specification problem')? How does one wean them from support once they have grown up? How does one stop the process of selection from becoming politicised? The economic landscape is littered with examples of infant industries which have never fulfilled their promise. It is easy to 'target' this or that economic sector for special treatment – but it is difficult to make money in competitive world markets. And this is the acid test of whether or not the infant has 'grown up' – see El-Agraa (1983b; 1984b; 1989b).

8.2.4 Positive externalities

The infant industry argument for state intervention can be buttressed by an appeal to positive externalities, that is, inappropriate returns (i.e. benefits to the economy at large for which the firm producing them cannot make us pay). Thus it may be argued that support for, say, the aeronautical industry will generate a large pool of skilled engineers to which other industrial sectors will also have access – because they cannot be indentured exclusively to the aeronautical industry. In these circumstances, one could argue in favour of supporting the aeronautical industry, even if it operated at a loss, because of the indirect benefits accruing to employers of engineers in the rest of the economy. Left to its own devices, the aeronautical industry would not reach the 'right' size because the whole cost of training specialised engineers could not be recovered, since some benefit would accrue to firms which had not spent a penny on training and could not be forced to contribute.

The Apollo space programme is often credited with having generated many industrial spin-off benefits, especially in the field of electronics and miniaturisation. Countless firms (and not just American ones) sprang up to take advantage of licensed technology at a fraction of the cost of developing it for themselves. Before jumping to the conclusion that we should all rush off and support a man-to-Mars programme, however, it must be remembered that if the positive externalities could be spotted in advance, the market would finance them (the engineers would borrow to study, the technicians would borrow to do the research and take out patents). In reality, positive externalities are rare. Either they have been spotted, and then it is worth something to someone to appropriate them, or they have yet to be discovered, and we are back to the old problem of how to select the economic sector which will generate the best externalities (the 'specification problem'). At the frontiers of knowledge (and this is where we often are in the externalities debate) it is very difficult to avoid costly mistakes.

8.2.5 Public goods

This argument states that people derive pleasure from the knowledge that their country is active in some 'strategic' branches of industry. Since this pleasure adds to national welfare, but cannot be appropriated by the producer of, say, cars, or ships, or steel, state intervention in support of the desired activities is justified, even if they operate at a loss. Since there is no way of measuring the intensity of this pleasure, or even of ascertaining that it really exists at all, this argument needs to be treated with caution. It will most often be found in the policy statements of important lobbies, which can be relied upon to argue that their industry is 'strategic' and its continued good health in the national interest. In fact, this argument comes very close to belonging to the next group of justifications for industrial policy.

In this and previous arguments in favour of state intervention, a common theme is that there is a hierarchy of economic activities which anyone of reasonable intelligence can establish, but which the market refuses to endorse because it is too concerned with short-term profits, or even with profits *tout court*. Yet very few economists would agree that such a hierarchy in fact exists, the only hierarchy worth retaining being that which measures the efficiency of a particular allocation of resources in terms of its ability to cover its costs and attract new resources into the business, i.e. profits. Economists tend to argue that today's pattern of profits (or lack thereof) are reliable *signals* for the future allocation of resources and while not necessarily rejecting arguments for active state intervention, challenge its proponents to provide a better system of establishing a hierarchy of economic activities. Since it is logically impossible to subsidise all activities at once choices have to be made and hierarchies established.

8.2.6 Employment

Subsidisation of declining industries in order to prevent unemployment is one of the least respectable arguments for state intervention but one of the most frequently used in practice (but not always admitted to). In terms of straightforward general-equilibrium economics, it is simply wrong to argue that a subsidy can reduce unemployment. The subsidy has to come from somewhere, and the non-subsidised sectors of the economy 'pay' (in terms of lost investment opportunities, fewer new jobs, lost market share and higher taxes) for every job 'saved' in the subsidised areas. And there is a strong presumption that the jobs 'saved' in the declining sectors will be less numerous, will pay less well and will have a dimmer future than those lost in the non-subsidised sectors.

Sheer political expediency and the fact that the jobs at risk in the stricken industries were highly visible, often regionally concentrated and industrially focused, explain why governments in Western Europe resorted to numerous bail-outs from 1975–85. But wholesale subsidisation of loss-making industries in the end shocked the voting and working public, who did not need general-equilibrium theories to see that this was make-believe economics, and the worst abuses were gradually reversed – see El-Agraa (1984b).

8.2.7 Balance of payments

The public has been taught to worry about the balance of payments, so mercantilistic arguments in favour of reducing imports and/or increasing exports always get a good hearing. Import substitution used to be considered a sensible guide for industrial policy, since it not only resolved the specification problem (one just had to run one's eye down the list of imports and select those products on which much foreign exchange was spent and which also looked easy to make) but, as an added bonus, it 'helped' the balance of payments. Practical application of these notions has since discredited them completely, not least because *import substitution does not 'improve' the balance of payments*. Again, reference to a general-equilibrium framework of analysis will quickly confirm that resources drawn into import substitution have to come from somewhere, and if the aim of the government is really to reduce imports, then they will come from the export sector, and exports will fall by at least as much as imports. Export promotion, if carefully managed, might prove a sounder policy, not for balance of payments reasons, but as a general method of enlarging the traded-goods sector if it is deemed 'too small' (see the second best argument above).

Mercantilist arguments take many forms, among the most prevalent at present being calls for sectoral reciprocity. Thus the European automobile industry argues that it is willing to face (fairly) free competition from Japanese cars on condition Japan opens its own markets to European automobiles. Since Japan, in its eyes, remains protectionist, restrictions on Japanese automobiles are justified. On the face of it, nothing sounds more reasonable. But such bilateral/sectoral arguments are unfounded in both fact and theory; here is not the place to expand on this theme – on the threat to multinational trade of 'strict' reciprocity, see Curzon and Curzon Price (1989).

Balance of payments and employment arguments together form an unbeatable combination, as in the furious 'local content' debate over the definition of what is a 'European' and what a 'Japanese' automobile. In fact, both are pseudo-economic arguments masking special pleading by powerful interest groups (see below).

8.2.8 National defence

This is the most noble of the non-economic justifications for industrial policy, but we know that as an argument it is frequently abused. In principle, the problem of specifying *what* should be produced, *by whom*, *how* and *for whom* (the 'specification problem' referred to above) is resolved politically, since the state and the military are delegated to make the necessary choices for us. But as there is no market for national defence, what is 'essential' is largely a matter of opinion, varies over time and runs the danger of becoming politicised. Note, however, that the argument is not based on the 'public goods' nature of defence (see 8.2.5) but on a perceived need for a degree of self-sufficiency. In an increasingly interdependent world economy, the plausibility of the national defence argument is reduced daily.

8.2.9 Other non-economic objectives

Besides defence, many other socio-political objectives may be pursued via industrial policy: for example, regional development, income redistribution, environmental protection, zoning (land-use) policies and even, perhaps, something as hard to specify as 'European unity'. While economics is of no use in judging whether these *ends* are valid or not (these being collective value judgements, to be decided upon by the political process) economic analysis can be applied to the *means*. Generally speaking, the shortest and most direct route is to be favoured: if raising incomes in poorer regions is the *end*, the best *means* would be a cheque through the post. Landing a poor region like Calabria with a loss-making steel mill is not necessarily a kindness in the long run. Making European industry (or agriculture for that matter) bear the burden of European political integration is also hard on industry and not necessarily good for 'Europe'.

8.3 The 'new trade theory' and its relevance to industrial policy

The 'new trade theory' was developed in the 1980s in response to the observed fact that two-thirds of world trade took place between developed countries and that most of this was of an 'intra-industry' nature. From this observation flowed a series of hypotheses explaining trade flows on the basis of imperfect competition; duopolistic competition (Brander 1981); oligopolistic competition (Brander and Spencer 1984); monopolistic competition (Helpman 1981 and Lancaster 1980); and declining marginal costs (Krugman 1979; 1983). The policy implications of this new approach were to add a *strategic* dimension to the economic case for state intervention in industry.

In a world where technology is paramount and very costly to produce, dynamic economies of scale (learning-curve effects) may determine where a particular economic activity is located, rather than traditional factor endowments. Comparative advantage becomes man made, hence subject to policy. The case of Japan is frequently cited: for example, microprocessors having been identified in the early 1980s as 'strategic', government direction under MITI (Ministry of Trade and Industry) did the rest, not so much by making large funds available to firms in the industry, but by a specifically Japanese combination of consensus and emulation. The point is that the 'first mover' has an advantage, since he is the first to travel down the learning curve, which is related to *accumulated* experience. Also, the larger his initial market, the faster he will travel down the learning curve, since sheer repetition is also important. Time and market size are therefore of the essence and will allow the 'first mover' to reap monopoly rents, which in turn will allow him to invest in the next cycle of techno-logical innovation and so on.

It is easy to see that we have here a good case for state intervention in either of two cases:

1. If one can spot a strategic new industry for the future, possessing the above characteristics, one should seriously consider supporting it, in order to gain 'first mover' advantages.
2. If others have developed a man-made comparative advantage in an industry and are enjoying monopoly rents, another state might be able to share those rents if it developed its own industry in competition. At the very least, it could ensure, through competition, that the 'prime mover' shared his lower unit costs arising from the learning-curve effect.

Case 1 suffers from the specification problem already outlined: it is not that easy to foretell the future and as Kierzkowski (1987) warns: 'New industrial ... policy towards "strategic" industries would involve many policy misses, just like betting on horses'. Case 2 is altogether more attractive. It proposes, in essence, to speed up the Schumpeterian process of creative destruction, spreading the benefits of techno-logical innovation throughout the world in the form of lower prices and lower monopoly rents. The example most frequently cited is that of the European Airbus, which exists only thanks to subsidies, but which presumably has held down the price of Boeings and DC-10s.

8.4 Problems with the new strategic industrial policy

We shall select two which strike us as being particularly noteworthy.

8.4.1 A typical prisoner's dilemma

When discussing strategic industrial policy, we are cumulating two levels of imperfect competition: firstly, the industry itself possesses the attributes of imperfect competition: economies of scale, tendency towards monopoly or at least oligopoly, etc.; secondly, state intervention is proposed not, as is customary, to limit the negative effects of imperfect competition via anti-trust legislation, but to actively promote a rival monopoly *because it is reacting to a monopoly in another country*. In fact, implicit in the whole discussion is the idea that if state industrial policy produces home country monopoly that is fine. Rivalry therefore takes the form of competition between different countries' industrial policies and the final outcome may be negative for all players.

A good parallel can be found in the world of sport. If *A* takes anabolic steroids, and her rivals do not, she is bound to win. If her rivals take anabolic steriods and she does not, she is bound to lose. So everybody takes them, the race is as indeterminate as ever, but everybody's health is impaired.

In the world of strategic industrial policy, if all major players consider that telecommunications are 'strategic', the world as a whole may end up investing far too much in this particular activity and duplicating efforts uselessly. If there is a case to be made for strategic industrial policy in terms of consumer welfare (scale economies, lower average unit costs, etc.), then it is more a case for *global* industrial policy at an international level, than for national industrial policy at a local level.

8.4.2 The problem of rent seeking

The case for state intervention has not been the same since 1967, when Tullock (1967) took a new look at the economics of rents derived from the artificial scarcity caused by tariffs, and suggested that entrepreneurs might compete for them as enthusiastically as they searched for other (more productive) ways of making profits. This apparently simple alternative approach opened up a broad new avenue for economic investigation. Until then, economists had treated transfers between members of the same community as 'neutral' or, if they worried about the distribution effects of tariffs, they did so in terms of the illegitimacy of using community indifference curves to assess 'national' welfare, both of which were effective conversation stoppers.

Tullock's approach, on the other hand, suggested that economic agents had an incentive to waste resources lobbying the state for artificial scarcity rents. These rents could therefore no longer be considered 'neutral', since part of them – and under certain constrained circumstances *all* of them – would be 'dissipated' by the competing rent seekers. In short, this constituted a substantial hidden cost of state intervention – see *inter alia*, Kreuger (1974).

Rent seeking is part of normal profit-seeking entrepreneurial behaviour; it becomes wasteful only when phoney, state-contrived rents are being competed for, and it is in this sense that the term is generally used (and will be used here). Rent seeking can take many forms: lobbying for tariff or non-tariff protection from import competition is a subtle form, usually well-accepted by the general public, especially if presented as being in the national interest (see above). Lobbying for outright subsidies, or a tax break, is rather more obvious and needs a stronger case (perhaps in terms of 'strategic' industrial policy, or a good non-economic objective like employment – see the case of steel discussed below). Obtaining the right to speak to one's direct competitors (something normally frowned upon under most anti-trust laws) can prove to be a well-disguised source of rent. Finally, a good domestic regulation, properly inspired by the industry which the regulation is supposed to constrain, can become a powerful barrier to entry, thus ensuring a permanent flow of rents to the established members of the group: see *inter alia*, Stigler (1971) and El-Agraa (1989b).

All this puts microeconomic state intervention in the economy in a new, rather cynical, light. At the very least, every state intervention must be evaluated for:

1. The open and hidden rents that it generates.
2. The private resources wastefully devoted to obtaining them.
3. The incentive that they provide to other economic agents to waste another round of resources in order to obtain similiar rents for themselves.

8.5 Conclusion

If any general conclusion is to be drawn from this brief summary of the intellectual case for state intervention in the economy it is this: it is not enough to demonstrate market failure to justify government action. The direct and indirect costs of government action may be far greater than the original market imperfection. This is not to say that no industrial policy is the best policy, but to make a plea for very close scrutiny of what is advanced under this banner.

8.6 Industrial policy in the EC

8.6.1 The early years

The Treaty of Rome does not provide for a 'Common Industrial Policy' in the same way as it provides, for instance, for a Common Agricultural Policy, a Common Transport Policy and a Common Social Policy. It does not even provide for a 'Common Regional Policy'. This is no accident. Common policies were necessary between the member nations only in sectors where extensive state intervention by all members made it necessary to avoid wholesale distortions and policy wars. Where these loomed, the founding fathers elevated the problem to Community level and a 'common' policy was born. Where potential problems could be covered up (transport) or where state intervention was sporadic, individualistic or insignificant, there was no need for a common policy.

Articles 92–94 (aids granted by states) were deemed to be sufficient to cope with such problems, and gave the Commission powers of supervision to ensure that state aids did not distort competitive conditions. It was, however, some time before the Commission developed these powers into a 'policy' (see below), since the role of gendarme was not an easy one to assume when the miscreants were member states. And even then the policy was still only one of supervision and control. The Commission had to wait until the 1980s for a proactive industrial policy with a budget to match.

Nevertheless, in one area state intervention was already extensive in the 1960s and threatened the stability of the nascent common market: the regional aid policies of various member states. To persuade member states to agree on guidelines for regional aid was therefore a first priority. The process started in 1968 and by 1971 the Council of Ministers agreed to a series of rules which defined:

1.   The difference between 'central' and 'peripheral' regions.
2.   The establishment of aid 'ceilings' depending on the classification of the region.
3.   Methods of ensuring the transparency of aids.
4.   *Ex post* notification of regional aids to the Commission, which was then entrusted with their evaluation in the light of the preceding guidelines – see EC Commission (1972b).

The first of the Community's 'common policies' not based specifically on the Treaty of Rome was born.

On the whole, however, the 1960s and early 1970s were good years and there was little excuse for state intervention: the only sectors in trouble (if the Commission's *First Report on Competition Policy* is any indication) were shipbuilding, textiles and films, and the Commission limited itself to exhortations to keep national aids within rather vague 'guidelines'. General aid schemes to promote investment and new industries were generally approved of and dowries for industrial weddings in the French electronics industry (Machines Bull and CII) were agreed to without difficulty.

In fact, in the 1960s and early 1970s the term 'industrial policy' was either not in use at all or subsumed under the generic term 'completion of the internal market' (see, for instance, Toulemon 1972) and considered to include the elimination of non-tariff barriers, the reduction of discrimination in government purchasing and the creation of a harmonised legal, fiscal and financial environment for European industry. In a word, industrial policy took the form of an *absence* or reduction of state intervention (see the previous chapter). True, it was felt that a Community science and research programme would be sensible; but the lack of cooperation on nuclear energy in the Euratom framework had proved disappointing – and the Commission had been told in no uncertain terms by General de Gaulle in 1965 not to overstep its limits.

8.6.2 The 1970s

By contrast, the 1970s and early 1980s saw interesting developments on several fronts. The Community matured, increased its membership, but above all experienced several years of unprecedented recession, industrial restructuring, high rates of unemployment and inflation, and low growth. Member states found that their traditional methods of macroeconomic demand management were useless in these circumstances: if they fought inflation with restrictive policies, unemployment figures deteriorated, while if they tried to combat unemployment with expansionary policies, inflation took off. They reacted with a ragbag of microeconomic measures: wage 'policies' (i.e. controls), price controls, credit controls, import controls – anything which might appear to manage the situation, however briefly – none of which worked. Firms continued to fail, unemployment continued to rise. Finally, wholesale direct subsidisation of loss-making industries became the only answer. For this most member states did not have to set up new machinery – they just used pre-existing general aid schemes, increased the funds available and extended their scope.

This was extremely dangerous for the future of the EC. Not only had the internal market not been completed by the mid-1970s, but what had been achieved was now under direct threat from the fatal combination of reinforced non-tariff protection between member states (frequently based on technical barriers) and subsidisation. To begin with the Commission did not appreciate the extent of the danger:

> [It] concluded that Member States, in an attempt to protect employment, were justified in boosting investment by granting firms financial benefits (in the form of tax deductions or low-interest loans) on an automatic or quasi-general basis for a limited period. Similarly, it agreed to financial aid being granted to ensure the survival of firms which have run into difficulties, thereby avoiding redundancies. (EC Commission, 1976a, para. 133)

Thus plain operating subsidies were permitted to safeguard employment, subject to two criteria: that capacity should not be increased and that subsidies should 'benefit firms which are basically sound' (EC Commission 1976a, para. 134). The logical inconsistency of this last criterion was quite lost on the Commission. It was obviously confident that it could, without difficulty, distinguish between sound and unsound firms. In fact, the market normally does this quite simply: if firms are 'basically sound' then they can raise money in the market; if they need subsidies because they have failed to find lenders, then the market has judged them unsound. In the event, the Commission would inevitably be approving aids to unsound firms, no matter how the definition was stretched and twisted – unless, of course, it invented its own (non-market) definition of 'soundness'.

On the enforcement front, member states agreed to prior notification of all general aid schemes and to concurrent or *ex post* notification 'of the more important specific cases where aid is granted'.

The list of sectors 'in difficulty', which until then had been limited essentially to shipbuilding and textiles, expanded to include motor cars, paper and board, machine tools, steel, synthetic fibres, clocks and watches and chemicals. The number of subsidy schemes notified to the Commission rose from a mere handful in the early 1970s to well over a hundred a year at the end of the decade (see Table 8.1). The race for subsidisation was in full swing.

Finally waking up to the danger, the Commission and Council in April 1978

Table 8.1 Accumulated data on state subsidies 1970–87[a]

1	2	3	4	5	6
Year	Total positions	No objection	Objection	Of which final negative decision	Objections/ no objections (col. 4/col. 3)
1970	21	15	6	1	0.29
1971	18	11	7	3	0.39
1972	35	24	11	3	0.31
1973	22	15	7	4	0.32
1974	35	20	15	—	0.43
1975	45	29	16	2	0.35
1976	47	33	14	2	0.30
1977	112	99	13	1	0.12
1978	137	118	19	—	0.14
1979	133	79	54	3	0.14
1980	105	72	33	2	0.31
1981	141	79	62	14	0.43
1982	233	104	129	13	0.55
1983	195	101	94	21	0.48
1984	314	201	113	21	0.36
1985	178	102	76	7	0.43
1986	181	98	83	10	0.46
1987*	274	205	69	10	0.25

Note
[a] According to the *17th Report on Competition Policy*, 'The increase in the total number of notifications (in 1987) is not considered to represent any significant change in the trend of the total value of State aids granted in Member States. It reflects the increasing efficiency of Commission policy in controlling such aids' (para. 174).

Source: EC Commission, *Reports on Competition Policy*, various years.

decided to take a less lenient view of subsidies to preserve employment (EC Commission 1979e, paras 173–4), putting more emphasis on the 'need to restore competitiveness' and to 'face up to worldwide competition'. The change in policy emerges quite clearly from Table 8.1, which lists the number of 'positions' taken by the Commission on state subsidies, dividing them into those to which no objection was raised – and the others. The rate of 'objections' (column 6) fell from about one-third in the early 1970s to a mere 12–14 per cent in 1977–9, but rose again to over 40 per cent thereafter. The number of 'final negative decisions' (where member states were told to withdraw the subsidy scheme altogether) was negligible throughout the 1970s (although the cases reviewed increased substantially), but rose significantly in the 1980s.

The final test of the effectiveness of the Commission in containing the subsidy crisis, and the willingness of the member states to submit to common guidelines, is whether the Commission can force the member states to recover subsidies granted illegally. This has been ordered in 22 cases (see Table 8.2), many of which have been subject to appeals to the European Court of Justice.

Table 8.2 Repayment of subsidies ordered by the Commission (cumulative data up to 1987)

	Cases	Amounts involved (million ECU)
Belgium	10	300
France	5	565
W. Germany	4	14
Netherlands	2	118
United Kingdom	1	2

Source: EC Commission (1988) *Seventeenth Report on Competition Policy*, para. 173, Brussels and Luxemburg.

Steel

Steel became a special case partly because the crisis in this sector proved both excessively deep and widespread (major steel producers in the Community lost some $3 billion in 1977 and the same again in 1978; at a time when a ton of raw steel cost about $250, firms like Sacilor and BSC were losing between $46 and $78 per ton – see *Financial Times*, 5 July 1978), and partly because Community policy was governed by the Treaty of Paris which, by some embarrassing oversight, prohibited specific state subsidies to steel firms without any possibility of derogation (Article 67).

Viscount Etienne Davignon, then EC Commissioner for Industrial Affairs, after consultation with the main firms in the industry, set up a stream of 'voluntary' quotas and 'guideline' prices in May 1977 in accordance with Article 57 of the Treaty of Paris (the qualifying adjectives were necessary because Article 65 of the Treaty of Paris, like Article 67, did not permit agreements between firms, in particular those which fixed prices and/or restricted production).

This first attempt to manage the steel sector in the EC did not prove successful because imports disrupted the guideline prices, forcing Community firms to break the guidelines themselves. In January 1978 the Commission accordingly introduced a minimum price for steel imports and negotiated a series of voluntary export restraints with its principal external suppliers. This worked for a time, but as small steel producers in Northern Italy refused to respect the voluntary quota system, and as the demand for steel continued to fall, discipline in the steel market evaporated. The London *Economist* (8 November 1980, p. 56) described conditions as 'chaotic' as steel firms 'resorted to frantic price-cutting to grab a share of the shrinking market'; losses amounted to $20 million a day. Finally, the Commission invoked the emergency provisions of Article 58 of the Treaty of Paris and introduced compulsory production quotas as from October 1980.

In the meantime, the Commission introduced a code for aids to the steel industry in February 1980 in view of 'the need for all aid to steel to be subject to a coherent Community discipline' (EC Commission 1980c, para. 194). It insisted on prior notification of all subsidies on 'a genuine contribution to the restructuring of the industry' (the intensity of the aid being proportional to the amount of restructuring),

Table 8.3 Subsidies and capacity cuts in the Community steel industry 1980–6

	Accumulated subsidies since 1980 (million ECU)	% of total	Accumulated capacity cuts (million tonnes)	% of total
Belgium	4,259	11.0	3.4	11.0
W. Germany	4,522	11.5	6.7	21.0
France	9,222	23.6	6.1	19.7
Italy	13,893	35.5	7.2	23.0
United Kingdom	5,768	14.7	5.4	17.4
Other	1,438	3.7	2.3	7.9
Total	39,102	100.0	31.1	100.0

Source: EC Commission (1986) *Fifteenth Report on Competition Policy*, Brussels and Luxemburg.

on the minimisation of distortions of competition – and on 'complete transparency'.

Six years and 40 billion ECU later the Community's steel industry had cut capacity by 18 per cent (see Tables 8.3 and 8.4). Despite the Commission's attempts to prevent distortions of competition, it is quite clear from the record that Italian and French steel producers received between four and four and a half times as much help as German steel firms (Table 8.4) and that the latter, although by far the most efficient of the EC's steel producers, had had to cut capacity by almost as much as the notoriously inefficient state-owned Italian steel industry.

In the meantime, the Community's steel-using industries, such as automobiles and shipbuilding, were forced to contribute indirectly to subsidising the steel industry via higher prices, due to the artificial scarcity created by import restrictions and production quotas.

Little wonder that the European steel industry has been most reluctant to accept the gradual unwinding of the Davignon Plan and that it still benefits from voluntary export restrictions from competitive world suppliers – a classic case of rent seeking.

Table 8.4 Relative rates of subsidisation and capacity reductions 1980–6

	Accumulated cuts as % 1980 capacity	Accumulated subsidies per tonne of 1980 capacity (ECU)
Belgium	21.4	266
W. Germany	13.0	87
France	22.9	343
Italy	19.8	383
United Kingdom	23.8	250
EC average	18.1	227

Source: EC Commission (1986) *Fifteenth Report on Competition Policy*, Brussels and Luxemburg.

Synthetic fibres

An account of these dark days would be incomplete without a brief reference to the development of the Community's policy towards the synthetic fibres industry, since it prompted a novel interpretation of Article 85 (cartels) and cleared the legal ground for horizontal agreements between firms to reduce 'structural overcapacity'.

In parallel with the problem of over-capacity which developed in the steel industry, a similar crisis emerged in the synthetic fibre sector in the latter 1970s. Believing that something like the Davignon Steel Plan was called for, the directorate-general for industrial affairs in 1978 sponsored an agreement between the Community's eleven principal fibre producers to share out the existing market according to the pattern of deliveries in 1976 (see *Financial Times*, 23 June 1978). Any loss in demand would be shared equally, as well as any growth, an exception being made for Italy on the grounds that because it was a late starter, it had a 'right' to a larger share.

This agreement was no more and no less than a good, old-fashioned crisis cartel, for which the Treaty of Rome did not provide. Article 85(3) permitted only cartels which contributed 'to improving the production or distribution of goods or to promoting technical or economic progress'. The competition directorate of the Commission duly condemned the agreement among synthetic fibre producers, enjoining them to either discontinue their arrangement or modify it to meet the terms of Article 85(3). In particular, producers were asked to eliminate the quota system (EC Commission, 1979e, para. 42).

What was the industry to do? One Commission directorate told them to set up a cartel, another told them to dismantle it! The lack of agreement within the Commission on the question of (temporary) 'crisis cartels' was obvious. The synthetic fibre cartel continued (shorn of its most blatant quota clauses) in a legal twilight until 1982, when the Commission produced its 'policy' on the matter.

The statement on the application of competition rules to agreements aimed at reducing 'structural over-capacity' reads as follows:

> The Commission may be able to condone agreements in restraint of competition which relate to a sector as a whole, provided they are aimed solely at achieving a coordinated reduction of overcapacity and do not otherwise restrict free decision-making by the firms involved. The necessary structural reorganization must not be achieved by unsuitable means such as price-fixing or quota agreements, nor should it be hampered by State aids which lead to artificial preservation of surplus capacity. (EC Commission 1983b, para. 39)

The synthetic fibre producers duly sought and obtained exemption for their less structured agreement to cut capacity in 1984 (EC Commission 1985e, paras 81–2).

The case is interesting, for it shows among other things that the generally accommodating stance of the Commission towards state subsidies during the crisis years was essentially extended also to firms. It also shows the degree of latitude which the Commission enjoys in the interpretation of the Treaty of Rome. Thus (remembering that exemptions to the prohibition of cartels under Article 85 hinge on strict *economic* criteria, in particular on improvements to production), the Commission justified its new policy towards crisis cartels on the following grounds: 'production can be considered to be improved if the reductions in capacity are likely in the long run to increase profitability and restore competitiveness'.

If *concerted* reductions in capacity are deemed to improve production, we are some way from the original meaning of Article 85. The rent-seeking interest of the industrial groups concerned is obvious: managed, or coordinated, reductions in capacity mean that all firms in the industry share out the agony 'equitably' – not on the basis of efficiency. They are spared the full implications of previous errors of judgement, while the efficient go unrewarded... Is it not a 'fatal conceit' (see Hayek, 1989) that the Commission should believe that it can enforce anything like competitive conditions on an oligopolistic industry, once it has allowed it to form an 'agreement in restraint of competition' (to use its own words)?

In fact, the less said about this whole disastrous decade the better. The Commission should have upheld competitive market principles at Community level much more forcefully, instead of accommodating member states' inglorious capitulation before political pressure from special interest groups and adding its own brand of *clientelisme* at European level. The end result, by mid-1985, was a palpable loss of competitiveness of European industry and loss of confidence in the future: the word 'Eurosclerosis' (attributable to Herbert Giersch) was on every lip.

8.6.3 The 1980s and beyond

So much has happened since those dark days (not so long ago) that it is difficult to know where to start. The adoption of the Commission's White Paper on completing the internal market in June 1985, the signing and later ratification of the Single European Act (SEA) in 1986 and 1987, have changed the Community entirely.

If we were to return to the Bayliss/El-Agraa definition of industrial policy (see above), we would have to discuss the entire single-market programme, since it is a grand (positive) industrial policy in its own right – a huge exercise in the withdrawal of the state from intra-European frontiers and many other spheres of the European economy (but this is not necessary since the penultimate chapter is devoted to this). For this very reason we took a more restrictive view of industrial policy.

Let it nevertheless be said that the main reason why the single market, as a concept, has fired people's imagination and awakened the 'animal spirits' of entrepreneurs is that a major restructuring of the European economy is under way, fuelled by competition and market forces. State intervention at the EC level to guide this process is therefore our subject. Whereas in the 1970s the Commission tried to limit and coordinate subsidies to dying industries, in the 1980s and beyond it sees its task as encouraging and coordinating subsidies to 'high-tech' industries. This is not to say that the problem of subsidies to declining industries has gone away, nor that aid to research and development was absent in the 1970s, but just to point out that there has been a radical shift in emphasis since 1985.

We shall not discuss regional, agricultural or social policy since these are tackled elsewhere in the book, although it should be remembered that each of these is entrusted with softening the impact of the radical restructuring of European industry implied by the single market. We shall instead concentrate on the Community's drive to promote new, technology-intensive sectors.

8.7 Development of the Commission's policy towards R&D

8.7.1 Commission's attitude to private joint ventures in R&D

From its inception, the Community's competition policy has favoured cooperative research and development by the private sector, as well as state support for private R&D. And indeed, as Articles 85–94 of the Treaty of Rome make quite clear, positive benefits are expected to flow from the direct and indirect help implied in R&D subsidies and the pooling of private R&D efforts.

Already in 1968 the Commission had established guidelines for the application of Article 85, which allowed agreements between firms (even large ones) for the exclusive purpose of developing joint R&D, providing the cooperation did not extend downstream to actual production and on condition that the results of the R&D were freely available at least to members of the consortium, and preferably to outsiders as well on a licensing basis (EC Commission, 1972b, paras 31–2).

In December 1984 the Commission adopted a 'block exemption' regulation for R&D agreements between firms which defined a new, more favourable policy. In particular, the adoption of the 'block exemption' approach meant that cooperative R&D agreements, in principle, no longer needed to be individually notified to the Commission, on condition that they met the terms of the 'block exemption'. Secondly, the exemption also applied to R&D agreements which provided for the joint exploitation of the results. This meant that cooperation could now extend to the manufacturing stage (but not marketing).

This represented a considerable shift in policy for which European industry had been asking for some time, on the grounds that it made little sense to pool R&D resources if, once they were successful, competition between the members of the pool wiped out all potential monopolistic rents: under such circumstances, firms would prefer not to pool R&D resources at all, but take the risk of going it alone – see Jacquemin (1988).

8.7.2 The Eureka initiative

The modification of Commission policy coincided with the adoption of the Eureka (European Research Cooperation Agency) initiative by the then ten member states of the EC as well as Spain, Portugal, Austria, Finland, Norway, Sweden and Switzerland. Eureka was launched in April 1985 by President Miterrand as a European response to President Reagan's Star Wars (or what is technically referred to as

Strategic Defence Initiative – SDI) initiative. It involved public support (in the form of subsidies) for substantial cooperative ventures between European firms to develop and launch new, high-technology products (i.e. beyond the R&D stage). As Eureka is not a Community body, but a pan-European one (even including Turkey in some projects), and as it has appropriated for itself the sphere of high-visibility, high-technology, variable-geometry, inter-state cooperation (like Arianespace or Airbus), there is palpable disapproval on the part of the Commission. By some appalling accident this industrial policy plum has escaped its portfolio. In June 1988 the Commission accordingly made several proposals to reinforce its supervision of Eureka projects (see EC Commission, 1988i, para. 352), but it is not yet clear whether this take-over bid has been successful. The easy launching of the Eureka project by seventeen countries, its light institutional and bureaucratic structure (just a small secretariat), its immediate popularity with industry and the bypassing of the EC are all part of an interesting chapter in the broader story of European industrial policy which regret-fully cannot be fitted into the scope of this chapter.

8.7.3 Commission's attitude to state subsidies for R&D

In the meantime the Commission adopted a 'Framework on State aids for research and development' (which had been some time in the making) in 1986, which again emphasised its favourable attitude towards such help but warned of the dangers of fruitless duplication of effort and hence the need for proper coordination by the Commission. It therefore called for the notification of all subsidies in excess of 20 million ECU. A good part of the increase in the number of subsidies investigated by the Commission in 1987 (see Table 8.1) was due to the adoption of this new frame-work. But part was also due to the general increase in state support for R&D, in particular collaborative R&D in the context of the Eureka initiative.

8.8 A real EC industrial policy at last

Despite clear advantages of pooling research efforts at a European level in areas where the costs obviously exceeded the ability of any single country, or company, to defray, member states have been traditionally hesitant to relinquish such an important instru-ment of policy to the Community (hence, in fact, Eureka). Their loss would be the Commission's gain, and this was tolerable only under the most extreme duress.

Thus, until the first energy crisis in the mid-1970s, the Community's industrial research activities were kept on very short rations.[1] Programmes, such as they were, had to be based on Article 235 of the Treaty of Rome[2] and it is significant that it was not until the crucial Hague meeting of heads of state or government in December 1969 that the member states confirmed their readiness 'to coordinate and promote indus-trial research and development in the principal pacemaking sectors, in particular by means of common programmes, and to supply the financial means for these purposes'

(The Hague Summit Communiqué, 1–2 December 1969, point 9). Even then, non-repayable 'free' money available for R&D under the EC did not amount to more than 235 million EUA for the entire period 1974–9. According to Mr Daniel Strasser, at the time Director-General for Budgets, who was in a good position to judge the situation: 'The term "industrial policy" is a euphemism. Community achievements to date in this [industrial policy, R&D] field are so limited that they would scarcely deserve a mention were it not for the ECSC's role in the steel industry' – see Strasser (1981) – (to which we have already alluded).

Since failures are sometimes as revealing as achievements, it may be worth recalling briefly the fate of the Commission's 1977 proposal to research, develop, build and market a large civil transport aircraft, on the grounds that no one member state could carry out such a project on its own because of its cost. The Commission proposed that individual national subsidies in this area should be pooled and replaced by Community financing for all four phases (see Strasser 1981, p. 256). The Commission would then manage the project, of course in constant collaboration with the member states. Despite the obvious logic of the proposal, it was never adopted. Instead, the member states preferred the variable-geometry method of Airbus Industrie.

As the technological weaknesses of European industry became more and more apparent, however, it became harder for governments to maintain their go-it-alone attitudes. In one particular area – information technology – industrial pressure for a pooling of resources became particularly insistent. Twelve prominent firms active in the information technology sector (Bull, CGE, Thomson from France, AEG, Nixdorf, Siemens from Germany, GEC, ICL, Plessey from the United Kingdom, Olivetti and Stet from Italy and Philips from the Netherlands) formed 'The Round Table' and effectively lobbied the Commission and their respective national governments for the adoption of a European Programme for Research in Information Technology (subsequently known as ESPRIT). ESPRIT was proposed by the Commission in May 1983 and adopted unanimously by the Council of Ministers in February 1984.

The motivations behind this move were, in the words of the ESPRIT Review Board:

> The undiminished poor competitiveness of the European IT industry in the face of increasing market penetration from the US and Japan... The importance of economies of scale and the ensuing need for the European IT industry to act together in a collaborative manner in innovative technologies without restraining competition (ESPRIT Review Board, 1985, p. 1)

ESPRIT was in many ways a trail blazer: it established a pattern for creating an industrial policy partnership between the Community, the member states and industry which has since been used in many other fields. Very briefly, the Community would call for projects from industry. These would have to emanate from two or more firms from two or more countries in the EC and they would have to fit the broad terms of reference agreed to after much consultation by the Council of Ministers. The

Community would finance half the cost of the project, while the other half would come from national sources, including private companies participating in the research. In fact, a substantial private sector contribution was considered necessary to guarantee both commitment on the part of industry and a correct allocation of public resources. Finally, it was always made very clear that only pre-competitive R&D fell within ESPRIT's terms of reference.

The reason for this limitation was quite clear: cooperation between European firms was to be encouraged, but not to the point where it might constitute a threat to competition. It is to be remembered, however, that the Commission's block exemption on R&D agreements between firms was at this very moment in the process of being revised in order to permit joint production of the fruits of joint R&D projects. What the Commission refused to do was in fact to *subsidise* joint production activities.

There was a very simple reason for this: to avoid being accused by the United States of subsidising industry. The more general the programme and the further removed it was from the market-place, the easier it was to refute such objections. Indeed, the Community, to this day, is at pains to point out that it does not operate any industrial policy as such, only a series of R&DT (research and technological development) programmes. 'Industrial policy' is a bad phrase.

The first phase of ESPRIT (1984–8) covered R&DT projects amounting to 1,500 million ECU, half financed by the Community. Calls for proposals produced almost a thousand projects, of which 240 were approved by the Commission after consultation with the Round Table representatives. A mid-term review, published in 1985, confirmed that industry was very enthusiastic about the programme, wanted more money, more coverage and was anxious that continuity should be assured. Respondents to the review's questionnaire added that they would have liked fewer but larger projects and that 'ESPRIT alone is not sufficient': in particular, they argued that the programme should be extended to cover prototype development, production engineering, manufacture and marketing (ESPRIT Review Board, 1985, p. 37). ESPRIT projects should be 'more focused' (coded language for actual manufacturing subsidies) – naturally enough! The rent-seeking instinct, once stimulated, expands to cover the ground available.

By now other European industries had awoken to the fact that if financial support for joint R&D was available for the information technology sector, it might also be forthcoming for other sectors as well. One can only speculate on the industrial representations being made at all levels of Community decision-taking structures in the early 1980s, but they must have been considerable, for in 1983 the Council of Ministers adopted what is now called the 'First Framework Programme' for Community R&D policy, running from 1984–7. The purpose of this programme was to integrate all Community aid to R&D into a single, coherent (it was hoped) system, capable of ensuring continuity beyond twelve months. It included all past aid to nuclear and non-nuclear energy, but added research in raw materials, recycling of industrial waste, wood, basic research in industrial technologies, high-temperature materials, metrology, agriculture, the environment, health and safety and science and technology for development (see *inter alia* EC Commission, 1984a, paras 552–83). This first

Framework Programme was given an overall budget of 3,750 million ECU over 4 years.

In the meantime, an important institutional change in the European industrial policy scene occurred in 1987 with the ratification of the SEA, Title VI of which was devoted to technological research and development. Under its terms the Community's sphere of action was significantly enhanced by comparison with the Treaty of Rome. The Commission was urged to coordinate member states' R&D programmes (Article 130H); the Council, the Parliament and the Commission together were urged to establish a 'multiannual framework programme' for Community R&D (Article 130I); in broad terms, they were to establish (subject to unanimous Council vote) both priority areas and the degree of Community financial support for each of the specific programmes decided upon; specific programmes could be decided upon by qualified majority vote; finally, the Community could initiate technological cooperation agreements with third countries or international organisations (i.e. coordination with Eureka was provided for) (Article 130N).

This modification of the Treaty of Rome has put the Community's proactive industrial policy on a firm legal footing for the first time. It institutes a three-stage decision-making process: the Council, acting unanimously, decides (on the basis of a proposal from the Commission) on the broad allocation of resources in the 'multi-annual framework programme' (lasting four years), specific programmes are then decided upon by qualified majority vote (again on the basis of proposals from the Commission), then actual projects are finally selected by the Commission, acting in concert with industry and national civil servants.

A second Framework Programme, running from 1987 to 1991, was duly adopted and provided with a budget of 6,480 million ECU over four years. Its scope has been expanded to include medical research on AIDS, radiation protection and occupational medicine, pollution and climatology (greenhouse effect), pre-standardisation research (to establish European norms and standards more easily) and biotechnology.

8.9 The two Framework Programmes in greater detail

By now it is not easy to summarise the content of the Community's R&DT programmes, so wide-ranging have they become. This section nevertheless will attempt to list in a comprehensive manner the main projects in order to show where resources are being allocated.

8.9.1 Information technologies

These are covered by the ESPRIT programme already referred to. This is now in its second stage. ESPRIT II, running from 1988–93, has a budget of 3,200 million ECU (double the sum allocated to ESPRIT I), half of which is financed by the EC.

Participation by EFTA countries is expected to raise the total of public funding beyond this amount.

Information technologies (of which there are many)[3] are clearly being aggressively targeted by the Community. The ESPRIT budget is by far the largest of all the programmes receiving Community support. The strategic importance of the sector is constantly stressed in the Commission's documentation. For instance: 'Japan currently dominates the world market for domestic electronics with 60% of production, a field where Europe has a persistent trade deficit of about 8 billion ECU per year; while the USA maintains its long-standing strength in data-processing' (EC Commission, 1989d, para. 11). Information technologies are also seen to be 'pervasive' – 'seeping deeply and broadly into the economic and social fabric of all industrial countries' (*ibid.*, para. 21). The interaction between different spheres of scientific and technical knowledge is also stressed, suggesting that one thing leads to another in these high-technology areas. Thus 'in the aerospace industry, for example, electronics, materials, optical technologies and hydrodynamics have to be engineered together into new design and operating systems' (*ibid.*, para. 23). Finally, 'a growing interaction and proximity between more basic and applied R&D' is noted, suggesting that drawing the line between pre-competitive and applied research and development of new products is becoming difficult. (This may be to prepare us for the next stage in the development of the Community's industrial policy, downstream towards production and marketing.)

There is no doubt, therefore, that in information technologies the Community is convinced that it has 'picked a winner': it certainly seems to meet the criterion of strategic importance for the European economy, as well as excessive cost for any single player. One would, however, be happier with the programme were it not so obviously dominated by the twelve firms forming the Round Table, which are all represented on the supervisory board selecting the deserving projects.

8.9.2 Thermonuclear fusion

The Joint European Torus (JET) programme (current phase 1988–92, budget 745 million ECU) is a 'prime example of the benefits of European cooperation: the Twelve are making spectacular progress towards harnessing fusion energy (EC Commission, 1988j, p. 6). This is good to know. However, a great deal more work still has to be done and the earliest practical application of the research is not expected before 2025.

This is a field which will typically be ignored by the market because the pay-off is too far ahead and risky, and the current costs enormous. Furthermore, the costs far exceed what a small European country such as France, Germany or Britain would care to devote, individually, to such a risky project. The JET programme thus meets two criteria for Community action: market failure and suboptimal investment by nations acting individually. It can perhaps be agreed that this is a 'prime example' of what is best tackled collectively at a European level, rather than individually at the nation state level: i.e. the principle of subsidiarity is respected.

8.9.3 Telecommunications

Research and development in advanced communications for Europe (RACE: current phase 1987–91, budget 550 million ECU), 'is designed to ensure that the advanced telecommunications infrastructure which will "irrigate" Europe in the XXIst century is put in place'. The objective: sound, images and data to be freely transmitted throughout Europe (it is hoped at reasonable cost). The means: coordination of national PTT's policies and specifications, standardisation to guarantee compatibility – and recognition that 'no one European country on its own is big enough to face up to international competition'. Here is another winner: strategic, pervasive, too much for any single country – a clear candidate for Community action.

8.9.4 Traditional industries

Basic research in industrial technologies for Europe (BRITE: current phase 1988–92, budget 439.5 million ECU) aims to rejuvenate traditional sectors by applying new technologies. BRITE I (1985–8) was so successful that its budget had to be increased in mid-stream. Some 215 projects, each involving firms from at least two EC member states, were thus financed. Enthusiasm for BRITE shines through even the driest Commission prose:

> it has enabled transfrontier industrial alliances to be consolidated and fresh ones to be forged, the gap between industry and universities to be bridged and multidisciplinary exchanges to be promoted... BRITE meets a real need. The participants feel that without Community funds 85% of the projects would never even have seen the light of day (*ibid.*, p. 9).

One feels the need for an exclamation mark. But is this area 'strategic'? Is there a clear case of market failure? If so, is it beyond the purse of national governments to correct? Is there not a hint of rent seeking in industry's enthusiasm for the BRITE programme? Questions, questions...

8.9.5 Biotechnology

As far as the biotechnology action programme (BAP: current phase 1985–9, budget 75 million ECU) is concerned, the strategic nature of the sector is not in doubt for the Commission:

> with programmed bacteria, enzymes and microorganisms serving mankind many things are at stake in the biotechnological revolution: improving the competitiveness of agriculture and industry and the quality of life and ultimately resolving the burning issues of our time: disease, malnutrition, pollution, genetic equation, etc. ... the last technological revolution of the century is in full swing (*ibid.*, p. 11).

Since we are here at the interface between industry and agriculture, BAP is not alone in taking up the challenge: it can rely on the European Collaborative Linkage of Agriculture and Industry through Research (ECLAIR: 1988–93, budget 80 million ECU) for some help in resolving the burning issues of our time. Without a doubt, another winner.

8.9.6 Science

A plan to stimulate the international cooperation and interchange needed by European research scientists (no acronym, just 'Science': 1988–92, budget 167 million ECU) has been adopted as a 'simple means of improving the level of European research to a truly spectacular extent and of stemming the brain drain' (*ibid.*, p. 13). By the end of the first plan (1985–8) over 3,000 European scientists belonging to 1,000 teams had taken part in 400 joint projects. By 1992 it is expected that 7,000–8,000 researchers will be thus involved.

Why not? Basic science is a public good which needs public funding. Encouraging free trade in scientific ideas is surely beneficial. The only question is the cost–benefit ratio. While the cost is clear enough, one has to take on trust the 'truly spectacular' benefit.

8.9.7 Road safety

Dedicated road infrastructure for vehicle safety in Europe (DRIVE: 1988–90, 60 million ECU), aims to use the innovations emerging from the ESPRIT, RACE and EUREKA programmes in order to reduce deaths (55,000 a year) and injuries (1.7 million) on European roads. DRIVE is also expected to make a major contribution to the European integrated road transport environment (IRTE), to link up with the PROMETHEUS project (the 'intelligent car'), etc. The possibilities are infinite (*ibid.*, p. 14).

The reference to Europe's appalling death toll makes it almost immoral to question the usefulness of DRIVE, but as it aims to reduce some of the strong negative externalities associated with one of our most important industries perhaps it should be financed by a tax on driving, or on the automobile industry itself, rather than out of general taxation. Unless the automobile industry were to object, of course...

8.9.8 Learning technologies

Developing European learning through technological advance (DELTA: pilot phase 18 months, budget 20 million ECU), is 'tackling head on one of the social ills of our century: unemployment' (*ibid.*, p. 15). It aims to investigate advanced technology (distance learning techniques) for educating, training and retraining.

Why not? The appeal to the social ill of unemployment makes this project irresistible. Besides, anything which speeds up the flow of information and improves the level of education is 'a good thing'. But is the sector 'strategic'? Is it beyond the purse of individual governments to support? The direct beneficiaries will be the computer, IT and telecommunications industries, and we can be sure that DELTA's pilot phase will be deemed a great success.

8.9.9 Unconventional energy

Joint opportunities for unconventional or long-term energy supply (JOULE: 1989–92, budget 122 million ECU) aims to ensure more secure energy supplies while at the same time respecting the environment. The oil crisis is 'now just a bad memory but the Twelve are still on their guard' (*ibid.*, p. 16). Universities and industries will be partners in joint research projects, which will tackle, *inter alia* the rational use of energy and energy-saving devices, wind power, photovoltaic, solar and geothermal energy, etc.

Enthusiasts for industrial policy have, ever since 1973, always claimed that market failure permeates the whole energy scene, but especially the area of unconventional (renewable and ecological) new sources of energy. Perhaps this is so. Perhaps we need to support all this at a European level to avoid wasteful duplication of effort. Who knows? One thing is sure: the market has discovered for itself most if not all currently efficient forms of energy saving, and new sources of energy as well – and for the remainder, avoids this area like the plague as being too removed from market realities. Our fearless leaders have therefore assumed these risks on our behalf.

8.9.10 Food science

Food-linked agro-industrial research (FLAIR: 1989–93, 25 million ECU) aims to 'promote the food industry's competitiveness and to improve the quality of the food-stuffs available to the single European market of 320 million citizens' (*ibid.*, p. 17). FLAIR is concerned with the 'processing–distribution–consumer' part of the food chain and therefore complements the ECLAIR programme.

One must assume that the Common Agricultural Policy, ECLAIR and FLAIR are all part of the same 'strategic' policy to support the farm sector and its close ally, the agro-industrial sector. It would be surprising if they were not on our list.

8.9.11 X-ray examination of research

The Community programme in the field of strategic analysis, forecasting and evaluation in matters of research and technology (MONITOR: 1988–92, 22 million ECU) aims to research research. The Commission puts it this way:

> The Community is stepping up its research activities in order to remain in control of its future. Even so there is a need to detect the new paths emerging from the work in progress, to make an accurate evaluation of the medium-term impact of the programmes and to endeavour to look far ahead into the future. For the sake of effectiveness. (*ibid.*, p. 18)

Oh fatal conceit ... but we wish you luck in remaining in control of the future, in being able to detect new paths, in evaluating accurately the medium-term impact of all your good works, in looking far ahead into the future.

At this point, the reader will forgive us if we sign off before describing in any detail:

1. Advanced informatics in medicine (AIM: pilot phase, 20 million ECU).
2. Action programme of the Community in education and training for technology (COMETT: 1986–9, 45 million ECU).
3. European action scheme for the mobility of university students (ERASMUS: 1987–90, 85 million ECU).
4. Measures to encourage the development of the audiovisual industry (MEDIA: pilot phase 1988–9, 5.5 million ECU).

In the pipeline as future Commission proposals are:

1. Promoting European HDTV ('Are the Twelve going to lose the high-definition television battle which they are fighting against the Japanese? No ... says the Commission' (*ibid.*, p. 26)), but there is no budget as yet.
2. Space EC/ESA cooperation.
3. Aeronautics, i.e. the pooling of research talents to support Airbus.

Is this a trickle or a flood? Where is it leading us?

8.10 Conclusion

There is no doubt that the Community's industrial policy has come a long way in a short time. It has switched from being essentially backward looking in the 1970s to being resolutely forward looking in the 1980s and beyond. It has graduated from having a mainly coordinating and supervising function in the 1970s to possessing its own resources for fostering its own ideas in the 1980s (while still maintaining the traditional coordinating and supervising roles). It has gained legitimacy since its explicit inclusion in the 1987 Single European Act. In short, the Community's industrial policy has arrived.

The driving force behind this rapid development of EC industrial policy is the single-market project. While recognising the need for the single market, our governments and industrialists are very worried that US and Japanese firms will run off with most of the opportunities it offers. They recognise Europe's relative backwardness,

especially in hig...
'European' firms,...
spectives. Encouragin...
technology research and...
outlined above. There is e...
gramme: after all, the single m...

This is why certain industries...
rules, for a buy-European public pr...
national dumping, for protection of ...
careful scrutiny of Japanese greenfield di...
foreign markets or else for Community subsi...
pre-competitive stage and so on. And it would ...
most of what they are asking for.

As will by now be clear, I approach this whole con...
Krugman–Brander–Spencer theories are correct, the C...
certain 'strategic' industries. Perhaps information technolog...
be the first to admit the possibility. What is more worrying,...
that the Community's industrial policy is already in the process...
rent-seeking special interest groups. The sheer number of projects,...
in funds available, the unbelievably wide spread of industries deemed ...
are not encouraging symptoms. If we add in the subtle non-tariff barriers...
for daily by powerful interest groups, one wonders how long the Community...
trade and industrial policy can remain clean.

If the single market is used to shield our large corporations from global c...
petition few of the much-vaunted economies of scale will in fact be realised. Nurturing...
national champions did not produce world-scale competitive industries in the past,
and nurturing European champions behind tariff and non-tariff barriers will not do so
in the future. A protectionist single market would simply repeat our old mistakes at a
higher level.

It cannot be said often enough that the sheer size of one's domestic market is not
the only, or even the main ingredient in economic growth and prosperity, otherwise
Switzerland and Sweden would not be among the world's wealthiest countries,
Taiwan and Korea would not be among its fastest growing and China, India and
Brazil would not be among its poorest. The only long-term method of ensuring
continued viability of one's industries, year after year, is to make sure that they are
constantly exposed to world-scale competition *and have access* to knowledge, goods,
capital and people from abroad: in other words, to have as open a trade and industrial
policy as possible.

This leads me to a modest plea: the programmes described above are aimed at
European industry. They may sometimes include firms from EFTA countries, if the
latter contribute to the project financially. They may even sometimes include 'European firms of foreign parentage', as the current expression goes, because it is difficult
to exclude them on any but the most mercantilistic and sectarian grounds. But they do
not include non-European firms. Fair enough, one might say. After all, one is talking

-technology industries, and the fact that there are, as yet, no truly
but French, German, Italian firms, limited by national per-
g transnational inter-firm cooperation and supporting high-
development are therefore the general aims of the policies
ven a considerable sense of urgency in the whole pro-
market is not far off and there is a long way to go.
are lobbying, additionally, for special local-content
curement policy, for strong action against inter-
European firms against foreign takeovers, for
rect investments, for 'strict reciprocity' in
disation programmes that go beyond the
e naive to think that they will not get

plex with mixed feelings. If the
ommunity is right to support
gies *are* strategic. I would
however, is the feeling
of being hijacked by
the rapid increase
o be 'strategic'
being called
's general
om-

9 The Common Agricultural Policy

A. M. El-Agraa[1]

The EC, unlike EFTA, extends its free trade arrangements between member states to agriculture and agricultural products. The term 'agricultural products' is defined as 'the products of the soil, of stockfarming and of fisheries and products of first-stage processing directly related to the foregoing' (Article 38), although fisheries has developed into a policy of its own – see Chapter 10. Moreover, the EC dictates that the operation and development of the common market for agricultural products must be accompanied by the establishment of a 'common agricultural policy' among member states (Article 38).

One could ask: why should the common market arrangements extend to agriculture? Such a question is to some extent irrelevant. According to GATT – see appendix to Chapter 1 –

> a customs union shall be understood to mean the substitution of a single customs union territory for two or more customs territories, so that ... duties and other restrictive regulations of commerce are eliminated with respect to substantially all the trade between the constituent territories of the union. (Dam, 1970)

It is quite obvious that excluding agriculture from the EC arrangements would be in direct contradiction with this requirement (see next section). In any case:

> a programme of economic integration which excluded agriculture stood no chance of success. It is important to appreciate that the Rome Treaty was a delicate balance of national interests of the contracting parties. Let us consider West Germany and France in terms of trade outlets. In the case of West Germany the prospect of free trade in industrial goods, and free access to the French market in particular, was extremely inviting. In the case of France the relative efficiency of her agriculture ... as compared with West Germany held out the prospect that in a free Community agricultural market she would make substantial inroads into the West German market... Agriculture had therefore to be included. (Swann, 1973, p. 82)

187

The purpose of this chapter is to discuss the need for singling out agriculture as one of the earliest targets for a common policy; to specify the objectives of the Common Agricultural Policy (CAP); to explain the mechanisms of the CAP; to make an economic evaluation of its implications and to assess the performance of the policy in terms of its practical achievements (or lack of achievements) and in terms of its theoretical viability.

Before tackling these points, it is necessary to give some general background information about agriculture in the EC at the time of its formation and at a more recent date.

9.1 General background

The economic significance of agriculture in the economies of member states can be demonstrated in terms of its share in the total labour force and in GNP. Table 9.1 gives this information. The most significant observations that can be made regarding this information are as follows:

1. At the time of the signing of the treaty many people in the original six were dependent on farming as their main source of income; indeed, 25 per cent of the total labour force was employed in agriculture – the equivalent percentage for the United Kingdom was less than five.
2. The agricultural labour force was worse off than most people in the rest of the EC.[2]
3. A rapid fall in both the agricultural labour force and in the share of agriculture in GNP occurred between 1955 and 1975.[3]

It is also important to have some information about the area and size distribution of agricultural holdings. This is given in Table 9.2. The most significant factor to note is that in the original six, around 1966, approximately two-thirds of farm holdings were between 1 and 10 hectares in size. At about the same time, the equivalent figure for the United Kingdom was about one-third.

A final piece of important background information that one needs to bear in mind is that, except for Italy and the United Kingdom, the EC farming system is an owner occupier system rather than one of tenant farming.

9.2 The problems of agriculture

The agricultural sector has been declining in relative importance and those who have remained on the land have continued to receive incomes well below the national average. Governments of most developed countries have, therefore, always found it necessary to practise some sort of control over the market for agricultural

Table 9.1 Share of agriculture in total labour force and national output (per cent)

		Belgium	France	W. Germany	Italy	Luxemburg	Netherlands	Denmark	Ireland	UK	Greece	Portugal	Spain
Labour force	1955	9.3	25.9	18.9	39.5	25.0	13.7	25.4	38.8	4.8	—	—	—
	1970	4.1	12.7	5.6	13.1	11.0	5.8	9.0	25.7	2.7	—	—	—
	1975	3.4	10.9	7.1	15.5	6.1	6.5	9.3	23.8	2.7	33.2[b]	—	—
	1981	2.9	8.4	5.8	13.0	5.6	4.5	8.4	18.9[a]	2.8	30.3[a]	—	—
	1986	2.9	7.3	5.3	10.9	4.0	4.8	6.2	15.8	2.6	28.5	21.9	16.1
National output	1955	8.1	12.3	8.5	21.6	9.0	12.0	19.2	29.6	5.0	—	—	—
	1970	4.2	6.6	3.3	9.8	3.3	6.1	6.4	16.9	2.7	—	—	—
	1975	3.2	5.6	2.9	8.7	3.5	4.7	7.4	18.1	1.9	19.0	—	—
	1981	2.5	4.0	1.9	6.4	2.8	4.3	5.0	11.3[a]	2.1	16.3	—	—
	1986	2.0	4.0	2.0	5.0	—	4.0	6.0	14.0	2.0	17.0	10.0	6.0

Notes
[a] 1980.
[b] 1973.

Source: The Agricultural Situation in the Community: 1988 Report, EC Commission, Brussels and World Bank's World Development Report, 1988.

Table 9.2 Size distribution of agricultural holdings (per cent)

Year	Hectares	Belgium	Denmark	France	W. Germany	Greece	Ireland	Italy	Luxemburg	Netherlands	Portugal	Spain	UK
1960	1–under 5	48.5	18	26	45	—	20	68	32	38	—	—	29.5
	5–under 10	26.5	28	21	25	—	24	19	18	27	—	—	13
	10–under 20	18	28	27	21	—	30	8.5	26	23	—	—	16
	20–under 50	6	23	21	8	—	21	3	22	11	—	—	22.5
	50+	1	3	5	1	—	5	1.5	2	1	—	—	19
1967	1–under 5	37	13	24	40	—	21	69	24	35	—	—	30
	5–under 10	27	23	20	23	—	22	18	16	24	—	—	13
	10–under 20	24	31.5	26	24	—	30	8	25	27	—	—	15
	20–under 50	10	27.5	24	12	—	22	3	32	13	—	—	22
	50+	2	5	6	1	—	5	2	3	1	—	—	20
1973	1–under 5	31	12	22	36	72[a]	15[c]	68[c]	21	25	78[d]	56[e]	16
	5–under 10	23	20	16	20	20.5	16.5	17.5	13	22	12.5	18	13
	10–under 20	27	29	24	24	6	31	8.5	20	31	5	12	16
	20–under 50	16	32	28	18	1.5	29	4	41	20	2.5	8.5	26
	50+	1	7	10	2	0.0	8.5	2	7	2	2	5.5	29
1980	1–under 5	28	11	21	32	71[b]	15[b]	68.5[b]	19	24	—	—	12
	5–under 10	20	17.5	15	19	20	16.5	17	11	20	—	—	12.5
	10–under 20	27	26.5	21	23	7	30	8.5	14.5	29	—	—	16
	20–under 50	21	35	30	22	2	30	4	38.5	24	—	—	27
	50+	4	10	13	4	0.0	8.5	2	17	3	—	—	32.5
1986	1–under 5	28	2	18.5	31	69.5[f]	24[f]	69[f]	19	24	—	—	13
	5–under 10	18	16.5	12.5	18	20	26	17	10	19	—	—	12.5
	10–under 20	25	26	19	22	7.5	15	9	12.5	26	—	—	15
	20–under 50	23.5	39.5	31.5	23.5	2.5	27	5	33	27	—	—	26
	50+	5.5	16	18.5	5.5	0.5	8	2	25.5	4	—	—	33.5

Note
[a] = interpolation between the surveys of 1971 and 1977–8; [b] = 1977; [c] = 1975; [d] = 1979; [e] = 1975; [f] = 1985.

Source: Calculated from EC Commission, *The Agricultural Situation in The Community: 1982 Report*, and from *Eurostat Review 1977–86*, but the figures were adjusted to cater for mistakes in the totals.

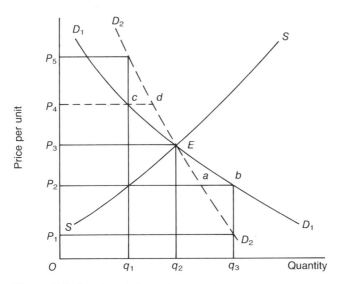

Figure 9.1 Supply and demand in agriculture

commodities through price supports, subsidies to farmers, import levies, import quotas, etc. In this section I shall analyse the background to such practices.

It should be plain to all that the production of many agricultural commodities is subject to forces that lie beyond the direct control of the farmers concerned. Drought, floods, earthquakes, and to some extent invasions of pests, for instance, would lead to an actual level of agricultural production far short of that *planned* by the farmers. On the other hand, exceptionally favourable conditions could result in *actual* production being far in excess of that *planned* by farmers. It is therefore necessary to have some theoretical notions about the effects of such deviations between planned and actual agricultural produce on farmers' prices and received incomes.

The predictions of economic theory can be illustrated by reference to a simple diagram. In Figure 9.1, *SS* represents the range of quantities that farmers plan to supply to the market at various prices in a particular period of time given a certain set of 'market circumstances', for example, agricultural input prices, farmers' objectives for production, agricultural technology, etc. *DD* represents the various quantities that consumers of agricultural products plan to purchase at alternative prices in a specific period of time given a certain set of 'market circumstances', for example, consumers' tastes for agricultural products, their incomes, population size and composition, etc. D_1D_1 and D_2D_2 represent two such demand curves, with D_2D_2 being less elastic than D_1D_1.

If consumers' plans and producers' plans actually materialise, P_3 will be the equilibrium price which will clear the equilibrium output Oq_2 off the market. As long as this situation is maintained, agricultural prices (represented by P_3) will remain stable and agricultural incomes (represented by the area OP_3Eq_2) will also remain stable. However, actual agricultural production may fall short of, or exceed, the equilibrium planned production Oq_2 for any of the above-mentioned reasons. If a shortage occurs such that actual output is Oq_1, the price will rise above the equilibrium level to P_5 (for D_2D_2) or P_4 (for D_1D_1). In the case of an actual supply of Oq_3, the price will fall to P_1 or P_2 respectively. Therefore, when actual agricultural production deviates from the planned output, fluctuations in agricultural prices will result such that an excess actual output reduces prices and a shortage in output increases prices. The extent of these price fluctuations is determined by the price elasticity of demand: the more (less) price inelastic the demand curve, the wider (narrower) the margin of price fluctuations.

Moreover, as long as the demand curve does not have a price elasticity of unity, agricultural incomes will fluctuate from the planned level OP_3Eq_2: with a price elastic (inelastic) demand curve, an actual shortage will result in a lower (higher) income for the farmers and an actual excess supply will lead to higher (lower) incomes.

At this point it is appropriate to mention two further characteristics of agriculture in advanced economies. Firstly, as people's incomes rise they tend to spend a smaller proportion of it on agricultural products: the income elasticity of demand is low. (People spend relatively less on food as their incomes rise, therefore they spend even less on agricultural products because a higher proportion of the expenditure on food goes on processing, packaging and presentation.) Hence poor (rich) nations tend to spend a large (small) proportion of their income on agricultural products. The data given in Table 9.3 give an approximate representation of this point for food (as a representative of agricultural products).

Secondly, because of advances in technology and growth of factors of production, average incomes have been rising in developed economies. Agricultural economists would argue that for the same reason, agricultural outputs tend to rise at at least the same rate as those of the non-agricultural sector. Once it is realised that consumers

Table 9.3 Relationship between the proportion of income spent on food in a household and the income group to which the household belongs in the United Kingdom (1971)

Income group (given by gross weekly earnings of the head of the household only)	Expenditure of the household on food as a % of the gross earnings of the head of the household
Over £69 per week	Less than 13
£45–£69 per week	12–18
£27–£45 per week	18–29
£14–£27 per week	27–52
Under £14 per week (non OAP)	More than 37
Under £14 per week (OAP)	More than 20

Source: Ritson (1973), p. 97.

would want to spend relatively more on non-agricultural products as their living standards rise (the income elasticity of demand is high for these products), it is inevitable to conclude that there would be a relative tendency for a fall in the demand for farm products. Hence farm incomes would tend to lag behind the incomes of those engaged in the non-farm sector.

Furthermore, once one appreciates that the demand for most agricultural (non-agricultural) products has a low (high) price and income elasticity and that agriculture as an industry is becoming at least as efficient as the national average (because of technological progress in the agricultural sector, the supply curve is moving to the right all the time), then it is easy to understand that agricultural (non-agricultural) price levels and incomes have a tendency to relative decline (rise) with economic growth. This adds a new dimension to the problem in that an 'agricultural stabilisation policy' must be introduced with the aim not simply of stabilising agricultural prices and incomes, but also of raising agricultural incomes to the national average – if only for equity reasons.

However, the assumption that agricultural outputs tend to rise at at least the same rate as those of the non-agricultural sector does not stand up to close scrutiny. In the United Kingdom, according to the Cambridge Department of Applied Economics Programme for Growth 12, agricultural productivity grew at a rate of 1.6 per cent per annum compound during the period 1948–68, as against 1.8 per cent for manufacturing. In the United Kingdom, manufacturing productivity growth has been low and agricultural productivity growth, because of the form of policy, high. In the rest of Europe the disparity will be much greater. Since agriculture started as a low productivity industry, the disparity has indeed worsened – the impact of science and technology on farming is less than on manufacturing for two reasons: firstly, agriculture is characterised by decreasing returns to scale while manufacturing is characterised at least by constant returns to scale; secondly, there are severe institutional constraints on increasing the size of farms, therefore technology can make its impact only from specialisation within the existing farm structure. Economies of specialisation are limited within this constraint and furthermore there are offsetting losses of economies of joint production (from rotations, etc.) which are more pronounced in agriculture than elsewhere and are virtually lost from specialisation. Hence the problem of agricultural incomes stems from declining agricultural productivity (in comparison with manufacturing productivity) rather than from inelastic demand for agricultural products. In any case, the elasticity has not been so low once population growth is taken into account. (For a forceful and detailed explanation of these points, see Bowers, 1972.)

This is a more convincing argument in that it suggests that the setting of reasonable agricultural prices, given the declining relative efficiency of agriculture, ensures declining agricultural incomes. Hence, the way to increasing agricultural productivity is to encourage the marginal agricultural labour to seek alternative employment. This view is consistent with the structural problem of the EC, where declining farm incomes are attributed to the fact that labour does not flow out of agriculture quickly enough (trapped resources with low salvage values).

The above suggests why most advanced mixed economies have been adopting some kind of agricultural support policies. Other arguably more important considerations include historical factors, strategic considerations and the strengths of the agricultural lobby; indeed, it is commonly accepted that the latter is the main determining factor of these apparently uneconomic policies.

9.3 Agricultural support policies

With the foregoing analysis and observations, we are in a position to attempt a specification of the necessary elements in an agricultural policy and to point out the difficulties associated with such a policy.

In most advanced mixed economies where living standards have been rising, an agricultural policy must:

1. As a minimum requirement, avoid impeding the *natural* process of transferring resources from the agricultural sector to the non-agricultural sector of the economy, and if necessary promote this process.
2. Aim at protecting the incomes of those who are occupied in the agricultural sector. The definition of the farm sector raises a number of problems, for instance:

    > should one's policy be devised to guarantee prosperity to any who might wish at some future date to enter agriculture – and moreover to assure a reasonable rate of return for any amount of capital that they may wish to invest in farming? Or should one's policy be geared to those already in the industry who have made resource allocation decisions based on expectations of the future which governments then feel under an obligation to realise? (Josling, 1969, p. 176)

3. Aim at some kind of price stability, since agriculture forms the basis of living costs and wages and is therefore the basis of industrial costs.
4. Make provision for an adequate agricultural sector since security of food supplies is essential for a nation.[4]
5. Ensure the maintenance of agriculture as a family business, and the maintenance of some population in rural villages.

Unfortunately these objectives are, to a large extent, mutually contradictory. Any policy which aims at providing adequate environmental conditions, secure food supplies and agricultural incomes equal to the national average interferes with the economy's natural development. Moreover, the provision of stable farm incomes, let alone rising farm incomes, is not compatible with the provision of stable agricultural prices. This point can be illustrated by reference to Figure 9.1.

Suppose that D_1D_1 is a demand curve which has unit price elasticity along its entire range. In order to keep farmers' incomes constant it would be necessary to operate along this curve, keeping farmers' incomes equal to OP_3Eq_2. If agricultural production deviates from Oq_2, the following will ensue:

1. When output is equal to Oq_3, the authority in charge of the policy must purchase *ab* in order to make certain that the price level falls only to P_2 rather than P_1, therefore ensuring that farmers' incomes remain at the pre-determined level.
2. When output is equal to Oq_1 the authority must sell *cd* in order to achieve the price level P_4 rather than P_5.

Hence a policy of income stability can be achieved only if the price level is allowed to fluctuate, even though the required level of fluctuation in this case is less than that dictated by the operation of the free market forces.

On the other hand, a policy of maintaining constant price levels (constant P_3) will give farmers higher incomes when output is Oq_3 (by $q_2q_3 \times OP_3$) since the authority will have to purchase the excess supply at the guaranteed price, and lower incomes when output is Oq_1 (by $q_1q_2 \times OP_3$). Therefore, a policy of price stability will guarantee income fluctuations in such a manner that higher (lower) agricultural outputs will result in higher (lower) farmers' incomes.

This throws light on another aspect of agricultural policies: if average farm prices are set at too high a level this will encourage farmers to increase production, since at the guaranteed price they can sell as much as they can produce. This, in effect, results in a perfectly elastic supply curve at price level P_3. In such circumstances, an excess supply of these commodities could result. This is a point that has to be borne in mind when assessing the CAP.

9.4 EC member policies

Prior to the formation of the EC, member countries (except for Holland) had adopted different practices in their agricultural stabilisation policies. This is an appropriate point to turn to a discussion of these policies.

Agricultural policies in Western Europe as a whole since the Second World War have been rather complicated, but a substantial element of these policies has been the support of prices received by farmers for their produce. In this respect, a variety of methods have been practised:

1. *Deficiency payments schemes* (supplements to market determined prices): these refer to policies of guaranteed farm prices which the government ensures by means of deficiency payments. These prices become the farmers' planning prices. This system was used in the United Kingdom before it joined the EC; however, the United Kingdom was moving away from this system for budgetary reasons, not as a preparation for joining the EC.
2. *Variable levies or import quota systems*: these systems are concerned with policies which effectively impose threshold prices and charge levies on imports equal to the difference between world prices and the threshold prices.
3. *Market control systems*: these aim at limiting the quantities of agricultural produce

that actually reach the market. This can be achieved by ensuring that the produce is marketed by single private authorities (agencies) or by certain government departments. The quantity that is not allowed to reach the market can

> either be destroyed, stored (to be released when prices rise), exported, donated to low income countries or needy groups within the home economy, or converted into another product which does not compete directly with the original one. Examples of this last course of action are 'breaking' of eggs for use as egg powder and rendering some cereals and vegetables unfit for human consumption (usually by adding a dye or fish oil) but suitable for animal feed. (Ritson, 1973, p. 99)

This system was widely used in the original six.

4. *Direct income payments*: this term describes schemes whereby incomes are transferred to the farmers without these bearing any relationship to the level of output. The nearest to this system is the Swedish system.
5. *Non-price policies*: a miscellaneous set of policies such as import subsidies on both current and capital inputs, output increasing measures (R&D), export subsidies and production quotas. Of course, input subsidies do add to the effective protection afforded to agriculture.

Let us now turn to an analytical consideration of these schemes. The analysis of 1., 2. and 4. is slightly different from that illustrated by Figure 9.1 in that one needs to deal with products which compete with imports. This is because most Western European countries were net importers of most agricultural products at the time of the inception of the EC.

Assume (unrealistically in the context of the EC since Western Europe is a large consumer) that the level of imports does not influence the world prices of agricultural commodities and that, allowing for transport costs and quality differentials, the import price level is equal to the domestic price. Then consider the different support systems with reference to Figure 9.2.

In Figure 9.2, P_w is the world price, Oq_1 is the domestic production level and q_1q_4 is the free trade level of imports. When a deficiency payment scheme is in operation, P_d becomes the guaranteed farmer price. This leads to an increase in domestic production (from Oq_1 to Oq_2) which guarantees the farmer a deficiency payment of $P_w P_d bc$ (equal to $(P_d - P_w) \times q_1q_2$) and which results in foreign exchange savings of q_1acq_2. On the assumption that the supply curve is a reflection of the marginal social opportunity cost of resources used in production (for a detailed discussion of this see El-Agraa 1978 and El-Agraa and Jones 1981) it is possible to make some significant remarks regarding this new farm revenue.

The area q_1abq_2, in an extremely simple analysis, approximates the value of the extra inputs attracted into agriculture by the deficiency payment policy. The area $P_w P_d ba$ represents the additional producer's surplus, or economic rent.[5] This can be thought of as an income transfer in favour of the farming sector.[6] Area abc represents the net loss to the society for adopting this policy; this is because the price for the consumer remains at P_w and therefore the level of imports is equal to cf.

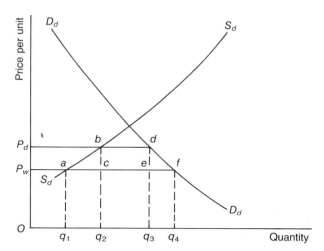

Figure 9.2 Economic effects of different agricultural support schemes

When a variable levy scheme is in operation, the relevant farmer price equals the threshold price so that P_d becomes the price facing both farmers and consumers. Hence, the effects on the agricultural producing sector are exactly the same as in the previous case. However, the foreign exchange savings would now be equal to $q_1 a c q_2$ plus $q_3 e f q_4$ due to the fall in consumption by $q_3 q_4$ (from Oq_4 to Oq_3) – imports fall to bd. The loss of the policy is therefore equal to the areas abc and def. Area $bced$ represents a transfer from the consumers to the government.

Under extremely restrictive assumptions, it can be demonstrated that the operation of a quota system equal to $q_2 q_3$ produces the same result as a variable levy of the same equivalence.[7] There is another problem here relating to who gains the area $bced$, which in the variable levy system represents government revenue: if the government assumes responsibility or if the importers are well organised there is no problem, but if the foreign exporters are well organised they can absorb this area in the form of economic rent or excess profit – see El-Agraa (1983b, Chapters 8–10).

In a purely static theoretical analysis, direct income subsidies have no economic costs (see Johnson, 1965a), particularly since they do not harm the consumer or the foreign supplier. However, for these subsidies to be strictly neutral in their economic impact, they should be paid in such a manner as to 'allow the recipients to leave farming without prejudice to their income from the payment scheme'.[8]

From the foregoing analysis it is evident that the income transfer system is the most efficient mechanism for farm support and that the variable levy or import quota system is the least efficient in this respect.[9] This is because the income subsidies and deficiency payment schemes allow the consumer to decide according to the cheapest international prices available, while the variable levy and import quota systems interfere with both producers and consumers. This comparison should be borne in mind when reading the conclusions of this chapter.

9.5 Objectives of the CAP

Due to the variety of agricultural support policies that existed in Western Europe at the time of the formation of the EC, it was necessary to subject agriculture to equal treatment in all member states. Equal treatment of coal and steel (both necessary inputs for industry and therefore of the same significance as agriculture) was already under way through the ECSC and the importance of agriculture meant that equal treatment here was vital.

The objectives of the CAP are clearly defined in Article 39 of the Treaty. They are as follows:

1. 'To increase agricultural productivity by promoting technical progress and by ensuring the rational development of agricultural production and the optimum utilisation of all factors of production, in particular labour'.
2. To ensure thereby 'a fair standard of living for the agricultural community, in particular by increasing the individual earnings of persons engaged in agriculture'.
3. 'To stabilise markets'.
4. 'To provide certainty of supplies'.
5. 'To ensure supplies to consumers at reasonable prices'.

The Treaty also specifies that in:

> working out the Common Agricultural Policy, and any special methods which this may involve, account shall be taken of:
> (i) the particular nature of agricultural activity, which results from agriculture's social structure and from structural and natural disparities between the various agricultural regions;
> (ii) the need to effect the appropriate adjustments by degrees;
> (iii) the fact that, in the member states, agriculture constitutes a sector closely linked with the economy as a whole.

The Treaty further specifies that in order to attain the objectives set out above a common organisation of agricultural markets shall be formed:

> This organisation shall take one of the following forms depending on the product concerned:
> (a) common rules as regards competition;
> (b) compulsory co-ordination of the various national marketing organisations; or
> (c) a European organisation of the market.

Moreover, the common organisation so established:

> may include all measures required to achieve the objectives set out ... in particular price controls, subsidies for the production and distribution of the various products, stock-piling and carry-over systems and common arrangements for stabilisation of imports and exports.

> The common organisation shall confine itself to pursuing the objectives set out ... and shall exclude any discrimination between producers and consumers within the Community.
>
> Any common policy shall be based on common criteria and uniform methods of calculation.

Finally, in order to enable the common organisation to achieve its objectives, 'one or more agricultural orientation and guarantee funds may be set up'.

The remaining articles (41–7) deal with some detailed considerations relating to the objectives and the common organisation.

The true objectives of the CAP were established after the Stresa conference in 1958 which was convened in accordance with the Treaty. The objectives were in the spirit of the Treaty:

(i) to increase farm incomes not only by a system of transfers from the non-farm population through a price support policy, but also by the encouragement of rural industrialisation to give alternative opportunities to farm labour;

(ii) to contribute to overall economic growth by allowing specialisation within the Community and eliminating artificial market distortions;

(iii) preserving the family farm and ... ensuring that structural and price policies go hand in hand.

It can be seen, therefore, that the CAP was not preoccupied simply with the implementation of common prices and market supports; it also included a commitment to encourage the structural improvement of farming, particularly when the former measures did not show much success (see the later section on assessment). Regarding the latter point, the main driving force has been the Mansholt Plan of 1968.[10] Dr Sicco Mansholt, who was the Agricultural Commissioner at the time, emphasised that market supports by themselves would not solve the agricultural problem. The plan, which basically relates to the guidance aspects of the CAP, proposed the following principal measures:

(a) A first set of measures concerns the structure of agricultural production, and contains two main elements:

(i) One group of measures, varying widely in character, must be taken to bring about an appropriate reduction in the number of persons employed in agriculture. Older people will have to be offered a supplementary annual income allowance if they agree to retire and thereby release land; younger farmers should be enabled to change over to non-farming activities; the children of farmers, finally, should be given an education which enables them to choose an occupation other than farming, if they so desire. For the two latter categories, new jobs will have to be created in many regions. These efforts at reducing manpower should be brought to bear with particular force on one group of persons within agriculture, namely, those who own their farm businesses, inasmuch as the structural reform of farms themselves ... largely depends upon the withdrawal of a large number of these people from agriculture.

(ii) Secondly, far-reaching and co-ordinated measures should be taken with a view to the creation of agricultural (farming) enterprises of adequate economic dimensions.[11] If such enterprises are to be set up and kept running, the land they need will have to be made available to them on acceptable terms; this will require an active and appropriate agrarian policy.

(b) A second group of measures concerns markets, with the double purpose of improving the way they work and of adjusting supply more closely to demand:

　(i) Here a major factor will be a cautious price policy, and this will be all the more effective as the enterprises react more sensitively to the points offered by the market.

　(ii) A considerable reduction of the area of cultivated land will work in the same direction.

　(iii) Better information will have to be made available to all market parties (producers, manufacturers and dealers), producers will have to accept stricter discipline and there will have to be some concentration of supply. Product councils and groupings of product councils will have to be set up at European level to take over certain responsibilities in this field.

(c) In the case of farmers who are unable to benefit from the measures described, it may prove necessary to provide personal assistance not tied either to the volume of output or to the employment of factors of production. This assistance should be payable within specified limits defined in the light of regional factors and the age of the persons concerned.

After a lengthy discussion the Council issued three directives (72/159–61) in April 1972. These related to proposals similar to those suggested in the Mansholt Plan. However, although the precise method of implementation of these proposals was left to the discretion of national governments, about a quarter of the necessary outlay would be borne by the CAP guidance section. Since 1972 further efforts have been made and some success has been achieved. However, the EC expenditure on the structural aspects of the CAP remains very small indeed – see Fennell (1979) for a detailed specification of these changes.

9.6 The CAP price support mechanism

The CAP machinery does not apply to every product and, in the cases where it does, it varies from one product to another. The following illustration therefore applies to just a few products, mainly cereals – see Fennell (1979) for detailed specification. The farmers' income support is guaranteed by regulating the market so as to reach a price high enough to achieve this objective. The domestic price is partly maintained by various protective devices. These prevent cheaper world imports from influencing the EC domestic price level. But in addition, certain steps are taken for official support buying within the EC, so as to eliminate from the market any actual excess supply that might be stimulated by the guaranteed price level. These surpluses may be disposed of in the manner described in the section on the policies of the EC member nations.

More specifically, the basic features of the system can be represented by that originally devised for cereals, the first agricultural product for which a common policy was established.

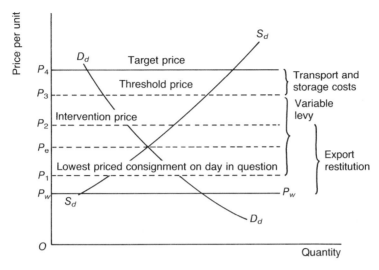

Figure 9.3 CAP product prices

A 'target price' is set on an annual basis and is maintained at a level which the product is expected to achieve on the market in the area where cereal is in shortest supply – Duisburg in the Ruhr Valley. The target price is not a producer price since it includes the costs of transport to dealers and storers. The target price is variable, in that it is allowed to increase on a monthly basis from August to July in order to allow for storage costs throughout the year.

The 'threshold price' is calculated in such a way that when transport costs incurred within the EC are added, cereals collected at Rotterdam should sell at Duisburg at a price equal to or slightly higher than the target price. An import levy is imposed to prevent import prices falling short of the threshold price. The import levy is calculated on a daily basis and is equal to the margin between the lowest priced consignment entering the EC on the day – allowing for transport costs to one major port (Rotterdam) – and the threshold price. This levy is then charged on all imports allowed into the EC on that day. All this information is illustrated in Figure 9.3.

It is quite obvious that as long as the EC is experiencing excess demand for this product, the market price is held above the target price by the imposition of import levies. Moreover, import levies would be unnecessary if world prices happened to be above the threshold price since in this case the market price might exceed the target price.

If target prices result in an excess supply of the product in the EC (see Figure 9.3), the threshold price becomes ineffective in terms of the objective of a constant annual target price and support buying becomes necessary. A 'basic intervention price' is then introduced for this purpose. This is fixed for Duisburg at about 7 or 8 per cent below the target price. Similar prices are then calculated for several locations within the EC on the basis of costs of transport to Duisburg. National intervention agencies are then compelled to buy whatever is offered to them (provided it conforms to standard) of the 'proper' product at the relevant intervention price. The intervention price is therefore a minimum guaranteed price.

Moreover, an export subsidy or *restitution* is paid to EC exporters. This is determined by the officials and is influenced by several factors (world prices, amount of excess supply, expected trends) and is generally calculated as the difference between the EC intervention price (P_2) and the world price (P_w).

For the latest position on this mechanism and the new methods that the EC has introduced to tackle the problems of excess supply, see the section below on assessment.

9.7 The green money

The various agricultural support prices are fixed by the Council in units of account. For each member country there is a 'green rate' at which the support prices are translated into national prices. The unit of account originally had a gold content equal to a US dollar, but in 1973 was linked to the 'joint float'; since the introduction of the European Monetary System (EMS) in March 1979 it has been given a value equal to the European currency unit (ECU). This implies that if a member country devalues (revalues) its currency, its farm prices expressed in terms of the national currency rise (fall). It should also be noted that the scope for changing green currency rates gives the member countries scope for altering internal farm prices *independently* of price changes determined at the annual reviews for the EC as a whole. In August 1969 the French franc was devalued by 11.11 per cent, which obviously disturbed the common farm price arrangements in favour of the French farmers, and the rise in their price level would obviously have stimulated their farm production and aggravated the excess supply problem (see next section). Moreover, the devaluation of the unit of account would not have improved matters in such a situation, since it would have depressed the price level for the farmer in the rest of the EC, even though it would have nullified the effects of the devaluation of the French franc. Therefore, a more complicated policy was adopted: the French intervention price was reduced by the full amount of the devaluation so as to eliminate the unfair benefit to the French farmer; French imports from and exports to the rest of the EC were to be restored by asking France to give import subsidies and levy duties on its exports to compensate for the effects of the devaluation. The term 'monetary compensatory amounts' (MCAs) was coined to describe this system of border taxes and subsidies. Since then, the MCA system has become general in application and more complicated with the changes in the rates of exchange of the currencies of other EC members.

Even though the EC continues to announce (see below) its intention to discontinue the MCA system, it seems that it will be with us for some time yet. The system therefore warrants some further explanation. It should be remembered that one of the basic aims of the CAP is to establish a uniform set of agricultural prices for all the participating nations. Since these prices are expressed in units of account, when a member country decides to devalue its currency (i.e. its official rate), the prices of agricultural products will rise in terms of the domestic currency by the full percentage of devaluation (given a simple analysis). This increase in the domestic prices will distort trade between the member nations and its effect on intra-EC trade can be fully eliminated (again in a simple analysis) by imposing equivalent taxes on the export of these products and by granting equivalent subsidies to the imports of the products. This in effect amounts to operating a system of multiple exchange rates. On the other hand, when a member of the EC decides to revalue its currency, it will have to tax intra-EC imports and subsidise intra-EC exports to eliminate a fall in agricultural prices. Since the 'green rates' of exchange – known as 'representative rates' – are officially used for converting prices expressed in units of account into national currencies – official rates – it follows that when the 'green rate' deviates from the official rate, these taxes on, and subsidies to, intra-EC traded agricultural products are used to maintain uniform agricultural prices. This is the MCA system which, once adopted by a member of the EC, will remain until that country is able to restore its 'green rate' to that on the foreign exchange market.

The MCA system is therefore basically simple; it became complicated because of several factors. First, the French devaluation of 1969 was followed almost immediately by the German revaluation and the French and the Germans asked for the adoption of MCAs which were to be eliminated within periods of two and three years respectively. Secondly, the EC agreed to these arrangements and met part of the cost, hence increasing the financial burden of the CAP. Thirdly, the later weakness of the US dollar was used as a reason by the EC to introduce MCAs in order to protect its farmers from 'worldwide unfair competition' – the EC claimed this was because the United States, being a net exporter of agricultural products, was able to determine the world price level for agricultural products and this was in spite of the fact that the unit of account was fixed in terms of dollars. Finally, the floating of the pound sterling in 1972 and the Italian lira in 1973, which led to the sinking of both, encouraged the use of MCAs to protect the stronger EC currencies from agricultural price increases.

The reader who is particularly interested in this area of the CAP is advised to read Irving and Fearne (1975), Josling and Harris (1976), Mackel (1978), Hu (1979), Fennell (1979) and Marsh and Swanney (1980; 1983). Hu demonstrates that Germany has recently been the main beneficiary of this system.

9.8 Financing the CAP

Intervention, export restitution and the MCA system need to be financed. The finance is supplied by the EC central fund called FEOGA (Fonds Européen d'Orientation et de Garantie Agricole), the European Agricultural Guidance and Guarantee Fund (EAGGF), so named to incorporate the two basic elements of the CAP: support and guidance. At the time of inception of the CAP it was expected that the revenues collected from the imposition of extra area import levies would be sufficient to finance

FEOGA. Since then, the rapid rise in agricultural output has led to a reduction in EC imports and therefore to a reduction in receipts from levies. Also, the cost of the support system has increased beyond expectation (see the McDougall Report, 1977, and Chapter 14). Thus the EC deemed it necessary to make provision for direct budgetary contributions from national governments on the basis of a formula which is discussed in some detail in the McDougall Report. However, in 1970 the EC switched to a system of own resources, which became fully operative in 1980 – see Chapter 14.

In order to put the expenditures in their proper perspective, it should be noted that the general budget of the EC makes provision for the administrative expenses of the European Parliament, the Council of Ministers, the Court of Justice, the ECSC, and the European Development Fund, and for the administrative costs and the other operational expenditures of the Commission, which include the Agricultural Guarantee and Guidance Funds, the Social Fund, and the Regional Development Fund. For the financial year 1989 the budget is expected to amount to some 46 billion ECU or, roughly, £31 billion (which is equal to $50 billion), of which agricultural expenditure accounts for about 61 per cent. The revenue from agricultural levies is estimated at about 2.5 billion ECU, approximately 5.4 per cent of the total budget.

9.9 **Assessment**

Judged in terms of its own objectives, the CAP would seem to have had several successes. Firstly, the various agricultural support systems that existed prior to the formation of the EC have been liquidated and a common, although highly complicated, system has been achieved. Secondly, to a qualified extent, intra-EC free trade in agricultural products has been accomplished through the removal of all intra-EC trade impediments. Thirdly, the EC as a whole has become more or less self-sufficient in farm products going to the final consumer even though the Community still depends a great deal on imported agricultural raw materials, for example, fertilisers and animal feed. Fourthly, Directive 75/268, which deals with mountain and hill farming in certain disadvantaged areas, was adopted in 1975 and this amounted to a recognition of the fact that special provision would have to be made for these areas. Fifthly, it should be mentioned that agriculture has experienced a high rate of technical progress and increased productivity and that the CAP has resulted in stability of EC agricultural markets and in increasing self-supply; these achievements are consistent with the objectives set out in Article 39. Finally, it could be claimed that the CAP has achieved much progress in increasing the size of farm holdings and in reducing the number of farm businesses – see Table 9.2.

On the debit side, the CAP has failed to achieve any progress on the structural aspect of encouraging farmers to seek alternative occupations (even though the drift from land to industry is a natural process), etc. – hence the Mansholt Plan. Moreover, the CAP has been the cause of embarrassing surpluses: the butter and beef mountains; the wine lakes; earlier on, the grain and sugar surpluses; and more recently the milk lake. However, it should be noted here that a 'co-responsibility levy' was introduced in 1977, the purpose of which was to hold the farmers partly responsible for the surpluses they had created. The CAP has had the effect of making the prosperous farmers richer, but has not helped the poorer farmers as it has retained them in the industry through high intervention price levels. Finally, the CAP has failed to provide reasonable and stable prices for the consumer; indeed, the initial prices were set at the high German level.

These successes and failures have to be examined more carefully. Firstly, most economists would agree that the embarrassing surpluses are caused by the high level of intervention prices. This of course has serious consequences for the financing of the policy.

However, it should be added here that the member nations of the EC agreed on 31 March 1984 on a package which reduced the EC's common farm prices by 0.5 per cent and relied on a system of quotas to restrict milk production from 103 million tonnes in 1983 to 99.2 million and 98.4 million tonnes in 1984 and 1985 respectively; thereafter it was to be pegged for a further three years. Moreover, the quotas which had already been applied to sugar beet were extended to other surplus products such as cereals, oilseeds and processed tomatoes. In order to reduce wine production, new vine plantings were banned until 1990. Finally, various production and consumption subsidies to livestock, butter, fruit and vegetables were reduced, and the MCAs were to be phased out over four years. It should also be added that the EC Council of February 1988 decided that the annual growth rate of EAGGF guarantee expenditure shall not exceed 70–80 per cent of the annual growth rate of EC GNP. New agricultural stabilisers are to be introduced. For example, the threshold for cereals will be set at 155 to 160 million tonnes per year for the period 1988–91, and an additional co-responsibility levy of 3 per cent will be provisionally charged at the beginning of each marketing year to ensure that agricultural expenditure stays within specified limits. Similar quotas are set for oil seeds and protein products, existing stabilisers will continue for olive oil and cotton, the quota system for milk will be extended for another three years, etc. What is significant, however, is that the Council agreed to adopt provisions to limit supply by withdrawing agricultural land from production. This 'set-aside' programme is devised to complement policy measures, and will be compulsory for member countries but optional for producers. The EC has therefore made very serious attempts to tackle the problems of surplus. (The reader should note that these developments and their implications are discussed more fully in Chapter 14.)

Secondly:

> low earnings in agriculture are the consequence of low alternative earnings arising from disparities in education levels in rural areas. But in these circumstances any price policy based on some concept of giving to farm resources the ability to achieve parity incomes with the non-farm population is doomed to failure. Higher prices are largely translated into the purchase of more inputs from the non-farm sector (fertilisers and machinery) and into the values of assets the supply of which are fixed (mainly land). Input suppliers and landlords gain, but the new entrants get no benefit. This accounts for the seemingly insatiable appetite of farm

programmes for public money and the desire to hide the appropriations in the form of higher food costs even if the same transfer could be made more efficiently by direct payments. Agriculture adjusts in size to the level of support it is given; price support policies have never influenced long-run resources returns appreciably. The implication of this is that the only way to raise farm incomes is to control the inflow of resources into agriculture, or to increase the level of education in rural areas. (Josling, 1969, pp. 268–9)

Thirdly, the MCA system which most observers had thought was a temporary phenomenon has become very well established in the mechanism of the CAP; indeed, the MCA system and the 'green money' have been used in a very sophisticated way to enable farmers to accommodate their national interests within the CAP (Ritson and Tangermann, 1979). The MCA system seems a positive deterrent to intra-EC trade – traders have great difficulty in predicting MCAs and would presumably offset this by adding them to their margins. This has created unequal prices and has justifiably led to the use of the term 'the uncommon market'.

In global terms, the CAP has been seen as undermining the interests of the Third World. This point has two elements to it: firstly, by disposing of surpluses at subsidised prices to countries like the USSR, the EC is depriving the developing world of potential export earnings; secondly, and most importantly, the EC, in protecting its own agriculture, is competing unfairly against imports from these same countries. Indeed, some economists would argue that under free international trade conditions, Western Europe would have no comparative advantage in agriculture and that the industry would virtually disappear under such circumstances. However, this is not entirely correct since it could be argued that even with perfectly free agricultural trade there would be a cost advantage in providing nearly all dairy products, much meat (grass-based) and a good deal of cereals, fruit and vegetables within the EC.

A possible response to these claims is that 'it would be churlish to question such a goal of a prosperous agriculture contributing to economic growth in the community,' (Josling, 1969, p. 268) particularly in a world where agriculture is a highly protected industry, as is the case in the EC's most eminent competitors like the United States and Japan. Moreover, agriculture should be seen as an industry for which the EC has a socio-political preference (secure food supplies and pleasant environmental conditions?) in terms of output and employment; this is the case of a preference for a collective good discussed in detail elsewhere (see, for example, El-Agraa, 1978 and El-Agraa and Jones, 1981) and in Chapter 4. Additionally, absolutely free trade in agriculture would be detrimental to the interests of countries like France and Italy, unless the argument for free trade was applied simultaneously to *all* industries. Finally, the EC does not produce the same range of agricultural products as does the developing world.

However, these responses have no solid foundation. It is difficult to see why it is churlish to question the goal of a prosperous agriculture, particularly when this goal can be achieved, if at all, only at the expense of alternative goals – it is a question of priorities. Moreover, the EC *does* compete with countries like Argentina, Australia, Canada, New Zealand, United States, etc., in terms of sugar, cereals, vegetables and beef; the self-sufficiency figures published by the Commission do not reflect this because they are a manifestation only of the protectionist nature of the CAP. It is nonsensical to compare the EC with the United States when the United States is a net exporter and the EC is basically (under free trade conditions) a net importer of agricultural products. Of course, this is not meant to suggest that the United States has a true comparative advantage in *all* the agricultural products (since the subsidies provided by the United States to some of its farmers may be the main reason for their exports), only in some of its exports. Finally, the argument for a social preference for employment in agriculture is not very appealing in the context of the EC, particularly since the world supplies are cheaper and the movement away from agricultural employment, which is what the CAP structural policies are trying to promote, is a 'natural' phenomenon.

The gist of this argument is that some agricultural economists seem preoccupied with the 'trade creation' elements of the CAP and seem to ignore completely the 'trade diversion' aspects of it. (For a detailed discussion of these concepts see El-Agraa, 1978 and 1989; El-Agraa and Jones, 1981; Chapter 4.) Because trade diversion has been ignored, the successes have been exaggerated and the failures have been under-estimated.[12] The reader who is interested in a full survey of the actual cost estimates of the CAP should consult Chapter 12 of El-Agraa 1989a, Baldwin *et al.*, 1988 and the references given there. To conclude this section, we shall concentrate on a summary of the latest estimate since it is the most comprehensive in both coverage and scope.

Stoeckel (1985) and Breckling *et al.* (1987) made estimates using a simplified general-equilibrium approach. Since the Breckling *et al.* study was a more sophisticated version of the Stoeckel work, this section is devoted to this later attempt; Stoeckel himself was a joint author of the Breckling *et al.* study.

The study commenced by stressing the three major problems facing the EC:

1. The excessive surpluses created by the CAP in most (?) agricultural products necessitating huge restitution costs to enable their disposal on the international market.
2. The high level of unemployment which in 1987 reached about 11 per cent of the total labour force.
3. The declining competitiveness of the EC manufacturing sector – the share of the EC in OECD exports of equipment goods having declined by more than 25 per cent since 1964 and its imports share having risen by more than the same percentage; it is the traditional industries that have lagged behind while the new technology industries and products with high growth in demand are lacking.

The authors correctly believed that these problems were interrelated, hence their employment of a general-equilibrium approach. They conceded that the causes were numerous and complex but they were certain that the CAP 'has contributed significantly to the EC's relative economic malaise' (Breckling *et al.*, 1987, p. 2).

The model specified a general-equilibrium structure for each of the largest four EC economies and estimated the effects of protecting the agricultural and food processing sectors on the rest of the economies in terms of exports, factor markets and total unemployment. The four economies accounted in 1982 for 86 per cent of the GDP of the EC; hence they were fairly representative of the EC as a whole. They were, in ranking order: West Germany (28 per cent), France (23 per cent), the United Kingdom (19 per cent) and Italy (16 per cent). The reason for concentrating on these four was simplicity.

Each of these countries had large *services* and *manufacturing* sectors, representing about 55 per cent and 25 per cent of their respective GDPs. Agriculture accounted for a small percentage of GDP, ranging from 2 per cent in the United Kingdom and West Germany to 6 per cent in Italy. The food processing sector (which was subject to CAP support) represented about 4–6 per cent of the GDP of these countries. About 26 per cent of the agricultural production of the EC came from France, about 21 per cent from Italy, 17 per cent from West Germany and about 12 per cent from the United Kingdom.

A basic feature of EC agriculture was the co-existence of small- and large-scale farm enterprises. Within the EC of ten, large-scale farms represented about 10 per cent of the total number of farm enterprises but accounted for 40 per cent of the total agricultural output. The large-scale farms were mostly (in ranking order) in the United Kingdom, West Germany and France – see Table 9.2. It was always recognised that, *on the whole*, the large-scale farms tended to be more capital intensive relative to the small-scale ones.

The authors believed that the least controversial explanation for the high level of unemployment in the EC and its sharp rate of increase in the United Kingdom between 1975 and 1982 was rigidity of real wages. This belief was based on the study by Klau and Mittelstädt (1986) which showed the United Kingdom, France and Italy to have the highest real wage rigidities of all the members of the OECD. The same study showed West Germany to have a low level of real wage rigidity despite narrow wage differentials reflecting minimum wage legislation and cost-of-living adjustments.

The formal model incorporated all these features. It was based on a linearised Samuelson–Heckscher–Ohlin general-equilibrium framework first advanced by Woodland (1982) and adapted for the EC by Stoeckel (1985); the present study extended it to a multi-country representation of the EC.

As indicated before, the EC was represented by its four major producers. For each of these, four production sectors were distinguished, reflecting the authors' focus on the CAP: agriculture, being the supplier of the products and the main recipient of financial support; food processing, being an intensive user of agricultural inputs and the second major recipient of financial support; manufacturing, being representative of all other tradable goods; and services, being the labour intensive and mostly non-traded goods sector. The agricultural sector was disaggregated into small- and large-scale farm enterprises. The main instruments used in the approach to reflect CAP support were production subsidies, export restitutions, variable levies and the VAT tranche forming an own resource of the EC budget.

The authors felt that agriculture warranted special treatment, given the study's focus on it. A common agricultural sector, encompassing the four EC countries, was specified, and the agricultural products of these countries were treated as a single homogeneous product, which was exported, in aggregate, to the outside world. However, non-agricultural commodities produced in the EC were assumed to be not only exported to the rest of the world but also to other members of the EC. Except for the composite agricultural product, all EC commodities were distinguished by both country of origin and destination. All four countries were assumed to import both agricultural and non-agricultural commodities from the outside world. Each of the four countries was seen to be large enough to influence the world price of its traded goods.

Each industry was assumed to use domestic and imported intermediate imports as well as primary factors in the production process. The model incorporated four factors of production: capital, labour and land use in both the agricultural subsectors, and land specific to the large farms. All factors other than labour were assumed to be fully employed, while labour could be either so or unemployed. Both capital and labour were assumed to be mobile domestically but immobile within the EC, in spite of the *economic union* nature of the EC.

All factor endowments were assumed to be determined exogenously, implying, for the capital stock, that sectoral investment could take place only through the reallocation of capital (other than large-scale land) amongst the sectors, i.e. at the margin, capital was 'malleable and . . . usable' by all sectors. Another implication was that all commodities were used in current production and could not be reproduced.

The main behavioural assumptions were that producers minimise costs subject to technological constraints, with each sector producing a single product; there was a single consumer in each country maximising utility subject to a budget constraint; perfect competition ensured that all factors, except labour, received their marginal products and were fully employed; and *Walras' law* applied with results being independent of the choice of reference price – this being the consumer price index for each country – hence only 'real' changes took place with movements in real income acting as a welfare indicator.

The basic model was non-linear. The solution procedure involved first linearising it using logarithmic differentiation. The resulting elasticity version was then solved by matrix inversion. The linear approximation is valid for the estimation of small changes in the endogenous variables from exogenous stimuli, but due to the large exogenous changes in the export restitutions and import levies, the authors conceded that the linearisation errors were substantial, particularly in the case of trade parameters.

Given the Samuelson–Heckscher–Ohlin nature of the methodology employed, the authors' (Breckling *et al.*, 1987, p. 11) expectation with regard to the CAP (agricultural protectionism) was that it would have adverse effects on the other traded goods sectors and the economy as a whole by:

1. Distorting the pattern of trade through agricultural import taxes (export taxes on non-agricultural goods) and agricultural export subsidies (import subsidies on non-agricultural goods).
2. Worsening the terms of trade for the EC, thus reducing EC welfare.

3. Increasing unemployment in the relatively labour-intensive industries, given the assumption of real wage rigidities.
4. Promoting research into and investment in relatively inefficient industries.

The aim of the study was to establish the magnitude of each of these expected effects. The results were obtained through simulation. 1979 was chosen as the base year for calculating the impact of CAP support, modelled as exogenous shocks, on member countries since it was the year when the own resources system for financing the EC budget was formally phased in. The full absorption time for such shocks was thought to be typically a five-year period; thus the authors interpreted the results as changes covering the period 1979–83.

The data base was the *Standard Input-Output Tables of ECE Countries for Years around 1975* (UN, 1982) augmented by trade shares obtained from OECD trade tapes used in their *INTERLINK Model* (OECD, 1983). Unemployment figures were obtained from OECD country-specific statistics for 1979 (OECD, 1985). The ratio of unemployment benefit to employment wage was set at 0.5 in the four EC nations, and

Table 9.4 Behavioural elasticities

Description	Elasticity
Production and consumption substitution elasticities (CES)	
Between domestic and imported goods and primary factors for all countries	0.8
Between imported goods and domestic goods for all countries	2.0
Consumer income elasticities	
Agricultural products for all countries	0.2
Food processing products for all countries	0.4
Manufacturing products for all countries	0.8
Service sector products[a]	
W. Germany	1.18
France	1.17
United Kingdom	1.17
Italy	1.23
Export price elasticities of demand by rest of world	
Agricultural and agrifood products for all countries	2.0
Manufacturing products for all countries	1.0
Service sector products for all countries	4.0
Import price elasticities of supply by rest of world	
Agricultural and agrifood products for all countries	2.0
Manufacturing products for all countries	4.0
Service sector products for all countries	5.0

Note
[a] These settings ensure that the weighted sum of expenditure elasticities is unity in each country. Leisure demand (unemployment supply) elasticity for all countries was set to 1.0.

Source: J. Breckling *et al.* (1987), *Effects of EC Agricultural Policies: a General Equilibrium Approach* (Canberra: Bureau of Agricultural Research), p. 23.

real wages were assumed to be fixed. The input–output shares of the agricultural subsector were derived from the *Farm Accountancy Data Network* (*Eurostat*, 1982) since their preliminary tables for 1986 suggested no change from their 1975 calculations.

Behavioural elasticities were taken from Whalley (1985), Stern, Francis and Schumacker (1976) and Deaton and Muellbauer (1980b); these are given in Table 9.4. The authors claimed that although the calculations may have varied considerably, 'a preliminary sensitivity analysis has indicated that, except on the trade side, the results are fairly robust and that the effect on the economy is negligible' (Breckling *et al.*, 1987, p. 22).

The CAP support was modelled by four exogenous shocks:

1. A 12.32 per cent agricultural production subsidy.
2. Subsidies of 80 per cent on all agricultural and food processing products exported to the rest of the world.
3. Import levies of 40 per cent on all agricultural and food processing products imported from the rest of the world.
4. A 0.75 per cent VAT tax on all consumer goods in the EC countries.

The sizes of these shocks were chosen by reference to the FEOGA accounts. All storage costs were treated as implicit export subsidies and production aids were regarded as implicit production subsidies. The precise value of the agricultural production subsidy was selected to guarantee that the EC budget constraint was met. Note that the measurement of these shocks assumed a distortion-free base in 1979, i.e. 1979 was the year of equilibrium.

On the expectation that CAP support may have promoted investment in agricultural research and development (by assumption, to the advantage of large, capital intensive farms), two shocks were used to capture this effect:

1. A 5 per cent increase in total factor productivity on large farms.
2. A 5 per cent decrease in total factor productivity on small farms.

Finally, the simulations were carried out on the assumptions that the MCAs and national government supports were held constant.

The simulation results, given in Table 9.5, indicated the following:

1. The agricultural production subsidy and the VAT tax necessary to finance agricultural support were more important instruments than the border measures.
2. EC agricultural production increased by 18 per cent, mainly due to the production subsidy. Output grew fastest in the United Kingdom (about 54 per cent), and least in Italy (about 7 per cent) with West Germany's growing by about 20 per cent and France's by about 12 per cent. Since the average growth rate for the EC was just under 20 per cent, the British and West German agricultural enterprises increased their share of total EC production.
3. The increase in agricultural production was associated with price rises for the

Table 9.5 Country-specific simulation results[a]

Variable	W. Germany (%)	France (%)	United Kingdom (%)	Italy (%)
Gross output				
Agriculture – small farms	−1.1	0.3	−35.4	−1.2
– large farms	51.2	27.0	98.5	29.3
– total	20.2	11.7	53.7	6.8
Food processing	8.0	13.7	15.9	5.1
Manufacturing	−1.4	−1.9	−2.5	−1.1
Services	−1.3	−0.6	−3.1	−0.7
Producer prices				
Agriculture	−2.6	−4.6	−3.8	−2.9
Food processing	0.2	−2.0	1.3	−0.9
Manufacturing	−0.5	−0.7	−0.4	−0.6
Services	−0.3	−0.2	0.3	−0.4
Domestic consumer demand				
Agriculture	11.1	6.0	7.8	3.2
Food processing	0.9	2.9	1.6	1.6
Manufacturing	−0.8	−0.2	−2.0	−0.1
Services	−0.6	0.4	−1.5	0.2
Primary factor returns				
Labour	0.0	0.0	0.0	0.0
Capital	−0.5	0.4	1.7	−0.3
General land	17.6	11.7	14.0	9.5
Large scale land	72.5	40.2	130.4	44.8
Labour movement				
Employment	−0.9	−0.4	−1.8	−0.6
Unemployment	7.8	3.4	16.0	5.2
Exports to rest of world				
Food processing	149.9	150.2	145.3	151.5
Manufacturing	−4.4	−6.2	−5.7	−4.6
Services	−18.3	−26.7	25.4	−19.4
Imports from rest of world				
Agriculture	−32.1	−34.0	−26.8	−33.6
Food processing	−33.1	−32.4	−28.4	−33.3
Manufacturing	5.1	7.3	5.8	5.4
Services	6.2	9.0	0.0	6.0
Real income	−0.1	0.8	−0.6	0.4
Exchange rate	4.9	6.9	6.1	5.2
Terms of trade	−0.4	1.9	−0.5	0.2

Note
[a] All price changes are relative to the consumer price index in each country.

Source: J. Breckling *et al.*, 1987, *Effects of EC Agricultural Policies: a General Equilibrium Approach* (Canberra: Bureau of Agricultural Research), p. 14.

factors used most intensively in agriculture, especially land. These increased land costs favoured the countries least intensive in the use of land, i.e. the United Kingdom and West Germany.

4. Given the assumptions made about technology, it was not surprising to discover that the large farms were the main beneficiaries. Indeed, output growth on small farms actually declined by about 35 per cent in the United Kingdom and remained almost constant in the rest of the EC.

5. The food-processing sector expanded, on average, by about 10 per cent throughout the EC. Most of this growth was attributed to the 80 per cent export subsidy, since the export sector accounted for 10 per cent total demand. The differences in growth rates in the EC countries were attributed to their different export shares.

6. The manufacturing and services sectors contracted by about 1 per cent in each country, except in France where manufacturing declined by about 2 per cent and the United Kingdom where manufacturing declined by 2.5 per cent and services by 3.1 per cent. However, except for the United Kingdom, manufacturing was more adversely affected relative to the services sector, a situation which was to be expected since in this model agricultural protection resulted in an appreciation of the real exchange rates, which depressed exports; this was not so in the case of services since they were, by assumption, non-traded, but this left unexplained the UK reverse position.

7. As expected, unemployment increased throughout the EC, given the assumption of rigid real wages and the fact that the declining non-agricultural sectors were relatively intensive employers of labour. Calculations showed that the unemployment rate would become higher than in the absence of the CAP by 1.8 per cent (450,000 fewer persons employed) in the United Kingdom, 0.9 per cent (220,000 fewer persons employed) in West Germany, 0.6 per cent (110,000 fewer persons employed) in Italy and 0.4 per cent (80,000 fewer persons employed) in France. The rationale for greater job losses in the United Kingdom and West Germany was attributed to the lower contraction rate in the non-agricultural sectors of France and Italy, implying that jobs in the United Kingdom and West Germany were being lost in favour of France and Italy, reflecting the fact that labour was assumed to be immobile between members of the EC. It should not come as a surprise to learn that the relative effect of the CAP on unemployment followed an almost identical pattern to that in the non-agricultural sectors.

8. The CAP was found to create substantial changes in the pattern of consumer expenditure. For instance, consumer demand for locally produced manufactured goods declined in all four countries in the sample, particularly so in the case of the United Kingdom. The demand for services contracted in the United Kingdom (1.5 per cent) and West Germany (0.6 per cent), but marginally increased in France and Italy.

9. Exports of both processed and unprocessed products by the EC to the rest of the world rose by about 150 per cent – see also Table 9.6. This largely reflected the size of the export subsidy, and the authors claimed that this result was consistent with 'the evidence of massive surplus production' (Breckling et al., 1986, p. 15).

Table 9.6 Aggregate EC simulation results for agriculture

Variable	Change (%)
Gross output	+18.3
Producer price	−2.3
Exports to rest of world	+155.4

Source: J. Breckling *et al.*, 1987, *Effects of EC Agricultural Policies: a General Equilibrium Approach* (Canberra: Bureau of Agricultural Research), p. 15.

Table 9.7 Intra-EC transfers

Variable	W. Germany (%)	France (%)	United Kingdom (%)	Italy (%)
Value of exports	−1.9	−2.4	−0.4	−4.8
Value of imports	−1.0	+0.6	−0.8	−0.8
Consumption tax	3.3	4.1	3.2	3.8
Production subsidy	4.2	7.1	2.8	7.8
Import tariffs on agriculture	2.7	0.6	2.3	0.8
Import tariffs on food processing	2.3	2.0	4.3	2.6
Agricultural export subsidy	−1.0	4.2	0.0	0.3
Agrifood export subsidy	1.6	3.4	2.6	0.8
Net transfers	−3.5	8.0	−4.4	1.7

Source: J. Breckling *et al.*, 1987, *Effects of EC Agricultural Policies: a General Equilibrium Approach* (Canberra: Bureau of Agricultural Research), p. 16.

On the whole, the EC exports of manufactures and services declined by about 5 per cent and 23 per cent respectively. On average, intra-EC trade in processed agricultural products increased by about 7 per cent. The terms of trade worsened for the United Kingdom and West Germany, were almost unchanged for Italy and improved for France by about 2 per cent.

10. As Table 9.7 shows, the simulations suggested that France was the main beneficiary from EC budgetary transfers by 8 per cent of its gross export income. The loss by the United Kingdom and West Germany is attributed to their relatively small agricultural sectors.

This approach is to be applauded since economists should be interested in the total economy-wide effects of any protectionist policy. Moreover, the approach improves on the five areas identified by Stoeckel (1985) as requiring more attention: the need to incorporate an agricultural sector, to specify a multi-country framework, to model explicitly the transfers within and between countries, to model a heterogeneous agricultural sector where just over 10 per cent of farms produce almost half the total output and to specify labour market rigidities in an acceptable model of unemployment.

However, both the model specification and some of the assumptions employed here leave a lot to be desired. Theoretically, the model is inappropriate for dealing with large changes, as is the case with the CAP. The authors concede this point and are presently working on an improvement of the solution procedure in order to remove the linearisation error, but until those errors are eliminated, one should not have much faith in their preliminary results.

This point is reinforced when one carefully examines the assumptions built into the model. First, factors of production are not allowed to move across the borders of the EC. Of course, factor mobility has not been enhanced to any substantial extent by the formation of the EC, but there is evidence to suggest that some labour mobility does take place, and substantial amounts of capital and technology do move about within the EC – see Chapter 19. Second, large farms are not only intensive in their use of capital but also have access to land not available to small farms, the implication being that *all* large farms are more efficient than small farms. There is much evidence to suggest that some small farms are more efficient than large farms, depending on the agricultural product under consideration. This takes one to the third point: because all agricultural products are counted as one aggregate, no such disaggregation is possible, hence this reality is completely ignored in the calculations. Related to this is another point: in the EC, surpluses have been confined to certain products only, mainly milk and wine, and occasionally other products; but because there is no room for disaggregation, the estimates of this model suggest surpluses all round. The authors, realising this result, began by claiming that there have been surpluses in most agricultural products; there are no statistics to support such a claim. Also, and more importantly, a model which incorporates such assumptions is bound to produce the sort of results obtained, i.e. the model has been specified in such a manner as to produce these results; therefore both the formulation of the model and its application leave one unmoved. However, this does not diminish the need for a general-equilibrium approach.

9.10 Conclusions

Having explained the CAP, its mechanisms, financing, successes and failures, it is now possible to attempt some final conclusions.

Firstly, the structural problems and the embarrassing surpluses still remain, partly because the intervention prices are set at too high a level. The only justification for such high prices is that the authorities are not in a position to know the shapes of the relevant supply and demand curves for agricultural products, but when the authorities err consistently, it must be because they wish to do so, i.e. they are under great pressure to accede to the wishes of the farming lobby.[13] A lower level of intervention prices should dispose of the surpluses problem and should encourage people who are inefficiently engaged in the farm sector to seek alternative employment. As we have seen, the EC has recently attempted this, but it remains to be seen whether or not the end result will be success.

Secondly, the CAP has failed to adopt the most efficient method of implementing its own objectives. It was clearly demonstrated that direct subsidies and deficiency payments are, in that order, economically superior to the variable levy system. Presumably the reason for not using subsidies in the first place was the problem of finding sources of finance. But with the surpluses and the substantial requirements for supporting artificially high prices draining the finances of FEOGA, a central budget finance system (more on this in the McDougall Report) which would make subsidies possible is inevitable, particularly now that Portugal and Spain have become members of the EC and both have large agricultural sectors – see Table 9.1.

Thirdly, the CAP has been a success for the EC in that one system has been adopted to replace the elaborate support systems that had existed before. (Some commentators have gone to the extent of stating that the only success of the CAP is that it exists.) However, it can be argued that the common system contains the worst features of all the others. It is arguably also more protective than any member state on its own would contemplate being.

It is time that the CAP system was reformed with the object of adopting the most efficient support system and incorporating into it elements for the removal of any possible damage to the developing world. An income subsidy system accompanied by the appropriate intervention price levels should produce the desired effect: no single policy measure can be expected to tackle the sort of problems facing the agricultural industry. In fairness, it should be added that the Commission has been working very hard for a proper reform of the CAP; it would seem that the strength of the agricultural lobby has been the main deterrent.

Notes

1. I wish to express my thanks to Dr Allan Buckwell and to Professor A. J. Brown for helpful comments on an earlier draft of this chapter. They are, of course, not to be held responsible for any shortcomings that remain in my argument.
2. A rough indication of average levels of income of people working in agriculture, relative to incomes of people in other occupations, can be obtained by comparing agriculture's share of the total workforce with its share of national output. Such a comparison suggests that, when the EEC was formed, average agricultural incomes in the three largest countries, France, Germany and Italy, were only about half those of other occupations. (Ritson, 1973, p. 96)
3. 'Agricultural incomes have risen, but in France, Germany and Italy there is little evidence that the gap in incomes between agriculture and other occupations has diminished' (Ritson, 1973, p. 69).
4. It is argued by some that the provision of an adequate agricultural sector incidentally helps to ensure a pleasant environment for the nation's inhabitants. However, there is considerable argument that intensive agriculture is detrimental to the environment, e.g. removal of hedges, odours from intensive livestock, etc. (see Bowers, 1972).
5. 'This does not, however, accrue to farmers alone: in fact it represents increased return to fixed factors in both farming and in the purchased input industries' (Josling, 1969, p. 296).

6.   It is possible to derive expressions for the *average* cost (in terms of extra resources or budget payments) of achieving a unit of objective in this case income transfer. Such calculations are meaningful if comparing the policy with a free market. More relevant in the case of a policy where the level of guaranteed price can be changed from year to year is the *marginal* cost of gaining an additional unit of objective. (Josling, 1969, p. 272)

7. Bhagwati (1965) demonstrates that tariffs and quotas can be equivalent in their effects only if it is assumed that free competition exists in both the importing countries and in the industry under consideration – see El-Agraa (1983, Chapters 8–10 and 1989, Chapters 8–10).

8. Josling, 1969, p. 277. For a more detailed discussion of distortions, the reader should consult Johnson, 1965a and Chapter 4.

9. For an estimate of the average and marginal costs of some of these policies the reader should consult Josling, 1969, pp. 278–80.

10. This refers to a series of six documents which were submitted to the Council in December 1968. The first of these was called 'Memorandum on the Reform of Agriculture in the European Community', in *Bulletin of the European Community*, 1969, Supplement. The series is available in one volume as *Le Plan Mansholt*, Brussels, July 1969 – see Fennell (1979) for details.

11. The average size of holding in the United Kingdom in 1970–1 was in excess of three times that in the original six – if one were to include farms of less than one hectare, the difference would be more extreme.

12. Using 1953–69 annual observations, Thorbecke and Pagoulatos, 1975 (p. 322) reached the conclusions that 'the formation of the CAP has affected the pattern of international trade flows by inducing a shift from extra-EEC producers to partner countries or domestic sources of supply for nine out of ... fourteen individual commodity groups'; and that 'agricultural protectionism in the Community has slowed down the rate of labour out-migration'.

13. Mr Roy Jenkins, when he was President of the EC Commission, was unable to clarify this position.

        I mentioned a minute ago the question of surpluses. They are not always a bad thing. *It is better for the consumer to have a small surplus than a small shortage*. But that is not the same with European milk production. One-sixth of milk output is already surplus to requirements, while total consumption of milk products is declining. We shall not be able to persuade Europe's taxpayers and consumers to support that indefinitely. We cannot expect importers and other exporters of milk outside Europe to relieve us of that burden, even though we can dispose of some part outside the Community. In *European Community*, September 1978, p. 9. The emphasis is not in the original text.

10 The Common Fisheries Policy

A. M. El-Agraa

It was stated in the previous chapter that in the Treaty of Rome fisheries were included in the definition of agricultural products; but in 1966 an effort was made by the EC Commission for the establishment of a Common Fisheries Policy (CFP – in its *Report on the Situation of the Fisheries Sector in the Member States of the EEC and the Basic Principles for a Common Policy*, 1966); prior to that, many fish stocks in what are now EC waters were controlled by the NE Atlantic Fisheries Commission (NEAFC). However, agreement on the CFP was not reached until 1983, after six years of negotiations and hard bargaining. The purpose of this chapter is briefly to examine the background to these developments and to explain the nature and implications of the CFP. The reader who is interested in a detailed account of the developments leading to the creation of this policy together with its geographical and political implications is advised to read Wise (1984).

10.1 Background

It could be argued that what prompted the emergence of a CFP was the situation in 1966. Then, production in the original six began to stagnate, the attitude of non-menber nations regarding their twelve-mile limits became increasingly restrictive and there was a sharp decline in the Community's self-sufficiency rates for the major fish species. As a consequence of this, proposals were advanced in June 1968 which amounted to a set of basic ingredients for a CFP. These proposals were adopted by the Council in October 1970 and came into force in February 1971.

The striking feature of this policy was the recognition by all six member states of the principle of 'equal access' for all EC fishermen to the territorial waters of the EC together with a free EC market for fish. This was opportune, given the fact that the waters of the three imminent member countries of the EC (as well as those of Norway, which finally decided not to join the EC, arguably because of this very issue) were rich in fish: the total catch of the original six was half that of the three imminent partners. Hence, the negotiation of 'access' was vital if the CFP were to become a reality.

It should be added that the agreements reached between the original six and the three new member nations included arrangements for fisheries which entitled the fishermen of coastal countries (those countries highly dependent on fishing for their livelihood) to a general and exclusive six-mile zone and to a twelve-mile exclusive zone in some areas with the proviso that these zones would become EC waters after 1982 if no review of the CFP took place in the meantime. However, the three nations did not view this as a permanent solution since they felt that they were losing more than they expected to gain. Thus an atmosphere ripe for conflict was created.

However, during the period 1974–6, the United Nations Conference on the Law of the Sea (UNCLOS III) was in session and one of the points which occupied a large part of its deliberations was the issue regarding the extension of national fishing zones to 200 miles. The nine member nations of the EC were actually about to implement such an exclusive zone limit, but preferred to await the outcome of the conference. In the end, UNCLOS III failed to reach agreement on this issue, and when Canada, Norway and the United States announced their intention of adopting a 200-mile zone, the EC decided (in The Hague in October 1976) to follow suit and implement what it had already intended, especially since the United Kingdom was threatening to do so unilaterally. In The Hague meeting, it was also decided to ask the EC Commission to proceed with negotiations with third countries. Obviously, without specific agreements, the 200-mile zone limit was bound to exclude countries which had in the past fished in what came to be known as the 'Community pond'. It should be clear that whether or not these countries should be allowed access to the EC pond would depend on the size of catch granted and the extent of reciprocity extended to the EC in terms of EC fishermen having access to the waters of such countries. Not surprisingly, the EC Commission, for this purpose, classified third countries into three categories:

1. Possible reciprocators such as Iceland and Norway.
2. Countries like Canada and the United States which have no interest in the EC pond but which might have surpluses in their waters to which the EC fishermen might want to gain access.
3. Countries which would like access to the EC pond but could not reciprocate, such as the nations of Eastern Europe.

By 1976 the same old questions began to surface again. Were the member nations to have completely free access to the EC pond or would they be granted exclusive zones on a permanent basis? Would the EC go for a maximum catch, partly determined with conservation in mind, which would be shared out between the member states on a percentage basis? Would the EC perhaps opt for both these possibilities? What compensation would Ireland and the United Kingdom receive, in terms of access to the EC pond, for losing some of their own waters to countries like Iceland because of the common 200-mile zone?

The position of the United Kingdom was that the twelve-mile limit was unacceptable, and the British government started by demanding a 100-mile exclusive zone, but later dropped this limit by 50 per cent. During the negotiations that followed, more emphasis was laid on a limit on the total catch to be divided into national quotas and less on exclusive zones. Late in 1977, the EC Commission proposed possible national quotas, giving about 30 per cent to the United Kingdom; but this was only two-thirds of what the United Kingdom had hoped for.

The first detailed proposals of a CFP went to the Council in September 1976. These comprised measures for 'conserving fishery resources (total allowable catches – TACs – and quotas), for safeguarding, as far as possible, employment and incomes in coastal regions, and for adjusting fleet size in the light of the catch available' (*Bulletin of the European Communities*, no. 1, 1983, p. 1). In October 1976 the six agreed to extend their fishing limits to 200 nautical miles as from 1 January 1977 (North Sea and North Atlantic). It should therefore not be surprising to learn that the negotiations were very tense and difficult since it was not just that the question of access had to be solved but also that TACs had to be fixed and then allocated to each member country of the EC on a quota basis at a time when there was evidence of over-fishing. Indeed, final resolution of the matter was not reached until 25 January 1983 when the ministers in charge of fisheries in the ten member nations of the EC agreed on the new CFP. This was based on the proposals that the EC Commission had itself initiated. The relief expressed by the EC Commission on reaching an agreement, after six years of hard bargaining, should not be underestimated.

10.2 The policy

The delight of the EC Commission with the new CFP can be clearly captured from their statement that a Blue Europe had been born (EC Commission, 1983c, p. 193).

In that Report, the EC Commission states that the following groundrules were laid down for EC fishery activities:

1. 'Equality of access to resources in Community waters except, by way of derogation and for a renewable period of 10 years, for the preferential arrangements for in-shore fishermen within the 12-mile limit'.
2. 'Compliance with a common policy for the conservation of resources, including both technical measures concerning the different fisheries and such stock management measures as the fixing of total allowable catches ... and annual quotas'.
3. 'The scope of agreements with non-Community countries to be reinforced and extended so as to safeguard fishing possibilities in their waters'.
4. 'Market support by implementation from 1 January 1983 of a common organisation of the market, with the changes decided upon on 29 December 1981'.
5. 'Modernization of development of the fishery and aquaculture sector, through measures financed by a Community budget of 250 million ECU over three years'.

The Report added that in 1983, the Blue Europe was experiencing some difficulties in settling down with the new groundrules. To cater for this, 'structural rules' were

Table 10.1 Allocations for 1984 and 1985 catch quotas in EC waters and in waters managed in cooperation with non-member countries and TACs for 1982 and 1983–6 (tonnes)

	Cod	Haddock	Saithe	Whiting	Plaice	Redfish	Mackerel	Herring[a]
Belgium								
1984	8,230	1,670	80	3,680	12,030	—[b]	100	—
1985	9,030	1,830	90	3,970	12,990	—	400	8,920
Denmark								
1984	234,350	18,615	7,550	34,190	46,110	4,890	7,400	43,770
1985	166,420	11,690	8,390	15,870	42,100	—	8,000	90,260
France								
1984	36,390	19,340	69,850	37,510	7,250	2,410	17,100	1,930
1985	39,540	20,270	95,020	41,400	7,500	4,410	14,930	35,430
W. Germany								
1984	84,380	7,110	21,110	3,900	9,860	62,820	25,600	22,180
1985	87,840	7,530	25,260	4,330	10,780	62,535	22,190	65,760
Ireland								
1984	11,520	4,370	3,060	17,800	3,070	—	85,300	27,170
1985	11,520	3,820	3,730	22,700	3,730	—	72,640	31,900
Netherlands								
1984	23,230	1,120	190	8,630	66,890	—	37,300	7,850
1985	25,950	1,270	210	9,290	71,810	—	32,180	82,900
United Kingdom								
1984	117,910	140,840	20,860	79,480	53,710	380	234,700	38,800
1985	129,550	151,540	27,400	92,890	59,570	375	200,160	98,180
EC[c]								
1982	524,700	201,700	101,760	208,120	159,960	70,500	375,000	219,400
1984	516,010	193,065	122,700	185,190	198,920	70,500	407,500	141,700
1985	469,350	197,950	160,100	191,450	208,480	65,320	350,500	413,350
1986	377,470	245,630	157,000	176,200	212,690	—	349,000	514,415

Notes
[a] The herring quotas excluded provisional North Sea allocations to six of these countries – Belgium (1,570), Denmark (6,920), West Germany (4,350), France (4,520), Netherlands (9,030) and the United Kingdom (7,910).
[b] – means zero allocation.
[c] Both Greece and Italy are not involved in the TACs simply because they conduct all their fishing in the Mediterranean.

Source: *Bulletin of the European Communities*, no. 1, vol. 17, 1984, p. 37.

introduced on 4 October and TACs and catch quotas for 1983 were determined on 20 December of the same year, thus reinforcing the agreement.

In short, the new CFP covers four aspects. Firstly, the policy has a 'system' for the conservation of sea resources within the EC. Secondly, the policy has a common organisation of the market. Thirdly, the policy includes 'structural' measures. Finally, the policy asks for fisheries agreements with non-EC countries and for formal consultations between EC nations so that they can act in concert in the context of international agreements.

With regard to the conservation of resources, the Council has adopted a regulation which establishes an EC system which provides for measures to curtail fishing activities, sets rules for utilising resources and makes special provisions for coastal fishing. More specifically, a conservation box has been established around the Orkney and Shetland islands and the number of licences offered to EC fishermen over-fishing endangered species has been made more limited. Hence both 'access' and TACs are aspects of crucial importance here.

Table 10.1 provides information on the 1984 and 1985 TACs and the individual country quotas together with the TACs for 1982 and 1986. I have provided fuller data for 1984–5 simply for ease of exposition. This is because the Council decided that fishing during the first few months of 1983 should be conducted on the basis of the 1982 TACs and quotas (due allowance being given to normal seasonal fluctuations), thus making the 1982 figures (the 1982 TACs and shares available to the EC are given in full in the appendix to this chapter) provisional in nature. Moreover, the levels for 1984 can easily be compared with those of 1983: the 1984 figures were slightly lower for cod, haddock and whiting and slightly higher for mackerel, plaice and saithe, with the TAC for redfish remaining unchanged at 70,500 tonnes. Thus there is enough information to compare the TACs in the three years, but such a comparison is too obvious to warrant specification. However, attention should be drawn to the fact that although the TAC for cod has declined over the period 1983–5, Denmark has absorbed more than the total decline since all the countries in the table have increased their share, with Ireland maintaining its quota. A more drastic situation also applies to Denmark with regard to haddock, plaice and whiting since the TACs have increased relative to 1984. The reader who is interested in following the detailed yearly changes in the TACs and their allocation between the member nations of the EC is advised to consult the *Official Journal of the European Communities*; these yearly comparisons will not be pursued here simply because the variations in them are not determined just by the bargaining position of the individual nations: changes in conservation criteria and in the natural catch environments are most crucial.

The market organisation covers fresh fish and frozen and preserved products and its main objective is to apply common marketing standards and to facilitate trading between the member nations of the EC. More precisely, however, it should be stated that the objectives of the marketing aspect are to guarantee an adequate income to the producers, to enhance rational marketing, to alter supply in accordance with market requirements, to ensure that consumer prices are reasonable and to promote common marketing standards – see Cunningham and Young (1983, p. 2).

The structural measures can be described more precisely by stating their aims. The main objectives are to ensure that the resources of the sea are rationally utilised; to ensure that the fishermen of the different member nations of the EC are treated on an equal basis; and to conserve resources or reduce over-capitalisation (Cunningham and Young, 1983, p. 3). With regard to these aspects, the Council agreed on 25 January 1983 to activate, within six months, special EC measures which were

Table 10.2 EC funds to assist the fisheries sector 1983–6

Proposed measures	Total expenditure (million ECU)
1. Directive on adjusting capacity	
(a) temporary withdrawal	44
(b) permanent withdrawal	32
2. Regulation on exploratory fishing and joint ventures:	
(a) exploratory fishing	11
(b) joint ventures	7
3. Regulation on a common measure for restructuring, etc.	
(a) construction and modernisation of fishing vessels	118
(b) aquaculture	34
(c) artificial structures intended for restocking	4
Total expenditure over three years	250

Source: *Official Journal of the European Communities*, 26, C28, 3 February, 1983, 1.

designed to 'adjust capacity and improve productivity of fishing and aquaculture'. These measures consist largely of proposals put forward by the EC Commission between 1977 and 1980 and include 'aids for laying up, temporarily or permanently, certain fishing vessels so that capacity can be adjusted in the light of the conservation needs'; 'aids for exploratory fishing and cooperation with certain non-member countries in the context of joint ventures in order to encourage the redeployment of the Community's fishing activity'; and 'aids for the construction and modernisation of certain fishing vessels and aquaculture facilities and for the installation of artificial structures to facilitate restocking and develop the fishing industry generally' (*Bulletin of the European Communities*, no. 1, 1983, p. 2). As stated above, these measures are to apply for three years and are to qualify for EC financing to the total of 250 million ECU: 76 million ECU for capacity adjustment; 18 million ECU for exploratory fishing and joint ventures; and 156 million ECU for restructuring, i.e. for encouraging investment in the fishing industry (see Table 10.2 for details). It should be added, however, that the EC's financial contribution to any approved project is generally limited to 50 per cent of its total cost, and that these are EC monies for which EC citizens can apply irrespective of their nationality. With regard to the latter point, Wise (1984, p. 244) argues that since a large percentage of these funds was 'designed to help fleets adjust to nearer-water fishing following the loss of rights in far-off grounds, Britain could expect to continue as a major recipient of [EC] structural aid following a pattern established over the previous 10 years'. The United Kingdom received about 40.8 million ECU during 1973–82 for the construction and modernisation of vessels from EAGGF; this amounted to 35.8 per cent of total EAGGF expenditures on this item over the specified period – see below.

Finally, with regard to agreements with non-EC countries, framework fisheries agreements were signed with the Faeroe Islands, Guinea, Guinea-Bissau, Norway, Spain, Sweden and the United States. Moreover, talks were in progress with Mauritania and were to be resumed with some other African countries. The EC Commission was also authorised to negotiate fisheries agreements with the Caribbean countries of Antigua, Dominica, Saint Lucia and Suriname. Multilateral agreements were concluded with a view to the Community's participation in international agreements covering the north-east and north-west Atlantic, the Antarctic and salmon in the north Atlantic, and talks were in progress with regard to the EC's participation in international agreements on tuna and whaling and to its joining the organisations which control fishing in the Baltic, and in the central and south-east Atlantic.

10.3 Developments in the CFP

The progress of the CFP has been almost along the expected lines, especially when, two years after the inauguration of the CFP, the EC began to take decisions on TACs and their country allocation in December so as to inform the EC fishermen of their expected catches well before they started fishing. Although later agreements on the TACs and individual country quotas have been taking longer to reach than expected, the delays have been mainly for technical reasons and have been no longer than two or three months, which is natural, given the bargaining nature of the situation.

With regard to the promised assistance for the restructuring of the fishing industry, Table 10.3 gives some indication of the progress made in this regard. The table shows that for the period 1983–6 the EC intended to extend aid totalling about 219 million ECU, but for the first three years the total was only about 174 million ECU. Thus it would seem that the aid for the restructuring of the fisheries industry fell short of the promised of 250 million ECU for the first three years of the CFP. If,

Table 10.3 Aid granted under the common measures for the restructuring, modernising and developing of the fisheries industry and for developing aquaculture under Regulation (EEC) no. 2908/83 (million ECU)

Appropriations	1983	1984	1985	1986	1987	1988
Belgium	0.35	3.95	2.41	2.38	0.41	0.10
Denmark	2.71	4.60	4.09	7.69	1.21	3.29
France	6.07	12.80	5.86	13.78	12.42	4.74
W. Germany	3.13	3.18	1.12	4.92	4.41	1.39
Greece	6.70	2.44	3.95	9.51	6.37	5.41
Ireland	5.91	3.07	1.45	3.50	1.84	4.99
Italy	10.68	22.11	11.22	18.99	16.12	11.40
Netherlands	1.87	2.06	0.46	2.68	0.66	0.57
Portugal	—	—	—	—	11.22	2.85
Spain	—	—	—	—	32.20	18.11
United Kingdom	7.39	9.90	5.04	11.07	7.23	7.50
Total	44.81	64.11	35.60	74.52	94.09	60.35

Source: calculated from various issues of the *Bulletin of the European Communities*.

Table 10.4 Allocation from the EC General Budget for the restructuring of the fisheries industry

Year	Million ECU
1983	107.24
1984	112.35
1985	111.73
1986	189.62
1987	197.29
1988	325.89

however, one were to include aid amounting to about 68 million ECU granted under regulation (EEC) no. 355/77, which was adopted on 15 February 1977 and which comes under the EAGGF structural fund, then the latter sum is only about eight million ECU short of the target.

Another way of looking at the finances provided by the EC to support the restructuring of the fisheries industry is simply to quote the figures from the EC General Budget which come under the heading of fisheries (Chapters 40 to 47). These are given in Table 10.4. It does not matter which three years cover the appropriate sum mentioned in the CFP since it is evident that the total of 250 million ECU was exceeded between 1983 and 1986. The comparison is made even more difficult by the EC's decision to inject a further 850 million ECU for restructuring over the five-year period 1987–91.

It should be added that the projects covered by the 1983 regulation amounted to 4,271 while those covered by the 1977 regulation added a further 299 to this total. Also, that Wise's expectation of the United Kingdom getting about 36 per cent of the total aid is way off target since the average percentage received by the United Kingdom between 1983 and 1986 was about 15 per cent – see above.

These figures also point to the most significant development in the CFP: the accession of Portugal and Spain. These countries were expected to increase the number of EC fishermen by 90 per cent, the fishing capacity by 80 per cent and fish consumption by EC citizens by about 50 per cent. The changes in these totals reflect this reality. It should be added that as a result of the Iberian enlargement the EC has become the third largest fishing area in the world.

Finally, it should be mentioned that the EC continues to negotiate agreements with third countries, the latest of these having been concluded on 3 May and 23 June 1988 with, respectively, the Comoros and Morocco.

10.4 Reservations

Although the agreement on the CFP has been much applauded, a great deal of caution should be exercised. Firstly, the use of such words as 'rational' and 'fair' immediately reminds one of the problems of the CAP where similar terminology came to mean self-sufficiency and an income to farmers much closer to, if not in excess of, the national average. Indeed, one aspect of the CFP is that when the price of fish falls, the fishermen can withdraw their excess stocks from the market in return for the receipt of financial assistance from the funds designated for the purpose. Secondly, there is the apparent conflict between the structural aspects and the market organisation, since the structure seeks conservation, while the market organisation encourages larger catches by giving price supports which are directly related to the size of the catch. Thirdly, it is inevitable that TACs will be negotiated annually; hence a tense bargaining atmosphere is likely to be generated over quota allocations. This reminds one of the classical case where it is desirable for oligopolists to pursue a policy of joint profit maximisation, but where the outcome is for each oligopolist to try to maximise his share of the profit. Fourthly, as Cunningham and Young (1983, p. 3) rightly state, even if the structural measures could be achieved

> almost complete reliance is placed on management methods which might be termed 'biological' in that, while they generally improve the condition of the fish stock itself, they will not result in any long-term improvement in the economic health of the [fishing industry]. Typical of such biological techniques are net mesh size restrictions, closed seasons, closed areas and limitations on the use of certain efficient methods of capture.

10.5 Conclusion

Although the CFP is six years old and the accession of Portugal and Spain has gone rather smoothly, it is still too early to make firm predictions about the appropriateness or otherwise of this policy. This is because the points mentioned in the previous section do indicate that there are potential problems which the EC Commission must keep constantly in mind if the situation is not to be potentially explosive. Having stated all that, one must conclude by sharing in the applause for the reaching of agreement in 1983 after negotiations which took six years of hard bargaining and mackerel wars with Denmark, and for the smooth incorporation of the Iberian countries into the agreement.

Appendix: TAC by stock and sector envisaged for 1982 (Table A10.5)

Table A10.5 TACs by stock and sector envisaged for 1982 (tonnes)

Species	ICES[a] division or NAFO[b] sub-area or division	TAC 1982	Share available to the Community for 1982
Cod	III a) Skagerrak	20,000[c]	16,500
Cod	III a) Kattegat	16,400	9,900
Cod	III b), c), d) (EC zone)	117,000	115,000
Cod	IV, II a) (EC zone)	255,000	244,100
Cod	VI, V b) (EC zone)	31,500	31,500

Table A10.5 (Con't)

Species	ICES[a] division or NAFO[b] sub-area or division	TAC 1982	Share available to the Community for 1982
Cod	VII except VII a), VIII (EC zone)	15,700	15,700
Cod	VII a)	15,000	15,000
Cod	XIV (EC zone), V a) (EC zone), XII (EC zone)	15,000	15,000
Cod	NAFO 1	62,000[d]	62,000[d]
Cod	NAFO 3 Ps	28,000	5,170
Haddock	III a), III b), c), d) (EC zone)	10,400[e]	9,100
Haddock	IV, II a) (EC zone)	180,000	150,000[f]
Haddock	VI, V b) (EC zone)	38,000[e]	38,000
Haddock	VII, VIII (EC zone)	4,500[e]	4,500
Saithe	II a) (EC zone), III a), IV, III b), c), d) (EC zone)	128,000	67,940
Saithe	VI, V b) (EC zone)	26,000[e]	26,000
Saithe	VII, VIII (EC zone)	7,820[e]	7,820
Whiting	III a) Skagerrak	4,650[e]	3,850
Whiting	III a) Kattegat	17,500[e]	15,800
Whiting	III b), c), d) (EC zone)	2,600[e]	2,600
Whiting	IV, II a) (EC zone)	170,000	130,800[g]
Whiting	VI, V b) (EC zone)	16,400	16,400
Whiting	VII a)	18,170	18,170
Whiting	VII except VII a)	20,500[e]	20,500
Plaice	III a) Skagerrak	10,000[e]	9,400
Plaice	III a) Kattegat	7,000[e]	6,300
Plaice	IV, II a) (EC zone)	140,000	130,000
Plaice	VI, V b) (EC zone)	1,810[e]	1,810
Plaice	VII a)	4,500	4,500
Plaice	VII b), c)	200[e]	200
Plaice	VII d), e)	5,500[e]	5,500
Plaice	VII f), g)	1,450	1,450
Plaice	VIII (EC zone)	250[e]	250
American plaice	NAFO 3 Ps	5,000	550
Witch	NAFO 3 Ps	3,000	410
Sole	III a), III b), c), d) (EC zone)	600[e]	600
Sole	IV, II a) (EC zone)	21,000	21,000
Sole	VI, V b) (EC zone)	50[e]	50
Sole	VII a)	1,600	1,600
Sole	VII b), c)	60[e]	60
Sole	VII d)	2,600[e]	2,600
Sole	VII e)	1,700[e]	1,700
Sole	VII f), g)	1,600	1,600
Sole	VIII (EC zone)	3,100[e]	3,100

Table A10.5 cont'd

Species	ICES[a] division or NAFO[b] sub-area or division	TAC 1982	Share available to the Community for 1982
Mackerel	III a), IV, II a) (EC zone), III b), c), d) (EC zone)	25,000	0
Mackerel	VI, V b) (EC zone), VII, VIII (EC zone)	401,000	375,000
Sprat	III a)	77,000[e]	48,000
Sprat	III b), c), d) (EC zone)	3,400[e]	3,400
Sprat	IV, II a) (EC zone)	400,000[e]	325,000
Horse mackerel	IV, VI, VII, VIII (EC zone)	250,000[e]	244,000
Hake	III a), III b), c), d) (EC zone)	1,300[e]	1,300
Hake	IV, II a) (EC zone)	2,750[e]	2,750
Hake	VI, VII, VII (EC zone), V b) (EC zone)	35,750	26,250
Anchovies	VIII	32,000[e]	3,000
Norway pout	III a), IV (EC zone), II a) (EC zone)	371,000[e]	321,000
Blue whiting	IV (EC zone) VI, VII, XII (EC zone), XIV (EC zone)	580,000[e]	415,000
Sand-eel	XIV (EC zone), V a) (EC zone)	0	0[h]
Sand-eel	NAFO 1	0	0[h]
Redfish	V (EC zone), XIV (EC zone)	43,500	43,000
Redfish	NAFO 1	10,000	9,500
Redfish	NAFO 3 Ps	18,000	2,000
Greenland halibut	V (EC zone), XIV (EC zone)	3,950	3,200
Greenland halibut	NAFO 1	20,000	7,250[i]
Halibut	XIV (EC zone)	220[e]	220
Halibut	NAFO 1	1,000[e]	1,000
Shrimp	XIV (EC zone), V (EC zone)	5,500[e]	3,050
Shrimp	NAFO 1	30,000	28,650
Shrimp	French Guyana	j	j
Herring	III a)	60,000	25,400
Herring	III b), c), d) (EC zone)	34,900	33,900
Herring	IV a), II a) (EC zone)	0	0
Herring	IV b)	0	0
Herring	IV c) (Blackwater stock excepted), VII d)	72,000	68,000[k]

Table A10.5 (Con't)

Species	ICES[a] division or NAFO[b] sub-area or division	TAC 1982	Share available to the Community for 1982
Herring	IV c) (Blackwater stock)[l]	0[m]	0[mn]
Herring	VI a) (North)[o], VI b), V b) (EC zone)	80,000	66,200
Herring	VI a) (South)[p], VII b), c)	11,000	11,000
Herring	VI a), (Clyde stock)[q]	2,500	2,500
Herring	VII a)[r] (Mourne stock)[s]	600	600
Herring	VII a)[r] (Manx stock)[t]	3,200	3,200
Herring	VII e)	500[e]	500
Herring	VII f)	0	0
Herring	VII g) to k)[u]	8,100	8,100[v]
Catfish	NAFO 1	6,000	6,000
Capelin	II b)	0	0
Capelin	XIV (EC zone), V (EC zone)	10,000	0
Salmon	III b), c), d) (EC zone)	920	920
Salmon	NAFO 1: west of 44°W	—	1,253

Notes
[a] ICES is the International Council for the Exploration of the Sea.
[b] NAFO is the North-West Fisheries Organisation. For the zonal details, consult the *Official Journal*.
[c] Excluding 1,600 tonnes attributed to the Norwegian coastal zone.
[d] *Ad hoc* solution for 1982.
[e] Precautionary TAC.
[f] Excluding estimated 5,600 tonnes of industrial bycatch.
[g] Excluding estimated 22,180 tonnes of industrial bycatch.
[h] Except for certain catch possibilities for experimental purposes.
[i] 12,000 tonnes not allocated.
[j] See Regulation (EEC) no. 1177/82.
[k] For the period 1 October 1982 to 28 February 1983.
[l] Maritme region of the Thames estuary between Felixstowe and North Foreland within six miles from the UK baselines.
[m] Subject to revision following scientific reassessment.
[n] TAC and quota are for the period 1 October 1982 to 31 March 1983.
[o] Reference is to the herring stock in ICES division VI a), north of 56°N and in that part of VI a) which is situated east of 7°W and north of 55°N, excluding the Clyde as defined in note q.
[p] Reference is to the herring stock in ICES division VI a), south of 56°N and west of 7°W.
[q] Maritime area situated to the north-east of a line drawn between the Mull of Kintyre and Corsewall Point.
[r] ICES division VII a) is reduced by the zone added to the Celtic Sea bounded: – to the north by latitude 52°30'N, – to the south by latitude 52°00'N, – to the west by the coast of Ireland, – to the east by the coast of the United Kingdom.
[s] Reference is to the herring stock within 12 miles of the east coast of Ireland and of Northern Ireland between 53°00'N and 55°00'N.
[t] Reference is to the herring stock in the Irish Sea (ICES division VII a)) excluding the zone referred to in note s.
[u] Increased by zone bounded: – to the north by latitude 52°30'N, – to the south by latitude 52°00'N, – to the west by the coast of Ireland, – to the east by the coast of the United Kingdom.
[v] From 1 October 1982 to 31 March 1983.

Source: *Official Journal of the European Communities*, No. L24, 27.1.1983.

11 The Common Transport Policy

K. M. Gwilliam

The extension of the European Community from the original six to the present dozen member states has already brought about major reconsideration and realignment of its internal policies. In transport terms the entry of the United Kingdom in 1973 injected a much more liberal attitude towards both national and international transport markets. The entry of Greece in the early 1980s and Spain in the mid-1980s raised those problems of peripherality in the transport sense parallel to those that they raised in the general wealth and welfare context. The next major watershed, much heralded, is the 'completion of the internal market', scheduled for 1992. The purpose of this chapter is to consider the implications of this latest step for the development of the Common Transport Policy.

The chapter falls in three parts. Firstly, we consider the development of the general philosophy of the Common Transport Policy from the Treaty of Rome through to the requirements of a completed internal market. Secondly, we examine the implications of this development in individual subsectors of the transport market. Finally, we attempt to identify those remaining steps which are likely to cause the greatest difficulty, and suggest ways in which they might be confronted.

11.1 Transport and the Treaty of Rome

Any costs which are peculiarly associated with the international transport of people or goods have potentially the same effect as tariffs on international trade. The Treaty of Rome recognised this by including a chapter on transport. It adopted provisions previously contained in the Treaty of Paris aimed at the elimination of conscious national discrimination as an initial step, looked to the progressive approximation of national transport policies as an intermediate requirement, and saw the application to the transport sector of the general rules of the free internal market as the ultimate end.

By identifying transport as a sector requiring separate treatment, however, the Treaty implicitly accepted that there were some special characteristics of the sector which made it inappropriate, or impractical, to apply the general trading conditions of the Community, at least in the first instance. In particular, the traditional use of transport sector policies in the member states as an instrument of regional and national economic development policy, and as an instrument in social policy, had produced complex, but diverse, sets of internal regulations of the sectors in the member states. An immediate introduction of a liberal transport regime could only have been achieved at the expense of these other objectives – see Gwilliam (1980).

The transition path from the highly regulated national transport markets to a liberal Community transport market was thus seen to require progressive harmonisation of the conditions of operation and constraints in the national transport markets. At the behest of the Council of Ministers the Commission prepared a strategy for this transition which was embodied in the Schauus Memorandum (EC Commission, 1961) followed by a plan for a legislative programme to achieve its objectives – the Action Plan of 1962.

The nature of that strategy has been described as a rational comprehensive approach to policy making. The memorandum set out to provide a complete logical structure on which a new policy could be founded. The legislative programme was directed at the ultimate implementation of this structure through the elimination of any elements of national policy variation which might act as a distortion within it. Whilst logically elegant, the weakness of this approach was that, given the impossibility of doing everything at once, the path of transition would inevitably involve upsetting existing, delicate, balances of policy instruments in the member states (see Gwilliam, 1980).

The elements of that strategy were very wide ranging. Firstly, it was aimed at eliminating such direct obstacles to the achievement of the common market as a whole as conscious national discrimination in rates and unnecessary physical and administrative barriers to crossing internal frontiers. Secondly, it aimed at the integration of international movement within the Community through the harmonisation of fiscal, social and technical conditions of operation as the basis for fair and free competition between modes and between countries. Thirdly, and ultimately, it aimed at the establishment of a common national transport regulation system within the Community through such measures as a common licensing system for entry to the transport markets, mandatory transport price regimes, and common charges systems for infrastructure (see Gwilliam, 1980, 1985).

11.2 Transport policy development in the incomplete market

The stance adopted by the Commission was widely described as 'harmonisation before liberalisation'. Given that implementation of the policy required legislation by the Council of Ministers which operated on the convention of unanimity on major issues, and that changes in the direction of harmonisation might well have very significant effects on the member state which had to move furthest to harmonise, there was a great deal of inertia in the system. Even such apparently apolitical matters as maximum permissible road vehicle weights and dimensions became great stumbling blocks and Commission draft regulations on the topic lay on the table, without implementation for over a decade.

A further very important impediment to the development of an effective policy arose in the area of implementation. Much of the early policy emphasis concerned the road transport sector, which was very fragmented in all member states. Even if there was a whole-hearted commitment to common policy development, controls over vehicle dimensions, pricing regimes, working hours and the like required enormous administrative effort. Where the whole-hearted commitment did not exist it was very easy for member states to make legislation a dead letter. That appears to have been the case in the control of drivers' hours and the enforcement of the mandatory bracket tariff for international road haulage.

Growing realisation by the Commission of its impotence in these areas led to a change of emphasis, away from harmonisation in the field of operations to harmonisation in the field of infrastructure. In this respect the European Parliament's formal powers over the budget did enable a small Community transport infrastructure budget to be allocated. But it was too small to be of any real effect. On common infrastructure charging regimes there was much study and a little preparatory regulation (such as the enforcement of a common basis of assessment for road vehicle taxation) but little effective common action.

The entry of the United Kingdom in 1973 introduced into the EC a transport regime which was in some respects already very liberal. Entry to the domestic road haulage market had been deregulated prior to UK entry and, partly as a corollary to this rail charges were also, at least in principle, free of any government control. The balance of argument about both the path and the pace of movement to full liberalisation was inevitably changed. The election of the first Thatcher government resulted in the extension of this liberalisation to first the long distance and then the local bus sectors, and resulted in a much more critical approach to subsidy of transport operation. Insofar as harmonisation tended to be towards the most liberal of the existing members regimes that reference point shifted dramatically.

The entry of Spain and Greece to the EC added a new dimension to the problem of peripherality. Not only were these relatively low income members, but they were also physically peripheral. The tension between economic liberalism and income redistribution which resulted will almost certainly add to the calls both for an increased Community transport infrastructure investment budget and for allocation to be based on the criterion of reducing peripherality rather than eliminating bottlenecks.

11.3 Infrastructure policy

The Community turned its efforts to securing a common policy on transport infrastructure at a time when the efforts to secure a common set of regulations on operation were failing. It appeared to be felt that the fact that infrastructure activity was primarily undertaken directly by governments would make it easier both to secure agreement on a policy and to ensure effective implementation. Two major thrusts were made, concerning charges for the use of infrastructure and a common investment budget. The development of those initiatives, and the problems they faced have been discussed in detail elsewhere (Gwilliam, 1984). As feared, neither has come to fruition. The important issue now is whether that failure is likely to be a crucial hindrance to the completion of the internal market.

The first element of the infrastructure initiative concerned charging for the use of roads. Early theoretical studies undertaken by the Community reached the conclusion that charges should be related to marginal social costs of use, but should also cover the total costs of provision in each member state. This work was supplemented by case studies to clarify the implications for levels and structures of charges and to establish the practicability of the principle. Some groundwork for the implementation of a common regime was laid by the creation of a common approach to defining vehicle weights for taxation purposes. But that is as far as matters have gone.

More recently the Commission has examined the differences in road haulage operating costs between member states and has argued that despite differences in wage levels and taxation structures there exist only relatively small differences in costs of operation between states. Only Greece and Spain appear to have about a 15 per cent advantage, and this is attributed primarily to labour costs. The attitude which now appears to prevail is that the United States's inter-state haulage business has been successfully deregulated despite differences in state taxation levels, and there is no reason to expect the absence of a common taxation structure to be a serious impediment in EC.

That view is not accepted by all. In particular, there is a growing resistance to the unilateral imposition of new charges, or types of charge, which appear to impinge differentially on international hauliers. For example, a greater reliance on tolls or direct charges on transit traffic exercised by some member states only (for example by West Germany in 1988) is seen as a significant new distortion.

A procedure for consultation between member states on major infrastructure proposals has existed since the mid-1960s, amended in 1978 to extend its coverage and ensure that consultation took place at an early enough stage to be effective. Without a common infrastructure budget this was at best a very weak instrument and appears to have had little practical effect.

In 1980 the Commission attempted to overcome this weakness by proposing a special financial instrument for the support of infrastructure investment of EC interest. That initiative was helped along by two essentially incidental events. Firstly, the European Parliament chose to use this particular channel to test its power over the Community budget. Although the budget involved was minute the Parliament did succeed in creating a budget head and the first allocations under it were made in 1984. Secondly, as part of the political process of renegotiating the British contribution, means were sought to allow Britain to claw back contributions within the existing institutional procedures. EC contributions to British road investment formed part of the deal.

Further formal steps have included a study of bottlenecks within the transport system of the Community, and the commissioning of studies of means of identifying and measuring the Community interest in infrastructure projects. But these have not led to any increase in the size of the budget, or the establishment of agreement on the basis on which progress might be made. In particular, there remain unresolved questions about the criteria on which investment should be allocated. On the one hand a bottlenecks approach would imply the use of some form of cost–benefit analysis in which the returns on projects (either gross or net of the benefits to the country in which the project was located) is used as the touchstone. On the other hand a peripherality approach would view transport infrastructure as an instrument for achieving greater physical integration in the Community and a reduction in the transport cost disadvantage of the peripheral countries. Clearly the different approaches would select very different programmes.

That conflict does exist, of course, even at the national level. It is typically resolved by high level political judgements on programme priorities. In the absence of any central political institution in the Community capable of making those kind of judgements, several member states remain opposed to an EC programme for infra-structure investment and, by the end of 1988, there was little sign of the deadlock being broken.

11.4 The road freight market

The Commission has always seen the route to the liberalisation of international road freight movement coming through the progressive expansion of the number of EC-wide licences available, and the availability of those licences for all activities including cabotage. The Community quota was first introduced in 1969 and has been increased slowly since. In June 1988 the Council finally reached the momentous decision to eliminate all quantitative restrictions by the end of 1992. To that end a regulation increased the Community quota by 40 per cent for 1988 and 1989 and gave an uncon-ditional legal commitment that from 1 January 1993 access would be based on qualitat-ive considerations only, and would not be subject to quota. Moreover, the commitment was not made dependent on any other accompanying steps of harmonisation.

The slow progress to technical and social harmonisation continues. In the technical field the weight and dimensions for five- and six-axled vehicles have already been harmonised, but discussions on the regulations to apply to two-, three- and four-axle vehicles are continuing. In the social field working hours and rest periods for professional drivers have been agreed for some time; the problem here is that even the Commission concedes that these conditions are implemented with very differing degrees of commitment in some states compared with others.

It is clear that the Commission recognises the importance to the completion of the internal market of having freedom of establishment throughout the market. They have therefore put forward proposals to allow non-resident undertakings to operate temporarily in any other member state subject only to the same conditions as national undertakings. Such proposals are consistent with the Treaty of Rome, have been confirmed by the Court of Justice and identified explicitly as part of the necessary requirements for completion of the internal market. But to be effective such freedom would depend on sufficient degree of similarity in the conditions of entry to the national markets, or sufficiently liberal derogations for non-resident enterprises, for the nationality of origin not to be a serious impediment. So far little progress appears to have been made on this front and the road haulage industry appears to have come to the conclusion that it will be much more effective to get round any residual impediments by buying local subsidiaries in countries where they wish to engage in cabotage rather than rely on resolution of the formal problems.

The EC is rapidly retreating from control of rates. Introduced originally on a mandatory basis for international road freight in 1968, it was envisaged that the forked tariff, specifying upper and lower permissible rates, would ultimately be extended to all long distance road haulage. In the event it was replaced first of all by the reference tariff, and, with the expiry of the existing tariff regulations at the end of 1989 it may well be that no tariff rules of any kind may thereafter be specified.

11.5 Road passenger transport

Long distance coaching has been severely discriminated against in most member states in the interests of protecting the preferred, rail operator in the long distance passenger market. Britain was in the lead in eliminating this protection by deregulating the express coach sector entirely in 1980. It is a sign of the magnitude of change in Community thinking that the Commission should now be urging on the Council measures to introduce freedom to provide international road passenger transport services and to simplify administration in this area. A proposal to this end was presented to the Council in December 1988, though no action was immediately taken.

The Community has never had an urban transport policy as such. Nor, indeed, have some of the member states, urban policies being seen as a matter of local determination in response to local variation both of circumstances and objectives. It is difficult to see any reason why that should change. The major recent exception to this position appears to be the move, exemplified in the DRIVE initiative, for EC to take the lead in stimulating collaborative research on roads and urban transport issues. The DRIVE programme is involving academic and research institutions throughout the EC in technical studies on matters as disparate as road safety and automatic vehicle guidance.

11.6 Rail transport policy

Rail transport policy has always been a difficult area for the formulation of a common, liberal, policy because of the role which it has traditionally been given in many member states as an instrument in the implementation of government policies both on regional development and on income distribution. As the corollory of the attribution of these roles rail transport has typically been provided by a statutory, nationally owned undertaking, either directly or indirectly subsidised. This approach to rail transport conflicts with Community aspirations about fair competition both within the transport sector between modes, and externally between locations.

The initial attempt to square this circle was embodied in a Council decision of May 1965 that railway undertakings should be treated as financially autonomous, and that any special obligations which were imposed on them should be the subject of explicit subsidy. A series of regulations legitimised direct compensation for public service obligations (1191/69), employment and pension obligations (1192/69) and to countervail undercharging for infrastructure by other modes (1107/70). Subsequent regulations on common rail accounting systems (2830/77) and uniform principles for the costing of international rail traffic (2183/78) added little to the reality of the regime. In the event the compensatory principles were not converted into an *ex ante* determination of the level to which state support could legitimately be allowed to rise. Instead, they appear to have been used, *ex post*, in an arbitrary way, to allocate the deficits that arose from essentially unconstrained government rail-financing policies. Rail deficits rose despite rather than because of the regulations on rail finance.

The Commission itself recognised the irrelevance of its existing legislation when it published, in 1980, a new memorandum on rail policy in the eighties (COM (80) 752f). It argued that the railway managements had been unable to adapt to new needs because of the nineteenth-century rigidity of both their structures and their technology, the intervention of governments preventing them from abandoning traditional but no longer sensible activities, inadequate investment funding, low operational efficiency and lack of a Community dimension in policy formation. It therefore proposed that a number of new directions should be pursued in an attempt to establish a sound basis for future rail development. Some, such as greater cooperation between railways and the promotion of combined transport, were strictly matters for rail management. Others, such as a better separation of the commercial and the social activities of railways, a clearer definition of the respective roles of the railway management and the state, and the writing off of historic debts so that railways could better finance investments for the future, had already been implemented to a large degree in the United Kingdom. Perhaps the most radical proposal was that to separate responsibilities for planning and investing in the network, which would rest with government, from that of operating services on the network, which would be the responsibility of rail management.

Following a further memorandum in January 1984 the Council of Ministers reached agreement in December 1986 on the principles to be adopted for the future financing of the railways. Current charges representing the servicing of past debts were to be reduced; differences between the systems of payment for infrastructure by rail and other modes were to be eliminated; compensation for public service obligations was to be in the form of contract payments; and a suitable discipline should be imposed on deficits outside these arrangements. By the end of 1988, however, no concrete progress had been achieved towards the implementation of the principles.

In rail transport as for other modes the Commission has from time to time identified and reconsidered the definition of a trunk network of major EC interest. Looked at from the point of view of the national systems the major networks defined have looked curiously unrealistic. For example the routes selected in the United Kingdom did not appear to take any cognisance at all of the current configuration of rail flows. Looking to the future, the Commission has now identified, in a report of June 1986, a European high speed network. Insofar as it is more restricted, and more closely based on projects under consideration by national rail systems, it looks more realistic. But it would still appear to be the case that the Community institutions themselves have neither the competence nor the skills to progress the plans, the future of which seems to be essentially dependent on the commitment of the national governments.

11.7 Air transport policy

Because of its highly international character, and the complexity of the interaction between international and inter-EC air transport activities, the development of a Community air transport policy has to be seen against the background of the international regulatory framework.

There are two central elements to this international framework. Firstly, because governments view their airspace as well as their landspace as part of the national sovereignty, any movements between and over national states must have the agreements of the governments concerned. A framework for those agreements was established by the Chicago Convention in 1944, built upon by a series of essentially bilateral agreements of which those between the United States and the United Kingdom (Bermuda 1 and Bermuda 2) have been particularly significant as the models on which many others have been based. Despite a trend to increasing liberality within these agreements, national governments retain the essential rights over access to their territories and hence the power to bargain over the exchange of those rights.

The second element to the international regime has been the agreements between operators through the International Air Transport Association (IATA) concerning fares and other commercial aspects of international aviation. In this aspect of international regulation what has historically been a very tight cartel enforcing common standards of service, high availability, and relatively high fares has come under increasing pressure from a number of directions. The development of charter and inclusive tour operations, sanctioned bilaterally by mutually benefited governments, has almost totally eroded the traditional IATA tight control and has encouraged schedule airlines to protect themselves by increasingly complex promotional and discriminatory pricing arrangements. The whole-hearted commitment of the United States to liberalisation since 1978 has contributed greatly to the break-up of the international cartel power.

Given the nature of the control mechanisms liberalisation of air transport within the EC could take place only insofar as individual countries deregulated their domestic transport, pairs of member states by mutual agreement liberalised the trade between them, or the Community adopted regulations enforcing a liberal policy on all member states. These three routes to liberalisation will now be discussed in turn.

By very definition domestic action is confined to air routes wholly within a member state. The direct significance of action on this front for Community-wide movements is thus limited, though it may have indirect significance as an indicator of the direction of intent.

The general position in the member states of the EC is that the air transport sector has been specifically excluded from the applications of national rules on competition. The exercise of limitations on entry and on prices, often associated with the reservation of the market for a state-owned monopoly operator, has thus been unchallenged. In April 1986 the European Court of Justice ruled, in the Nouvelles Frontières case that Community competition rules did apply to air transport and that it was thus illegal for governments to control fares. But it also observed that air transport had been specifically excluded from the application of Regulation 17, and that it would thus require a special procedural regulation to enable the Commission to effectively implement Articles 85 and 86 in this sector. As a consequence, liberalisation in domestic markets has taken place only where the national government wished it to.

Of the member states only the United Kingdom has had both a sufficiently large domestic air transport sector and sufficient will to liberalise for effective action to have occurred. The formal position existing in the United Kingdom since the Civil Aviation Act of 1971 has been that licences were issued by the quasi independent Civil Aviation Authority (CAA) within the general policy directions set out in published government policy guidelines. In April 1981 a pro-competitive policy guidance statement specified the objectives of increasing choice, improving efficiency, and stimulating innovation by incumbent carriers, with the implication that this might be achieved through sanctioning competitive entry. A CAA report on Airline Competition Policy in July 1984 proposed the introduction of area licensing, which would enable approved carriers to fly any route of their choice within the total market and the replacement of specific approval of air fares with fare filing. A subsequent policy guidelines paper of January 1985 recommended free access to some domestic routes, and although this was dropped in July of the same year, fare filing was introduced and much freer entry also ensued.

The first effective direct competition occurred in October 1982, when British Midland were licensed on the Heathrow to Glasgow route in competition with BA; subsequent direct competition has occurred on the routes from Heathrow to Edinburgh, Belfast and Manchester, and through licences granted to the same destinations from different London airports. The effects of this partial deregulation have not been dramatic. Full fares do not appear to have been reduced. Discount fares appear to have received a once-for-all reduction at the time of new entry which, together with more sophisticated forms of price discrimination appears to have generated extra traffic and enabled higher combined frequencies to be maintained. The number of operators, even on the most attractive routes remains small (two or three).

In addition to the United Kingdom the Netherlands government has also adopted a broadly liberal view on air transport through the achievement of a new liberal agreement for air travel between the two countries in July 1984. The new agreement provided for extension of the range of operations licensed and gave carriers much greater freedom to determine fares. In a recent OECD review it was estimated that this liberalisation had increased the traffic growth rate by 3–5 per cent per annum. Full fares appear to have increased slightly, but there has been a proliferation of discount ticket types, with the lowest fares available being very substantially reduced.

Article 84 of the Treaty of Rome apparently left it for subsequent determination by the Council of Ministers the extent to which, and procedures by which, provisions should be laid down for sea and air transport. The implication that these modes of transport need not be incorporated in the Community integration process was always disputed by the Commission, whose views were upheld by ruling of the Court of Justice in 1974 and 1978 to the effect that sea and air transport were governed by the general rules of the Treaty unless the Council positively decided otherwise.

Early initiatives in air transport policy included little more than the creation of a consultation procedure over member states' negotiations with third parties in 1979 and a directive on accident investigation in 1980. The first real sign of liberalisation came in the directive on inter-regional air services in 1983. This directive provided for a greater freedom of fare setting on services using small aircraft between non-major airports. As a step towards a more thorough liberalisation it was overtaken in substance by the bilateral arrangements particularly that between the United Kingdom and the Netherlands, and it was subsequently modified to allow its applications to flights from regional airports into major airports.

The combination of increasing external pressures to deregulate and the approach of 1992 has more recently produced some much more significant action in the wide-ranging package of measures adopted in December, 1987. Regulations 3975 and 3976 laid down a procedure for the application of the rules of competition to the air sector and provided for the application of Article 85 of the Treaty to some types of agreement in the sector. Block exemptions from the application of competition policy would be subject to strict control. These were accompanied by a directive on fares and a decision on the sharing of capacity which substantially reduced the scope for the exercise of national sovereignty by setting objective criteria for the range within which fares and the protection of the national share of markets could be limited. Multiple designation was provided for on some of the major intra-EC routes, while the creation of new traffic rights between regional and major airports opened the way for more extensive competition between the major hubs. The package also committed the Community to further measures of liberalisation.

At this stage it is difficult to tell how far these new initiatives will go. Certainly the thrust is to increase competition both by direct entry on to existing routes and by the creation of new competing network structures. Commercial freedom is to be increased. But the state-owned carriers in most of the member states will retain interests in maintaining some degree of restriction, which at least some of the governments will not wish to see jeopardised.

11.8 Shipping policy

As for air transport, it was not really until the Court of Justice decisions of 1974 and 1978 that a comprehensive Community policy began to be developed. The move to develop a maritime policy was accelerated by the entry of Britain and Denmark, which made sea transport an important part of the internal transport system of the Community, by the subsequent entry of Greece as a major shipping nation, and by the increasing impact of flags of convenience since 1975. Thus from the mid-1970s the Community began to take *ad hoc* measures in the maritime field, and in April 1985 set out the framework in a policy document.

The EC is the biggest trading block in the world, its trade with third countries accounting for about 20 per cent by value of both world exports and imports. About 95 per cent of Community trade with third countries and 30 per cent of intra-EC trade is carried by sea. Despite increasing trade, the size of the EC flagged fleet and its share of trade had fallen by about a quarter in the first half of the 1980s. This loss of share was associated with the expansion of national intervention in other countries both in the form of direct subsidy and cargo reservation, particularly by the state-trading countries, and with the increasing practice of shipping being operated under flags of convenience to secure lower labour costs, less strict operating conditions and more favourable tax treatment. The essential problem facing the EC is therefore that of reconciling the wish to secure a free market in shipping with the existence of an external environment in which there is already much discrimination and distortion.

Historically, much general cargo shipping, throughout the world, has been handled by the liner conferences. These are cartels of operators agreeing, on an area of trade basis, a schedule of services, a tariff, and forms of traffic protection such as loyalty rebates, etc. As such they appear to be clearly contrary to the spirit of the competition rules of the Community, though the doubts about the applicability of the Treaty to the maritime sector appears to have deferred for a long time any formal challenge to their legality.

In a draft regulation in 1981 the Commission set out to regularise this. It was proposed to grant an exemption to liner conferences and loyalty agreements from the conditions of Article 85 of the Treaty conditional on the good conduct of parties, with the Commission, and ultimately the Court of Justice, monitoring and enforcing reasonable behaviour. The thrust of policy here was to recognise the existence of benefits arising from cartelisation in this particular trade, but to ensure that procedures existed to prevent the exploitation of such cartelisation.

A further set of problems remains to be faced. The entry into the Community of members with substantial amounts of domestic shipping opens up the possibility of cabotage activity on a grand scale. It remains to be seen whether the member states can be moved quickly to the situation in which there are no effective barriers to entry in these trades within the EC.

The major external problem facing the EC was cargo reservation, which not only discriminates against the activities of cross-traders in the shipping markets, but also increases shipping costs by protecting at least part of the trade for operators who would not be able to obtain it in a freely competitive market. Cargo reservation was effectively being operated by the state-trading nations through the imposition of conditions of purchase and sale of commodities and through direct shipping subsidy. It was also being claimed extensively by Third World countries as a means of assisting their development, based on the United Nations Liners Code agreement that it was permissible for developing countries to require a 40:40:20 split of liner-borne trade between themselves, their trading partners and cross-traders. A coordinated EC policy to these matters was agreed in 1983, known as the Brussels package.

The Brussels package agreed to the 40:40:20 rule only for liner trade with the Third World, and insisted that for trades with other nations multilateralism should apply. Moreover, the extension of the code to the bulk trades, as proposed in UNCTAD V at Manila, was subsequently opposed. In a Council decision of December 1983 member nations were required to consult with each other before introducing countermeasures in retaliation against discrimination by third parties. The thrust of the policy in this area was thus to limit the extension of constraints on free trading in shipping services to liner trade with developing countries, and to progressively develop effective means of enforcing that approach.

Internally, within the inland waterway system the problem for the last twenty years has been perceived as that of structural over-capacity. In an attempt to resolve the problem the Commission presented to the Council in May 1988 a proposal for a two-part system involving measures to harmonise national capacity scrapping schemes, along with arrangements to avoid the impact of this being cancelled out by new vessels being brought into service.

The maintenance of appropriate controls on safety and environmental pollution standards for all shipping involved in EC trades is seen as important both for its own sake, and because failure to apply standards equally would have the effect of discriminating in favour of those, whether within the EC or external to it, who applied the lowest standards. It is, however, a very complicated one since the country of registration of a ship (the flag carried) often differs from the country in which it is owned. Hence action to tighten enforcement on flags of convenience might in some respects be militating against some internal interests within the EC.

Following the Amoco Cadiz disaster a series of recommendations and directives were adopted in 1978 to improve safety at sea for Community vessels. In 1980 the Commission proposed a directive to improve the enforcement of international standards of safety and pollution prevention for all shipping using EC ports, which, although not adopted, was the basis of a memorandum of understanding signed in 1982, and a further ministerial conference on the matter in April 1986. The thrust of the policy is thus to agree common standards internally and to enforce, for all shipping entering EC ports, international standards. Whether the enforcement capability exists to make this effective is less certain.

11.9 Conclusions

Despite some initial progress in eliminating conscious national discrimination, transport policy in the Community has subsequently developed very slowly. In particular, liberalisation of the transport market has always been retarded by the philosophy which called for harmonisation of the conditions under which competition would take place before the liberalisation of markets to that competition could be allowed.

That is not surprising. The regulatory regimes in the separate national transport markets were subtly different, and involved delicate balances of instruments. Measures to secure uniformity in any one particular dimension might well upset these regulatory balances in very significant ways in individual countries. Thus, for example, the United Kingdom has been very loth to agree to technical harmonisation of heavy goods vehicle weights and dimensions because these played a much more important role in determining modal split in the United Kingdom than elsewhere because of the much greater freedom of entry to the road haulage market. The attempt to make progress by concentrating on infrastructure policy rather than operational controls was also unfruitful for rather similar reasons.

Many of the problems of harmonisation are unresolved and look likely to remain so until after 1992. Curiously, however, that looks to be less of a problem now than at any time hitherto. There are a number of reasons for this. Firstly, the world transport environment is now much more liberal than it was, and there seems to be some evidence that differences in conditions of operation between locations are both smaller than was imagined and likely to be less significant as distortions. Secondly, within the Community itself several member states have a much greater commitment to liberality in their domestic transport markets than hitherto; in such circumstances it is much more difficult to resist liberalisation at the Community level. Finally, the increasing multinationalisation of business has offered the aspiring entrepreneur an alternative route of escape from differential national restrictions on his freedom of operation.

In those circumstances it is likely that the emphasis in the common transport effort will move back to the much more pragmatic level of responding to situations where there exist blatant distortions of significance, and to attempting to positively identify actions in which there is a common interest. It will be all the better for that.

12 EC energy policy

F. McGowan

Since the early 1950s, the idea of a Common Energy Policy (CEP) for the EC has been on and off the political agenda many times. In the years since the EC was founded numerous policy proposals have been made by the Commission, although they have been marked by a shifting balance of priorities and a range of proposed mechanisms, depending on the conditions in the energy markets and the influence of the Commission. For the most part, these attempts have come to nothing, with member states variously rejecting or ignoring them. However, there has, in the last few years, been a renewed focus on energy issues, as the momentum of the single-market debate has gathered pace and environmental concerns have intensified. As a result, a CEP looks more likely now than for many decades.

This chapter seeks to analyse why current developments may result in a CEP and what that policy may mean for the energy sector as a whole. It notes past attempts to create a CEP and assesses the factors behind their failure. After discussing the current policy proposals and the context to them, the chapter reviews the situation in the different energy industries of the EC, noting their main characteristics and the balance of past and present EC policy towards them. Finally it assesses some of the difficulties the Commission faces in developing a credible energy policy.

12.1 Past attempts and present successes

12.1.1 The Treaties and energy

That the EC attached great importance to the energy sector is demonstrated by the fact that two of the three treaties on which the EC is based are concerned with energy specifically: the ECSC and Euratom Treaties were devoted to the coal and nuclear sectors. The details of these treaties (and their rationale) are covered elsewhere, but their significance for energy policy is clear enough. The 1951 ECSC Treaty reflected the dominance of coal in the energy balances of member states (as well as its role in the steel industry); by tackling coal, most EC energy supply and demand issues were addressed. The 1957 Euratom Treaty sought to foster cooperation in the development of civil nuclear power, then perceived as the main source of future energy requirements (Lucas, 1977). Both treaties, moreover, were in principle geared towards the creation of free and integrated markets in these sectors: the ECSC sought to abolish all barriers to trade between member states while controlling subsidies and cartel-like behaviour amongst producers; Euratom also paid lip-service to the idea of a common market in nuclear products.

A common market for other energy sectors was addressed in the Rome Treaty. While the EEC was orientated towards more or less competitively structured sectors, it was also intended to cover the more oligopolistic or monopolistic sectors such as oil, gas and electricity. Accordingly in addition to being subject to the EEC Treaty's general provisions on opening up markets, these energy industries' special characteristics were covered by the Treaty's provisions on state enterprises and their conduct.

12.1.2 Policy efforts 1951–73

The gap between intentions expressed in the treaties and the outcomes, however, has been a large one for energy, more so than for most other parts of the economy. The Commission's attempts to develop an energy policy of any sort, let alone one reflecting the ideals of the treaties, have proved to be only of limited success.

From the 1950s on the Commission or its equivalents sought to develop a policy first for coal and then for energy more broadly. On coal, the High Authority was unable to impose the spirit of the Paris Treaty on national industries; it was mainly involved in tackling the crises which beset the European coal industry from the mid-1950s on (Lindberg and Scheingold, 1970). In the sphere of energy more generally, initial efforts took place as the negotiations for the EEC were progressing. The Messina conference recommended that the potential for coordinated energy policy be considered but the Spaak Committee determined that this would not be necessary (von Geusan, 1975).

Following the establishment of the new Communities, there was a renewed attempt to develop a CEP. The formation of an inter-executive committee on energy in 1959 sought to develop a policy focusing on the creation of a common energy market. The main concerns of the committee were with the effect of energy prices on industrial competitiveness and, to a lesser extent, security of energy supply (PEP, 1963). However, governments largely rejected the committee's attempts to gain access to energy policy; instead they exercised benign neglect towards the energy sector. This inertia on energy policy reflected the largely untroubled energy markets of the period. However, when there was concern over supply in the 1950s and 1960s (such as in the wake of the Suez crisis), governments were keen to retain their autonomy.

The merger of the Communities in 1968 saw the Commission renew its efforts to develop a CEP. In its document 'First Guidelines Towards a EC Energy Policy' (EC

Commission, 1968), the Commission noted that barriers to trade in energy persisted and stressed the necessity of a common energy market. Such a market, based on the needs of consumers and competitive pressures, would help obtain security of energy supplies at the lowest cost. To this end the Commission suggested three broad objectives: a plan for the sector involving data collection and forecasting as a means of influencing members' investment strategies; measures to bring about a common energy market (tackling issues such as tax harmonisation, technical barriers, state monopolies, etc.); and measures to ensure security of supply at lowest cost.

The proposals proved difficult to put into practice in part because of the scale of objectives and the contradictions between the substance of different goals but mainly because of the resistance of member states to the goals. Even though the Council approved the strategy, it ignored most of the Commission's attempts to enact the proposals. The principal measures adopted in the wake of the Commission's proposals concerned oil stocks (following OECD initiatives) and some requirements for energy investment notification. These actions owed more to growing concern about security of supply than the creation of a common energy market, and presaged a wider shift in Commission and member state perceptions of the priorities of energy policy.

Table 12.1 Primary energy production, consumption and net imports in the EC 1950–85

	1950	1955	EC(6) 1960	1965	1970	EC(9) 1975	EC(10) 1980	EC(12) 1985[b]	Million Tonnes oil equivalent EC(12) 1987[c]
Primary energy production									
Coal/solid fuels	243	277	267	253	200	274	269	248	168
Oil	3	8	17	24	21	18	138	230	148
N gas	1	6	14	24	86	209	199	189	128
Nuclear/hydro	6	9	13	14	16	26	39	79	155
Total	253	300	311	314	323	526	645	744	599
Total net imports[a]	22	70	129	273	480	607	609	587	461
Inland energy consumption									
Coal/solid fuels	238	291	285	270	235	286	324	342	232
Oil	30	64	128	278	464	598	630	631	473
N gas	1	6	14	24	86	221	259	278	199
Nuclear/hydro	6	9	13	15	18	28	41	81	156
Total	275	370	440	588	804	1,133	1,254	1,331	1,060

Notes
[a] Net imports includes bunkers and stocks.
[b] 1985 uses EC(12) to indicate current Community energy conditions.
[c] The figures in this column are not comparable with the rest of the table due to different sources and the use of 'oil' rather than 'coal' equivalence.

Source: UN *World Energy Supplies* and *Statistics of World Energy*, various years, and Eurostat, various years.

The reaction to the 1973–4 oil crisis confirmed the change in orientation of energy policy proposals away from markets and towards security.

12.1.3 Energy crises

The backdrop for the new emphasis on security of supply was the development of the Community's energy balances and the changes in global energy markets generally. Since the 1950s the member states had become less reliant upon domestically produced coal and more on imported resources, primarily oil. This shift in demand reflected the growth in energy demand overall but also a gradual but absolute decline in energy resources among the then member states. By 1970 over 60 per cent of the EC's needs were imported, leaving it highly vulnerable to the supply disruptions and price increases of 1973–4 (see Table 12.1).

In the midst of the first oil shock, the EC attempted a crisis management role but failed even to provide a united front *vis-à-vis* OAPEC over their oil embargo of the Netherlands (Daintith and Hancher, 1986). Member states pursued their own policies or worked through the International Energy Agency (IEA). Formed in 1974, the IEA overshadowed the EC both in breadth of membership (covering all the OECD countries except France) and in terms of its powers on oil sharing in a new crisis (van der Linde and Lefeber, 1988).

Even so the shock of oil price increases reinforced the reassessment of energy policies in member states and the Commission. The Commission attempted to develop a more strategic approach to the management of energy supply and demand. The 'New strategy' (*Bulletin of the European Communities*, Supplement 4, 1974), which was agreed to only after much wrangling and dilution (a proposal for a European energy agency was abandoned after member state opposition – see Lucas, 1977), envisaged a number of targets to be met by 1985 (COM (74) 1960). These included the reduction of oil imports, the development of domestic energy capabilities (notably nuclear power) and the rational use of energy (see Table 12.2). The policy, while only indicative, mobilised resources for R&D and promotional programmes on energy, covering conventional and nuclear technologies but also renewables and energy-efficiency technologies. The new strategy also provided the basis for a handful of directives designed to restrict the use of oil and gas.

The policy clearly entailed a change in emphasis for energy policy and the goal of a common energy market was demoted, although it was alluded to in areas such as pricing policies and some measures directed at the oil sector (see below). Overall, policy was concerned with changing the structure of energy balances rather than the structure of energy markets. The condition of energy markets (notably after the second oil shock) and concern over energy prices and security in the early 1980s was such that the policy was sustained into the decade. Further rounds of energy policy objectives were agreed in 1979 (to be met by 1990) and 1986 (for 1995). The 1995 objectives included a number of horizontal objectives, aimed at more general energy policy concerns, such as its relationship with other EC policies. Each round sought to

Table 12.2 The Community's energy objectives for 1985, 1990 and 1995

1985 objectives
To increase nuclear power capacity to 200 GW.
To increase Community production of oil and natural gas to 180 million tonnes oil equivalent.
To maintain production of coal in the Community at 180 million tonnes oil equivalent.
To keep imports to no more than 40 per cent of consumption.
To reduce projected demand for 1985 by 15 per cent.
To raise electricity contribution to final energy consumption to 35 per cent.

1990 objectives
Reduce to 0.7 or less the average ratio between the rate of growth in gross primary energy demand and the rate of growth of gross domestic product.
Reduce oil consumption to a level of 40 per cent of primary energy consumption.
To cover 70–75 per cent of primary energy requirements for electricity production by means of solid fuels and nuclear energy.
To encourage the use of renewable energy sources so as to increase their contribution to the Community's energy supplies.
To pursue energy pricing policies geared to attaining the energy objectives.

1995 objectives
To improve the efficiency of final energy demand by 20 per cent.
To maintain oil consumption at around 40 per cent of energy consumption and to maintain net oil imports at else than one-third of total energy consumption.
To maintain the share of natural gas in the energy balance on the basis of a policy aimed at ensuring stable and diversified supplies.
To increase the share of solid fuels in energy consumption.
To pursue efforts to promote consumption of solid fuels and improve the competitiveness of their production capacities in the Community.
To reduce the proportion of electricity generated by hydrocarbons to less than 15 per cent.
To increase the share of renewables in energy balances.
To ensure more secure conditions of supply and reduce risks of energy price fluctuations.
To apply Community price formation principles to all sectors.
To balance energy and environmental concerns through the use of best available technologies.
To implement measures to improve energy balance in less developed regions of the Community.
To develop a single energy market.
To coordinate external relations in energy sector.

build on the previous one and although in general the goals appeared to be on target in some cases they reflected a degree of failure either across the EC or in certain member states, and subsequent rounds would adopt a rather less ambitious agenda (COM (84) 88 and COM (88) 174).

By the mid-1980s, therefore, the Commission had succeeded in establishing a place in energy policy making, but it was far from being central to member states' energy policy agendas, let alone one being effectively influential enough to dictate the development of a common energy market. Instead it consisted of information gathering, target setting and enabling activities (the latter had a substantial budget for energy R&D and promotion). While these measures ensured that the Commission had an influence on policy, they still had many problems: some of the objectives were showing few signs of achievement while aspects of the Commission's funding strategies were also open to criticism (Cruickshank and Walker, 1981). Moreover, aside from a few legislative measures, the Commission's policy had few teeth. The locus of power remained with national governments which generally chose to follow their own energy policies, resisting too strong a Commission role.

12.1.4 The new energy agenda

In the course of the 1980s, however, the agenda for energy policy began to change. Developments in energy markets, the attitudes of governments towards the energy industries and the overall position of the Commission in policy making contributed to a turnaround in the concerns of EC energy policy.

A key factor in this changed regime was the shift in energy markets. Prices stabilised and faltered in the early 1980s and continued to weaken until the 1986 oil price collapse. The reasons for this were more fundamental than the rows within OPEC which precipitated the fall in prices. The price increases of the early 1980s had had the effect of boosting output in OPEC countries, as well as fostering exploration and production in the rest of world. Furthermore, many countries had sought to improve energy efficiency and diversify sources of energy (if not to the levels sought by the Commission). The economic recession of the 1980s also dampened demand. The combined effect of these factors was a massive over-capacity in supply and minimal demand growth (see Table 12.1) which forced down prices. The effects were not only confined to oil: gas and coal were also in plentiful supply, while the consequences of past over-investment in electricity capacity also boosted the energy surplus.

The combined effect of these developments was to weaken the scarcity culture which had prevailed among suppliers, consumers, governments and the Commission. As prices fell and markets appeared well supplied so the concerns of policy focused less on energy supply *per se* and more on the price of supply and existence of obstacles to the lowest price.

This change in market conditions made many energy policies, especially those fostering conservation or diversification from high price fuels, hard to sustain. In any case, in some countries, governments were abandoning energy policy. The United Kingdom was the most notable example, making an explicit move to rely on market forces for determining supply and demand. A major plank of that policy was deregulation, with attempts to introduce competition to gas and power, and privatisation, with the sale of oil interests and then the gas and electricity industries (Helm, Kay and Thompson, 1989). Similar policies were under review in other parts of the EC (Helm and McGowan, 1989), although these were often conceived at a less ambitious level or pursued for rather different reasons.

The deregulatory thrust was not confined to the energy sector – indeed it was probably more widely spread initially in other areas of the economy. It was, for example, to the fore in the Commission's plans for the single European market (SEM) as covered in the White Paper (EC Commission, 1985a). Partly as a reflection of past energy policy failures, the Commission did not include energy in the initial agenda for the SEM. However, areas where energy was affected indirectly by more general SEM measures (such as indirect taxation and procurement policies) meant that the sector was not untouched by the proposals.

However, there were signs of a different policy towards energy even in this period. The issue of price transparency was extended across the energy industries with attempts to agree a directive on the issue. While the moves failed, they indicated a greater interest in the issue by the Commission. The Commission was also taking a greater interest in energy subsidies (as in the case of Dutch support to its horticultural industry through the provision of cheap gas). Other indications of change included moves to tackle state oil monopolies and the types of support given to the coal industry in a number of member states.

The potential for more radical action was indicated by a number of moves taken by the competition directorate of the Commission towards other 'utility' industries. It sought the introduction of more competitive arrangements in the civil aviation industry and was able to threaten use of legal powers to this end. In the field of telecommunications it sought open access for equipment and service sales, using powers under Article 90 to do so. These moves not only demonstrated a willingness to act but also a range of mechanisms which could be used in other sectors. The further the policy went in one industry the more likely it would be applied to others.

This changing agenda meant that the idea of an internal energy market (IEM) was once again an issue for the EC. While the 1985 goals were largely flavoured by energy security concerns, one of the 'horizontal' objectives was the creation of an IEM. As the prospect of a SEM became realisable with the 1992 campaign the idea of extending it to energy took root, and in 1987 Energy Commissioner Mosar announced a study of the barriers to an IEM.

12.1.5 The internal energy market

The Commission's thinking was revealed in 'The Internal Energy Market' (COM (88) 238), a review which set out the potential benefits of an IEM and the obstacles which faced it. The IEM would cut costs to consumers (particularly to energy-intensive industries), thereby making European industry as a whole more competitive; it would increase security of supply by improving integration of the energy industries; it would rationalise the structure of the energy industries and allow for greater complementarity among the different supply and demand profiles of member states. The benefits would stem from a mixture of cost-reducing competition and the achievement of scale economies in a number of industries. Taken together these would more than recover the 0.5 per cent of EC GDP which the Commission claimed was the 'cost of non-Europe' in the energy sector (although, as noted, energy was not part of the original SEM debate nor of the 'cost of non-Europe' exercise which assessed the benefits of the SEM – see Cecchini, 1988 and Emerson *et al.*, 1988).

According to the Commission, the obstacles to the IEM were to be found in the structures and practices of the energy industries. These ranged from different taxation and financial regimes to restrictive measures which protected energy industries in particular countries and conditions which prevented full coordination of supplies at the most efficient level (the latter applying to the gas and electricity industries). However, as the Commission admitted, the effects of particular practices were difficult to assess, given the special nature of the energy industries. Indeed, in certain cases, the Commission appeared hesitant over the extent of the IEM.

None the less the document demonstrated that the Commission was determined to implement an IEM and would examine all barriers to its development. It set out a timetable for implementing the IEM: the implementation of the White Paper proposals (on taxation and procurement); the application of EC law to the sector and the resolution of issues peculiar to the energy sector.

In the period since the IEM document was published, the Commission has begun to implement the agenda, pushing forward proposals on public procurement and revising those on indirect taxation, presenting a draft directive on energy price transparency, announcing an investigation of restrictive practices in relationships between coal and electricity industries and setting forth its ideas on electricity trade. The pace of the debate has not only beeen helped by changes in EC decision-making procedures, notably the majority voting procedures allowed by the Single European Act (SEA), but also by the prospect of the Commission using its powers to investigate the energy sector from a Treaty of Rome perspective.

Since 1988, the IEM has dominated Commission proposals on energy policy. However another element has gained a higher profile in deliberations on the sector – the environment.

The Commission's interest in environmental issues is not new. The formal commitment of the EC to environmental policy dates from early 1972 when, in the wake of the Stockholm conference, the Council agreed a programme of action, while some measures on environmental problems predated even this initiative (Haigh, 1987). While the Commission's concerns on environment are very wide ranging, covering issues such as chemical wastes, water quality and noise pollution, the consequences of energy choices are a major part of the policy. Two areas have been to the fore: the content of, and emissions from, particular fossil fuels and nuclear waste management (Berkhout, Boehmer Christiansen and Skea, 1989).

The importance of EC environmental policy for the energy sector has paralleled the ascent of the issue up the political agenda in an increasing number of member states, particularly as the Greens have become a political force. In those cases where governments have been obliged to introduce new controls on pollution, they have sought to have them generalised across the EC so as not to lose competitiveness. The best example has been the acid rain debate where the West German government, forced to introduce major controls on domestic emissions from industrial and electricity plant, has pressured for similar controls in all member states.

With this debate, the Commission has gained a higher profile and another lever on energy policy (Owens and Hope, 1989). The importance of the issue to energy policy was demonstrated in the 1995 objectives, where environmental concerns were identified as a major consideration in policy. The status of environmental issues overall was confirmed in the SEA where it was given its own provisions (allowing it to enforce decisions on a majority vote). The SEM proposals also identify the need for high standards of environmental protection in the EC and this has impacted on the IEM debate. The issue is likely to grow in importance as the issue continues to gain political importance in member states (belatedly in the United Kingdom as well as consolidating its hold elsewhere), particularly with growing concerns over issues such as the greenhouse effect. (See Chapters 17 and 18 for a fuller coverage of EC environmental policies.)

12.2 The Community and the energy industries

12.2.1 Coal

The coal industry in the EC has undergone a major restructuring since the 1950s when it was the mainstay of the industrial European economy. Indigenous production of hard coal has been in more or less constant decline (lignite and peat have actually shown a slight increase but they are relatively unimportant due to their low thermal value). In 1960 coal production in the original six totalled 235 million tonnes (in the countries which now make up the EC it was 450 million tonnes); by 1987 production was less than 230 million tonnes in the EC of the twelve (see Figure 12.1). Many countries have effectively wound down their industries while others have rationalised substantially (either capacity or manpower).

The coal market has been more stable but the balance of that market has changed. For much of the intervening period coal demand was also in decline, as the household market disappeared and industrial demand diminished, although from the late 1970s on demand recovered slightly as coal use in power stations expanded. Increasingly, however, demand is met by imports: in 1960, 15 million tonnes were imported; by 1987 imports accounted for 90 million tonnes.

Imports might account for an even greater amount of coal consumed were it not for the barriers to entry in a number of member states which maintain a domestic industry. The restructuring of the sector has seen some countries close down industry, while some have maintained capacity, often on a large scale. In almost every country the industry is at least partly publicly owned. The competitiveness of these industries varies considerably, depending on developments in world coal prices, although some are clearly maintained only by a mixture of direct subsidy and government-backed agreements with electricity utilities (such as the Jahrhundertvertrag in Germany which obliges utilities to buy from high cost local suppliers but allows them to pass on the burden to the consumer – see IEA, 1988a; 1988b). In a number of countries these measures have come under increasing criticism, from consumers (who have to bear the higher cost of electricity production) and suppliers of other forms of energy whose position is also affected by them.

Considering the major restructuring under way in the industry and its position in

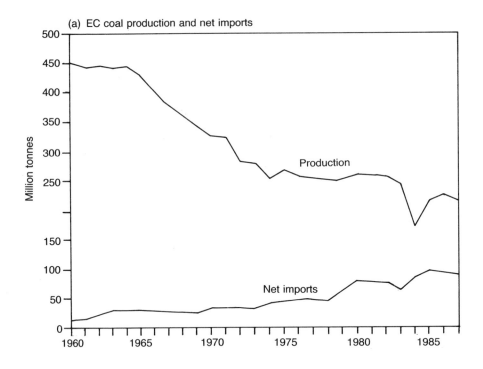

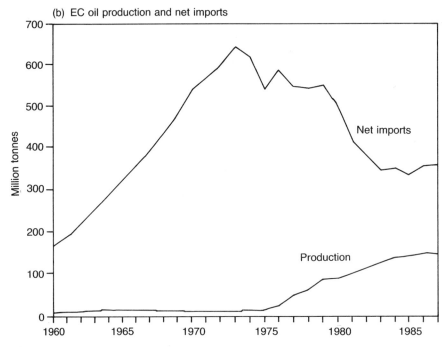

Figure 12.1 EC energy production and imports 1960–87. (Data used in this figure are given in Table A12.3.)

(c) EC gas production and net imports

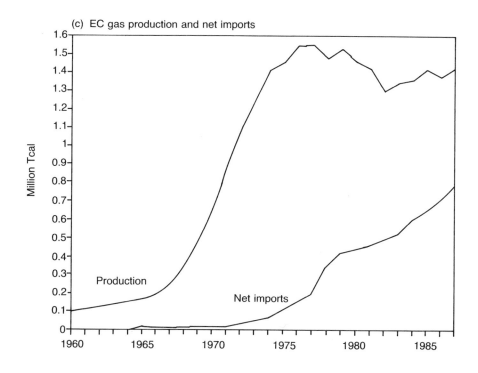

(d) EC electricity production by generation source

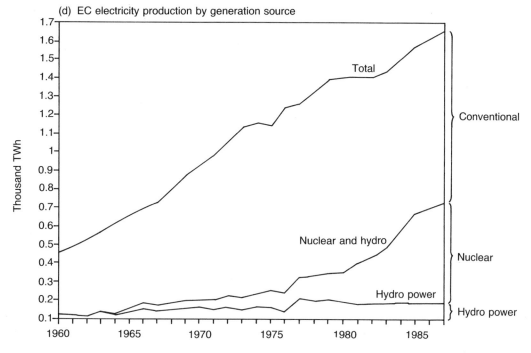

the EC's treaties and institutions, the role of the Commission in coal policy has been limited. As noted, many of the attempts to develop policy from the 1950s on came to little as the industry entered successive crises and the Commission grew concerned over the EC's vulnerability to imported energy.

The impotence of the Commission is demonstrated by the case of subsidies. The Paris Treaty effectively ruled out the state aids to the industry. The Commission sought to rectify this conflict by permitting such programmes, although there were certain controls placed upon them (Lucas, 1977). Since then these policies have expanded across the EC, helped in the 1970s by the Commission's concerns over energy security raising the profile of EC energy reserves.

The Commission attempted to adopt a tougher policy towards the sector in the 1980s. In 1985 the Commission proposed much more stringent controls of government policies, including a major reduction in the level of subsidy to the industry. As the Commission noted, whereas the old rules were dominated by supply concerns, the new ones would emphasise 'the need to achieve viability . . . and reduce the volume of aid even if this means substantial reductions in uneconomic capacity' (EC Commission, 1985d, p. 130).

The proposals were opposed by most coal-producing countries and the Commission was obliged to accept a less ambitious policy. The policy set a framework for continuing aid until 1993 on the basis of three criteria: to improve the industry's competitiveness; to create new economically viable capacity; and to solve the social and regional problems related to developments in the coal industry. In addition, the Commission developed a more detailed procedure for approving those aids and for reviewing progress made on improving the industry's financial and economic position and for bringing into line the different forms of aid offered by member states.

The effect of the Commission's scrutiny policy has been difficult to assess since many countries were already pushing their own rationalisation policies; but progress does appear to have been made. In its most recent review, the Commission noted that the level of aid had been falling in real terms. In addition, the transparency of aid procedures had increased, although this only exposed the complexity and diversity of the measures taken (COM (88) 541). The report, however, looks only at direct and indirect subsidies (i.e. subsidies to the industry and to the regions where mines are located), not at other forms of distortion which might affect the position of coal vis-à-vis other fuels and imports. It is these other distortions which have raised most controversy in recent years.

Given that this process of rationalisation is under way, the Commission's IEM proposals do not tackle the sector as robustly as might have been expected. The document stresses that the Treaty of Paris prevails over the SEA (notably in the area of commercial policy where the ECSC leaves member states to determine their own). In addressing the issue the Commission then notes three areas as sources of potential obstacles to a single market: the internal trade in coal, agreements between producers and consumers of coal, and import policy.

The Commission is not particularly concerned with trade in coal within the EC (in contrast to all other elements of the European energy economy). The vertical agreements between producers and consumers are of greater interest. These agreements are ostensibly of mutual benefit to both sides, providing producers with a guaranteed market and consumers with a protected supply of coal outside of price and supply fluctuations. Such agreements may not reflect market prices and will favour coal over other fuels. According to the Commission they do not themselves block EC trade in coal. Restriction of imported coal is a real enough obstacle but it is one permitted by the ECSC by commercial policy and therefore not directly subject to the IEM process. The combined effect of these measures is to restrict competition in coal supply.

Although the Commission did not set any goals for coal specifically in the IEM document, it has subsequently taken a stronger line. It has begun investigation of the relationship between the coal and electricity industries, which will inevitably question the compatibility of these long-term agreements with the goal of the IEM. In large part this has been prompted by French criticism of the Jahrhundertvertrag, which they regard as a block on energy trade (not least of French nuclear electricity).

The Commission will face opposition from few governments in its policy. The only forceful defence is likely to come from Germany, which argues that the social cost (quite apart from the energy balance implications) of abandoning its support is too high. (The German coal industry is already taking the Commission to court on the terms of its study.) The Commission's attitude on the social issue is that there should be compensation from other sources but not in the form of such a major market distortion. Its response to any security-of-supply concerns is less clear. These may increasingly be outweighed by environmental considerations as worries over acid rain and greenhouse emissions target coal as a culprit.

12.2.2 Oil

As in the rest of the world, the importance of oil in EC energy balances has increased dramatically since the 1950s, even allowing for the levelling off which has occurred since the 1980s. By 1960 oil accounted for 25 per cent of energy requirements in the original six. By the early 1970s it had risen to over 60 per cent before gradually declining and stabilising at just over 45 per cent in the mid-1980s. The bulk of these requirements was met by imports, since EC production was limited until the mid-1970s, when North Sea oil came on stream (see Figure 12.1b). (Dependence on refined products has always been notionally much smaller, given refinery capacity in the EC, although of course this has been ultimately dependent on the flow of crude oil.)

The major factors controlling demand have been the oil shocks of the 1970s, which demonstrated the EC's vulnerability to supply disruptions and price increases. In response member states shifted polices (at different intensities), with some attaining major reductions in oil dependency (e.g. Denmark cut its reliance on oil from nearly 90 per cent of energy requirements in 1973 to 57 per cent in 1986). However, oil remains the largest single element of primary fuel requirement.

The structure of the industry is quite diverse, reflecting in part the existence or otherwise of indigenous reserves. Where a production capability emerged (either at home or in colonies or dependencies), there has been a strong domestic element – often publicly owned – involved in the industry. In others the multinationals have dominated through their subsidiaries and have played a part in the development of almost every industry. The picture is not as clear cut as this: in many of the Mediterranean countries, with little or no production capacity, the state monopolies dominate imports, refining and distribution (Osborne and Robinson, 1989).

Given this diversity, and particularly the influence on international companies and markets, the industry is apparently more competitive than other energy industries. There is not the same natural monopoly element in distribution and marketing found in other sectors, while production and refining is notionally competitive. However, the close-knit structure of the international industry has prompted fears of collusion, while the dominance of state firms in some countries also raised fears of unfair trade practices.

As noted, much of EC policy on energy has been focused on the oil sector, with policies aimed at reducing vulnerability and maintaining security of supply. The objectives set in the 1970s and 1980s have been supplemented with actions to restrict use in power stations and encouraging stockpiling arrangements. Another aspect has been the encouragement of oil exploration in the EC and supervising the restructuring of the refinery industry which developed severe over-capacity when demand turned down in the 1970s and 1980s (COM (88) 491). Finally policy has sought to maintain a diversified source of supply and to continue a dialogue with major supply countries. More ambitious policies such as the attempts to develop a minimum support price have largely failed (Weyman Jones, 1986).

Pricing policies have also been a component of measures to control the industry's conduct. The Commission has sought to increase the transparency of oil industry pricing. It also sought to tackle the practices of state oil monopolies in a number of member states (notably the new Mediterranean members).

In applying the IEM to oil, the Commission tries to maintain these two aspects of past policy, but with the emphasis on market conduct. The Commission accepts that the oil industry is structured differently from other energy industries; nevertheless it sees a series of barriers persisting, including exploration and production monopolies; exploration and production-licensing procedures; oil field development conditions; taxation of oil production; landing obligation; restrictions on imports of oil and its byproducts; flag protection for shipments of oil; restrictions on refining and marketing rights; differences in technical norms and rules; pricing systems; and indirect taxation conditions.

The Commission's initial target is the implementation of the White Paper goals on taxation (harmonising excise duties and VAT and abolishing other taxes – see Chapter 13), standards (uniform standards on product quality and equipment) and procurement (open up markets for offshore exploration equipment). In tackling these issues, however, the Commission maintains its concerns over oil dependence, (for example it fears that too lax a tax regime might discourage energy efficiency and the shift from oil).

12.2.3 Natural gas

The EC gas industry has seen dramatic growth in the last twenty years considering that the industry has been rooted in town gas for most of its history and seemed in definite decline. The discovery of natural gas first in Groningen after the war and then in the North Sea indicated its potential to supply Europe with energy. Production has risen from 0.1 million Tcal in 1960 to 1.4 million Tcal in the 1980s. Demand has outpaced supply and imports have met a steadily rising proportion of consumption (currently approximately a third – see Figure 12.1c). While natural gas accounted for 3 per cent of energy requirements for the EC in 1960, it had risen to just under 20 per cent by the mid-1980s.

The gas industry shares the characteristics of the exploratory production industries such as oil and the network utility industries such as electricity. On balance the industry is dominated not so much by production companies but by the transmission companies which import and carry gas. Production is widespread (with the Netherlands and United Kingdom dominating) and is carried out by oil exploration companies. Transmission and imports are normally carried out by national monopolies (Germany is the exception where the monopolies are organised regionally). Distribution is also a monopoly and is generally carried out by local companies. Ownership is largely public with the exception of Germany and the United Kingdom. The extent to which monopoly or oligopoly prevails is reinforced by the substantial degree of vertical integration in the industry thanks to long run contracts between the suppliers and transmission companies and between the transmission companies and the distributors. Some attempts have been made to introduce competition into the industry, with the United Kingdom the most advanced; but they are not widespread in the EC (Stern, 1989).

The EC's past policy towards the gas industry has mainly been directed towards ensuring adequate supplies and controlling its use in non-premium markets (with the gas in power stations directive the main policy element). The other concern has been on pricing for large consumers (as demonstrated in the Dutch horticulture case).

The first signs of a wider agenda for gas came with the publication of the Commission's review of the natural gas industry in the EC (COM (86) 518). This not only indicated that the prospects for supply and demand appeared healthy (and underscored the fuel's relatively benign environmental effects) but that the industry should move towards a European structure with as much competition as possible in the system.

The IEM objectives for the gas market straddle the two components of the industry. To the extent that the gas is produced in the EC, then considerations related to oil production and barriers to that market would also apply to the gas industry. To the extent that the gas industry at the distribution level approximates to natural monopolies such as electricity, it is subject to similar proposals on extending grid integration, encouraging competition and determining regulation.

One of the Commission's main objectives is to see the creation of an EC-wide gas network. While applauding the widespread integration of the system of continental Europe and the joint ventures created, the Commission sees scope for greater links; a number of countries are still not fully integrated into the European grid while one (Portugal) does not yet have natural gas supply. It wants direct access by transmission and distribution companies to the grid and possibly to large consumers. This latter option opens the prospect of common carriage in the EC industry (and with it the possibility of a pan-EC regulator for access issues).

The idea of complete integration is not directly opposed by member states or the industry (as long as it is economically feasible). However, there are plans to give large consumers access to that system and this is opposed by many utilities. The industry argues that such a system (by introducing competition) would not provide the certainty required for the long-run investment needed in the sector. Industry and governments are united in opposing a regulatory agency at the EC level.

How far and how quickly the Commission will move on the issue of competition is still unclear, but there are signs that the structure of the industry may be shifting toward more competitive forces in at least some parts of the EC.

12.2.4 Electricity

Electricity has seen the most rapid growth in the post-war period. Electricity demand and production in the EC rose rapidly for many years (in the 1950s and 1960s by an average of 8 per cent annually). Although the mix of production technologies has changed over the years (see Figure 12.1d), for many decades, the industry has benefited from a virtuous circle of improving supply technologies reducing costs and prices and rising demand.

The electricity supply industry (ESI) retains a wide diversity of institutional forms with differing levels of public and private participation and/or centralised or decentralised organisation. The diversity owes much to the origins of the industry in each country, whether in rural cooperatives, municipal companies or industrial firms selling surplus power. The determining factor in shaping the development of the ESI, however, has been the political–economic structure of the country; much of the way in which industries have evolved can be attributed to the balance of power between public authority and private enterprise in the economy and between central and local government in the political realm (Hughes, 1983).

The shared position of the utilities has extended to international contacts. Despite the different structures and practices of the industry, for the most part they share a common perception of their obligations and future options and are organised within a common pressure group for international issues. Cooperation has also extended to operational aspects – most EC utilities are linked into common despatch systems for optimising the use of peak and reserve capacity (Bruppacher, 1988).

In more recent years, the pattern of steady improvement and the status of the utility has faltered. Technological improvements have turned out to be harder to obtain and (in scale economies) self-defeating, demand has faltered, and costs and prices have risen. The industry's record on environmental affairs also came under criticism in the 1970s and 1980s. However, the most important factor in change was in the relationship between the utilities and the consumers (particularly the largest industrial users).

In the 1980s, a number of large consumers sought to gain access to the national systems in various member states (either to buy from private producers or from exporters), but without success. In this environment, tensions between utilities also increased, and in the face of irreconcilable positions a number of consumers (primarily large German industrial users seeking to purchase cheap nuclear surplus power from France) threatened the use of the Rome treaty to support their goals (Lippert, 1987).

As noted, the idea of a European component to the ESI predates the EEC, and figured in the debate on the development of the EC at some stages. However, an EC role was rejected in the 1950s and most moves on integrating systems have occurred outside the EC framework. Commission interest has intermittently focused on the EC (e.g. on investment notification and rules for equipment procurement) but mostly these interventions have been unsuccessful or have reinforced the autonomy of member states and of the utilities.

Certainly there has been little in EC policy on electricity prior to the IEM which would indicate such a transformation. While the Commission indicated that an integration and liberalisation of the ESI was desirable, the idea did not receive any serious consideration. Policy has for the most part been developed in the 1970s and was largely informed by the need to diversify fuel types in power production by discouraging and encouraging various forms of power generation. The use of gas and oil was limited in 1985 (though it has been largely honoured in the breach), while incentives for coal, nuclear and renewables have also been devised.

The Commission's view of how the IEM should affect electricity seeks to balance the special characteristics of the sector with the drive to integrate and liberalise its structure. Integration of the electricity market is the Commission's principal objective. The Commission sees the development of international interconnection in Europe as very limited by comparison with the potential of an EC-wide electricity pool. The system of interconnection is balkanised between different groupings of countries, none of which has any executive power. Within each grouping, moreover, trade is conducted on a bilateral basis on terms agreed by the utilities. The Commission views the structure of the system as a major constraint in the emergence of more competitive pressures in electricity production. It fails not only to take advantage of the potential downward pressure on costs which a more competitive market might provide, but also, and more importantly, to exploit the comparative advantages of a mix of supply sources and the economies of a fully integrated system.

The Commission's view implicitly criticises the dominance of national systems in the ESI by identifying a number of distortions and barriers to trade within and between these systems. According to the Commission these differences in treatment of the industry between countries are key obstacles to an economically efficient ESI. Fiscal and financial treatment is one area where there are wide disparities between countries. Further differences arise in terms of the planning procedures which utilities confront. Consent processes are very different, with a range of criteria to be satisfied. Differences in safety standards and environmental protection are a further catalogue of different conditions facing utilities. In terms of the industry's operation, the critical factor which has distorted the emergence of a market is the influence of governments on utility purchasing. This not only affects the purchase of new power plant but also the options available in fuel supply.

The main obstacle to these developments is the organisational structure of the ESI in most member states. According to the Commission the close organisational links between production on the one hand, and transmission and distribution on the other, has tended to favour national supply solutions for electricity. A change in the relationship between these constituent parts of the ESI would help foster the development of trade in power. The Commission hints at a radical transformation of the industry when it suggests 'whether a change in the operational (as distinct from the ownership) system would be conducive to further opening of the internal market' (EC Commission, 1988b, p. 72).

In contrast to this radical proposal, the Commission's attitude to the issue of open access or common carriage is more cautious. While it sees potential benefits from opening the market up to both large consumers and cogenerators, it admits that there are major technical and security issues to be resolved.

The Commission's first initiative under the IEM was to rekindle its pricing policy proposals and to increase the transparency of electricity prices. In a review of transparency in the energy sector (EC Commission, 1989a), it considers the lack of publishable information on prices to large consumers as unacceptable. It wants to devise reference tariffs against which consumers across the EC can assess and compare their own prices.

The Commission is also currently assessing the scope for increasing access and trade in electricity markets. It now proposes a three-stage programme. In the first stage the Commission wants to establish the right to trade between utilities across the EC. All producing utilities would be able to trade with one another. Behind this seemingly unobjectionable proposal is the problem of transport of electricity between two countries by an intermediary. To the extent that this measure created greater trade in electricity (and it is not clear whether it would) the Commission's proposal then envisages that the EC interest in new investments by European utilities be considered. In effect this would mean that a country planning new capacity would more fully assess the potential for obtaining that capacity from trade rather than new construction. To the extent that these measures created a common electricity system, and possibly moves towards a European power pool, the last stage of the Commission's proposals would lead to an electricity market. At this stage the Commission proposes measures to allow for open access to the electricity system for non-utility generators on the one hand and large consumers and distribution companies on the other.

The Commission is taking a softly softly approach to the issue since its more radical approach had prompted opposition from the industry and governments wary of losing their autonomy on operation and investment. In the longer term, however, it appears determined to achieve its goal of a European electricity market (not least because it anticipates major economic and environmental benefits, the former consisting of savings of between 1.5 and 3 billion ECU per year, possibly much higher in the long run if the full proposal on electricity trade were introduced).

12.2.5 Nuclear power

The growth of nuclear power in the EC has been rapid, but not dramatically so. Its contribution to electricity input in the EC has risen from almost zero in 1960 to nearly one-third in the mid-1980s (see Figure 12.1d). The position varies widely from country to country, reflecting the different political climates within which the industry has developed: some, like France, obtain 80 per cent of electricity from nuclear power while others, like Denmark, have none. The industry has been badly shaken by scandal (Transnuklear) and crisis (Chernobyl) and the variable operating record and cost levels experienced in many countries (Thomas, 1988). Now nuclear power is promoted less for its economic than for its environmental benefits (since it does not emit greenhouse gases). None the less, not even its proponents persist with the optimistic forecasts made in the 1950s and which persisted into the early 1980s.

The EC nuclear industry is broadly composed of utilities, national authorities and fuel agencies. In almost every case the industry is predominantly publicly owned. Advanced nuclear technologies (such as the fast breeder reactor and fusion) are even more the preserve of the public sector. As part of the ESI, and given its special characteristics, the industry has not been subject to competitive pressures.

Commission policy on the sector has never lived up to the expectations of the Euratom treaty. Too many countries have sought to maintain autonomy over the industry. Yet the Commission has sought to sustain the industry as much for its industrial policy implications as for energy concerns (EC Commission, 1970b). Considerable resources have gone into promoting nuclear power and particularly joint ventures on advanced technologies: of the 800 million ECU of grants made to energy research development demonstration and promotion, over 340 million were allocated to the nuclear sector (EC Commission, 1989b).

The Commission's treatment of nuclear power and the IEM is separate from that of electricity, and as a result focuses less on the economics of nuclear power as a source of electricity than on the characteristics of nuclear fuel, plant and services. As in the case of coal, the Commission notes the wide disparities in policy and practice across the EC and the relative weakness of Euratom, the treaty guiding the sector's development, and the obstacles facing the development of a European and competitive market for nuclear fuels and equipment. In the first case, the long-term nature of contracts for enrichment and reprocessing means that any moves towards an internal market will have to wait for their expiry. Moves towards a liberalised market for nuclear plant and services should be covered by the procurement proposals.

12.2.6 Renewables and conservation

The sectors already examined are all substantial components of the energy sector. However, there are other energy industries and services which, while marginal in their contributions to energy balances, are critical to strategic views of energy policy, both at the national and the EC levels. The key sectors are the renewables and conservation industries.

The most established renewable energy industry is hydroelectric power, which accounts for a sizable, if relatively declining, proportion of electricity (most major sites are in use and new developments face considerable opposition). The 'new' renewables such as mini-hydro, solar power, wind and wave have largely developed in the aftermath of energy crises and growing environmental concerns. While still small in terms of power contribution, they are a fixture in many utilities and their role is set to grow in most, as their reliability and competitiveness improves. The sector industries largely consist of joint ventures between governments, utilities and manufacturers.

The importance and structure of conservation industries are even harder to discern. While advisory, architectural and control systems companies (each offering ways to reduce energy consumption) proliferate, their impact is difficult to assess (given that they are aiming to help consumers forgo energy usage). The overall improvement in energy efficiency must be partly due to these companies but also to other factors such as economic restructuring and price effects. Largely private, these companies have received varying degrees of support from governments, while the energy industries have for the most part been lukewarm, perceiving them as a threat to growth of their market. More recently, however, some large energy companies have adopted a higher profile on conservation issues as means of developing their market and diversifying.

Commission policy has been favourable towards both sectors, mainly through funding for R&D and promotional projects. In 1987 grants of just over 160 million ECU were provided for projects in renewables and conservation. Policy initiatives have also intensified. On renewables, the Commission announced in 1988 a recommendation to allow favourable access for such supplies (on the basis of their environmental benefits) to public grid systems. On conservation it is developing a programme of efficiency measures for the electricity sector, and further measures are likely, given the pressure of environmental concerns.

Despite their potential importance and the Commission's support for them, neither sector is covered directly by IEM. This may be due to their intangibility and their status as 'infant industries' not to be exposed to full rigours of competition. It may also, however, indicate difficulties in integrating or reconciling such goals and suggest fundamental problems with the IEM proposals in the context of a wider energy policy.

12.3 Conclusion

After more than thirty years the Commission is once again developing a CEP, and it may be more successful than before. Each of the mainstream energy sectors will be affected by the IEM proposals, providing a means for the Commission to address broader policy issues for these sectors and for energy as a whole.

The problem of trying to reconcile an interventionist policy with the goal of a free integrated market persists. From 1951 to 1973 energy policy efforts tried to balance the goal of a common competitive energy market with the need to maintain security of supply. For the next ten years, the security goal predominated. Now the balance between the two agendas is harder to assess. While the current debate and the nature of the proposals suggest that the SEM appears to be in the ascendant, the 1995 goals remain part of policy. The Commission sees no problem in this: as noted, the 1995 goals include the SEM, while the IEM document calls for a balance between the two components of policy. Indeed, it might be argued that the two agendas are separate and can co-exist. However, decisions in one agenda affect outcomes in the other one. If one is about imposing the logic of the market-place on the energy industries, the other is about the market failures, which abound in the sector.

In its extreme form, the IEM would indicate that the lowest cost source of supply should be obtained, and that this goal should prevail over any other policy considerations, notably that of controlling energy vulnerability. As the following examples demonstrate, this brings the two agendas of energy policy into conflict.

Energy conservation is an aim well to the fore in the 1995 objectives. While it is not in principle in conflict with the idea of a single market, many of the mechanisms which are used to achieve it are (e.g. high levels of taxation on energy products or subsidies to encourage energy efficiency). More generally, such policies are hard to reconcile with low energy prices, as the experience after the 1986 oil shock demonstrated.

The development of renewable sources of energy is another goal of the EC under the 1995 objectives. Again there is no conflict in principle; but in practice there may be difficulties. If, for example, we pursue the goals of lowest possible unit costs, then development of scale economies at a plant and at a network level may well be the best option. It seems probable that renewables will face a hard fight against existing large-scale plant. Similarly, the low price energy regime may squeeze out renewables. Of course, special arrangements could be made, but these may be regarded as a restraint on trade.

There are also problems for more mainstream technologies, notably nuclear power. Increasingly, the economies of nuclear power have been called into question, so much so in the United Kingdom that the government has encountered a number of difficulties in including it in its privatisation programme. The arguments have, moreover, shifted from the economic attractiveness of the option to its strategic role in reinforcing security of supply and aiding the environment. The strategic arguments are ones which the EC would echo – indeed the EC may see nuclear as still the most economically attractive option for power generation. But in the light of the difficulties in convincing investors, what measures are justified in sustaining the programme?

It is not difficult to see contradictions between the market-failure perspective of 1995 and the myopic perspective of 1992 which seems to leave all to the market, in a host of energy issues (many of them involving technologies or policies close to the core of EC energy activities). Determining how each is settled will be an extremely delicate task. The easy answer to these problems is to admit the existence of such contradictions and to allow for derogations where one policy is seen to be more important. But how to devise criteria for choosing priorities?

This raises a number of institutional problems. It is only to be expected that different parts of the Commission will have rather different views of what energy policy should entail. Because of its fundamental importance and unique characteristics, energy more than most other sectors will be the focus of a host of directorates' attention. This will multiply with the IEM. Whereas before energy largely linked into environment and R&D issues, after 1992 the interaction of energy concerns with other policy areas will increase. While Directorate General 17 (DG XVII) will be playing the lead role in determining the debate (and there may be competing claims within that agency as well), directorates pushing for the achievement of competitive energy markets (principally single market and competition respectively) and directorates concerned with the wider ramifications of the IEM (such as social affairs and regional policy and, of course, environment) will also play a role.

In theory all are pushing for the same objective; but their views are inevitably shaped by their own remit, with DGXVII acting as a clearing house for competing concerns and moderating some of the enthusiasms of other parts of the Commission. It is clear that moves to tackle certain barriers to the IEM will require some compensating mechanisms; but there remain a number of areas where different aspects of policy (and the different interests reflecting them) will be difficult to reconcile. Moreover, such intra-Commission tensions will be as nothing compared with the potential difficulties between the Commission and member states. While it may be that the impasse on policy of the past will no longer be possible, disputes between the Commission and governments in this area may prove to be the spark for more fundamental conflicts.

Where does this leave the CEP? Three solutions are possible. One solution is that the IEM debate gets bogged down and that things carry on as they are. Countries pursue their own policies with occasional conflicts, largely resolved without recourse to the Commission. Another possibility is that, in creating an EC energy market, an EC energy policy will be developed to cope with the market failures that emerge. It would be the Commission that made this decision. In other words, in the process of arbitrating between policy measures the Commission would effectively take control of energy policy. A final option is that the agendas are swept aside by a more pressing set of concerns. This appears quite likely given the pressures of environmental concerns. These may become so overwhelming in the next few years that they supplant other issues. The consequence of such a change would be that IEM-type concerns would be less important and it would probably mean that issues similar to those raised on security of supply grounds would come to the fore, but with rather more force than they have done in the past.

It may be that a combination of all three will emerge. Certain highly controversial aspects of the IEM may be neutered and member states will retain autonomy in those areas, leaving the IEM to be applied to other policies. Where the IEM prevails, the

Commission may have to resolve the competing and conflicting claims of, for example, competition and supply security, with perhaps the environment being the determinant of any decision. This balancing of policies is under way in the Commission as it reviews energy market and policy prospects after the year 2000. Whether it will be more successful in developing a full CEP in the next century than it has been in this remains to be seen.

Appendix: Data used in drawing Figure 12.1 (Table A12.3)

	Electricity			Coal	
	Production	Hydro	Nuclear + Hydro	Production	Imports
1960	454	124	126	451	15
	486	119	122	444	16
	529	113	117	447	22
	575	134	141	442	31
	619	118	129	445	29
1965	659	137	157	428	31
	697	155	181	401	28
	731	142	173	377	27
	794	148	182	361	25
	872	155	197	342	26
1970	929	160	202	326	35
	984	151	200	324	34
	1,053	159	221	283	35
	1,132	149	214	280	33
	1,153	163	238	253	41
1975	1,137	162	253	268	45
	1,235	140	241	258	48
	1,260	207	327	253	49
	1,322	198	330	250	46
	1,390	204	349	251	64
1980	1,403	186	352	260	80
	1,400	179	405	259	76
	1,403	182	434	257	76
	1,437	183	487	245	64
	1,501	187	586	173	85
1985	1,573	183	668	217	96
	1,612	178	701	228	92
	1,659	186	724	217	90

	Oil			Natural gas	
	Net Imports	Production		Production	Imports
1960	167	11	1960	99	0
	188	13		115	0
	219	13		127	0
	253	14		134	0
	289	15		149	0
1965	324	16	1965	164	18
	358	15		192	10
	390	15		243	12

Table A12.3 (Con't)

	Oil			Natural gas	
	Net Imports	Production		Production	Imports
	433	14		345	14
	478	14		482	17
1970	540	13	1970	657	16
	567	13		857	16
	597	13		1,086	36
	645	13		1,238	51
	619	14		1,413	67
1975	537	14	1975	1,457	107
	586	24		1,544	150
	546	50		1,550	196
	541	64		1,478	348
	549	88		1,526	421
1980	497	90	1980	1,459	441
	415	100		1,420	458
	381	114		1,302	488
	346	128		1,349	529
	351	138		1,363	603
1985	335	142	1985	1,424	644
	357	149		1,381	706
	358	147		1,434	792

Part IV

Macroeconomic policies

This section completes the analysis of the economics of the EC by tackling its macroeconomic policies. As stated in the introduction, however, the dividing line between microeconomic and macroeconomic policies is in some cases not so clear; but this should not create any serious problem since what really matters is that the grouping of EC policies should on the whole be a fairly logical one.

13 Tax harmonisation

A. M. El-Agraa

13.1 The meaning of fiscal policy

Very widely interpreted, fiscal policy comprises a whole corpus of 'public finance' issues: the relative size of the public sector, taxation and expenditure, and the allocation of public sector responsibilities between different tiers of government (Prest, 1979). Hence fiscal policy is concerned with a far wider area than that commonly associated with it, namely, the aggregate management of the economy in terms of controlling inflation and employment levels.

Experts in the field of public finance (Musgrave and Musgrave (1976) rightly stress that 'public finance' is a misleading term, since the subject also deals with 'real' problems) have identified a number of problems associated with these fiscal policy issues. For instance, the relative size of the public sector raises questions regarding the definition and measurement of government revenue and expenditure (Prest, 1972), and the attempts at understanding and explaining revenue and expenditure have produced more than one theoretical model (Musgrave and Musgrave (1976) and Peacock and Wiseman (1967)). The division of public sector responsibilities raises the delicate question of which fiscal aspects should be dealt with at the central government level and which aspects should be tackled at the local level. Finally, the area of taxation and expenditure criteria has resulted in general agreement about the basic criteria of allocation (the process by which the utilisation of resources is split between private and social goods and by which the 'basket' of social goods is chosen), equity (the use of the budget for achieving a fair distribution), stabilisation (the use of the budget as an instrument for achieving and maintaining a 'reasonable' level of employment, prices and economic growth and for achieving equilibrium and stability in the balance of payments), and administration (the practical possibilities of implementing a particular tax system and the cost to the society of operating such a system). However, a number of very tricky problems are involved in a consideration of these criteria. In discussing the efficiency of resource allocation, the choice between, e.g. work and leisure, or between private and public goods, is an important and controversial one. With regard to the equity of distribution, there is the problem of what is meant by equity: is it personal, class or regional equity? In a discussion of the stabilisation of the economy, there exists the perennial problem of controlling unemployment and inflation and the trade-off between them. A consideration of administration must take into account the problem of efficiency versus practicality. Finally, there is the obvious conflict between the four criteria in that the achievement of one aim is usually at the expense of another; for example, what is most efficient in terms of collection may prove less (or more) equitable than what is considered to be socially desirable.

These complex considerations cannot be tackled here, given the level of generality of this chapter. The interested reader is, therefore, advised to consult the very extensive literature on 'public finance'.

The above relates to a discussion of the problems of fiscal policy in very broad national terms. When considering the EC fiscal policy, there are certain elements of the international dimension that need spelling out and there are also some interregional (intra-EC) elements that have to be introduced.

Very briefly, internationally, it has always been recognised that taxes (and equivalent instruments) have similar effects to tariffs on the international flow of goods and services – non-tariff distortions of international trade (generally referred to as non-tariff trade barriers – NTBs – Baldwin, 1971). Other elements have also been recognised as operating similar distortions on the international flow of factors of production (Bhagwati, 1969; Johnson, 1965a; 1973).

In the particular context of the EC, it should be remembered that its formation, at least from the economic viewpoint, was meant to facilitate the free and unimpeded flow of goods, services and factors (and the other elements discussed in Chapter 1) between the member nations. Since tariffs are not the only distorting factor in this respect, the proper establishment of intra-EC free trade necessitates the removal of all non-tariff distortions that have an equivalent effect. Hence, the removal of tariffs may give the impression of establishing free trade inside the EC, but this is by no means automatically guaranteed, since the existence of sales taxes, excise duties, corporation taxes, income taxes, etc., may impede this freedom. Indeed, this is precisely what has happened in the EC: the removal of tariffs immediately highlighted the significance of NTBs. This is also the reason why the EC Commission has been able to persuade the member nations to adopt the Single European Act (SEA) to enable the creation of one internal market free of such distortions by 1992 – see below. The moral is that not only tariffs, but all equivalent distortions, must be eliminated or harmonised. (See Table 13.1 for the EC tax structure in 1955.)

At this juncture it becomes necessary to emphasise that there are at least two basic elements to fiscal policy: the instruments available to the government for fiscal policy purposes (i.e. the total tax structure) and the overall impact of the joint manoeuvring of these instruments (i.e. the role played by the budget). The aim of this chapter is to discuss the meaning of and the need for tax harmonisation and to assess the progress made by the EC in this respect. The other element of fiscal policy, the general budget of the EC, is discussed in the following chapter. Hence, the two chapters com-

Table 13.1 Percentage composition of tax receipts and tax burden in the EC 1955

	Income and property taxes	Turnover taxes	Consumption taxes	Tax receipts as % of GNP
Belgium	50.7	26.5	22.8	17.1
France	38.4	41.5	20.1	19.6
W. Germany	52.4	26.9	20.7	21.9
Italy	32.3	21.1	46.6	22.9
Luxemburg	66.4	15.4	18.2	23.6
Netherlands	60.0	20.1	19.9	26.6

Source: Balassa, 1961.

plement each other in that, taken together, they cover the two basic elements of EC fiscal policy.

13.2 The tax structure and its implications

In case it is not obvious why taxes should give rise to trade distortion (Swann, 1978), it may be useful to examine the nature of taxes before the inception of the EC, as well as to consider the treatment given at the time to indirect taxation on internationally traded commodities.

Before considering these aspects, however, it may be useful to state that there are two basic types of taxation: direct and indirect. Direct taxes, like income and corporation taxes, come into operation at the end of the process of personal and industrial activities. They are levied on wages and salaries when activities have been performed and payment has been met (income taxes), or on the profits of industrial or professional businesses at the end of annual activity (corporation taxes). Direct taxes are not intended to play any significant role in the pricing of commodities or professional services. Indirect taxes are levied specifically on consumption and are, therefore, in a simplistic model, very significant in determining the pricing of commodities given their real costs of production.

Historically speaking, in the EC there existed four types of sales, or turnover, taxes (Dosser, 1973; Paxton, 1976): the *cumulative multi-stage cascade system* (operated in West Germany until the end of 1967, in Luxemburg until the end of 1969 and in the Netherlands until the end of 1968) in which the tax was levied on the gross value of the commodity in question at each and every stage of production without any rebate on taxes paid at earlier stages; *value-added tax*, which has operated in France since 1954 where it is known as TVA – *Taxe sur la Valeur Ajoutée* – which is basically a non-cumulative multi-stage system; the *mixed systems* (operated in Belgium and Italy) which were cumulative multi-stage systems that were applied down to the wholesale stage, but incorporated taxes which were applied at a single point for certain products; and finally, *purchase tax* (operated in the United Kingdom) which was a single-stage tax normally charged at the wholesale stage by registered manufacturers or wholesalers, which meant that manufacturers could trade with each other without paying tax.

Although all these tax systems had the common characteristic that no tax was paid on exports, so that each country levied its tax at the point of entry, one should still consider the need for harmonising them.

A variety of taxes also existed in the form of excise duties. The number of commodities subjected to this duty ranged from the usual (or 'classical') five of manufactured tobacco products, hydrocarbon oils, beer, wine and spirits, to an extensive number including coffee, sugar, salt, matches, etc. (in Italy). The means by which the government collected its revenues from excise duties ranged from government-controlled manufacturing, e.g. tobacco goods in France and Italy, to fiscal imports based on value, weight, strength, quality, etc. (Dosser, 1973, p. 2).

As far as corporation tax is concerned, three basic schemes existed and still exist, but not in any single country at all times. The first is the *separate system* which was used in the United Kingdom – the system calls for the complete separation of corporation tax from personal income tax and was usually referred to as the 'classical' system. The second is the *two-rate system* or *split-rate system* which was the German practice and was recommended as an alternative system for the United Kingdom in the Green Paper of 1971 (HMSO, Cmnd. 4630). The third is the *credit* or *imputation system* – this was the French system and was proposed for the United Kingdom in the White Paper of 1972 (HMSO, Cmnd 4955) – see Kay and King (1983) for how the imputation system works within the United Kingdom context.

Generally speaking, corporation tax varied from being totally indistinguishable from other systems (Italy) to being quite separate from personal income tax with a single or a split rate which varied between 'distributed' and 'undistributed' profits, to being partially integrated with the personal income tax systems, so that part of the corporation tax paid on distributed profits could be credited against a shareholder's income tax liability (Dosser, 1973, p. 2).

The personal income tax system itself was differentiated in very many aspects among the original six, not just as regards rates and allowances, but also administration procedures, compliance and enforcement.

Finally, the variety in the para-tax system relating to social security arrangements was even more striking. The balance between sickness, industrial injury, unemployment, and pensions was very different indeed, and the methods of financing these benefits were even more so – see Chapter 17.

In concluding this section, it is useful to discuss certain problems regarding these taxes. Since VAT is the EC turnover tax (see the section below on EC progress on tax harmonisation), I shall illustrate the problems of turnover taxes in the context of VAT.

The first problem relates to the point at which the tax should be imposed. Here, two basic principles have been recognised and a choice between them has to be made: the 'destination' and 'origin' principles. Taxation under the destination principle specifies that commodities going to the same destination must bear the same tax load irrespective of their origin. For example, if the United Kingdom levies a general sales tax at 8 per cent and France a similar tax at 16 per cent, a commodity exported from the United Kingdom to France would be exempt from the United Kingdom's 8 per cent tax but would be subjected to France's 16 per cent tax. Hence, the UK export commodity would compete on equal tax terms with French commodities sold in the French market. Taxation under the origin principle specifies that commodities with the same origin must pay exactly the same tax, irrespective of their destination. Hence, a commodity exported by the United Kingdom to France would pay the United Kingdom tax (8 per cent) and would be exempt from the French tax (16 per cent). Therefore, the commodity that originated from the United Kingdom would compete unfairly against a similar French commodity.

The choice between the destination and origin principles raises a number of technical issues which cannot be tackled here. Those interested should consult the voluminous literature on the subject (Shoup, 1966; 1972; Dosser, 1973; Paxton, 1976; Pinder, 1971).

The second problem relates to the range of coverage of the tax. If some countries are allowed to include certain stages, e.g. the retail stage, and others make allowances for certain fixed capital expenditures and raw materials, the tax base will not be the same. This point is very important, because one has to be clear about whether the tax base should be consumption or net national income. To illustrate, in a 'closed' economy:

$$Y \equiv W + P \equiv C + I$$

where Y = gross national product (GNP), W = wages and salaries, P = gross profits, C = consumption and I = gross capital expenditure. If value-added is defined as $W + P - I$ (i.e. GNP minus gross capital expenditure), then consumption will form the tax base. If instead of gross capital expenditure one deducts only capital consumption (depreciation), then net national product will become the tax base. Obviously, the argument holds true in an open economy. It is therefore important that members of a union should have a common base.

The third problem relates to exemptions that may defeat the aim of VAT being a tax on consumption. For example, in a three-stage production process, exempting the first stage does not create any problem, since the tax levies on the second and third stages together will be equivalent to a tax levied at all three stages. Exempting the third stage will obviously reduce the tax collection, provided of course that the rates levied at all stages were the same. If the second stage is exempt, the tax base will be in excess of that where no exemptions are allowed for, since the tax on the first stage cannot be transferred as an input tax on the second stage, and the third stage will be unable to claim any input tax from items bought from the second stage. The outcome will be a tax based on the total sum of the turnover of stages one and three only, rather than a tax levied on the total sum of the value-added at all three stages.

With regard to corporation tax, a proper evaluation of any system raises national as well as intra-regional (intra-EC) questions. The national questions relate to the standard criteria by which a tax system can be judged: its effect on budget revenue and effective demand, on income distribution, on the balance of payments, on the rate of economic growth, on regional differences and on price levels. It is obvious that what is very efficient for one purpose need not be so efficient for the other purposes.

The intra-EC questions relate to the treatment of investment, since, if capital mobility within the EC is to be encouraged, investors must receive equal treatment irrespective of their native country (region). Here, Dosser highly recommends the separate system since it is 'neutral' in its tax treatment between domestic investment at home and abroad, and between domestic and foreign investment at home, provided both member countries practise the same system (Dosser, 1973, p. 95). Prest (1979, pp. 85–6) argues that even though a separate system does not discriminate against partner (foreign) investment, it does discriminate between 'distributed' and 'undistributed' profits, and that the imputation system, even though it is 'neutral' between 'distributed' and 'undistributed' profits, actually discriminates against partner (foreign) investment. Prest therefore claims that neither system can be given 'full marks'.

Again, at this level of generality, one cannot go into all the complications raised by such questions. The interested reader is therefore advised to consult Dosser (1966; 1971; 1973; 1975), Dosser and Han (1968), Paxton (1976) and Pinder (1971), or the vast literature on the subject.

Excise duties are intended basically for revenue-raising purposes. For example, in the United Kingdom excise duties on tobacco products, petroleum and alcoholic drinks account for about a third of central government revenue (Kay and King, 1983). The issues raised by the harmonisation of these taxes are specifically those relating to the revenue-raising function of these taxes and to the equity, as opposed to the efficiency, of these methods.

Finally, the income tax structure has a lot to do with the freedom of labour mobility. Ideally, one would expect equality of treatment in every single tax that is covered within this structure; but it is apparent that since there is more than one rate, the harmonisation of a 'package' of rates might achieve the specified objective.

13.3 The meaning of tax harmonisation

Having discussed the problems associated with taxes in the context of economic integration, it is now appropriate to say something about the precise meaning of tax harmonisation.

In earlier years, tax harmonisation was defined as tax coordination (Dosser, 1973). Ideally, in a fully integrated EC, it could be defined as the identical unification of both base and rates, given the same tax system and assuming that everything else is also unified. Professor Prest (1979, p. 76) rightly argues that 'coordination' is tantamount to a low level meaning of tax harmonisation, since it could be 'interpreted to be some process of consultation between member countries or, possibly, loose agreements between them to levy tax on a similar sort of base *or* at similar sorts of rates'. It is therefore not surprising that tax harmonisation has, in practice, come to mean a compromise between the low level of coordination (the EC is much more than a low level of integration – see Chapter 1), and the ideal level of standardisation (the EC is nowhere near its objective of complete political unity). However, the SEA asks for the creation of one internal market, and this has been interpreted to mean a market without fiscal frontiers which the EC Commission insists must be one where taxes are near equal – see below.

13.4 EC tax harmonisation experience

To discuss the experience of the EC with tax harmonisation meaningfully, it is sensible to consider the developments before the adoption of the SEA separately from those after it.

·13.4.1 The period leading to the SEA

During this period, the main driving force was Article 99 of the Treaty of Rome, which specifically calls for the harmonisation of indirect taxes, mainly turnover taxes and excise duties. Harmonisation here was seen as vital, particularly since the removal of tariffs would leave taxes as the main source of intra-EC trade distortion. However, given the preoccupation of the EC with the process of unification, the Treaty seems to put very little stress on the harmonisation of its initial tax diversity. Moreover, the Treaty is rather vague about what it means by 'harmonisation': for example, in Article 100 it does not specify more than that laws 'should be approximated' with regard to direct taxation. The whole development of tax harmonisation during this period has been influenced by the work of special committees, informal discussions, etc., i.e. the procedure detailed in Chapter 2. This, however, should not be interpreted as a criticism of those who drafted the Treaty. On the contrary, given the very complex nature of the subject and its closeness to the question of political unification, it would have been short-sighted to have done otherwise.

Given this general background, it is now appropriate to describe the progress made by the EC with respect to tax harmonisation during this period.

In the area of indirect taxation most of the developments have been in terms of VAT, which the EC adopted as its turnover tax following the recommendations of the Neumark Committee in 1963, which was in turn based on the Tinbergen study of 1953 – particularly since it was realised that the removal of intra-EC tariffs left taxes on traded goods as the main impediment to the establishment of complete free trade inside the Community. Between 1967 and 1977, six directives were issued with the aim of achieving conformity between the different practices of the member countries. These related, apart from the adoption of VAT as the EC sales tax, to three major considerations: the inclusion of the retail stage in the coverage of VAT; the use of VAT levies for the EC central budget (see the following chapter); and the achieve-

Table 13.2 Taxes and actual social contributions, VAT and corporation tax

	Taxes and actual social contributions (% of total), 1980				Effective rates of VAT (%), 1982[c,d]			Corporation tax[e,f]		
	Taxes linked to production and imports	Current taxes on income and wealth	Capital taxes	Actual social contributions	Standard	Reduced	Increased	Rate (%)	System	Imputation credit (%)
Belgium	27.1	41.8	0.8	30.3	17	6	25	48	Imputation	49.8
Denmark	41.5	56.3	0.4	1.8	22	—	—	37	Imputation	25.5
France	35.5	20.4	0.6	43.6	18.6	5.5, 7	33.3	50	Imputation	50
W. Germany	32.0	32.7	0.2	35.1	13	6.5	—	56.36	Imputation	100
Ireland[a]	49.1	35.6	0.4	14.9	30	0, 18	—	45	Imputation	52.4
Italy[b]	30.9	32.3	0.2	36.6	15	2, 8	18.35	36.25	Imputation	58.6
Luxemburg	27.2	43.5	0.2	29.1	10	2, 5	—	40	Separate	None
Netherlands	25.6	34.5	0.5	39.5	18	4	—	45	Separate	None
United Kingdom	43.6	38.5	0.5	17.6	15	0	—	52	Imputation	39.6

Notes
[a] 1979.
[b] 1978.
[c] The effective VAT rate is that on the price net of tax.
[d] Greece is still to introduce VAT.
[e] Proposals were made in August 1982 for increasing Italy's to 35–8 per cent.
[f] The West German system is a two-rate one.

Sources: Eurostat, 1982 various publications, and *Bulletin of the European Communities*, Supplement 1/80.

ment of greater uniformity in VAT structure. These directives have been supplemented by several minor ones and by a series of draft-directives.[1]

What, then, is the state of play? (See Table 13.2 for information covering this period and Tables 13.3 and 13.4 for the latest information for all twelve EC member nations.) Having adopted the VAT system and having accepted a unified method of calculating it, the EC has also acceded to the destination principle which, as we have seen, is consistent with free intra-EC trade. It has been agreed by all member states that the coverage of VAT should be the same and should include the retail stage (now the normal practice), that crude raw materials, bought-in elements and similar components are to be deductible from the tax computation, and that investment stock and inventories should be given similar treatment by all member nations. There is agreement about the general principle of VAT exemptions, but the precise nature of these seems to vary from one member country to another, thus giving rise to the problems concerning the tax base discussed earlier.

On the other hand, this similarly of principles is, in practice, contradicted by a number of differences. The tax coverage differs from one member country to another, since most seem to have different kinds, as well as different levels, of exemptions. For example, the United Kingdom applies zero rating for foodstuffs, gas and electricity (zero rating is different from exemptions, since zero rating means not only tax exemption from the process, but also the receipt of rebates on taxes paid at the preceding stage – see Prest (1979), Dosser (1975) and Paxton (1976)). There is a wide difference in rate structure.

With respect to corporation tax, the Neumark Report of 1963 recommended a

Table 13.3 Corporation tax structure and rates 1986

	System	Corporation tax rate (%)	Imputation credit (%)
Belgium	Imputation	45.00[a]	40.87
Denmark	Imputation	50.00	25.00
France	Imputation	45.00	61.11
W. Germany	Imputation	56.00/36.00[b]	100.00
Greece	Imputation[c]	34.00 to 47.20	100.00
Ireland	Imputation	50.00[a]	53.85
Italy	Imputation	46.368[d]	100.00
Luxemburg	Separate	40.00[a]	0.00
Netherlands	Separate	42.00	0.00
Portugal	Imputation[c]	42.20 to 47.20	100.00
Spain	Imputation	35.00	18.57
United Kingdom	Imputation	35.00[a]	75.81

Notes
[a] Reduced rates are applied to low income.
[b] The 36 per cent is levied on distributed profits.
[c] Greece and Portugal have no corporation tax on distributed profits. This is tantamount to a 100 per cent imputation credit.
[d] This is the sum of both central and local taxes.

Source: Various publications by the EC Commission and national sources.

Table 13.4 Excise duties, proposed and current (ECU)

Excisable goods	Proposed rate	EC average arithmetic	EC average weighted	Netherlands	Belgium	Denmark	West Germany	France	Greece	Ireland	Italy	Luxembourg	United Kingdom	Spain	Portugal
Alcoholic beverages															
Pure alcohol (1 hl)	1,271	1,271		1,298	1,252	3,499	1,174	1,149	48	2,722	230	842	2,483	309	248
Intermediate products (1 hl)	85[b]	103		63	61	292	70	6	2	404	10	41	286	0	0
Wines (1 hl)	17[b]	58		33	33	157	20	3	0	279	0	13	154	0	0
Beers (1 hl)	17	22.5		20	10	57	7	3	10	81	17	5	49	3	7
Mineral oils															
Petrol, leaded (1,000 l)	340	340	336	340	261	473	256	369	349	362	557	209	271	254	352
Diesel (1,000 l)	177	153	177	109	123	236	213	190	106	279	178	100	229	124	162
Heating gas oil (1,000 l)	50	62	50	44	0	236	8	53	109	48	178	0	15	38	23
Heavy fuel oil (1,000 kg)	17	26	17	15	0	266	7	25	93	10	7	2	11	1	11
LPG (1,000 l)	85	85	61	0	0	163	160	138	40	222	96	21	(1,353)	27	17
Cigarettes															
Specific excise (per 1,000)	19.5	19.5		26	2	77	27	1	1	49	2	2	43	1	2
Ad valorem duty + VAT (%)[c]	52–4	53		36	66	39	44	71	60	34	69	64	34	52	65
Other manufactured tobacco[c]															
Cigars (%)	} 34–6	35		20	22	} 40	26	50	} 31	} 56	} 39–63	} 23	} 50	} 21	} 40
Cigarillos (%)				25	27		29	54							
Smoking tobacco (%)	54–6	55		56	37	58–83	36–54	65	63	70	71	38	65–70	31	26
Other (%)	41–3	42		56	37	41–57	20	37–59	64	20–70	42	38	13–50	36	30

Notes
[a] Rates as at 1 April 1987, in ECU.
[b] Sparkling wines: 30 ECU/hl.
[c] *Ad valorem* duty + VAT, as a % of the retail price.

Sources: European Commission, *Europe without Frontiers* (Information 1987 P 51); COM (87) 325–8.

split-rate system, the van den Tempel Report of 1970 preferred the adoption of the separate or classical system and the draft directive of 1975 went for the imputation system. Moreover, the method of tax harmonisation which is accepted is not the ideal one of a single EC corporation tax and a single tax pattern, but rather a unified EC corporation tax accompanied by freedom of tax patterns. Hence, all systems have been entertained at some time or another and all that can be categorically stated is that the EC has, at this stage, limited its choice to the separate and imputation systems – see Table 13.3.

As far as excise duties are concerned, progress has been rather slow, and this can be partially attributed to the large extent of the differences between the rates on the commodities under consideration in the different member countries – see Table 13.5 for information covering this period and Table 13.4 for the most up-to-date information on all twelve EC member nations. This is a partial explanation, however, because, as was pointed out earlier, these taxes are important for government revenue purposes and it would be naive to suggest that rate uniformity can be achieved without giving consideration to the political implications of such a move.

The greatest progress has been achieved in tobacco, where a new harmonised system was adopted in January 1978. The essential elements of this system are the abolition of any duties on raw tobacco leaf and the adoption of a new sales tax at the manufacturing level, combined with a specific tax per cigarette and VAT. Prest (1979) argues that the overall effect of this will be to push up the relative prices of the cheaper brands of cigarettes.

It has been suggested (Prest, 1979) that the harmonisation of tax rates here is misguided, since the destination principle automatically guarantees fair competition. This is a misleading criticism, however, since the harmonisation of the tax structure should be seen in the context of the drive in the EC for monetary integration and political unification, processes which become increasingly difficult without tax harmonisation – see next section.

Some progress has been achieved with regard to stamp duties. Harmonisation

Table 13.5 Excise duty application in each member state as a percentage of Community average (July 1979 = 100)

	Cigarettes	Spirits	Wine	Beer	Petrol (high grade)	Gas/oil
Belgium	86	62	69	46	99	85
Denmark	299	289	240	272	132	51
France	42	89	4	7	127	156
W. Germany	118	63	0	29	92	203
Ireland	74	147	218	289	76	72
Italy	57	18	0	34	140	27
Luxemburg	54	34	34	33	74	44
Netherlands	77	62	69	46	91	82
United Kingdom	92	136	265	144	68	180

Source: Bulletin of the EC, Supplement 1/80.

here is necessary for promoting the freedom of intra-EC capital flows. The 1976 draft directive recommended a compromise between the systems existing in the member countries. This recommendation has been accepted, with the proviso that time will be allowed for adjustment to the new system.

Nothing has been attempted in the area of personal income taxation and very slight progress has been achieved in social security payments, unemployment benefits, etc., the only exception being the draft directive of 1979 which deals with equity in the taxation of migrant workers; but this is still to have any serious impact. These issues are discussed in some detail in Chapter 17.

13.4.2 The period beginning with the SEA

The aim of the SEA is to transform the whole of the EC into a single internal market by 1992, i.e. the EC will become 'an area without internal frontiers in which the free movement of goods, persons, services and capital is ensured'; thus the SEA reiterates the original objectives of the Treaty of Rome. The EC Commission emphasises the 'Europe without frontiers' since it is convinced that frontiers are the clearest symbol of divisions within the EC. It insists that if frontiers persist, they will be used as convenient locations for practising some protectionist measure or another.

The most significant features of frontiers are the customs posts, and, as we have seen, these crucially relate to taxes. Of course, as Mrs Thatcher has persistently claimed, they may be very important for controlling the movement of terrorists; but our concern here is with the free movement of goods and factors of production. As our earlier discussion has demonstrated, customs controls protect the indirect taxes of one EC member country from relative tax bargains which are obtainable elsewhere within the EC. Moreover, customs controls guarantee that governments can collect the VAT that belongs to them. A frontier-free EC would undermine these factors unless the rates of indirect taxation within the EC were brought much closer to each other. They do not have to be equalised (see above) since the experience of the United States indicates that contiguous states can maintain differentials in sales taxes of up to about 5 percentage points without the tax leakage becoming unbearable. The EC Commission would ideally like to see an equalisation of the rates, but given the US experience and the obsession of the EC member nations with (illusory?) sovereignty, it has decided to aim for a position similar to that of the United States.

Given the brevity of this chapter, it is unjustifiable to devote space to the development of the position that the EC Commission would like the member nations to adopt. Those interested in a full description and some analysis of this development are advised to consult Guieu and Bonnet (1987), Bos and Nelson (1988) and Smith (1988). Here we shall concentrate on the latest position adopted by the EC Commission.

In the 1985 White Paper, the EC Commission reached the conclusion that to treat EC transactions crossing frontiers within the EC in exactly the same manner as transactions within an EC member state certain measures will have to be adopted with regard to VAT and excise duties. For VAT, these are as follows:

1. The replacement of the present system of refunding tax on exportation and collecting it on importation by a system of tax collection by the country of origin.
2. The introduction of an EC clearing mechanism to ensure that revenues would continue to accrue to the EC member nation where consumption takes place so that the 'destination principle' remained intact.
3. The narrowing of the differentials in national VAT rates so as to lessen the risks of fraud, tax evasion and distortions in competition.

With regard to excise duties, three conditions are deemed necessary:

1. An interlinkage of the bonded warehouse systems (these are created to defer the payment of duty since, as long as the goods remain in these warehouses, duties on them do not have to be paid; recall that excise duties are levied only once on manufacture or importation).
2. Upholding the destination principle.
3. An approximation of the national excise duty rates and regimes.

The initial recommendations advanced by the EC Commission regarding how to achieve these requirements were examined by an *ad hoc* group invited by the Council of Ministers for Financial Affairs (ECOFIN). The group reported (see Council of the European Communities, 1986) that some of its members did not endorse the need for abolishing fiscal frontiers. However, they felt that if frontiers have to be removed, the proposals put forward by the EC Commission were necessary, but inadequate: the group advanced a number of serious problems with respect to the clearing mechanism and the system of interlinked bonded warehouses.

The EC Commission responded in August 1987 – see EC Commission (1987b) – by mainly elaborating on the proposals put forward in the White Paper and by advancing different recommendations concerning the VAT clearing mechanism and the approximation of excise duties; thus it has responded in precisely the way it has been instructed. These recommendations are as follows:

1. The creation of a central account, in ECUs, to be administered by the EC Commission and to which net exporting member nations will contribute on a monthly basis and from which net importing member nations will receive payment.
2. The settlement of accounts on the basis of statements made by each member state about its net position (the balance of its VAT on intra-EC input and output).

The new clearing mechanism differs from the one suggested by the *ad hoc* group in that, apart from the proposal that the EC Commission should administer it, it asks for a clearing of net VAT flows, not a clearing of claims based entirely on input VAT data. The EC Commission justified this new proposal by stating that it is soundly based; reliable; guarantees each member nation its correct VAT allocation; minimises the extra burden on traders; ensures the system's compatibility with the existing VAT administrative structure, bases clearance on data on individual transactions; and ensures that the mechanism is self-financing.

The EC Commission is also of the opinion that the removal of fiscal frontiers is impossible unless the approximation of VAT rates is achieved first. It therefore put forward proposals for both the number and levels of rates and the allocation of products to the rates. Being well aware that the SEA does not extend the system of majority voting to taxation (see Chapter 1), due to the obsession with national sovereignty mentioned above, the EC Commission stuck closely to the present system: it has suggested a dual-rate structure consisting of a standard (normal) and a reduced rate. The reduced rate is to cover basic necessities such as foodstuffs, energy products for

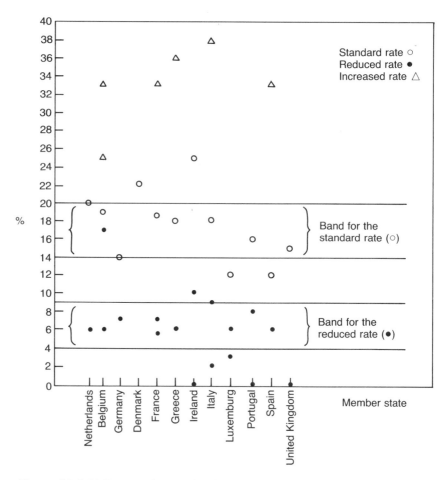

Figure 13.1 VAT rates in the EC – bands proposed by the European Commission and current rates in the member states (April 1987). (Source: European Commission, Europe without frontiers (Information 1987, p. 51); COM (87) 325–8.)

heating and lighting, water supplies, pharmaceuticals, books, newspapers, periodicals and passenger transport. To discourage excessive tax-induced distortions on competition, it has proposed a six-point band for the standard rate (14 per cent to 20 per cent) and a five-point band for the reduced rate (4 per cent to 9 per cent) – see Figure 13.1.

Precise rates have also been proposed by the EC Commission for excise duties. These rates are fixed amounts, specified in ECUs, for the various excises (on alcoholic beverages, mineral oils and tobacco products). Only for the sum of the *ad valorem* elements of excise duty and VAT (on tobacco products) is an optional margin allowed, the impact of which on retail prices will equal the VAT band for non-excisable products – see Table 13.4. The approximation of excise duties is tantamount to an equalisation of rates which the EC Commission deems to be necessary because VAT is also charged on excisable products, and the combined effect of differentials in excise and VAT rates might otherwise result in unreasonably high tax-induced differences in prices.

Of course, as mentioned above, some of these developments are not necessary if all that is being sought is an internal market. For example, the factors that influence prices are both numerous and diverse, and differentials in tax rates are only one such factor. That is why some authorities argue that it is only when frontiers are abolished, without prior harmonisation of tax rates, that the distortions arising primarily from fiscal factors can be measured. We have also seen that even in a federation as strong and as old as that of the United States, the equalisation of tax rates has not been necessary. Moreover, in the case of excise duties, the present system ensures that duties are charged where the goods are sold since exports are duty free; thus, for those dutiable goods mainly purchased by consumers, such as alcoholic drinks and tobacco products, the existing system provides fiscal neutrality with respect to the location of production, even though the member states apply very different levels of duty (Smith, 1988, p. 154). Be that as it may, the relevant criterion for judging the position of the EC Commission is the dynamic one concerning where the EC will want to go after 1992, and the EC has recently agreed to go for an EMU to be achieved in three stages (see Chapter 5). Thus it is perfectly in order for the EC Commission to ask for an approximation of rates. The piecemeal analysis carried out by most economists seems to centre around what is happening at a particular moment in time, but the EC Commission is entrusted with initiating efforts for the further integration of the Community; hence its perspective is, rightly, much wider and goes further into the future: reaching the summit requires looking out for the precipices.

13.5 Conclusions

In conclusion, it must be emphasised that the lack of fundamental progress in EC tax harmonisation during the period prior to the adoption of the SEA should not come as a surprise. There are three basic reasons for this. First, lest it be forgotten, the EC stands for the harmonised integration of some of the oldest countries in the world, with very diverse and extremely complicated economic systems, and this diversity and complexity is increasing with the enlargement (and potential enlargement) of the EC. Secondly, tax harmonisation is intimately connected with the role played by the government in controlling the economy and since this role depends on a complicated package of taxes, it should be apparent that the separate harmonising of the different components of the package is extremely difficult and probably also misguided. Finally, and more importantly, tax harmonisation, or at least the complex and sensitive elements within it, is very closely linked with the question of monetary integration and political unification. It is argued in Chapter 5 that these matters are very closely related. It would therefore be naive to expect substantial progress in tax harmonisation, without similar progress in these other fields. That is the reason why the EC Commission has fought hard to get the member nations to accept the Delors Report and thus to commit their governments to an EMU, and in the process hasten the need for fiscal harmonisation, but not necessarily for tax-rate equalisation.

Note

1. The first (67/227/EEC) and second (67/228/EEC) VAT directives (all the directives in this note are issued by the EC Council) were issued on 11 April 1967; they related to the harmonisation of legislation in EC member states – see *Official Journal of the European Communities* (*OJ*, hereafter), no. 71, 14 April 1967. The sixth (77/388/EEC) VAT directive of 17 May 1977 was also concerned with harmonisation in the member states – see *OJ* no. L 145, 13 June 1977 and no. L 149, 17 June 1977.

   The minor directives include: the eighth (79/1072/EEC) VAT directive of 6 December 1979 which is concerned with foreign taxable persons (*OJ*, no. L 331, 27 December 1979); and the tenth (84/386/EEC) VAT directive of 31 July 1984 concerning the application of VAT to the hiring out of movable tangible property (*OJ*, no. L 208, 3 August 1984).

   The latest act of draft directives is rather complex, thus the following is just a sample; the reader who is interested in the full list and its contents is advised to read the *OJ*.

   1. Proposal for a twelfth VAT directive concerning a common system of VAT, expenditure on which tax is not deductible (professional and private usage), COM(82)870, 25 January 1983 and COM(84)84, 16 February 1984 – see *OJ*, no. C 37 of 10 February 1983 and no. C 56 of 29 February 1984.
   2. Proposal for a thirteenth VAT directive relating to the refund of VAT to taxable persons not established in EC territory (in parallel to the eighth VAT directive), COM(82)443 of 15 July 1982 and COM(83)413 of 24 June 1983 – see *OJ*, no. C 223, 27 August 1982 and no. C 196, 23 July 1983.
   3. Proposal for a seventh VAT directive concerning a common system of VAT for used goods, COM(78)735 of 6 January 1978 and COM(79)249 of 4 May 1979 – see *OJ*, no. C26, 1 February 1978 and no. C 136, 31 May 1979.
   4. Proposal for a sixteenth VAT directive concerning the implementation at the EC level of the ruling by the Court of Justice regarding the avoidance of double taxation of used goods imported by a consumer in one EC member nation from a consumer in another, COM(84)318 of 18 July 1984 and COM(86)163 of 25 March 1986 – see *OJ*, no. C 226, 28 August 1984 and no. C 96, 24 April 1986.
   5. The eighteenth VAT directive concerning the abolition of certain derogations, which are still authorised within the framework of the sixth VAT directive, by 1 January 1992 at

the very latest, COM(84)649 of 30 November 1984 – see *OJ*, no. C 347, 29 December 1984.

6. Proposal for a nineteenth directive regarding clarifications to the sixth VAT directive, COM(84)648 of 22 November 1984 and 6 December 1984 – see *OJ*, no. C 347, 29 December 1984.

$\boxed{14}$ The General Budget

A. M. El-Agraa

As stated in the previous chapter, the General Budget of the European Communities (EC Budget hereafter) forms an integral and very important part of the Community's fiscal policy. Recall that, very widely interpreted, fiscal policy comprises a whole corpus of public finance issues, and that there are at least two basic elements to fiscal policy: the instruments available to the government for fiscal policy purposes (the total tax structure) and the overall impact of the joint manoeuvring of the instruments (the role played by the budget). The former was tackled in the previous chapter; the purpose of this chapter is to explain briefly the nature of the EC Budget; to discuss recent developments concerning it, to demonstrate why it has been inequitable and to suggest ways in which it could be made less so.

14.1 Expenditures

The EC Budget expenditures are grouped into two categories: compulsory and non-compulsory. The former is the expenditure emanating essentially from commitments in the treaties (such as the price support provided by the European Agricultural Guarantee and Guidance Fund – EAGGF, or FEOGA in French – and certain types of foreign aid to third countries) while the latter arises from the operational areas of the EC Budget (such as some of the expenditures of the European Regional Development Fund – ERDF – and the European Social Fund – ESF). Compulsory expenditures have a priority claim, which is why the EC Budget is necessarily 'functional', i.e. the EC has been endowed with revenues to discharge certain specific functions arising from well-defined activities it was required to undertake either in the original treaty or as subsequently agreed by the EC Council, including, of course, any financial commitments arising from the adoption of the Single European Act (SEA).

It should also be pointed out that the EC Budget expenditures are classified into two other types: payment appropriations and commitment appropriations. Payment appropriations define expenditure to be actually incurred during the financial year under consideration. Part of the payment may be in settlement of commitments made previously. Commitment appropriations define the ceiling on resources to be pledged in the current financial year. Part of the payment of commitment appropriations may be spread over subsequent years. As one would expect, the 'commitments' have always been in excess of the actual 'payments'. Note that the distinction originated in the Euratom Treaty (Article 176), but was not applied to other areas of expenditure until Regulation 76/919/ECSC, EEC, Euratom of 21 December 1976 was approved. Even then it was agreed as applicable only in some areas of expenditure, with many other areas dependent on a single set of 'undifferentiated' appropriations for payment during the year under consideration. In addition, special exemptions from the payment rules apply, for example, to EAGGF guarantee section in case of difficulties in disbursing actual payments within the financial year.

The EC Budget provides for two types of expenditure. First, there are the administrative expenses (staff salaries, costs of providing and disbursing information, etc.) of the institutions of the EC: the Commission, the Council, the European Parliament, the Court of Justice, the European Coal and Steel Community (ECSC), the ESF and the ERDF. Second, there are the operational expenditures of the EC Commission, such as the intervention and guidance expenses of EAGGF, ERDF support grants, 'food aid', etc. The EC Budget also provides for a miscellaneous collection of 'minor' expenditures.

In 1985, the EC Budget amounted to about 28.4 billion ECU (see Table 14.1), which was roughly equivalent to 18 billion pounds sterling (then, 1 ECU = £0.567748) or $21 billion (then, 1 ECU = $0.734949) or Y5,206 billion (then, 1 ECU

Table 14.1 The General Budget of the EC 1973–88

Year	Total payments (million ECU)	EAGGF guarantee (%)
1973	4,641	77.4
1974	5,037	67.3
1975	6,214	69.6
1976	7,993	71.8
1977	8,483	76.8
1978	12,363	70.2
1979	13,716	69.3
1980	16,182	73.0
1981	18,441	66.6
1982	21,987	59.7
1983	25,061	63.1
1984	27,248	67.3
1985	28,433	69.3
1986	35,174	62.9
1987	36,675	63.5
1988	43,820	62.8

Sources: Bulletin of the European Communities, various issues, *General Report on the Activities of the European Communities*, various issues, and various Eurostat publications.

= ¥183.113). The total for 1986 was 31.8 billion ECU for the EC of nine and 35 billion ECU for the EC of twelve, with the expenditure on the EAGGF guarantee section of the Common Agricultural Policy (CAP) falling to 62.9 per cent; the 59.7 per cent for 1982 was the smallest ever expenditure on this section of EAGGF. Note that the more than usual increase in the total EC Budget between 1983 and 1984 was due mainly to a substantial increase in agricultural spending, while the increases since 1986 are mainly due to the accumulation of commitments which must now be paid, and to some recent developments in the EC Budget itself – see below.

The total size of the EC Budget is of the same order of magnitude as that of a large UK department such as Health and Social Security or Education and Science. In US terms, it is equivalent to just under 8 per cent of total US 'national defence and veterans outlay', itself equal to 6.7 per cent of US GNP in 1984. In terms of Japan, the EC Budget is equivalent to the country's total expenditure on Culture, Education and Science Promotion in 1984, which was under 10 per cent of Japan's total government expenditure for that year. These comparative percentages have not changed much since 1984. The allegations regarding a very powerful EC Commission are thus ill founded. Moreover, the suggestion that the EC has a large bureaucracy is also incorrect since only about 4.5 per cent of the EC Budget is expenditure on adminis-tration and the EC Budget itself is less than 1 per cent of EC GDP (more on this below). However, this is not a justification for the vast number of translators and interpreters employed by the EC to assist with its official publications and meetings; it is high time the EC decided to reduce its official languages to a sensible number instead of the present system of using all the main EC languages.

14.2 Revenues

Turning to the financing side, the EC Budget revenues come from gross contributions termed 'own resources', i.e. the EC has its own independent and clearly defined revenue sources such that the EC member nations pay to it what actually belongs to it. This principle of 'own resources' was adopted after the Council Decision of 21 April 1970, and in 1980 fully replaced the previous system which was entirely based on national contributions determined largely in accordance with the member nations' relative economic strength.

Before the introduction of more radical changes in the EC Budget in 1987 there were three basic categories of own resources:

1. Agricultural and sugar levies.
2. Customs duties, i.e. the proceeds from industrial tariffs on imports from third countries.
3. Until 1984, up to 1 per cent of the common VAT base yield (see Table 14.2).

If more than 1 per cent of the VAT base yield is required, further legislation ratified by all the member nations becomes necessary – see below.

Table 14.2 Revenues of the EC General Budget 1982–8 (per cent)

Revenue	1982	1983	1984	1985	1986	1987	1988
Agricultural and sugar levies	12.2	11.7	9.1	7.4	7.0	8.6	6.1
Customs duties	31.6	34.6	30.1	30.2	24.3	24.7	21.4
VAT	54.6	52.0	55.2	54.4	66.2	64.7	55.1
Financial contributions	0.9	0.8	—	—	0.6	0.6	0.5
GNP based own resources	—	—	—	—	—	—	14.0
Miscellaneous revenue	0.7	0.9	1.8[a]	1.0	0.9	1.1	0.9
Advances from member states	—	—	3.8	7.0	—	—	1.2
Balance of VAT from previous financial years and adjustments to financial contributions	—	—	—	—	1.3	0.3	0.9
Total	100.0	100.0	100.0	100.0	100.0	100.0	100.0

Note
[a] The figure includes the surplus from 1983 (307.1 million ECU) and VAT/GNP balances corrections (−111.7 million ECU).

Sources: Bulletin of the European Communities, various issues; *General Report on the Activities of the European Communities*, various issues; and various Eurostat publications.

14.3 Net contributions

Table 14.3 gives gross contributions and gross receipts in 1980, together with net receipts for the period 1979–81, broken down by member nation; the choice of this period is to highlight the reasons for the budgetary battles during the early 1980s (later developments are considered below). It should be clear from the table that the United Kingdom and West Germany provided the largest share of gross contributions with regard to all three categories of the EC Budget revenues; the levies and tariffs categories are easily explained in terms of the two countries' large extra-EC trade. The table also shows Germany and the United Kingdom to have been the only net losers with regard to net receipts; this was the main reason for the UK budgetary battles with the EC, particularly since the United Kingdom was the second largest net contributor when its position in the league of EC GDP was third from the bottom. This anomaly arose simply because a large percentage of the EC Budget expenditures falls on agriculture when the size of the agricultural sector is not strictly related to GDP (Denmark with a large agricultural sector has the highest per capita income within the EC) and because VAT contributions, which are to a large extent related to GDP (see the previous chapter and Nevin, 1988), form only just over half of the total EC Budget revenues.

Finally, although the EC Budget is meant to be balanced, it is not true that gross contributions and expenditures always sum to zero; earlier on, there was a small increase in cash balances held by the EC 'which exercises a small deflationary effect' on the EC (Godley, 1980b, p. 76). However, in later years the EC has become short of funds and has had to seek special financing arrangements from the member nations in

Table 14.3 EC General Budget

	Gross contribu-tions, 1980 (% share)	Gross by source, agricul-tural levies	Contribu-tions 1980 industrial tariffs	VAT	Gross receipts 1980 (% share)	Net receipts (million ECU)		
						1979	1980[a]	1981[a]
Belgium and Luxemburg	6.1	11.0	7	5	11.9	+394	+250	+351
Denmark	2.4	2.0	2	3	4.4	+246	+174	+157
France	20.0	13.0	15	24	20.0	−50	+41	+102
W. Germany	30.1	20.0	30	31	23.5	−924	−1,177	−1,260
Ireland	0.9	0.5	1	1	3.8	+352	+372	+340
Italy	11.5	20.5	9	14	16.8	+345	+329	+215
Netherlands	8.4	15.0	9	6	10.5	+186	+215	+81
United Kingdom	20.5	19.0	27	16	8.7	−549	−203	−56

Note
[a] The 1980 and 1981 'Net receipts' allow for refunds to the United Kingdom (see Table 14.4 for further details).

Sources: Wallace, 1980, and various publications by the EC Commission.

order to pay for overdue expenditures on the CAP – see Table 14.2. Does this mean that inflationary pressure is being exerted on the economies of the EC? The answer depends on how these deviations from a balanced EC Budget are financed and on whether or not one is a 'Keynesian' or 'monetarist'; but this is not the place to discuss this issue.

14.4 Budgetary transfers

If the EC Budget is to be regarded as the 'embryo centre of a federal system' (Brown, in the first two editions of this book), its size relative to EC GDP (less than 1 per cent) means that it is at a very early stage in its development – more on this below. However, because the EC Budget expenditures are dominated by agricultural spending, it does play a significant role in the transfer of resources between the member nations; hence the British budgetary quarrels with the rest of the EC during the early 1980s. Discussion of this aspect has been very disappointing indeed; it concentrates on the CAP when a 'proper' evaluation of the extent of transfers should include a similar treatment of industrial products. For example, if a member nation ceases to import a manufactured product from outside the EC and replaces it by imports from a partner nation, that country will contribute less to the EC Budget revenues (reduced proceeds from industrial tariffs); but since this act is one of 'trade diversion' (see Chapter 4), the country will pay more per unit of that product in comparison with the pre-membership situation. This element of transfer of resources must surely be included in any proper evaluation – simply to allege that, on balance, this element is 'mutually advantageous' to all the member nations (*Cambridge Economic Policy Review*, no. 5,

April 1979) and hence that it is appropriate to ignore it, is to bypass the intricate issues raised with regard to the elimination of such effects – see El-Agraa (1989b), Mayes in El-Agraa (1982; 1988) and Chapter 6. In short, in order to assess the budgetary effects of the transfer of resources between the member nations, one needs to take into account *all* the elements that enter into such calculations.

14.5 Developments prior to the SEA

The inequity of the EC Budget was the main reason for the heated quarrels between the United Kingdom and the rest of the EC during the early 1980s. Through protracted discussions and compromises, the United Kingdom managed to reduce its net contribution (see Table 14.4) – note that 2.0 billion ECUs were equivalent to 1.1 billion pounds or $1.5 billion or Y366 billion. The 24–25 June 1984 Fontainebleau settlement, which asked for the raising of VAT to 1.4 per cent in 1986, included paying the United Kingdom 1.0 billion ECUs in 1984 and 66 per cent of the *difference* between its VAT contribution and the EC Budget expenditures in the United Kingdom in subsequent years. This was later interpreted to mean rebates of 1.0 billion ECUs for 1985 and 1.4 billion ECUs for 1986. These provisions were conditional on agreement regarding some changes in the CAP. First, the agriculture ministers agreed on 31 March 1984 on a package which reduced the EC's common farm prices by 0.5 per cent and relied on a system of quotas to restrict milk production from 103 million tonnes in 1983 to 99.2 million and 98.4 million tonnes in 1984 and 1985 respectively; thereafter it was to be pegged for a further three years. Ireland, whose dairy production is equivalent to 9 per cent of its GNP, was awarded a special dispensation in that its quota was actually increased (see Table 14.5); Greece (which was undergoing transition at the time) was the poorest EC member nation and was awarded treatment better than that of Ireland. Moreover, the quotas which already applied to sugar beet were extended to other surplus products such as cereals, oilseeds and processed tomatoes. In order to reduce wine production, new vines were banned until 1990. Finally, various production and consumption subsidies to livestock,

Table 14.4 UK net contribution to the EC Budget before compensation, compensation, and net contribution after compensation 1980–3 (million ECU)

Year	Net contribution before compensation	Compensation	Net contribution after compensation
1980	1512	1175	337
1981	1419	1410	9
1982	2036	1079	957
1983	1900[a]	750	1150[a]

Note
[a] These figures were approximate.

Source: Kindly supplied by Commissioner Christopher Tugendhat.

Table 14.5 EC changes in milk production 1984 (per cent)

	Milk quota
Belgium	−3.0
Denmark	−5.7
France	−2.0
W. Germany	−6.7
Greece	+7.2
Ireland	+4.6
Italy	0.0
Luxemburg	+3.5
Netherlands	−6.2
United Kingdom	−6.5

Source: EC Commission, 1984.

Table 14.6 Price changes for the 1984−5 farm year

	% Change in ECU	% Change in national currency	1985 inflation forecast
Belgium	−0.6	+2.7	+5.8
Denmark	−0.7	+1.5	+4.9
France	−0.6	+5.0	+7.1
W. Germany	−0.6	−0.6	+2.8
Greece	+0.4	+17.6	+19.8
Ireland	−0.6	+2.7	+7.8
Italy	−0.4	+6.4	+11.0
Luxemburg	−0.5	+2.8	+7.4
Netherlands	−0.5	−0.5	+2.0
United Kingdom	−0.6	−0.6	+5.3

Source: EC Commission, 1984.

butter, fruit and vegetables were reduced and the MCAs were to be phased out over four years.

The EC Commission felt that for 1985 the prices for most agricultural products should be kept unchanged, or if they were to change, that the changes should be modest and not exceed 2 per cent. For certain items, the Commission proposed significant reductions in prices, particularly for products where the guarantee threshold was exceeded. Indeed, the agreed package for 1985−6 included reductions in the prices of butter, beef/veal, sheepmeat and olive oil, with the target price for milk kept at the 1984−5 level.

These changes affected countries like Germany, the Netherlands and the United Kingdom by the full impact of the price cuts since they had positive MCAs. Countries with weak currencies found that the price cuts actually led to price rises ranging from 1.5 per cent for Denmark to 17.6 per cent for Greece (see Table 14.6). According to *The Economist* (7−13 April 1984), the outcome of the MCA changes 'is to turn the apparent 0.5 per cent cut in the ECUs into an average rise of 3.2 per cent in national currencies, which are the ones farmers get paid in'. Note that in all EC countries farmers experienced a fall in their real earnings when the 1984 inflation rates were taken into consideration; British farmers suffered the largest fall (5.9 per cent) and French farmers the smallest (2.1 per cent).

It may come as a surprise to learn that the agreed package did not reduce costs but actually raised them in 1984 and 1985. The package cost about 0.9 billion ECUs in 1984 and about 1.4 billion ECUs in 1985. However, in the longer term, relative costs are bound to decline, provided other things remained the same.

All these changes were formally adopted and ratified by the European Parliament and the EC member nations. The British government was pleased with them since a tightening of expenditures on the CAP was necessarily beneficial to countries like the United Kingdom. However, as we shall see in the final section, there is no reason for elation over this matter.

14.6 Most recent developments

The most recent developments in this area are to be found in the Decisions reached in the 11–12 February 1988 Council meeting. In order to fully appreciate them, it is necessary to have some background information first. This background is set out fully in the Commission's submission to the Council and Parliament on 28 February 1987 (COM(87)101 final).

In that report, the Commission drew attention to some disturbing developments concerning the EC Budget. Firstly, although the own-resource system was meant to provide financial stability so as to enable the Commission to concentrate on policy decisions, it had failed to do so due to the following:

1. The erosion in the traditional own resources (customs duties and agricultural levies) because of tariff reductions and increasing self-sufficiency in the EC.
2. The VAT base growing at a slower rate than economic activity because of the reduction in the share of consumption in total GNP.
3. The Fontainebleau mechanism actually decreasing the resources available insofar as the ceiling on VAT rates applied to the individual member nations which financed the abatement, not to the EC as such.

Secondly, as a consequence of the reluctance to provide additional finance to the EC, budgetary practices had arisen which disguised the real impact of expenditure decisions. These practices had to continue because new own resources were insufficient even by the time they were finally adopted. Thus, for the 1984 and 1985 EC Budgets, intergovernmental advances were needed to cover legal expenditure obligations, equivalent to an increase in the VAT rate of 0.14 per cent and 0.23 per cent respectively. For 1986 and 1987 underbudgeting of expenditure took place due to the exhaustion of the own resources then available, equivalent to 0.10 per cent and 0.23 per cent respectively. For all the years under consideration, the EC failed to provide a proper financial depreciation of agricultural stocks. The Commission argued that these, and similar developments led to a heavy burden weighing on the own-resources in future years. Thirdly, apart from the above, the system had not been adapted to more fundamental developments in the EC. This was because at best, VAT revenue produced little, if any, redistributive effect in relation to the relative prosperity of the member nations; the system as such provided no buffer for a structural decline in one of the components once the VAT ceiling had been reached – several types (not just two) of own resources are required to make the system sufficiently flexible; and VAT own resources were not in reality own resources of the EC, rather contributions by the member states – as such, EC expenditure was not subject to direct taxpayer control; the Commission argued that had the actual collection of VAT in member states been made on the harmonised VAT base, it would have been impossible for taxpayers to identify the EC share, and taxpayers would have been able to react similarly to other directly collected revenue by the EC.

The detailed analyses supporting these considerations cannot be tackled here, but it should be stressed that the Commission strongly argued that agricultural stocks represented a considerable potential liability on the EC Budget. Moreover, it pointed out an additional liability consisting of what had come to be known as the 'cost of the past'. This concerned in particular the EC's structural funds, but also related to development aid. Because of the marked increase in structural expenditure in recent years, mainly due to the two latest enlargements, the volume of outstanding commitments had risen rapidly. Indeed, the rapid build up of commitment appropriations had been stated policy as reflected in the annual EC Budget procedure. However, given the regulations and management practices, the scale of the rise had created some problems. Firstly, the underestimation of the time needed to complete the political, administrative and technical aspects of the operation had meant that commitments had translated into payments at a slower rate than had been expected. There had also been a tendency to inflate annual commitment appropriations to levels beyond the Commission's management capacity and the absorption capacity of the potential beneficiaries. Secondly, the failure to keep sufficient watch on the progress of operations had meant that a certain volume of commitments no longer had any real equivalent in terms of projects. These commitments should have been cancelled; but this was not always possible under the existing rules.

In short, one has to agree with the Commission's conclusion that to contain the growth of the 'cost of the past' and to return to proper EC Budget management, including its enactment in good time before the beginning of the fiscal year, the payment appropriations provided should flow from the commitments decided. Therefore, it was appropriate to apply budgetary discipline only to commitment appropriations and to do this only with due respect given to the political undertaking by the competent authority in the EC prior to the annual EC Budgetary process.

Given this background, the Commission put forward its own proposals for new EC own resources. These were largely endorsed by the Brussels Council of 29–30 June 1987. However, the finer details were left to the Copenhagen Council which met later in December; but since that Council ended in disagreement, the final decisions were left to the February 1988 Council. Since this is not the place to discuss the actual differences between the proposals suggested by the Commission and the final Council decisions, the interested reader is advised to consult El-Agraa (1990).

The Council decided (Council 1987) that there would be both an overall ceiling on own resources and annual ceilings for the period 1988–92. This would be done by laying down a ceiling for commitment appropriations in 1992 and determining an orderly evolution for them, maintaining a strict relationship between commitment appropriations and payment appropriations to ensure their compatibility and to enable the achievement of the ceilings for subsequent years as expressed in payment appropriations.

It also decided that the annual growth rate of EAGGF guarantee expenditure should not exceed 70 to 80 per cent of the annual growth rate of EC GNP. The expenditure on EAGGF guarantee was defined as that chargeable to Section III, Part B, Titles 1 and 2 (EAGGF Guarantee) of the EC Budget, less amounts corresponding to the disposal of ACP (the Afro-Caribbean–Pacific group – see Chapter 21) sugar, food aid refunds, sugar and isoglucose levy payments by producers and any other revenue raised from the agricultural sector in future years. For the financial years 1988–92, systematic depreciation costs for newly created agricultural stocks, commencing at their time of establishment, were to be financed from these allocations. The Council was to enter each year in its draft EC Budget the necessary appropriations to finance the costs of stock depreciation. Moreover, Council Regulation 1883/78 was to be modified so as to create a legal obligation to proceed to stock depreciation over the specified period in order to arrive at a normal stock situation by 1992.

The costs connected with the depreciation of existing agricultural stocks will be kept outside the guideline; 1,200 million ECUs will be inscribed in Title 8 of the EC Budget for this purpose for 1988, and 1,400 million ECUs per year, at 1988 prices, for the period 1989–92. Spain and Portugal will be treated in this respect as if their depreciation had been entirely financed by the EC in 1987; an appropriate restitution will be entered in Title 8 of the EC Budget for this purpose.

The reference basis for the definition of the annual allocations for EAGGF guarantee expenditure will be the 1988 figure of 27,500 million ECUs, at 1988 prices, adjusted in accordance with the points specified above regarding sugar, food aid, etc. The annual maximum allocation for any year after 1988 will be this figure multiplied by 70 to 80 per cent of the growth rate of EC GNP between 1988 and the year in question, again, given the above proviso.

In addition to this, new agricultural 'stabilisers' will be introduced. For example, the threshold for cereals will be set at 155 to 160 million tonnes per year for the period 1988–91, and an additional co-responsibility levy of 3 per cent will be provisionally charged at the beginning of each marketing year to ensure that agricultural expenditure stays within the specified limits. Similar quotas are set for oilseeds and protein products, existing stabilisers will continue for olive oil and cotton, the quota system for milk will be extended for another three years, etc. What is significant, however, is that the Council agreed to adopt provisions to limit supply by withdrawing agricultural land from production. This 'set-aside' programme is devised to complement market policy measures, and will be compulsory for member countries but optional for producers. Exceptions to compulsory application will be possible for certain regions 'in which natural conditions or the danger of depopulation militates against a reduction in production'. In the case of Spain, the exceptions may also relate, on the basis of objective criteria, to 'specific socio-economic circumstances, pursuant to the relevant' EC procedure. In the case of Portugal, the set-aside arrangements will be optional during the transition period. The set-aside period is a minimum of five years, but farmers may be allowed to terminate it after three years. The area involved must be at least 20 per cent of arable land used for cultivating products covered by the common market organisation, and the premium should cover the income lost by the farmer, the minimum level being 100 ECU/ha and the maximum 600 ECU/ha, rising to 700 ECU/ha in exceptional circumstances to be determined by the Commission. Farmers opting to set aside 30 per cent of their equivalent land will also be exempted from the basic and additional co-responsibility levy for 20 tonnes of cereals marketed. The EC contribution to the premiums will be 70 per cent of the first 200 ECUs, 25 per cent for ECUs between 200 and 400 and 15 per cent for ECUs between 400 and 600. The member states may grant farmers the possibility of using the land set aside for fallow grazing by means of extensive cattle farming or for producing lentils, chick peas and vegetables, but the conditions for these are still to be determined. The essential point, however, is that the EC undertakes to be responsible for only 50 per cent of the amount granted, with its contribution being 70 per cent for the first 100 ECUs, 25 per cent of the next 100 ECUs and 15 per cent of the third 100 ECUs; hence, the responsibility rests with farmers and the EC as well as the member nations. The EC contribution will be 50 per cent financed from the EAGGF guarantee section and 50 per cent from the guidance section. Finally, the possibility of fallow grazing and conversion will be introduced on a trial basis for three years; after that the Commission is asked to report to the Council and to submit appropriate proposals. In addition, the Council agreed to introduce optional EC arrangements for promoting the cessation of farming (early retirement). The necessary decision on this is expected during 1990.

In order to promote efficient budgetary management, the Council decided that EAGGF expenditure should be controlled by operating an efficient 'early warning' system for the development of the individual EAGGF expenditure chapters. Before the start of each budget year, the Commission is asked to define expenditure profiles for each budget chapter based on a comparison of monthly expenditure with the profile of the expenditure over the three preceding years. The Commission will then submit monthly reports on the development of actual expenditure against profiles. Given this early warning system, if the Commission finds that the rate of development of real expenditure is exceeding the forecast profile, or risks doing so, it will be entitled to use the management measures at its disposal, including those which it has under the stabilisation measures, to remedy the situation. If these measures prove insufficient, the Commission is asked to examine the functioning of the stabilisers in the relevant sector and, if necessary, present proposals to the Council calculated to strengthen their action. The Council is then required to act within a period of two months in order to remedy the situation.

To enable the Council and the Commission to apply the above rules, it was agreed that measures shall be taken to accelerate the transmission and treatment of data supplied by the member countries on agricultural expenditure within each marketing organisation in order to ensure that the rate at which appropriations in each chapter are used is known with precision one month after the expenditure has occurred. Existing agricultural legislation will be adapted to ensure this. The special provisions concerning the financing of the CAP decided for 1987 will continue to apply. However, the delay of the advances by the Commission to member states shall be extended from two to two and a half months. The existing system for payment of interest will be continued, but payment of EC advances is made conditional on member states complying with their obligation to make available to the Commission the information given above justifying EC payment.

The above decisions, together with the statement that the agricultural price proposals should be consistent with the specified limits and the provision of a 'monetary reserve' of 1,000 million ECUs to cater for movements in the ECU/US dollar rate, can be broadly described as decisions consistent with the Commission proposals for 1987.

With regard to non-compulsory expenditure, the Council reaffirmed its 1987 Brussels decision that budgetary discipline must be applied to all EC expenditure, both to payment appropriations and to commitment appropriations, and this must be binding on all the institutions which will be associated with the implementation. The Council, for its part, decided to apply the provisions of Article 203(9) of the Treaty in such a way as to ensure that two guidelines will be respected:

1. Progression of the non-compulsory expenditures which have been the subject of a multi-annual financing decision by the Council for the period 1988–92 (structural funds, IMP – Integrated Mediterranean programme – and research) ensuring that such decisions will be honoured.
2. Progression of non-compulsory expenditures other than that referred to in (1) equal to the maximum rate of increase communicated by the Commission.

The results of these guidelines should be considered as a maximum by the member states during all the budget procedure.

It was also decided that, in the interest of better budgetary management, carry-overs of differentiated appropriations shall no longer be automatic. However, it was also decided that the size of any future negative reserves in the EC Budget should be limited to 200 million ECU.

As to the structural funds, it was agreed that the member states shared the broad outlines of the Commission's general approach on the reform of the funds: they confirmed the conclusions of the Brussels Council concerning renationalisation of the funds' objectives, concentration of their measures in accordance with EC criteria, due account being taken of the relative underdevelopment of certain regions or of regions in industrial decline and recourse to the programme method. It was reiterated that the EC operations under these funds, the EIB (European Investment Bank) and the other financial instruments should support the achievement of the general objectives set out in Articles 130(A) and 130(C) of the Treaty by contributing to the achievement of five priority objectives:

1. Promoting the development and structural adjustment of the less-developed regions.
2. Converting the regions, border regions or part regions (including employment areas and urban communities) seriously affected by industrial decline.
3. Combating long-term unemployment.
4. Facilitating the integration of young people.
5. Speeding up the adjustment of agricultural structures and promoting the development of rural areas, all within the context of reforming the CAP.

The funds' finances are to be increased in a manner consistent with these objectives. The details of these increases are too elaborate to state here.

As to own resources, a limit of 1.25 per cent to 1.30 per cent of EC GDP is adopted, but before the end of 1991, the Commission is asked to report on the operation of the system and the application of the budgetary discipline. It was also affirmed that the EDF will continue to be financed outside the EC Budget. It was further agreed that the correction of budgetary imbalances would be carried out in such a way that the amount of own resources available for EC policies was not affected.

With regard to the details of own resources, the Council has decided to continue to use the agricultural levies and sugar and isoglucose duties as a source, together with the addition of ECSC duties, but has refused the Commission's suggestion regarding the elimination of the 10 per cent refund for collection costs in both cases. The Council also offered the Commission two options for remaining sources. The first option includes:

1. The application of a rate of 1.4 per cent, valid for all member states, to the assessment basis for VAT which is determined in a uniform manner for member states according to the EC rules.
2. The application of a rate to be determined under the budgetary procedure in the light of the total of all other revenue, but not exceeding 1.4 per cent, to an additional base representing the difference between the sum of GNP at market prices and the sum of the bases for VAT as stated in (1) of all member states. It was added that for each member state this additional base may not exceed 55 per cent of GNP at market prices.

The second option included:

1. As in first option, but with the specific rate being 1.4 per cent in 1988, 1.3 per cent in 1989, 1.2 per cent in 1990 and 1.1 per cent in both 1991 and 1992, and the assessment basis for VAT may not exceed 60 per cent of GNP at market prices for each member state.

2. The application of a rate to be determined under the budgetary procedure in the light of the total of all other revenue to an additional base representing the sum of GNP at market prices.

No logical explanation has been provided to justify these formulae.

As to the compensation mechanism for the United Kingdom, it was decided to continue with the Fontainebleau mechanism.

14.7 A proper budget?

Before concluding this chapter, it is interesting to ask whether the EC Budget can be made to perform proper fiscal policy functions, i.e. can it be used to reduce income disparities between the member nations? Can it perform stabilising functions? Even with the new and increased own resources, the budget will not do much in this respect, given the recommendation of the MacDougall Report (1977) for a minimum budget of about 2.5 per cent as a necessary precondition for EC monetary integration. However, even the MacDougall recommendations are in the nature of a compromise since a proper system must necessarily incorporate progressivity in order to ensure a narrowing of income disparities between the member nations and an equitable distribution of any possible gains and losses. In El-Agraa and Majocchi (1983) it was demonstrated how a progressive income-tax method can gradually be introduced in such a way that the EC Budget eventually approximates to the ideal. This section is devoted to a brief consideration of this vital issue.

To describe the nature of the proposed mechanism, an exercise can be developed with regard to fiscal year 1980 when the principle of own resources (a decision on which was taken on 21 April 1970) was fully operational – see Wallace (1980, pp. 54–8). 1980 is a convenient year since then Greece, Portugal and Spain were not parties to the inequity issue. However, the original figure given for that year (24.8 billion ECUs) has in reality come closer to the 1983 payment appropriations. The main hypothesis is that the size of the EC Budget is to be made equal to 2.5 per cent of EC GDP, in accordance with the recommendations of the MacDougall Report. EC Budget expenditures are, therefore, to increase to 49,687.5 million ECU. These expenditures are to be financed by the traditional resources plus an income tax. The first two sources of revenue (agricultural levies and customs duties) are provided according to the factors so far determining them. The differences between these receipts and payments appropriations is covered by VAT and the income tax.

The burden of income taxation must fall among the member states in a progressive way. To achieve this, the EC establishes at the beginning a proportional rate that can be fixed, say 50 per cent of the share of EC expenditures in EC GDP. The total yield of the proportional income tax is, therefore, 24,843.8 million ECUs (see Table 14.7). The yield for each country is obtained by multiplying the common rate (1.25 per cent) by the national GDP and is equal, as a share of the total yield, to the proportion of each country's GDP in EC GDP (see Table 14.8, columns 1 and 2).

Table 14.7 Financing an EC budget equal to 2.5 per cent of EC GDP

	Million ECU	% of total
Agricultural levies	1,535.4	3.09
Sugar levy	466.9	0.94
Customs duties	5,905.7	11.89
VAT	16,324.1	32.85
Miscellaneous	611.6	1.23
Indirect taxation	24,843.7	50.00
Income taxation	24,843.8	50.00
Total	49,687.5	100.00

Source: *Fourteenth General Report of the Activities of the European Communities* (Brussels, 1981), p. 57.

Table 14.8 National distribution of income tax burden

	1[a]	2[b]	3[c]	4[d]	5[e]	6[f]	7[g]
Belgium	1,048.4	4.22	1.1188	4.47	1,110.5	1.32	1.059
Denmark	598.8	2.41	1.2260	2.80	695.6	1.45	1.162
France	5,868.1	23.62	1.1489	25.71	6,387.4	1.36	1.088
W. Germany	7,373.6	29.68	1.2597	35.42	8,799.7	1.49	1.193
Ireland	159.0	0.64	0.4915	0.30	74.5	0.58	0.469
Italy	3,547.7	14.28	0.6536	8.85	2,198.7	0.78	0.620
Luxemburg	42.2	0.17	1.1903	0.19	47.2	1.43	1.145
Netherlands	1,508.0	6.07	1.1219	6.45	1,602.4	1.33	1.063
United Kingdom	4,698.0	18.91	0.8824	15.81	3,927.8	1.04	0.836
Total	24,843.8	100.00		100.00	24,843.8		

Notes
[a] $T_i = t_a Y_i$ with $\sum_{i=1}^{9} T_i = T = t_a Y$, $t_a = 0.0125$;
[b] $Y_i/Y = T_i/T = y_i$;
[c] $k_i = (Y_i/N_i)/(Y/N)$;
[d] $t_i = (k_i T_i)/(\sum_i k_i T_i)$;
[e] $T_i^\star = t_i T$;
[f] $t_{ai}^\star = t_a(t_i/y_i) = (T_i^\star/Y_i)$;
[g] t_i/y_i; where Y is GDP, t the tax rate, and T the total tax yield.

The parameter chosen for a progressive distribution of income taxation among EC countries is per capita income. Column 3 of Table 14.8 shows the ratio between each country's per capita income and the EC average. The amount of income tax attributed to each country under a progressive scale is determined by multiplying first the proportional yield (column 1) by the ratio of column 3(2). Thus the new share for each country of the total yield is established (column 4). By multiplying such a share by the total yield to be provided, the amount of income tax is determined for each EC nation (column 5). The per capita burden of income taxation is thus different in each country and a scale of rates follows ranging from 0.58 for Ireland to 1.49 for West Germany (column 6). The effective rate for each country equals the proportional rate multiplied by a progressivity coefficient (column 7), represented by the ratio between the effective share of each country in total yield (column 4) and the share of each country in EC GDP (column 2).

If the chosen size of the EC Budget is different, the effective rate for each country can be established by multiplying the proportional rate, fixed with regard to the level of expenditure to be covered by income taxation, by the progressivity coefficient of column 7.

The degree of progressivity, as measured by the elasticity of the yield with regard to the change in income, is very high and near 2 per cent. The implicit tax function, estimated by normal cross-section regression, has in fact the following exponential shape:

$$\lg T/N = \underset{(0.04463)}{-13.407} + \underset{(0.00501)}{2.004} \lg Y/N$$

where the figures in brackets are the standard errors of coefficients.

The distribution among the member states of the burden of income taxation is thus defined, and the target (of a progressivity hitting the richer countries more heavily than the poorer) is attained. The second step is the distribution within each country among its own citizens. In the proposed scheme, this is left for each country to determine in accordance with its income-tax progressivity scale. The distributive formula among the citizens is therefore considered to be beyond the boundaries of EC competence: what is important, from an EC viewpoint, is only the levelling of economic conditions for the member states such that a true economic and monetary union can be realised.

The gap between the amount of payments appropriations and the revenue accruing from income taxation, agricultural levies and customs duties is filled by VAT collections; hence VAT plays a residual role. The expected yield is divided by the VAT tax base to determine its rate.

The distribution of the total burden of financing an EC Budget equal to 2.5 per cent of EC GDP among the member nations is represented in Table 14.9. The share computed for each country by the Commission for fiscal year 1980 is adopted with respect to agricultural levies, customs duties and VAT. The values for the income taxation are taken from Table 14.8.

The result is shown in column 1, where the global share for each country of the total yield from the proposed scheme can be compared with the effective share in fiscal year 1980 (according to the Commission calculations) – column 2 – and with the share of each country's GDP in EC GDP – column 3. From the revenue side, a redistribution-oriented budget emerges, which should support a more balanced growth of the EC economy.

One should ask at least two questions about the proposed scheme. Is it a just and efficient one? Is it a feasible one? From the point of view of justice, it seems difficult, at first sight, to accept that the per capita burden of income taxation differs in the member states according to the level of average income in each state. It is important to

Table 14.9 National distribution of the total income tax burden

	Agricultural levies, etc.	VAT	Income tax	Total	1	2	3
Belgium	660.2	723.2	1,110.5	2,494.0	5.02	6.00	4.22
Denmark	168.7	419.5	695.6	1,283.8	2.58	2.40	2.41
France	1,238.7	3,943.9	6,387.4	11,570.0	23.29	20.00	23.62
W. Germany	2,319.9	5,259.7	8,799.6	16,379.2	32.96	30.10	29.68
Ireland	81.8	140.4	74.5	296.7	0.60	0.90	0.64
Italy	1,153.6	1,905.0	2,198.7	5,257.3	10.58	11.60	14.28
Luxemburg	5.1	34.4	47.2	86.6	0.17	0.10	0.17
Netherlands	874.1	1,025.2	1,602.4	3,501.7	7.05	8.40	6.07
United Kingdom	2,017.4	2,873.0	3,927.8	8,818.2	17.75	20.50	18.91
Total	8,519.6	16,324.1	24,843.8	49,687.5	100.00	100.00	100.00

Source: *Eurostat Review*, 1971–80.

recall here that the national income-taxation quota is distributed among the citizens according to the progressivity scale applied in domestic taxation. It is therefore, unlikely that the poor in a richer country will pay more than the rich in a poorer country. In any case, the difference in the burden of income taxation can be justified if one also takes into account the fact that the poor citizens of a richer member state can exploit many opportunities and enjoy benefits which are unavailable to those of a poorer member nation.

With regard to efficiency, this type of taxation introduces a strong fiscal incentive to reduce disequilibria within the EC. In particular, the stronger countries take an interest in the growth of per capita income in the weaker member nations insofar as, if convergence ensues, their own burden of income taxation is reduced. Indeed, if a perfect equalisation of per capita incomes is attained, the coefficient of progressivity will become one for all the member nations, and the distribution of income taxation among them will become proportional. Meanwhile, the weaker member nations have no incentive to slacken their efforts in reducing disparities in the level of income since, with a progressive income taxation, the elasticity of disposable income is less than one, but considerably larger than zero.

Concerning the political feasibility of the proposal, it is important to stress the need to clearly define an overall strategy relating to the growth of the budget. A plan for economic and monetary union involves a whole series of coordinated decisions spread over a long period of time. Since such decisions have to be taken at different times by more than one decision-making body, they are unlikely to be effective if there is no stated general frame of reference.

14.8 Conclusion

It should be apparent from the foregoing that a proper analysis of the future prospects for the EC Budget cannot be confined to its present structure. The EC Budget must be seen not, only in its proper context of public finance but also in the wider context of the ultimate objectives of the Community as a whole. Given its existing structure and the present stage reached in the EC integrative process, an equitable EC Budget, in the absence of forthcoming *fundamental* reform of the CAP, must aim at increasing the non-compulsory expenditures (regional, social and industrial aspects including employment generation, not just the so-called structural expenditures). This would require more than the mere strengthening of the recent changes in the EC Budget since the introduction of a progressive income tax facility for revenue-raising purposes (recall that VAT, which is still prominent in the new EC Budget structure, is regressive), especially now that the EC has agreed to introduce an EMU in three stages, with the first stage to begin in 1990 – see Chapter 5. The proposal put forward in El-Agraa and Majocchi (1983) is a practical one with very clear guidelines since it has a well-defined framework for reference. Moreover, it is not beyond the reach of the EC, given the present mood of the member nations and recalling that before the own-resource system was introduced in 1970, the EC Budget was financed by national contributions determined according to each member nation's relative prosperity within the EC.

Note

1. With the introduction of the progressivity coefficient the yield of income taxation does not change unless:
$$[t_a \sum_{i=1}^{6} Y_i(Y_iN/N_iY) + t_a \sum_{j=1}^{3} Y_j(Y_jN/N_jY)] - [t_a \sum_{i=1}^{6} Y_i + t_a \sum_{j=1}^{3} Y_j] = 0$$
where countries i have an above EC average per capita income and countries j a per capita income lower than the EC average. Rearranging the terms, the condition can be expressed as:
$$\sum_{i=1}^{6} Y_i(Y_iN/N_iY - 1) - \sum_{j=1}^{3} Y_j(1\ Y_jN/N_jY) = 0$$
Thus the condition shows that the yield increases if a progressivity coefficient larger than 1 is applied to countries i with a large (in absolute terms) cumulative national income and a progressivity coefficient lower than 1 to countries j with a small cumulative national income, the final result depending also on the values of the progressivity coefficients. This is what is happening in the numerical example in Table 14.8.

15 The European Monetary System

M. J. Artis

15.1 Founding and inception of the System

The European Monetary System (EMS) began operation on 13 March 1979 following a decision of the Council of Ministers meeting in Brussels in December 1978. The short delay between the Council's favourable decision and the actual inception of the EMS accommodated the negotiation of additional assistance to Italy and the Irish Republic, both of which were thought likely to encounter some difficulties in adjusting to the EMS. The initiative for the establishment of the EMS came, not from the EC Commission, but from the prime ministers of Germany and France, Helmut Schmidt and Giscard d'Estaing. Their decision was in turn guided by a perception that the United States was not capable at the time of exercising a responsible leadership in global monetary affairs and the proximate aim of the EMS was to create a zone of monetary stability in Europe – see Chapter 5. This aim accorded well with the strong, historically based aversion to inflation which governed German economic policy and the German interest in shielding its currency from the effects of irregular speculation against the US dollar together with the long-standing desire of successive French governments to break away from the global dominance of the United States in monetary affairs. The initiative happened also to fill what had been perceived as a disturbing deceleration in the momentum of political development of the EC and corresponded closely to a call made by the Commission's President in his speech at Florence in October 1977 for a corrective initiative along just these lines.

Preparations for the establishment of the EMS involved extensive discussions among the potential members from the moment when the idea was first floated in the Council of Ministers meeting at Copenhagen in April 1978 and in these the United Kingdom played a full role, although it was clear from the start that the British side had substantial reservations about the idea. (Ludlow (1982) gives a very ample account of the negotiations involved.) When the time for decision came, the EMS, although involving all the other members of the EC at the time, was launched without the full participation of the United Kingdom.

15.2 Provisions of the EMS

The most significant provisions of the EMS relate to the so-called parity grid of bilateral exchange rates or what is called the 'exchange-rate mechanism' (ERM). This is the vital aspect of the operation of the EMS and is the part to which the United Kingdom decided not to adhere on inception of the system, a position it maintains to this day.

Under the provisions of the parity grid, member countries – aside from Italy and Spain – undertake to maintain their exchange rates with each other within $\pm 2\frac{1}{4}$ per cent of a central rate of exchange. Italy negotiated a wider ± 6 per cent band for its currency to enable it to achieve a smoother transition from outside the previous snake arrangement, and in June 1989 Spain followed the Italian precedent, joining the ERM with a similar ± 6 per cent band.

Central rates of exchange are denominated for convenience in terms of a composite currency, the European currency unit (ECU) and may be changed by collective decision in a formal 'realignment'.[1] Table 15.1 shows the composition of the ECU which, as can be seen, comprises literally so many French francs, so many deutschmarks, so many pounds sterling, etc. These components were selected so as to provide a weighting of currencies in the ECU in accord with relative GNP and trade and are subject to review every five years; at the last review the ECU was changed to accommodate the inclusion of the drachma. It may be noted that representation of a country's currency in the ECU and its participation in the ERM are *not* coterminous, as, for example, neither the pound sterling nor the drachma belong to the ERM. The Spanish peseta and Portuguese escudo are to be included in the ECU with effect from 20 September 1989.

The use of a composite currency in which to denominate the central rate is not strictly necessary to the operation of the parity grid – participants in the ERM could

Table 15.1 Composition and weighting of the ECU and DI threshold

Country (currency)	Composition of the ECU (Units of national currency)		Percentage weight as of 31 December 1988	Divergence indicator threshold, % 31 December 1988
	13 March 1979–14 September 1984	From 17 September 1984		
Belgium/Luxemburg (franc)	3.80	3.85	8.8	1.54
Denmark (krone)	0.217	0.219	2.7	1.64
France (franc)	1.15	1.31	18.3	1.38
W. Germany (mark)	0.828	0.719	34.6	1.10
Greece (drachma)	–	1.15	0.7	nr
Ireland (punt)	0.00759	0.00871	1.1	1.67
Italy (lira)	109.000	140.00	9.5	4.07
Netherlands (guilder)	0.286	0.256	10.9	1.50
United Kingdom (pound sterling)	0.0885	0.0878	13.3	nr

simply have announced their adherence to a consistent set of bilateral central rates and bands. But the use of the ECU has useful symbolic connotations and may be felt to give the EMS an identity over and above that which would be commanded by a mere agreement to stabilise exchange rates – the identity, in fact, of a potential monetary union. EC transactions are denominated in ECU, as are the debts acquired by central banks intervening to support their currencies in the framework of the EMS.

In addition, the ECU did provide a necessary basis for what appeared at the time to be the most innovative technical feature of the EMS, that of the 'divergence indicator'. The essential role that the divergence indicator (DI) was designed to perform was that of enforcing timely and symmetrical adjustment. The idea of the indicator was that it should be designed so as to signal when a currency was becoming out of line with the rest of the system. Coupled with the injunction that the 'flashing' of the indicator gave 'a presumption' of corrective policy action on behalf of the country whose currency was singled out in this way, the DI would – it was hoped – enforce adjustment equally on a strong-currency country or on a weak-currency country, provided that the currency in question stood out from the pack. Combining this role with that of providing an early warning, the DI was to be triggered when a currency crossed a threshold set at 75 per cent of its permitted $\pm 2\frac{1}{4}$ per cent movement against all other currencies in the EMS. Because each currency is itself a component of the ECU, the DI threshold in terms of the ECU is less than $\pm(0.75 \times 2.25 = 1.675$ per cent) of the currency's central rate by an amount which is larger the larger is that currency's weight in the ECU (see the last column of Table 15.1).

Flanking these exchange-rate provisions, with the obligation to intervene at the bilateral limits and the 'presumption of action' created by a triggering of the DI threshold, the EMS also provided for credit mechanisms to enable weak-currency countries to borrow in order to defend their currencies. The principal such mechanism, called the VSTF (very short-term financing facility) provides for the extension of credit from one central bank to another, repayable over a term initially of 45 days; at the bilateral limits one central bank can call on another for credit in the partner's currency without prospect of a refusal, the amount being repaid under this mechanism. In the most recent extensions to the EMS negotiated in Nyborg in September 1987, the term of repayment under the VSTF was increased to 60 days and, more important, the provision for 'automatic' borrowing for intervention at the limits was extended to cover intervention *within* the limits (so-called intra-marginal intervention). In association with its credit mechanisms the founding of the EMS called for the central banks concerned to pool 20 per cent of their gold and dollar reserves in exchange for ECUs in a central fund, the EMCF (European Monetary Cooperation Fund).

15.3 Precursors of the EMS

The provisions and aspirations of the EMS reflected in part lessons felt to have been learnt from past endeavours among EC members to stabilise their currencies.[2] The recurrent failures marking these endeavours contributed to the absence of high aspirations to European monetary union (EMU) in the stated objectives of the EMS: by contrast, the Werner Report of 1972 had projected the achievement of EMU by 1980 – for a fuller discussion of this, see Chapter 5. Recent practical experience embodied in the failure of the so-called snake also contributed to the design of the DI and to a greater degree of self-consciousness about the need for multilateral decision making on such issues as realignments.

The snake took shape in April 1972 as a response to the acceptance by the EC of the Werner Committee's optimistic goal setting, and more immediately as a response to the Smithsonian Agreement of the previous December. That Agreement sought to extend the life of the Bretton Woods system by reinstating a global system of fixed but adjustable exchange rates on the basis of wider bands than had prevailed during previous decades; the dollar, although undergoing a discrete devaluation of its price in terms of gold, remained the numeraire key currency of the new system. Since the exchange rates of individual European currencies against the dollar were to be confined under the Smithsonian to $\pm 2\frac{1}{4}$ per cent, this implied that European currencies could move against each other by $\pm 4\frac{1}{2}$ per cent. The European countries sought to correct this and the snake agreement, which involved all six of the funding members, joined shortly after its inception by the United Kingdom, Ireland, Denmark and Norway (all countries which at that time anticipated becoming members of the EC), simply suggested that exchange rates between participating countries should also be limited to $\pm 2\frac{1}{4}$ per cent bands of fluctuation. It was from this period that the system earned the sobriquet 'snake in the tunnel', in that while the snake currencies were pegged within the Smithsonian margins against the dollar (the 'tunnel'), their variation against each other was more tightly constrained by the provisions of the snake agreement. The provisions of the snake continued to be pursued even after generalised floating against the dollar took place (in 1973), whereupon it became known as the 'snake outside the tunnel'. Just the same analogy can be applied to the EMS as the system as a whole floats against third currencies like the US dollar.

The snake agreement was a failure. Sterling left it as early as June 1972 and the lira left in February 1973. The French franc left the snake, rejoined it and left again. There were several other changes. It ended as a collection of smaller currencies heavily dominated by the deutschmark and including some non-EC currencies – a 'worm' or small deutschmark zone – and even within this grouping there were several changes of parity. The goal of establishing EMU by 1980 was officially abandoned by December 1974 – see Chapter 5.

One reason diagnosed for the calamity of the snake was that German dominance of the system was excessive and the invention of the DI was in part a result of this apprehension. Another was that decision making was unilateral (as it had been in the Bretton Woods system), so countries could change their parity agreement without feeling any restraining influence from other members of the system.

The EMS benefited from lessons learnt from this period to emerge as a better founded arrangement with more modest immediate objectives than its predecessor. Nevertheless, when it was launched, scepticism was widespread that the EMS could succeed where its precursors had failed. It was not difficult to greet the inauguration of the EMS as yet further evidence of the triumph of hope over experience.

15.4 The System in operation: the overall balance sheet in summary

The survival of the EMS has belied this early scepticism and although there are reasons for expressing renewed scepticism (see below) there is little dispute that the EMS has so far been something of a success. This success can be seen as embodied in three principal achievements.

First, despite occasional realignments and fluctuations of currencies within their pre-set bands, it seems that the EMS has succeeded in its proximate objective of stabilising exchange rates – not in the absolute sense but in the relevant and realistic sense of appearing to have brought about more stability than would have been enjoyed without it. Moreover, this has been done without provoking periodic speculative crises such as marred the demise of the Bretton Woods system.

Second, the claim is made for the EMS that it has provided a framework within which member countries have been able to pursue counter-inflationary policies at a lesser cost in terms of unemployment and lost output than would have been possible otherwise.

Third, while it is claimed that nominal exchange-rate stability has been secured it is also argued that the operation of the EMS has prevented drastic changes in *real* exchange rates (or 'competitiveness'). This is contrasted with the damaging experience in this respect of both the United Kingdom and the United States over the same period.

Finally, while not an immediate objective of the EMS as such, it is well worth mentioning that the ECU has become established as a significant currency of denomination of bond issues, which can be viewed as some testimony to the credibility of the EMS and the successful projection of its identity.

These achievements – which we detail and examine below – have not been without some qualifications. The DI mechanism does not appear to have withstood the test of time, for example, while sceptics would charge that the counter-inflationary achievements of the EMS in fact amount to little more than a bias against growth and expansion. Finally, the existence of exchange controls in some of the leading countries (notably France and Italy) means that hitherto the EMS has not significantly promoted financial integration and has shielded these countries from the need to contemplate the environment for policy making which will be brought about by their removal. Yet the 1992 project poses precisely such a challenge since it requires (and countries have, in fact, agreed to implement this by July 1990) the removal of exchange controls – for more on this, see Chapter 5. The EMS also faces the further challenge of how to integrate the United Kingdom fully into its mechanisms. Each of these considerations requires amplification.

15.5 Exchange-rate stability

As the EMS allows for realignments and for fluctuations of its currencies within the bands, absolute exchange-rate stability has not been achieved. However, realignments have been few in number, have not always involved the major currencies, have usually been small and have grown less frequent with the passage of time. Table 15.2 details all the realignments that have taken place, from which the support for these contentions is obvious. A particular feature of the realignment process is that, with some exceptions, it has been free from speculation. When the speculative crises which dogged the end of the Bretton Woods system are recalled, this is a remarkable achievement. An innovation of the EMS in this regard is the practice of carrying out a realignment in such a way that the central rate and bands are changed without disturbing the market rate. This device robs the market of the opportunity to make a one-way bet. The difference is illustrated in Figure 15.1. The one-way bet realignment is sketched in 15.1b: the discrete disturbance of the market rate, if correctly anticipated, affords huge gains to speculators. For example, if a currency is allowed to drift to the bottom of its band so that it can only be expected to be devalued by, say, 5 per cent, the gross gains from correctly anticipating the day on which this takes place substantially exceed, in annual interest rate terms, a rate of 1,500 per cent (5 × 365). Speculators could take advantage of this situation by borrowing the weak currency to buy the strong one in anticipation of the devaluation, thereafter redeeming the loan in cheaper currency: clearly interest rates in the weak currency country would have to be very high indeed to challenge the huge gains in prospect. The EMS technique of changing the central rate and thus the bands *around* the current market rate in a 'timely' realignment (15.1a) robs the speculator of the incentive of such large gains. In practice, EMS realignments have not always been 'timely' – Kenen (1988) estimates the proportion to be just over 70 per cent – and exchange controls have also played a role in deterring speculation. The demise of these controls will put a higher premium on the exercise of the non-provocative realignment procedure described.

Given that realignments have taken place and that currencies have fluctuated within the permitted bands, it cannot be assumed that the EMS has necessarily imparted stability to nominal exchange rates. This question can however be examined statistically. Investigators who have done this have taken to assuming as a counter-factual (or anti-monde) that in the absence of the EMS, exchange-rate stability would have evolved in the same way for the EMS currencies as it did for non-EMS currencies. Thus the examination proceeds by comparing a measure of exchange-rate stability for the EMS currencies with a similar measure for non-EMS currencies before, and after, the EMS period itself. By varying the precise measure of the exchange rate used (bilateral or effective; (log) level or (log) change), the data frequency (weekly, monthly, quarterly), and the precise measure of stability employed, this basic counterfactual assumption has supported a variety of estimates. From them, however, a strong consensus has emerged that the EMS has exerted a stabilising influence on the bilateral nominal exchange rates of its members and on their effective nominal rates.

Table 15.2 Realignments of EMS currencies (per cent changes)

| | \ | | | | | Dates of realignments | | | | | |
	24 September 1979	30 November 1979	22 March 1981	5 October 1981	22 February 1982	14 June 1982	21 March 1983	21 July 1985	7 April 1986	4 August 1986	12 January 1987
Belgian franc	0.0	0.0	0.0	0.0	-8.5	0.0	+1.5	+2.0	+1.0	0.0	+2.0
Danish kroner	-2.9	-4.8	0.0	0.0	-3.0	0.0	+2.5	+2.0	+1.0	0.0	0.0
German mark	+2.0	0.0	0.0	+5.5	0.0	+4.25	+5.5	+2.0	+3.0	0.0	+3.0
French franc	0.0	0.0	0.0	-3.0	0.0	-5.75	-2.5	+2.0	-3.0	0.0	0.0
Irish punt	0.0	0.0	0.0	0.0	0.0	0.0	-3.5	+2.0	0.0	-8.0	0.0
Italian lira	0.0	0.0	-6.0	-3.0	0.0	-2.75	-2.5	-6.0	0.0	0.0	0.0
Dutch guilder	0.0	0.0	0.0	+5.5	0.0	+4.25	+3.5	+2.0	+3.0	0.0	+3.0

Source: Ungerer *et al.* (1986), The European Monetary System: recent developments, *Occasional Paper*, no. 48, International Monetary Fund, Table 7, p. 35.

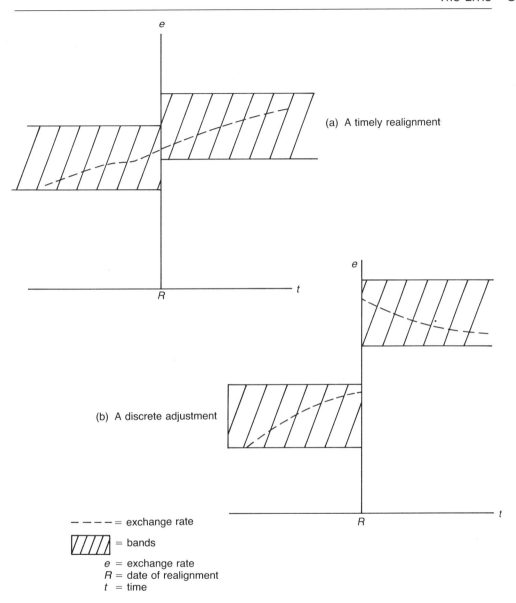

(a) A timely realignment

(b) A discrete adjustment

– – – – = exchange rate

▨ = bands

e = exchange rate
R = date of realignment
t = time

Figure 15.1 Exchange-rate realignments

A recent and authoritative example of this kind of approach is provided in a study for the IMF by Ungerer *et al.* (1986), an excerpt from which is shown in Table 15.3. The results quoted in this table are for nominal bilateral exchange rates against ERM currencies, the exchange rates being weighted together according to the pattern of weights implied by the IMF's multilateral exchange-rate model (MERM), which is

Table 15.3 Exchange-rate variability against ERM currencies 1974–85[a]

| | Period means | | | |
| | Levels | | Log changes | |
	1974–8	1979–85	1974–9	1979–85
France	31.6	15.9	16.8	7.6
W. Germany	29.2	16.3	14.7	7.0
Italy	36.0	19.3	19.3	8.8
Average ERM[b]	28.4	15.1	14.8	7.3
Japan	44.5	48.1	21.1	21.7
United Kingdom	32.7	37.8	16.8	20.9
United States	34.7	55.7	18.8	27.4
Average non-ERM[c]	34.5	35.9	17.2	17.9

Notes
[a] Weighted average of variability of bilateral nominal exchange rates against ERM currencies
(their log change), monthly data, IMF MERM weights. Variability is measured by the
coefficient of variation for levels, and by the standard deviation for log changes (in both
cases × 1000). Period means are unweighted.
[b] Including all ERM countries.
[c] Includes Japan, United Kingdom, United States, Australia, Canada, Norway, Sweden and
Switzerland.

Source: H. Ungerer *et al.* (1986) 'The European Monetary System: recent developments',
Occasional Paper, no. 48, IMF, Table 7, p. 35.

standard for this type of application. Two concepts of stability are then explored –
stability of the actual level and stability of the (log) change. The latter thus allows for
some regular change as the norm against which variability is to be assessed. For levels,
the authors use the coefficient of variation (the standard deviation divided by the
mean) and for log change the standard deviation itself (both scaled by 1,000) as a
measure of month-to-month variability. As can be seen, for both levels and log
changes, the index of variability rises for the three main non-ERM countries and falls
for the three main ERM countries. Including in addition the smaller ERM countries
in the coverage and a set of other developed countries in the non-ERM average, the
conclusion remains the same: where volatility falls sharply for the ERM countries
between the pre-EMS and the EMS period, it rises for the non-participant countries.

15.6 A framework for counter-inflationary policy

The inception of the EMS coincided with the second oil shock. Following a meeting
in December 1978, the OPEC countries raised oil prices in several stages through
1979 by some 130 per cent. On the face of it, such a shock, coming so soon after the
founding of the EMS, might have been supposed to ensure its early demise. After all,
the failure of the snake in the 1970s followed the disruption created by the first oil

shock in 1973–4, in the aftermath of which countries followed different adjustment policies incompatible with maintaining fixed exchange rates between themselves. It could well have been apprehended that the second oil shock would expose the EMS to similar strains. In fact, the EMS not only survived the shock but, in the eyes of some observers, proved to have some added advantages in providing for its members a framework within which to prosecute efficient counter-inflationary policies.

The first advantage the EMS proved to have over the snake was the provision for realignment. As Table 15.2 shows, the realignments at the beginning of the life of the EMS were quite frequent. It was important for the survival of the EMS that it should have been able to accommodate exchange-rate realignments at this stage and still continue as a system. This contrasted with the snake, where countries changing their exchange rates were deemed to 'leave' the snake. In the early period, then, as countries accommodated to the inflationary shock of the oil price rise in different ways, the EMS displayed sufficient flexibility to survive. Later on, countries in the EMS converged in their attitudes towards the inflationary problem, tending – in common with developments in other countries outside the system – to give first priority in their economic policy objectives to the defeat of inflation.

The claim is made for the EMS that it provided a particularly advantageous framework in this respect. The analytics of that claim are based on the modern theory of the value of reputation in economic policy and the important role played by expectations in the inflationary process. Both features are to an extent controversial and the empirical value of the claim made for the EMS is a matter of controversy. To take the two elements in the claim in reverse order: it is well known from work in the late 1960s by Phelps and Friedman that inflationary processes are capable of being sustained by self-fulfilling expectations. One of the things that a government intent on reducing inflation has to do is to break the climate of inflationary expectations. One way of doing this, of course, is to reduce demand so drastically that, despite the impetus given by strong expectations of inflation, actual inflation winds down and, as it does so, so also does the expectation of inflation. Such a process is potentially very costly in terms of the output which will be lost and the unemployment which will be created by the deflationary demand policy. The more stubborn the expectations are, the higher these costs will be. Another way of breaking the climate of inflationary expectations is for a government to find a direct means of persuading agents that inflation really will fall. In the 1960s and 1970s the device of incomes policies had been popular for this purpose but these policies fell out of favour and in the 1980s the principal counter-inflationary policy commitment was provided by the publication of targets for the reduction of the rate of growth of the money supply.

At this point we must take account of the theory of 'reputational' policies. This theory points out that the credibility of a government's commitment cannot just be taken for granted. For electoral and other reasons a government may be led to cheat on commitments it makes; if the apprehension of cheating is sufficiently widespread the commitment will be distrusted. If a government's announcements about its counter-inflationary intentions and policies are distrusted, perhaps because of a poor reputation acquired by past behaviour or simply because the electorate considers this to be the way of governments, the government will be unable to influence expectations directly. Inflation can then be brought down only by the costly route of demand deflation. But a government may be able to secure greater credibility in various ways: in particular, by committing to policies which are easy to monitor and by raising the visible costs to itself of cheating. The policies must, of course, be plausibly related to the goal. Membership of the EMS offers three important advantages in these respects for the control of inflation. First, the dominant economy in the EMS is Germany, which has a very secure and well-known record of low inflation; targeting exchange rates in the EMS involves targeting against the deutschmark and to the extent that exchange rates reflect relative inflation, a stable deutschmark exchange rate must imply low, German-like, rates of inflation. Second, an exchange-rate commitment is exceptionally easy to monitor; exchange rates are quoted every minute of the day and it is clear what an exchange rate is. Third, by committing itself to the EMS, a government puts its credibility on the line, not only with its own electorate but also with foreign governments; the commitment is the more credible for this reason.[3]

This is the theory. What are the qualifications and what is the evidence? An immediate qualification is that the argument takes for granted that EMS membership puts a heavy premium on exchange-rate fixity: yet, as we saw earlier, realignments are a part of the EMS and were not infrequently used in the early years. How do agents know that the rules have changed from permissiveness to a more disciplined approach and how can they be sure that their government will not go back to the earlier ways of the system?

The evidence does not really help to give a decisive verdict on the claim. It is not, of course, true that the EMS countries alone have brought inflation down; as Table 15.4 shows, inflation has fallen in the United States and the United Kingdom as well (obviously, for these purposes the United Kingdom is not counted as an EMS member because it does not belong to the critical ERM component of the system). But the claim that the EMS provides a superior counter-inflationary framework does not deny that other countries could bring inflation down – only that the costs of doing so are higher for them. A 'quick' indicator of the costs of disinflating is the ratio of the cumulative rise in unemployment to the reduction in inflation – the so-called sacrifice ratio. Table 15.4 gives estimates at three intervals for this ratio. It can be seen from this that Germany has the highest sacrifice ratio of all. However, this is not necessarily inconsistent with the hypothesis at issue in as much as it is the non-German members which are supposed to reap the benefit of Germany's extreme inflation aversion by targeting the deutschmark. Indeed, it can be seen that the sacrifice ratios for France and Italy are lower than those for the United Kingdom, consistent with the hypothesis. It is the United States, on the other hand, which seems to do best of all. While this might be treated as a special case, it is obvious that the evidence is far from un-ambiguous. At the moment, a position on the agnostic side of the question is probably the safest.

Whatever the position on the differential advantage of using the EMS as a counter-inflationary framework, it must certainly be acknowledged that it has, in fact,

Table 15.4 Inflation and the 'sacrifice ratio'

	USA	Consumer prices W. Germany	Inflation, % pa France	UK	Italy
1980	11.0	5.8	13.3	16.2	20.2
1981	9.3	6.2	13.0	11.4	17.9
1982	6.0	4.8	11.5	8.6	15.9
1983	3.5	3.2	9.7	5.0	14.8
1984	3.9	2.5	7.5	4.8	11.4
1985	3.1	2.1	5.7	5.2	9.3
1986	2.1	−0.5	2.5	3.6	6.1
1987	3.7	0.3	3.2	4.2	4.9
1988[a]	4.1	1.0	2.7	5.1	4.8
		Sacrifice ratios[b]			
1980−4	0.86	4.09	1.43	1.73	0.83
1980−6	0.66	3.37	1.51	2.33	0.95
1980−8[c]	0.51	5.77	2.33	3.18	na

Notes
[a] 1988 data partly estimated.
[b] The ratio of the cumulative increase in unemployment to the difference between inflation in 1980 and inflation in the terminal year (1984, 1986, 1988).
[c] Unemployment data for 1988 are average of the first three quarters.

Source: OECD *Economic Outlook*, December 1988.

been used as such. The DI has been an inevitable casualty of this, for a simple reason. Whereas the DI was designed, as explained above, with the purpose in mind of inducing symmetry of adjustment – and, in particular, of inducing adjustment by Germany – the counter-inflationary policies of the period ran counter to this conception. It was not desirable to induce Germany to raise its inflation to the EMS average (even supposing this could have been done); rather, the point was to bring the average down to the German level.[4]

15.7 Competitiveness

The *real* rate of exchange, the nominal rate corrected for relative prices, provides an index of competitiveness. Although the formal provisions of the EMS focus on nominal exchange-rate agreement, in a customs union exchange-rate arrangements must ensure a degree of stability in real rates of exchange. The reason is that because the real rate of exchange governs an economy's competitiveness, a sharp change – say a large appreciation in the real rate producing a large fall in competitiveness – will arouse protectionist pressures and thus threaten the reversal of the customs union's achievements in removing internal tariff barriers. Other, non-tariff barriers may be promoted and progress slowed on the removal of these and other obstacles to intra-union trade. Whether reflecting this 'inner logic' or not, the evidence does confirm

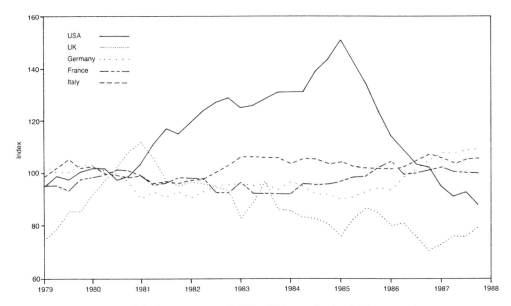

Figure 15.2 Competitiveness 1979–87 (normalised unit labour costs)

that whereas the real rates of exchange of both the United Kingdom and the United States have undergone large changes in the 1980s, changes in competitiveness of the EMS economies have been more muted. Thus it appears that among the achievements of the EMS might be included that of reducing the extent of exchange rate 'misalignment', deviations of real rates of exchange from equilibrium levels. By way of confirmation, Figure 15.2 displays measures of competitiveness for the United States, United Kingdom, Germany, France and Italy.

A qualification must be entered at this stage. It is one thing for the real exchange rates of EMS countries to show less evidence of misalignment than those of some key non-EMS (or non-ERM in the case of the United Kingdom) countries. It is another thing to be sure that the record of the EMS in stabilising real rates of exchange is adequate. A reason why it might not be adequate is the fact that, as argued above, countries have used the EMS as a counter-inflationary framework. Among other things, this has meant that realignments, although always changing central rates in the direction indicated by relative inflation, have been deliberately tardy and niggardly in doing so. The object has been to ensure that realignments do not accommodate and encourage inflation. A consequence of this is that an economy which persistently inflates above the EMS average rate will undergo prolonged pressure not to adjust its exchange rate to accommodate this and so will gradually lose its competitive edge. Because of the 'inner logic' of real rate stabilisation referred to earlier, such a situation could not be regarded as sustainable. The overall success achieved in reducing inflation among the EMS countries, however, means that this particular danger is perhaps less acute now than it seemed to be a little earlier.

15.8 The popularity of the ECU

As described above, the ECU is simply a 'composite currency', with no necessary role in the critical parity grid of the EMS. It has no central bank of issue and even its role as the foundation for the DI mechanism seems unimportant in light of the proven weakness of that mechanism.

Nevertheless, the ECU has proven quite popular as a currency of denomination of international bond issues; in 1985 it became the fifth most used currency of denomination of such issues outside the US dollar, its share rising to nearly 11.5 per cent (see Table 15.5). While the official transactions of the EC itself are denominated in ECU, the ECU is barely used as a means of payment by the private sector.[5] Its attraction is that of a 'currency cocktail', in that it offers some 'hedging' properties that agents find worthwhile. Thus, a trading company whose activities are concentrated in, say, three different markets may find that the best way of hedging its liabilities, if it needs to borrow, is to issue bonds which are denominated in a cocktail of the three different currencies used in those markets. The alternative of issuing bonds in one currency only (one of the three used in the markets where it trades or a fourth outside currency) inevitably involves the company in taking on the risk associated with changes in the exchange rates between the currency of denomination of the bond and the currencies used in the markets it operates in. While the risk, in itself, is as much a risk of gain as of loss, the trading company may not be interested in, or able to afford, to speculate in this way. For this reason, a demand for currency-cocktail borrowing arises from traders who are averse to risk. ECU-denominated bond issues appeal to businesses whose activities are concentrated in the EC for this reason. In a similar fashion, a demand for assets of this denomination arises from firms and institutions whose liabilities are of a similar nature. In fact, most of the bond issues have been made by EC organisations and national governments, although more recently corporate ECU borrowings have become significant. Both the Italian government (since 1987) and the British government (since 1988) have issued short-dated ECU-denominated debt instruments, helping to correct a deficiency in the market for short-term ECU assets. In addition to the ECU bond market there has also been a development of bank lending and borrowing in ECU.[6]

Table 15.5 Non-dollar international bond issues by currency of denomination (per cent)

	1981	1982	1983	1984	1985	1986	1987
Swiss francs	44.7	41.8	42.7	3.2	23.0	23.3	21.2
Sterling	7.3	7.3	8.8	14.0	10.1	10.9	13.2
Deutschmark	13.4	20.2	19.6	17.5	17.4	16.2	13.2
Yen	16.2	14.0	12.4	14.8	18.9	22.7	22.0
Canadian dollar	3.5	4.3	3.6	5.8	4.8	6.0	5.3
ECU	1.3	3.5	4.9	7.1	11.4	6.9	6.5
Others	13.6	8.9	8.1	7.7	14.4	14.0	18.5

Source: Computed from data shown in Walton (1988) 'ECU financial activity', *Quarterly Bulletin*, Bank of England.

The apparent success of the ECU depends on something more than its currency cocktail quality, however, since modern financial procedures readily allow cocktail mixing to take place and it does not seem difficult to imagine that for many purposes cocktails containing slightly different mixes of EC currencies (and perhaps including the Swiss franc, for example) would be preferable. Two main points should be mentioned.

One is that ECU borrowing can be seen in some countries of the EMS (France and Italy) as a reflection of exchange control. Certainly, the largest sources of ECU borrowing have been Italy and France, where the special status accorded to the ECU has permitted residents, in effect, to borrow from overseas in a way which would not be allowed if the borrowing was done in a single currency or, indeed, any other currency cocktail. At the same time, the comparatively high interest rates available on ECU-denominated loans have made these loans quite attractive to residents of some low interest rate countries. Viewed in this light, the prevalence of ECU-denominated borrowing and lending is a rather ambiguous advertisement for the EMS. Moreover, it suggests that as the controls are eliminated, the growth of the market will be reduced, as it has been since 1985 when liberalisation began. However, it does seem clear that the volume of private sector ECU issues is well above what can be attributed solely to such features and in itself this counts as a highly positive declaration of the credibility established by the EMS. So the second point to make is that the fact that the ECU is chosen rather than some other cocktail testifies to a perception of the credibility of the EMS and would pave the way, if other conditions permitted, for the ECU to become a genuine EC currency.

15.9 The position of the United Kingdom

The United Kingdom declined to participate in the operation of the EMS, to begin with, out of a belief that the system would be operated in a rigid way which would threaten the United Kingdom, with its high 'propensity to inflate', with a decline in its competitiveness, especially *vis-à-vis* Germany. This concern for the United Kingdom's freedom to determine or preserve its competitiveness still marks one strand of oppositional thinking on the question of British membership of the EMS today.

While opposition to full membership of the EMS was voiced on these grounds by the Labour government of Mr Callaghan, opposition on different grounds was voiced by the incoming Conservative government headed by Mrs Thatcher. The Thatcher government wished to run an experiment in monetary policy in order to bring inflation down and reasoned, correctly, that if the instruments of monetary policy (principally interest rates) were to be directed at reducing the rate of growth of the money supply, they could not simultaneously be used to target the exchange rate. Technically, this dilemma could be avoided by maintaining a suitably strong set of exchange controls; such controls would allow a government some freedom to maintain two different targets for monetary policy but the Thatcher government was keen to remove these controls in any case and did so not long after taking office.

Events were to turn out somewhat paradoxically. The first phase of the Conservative government's monetary experiment was associated with a very marked *appreciation* of the exchange rate – so competitiveness would have been *better* preserved inside the EMS – and the deep recession that soon set in was attributed by many observers to this cause. The view took root that while the Thatcher government was correct to say that membership of the EMS was incompatible with pursuit of an independent monetary policy and would involve a loss of sovereignty in this respect, better results would nevertheless be attained by adhering to the EMS. In particular, the exchange rate would be steadier and competitiveness more assured, while inflation would be dragged towards the modest German level (we have already described the claims made for the EMS as a counter-inflationary framework).

This view gained momentum as official British policy towards the exchange rate as a target changed and as it became clear that monetary policy was no longer aimed in single-minded fashion solely at controlling the supply of money. In fact, with practice preceding the public statement, the Chancellor of the Exchequer made this very clear in his 1983 budget speech. A House of Lords report on the question of entry into the EMS, published a little later in the same year, favoured 'early, though not necessarily immediate' entry into the system.

That report referred to four problems that the United Kingdom had had in relation to the EMS and noted that in each case events had moved in a favourable fashion. The first problem was the apprehension that the EMS would prove rigid and inflexible: the committee noted that the EMS had allowed a number of realignments. The second problem was that the United Kingdom had wanted to put the control of the money supply ahead of the goal of stabilising the exchange rate – where, as described, policy had already retreated somewhat. The third problem was related to the UK position as an oil exporter, with sterling subject to quite a different response than the EMS currencies to oil price shocks. The committee saw this as less problematic as the oil market had become less disturbed. The fourth problem arose from sterling's still persistent role as a vehicle currency, i.e. one widely held by agents other than those solely concerned with UK trade. The committee acknowledged that this might mean that it would not be so easy to stabilise sterling in the ERM.

The viewpoint of the House of Lords report appears to have been representative of a wide range of opinion. Although the later report of a subcommittee of the House of Commons Select Committee on the Treasury and Civil Service revived some of the earlier arguments against entry, the general climate of opinion had changed markedly in a favourable direction by the early 1980s. With the passage of time the lingering reservations over the exposure of sterling to oil shocks and over the problem of speculation diminished still further, while the case for exchange-rate management became more widely and firmly accepted. The initiative launched by the United States in 1985 to secure the coordinated actions of its major partners to bring the dollar down substantially reinforced the latter process.

In September 1986, at the meetings of the International Monetary Fund, the Chancellor of the Exchequer advertised the non-speculative realignment process of the EMS and not long afterwards followed this up with a policy of 'shadowing the EMS', keeping the sterling exchange rate closely in line with the deutschmark. This policy initiative lasted for just over a year; by the end of February 1988, following a well-publicised exchange of views between the Chancellor and the Prime Minister, sterling was uncapped. Higher interest rates, invoked as a means of dampening monetary growth and in response to forecasts of inflation, caused the exchange rate to appreciate through its previous working ceiling. The incident underlined the inconsistency between an independent monetary policy and an exchange-rate policy and at the same time served to confirm that sterling was unlikely to participate in the ERM during the prime ministership of Mrs Thatcher. Nevertheless, the probability of sterling's eventual full participation in the EMS seemed much higher by the end of the decade than it had at the outset – see Chapter 5 for Mrs Thatcher's latest position with regard to this issue.

15.10 The challenge of 1992

Full participation in the EMS is not a requirement of membership of the EC nor is it implied in the original Rome Treaty. The Single European Act (SEA), however, does add a section to the Treaty calling for member countries to take steps to ensure the convergence of economic and monetary policy, prefiguring the emergence of monetary union from the EMS and the ECU. However, the provisions of 1992 which are of immediate consequence to the EMS are those which require the dismantling of exchange controls. The consequences of this for the functioning of the EMS are profound and for its future, some sceptics suggest, possibly fatal.

Exchange controls of the type maintained by Italy and France throughout the first ten years of the life of the EMS have as their immediate object the prevention of the short-run export of capital. Controls of this type therefore forbid the direct export of financial capital, restricting or forbidding portfolio investment overseas, the holding of foreign-currency-denominated bank deposits and lending (and borrowing) overseas. These restrictions are not watertight but they are effective. They have two important effects. First, they prevent or slow down speculation. Agents anticipating a devaluation of a currency cannot, if they are residents of the country concerned, simply sell the currency for foreign exchange in the expectation of making a quick gain when buying it back after the devaluation; nor can they lend the currency to non-residents who could carry out the same speculative raid. Secondly, the controls break the link which holds currencies together when there are no obstacles to perfect arbitrage. The interest parity link states that the interest differential between two currencies is equal to the expected rate of change in the exchange rate between them. Thus, taking two countries, say France (F) and Germany (G), interest parity would have $r_F = r_G + d_{F/G}$ where r_F, r_G are interest rates on similar-maturity, similar-risk instruments denominated respectively in the French and German currencies and $d_{F/G}$ is the expected rate of depreciation of the French franc against the German mark.

The removal of exchange controls therefore poses two problems for the EMS. First, a protection against speculation will be lost. Second, because interest parity will no longer be prevented, interest rates everywhere will be tightly linked as the amount of expected depreciation is confined by the bands of permissible fluctuations of the currencies against one another. Because Germany is by far the largest economy in the EMS, this means that interest rates, and hence monetary policy, everywhere in the system will be dominated by Germany. Unless Germany in turn tempers its monetary policy by concern for the economic situation in other countries this could turn out to be an unacceptable state of affairs.

These problems have been realised and various solutions proposed. First, as regards the problem of speculation the mechanisms of the EMS have been improved by measures to accommodate automatic lending by a strong currency country to a weak currency country in the event of need; whereas previously this automaticity applied only when intervention was taking place at the edge of the band it has, since the deliberations of the EMS finance ministers in Nyborg in September 1987, applied also to so-called 'intra-marginal' intervention, i.e. foreign exchange operations taking place to support a currency before it has reached its limit. These new provisions were tested by a speculative run on the French franc in the autumn of 1987 and proved successful; the Bundesbank lent heavily to the Banque de France but the lending was rapidly repaid once the speculation subsided and confidence returned. The second problem – that of excessive German dominance – has yet to be as well resolved. The Nyborg provisions called for much closer monetary cooperation, implying more continuous exchange of information, and interest rate movements within the EMS have since that time displayed a high degree of synchronisation. However, the cooperation called for also seems to imply a degree of common decision making going beyond simply following a German lead in a prompt and well-prepared way. Progress on this front is less evident. The anxiety of France on this score has, however, led to important initiatives. First, France has called upon Germany to discuss economic policy on a regular basis and an economic council has been set up for this purpose. Second, it was on French initiatives that the EC was led to call for an investigation into the requirements of full monetary union, an investigation subsequently carried out by the Delors Committee, the recommendations of whose Report were endorsed by all twelve nations of the EC in June 1989 – see Chapter 5.

The path which the EMS participants have agreed to follow thus calls for increasing intervention resources and other devices to combat the threat of speculation and for increased economic and monetary cooperation between member countries, eventually leading to the creation of a European Central Bank – see Chapter 5. But we should note that there are alternative short-run solutions. Thus, one way in which countries could recover a greater measure of independence from the dominant power would be to enlarge the bands of exchange-rate fluctuation; another would be to compromise on 1992 by retaining a measure of exchange control. Either device has obvious counter-speculative advantages too. If maintained over the long term, these alternative solutions would be in effect a defeat for the higher aspirations of the EMS (more concretely, those of the Delors Report). But either one could, in principle, be adopted on a purely monetary basis until such time as the political prerequisites for greater cooperation were met.

The removal of exchange controls undoubtedly poses problems for the future of the EMS. Following the delicate path to which the member countries have agreed exposes the system to the hazards of speculation and poses political problems relating to the acceptance of German dominance in monetary affairs. The alternative short-run solutions have the disadvantage of taking the pressure off the search for a solution to the political problem, or perpetuating an obstacle to the integration of the European financial area. Despite this somewhat pessimistic statement, however, three valid claims can be made for thinking that the pessimism might be overdone: first, the reduction of inflation differentials across the EMS countries since 1979 has been substantial and this drastically reduces the need for realignments and the problems created by the speculative anticipation of realignments; second, the EMS has, in fact, survived what is already quite a large diminution in the extent of exchange controls maintained within the system, without any great difficulty; third, the provisions for counter-speculative inter-central bank lending and coordination of policy have so far been working very well. On this view, while the problems of continuing monetary cooperation, despite the Delors Report, remain to be fully resolved, there are reasons for thinking that time may resolve them.

15.11 Monetary union

A complete monetary union in Europe – an EMU – is an aspiration for the EMS which had advocates long before the EMS itself was founded – see Chapter 5.

In a complete monetary union, exchange rates are indissolubly locked so that currencies are complete substitutes. A common currency is the obvious next consequence and a single central bank and a common monetary policy a corresponding requirement.

The principal economic advantage of such a union is claimed to lie in the eradication of the uncertainty that prevails when rates of exchange are flexible. Of course, only one kind of uncertainty is removed by forming an exchange-rate union. The fact of monetary union does not eradicate any of the uncertainties that exist about the relative rates of return from investing in, say, Scotland as opposed to England, for example, although it does remove uncertainty about the exchange rate between the Scottish and English pounds. Because the facilities of the foreign exchange markets allow traders to insure themselves against the risk of exchange-rate fluctuation over short horizons, it is the reduction of long-period uncertainty and the beneficial effects of this on production location and investment decisions which are usually most emphasised. However, using the facilities of the forward markets is not inexpensive and the costs are not limited to pecuniary ones: time, trouble and inconvenience are involved as well, so the advantages accruing to trade from greater stability in exchange rates should not be overlooked. Advocates of monetary union will often suggest the United States as a model of the positive outcomes of the monetary union they have in mind, an example which emphasises that it is to a combination of the large internal market and monetary union that they are in effect looking: it is quite natural, then, to link the achievement of monetary union to that of the realisation of 1992.

Theoretical considerations suggest a number of caveats. When countries agree to lock exchange rates they agree to pool monetary policy. Although fiscal policy may be decentralised to some extent, at least in principle, a margin of national sovereignty is resigned in a monetary union in favour of a collective, union-level, sovereignty. This is why, as we noted earlier, France might hope to escape from the domination of Germany within an EMS without exchange control by forming a monetary union in which France would regain, through its input into union-level decisions, a portion of the sovereignty it resigns on agreeing to fix its exchange rate without the protection of exchange control.

In forgoing an ability to express national sovereignty directly and by way, if necessary, of a differential monetary and exchange-rate policy, a country in a monetary union forgoes some potential power to offset disturbances which impact differentially upon it. For this reason, a criterion of an optimum union is that its constituents should be asymmetrically, not differentially, open to or affected by disturbances; failing this, a high degree of intra-union factor mobility can offset the consequences of being unable to fight differentiated shocks with differentiated policy weapons. Alternatively, nationally differentiated policies must be evolved under the collective decision taking of the union – these are, in effect, regional policies – see Chapter 5.

All these considerations suggest that the political developments required to facilitate a movement towards a complete monetary union in Europe are very considerable. Willingness to cede national monetary sovereignty must be matched by willingness to innovate policy developments at the union level for dealing with erstwhile national, now 'regional' problems. None of this seems likely to be completed at all soon. Even though it is true that the speed at which the participants move from stage 1 of the Delors path to EMU to the later stages remains to be determined, the almost immediate endorsement of the Delors Report, subject to the minor provisos of Margaret Thatcher (see Chapter 5), thus comes as something of a surprise.

15.12 Conclusions

There have been a number of initiatives in the EC towards the locking of exchange rates and monetary union. Hitherto, these have been failures, even ludicrous failures. The EMS was on inception a less grandiose, more pragmatic and flexible construction. Perhaps not accidentally, it has also been strikingly successful.

The success nevertheless has not been without qualification and the EMS, before the adoption of the Delors Report, faced some severe challenges. A major qualification of the system's success and a challenge to its successful future was the fact that, until it accepted the Delors Report, the United Kingdom had stayed outside it. The integration of the United Kingdom was required before the EMS could be said to be complete, but this requirement will be met if the new EMU progresses as scheduled. The second major challenge was that provided by 1992. The creation of the internal market, with the removal of exchange controls implied, exposes the EMS to the risk of added speculative pressures and exposes the governments of France and Italy, the two biggest non-German members of the full EMS, to the full rigours of German policy domination. In the short to medium run a policy track involving more counter-speculative mechanisms and more policy coordination seemed to be proving viable; in the somewhat longer run, if the EMS did not settle for compromise (either by widening the bands or by reinstating exchange control), it seemed likely to be forced to proceed in the direction of the goal of monetary union. Hence, the Delors Report has in this respect come as a surprise: the longer-run expectation has arrived too soon.

Notes

1. Realignments in the EMS have only gradually become collective decisions (see Padoa-Schioppa, 1985).
2. The reader should refer to Swann (1988) for a useful summary and to Kruse (1980) for a detailed account of these past endeavours.
3. The title of the paper by Giavazzi and Pagano (1986) on this issue is indicative.
4. Thus a strong currency country should in these circumstances revalue, not inflate. This is very clear in the European Commission's evidence to the House of Lords (1983).
5. Walton (1988) notes that ECU invoicing accounts for 1 per cent of all foreign trade in Italy and France, where it is most popular.
6. The reader is referred to Bank for International Settlements (1989) for a detailed account.

16 Regional policy

E. T. Nevin

16.1 The nature of the regional problem

The expression 'regional policy' refers to the set of measures adopted by government, the primary aim of which is to influence the geographical distribution of economic activity. The object of the exercise is usually to increase output and incomes, in absolute and/or relative terms, in areas believed to be operating below their true potential, or to reduce them in areas considered to be over-congested or in danger of becoming so. Correspondingly, policy measures may be designed to encourage the growth of existing or prospective enterprises in 'depressed' regions or to restrict further expansion in congested ones. The regional 'problem', in other words, arises from the propensity of societies to spread their prosperity unevenly within their political boundaries and, in particular, to leave some of their regions noticeably behind others in terms of level and growth of income, population or environmental quality. Not everyone would describe this phenomenon as a 'problem'; there may be certain societies, after all, whose development positively requires some regional imbalance. It certainly becomes one, however – rightly or wrongly – if the political consciousness of any society declares it to be one. And most modern societies have in fact done so.

The origins of the phenomenon are closely bound up with four fundamental characteristics of a modern economy. First, the declining use of labour relative to capital in agriculture, and the corresponding urbanisation of society, has led to the continuing depopulation of (usually peripheral) regions whose only natural advantage is the availability of surface area for cultivation and whose environment is in other respects rather hostile to modern urban settlement.

The second element has been the decreasing reliance of manufacturing industry on natural materials, whether for processing or for power, and the consequent emphasis on proximity to a final market, rather than to mineral deposits or cultivable areas, as a determining factor in industrial location – and thus in population distribution. This, again, has tended to militate against regions in which deposits of coal, ore, 325 stone or slate underlay prosperity in an earlier stage of development, but whose exploitation has left a despoiled environment unattractive to contemporary settlement.

The third force at work has been the continuously increasing importance of service activities – as opposed to primary and manufacturing production – as income levels rise, and the apparently compulsive power of economies of scale in so many of those services, for example transport, health, distribution and perhaps education and entertainment. To this, some might even add the service of government, whose addiction to both growth and proximity to the other cogs of its own machine explains much of the sprawl and congestion of the capital cities of the developed world.

The fourth factor is the continuing displacement of the flexible prices and free markets of earlier stages of development (and the textbooks) by administered prices – fixed by unions or entrepreneurs – and imperfect markets. In such a market context, the response to disequilibrium tends to be expressed, at least in the medium run, in terms of quantity rather than price. In particular, a reduced demand for labour which arises when an industry is falling behind in the technological race results, not in a fall in relative wages and a rapid switch of capital, but in an increase in idle human and physical capacity. When the industry concerned is heavily concentrated in particular locations, as is the case with coal, steel or shipbuilding, the phenomenon of the 'depressed area' is automatically created.

All this is true, of course, at an international as well as a regional level; but there is one crucial respect in which the regional adjustment problem is more intractable than the international. This is the fact that in the context of international trade it is *comparative* cost which determines the long-run viability of any industry; differences in the *absolute* costs of production in different countries can be largely, if not wholly, eliminated by one or both of two powerful perquisites of sovereignty: on the one hand, a tariff (or other restrictions on trade having a comparable effect) and, on the other, the rate of exchange of the national currency, both of which affect the relative prices of foreign and domestic products. As between sovereign countries the impact of differing rates of technological change can be qualified, to varying degrees, by these instruments of national economic policy. Within any individual country, on the other hand, by definition there can be neither tariffs nor significant differences in general price levels; both product prices and wage rates now tend to be determined by central decisions or national negotiating arrangements which make significant regional differences in the prices of tradable goods and services increasingly improbable (Buck, 1975, pp. 368–9).

In theory, then, an uneven growth process within a country must lead to a movement of factors out of high cost regions and into low cost regions until cost differences are minimised. At first sight, any policy measures aimed at impeding this movement are bound to result in inefficiency in resource allocation. There are three reasons, nevertheless, why even the most *laissez-faire* government may be led to intervene. In the first place, given the quantity response referred to earlier, this factor-reallocation may work very slowly – too slowly to be tolerable to politicians who have to operate on the premise that in the long run we are all dead – or at least threatened with loss of office.

Secondly, it is not obvious that the process is a convergent one leading to a new equilibrium. Because of the operation of economies of scale, the movement of capital from A to B in search of relatively high returns may *increase* the efficiency gap between A and B rather than reduce it. (Hence, El-Agraa's emphatic conclusion in Chapter 5 that 'capital will always come to the rescue', while theoretically valid, may prove to be unduly optimistic as a matter of empirical reality.) Similarly, the migration of labour tends to be a highly selective business, drawing particularly on the younger, more able and more enterprising among the population; the population remaining behind in a declining region may be reduced not only in size, but in competitive ability, accentuating rather than correcting the initial cost disadvantage (Balassa, 1975, pp. 259–60).

Thirdly, the movement of labour and capital in response to market forces will be determined by private rather than social cost; where the two differ significantly a serious misallocation of resources may result. In the context of the location of industry and population, such differences are in fact probable. On the one hand, factor movement into an already densely populated area is likely to impose serious external diseconomies of congestion on enterprises already in the area; such costs will not enter into the calculations of the decision maker concerned. On the other hand, an opposite problem may be posed for the 'exporting' area where the usage of services may fall below the point at which their provision is viable: unused capacity is as much a recipe for increased unit costs as is excess pressure on capacity. Public transport or medical facilities are obvious examples.

All of this refers to the strictly economic aspects of regional development, but it would be unrealistic to ignore the fact that a regional 'problem' may be perceived to exist because of political and social, rather than purely economic, considerations. Regional policy is a particular manifestation of the general truism that overall prosperity enables countries to afford the luxury of a conscience regarding the less fortunate and the non-economic. This concern has been especially striking when the underprivileged groups involved have drifted from their place of origin to form congealed groups of squalid misery in the centres of increasingly congested cities, the centres themselves physically decaying as the more fortunate citizens retreat to the suburbs.

Hence, the motivation behind regional policy is a mixture of the political, social and economic. Underdevelopment has become a political issue within countries as well as internationally; like all such issues, it has tended to become a means of attack by 'them' and a necessity for defensive reaction on the part of 'us'. In the social context, the relative decay of particular regions frequently threatens (or is alleged to threaten) cultural patterns regarded by their defenders as being both valuable to society as a whole and irreplaceable. In some countries, the cultural patterns may involve language (as in Quebec, or Brittany, or Wales) or colour (as in the southern United States) or religion (as in Northern Ireland, or the Low Countries) or nothing more specific than a general lament about the passing of the rural way of life (a lament which, it has to be said, seems to increase in appeal as the familiarity of its audience with the realities of rural life grows weaker).

Leaving these rather elusive considerations on one side, however, the purely economic case for regional policy tends to reduce to the question of immobility of resources, although the external economies element (or diseconomies, as in the congestion issue) is an important one. Hence the case for regional policy can never be regarded as self-evident; in fact it rests on two crucial hypotheses concerning the real world. First, that these immobilities and external effects are of sufficient magnitude and of a sufficiently long-run nature to justify market intervention to deal with them. Second, that the costs of dealing with these factors by 'artificial' regional development at the losing end are less than the costs of eliminating them (by increasing mobility or removing external effects such as congestion) through action at the winning end.

There can be no *a priori* demonstration of the validity of these essentially empirical hypotheses; their validity will vary through time and from one society to another. The evidence, however, seems to suggest that the economic and social costs of the unrestricted gravitation of the population into a small number of large, densely populated conurbations are not only high, but rise rapidly as both the extent of urban concentration and the complexity of modern urban existence increase. One might add that as societies advance in affluence, their willingness to tolerate any given degree of environmental deterioration probably diminishes as steadily as the deterioration itself increases – see Chapters 17 and 18.

16.2 Integration and the regional problem

Put at its simplest, the effect of any movement towards a customs union, and *a fortiori* a common market, is to reduce the extent to which its member countries can conduct their affairs as sovereign, independent states and to increase the extent to which they acquire the characteristics of a single, unitary economy. On strictly *a priori* grounds, therefore, the likely consequences for the 'problem' regions of the participating countries are obvious enough.

In important respects, joining a customs union puts each individual member country in the position of a single region rather than that of a sovereign, independent state. The national power to levy tariffs against the rest of the union disappears; the power to vary exchange rates does not disappear necessarily or immediately, but it is inherent in the logic of most customs unions – and certainly in that enshrined in the Treaty of Rome – that one day it will. At first sight, therefore, economic theory would lead to two rather pessimistic predictions. First, that the mechanism of the EC, i.e. increased specialisation, fiercer competition and the exploitation of the economies of scale, is of its nature likely to accentuate, rather than reduce, the adverse pressures operating on areas in decline or in which industrial growth is at only an early stage. Second, that any centripetal tendencies in evidence within individual countries must *a fortiori* exert themselves at the customs union level. There are, however, two rather important reasons why this pessimism must be significantly qualified. The first is that generalisations about 'industries' may prove to be hopelessly inoperable as the basis for predictions concerning the actual course of national or regional events. In the real world, there is no such thing as an industry or a sector; rather, there are individual producers and individual products. In other words, it behoves economists to beware of generalisations here as everywhere else; the evidence suggests that the range of productive performance *within* any given country, be it on the farm or in the factory, is at least as great as that *between* countries. Of course, this cannot entirely dispose of the proposition that the comparative geographical remoteness of the less prosperous regions is likely to be accentuated by the expansion of 'domestic' market horizons so as to take in the whole of a customs union rather than merely the home territory. But it does suggest that broad generalisations concerning the regional impact on existing enterprises are on shaky ground.

The second reason why the pessimism of the predictions concerning regional consequences of integration needs to be tempered is certainly much more important. The simple (and rather obvious) lesson of experience is that policy intervention aimed at the improvement of the economic position of peripheral regions – certainly in absolute and possibly in relative terms – is invariably easier and more effective in the context of a national economy growing at a relatively high rate than in that of a stagnant economy. The reasons are plain enough. Insofar as policy relies on the use of bribery or cajolery to steer new development towards relatively depressed regions, it is obviously unlikely to work if industrial expansion generally is slow or zero. The most 'foot-loose' of industries must be faced with the need for expansion before it can be guided anywhere. Again, where regional policy takes the form of the direct use of public funds in the improvement of the infrastructure of depressed areas, or the active promotion of industrial development in them, the necessary intervention is liable to be politically easier and present smaller fiscal problems in a relatively prosperous environment than in recession conditions.

Given existing techniques of regional economic policy, in other words, it is axiomatic that a critically important factor in the determination of the pace of regional development must be the growth rate of the surrounding economy. Hence it follows that the impact of the formation of the EC on its problem regions will always be the outcome of two separate sets of forces: on the one hand, any special regional dimension its policies may or may not have and, on the other, its consequences for the EC economy generally – which means, predominantly, the prosperous central regions rather than the peripheral 'depressed' regions.

Such are the *a priori* predictions of theory. How far are they confirmed by the evidence of actual developments in the EC during the formative years between 1958 and 1972? Such evidence is unfortunately difficult to obtain with any great degree of accuracy. In the first place, the definitions of the constituent regional areas did not remain constant over the period.[1] Secondly, calculations of regional income and employment on a consistent basis are a relatively recent phenomenon and any attempt to measure movements over this earlier period of fourteen years must necessarily rely on statistical series of something less than complete comparability. The evidence assembled in Table 16.1 can therefore be interpreted as giving only broad orders of magnitude.

Bearing these provisos in mind, the evidence of Table 16.1 suggests that in the

Table 16.1 Per capita incomes in the EC[a]

	1950	1960	1970	1976	1982
	Internal regional variance (%)				
Belgium	22.9	14.2	19.9	22.7	22.0
France	30.6	30.2	27.6	32.8	24.0
W. Germany	21.0	15.8	14.0	13.8	14.2
Italy	34.0	35.5	27.4	29.7	24.6
Netherlands	12.3	9.5	10.1	10.8	15.5
EC (6)	24.5	21.5	11.0	17.8	9.2
Denmark	6.8	9.3	16.4	7.0	13.7
United Kingdom	18.0	11.6	13.8	9.3	11.7
EC (9)	26.6	18.7	9.7	23.4	24.8
	Per capita incomes (EC9 = 100)				
Belgium	146	109	102	119	105
France	120	112	101	110	109
W. Germany	82	110	117	126	111
Italy	63	61	85	69	87
Luxemburg	177	145	127	112	115
Netherlands	88	87	103	128	100
EC (6)	90	95	107	109	103
Denmark	135	112	118	140	111
Ireland	72	63	54	53	66
United Kingdom	129	118	95	78	92
EC (9)	100	100	100	100	100

Note

[a] Regional variance within countries is measured by the (population) weighted coefficient of variance around the average per capita income for the country concerned. Variance between countries is measured by the weighted coefficient of variance of national averages around the average for EC (6) and EC (9) respectively.

Sources: Results for 1950–60 compiled from Molle *et al.*, *Regional disparity and economic development in the European Community*, Saxon House, Farnborough, 1980. Income figures are in national currencies converted into $US at contemporary exchange rates. Results for 1970–80 compiled from *Yearbook of Regional Statistics*, 1981 and 1985, Commission of the European Communities, Luxemburg 1981 and 1985. The income figures used are in national currencies converted into ECU at purchasing-power parities as estimated by the Commission.

formative decade of the Community the more pessimistic predictions concerning the impact of economic integration on regional disparities were not well founded. In the three large member countries – France, Germany and Italy – overall internal regional disparity actually declined between 1960 and 1970, on average by around 15 per cent. In the two smaller countries – Belgium and the Netherlands – it would appear to have increased somewhat, but the fact that these countries are divided into only three and four regions respectively makes the estimate of regional disparity of somewhat dubious reliability. During the same period regional disparity in both Denmark and the United Kingdom appears to have widened. (Internal disparity cannot be measured for Luxemburg or Ireland since for the purposes of EC statistics both countries are treated as single regions.)

Superimposed on this internal narrowing was the fact that disparities *between* the member countries in the matter of average income also fell quite sharply over the same decade – they were in fact halved. In other words, regional inequalities in the EC as a whole were reduced not only because of a more even distribution of income internally but also because the relatively poor member countries – Italy and the Netherlands – experienced a noticeably high annual rate of growth in real per capita income (6.3 per cent) than did the remaining members of the six (5.5 per cent). This conclusion is confirmed by the definitive study of regional trends in Europe at this time; this found that during the 1950s and 1960s regional disparities in the EC were reduced by some 43 per cent, but about two-thirds of this narrowing was accounted for by the higher rate of growth in the relatively poor countries. The reduction in internal (i.e. national) variance, on the other hand, was primarily due to the movement of population out of the predominantly agricultural (and hence poorer) regions and into industrial areas – hardly the desired outcome of regional policy measures (see Molle *et al.*, 1980, Chapter 4, pp. 159–60). These two elements in the situation are obviously closely connected with each other; the switch of resources from agriculture to industry was in fact a major cause of the high rate of growth in the EC during this period.

All this being said, two important qualifications need to be stressed. First, the available evidence demonstrates clearly that being a poor region can mean very different things in different countries. The poorest German region in 1970, Schleswig–Holstein, enjoyed a per capita income which was in fact some 3 per cent *higher* than that of the richest Italian region, Lombardia. Secondly, while the relative position of the poorest regions improved somewhat during the 1960s, the gap between rich and poor remained wide. In 1960 the five poorest regions of the EC enjoyed an average per capita income which was only 22 per cent of that enjoyed in the five richest regions; in 1970 average income in the five poorest regions was still only 30 per cent of that in the five richest (see Molle, 1980, Table 10.2.C). The problem of southern Italy, the Mezzogiorno, was particularly acute; for the region as a whole, average income in 1970 was still less than half of the EC average. In short, progress towards economic integration may not have aggravated the 'regional problem' as had been feared by some; however, it had certainly not disposed of it.

16.3 The regional aid debate 1958–72

In June 1977 the European Commission submitted to the Council of Ministers a report on regional policy which began, 'The time has come for the Community to define clearly an overall approach to Community regional policy . . .' (EC Commission, 1977, p. 5). Since the member countries had then been arguing intermittently over regional measures for nearly twenty years, the phrase could fairly be described as a masterpiece of understatement.

The truth of the matter is that, prior to its amendment by the Single European Act (SEA), the Treaty of Rome contained no specific provision for a common regional policy comparable to that made for agriculture or transport. Indeed, it could reasonably be said that the spirit of the Treaty – and particularly its strong emphasis on the desirability of removing impediments to, or distortions in, trade between member countries – was inherently antagonistic to the sort of measures which have come to be associated with regional policy. Nevertheless, even the much-cited Article 92, which enunciated the basic doctrine that state aid which destroys competition should be deemed 'incompatible with the Common Market', immediately proceeded to admit the possibility of dispensation for 'aid intended to promote the economic development of regions where the standard of living is abnormally low or where there exists serious under-employment' (Article 92, section 3(a)).

Nor was this somewhat grudging dispensation from the perfection of undiluted market forces confined to the broad (and vague) generalisation of Article 92: it was repeated in several of the more detailed provisions of the Treaty. Title II, enshrining the concept of the Common Agricultural Policy (CAP), contained, for example, in Article 49, the specific caveat that due account would have to be taken of the 'structural and natural disparities between the various agricultural regions' (Article 39, section 2(a)). Similarly, the common rules to be laid down as part of the transport policy enshrined in Title IV were stated to be subject to qualification if their application 'might seriously affect the standard of living and the level of employment in certain regions' (Article 75, section 3). The financial agencies established by the Community were also exhorted to be concerned with regional problems. The 'guidance' section of the Agricultural Guarantee and Guidance Fund (FEOGA) was instructed to pay due regard to the regional impact of the CAP referred to in Article 39 and for this reason most of its finance of structural reform measures has been directed to Italy. This regional dimension of FEOGA received even greater stress in 1971, when the Council of Ministers approved the specific allocation of about £125 million from it over a period of five years to finance 'development operations' in priority areas.

Similarly again, the European Social Fund (ESF) was directed by Article 125 to assist workers whose employment had been reduced or suspended 'as a result of the conversion of their enterprise to other productions', an activity of direct and obvious relevance in the context of regional policy (Article 125, section 1B). In 1971 a directive by the Council of Ministers provided that 60 per cent of its resources should be devoted to increasing employment in 'problem' regions. Finally, the European Investment Bank (EIB) was given, as its first task, the financing of 'projects for developing less developed regions' (Article 130(a)) and has in reality operated as a regional development bank. The great bulk of its lending has been concerned with development projects in the poorer regions, most especially in Italy. Between 1958 and 1973, in fact, 46 per cent of its total lending related to projects in Italy (Woolley, 1975).

This motley collection of qualifications, derogations and exhortations, however, in no way added up to an integrated and coherent regional policy, or anything remotely like it. It enabled actions to be taken by individual member countries unilaterally, giving positive financial support to some and moral condonation to others, but provided no mechanism for ensuring that these separate actions were consistent with those being pursued by other member countries, or indeed followed any rational pattern over time within any individual member state. Nor, even less, did it comprise any kind of framework within which the EC as a whole could formulate or initiate regional policy measures for itself – nor, for that matter, did it ensure that the regional dimensions of its own separate policies were consistent with one another.

The overall result was that while the 1960s and the early 1970s were sprinkled with a dreary succession of conferences, reports, recommendations and ministerial pronouncements, the EC was very long on grandiose generalisations embodied in the tortured prose of the international civil service, but very short indeed on action. A Community regional policy, to have any meaning, required an enforceable agreement on two separate matters:

1. Criteria against which actions taken by individual member countries to assist their own regions could be adjudged, so as to determine whether they were compatible or incompatible with the rules of the club.
2. A mechanism by which the EC collectively could formulate its own regional policy measures independently of (or at least in addition to) measures being adopted by member countries individually.

It was only after 1975 that some vestige of progress could be said to have been made on the second of these elements; before that time, such debate as occurred was in practice concerned only with the first. Indeed, it would not be unfair to say that the arguments and actions nominally concerned with regional policy during the period 1958–72 were in reality one element of the EC's competition policy rather than part of a genuine regional policy.

It would be unduly tedious to attempt a chronological summary of the succession of reports and resolutions emerging between 1958 and 1973. (Excellent summaries are to be found in Vanhove and Klaassen, 1987, Chapter 10; Balassa, 1975, pp. 260–4; Flockton, 1970; McCrone, 1969.) In essence, three questions formed the bulk of the subject matter of the debate. First, what characteristics distinguished a 'problem' region (for which special measures of assistance were justified) from 'prosperous' regions (for which they were not)? Second, in assisting problem regions, which types of policy measure were to be deemed compatible with the principles of the common market and which not? Third, what, if any, was to be the maximum level of any such 'compatible' policy measures?

As far as the first question was concerned, it proved relatively easy to secure agreement on the matter in general, but less easy on matters in particular. As early as 1961, broad agreement was reached that 'problem' regions were those falling into one or other of four categories:

1. Those in which one or more basic industries were in long-run decline – the obvious examples being districts heavily dependent on coalmining, shipbuilding or (later) steel.

2. Those which had remained essentially rural and in which the infrastructure necessary to encourage industrial development did not exist – for example, Brittany or the south of Italy.
3. Those in which industry and population had become so congested that further expansion would generate serious diseconomies and/or environmental degradation.
4. Those peripheral regions through which ran the border between two (or more) member countries – the so-called 'frontier zones'.

While this classification was adequate enough for distinguishing between different *categories* of problem region, unfortunately it did not in itself provide criteria by which a decision could be made concerning whether a particular region was or was not a problem in the first place. The fact that a region is predominantly agricultural does not in itself render it depressed or declining – far from it, in the context of the CAP; nor does the mere presence of a border with another member country. Criteria of economic underprivilege were therefore needed in addition – a problem of particular delicacy when different national governments are involved, since criteria based on national averages (for example, of per capita income or unemployment) could result in identical situations being symptoms of regional underprivilege in one member country and regional prosperity in another.

It cannot be said that any real agreement had been reached on this issue prior to 1975 nor, indeed, that it has yet been attained. By common consent, the indicators of regional underprivilege included a level of income which was, by some standard, unduly low, an above average (but which average?) level of unemployment and an excessive tendency towards population migration. The various member countries had very divergent ideas, however, as to other appropriate criteria, the supreme example being perhaps the Belgian Minister of Regional Economy who managed to accumulate a total of 35 criteria for designating areas to be assisted under his country's regional policy legislation (including 'commuting under unfavourable conditions', which would strike a sympathetic chord in the hearts of many Londoners). What is worse, no agreement could be reached concerning the relative weight to be attached to the different criteria especially when – as must inevitably happen – they point in different directions.

An answer to the second question, i.e. which forms of regional aid were to be permissible and which not, was in fact much easier to obtain, since it is in reality implicit in what might be called the theology of the Common Market. On the one hand, the commitment to market competition – and the conviction that all state aids to industry are *prima facie* an interference with it – led to agreement that to be permissible all regional assistance measures should be 'transparent' – that is to say, that they should be open in nature and precisely calculable in value. Hence grants of a specific value – say, *x* per cent of initial capital cost – would be permissible, whereas special investment allowances against taxes on future profits would not, since the magnitude of future profits would be unknown. Secondly, anything amounting to a subsidy of current operations would be inadmissible. On the other hand, measures designed to correct an underlying deficiency in the general infrastructure – and which it was hoped would eventually result in an ability to compete unaided on the open market – would be acceptable. These general principles were agreed in 1971; since then, the Commission has proceeded on a case-by-case basis, challenging (usually with success) the validity of any measures which appear to it to conflict with one or other of these two principles.

The third question, i.e. what limits, if any, should be imposed on the magnitude of regional aid, was also resolved in 1971 through the rather simple expedient of fixing a ceiling so high as to cause discomfort to no one. The Council of Ministers (conscious of the folly of competitive bidding by member countries for the favours of overseas, and especially American, investors) resolved that after 1973 investment incentives should not exceed 20 per cent of the cash value of investments in the so-called central – i.e. prosperous – regions of the Community. Provided that the concept of the 'central' area was not constricted so far as to be meaningless, this was neither an unreasonable nor, in practice, a restrictive limit. (That considerable elasticity is possible is revealed by the fact that, under its 1971 law, the Belgian government was proceeding to treat 41 of its total of 43 regions as eligible for aid – a practice which the EC Commission sharply discouraged. See *The Economist*, 3 June 1972, p. 72.) For the frontier areas of Germany and some Danish regions, the limit was put somewhat higher, at 25 per cent. For the main development areas of the United Kingdom, France and Italy, the ceiling was even higher at 30 per cent, but even this limit could be exceeded in Southern Italy, Ireland and Greenland (Stewart and Begg, 1976, pp. 35–6).

By the early 1970s, then, some progress had been made towards the establishment of a degree of uniformity in the national policies of the six with regard to regional assistance. In a sense this was the negative requirement for a community regional policy – it substantially reduced the degree of conflict between the regional and other aspects of EC policy and between the efforts of one member country and another. But the positive requirements for an EC regional policy were as lacking in the early 1970s as they had been in the early 1960s.

16.4 The emergent community policy: phase 2, 1973–84

With the benefit of hindsight it is not difficult to see why, on the one hand, regional policy was pushed somewhat to the background during the first decade of the Community's existence nor, on the other hand, why it suddenly shot into prominence in the early and middle 1970s, a process which began with the celebrated declaration by the new President of the Commission before the European Parliament in May 1968 that an effective regional policy had become the *sine qua non* of further integration and should be in the EC 'as the heart is in the human body' (Flockton, 1970, p. 46). The heart, as it proved, had a good deal of waiting still ahead of it before its beat became audible, but times were manifestly changing.

In the first place, the opening decade of the EC was inevitably and necessarily dominated by the problems of what were unquestionably the crucial foundations of the whole edifice – the rapid movement to internal free trade, the establishment of a common external tariff (CET) and the creation of the common agricultural policy. Compared with these, questions of regional economic policy seemed a second-order triviality. By the end of the 1960s the situation was reversed: the foundations had been laid and, in a sense, the easy part was over. Further progress was likely to be politically very difficult, now that the first flush of enthusiasm was waning, if the interests of the hardest-hit regions within member countries were not visibly protected.

This was particularly the case once the EC had declared its intention of embarking on the path whose ultimate objective was the achievement of complete monetary union, a situation in which regional differences in output and income would be revealed most starkly (Stewart and Begg, 1976, p. 35). At the Paris summit of 1972, the creation was announced of the European Regional Development Fund (ERDF, discussed below) which, the ministers stated, was 'needed to correct the structural and regional imbalance which might affect the realisation of economic and monetary union'. The second holder of the office of Regional Policy Commissioner – a post originally created in 1969 – went so far as to declare, in 1973, that monetary union in Europe was 'inconceivable' without a strong EC regional policy (Thomson, 1973, p. 5).

Secondly, the 1960s had unquestionably been a decade of phenomenal growth in which, as the evidence given above has shown, the regions had experienced a marked improvement in both their relative and absolute standards of output, employment and income. The early 1970s saw a sharp reversal of the fortunes of both old and new members of the Community and it was one which was to prove distinctly intractable. Between 1958 and 1972, on the one hand, and 1972 and 1981 on the other, the annual growth rate of the real GDP of the six original member countries fell from 5.4 per cent to 2.5 per cent, while that of industrial production fell from 6.0 per cent to 1.7 per cent; the total number unemployed rose from 1.5 million in 1972, to nearly 6 million by 1981.

As was argued in 16.2 above, in such rather dismal economic circumstances regional policy becomes both more necessary and more difficult. It is more necessary precisely because recession (like prosperity) tends to have an uneven impact and the distress of the worst-affected regions (for example, the older steelmaking centres) was too obvious to be ignored. The evidence of Table 16.1 is persuasive. Between 1970 and 1976 the movement towards reduced internal variance characteristic of the 1960s was reversed in five out of the original six. This was reinforced by a similar and even more marked, reversal of the previous trend towards reduced disparities between the six. In the context of the integration of the EC, it would have been particularly unrealistic to suppose that further progress could be made while pockets of quite acute distress remained scattered through member countries. As the Commission was to remark in its 1977 report, the strengthening of EC regional policy was 'not only desirable; it is now one of the conditions of continuing European economic integration' (The European Commission, 1977d, p. 6). The pursuit of regional policy becomes more difficult, on the other hand, because measures aimed at attracting new development have little effect when no new development is occurring, while measures designed to improve regional infrastructure are more difficult to finance in the context of an economy growing only slowly or not at all. The coordination and strengthening of the Community's regional measures therefore took on a greater urgency.

The third stimulus to the development of regional thinking in the early 1970s was, quite simply, the political necessities of the prospective accession of three new members, in particular that of Britain. As the oldest of the industrial countries, British involvement in regional problems was far older and more extensive than in any other member country; Britain also had the longest acquaintance with a problem which the other member countries were now encountering for the first time – regional policy in the context of near-zero growth. What is more, this greater awareness of the regional problem had accentuated in British political thinking the potential threat to its already depressed regions implicit in their becoming even more peripheral than before as a result of membership of the EC.

Like God, therefore, even if the inclination towards a Community regional policy had not existed, it would have been necessary to invent it. Some prize had to be offered to the British (and Irish) and part of this took the form of the appointment as Regional Policy Commissioner of Mr George (later Lord) Thomson, together with the promise of resources for him to work with. This resulted, in 1973, in a report with which his name is customarily associated and which can fairly be described as the beginning of a genuinely collective regional policy in the EC.

The proposals of the Thomson Report, which were substantially adopted by the Council of Ministers in 1975, were subsequently replaced by 'new guidelines' set out in another Commission report in 1977 which was in due course approved by the Council of Ministers in 1978; hence there is little point in rehearsing its contents in detail. (For excellent summaries and comments see Balassa, 1975, pp. 267–71 and *The Economist*, 1973.) It opened a new era in the regional policy debate by establishing the concept of a comprehensive EC policy, with a Regional Development Committee to develop and apply it and a new financial source, the ERDF, through which Community resources, as contrasted with the budgetary allocations of individual member countries, were to be channelled into regional development programmes in the form of grants and rebates on loan interest charges. Certainly, it could be argued that an EC policy in the true sense had not yet emerged, since the resources of the ERDF were to be used only to contribute towards the cost of projects submitted by individual member governments – in general, to a maximum of 50 per cent of the amount of aid provided by the member government itself. The role of the ERDF, in other words, was wholly passive and the initiative in regional development remained with member countries. Nevertheless, an important principle had been established: EC resources were being allocated specifically to regional policy, rather than as a byproduct of the application of other policies.

The activities of the ERDF over the ten years 1975–84 are summarised in Table 16.2. The first point which has to be made concerns the relatively modest scale of the operation. The assistance provided by the fund averaged little more than the equivalent of 1,150 million ECU a year, although it has to be conceded that the running-in phase of 1975 makes this something of an understatement; for 1984 the actual total of grants approved was about 2,320 million ECU. Even this latter total,

Table 16.2 Grants from the ERDF 1975–84

Member state 1	Average quota (%) 2	Total (million ECU) 3	Assistance approved % of ERDF total 4	% of projects 5	ECU per capita 6
Belgium	1.22	114.4	0.99	15.4	11.7
Denmark	1.12	131.8	1.14	22.6	25.8
France	14.43	1,683.6	14.59	13.9	31.3
W. Germany	5.15	544.8	4.72	6.3	8.9
Greece	8.67	1,093.5	9.48	27.6	110.5
Ireland	6.11	712.9	6.18	6.6	209.7
Italy	36.88	4,352.8	37.73	20.3	77.5
Luxemburg	0.08	12.0	0.10	21.2	29.9
Netherlands	1.37	156.2	1.35	18.2	11.1
United Kingdom	24.98	2,735.6	23.71	13.1	48.6
EC (10)	100	11,537.5	100	14.4	42.7

Source: Based on Commission of the European Communities, *Eighteenth General Report*, Luxemburg 1985, Table 10, p. 148. The per capita figures are based on average populations over 1975–84 except in the case of Greece, for which the average for 1981–4 has been used. The average quotas shown in col. 2 are the allocations for the three periods 1975–8, 1979–80 and 1981–4 weighted by the total sums appropriated for the ERDF in each of those three periods.

however, represented less than 8 per cent of the Community budget for the year (compared with 65 per cent for agriculture) or somewhat less than 0.1 per cent of the total gross domestic product of the ten. For the three years 1975–7 the Commission itself had sought a total ERDF budget of 2,250 million EUA. The principal prospective beneficiaries – Britain, Ireland and Italy – had proposed a total of 3,000 million, while the likely principal contributor, Germany, suggested 1,000 million. In the final outcome, the agreed total of 1,300 million was far closer to the latter than to the former.

As a result, the relatively small contribution made by the ERDF made it unlikely that it was having any significant influence on the majority of regional development projects being initiated. Its activities during 1975–84 involved some 26,000 projects, but its contribution towards them amounted, on average, to only 14 per cent of their total value – although this average conceals a variation between 6 per cent in Germany and 28 per cent in Greece. (It has been estimated that total receipts by the United Kingdom from the ERDF in 1982 were equivalent to only 15 per cent of total UK expenditure on regional measures.) There was more than a suspicion, therefore, that the ERDF was being used by member countries as no more than a means of recovering part of the cost of projects which would have been undertaken in any event. This is scarcely what is meant by a positive and dynamic *Community* policy.

An awareness of these underlying weaknesses led to the 1977 Commission report on revised guidelines for regional policy referred to above (EC Commission, 1977a), somewhat modified by a further Commission communication in 1981.

The first major change introduced by the revised guidelines involved the redefinition of 'problem' regions, not so much in terms of the nature of the source of their weakness, but rather in terms of the appropriate level of policy action. The four categories were now defined as follows:

1. Underdeveloped regions which require long-run aid in order to acquire an economic and social infrastructure amenable to sustained growth – the Mezzogiorno, Ireland, Greenland and the French overseas territories.
2. Regions requiring short- or medium-term assistance in order to 'adapt' their structure (through productive investment) in order to replace declining industries or reduce dependence on agriculture – the typical 'depressed' regions of the highly industrialised countries.
3. 'Regional impact areas' – that is to say, those on which the changing world economic environment or, more importantly, other EC policies are having, or are likely to have, an unusually marked adverse effect.
4. Frontier regions, where national boundaries divide what are in fact natural economic entities and where an integrated and coherent policy involves the actions of two or more separate member governments.

The essential proposition advanced by the 1977 report was that while (1) and (2) represent regions for which sensible remedial action can and should be taken by and through individual member governments, (3) and (4) do not. Inherently, their situation calls for *Community*, not national, action.

Secondly, and following logically from this, the resources available to the ERDF had to make separate provision for (1) and (2) on the one hand – complementing but not displacing, it was stressed yet again, member government action – and, on the other hand, for cases falling under (3) and (4). Thus the funds of the ERDF were henceforth to be split between a 'quota' section, financing projects in (1) and (2) regions, and a non-quota section reserved for projects in (3) and (4) regions. While no precise figure was put on this 'non-quota' element in the 1977 Commission report, it was clearly envisaged that it would be allocated a fairly substantial fraction of the total ERDF budget and in the 1981 communication the share suggested was 20 per cent. Further, the specific recommendation that the approval of grants from the non-quota element should require only a 'qualified majority' among the Council of Ministers was a crucial element in establishing a *Community* policy as distinct from one dependent on the consent of every individual member country. In the event, both items received a severe mauling by the Council of Ministers before its approval was forthcoming. For the initial three-year period, 1978–80, the non-quota section was allocated only 5 per cent of the total ERDF budget – scarcely an overwhelming start. What was worse, a provision was inserted specifying that every project financed from non-quota funds would need unanimous approval by ministers – which meant, of course, that every ingredient of regional policy remained totally under the control of each member country concerned. This inevitably gave the apparently supranational character of the policy framework a somewhat superficial quality.

The third feature of the 1977 proposals – accepted by the Council – was the increased stress given to the coordination of the regional policy measures at both national and EC level. As far as the former was concerned, the Commission recognised the need to provide what had always been lacking – a system by which, through improved statistical information, the analysis and assessment of the state of the regional economies of the EC as a whole could be continuously undertaken. A two-yearly report on the state of the regions was proposed with the aid of this strengthened analytical system. This, in turn, it was proposed, would form the basis of comparison between the regional programmes of individual member countries, also to be prepared on a continuous and systematic basis. It is also noteworthy that the 1977 guidelines spelled out in more detail than hitherto the relevant indicators of 'regional imbalance' to be used in applying the resources of the ERDF and, by implication, in determining the regional policies of individual member countries. These were

1. The trend in regional unemployment rates over the preceding five years.
2. The proportion of the working population engaged in agriculture and in 'declining industrial sectors'.
3. The net regional migration rate during the preceding five years.
4. The level of, and trend in, regional GDP totals.

So far as the coordination of EC policy is concerned, the 1977 guidelines emphasised the need to assess and take due account of the 'spatial dimension' of all major policies of the Community. To this end, the Regional Development Committee was to be supplied with reports on the regional impact of EC policies and, in the light of these, to advance recommendations to the Council of Ministers concerning measures to be adopted to offset them when necessary – including, of course, projects to be financed from the non-quota section of the ERDF.

All this sounded impressive enough, but the outcome – in the view of the Commission, at any rate – proved to be disappointing. In its first periodic report on the social and economic position of the regions in 1980 it identified four matters giving rise to concern. First, far from narrowing, in its view, regional differences in the EC appeared to be widening; in 1970, average per capita income in Calabria (converted into ECUs at current exchange rates) had been 26 per cent of that in the Ile de France, but by 1978 it had fallen by 21 per cent. The comparison is undoubtedly distorted by the use of current exchange rates to convert into a common unit rather than purchasing-power parities; using income figures based on the latter, the deterioration was much more modest: from 30 per cent in 1970 to 28 per cent in 1978. What is more, a similar comparison for 1982 yields a relative income of 32 per cent in Calabria. The evidence of Table 16.1 suggests that by 1982 the magnitudes of internal variances in all member countries were quite similar to those of 1970. Much the same was true of external variances between the six; the sharp increase in variance between the nine (from around 10 per cent in 1970 to about 25 per cent in 1982) was essentially due to the abysmally poor growth record of the United Kingdom between 1970 and 1976. Over those six years, when real GDP per head was growing at an average rate of 2.5 per cent a year in the six, the United Kingdom had a growth rate of only 0.9 per cent.

But if the Commission was perhaps unduly pessimistic in speaking of a positive worsening in the regional position over the 1970s, it could argue with much greater justification that it had certainly not improved significantly.

The second Commission complaint was that far too much of the ERDF resources was being applied to individual projects in member states – roads, bridges, harbours and so on – and far too little to integrated development programmes. Over 1975–85 as a whole, in fact, no less than 97 per cent of the assistance granted by the ERDF was devoted to individual projects – more than 80 per cent of these being classified as Infrastructure and only 18 per cent being in 'industrial, service and craft industry sectors' – and only 2 per cent was used for general development programmes (EC Commission, 1985f, Table 10, p. 192). The drawback of the former is that they tend to generate employment during their constructional phase but little if any – at least directly – after their completion. What is more, the old problem of additionality arises: that is to say, the suspicion (to put it no higher) that grants towards infra-structure were merely helping to finance projects which would have gone ahead anyway. The ERDF was therefore making a contribution to general national budgets rather than stimulating additional regional development.

Thirdly, the Commission pointed out that, while the allocation of funds from the ERDF had been heavily weighted in favour of the relatively poor countries, a sub-stantial share was nevertheless still going to countries which could well afford to finance their own regional programmes. Indeed, Table 16.2 shows that over 1975–84 the six countries with above-average per capita incomes absorbed 23 per cent of the fund's total outlays. The Commission therefore proposed that the quotas should be abolished altogether for Belgium, France, Germany and the Netherlands.

Finally, the Commission noted that the take-up rate of the miniscule non-quota section of the ERDF had been very disappointing. Over most of the years since its inception, in fact, part of the non-quota allocation had to be transferred to the quota section for want of takers. The reason, it argued, was quite clear: in allocating non-quota funds the ERDF was able to emphasise the EC, rather than the national, dimension and to apply its own criteria in determining which were and which were not worthwhile projects. National governments found this submission to outside questioning and judgement unacceptable and therefore avoided exposure to it. The remedy, in the view of the Commission, was to introduce a progressive increase in the relative size of the non-quota section – beginning with an increase to at least 20 per cent of the total – and thus force member governments to, so to speak, choose between their pride and their pockets.

Put briefly, all was far from well in the Community's regional policy.

16.5 Community policy: phase 3, 1985 onwards

If the Commission had expected its proposals for revision to be greeted with unquali-fied enthusiasm it was doomed to disappointment. Any change involving a reduction in the flow of EC funds to any one member country is destined to receive a severe mauling in the Council of Ministers and is fortunate to survive at all, let alone un-scathed. The new regional policy which was finally agreed after three years of dis-cussion – embodied in Regulation 1787 of 1984 and coming into effect on 1 January 1985 – therefore reflected the thinking of the Commission to only a limited degree.

In the first place, the objectives of the ERDF were restated in somewhat simpler, if more general, terms. Its purpose was now declared to be the restructuring of areas most affected by industrial decline and the structural adjustment of regions ex-periencing delayed development. This falls far short of the Commission's proposal to exclude richer countries altogether but does at least imply the requirement that genuine relative poverty must be established before a region can qualify for assistance.

By implication the ministers confirmed what had in fact been a long-standing Commission practice. This was the replacement of detailed and complex criteria in order to establish qualification – and the more complex the criteria the greater the number of regions which would qualify – by a simple, if crude, objective 'problem index'. For each region a calculation was to be made of per capita GDP as a percentage of the EC average; its rate of unemployment was also to be related (inversely) to the EC average. If the arithmetic mean of these two figures was 75 or less, the region qualified for ERDF assistance. For example, suppose that for region A and the EC as a whole the relevant figures for a given year were:

	Per capita GDP (ECU)	Rate of unemployment (%)
EC average	10,000	8.0
Region A	8,000	12.5

The income index would be $[8,000/10,000].100 = 80.0$ while the unemployment in-dex would be $[8.0/12.5].100 = 64.0$. The overall index would thus be $[80.0 + 64.0]/2 = 72$, and the region would therefore qualify for assistance. The indicator was ad-mittedly crude and highly sensitive to relatively small changes in a single number. (In the example above, for instance, if the EC unemployment rate had been 9 per cent instead of 8 per cent the region's index would have been $[80.0 + 72]/2 = 76$ and it would therefore have ceased to qualify.) But it at least drastically reduced the scope for special pleading inherent in more sophisticated criteria systems.

Secondly, the Council of Ministers went some way towards the Commission's insistence that more emphasis should be placed on development programmes generating permanent employment and less on one-off projects. It was agreed that from 1985 onwards, and within three years, at least 20 per cent of assistance should go to integrated development programmes (compared with 1.6 per cent in 1984). Further, it was agreed that the maximum ERDF contribution should be raised from 30 per cent to 50 per cent for projects but even further to 70 per cent for development programmes. This attempt to switch emphasis seems to have had some limited success: in 1985 appropriations for programmes amounted to 7 per cent of the total and in 1986 to 8 per cent.

Thirdly, while the ministers found the Commission's proposals on ERDF quotas (i.e. their abolition for rich countries and their overall reduction to 80 per cent of the available funds) too much to swallow, they made some hesistant moves in the same direction. From 1985 the distinction between the quota and non-quota sections of the fund has been abolished. Instead, each country is allocated a minimum quota – much as before – but also a maximum quota. The difference between these two totals would be available for grants in support of proposals which would be appraised by EC (i.e. Commission) criteria rather than by those of the applicant governments. Thus the margin of just over 11 per cent of the total available each year would in effect be put up for competitive tender amongst member governments but would be subject to EC rather than national appraisal.

The details are shown in Table 16.3, from which it will be observed that the maximum quotas for 1985 were rather cleverly calculated so that with only one exception (Denmark) all member countries were theoretically able to obtain a larger share than under the previous regime – although obviously they could not all do so simultaneously. The quotas were rather drastically revised again in 1986 to allow for generous provision for the new entrants, Portugal and Spain. The outcome for 1986 shows that the degree to which individual countries availed themselves of the opportunity to obtain funds over and above the minimum quota varied considerably. Both Belgium and France showed considerable success in this regard, obtaining all, or nearly all, of the total available; at the other extreme, Denmark, Germany and Ireland made no use of the facility. Whether this reflects, on the one hand, the relative magnitudes of regional problems in different member states or, on the other, relative inclinations to be subject to Commission scrutiny and questioning must remain a matter of speculation.

Table 16.3 ERDF quotas 1985 onwards

Member state	Quota % old regime, 1981–4	Quotas %, 1985 onwards		Actual allocations % 1985–6[a]	% take-up of margin
		Minimum	Maximum		
1	2	3	4	5	6
Belgium	1.11	0.90	1.20	1.18	93
Denmark	1.06	0.51	0.67	0.51	—
France	13.64	11.05	14.74	12.91	50
W. Germany	4.65	3.76	4.81	3.46	—
Greece	13.00	12.35	15.74	15.12	82
Ireland	5.94	5.64	6.83	5.92	24
Italy	35.49	31.94	42.59	35.52	34
Luxemburg	0.07	0.06	0.08	0.07	50
Netherlands	1.24	1.00	1.34	1.01	3
United Kingdom	23.80	21.42	28.56	24.30	40
EC (10)	100	88.63	116.56	100	41

Note
[a] Excludes allocations in 1986 to Portugal, Spain and projects involving more than one country.

Source: Based on Commission of the European Communities, *Nineteenth General Report*, Luxemburg, 1986, Table 10, p. 192, and *Twentieth General Report*, Luxemburg, 1987, Table 11, p. 215.

16.6 Conclusion

What are the future prospects for an effective Common Regional Policy? The arguments originally advanced in its favour remain substantially unchanged over the
twenty years since the case for it was first seriously discussed. Regional disparities in
the nine do not appear to have changed significantly over that period, while the
accessions of Greece, Portugal and Spain have extended the EC to include countries
whose *average* per capita income is little, if at all, higher than the poorest regions of
Italy. Given the continuing plateau in the movement towards closer integration in
Europe, the case for monetary union takes on greater urgency than ever, since no
other policy initiative could possibly provide comparable impetus to the integration
process. And, as has been seen, monetary union without an effective regional policy is
scarcely conceivable. It is hardly surprising, therefore, that the architects of the SEA
in 1986 insisted that policies for regional development should be added to the formal
commitments of the Treaty.

Yet the EC remains as far removed from a genuinely common policy as in 1970.
The ERDF exists and is, doubtless, of value; indeed, at its Brussels meeting in 1988
the Council of Ministers resolved that the resources available to it should be doubled
between 1988 and 1993. Even so the resources of the ERDF remain almost trivial in
comparison with those deployed on regional affairs by national governments. It has
been estimated that in 1982 national governments allocated funds to regional development (*excluding* expenditures on infrastructure) which amounted to more than five
times the entire ERDF budget for that year (Vanhove and Klaasen, 1987, p. 474.)
And of those ERDF resources, nearly 90 per cent are in any event absorbed in quotas
which are little more than contributions to national budgets. Regional policy in the
EC remains effectively merely a collection of national policies pursuing national ends.

Nor is the EC itself beyond reproach in its own handling of regional matters. The
delay, bureaucratic procedures and vulnerability to the unremitting pursuit of national
self-interest for which Brussels has become renowned has not left Directorate-General
XVI for Regional Policy unscathed. Applications outside the minimum ERDF quota
require approval by the Council of Ministers and have been known to spend years in
the process. Only slowly is the EC groping its way towards some real coordination
between the ERDF and the other funds whose activities can have major regional
impact – the Guidance section of FEOGA, the ESF, the ECSC and the EIB. It
remains the case that other EC policies can and do have a regional impact far out-
weighing anything within the powers of the ERDF – most obviously the CAP, which
distributes 75 per cent of its largesse to the relatively prosperous farmers in northern
regions and a mere 25 per cent to their impoverished colleagues in the areas adjoining
the Mediterranean.

It would be both unjust and inaccurate to suggest that the EC is unaware of these
problems or making no effective moves to solve them. But the painfully limited
progress achieved after thirty years of EC existence must raise the question of whether
at the end of the day regional policy is in fact one of those areas for which the EC is the
appropriate level for effective operation. The case for giving an affirmative answer to

that question is powerfully and persuasively argued by Vanhove and Klaasen (1987, pp. 473–7). Certainly it is sensible that there should be agreed limits for investment incentives in order to avoid competitive bidding among member governments to attract outside enterprises. Certainly, also, the proposition that some form of inter-governmental compensation mechanism is an essential ingredient for a successful common market is beyond dispute, and if what is labelled a Regional Fund is used for this purpose, well and good. But that is a far cry from the EC seeking to construct and operate a common *policy* for the use of those funds in particular ways.

Strict uniformity throughout the length and breadth of twelve different nations makes sense only when there is unanimity concerning both the ends and the means. It is far from obvious that the relative costs and benefits of any technique of regional development will be the same in every country of the EC, nor, even less, that the social welfare rankings attached to those costs and benefits will be uniform. (Indeed, it is unlikely that they will be uniform for different regions within a single country.)

One must go further. The standard assumption that a reduction in regional inequality necessarily raises economic welfare (see Molle, 1980, Chapter 3, p. 70) is unduly simplistic. Such a reduction *may* conceivably raise the overall national growth rate, but it is at least equally conceivable that it may reduce it. In the latter case a difficult trade-off problem between relative and absolute levels of income will arise and the balance of advantage is unlikely to be identical – and even less likely to be evaluated as identical – in twelve disparate countries.

It is certainly fair to say, for example, that policy measures having a differential impact are frequently more effectively formulated at EC rather than national level. Pierre Mathijsen, the Director-General for Regional Policy, properly cites the cases in which almost all member countries wanted to expand their capacity for producing man-made fibres, thereby threatening vast over-capacity, and, similarly, seeking to maintain their steel industries with the same result (EC Commission, 1985b, p. 7). But in deciding between one location and another, how are the interests of regional inequality to be balanced against those of productive efficiency? And why should the balancing procedure be expected to produce the same outcome in every society? Might not the attempt to impose uniformity of policy result, in the end, in diminished rather than increased economic welfare?

The role of EC regional policy therefore seems likely to remain a highly marginal one for the foreseeable future and beyond. It is difficult to argue that any serious loss will be suffered as a result.

Note

1. An agreed definition of the regions of member countries was not formulated by the Commission until 1975 and given the characteristically ugly title of the Nomenclature of Territorial Units for Statistics. Students of regional economics will note without surprise that this is generally known by its acronym NUTS.

17 Social policies

C. D. E. Collins

The central core of Community social policy is to be found in questions relating to employment, industrial health and the social costs of industry, labour mobility and the role of social spending in economic affairs. In the early years of the EC, broader issues of social welfare seemed little related to the main task of removal of tariff barriers. In consequence, the Spaak Committee, whose report laid the basis for the Treaty of Rome, believed that there was a limited need for common policies in the social field, that the effect of social costs and state subsidies on the competitive system was a valid concern, but that social aid to individuals and social systems such as health and education lay outside the sphere of interest of the new organisation (Spaak, 1987, p. 58). In short, the EC has always been concerned with the impact of economic change, and in particular of integration, on the broad issue of living and working conditions, rather than with detailed consideration of the needs of particular individuals and the operation of personal social services. Thus its interests have only partially coincided with those of national governments which became increasingly involved, in the years since 1957, in services for social security, health care, education and personal welfare.

Nevertheless, over time, the overlap of interest in social policy has grown. The development of social security schemes in both coverage and costs has been a major concern of both national governments and the EC. The rapid increase in expenditure for which these schemes were responsible made it important to consider their effect on industrial competitiveness and the growing participation in them of the public sector meant that their contribution to public spending had to be considered. Furthermore, the wish for increased political legitimacy has led the Commission to press for a steadily increasing social role for the EC so that it can be seen to be responding to the needs of the ordinary citizen.

In any case, from the 1960s onwards, there was a broadening of interest in the social concerns of society in general. The need to deal with personal insecurities remained; but questions concerning the natural and urban environments, pollution, congestion, the growing interest in higher education and training came to be added to the original welfare questions. As social policy came to be seen far more in terms of the total quality of life it became more of a joint concern between the EC and member governments. This will become even more evident in the future. The 1980s have brought a rapid extension of Community interest in environmental issues (see Chapter 18) in youth training, aspects of education, tourism and culture with the recognition that many issues are transnational in their nature or are made so by integrative developments. This sharing process as yet leaves national governments primarily in charge and the prerogative is jealously guarded by them. Governments are far more important as sources of finance than the EC and the legitimacy of EC interest in new areas is constantly challenged. Policy on mainstream education, personal health care, the value of social security benefits and housing provision remains to be nationally determined. Even here, however, matters are changing. It is no longer novel for ministers of education and health to attend specialist Council meetings, and while these spend much time in the discussion of common problems there are signs of joint ventures and of a growing number of matters in which states recognise that the EC has a legitimate interest. The process of 'concertation' of national views and policies is slowly becoming more familiar even in circles, like the British, where the concept is strange. Nevertheless, it remains true that many EC issues in social policy, which seem so important from the Community point of view, appear marginal in interest and priority from the vantage point of national social policy which will remain the senior partner for a long time to come.

17.1 The basis of social policy

EC social policy is shaped by two factors. The first consists of the provisions to be found in the respective treaties, of which the Treaty of Rome creating the EEC is the most general in scope – see Chapter 2. The discussion in this chapter is mainly concerned with this treaty, but the Treaty of Paris, creating the European Coal and Steel Community (ECSC) and the Treaty of Rome, setting up Euratom, have also some significance for social policy. The Single European Act (SEA), Section II, Subsection III, brought supplementary provisions with the aim of ensuring that some elements of social policy progress in step with the development of the 'internal market'.

The social policy clauses of the treaties differ in their legal significance. Some provisions are specific, but some are general statements of intent and many express only the will of member states to collaborate in certain matters. However, such intentions may subsequently give rise to legally enforceable acts. Thus, at any given moment, there will be a wide variety of activity in the social field which stems directly from the treaties but which will demand varying degrees of commitment from the member states.

Secondly, there is nothing to prevent the member nations of the EC from taking a new political initiative in the social field and from time to time they do so. As a result, social policy is a mixture of acts deriving from the treaties and from subsequent political developments.

17.2 The Treaty of Rome

The charge has often been made that the Treaty of Rome is weak on the social side. Since it was believed that social policy had little direct relevance to immediate goals, it was logical to limit the treaty to the general cooperative sphere and to confine the more forceful parts of social policy to questions obviously related to the main aim of getting the common market started. The curiosity is that starting from a limited base, the EC has evolved a wide-ranging social policy whose impact in certain spheres has been considerable.

In the first instance, the Treaty of Rome has general objectives of a broadly social character. These include an accelerated raising of the standard of living, the free movement of people and a social fund to help with employment problems. Furthermore, Article 117 contains a recognition by the member nations of the need to improve living and working conditions and of their expectation that policies will gradually align under the impact of the new system. Thus, it was not the EC itself which was given the task of direct improvement, even though its existence was expected to have a beneficial effect and to encourage national policies to move in similar directions. The phraseology of Article 117 was designed to reassure the member nations that their welfare role was not to be usurped; but it also reaffirmed their commitment to the cause of social betterment (for more detailed analysis see Collins, 1975, vol. 2, pp. 21–2). State supremacy was reinforced by the agreement to collaborate in specific fields, such as labour legislation, working conditions, vocational training, social security, industrial health and welfare, and trade union and collective bargaining matters. Here the Commission was given the responsibility of promoting collaboration in various ways, such as study meetings and joint discussion (Article 118). In this way, scope for joint action was left open should the evolution of the EC require it; but it was not considered inevitable that common policies would be required.

A much clearer issue in 1957 was that of the effect of social costs on competition within the single market. The sensitivity of French industry to a competitive future made it imperative for the French government to insist upon certain provisions. The most important of these has proved to be the principle of equal pay for men and women (Article 119). Other clauses dealing with holiday and overtime pay, although in the treaty for the same reason, were less stringent in form and have been overtaken by events.

A special point had been made in the Spaak Report of the lack of effective utilisation of manpower in Western Europe. This led to the setting up of the European Social Fund (ESF) in Article 123. Its aim is to help to increase both occupational and geographical mobility, although the fund has never been on the scale which would be necessary to meet fully the tasks graphically described by the Spaak Committee. In addition, the treaty included an agreement to establish the common principles of vocational training.

Of far greater significance in 1957, and the great prize gained by Italy, was the adoption of the principle of the free movement of wage earners, along with rules to give it practical effect and to ensure equal treatment of migrants with indigenous workers. It was agreed, also, that rules would be necessary to allow the free establishment of the self-employed and for services to be provided across frontiers. This has given rise to separate programmes of great complexity. Even now, they are not complete, especially in relation to professional services.

The free movement policy, together with its supporting policies of employment-exchange collaboration, maintenance of social security rights and protection of equal working rights for migrants, must be considered as a major EC success, although it also owed much to the buoyant economic conditions of the time. Subsequent attempts to move the policy into the much more difficult areas of social integration and social equality and to evolve a policy towards migrants from outside the EC have not been so successful. Member nations resist EC intrusion into matters of great domestic sensitivity and can do so because of the limits of the treaty.

Special protective measures exist in the coal and steel industries which antedate the social policy of the Treaty of Rome. These relate, in particular, to the payment of cash benefits to workers losing their jobs, needing retraining, or having to move home for work elsewhere, and to the payment of grants to firms taking on workers from these industries. A second feature of the work of the ECSC has been the use of treaty provision to aid investment to help with housing construction, and this programme continues. Grand aid is also used for specific health and safety measures in the coal and steel industries. In the same way, Euratom has its own special concerns, notably in the obligation to establish basic health and safety standards, both for workers in the industry and for the general public.

17.3 The Single European Act

The SEA contains provisions which develop those of the past but at the same time clarify the position of the EC regarding matters of social concern which had not originally been considered at all. It is motivated, primarily, by the need to develop social provisions as a factor in making the internal market effective. In consequence, as will be seen, EC powers on the social side continue to be very variable in strength. Because of the breadth of the SEA, this chapter refers to a wide range of social policies and moves beyond the scope of the original treaties.

An important statement of principle is to be found in the preamble of the SEA. This affirms that member states accept the fundamental rights of citizens which are contained in the Convention for the Protection of Human Rights and Fundamental Freedoms and the European Social Charter, notably freedom, equality and social justice. Both are products of the Council of Europe. Although the European Court of Justice has drawn on the Convention in some of its judgements, this political declaration can only strengthen the moral basis of the EC. The second document, in particular, contains an expression of social rights which could, in future, be used for an extensive development of EC social policy should the political climate be ripe.

A special section of the SEA supplements the Treaty of Rome as part of the drive towards the internal market. Article 118 is expanded by Articles 118A and 118B (Articles 21 and 22 of the SEA). Member nations here agree to pay particular attention to the need for improvements in health and safety at work and to aim at harmonising standards while maintaining existing ones. The latter provision reflects considerable fears that firms will be tempted to make cuts as competitive pressures mount. Minimum standards will be introduced gradually by directives. Although these can be passed by qualified majority in the Council, Article 118A suggests that, in practice, Community action will be cautious in order to reflect the conditions in member states and the need to encourage the growth of small businesses. Once again, there is a possible base for the extension of EC interest in health matters should a broad interpretation of the health of workers become acceptable. Article 118B makes the Commission responsible for encouraging a dialogue between management and labour at the EC level which might, in turn, lead to formal agreements between the two sides of industry.

Although a wider use of qualified majority voting in the Council was thought necessary in order to implement the internal market, there are certain reservations written into the SEA about its application to the procedures for the necessary approximation of laws. In the social field, these relate to free movement, the rights and interests of employed persons and to the passing of directives which would require alteration in the methods of training for, and practice in, some professions. Article 100A refers to the need for the Commission to use high standards when regulating health, safety and environmental issues and when dealing with consumer protection.

Underlying these legislative provisions are considerable worries and uncertainties. Some member states fear that, by having EC standards imposed on them, their goods will be unable to compete; others fear that their own high standards will not be met by Community norms and may be reduced; and yet others fear that the import of goods, livestock and plants may introduce disease from which they have hitherto been free. Denmark has added a special declaration to the SEA designed to ensure it can continue to maintain its own high standards. The United Kingdom is not anxious to see provisions used to develop labour law in ways which would harm the growth of small firms and its Conservative government does not wish to see time and energy spent on developing consensus between management and unions. Although the SEA recognises that the internal market requires some alignment of national social legislation and stresses the importance of improving standards, there are considerable possibilities both for delay and for using the provisions to protect national markets rather than health standards. Such factors suggest that the application of Community norms is likely to take some time and may have a stormy passage.

A new subsection is introduced entitled economic and social cohesion. This inserts Title V into Part Three of the Rome Treaty. It primarily concerns the development of regional policy but affects the use to be made of the European Social Fund (ESF). Another addition is Subsection VI on the environment (see Chapter 18).

17.4 The development of social policy

Given the rather incoherent guidance of the early treaties, it is not surprising that the development of social policy was patchy. The first ten years of the EC saw the major steps taken to implement the policy on labour movement, a formal adoption of the equal pay policy, a narrow exploitation of the ESF and considerable discussion, study and research into labour questions; but it is difficult to avoid the conclusion that social policy hung fire.

A new impetus in social policy can be detected by the end of the 1960s. The reasons for this are not hard to seek. The essential elements of the transitional period had been completed by 1968. A recommitment to the existence and importance of the EC was necessary to fill a possible political vacuum and an emphasis upon the non-material aims of the group was in accord with the new concerns of Western Europe. A widespread unease was evident over environmental pollution, the problems of the disadvantaged and social inequalities. The lack of involvement of ordinary citizens in public processes, the difficulties of the old and handicapped and the stress problems of the cities were issues which were of concern to all member states. They were issues where political capital might readily be built but where the Community's social policy made little impact. The claim to a social conscience was the more appealing as the time of the first enlargement came nearer, for this revealed considerable public hostility to the EC in Denmark, Norway and Britain on the grounds of its social insensitivity. The West German Social Democrat government, too, was anxious to see the EC present itself in terms acceptable to its supporters at home, and the Brandt Memorandum on social policy development was a major source of inspiration for the summit meeting of October 1972.

The first sign of greater seriousness in social affairs had been expressed at the conference at The Hague in December 1969, when the existing six member nations accepted that the EC would go further towards the pursuit of common political and economic goals. They spoke of the need for a closely concerted social policy and the forward look was continued by the Paris summit conference of 1972. This asserted the importance member nations attached to vigorous action in the social field (*Bulletin of the European Communities*, no. 10, 1972.) The communiqué referred specifically to the need to widen participation in decision making and action to lessen inequalities and to improve the quality of life. Member nations accepted that Article 235 might be used in the social field. This allows the Council to develop policies necessary to fulfill the objectives of the EC even if the necessary powers are not to be found in the treaty. In this way, an acknowledged gap in procedures might be filled. Secondly, it was agreed that the Council, in contrast to its previous procrastination, should take a decision on the Commission's social proposals within six months.

The political momentum was followed by the establishment of a social action programme (SAP). These are now regularly issued to cover the work for consecutive four-yearly periods. The hopes of the first SAP were quickly dashed by the onset of recession and the burden of large-scale unemployment against which the measures seemed small scale and which destroyed the heady hopes of significant developments in social policy. Member nations became less ready to consider measures which required new finance for the EC and which, in prosperous years, they might have been ready to accept. Nevertheless, the SAP was designed to give social policy more bite than hitherto and this stage saw its establishment as a necessary part of EC development. A timetable for the introduction and application of measures was laid down and this was partially adhered to. However, social developments were steadily overshadowed by employment difficulties and unemployment became the dominant theme of subsequent SAPs (e.g. SAP 1984, *Official Journal of the European Communities (OJC)*, Legislation, no. 175, 1984). The EC began to experience large structural changes in employment patterns, large-scale unemployment and a formidable problem of youth unemployment. It proved impossible to adopt strong policies at the EC level but the effort of analysis and of encouraging cooperative action by states in the labour markets became a major preoccupation. Since member states differed in their views about the causes and cures for unemployment, an effective EC policy could not develop. The credibility of social policy was undermined since it now appeared it could only operate in good times.

A new impulse had to wait for the EC itself to gather momentum. The resolution of the European Parliament of July 1982 on the reform of the treaties and the achievement of European union recognised that a new policy for society was required (*OJC*, 238/82). The previous year, the newly elected French socialist government had urged a wide-ranging policy of social initiatives, including measures to adapt and reduce working time, improve vocational training, intensify the dialogue between management and labour and strengthen the rights of working people (*EC Bulletin*, 11/81). Much of the discussion about social policy revolved around the issues of adjusting to new employment circumstances and slower growth in addition to the strengthening of existing policies. A third question soon had to be added. With the entry of Greece, Portugal and Spain, the importance of devoting resources to their characteristic problems which included inefficiency on agricultural smallholdings, disguised unemployment in rural areas and lack of training for industrial work helped to turn attention away from the issues identified in the early 1970s which were associated with the urban problems of the more developed North.

The urge to establish the internal market by 1992, and the insistence that this must be accompanied by some steps towards cementing a European union, brought new initiatives. The previous section has explained that the SEA tackled two of them, namely the question of the powers the EC would require to harmonise certain social legislation and that of the need to establish economic and social cohesion. The third was the drive towards a 'people's Europe' (*EC Bulletin*, Supplement 7/85).

17.5 The people's Europe

In June 1984, the European Council set up an *ad hoc* committee under Mr Adonnino of Italy to look at ways of making the general public more aware of the importance of the EC and of strengthening its identity. Two reports were submitted to the European Council and accepted in 1985. They include many recommendations and, while some were new, others were either extensions of existing work or requests for current requirements to be pursued more rigorously. One group of suggestions related to the development of the free movement policy and included questions such as the need to speed up measures to recognise professional qualifications, the right of EC nationals to vote in local elections and opening up the right of residence to EC nationals who spend their working lives in the EC but would like to move to another member state on retirement. Bureaucratic regulations affecting settlers could be eased. The report argued that the rights of workers were not yet complete under the free movement policy. Tourists could be helped by the easing, or elimination, of frontier formalities, improved concessions on customs duties and simplified access to medical care when travelling. Ease of movement would be further helped by policies to develop intra-Community contacts, especially for young people. Border residents should be consulted over major works which were likely to affect them.

Symbolic acts would help to create an EC consciousness. These might include the speedy introduction of an EC passport, the adoption of an EC flag and anthem and Community signs, rather than national ones, at border crossings.

A growing interest in public health would be important. There could be an EC role in preventive education and in supporting medical research into problems of widespread concern such as drug abuse and the prevention of cancer.

Public awareness of the EC would be helped if there were more information programmes about its law, what it covers and its effect on the lives of ordinary citizens. An EC ombudsman, linked to the European Parliament, might help citizens obtain redress.

The Adonnino Committee was also interested in the development of radio and television services in the EC. Citizens should be able to receive a wider range of programmes, joint programmes could be developed and a greater use made of programmes produced within the EC. An EC cultural identity would be further strengthened by giving more attention to developing contacts between museums and libraries and putting on exhibitions.

Many of the ideas, of which these are a sample, were uncontroversial; but others are proving more difficult to implement. By June 1986, the European Council had to admit that the application of many of the proposals was already delayed, including the more 'meaningful proposals in terms of popular impact' (*EC Bulletin*, 6/86, point 2.1.130). Some of the recommendations hit hard at sensitive areas and this is particularly so for free movement issues. Member nations which have agreeable resorts fear an influx of the elderly who will put strains on care services; others are reluctant to recognise qualifications obtained in another member state while yet others are worried about the relaxation of frontier controls. As internal controls are removed, so it becomes more urgent that the EC adopts effective measures at all its external frontiers and that member states step up their collaborative efforts and joint measures in case they face worse problems than they do at present in surmounting the traffic in drugs, the movement of terrorists and the entry of illegal immigrants. Britain and Ireland have been particularly concerned about the possible consequences of the free movement policy for the spread of plant and animal diseases. In the coming years, much stronger EC action, and more joint member state action, will be necessary to forestall such difficulties and much of the foot dragging in the Council on the adoption of implementing measures has resulted from this miscellany of fears. Meanwhile, proposed directives on frontier procedures and the right of residence continue to provoke disagreement.

17.6 Employment

There have been striking changes in the labour force of the EC since 1957 (see the latest issue of *Eurostat Review*). It has expanded greatly, partly because of a general increase in population but also because of an increase in the number of women looking for work. The EC itself has also grown so that, by 1985, it had a working population of 136.6 million. At the same time, the employment structure has altered. Many millions of people have left agriculture, although a significant rural population remains in France, Germany and Italy. Agriculture is an even more important employer in the southern member states and in Ireland – see Table A3.1c. The EC now has a large number of migrant workers, the bulk of whom come from outside the EC; older industries such as shipbuilding, steel and coalmining have experienced great job losses, while service industries have grown as employers. The particular problems of adjustment that such changes occasioned have been complicated by the growing problem of general unemployment. In the late 1950s, only about 2.6 million people were unemployed and these were largely concentrated in the south of Italy where agriculture could not absorb them and for whom rather simple EC aids to mobility seemed the key to EC policy. Increasingly, however, from the 1970s, the major issue became that of industrial unemployment. By September 1987, 15.9 million people, or 11.6 per cent of the labour force of the twelve, were unemployed and many of them had little prospect of obtaining work. While problems varied between one member nation and another, three broad features have been noticeable. All have suffered from a particular incidence of unemployment among young people and women and have faced an intractable problem of the long-term unemployed.

Significant rates of unemployment have had an adverse effect on the aim of achieving an accelerated raising of the standard of living. As the Commission has pointed out, the goal has not been reached for the many citizens who belong to the new poor: the young unemployed, the long-term unemployed and the recipients of social security benefits in general. These groups form elements in the Commission's 'growing army of the deprived ... the persistence of such a situation is inconsistent with the ambitions and hopes of the founders and promoters of the European ideal' (*EC Commission*, 1984d, para. 20). Unemployment has been an important contributor to this situation, by increasing beneficiaries and decreasing contributors to social security schemes, by encouraging governments to change policies towards the poor and posing conflicts between economic and social policy. It is not, therefore, surprising that the Commission's views on the implementation of the SEA referred to unemployment as the central issue in social policy and that, in this sector of policy, it should direct its work primarily to the twin problems of young people trying to enter the labour market and of the long-term unemployed (Spaak Report, 1987, p. 8).

One of the consequences of a deteriorating situation was the inability of the

Commission to sustain the momentum of improvement in employment law. In the early 1970s, a particular form of job loss came through a spate of takeovers and mergers, often as a result of the development of multinational companies. Here the EC felt it could claim a particular interest. Directives were therefore passed on the procedures to be followed in the case of collective dismissals, the maintenance of employee rights when companies merged and the protection of rights when a firm became insolvent (*Agence Europe*, no. 1655, 19 December 1974; *EC Bulletin*, 12/76, p. 47; *OJL*, 283/80). Subsequent attempts by the Commission to pursue higher standards of employment law have, however, been unsuccessful. A succession of proposed directives relating to worker participation in decisions and disclosure of information to the workforce, to parental leave or leave for family reasons and to the protection of part-time and temporary workers on a basis equivalent to that provided for full-time workers have either been dropped or postponed. While this, in an immediate sense, seems related to the rise in unemployment and the consequent deterioration in employer–union relations, there is also some disenchantment with the effectiveness of directives which have to be applied in very different circumstances. Underlying the debates, however, have been ideological differences about the value of more protective legislation. Britain has been one member nation that has been generally against increased regulation and in favour of freeing employers as far as possible in order to encourage them to take on workers and to adapt to new patterns of work (HMSO, 1985, especially points 7.15–19. Britain continued to promote this view during its presidency in 1986. See also *The Times*, 16 June 1988).

A noticeable feature of recent years has been the growth of part-time work and much interest in it has developed as a means of reorganising the pattern of working time. A meeting of the ministers of finance, economic and social affairs in November 1982 accepted the need for measures to encourage its adoption, under safeguards; but the proposed directives intended to flesh out a policy and protect the position of part-timers failed to be adopted. In 1985, the Council did agree a number of specific employment measures (*OJC*, 165/85) while the economic guidelines adopted that year included the principle of a cooperative growth strategy for more employment creating growth. This document aims to reduce unemployment to 7 per cent by 1990 (*OJL*, 377/85). By the time of the Council meetings in December 1986, the broad lines of an employment strategy had been laid down; but it leaves wide scope for member nations to pursue their own particular priorities within it. The general approach accepts the importance of encouraging new businesses, the need for greater efficiency in labour markets, improved training and the need for more help for the long-term unemployed (*EC Bulletin*, 12/86, point 2.1.138. On policy conflicts see *Financial Times*, 4, 5, 6, 8, 12 December 1986). The emphasis is placed on encouragement to mobility, removing restrictions on part-time work and encouraging start-up schemes. The importance of special measures to aid the reintegration of the long-term unemployed has been generally agreed.

Employment difficulties have been particularly acute for the disabled and handicapped with the rise in unemployment. The Council passed a recommendation in 1986 stressing the importance of providing fair opportunities for training and employment and setting out a model code of action. Its terms are not particularly onerous, although it contains a number of useful suggestions for member states to pursue (*OJL*, 225/86). An action programme to encourage member nations to take more active measures is in operation (COM(87)342).

17.7 The European Social Fund

The principal weapon which the EC possesses to combat unemployment directly is the ESF. This has undergone several reforms and extensions. Having started in a limited way, primarily to help migrants from the Italian South move northwards into the main areas of industrial employment, a major reform was undertaken in 1971. This created a larger and more flexible fund which the EC would use more positively to help labour training and to concentrate on the needs of special groups of workers or of regions. Particularly deprived regions were singled out for extra help and, in later years, Greece, Portugal and large parts of Spain were added to the list. Not only is a percentage of total fund money reserved for these areas (at present 44.5 per cent) but the rate of grant is also more favourable (55 per cent of eligible expenditure instead of the more usual 50 per cent). Types of expenditure eligible for grant aid were also laid down and a small study and pilot scheme programme established.

During the 1970s the fund began to be seen as a means of contributing to broader EC policies and, over the years, the recognition that this was the way the fund should be used gained credence. The financing of the fund was altered and brought into the general budget of the EC. This meant that its objectives and use became of far greater political interest both to member states and to the European Parliament. Since the fund was deemed to be non-compulsory expenditure, the opportunity for Parliamentary pressure was considerable. Attempts made by Parliament to increase the size of the fund were, however, largely unsuccessful because of overall constraints on the budget and the fund continued to be hard pressed, with far more worthy applications than it could help. By 1986, the ESF was absorbing about 7 per cent of the EC budget (2,500 million ECU) for commitment appropriations (see Chapter 14), and nearly two and one half million people were receiving help from schemes drawing ESF aid (*European File*, 19/86, p. 3).

The reformed fund required the Commission to take on more sophisticated administrative tasks and its operation has never been without its critics. One major problem has always been the large gap between available finance and the pressure of demand. The agreement on budget reform reached in February 1988 should make the situation easier. It expressed a willingness to see the budget for the structural funds double by 1993 and increase, as a minimum, by 80 per cent. The ESF will, of course, only receive a part of this increase.

By the 1980s it was felt that the fund required further adaptation. It began to concentrate upon work to promote the employment and vocational training of young people under 25 years of age and to allocate 75 per cent of the budget to them. More recently, the long-term unemployed have been given a similar priority, while aid was extended to cover members of both groups wishing to set up as self-employed in 1985. Although finance is no longer earmarked for special groups such as women, migrants and the handicapped, it is intended that they should continue to receive help through schemes tailored to their particular needs. The fund also began to encourage employment in small- and medium-sized businesses and to give special aid to expand vocational guidance and placement services. The most deprived regions continued to receive special aid but otherwise the fund concentrated its efforts in areas of persistently high unemployment and where large, industrial reconstruction was required.

By now, however, it was coming to be seen as important that the ESF should adjust its work to follow the newer patterns of employment more closely and should be used as part of the Community's employment strategy. Similarly, it was seen that the ESF would be more effective if its grants could be coordinated with other sources of EC finance to aid broader schemes of area revitalisation rather than be used for individual schemes on an *ad hoc* basis. In laying down the goal of economic and social cohesion, the SEA stated that the ESF, the ERDF and the Guidance section of the EAGGF (as well as other sources of finance such as the EIB) should be used, their efficiency increased and their activities coordinated (Article 23 SEA adds a new Title V to Part Three of the Rome treaty). The City of Birmingham has been an early recipient of such integrated aid, being allocated a £203 million package over a five-year period (*The Times*, 7 June 1988).

The main lines of work for the next few years are now becoming clearer. The two major aims will be, firstly, to concentrate on the regions of greatest need and those suffering from large-scale industrial decline; secondly, to pay particular attention to the training and pre-training needs of young people and the long-term unemployed (COM(87)100; objectives 3 and 4). The selection procedures continue to be severe and, currently, preference is given to training for new technologies, encouragement to small businesses in developing sectors and to training for jobs whose prospects are good. Training for part-time work is acceptable (Guidelines for 1968–88, *OJL*, 133/85). Yearly guidelines publicise the changes in priority and in emphasis.

17.8 Vocational training and employment

The problem of unemployment has given new point to EC policy for vocational training. Support for short-term measures such as community service and job experience was overtaken as it became clearer that employment openings were to be found in new industries, often in small firms and in self-employment. As it was realised that EC training aims also required consideration of education, so the EC saw an opportunity to encourage greater awareness of the EC and its concerns amongst the rising generation.

By the late 1970s, the Commission had become aware of the particular problem of young people leaving school inadequately prepared for work. Not only did they lack useful skills, but many school leavers appeared psychologically unprepared to take their places in the labour market and a recommendation on vocational preparation for young people was agreed in 1977 (*OJL*, 180/77). The same year saw the establishment of the European Centre for the Development of Vocational Training (CEDEFOP), in Berlin, to encourage greater awareness about training needs and opportunities and to act as an information centre for experiences and learning experiments conducted across the EC.

Discussion in subsequent years developed the policy of the 'social guarantee', whereby member nations agreed to try to ensure that all school leavers go on to work, training or further education and in 1982 an agreement was reached on the importance of opening up classroom work to the workplace in order to ease the transition to working life. The EC has gone on to identify a range of issues requiring attention, including work experience, training, the special problems of girls and of young people from migrant groups. A Council decision following the Milan summit in June 1985 reinforced the importance of ensuring that school leavers have at least one year, and preferably two, of training and experience and deals with vocational training issues generally and preparation for adult and working life (Decision 87/569/EEC, *OJL*, 346/87). Aid is concentrated on innovative projects and schemes which encourage entrepreneurial skills.

In 1957 the Rome Treaty had referred to the desirability of exchange schemes for young workers (Article 50). Although there are some long-established exchange schemes, they have been on a small scale; but the theme of exchange has been taken up in the new education and training initiatives. During the 1980s, several resolutions showed the Council of Ministers grappling with the changes new information technologies were bringing and, following the Fontainebleau summit meeting in June 1984, the Commission submitted an action programme on education and training for technology (*OJC*, 234/85). This, which became known as the COMETT programme, was especially concerned with cooperation between higher educational establishments and industry. It aimed to help to foster an EC awareness by placements in firms in other member states, to encourage the joint organisation of programmes and to exchange experiences about cooperation between universities and industry. This was approved by the Council in July 1986 and obtained an initial budget of 45 million ECU. A comparable programme for cooperation between universities in research and innovation is followed by the ESPRIT programme.

The mobility of students in higher education is encouraged through the ERASMUS programme, which aims to promote more cooperation between establishments through student and teacher exchanges and joint courses. It is planned that, by 1992, at least 10 per cent of the student population should be spending more time in another member state so that a growing pool of graduates with direct experience of life abroad, and of intra-Community cooperation, should enter the labour force in the future (Decision 87/327/EEC, *OJL*, 166/87). To implement this programme requires considerable cooperative effort to ensure students can afford to participate, joint seminars can be run, joint curricula worked out, qualifications recognised and a system of credit transfer established if need be. Intensive language teaching will be necessary. In contrast, attempts to improve the quality of youth exchanges and to extend them under the 'Yes for Europe' programme met with delays in the Council although a modest programme was recently agreed (*OJL*, 158/88).

By 1986, the ministers of education had a wide-ranging programme of educational activities to be promoted across the EC. These included the special educational needs of the children of migrants, the need to promote equal access for boys and girls to all forms of education, to combat illiteracy, to ease the transition from school to adult life, to introduce information technology into education, to promote the teaching of EC languages, to ensure greater cooperation between higher educational systems through mobility and effective recognition of diplomas and training schemes.

Vocational training policy is not, of course, solely concerned with young people. The retraining of adults is now recognised to be of importance and the Commission's programme supports pilot training schemes, joint research and study programmes and study visits as well as the specific support for schemes through the ESF. Article 128 speaks of the common principles of vocational training. Originally agreed in 1963, these were of a very general nature; but a Council decision in 1985 took the matter further by agreeing that the mutual recognition of qualifications must be speeded up and providing directions on how to establish comparability (*OJC*, 264/83; *OJC*, 208/84; *OJL*, 199/85). A recent court case has made it clear that many university courses can be considered as vocational training and that students from all member states must be admitted on the same terms as nationals (*The Times*, Law Report, 4 April 1988). This ruling should help to increase the mutual acceptability of qualifications.

17.9 Industrial relations

Collective bargaining remains a matter handled within member states. Originally there was some expectation that the creation of a single market, greater mobility and the growth of the multinational company would require a Europeanisation of industrial relations but, in practice, changes have been modest. Some of the Commission's initiatives have met with fierce opposition. From the Community's point of view, three themes stand out which, in day-to-day affairs, are often tangled together. There is, firstly, the belief that it is important to involve employers' associations and unions in the operations of the EC; secondly, that consultation, or even cross-Community negotiation, may be essential in particular cases and, thirdly, that an integrated market may require some national changes.

The Paris and Rome treaties established certain formal structures, notably the ECSC Consultative Committee and the EEC Economic and Social Committee to associate representatives of employers and organised labour (and other groups) with EC affairs. Subsequently, the various advisory committees, such as that for the ESF, were constituted with joint representation: joint committees meet to deal with problems concerning a particular industry and, in recent years, a Standing Committee of Employment has been reactivated. From time to time, the members of the committee meet with the finance and social affairs ministers to form the Tripartite

Conference, which has wide-ranging discussions of socio-economic issues. The SEA provided the Rome Treaty with a new Article 118B which gives the Commission the duty to develop the dialogue between management and labour at European level which could, if both sides thought it desirable, lead to formal arrangements between them. To the original members of the EC, a central theme of social policy has always been the promotion of positive relations between employers and unions as a result of which improvements in working conditions and social security benefits would be agreed and implemented jointly.

Thus the Commission has promoted policies, such as encouraging asset holding by employees, which support this view. Two attempts have been particularly controversial and have not, so far, led to a definite conclusion. One long-standing attempt has been that of obtaining agreement on the appointment of worker directors in companies as a necessary precondition for creating a legal framework for a European company. Reaction to this idea in some states, notably the United Kingdom, has been hostile. A similar fate has met the so-called Vredling directive on information and consultation rights for employees. This was aimed at large companies, particularly multinational ones and required basic information about company affairs to be made available. Although it was revised in 1983, in an attempt to make it more palatable, discussion in the Council during 1986 could reach no agreement. The latest company proposals from the Commission (COM(88)320 final) have put forward various options in the hope that some agreement, which allows variable implementation, can be found. However, both issues are so far notable for displaying the extent of national sensitivities rather than movement towards common ground.

As unemployment rose in Western Europe, the climate for industrial relations worsened and the social partners increasingly adopted defensive positions. Thus the traditional Commission policy of establishing a consensus on its idea for the reduction and reorganisation of working time, the promotion of small businesses, formal job creation schemes and how to handle new technology ran into serious difficulties. During 1985 a set of meetings was held by the Commission with the social partners in order to establish some agreed lines and this initiative led to the setting up of a series of working parties on the implementation of the cooperative growth strategy and the introduction of new technologies. The President of the Commission, Jacques Delors, has been particularly outspoken in his view that trade union opinion must be carried along with EC developments. The European Council accepted that the social dialogue was important when it met in Luxemburg in December 1985 and, as has been seen, it is stressed in the SEA. Nevertheless, a different emphasis remains between those who see the future in terms of deregulation and free enterprise and those who believe in steps which have the prior agreement of the social partners.

17.10 Health, safety and environmental protection

The protection of industrial health and safety is a long-standing EC policy stretching back to 1951 when the ECSC established an active programme of research and standard setting. Special Commissions exist for the steel industry and for mining, the latter now includes offshore oil wells, and a large number of recommendations have been issued. The Euratom treaty gives the Commission power to establish precise standards of protection in the nuclear industry, while monitoring of the amount of radioactivity in the environment is carried out under Article 36. Industrial health and safety was included in the Treaty of Rome as one of the matters on which the Commission might encourage collaboration and it developed an active programme of research and recommendations as a result.

Over the years, EC interest has broadened. Its span has extended to include problems of environmental pollution and these, in turn, began to lead on to environmental protection and issues of conservation. Meanwhile, the EC has edged towards a clearer role in community health, interesting itself in questions such as the effect of modern industrial life styles on human welfare, the social costs of night work, the incidence of alcoholism and drug abuse and of social scourges such as cancer and, more recently, of AIDS. The ever increasing cost of social security, of which health care forms a large part, and its effect on competitive costs, has pushed the EC into taking a greater interest in the specific question of the costs of personal health care. Meanwhile, the drive to the internal market has renewed interest in industrial health and safety standards although, as previously explained, there are considerable uncertainties and loopholes left in the SEA.

The 1980s saw a renewed interest by the EC in matters of industrial health. There is a current stress on the importance of informational work, exchange of ideas and in establishing reference standards. Since the field is so vast, the EC will often proceed by means of an outline basic directive which is used later to tackle specific hazards. In 1980 basic standards to protect the health of the public and workers against ionizing radiation (Directive 80/836/Euratom, *OJL*, 246/80) were accepted and, following the Chernobyl accident, the Commission began work to update the standard. An outline directive on the protection of workers against the risks involved in the use of dangerous substances was agreed in 1980 (Directive 80/1107/EEC, *OJL*, 327/80) and was followed by a directive designed to protect against the hazards of a major accident in certain industrial sectors, often referred to as the Soveso directive (Directive 82/501/EEC, *OJL*, 230/82). More recently, a specific standard regulating the degree of exposure to noise at work was laid down (Directive 86/188/EEC, *OJL*, 137/86). Work on health and safety standards requires a faster momentum than it has had in the past if it is to keep pace with the plans for the internal market and raises issues of effective controls and monitoring and of dealing with complaints from the public in an increasingly urgent way.

In 1977 the ministers of health held their first meeting under the Rome treaty and they have continued to meet from time to time to discuss matters of common interest and to develop joint action where appropriate. Subsequently the Commission made considerable efforts to establish a public health programme and, despite some reluctance, the Milan summit meeting of June 1985 saw some strengthening of the EC's role in health matters. It was agreed to launch an anti-cancer programme and this was agreed the following year (*EC Bulletin*, 6/85, point 1.2.3; 5/86, point 2.1.66).

The same Council meeting in 1986 passed resolutions on alcohol abuse, the use of an emergency health care card and the protection of dialysis patients. A resolution on AIDS sought to find an educational role for the Commission and to establish joint initiatives to prevent its spread. The same year, the European Council asked for improved cooperation in public health matters. While such measures are far from creating a comprehensive EC health policy, the EC appears to be slowly defining an acceptable role in matters of public health.

An awareness of the environmental problems of modern society and the beginnings of an EC policy stretch back to 1972 when the Paris summit formulated principles of environmental protection which member nations would follow in their national policies and agreed on coordinating action – see Chapter 18. The SEA has strengthened this policy area through Subsection VI, solely devoted to environmental action. It aims, specifically, to preserve, protect and improve the quality of the environment, to contribute to the protection of human health and ensure a prudent and rational utilisation of natural resources. Action is based on the principles of prevention, rectification of damage at source and the belief that the polluter should bear the costs of rectification. Environmental protection is to be a component of other EC policies. Once again, the working of the SEA, with its reference to the need to adapt programmes to the varied environmental conditions existing within the Community, the need for balanced development and the recognition that some members may wish to adopt more stringent standards all show how widely the member nations differ, at present, in their priorities. EC action is designed to cover matters where individual action by the member nations would be inadequate and to undertake cooperative action with other member states and with international organisations. It is normally based on unanimous voting in the Council.

The environmental policy can be seen as a development of the basic aim of contributing to the improvement of living and working conditions but, during the recession, it appeared to weaken with the argument surfacing that it was an unaffordable luxury which must, if necessary, be sacrificed to encouraging renewed growth. The SEA argues that it is a necessary consequence of establishing the internal market but many would prefer to make the case in terms of the urgency of the task, to link policies with the possibility of creating new types of job and, more broadly, feel that it is time the EC accepted a greater responsibility for creating a better quality environment for the citizens of the area. Both policy and methods of implementation are still highly contentious politically. In 1985 the Council accepted, *inter alia*, directives on the reduction of air pollution, of the lead content in petrol and on methods of assessing the environmental impact of important projects such as for waste disposal or establishing large chemical plants (*33rd Review of the Council's Work*, paras 155–9). A fourth action programme on the environment, 1987–92, is now under way with a modest budget. Current policy emphasises the prevention of damage, prevention of pollution in air and water, the stricter enforcement of rules and the need to increase public awareness of environmental issues. The task of the Commission can be described as that of finding a way to reconcile environmental protection with lasting economic growth and to balance long-term benefits against short-term costs.

17.11 The free movement of people and citizen's rights

Arrangements to ensure free movement under the Treaty of Rome were centred on employees, the bulk of whom, in 1957, were unskilled. The essential structures were in place by 1968 or were settled not long afterwards. The rules protected the right to move for work and to remain in a country subsequently, gave rights of entry to families and elaborated a complex system for the maintenance of social security benefits, although there were still some gaps of coverage. The concept of equal treatment at work was applied through rules to protect the right to join a union and stand for office, the right of access to vocational training and to use the employment services. Broadly speaking, non-discrimination is an effective principle; but the application of rights is, inevitably, imperfect and individual cases may still require protection, quite frequently finding their way to the European Court of Justice.

Efforts to create a single labour market in order to aid migration through effective notification of job opportunities and labour offers had also been started in the early years and a system of inter-state notification of job vacancies (SEDOC) is in operation. Despite some gaps and difficulties, a general policy enabling workers and their dependants to move reasonably freely within the EC had been established by the 1970s.

The same principle of free movement was applied to the self-employed and to the supply of services across frontiers. Its application depended on the acceptance of programmes dealing with particular types of employment, including agreement on the appropriate conditions such as the standard of service, qualifications and training. Where necessary, these include special rules to ensure professional competence, as in the case of doctors and lawyers. Although a great deal of liberalisation has occurred, rules are not in place for all occupations. Difficulties relate to work of a professional nature, where states are reluctant to modify their own regulatory and training requirements; but action is being speeded up under the stimulus of the internal market drive. One significant impediment to the free movement policy has been the right to reserve employment in the public service for nationals. Although this has been exercised mainly with regard to professional and skilled work, it can be a serious obstacle if the term covers many activities. There are signs that this barrier is beginning to fall, along with existing requirements that a practitioner must be naturalised before practising.

The scale of migration during the 1960s made opinion everywhere acutely conscious of much broader problems of social integration for migrants and host populations alike. It exposed, too, the great difference between the formal possession of rights relating to work and effective social integration. The Rome treaty had ignored the question and member nations resisted attempts by the Commission to extend the scope of EC policy in a matter of such domestic sensitivity. The problem was the more difficult since the great influx of people into the cities of Western Europe did not come primarily from within the EC itself, although the scale of movement from the agricultural areas must not be overlooked. In the main, workers came from further afield and the EC now contains at least 12 million migrants, of whom 9 million come from outside the EC (*Social Report*, 1984, para. 9). Not only did the social problems of integration, housing, education and employment increase with the widening cultural gap between host communities and newcomers but the scale of the movement produced social tensions and pressures on the services in congested urban areas.

Against this difficult background, the EC had to face the free movement issue as part of the enlargement negotiations. The accession treaties for Greece, Portugal and Spain all contained transitional provisions. Greece is now fully part of the EC system but phased access continues for wage earners from the last two entrants, although most self-employed workers benefited from the policy immediately. The question of free labour movement has also been raised recently with regard to Turkey. It has sent large numbers of workers to the EC, especially to West Germany, and it is also the signatory to an early association agreement with the EC which foreshadowed free movement for Turkish labour by the end of 1986. In discussions over the possibility of moving to full membership, Turkey, in return for assurances of better treatment for Turkish workers already in the EC has not insisted upon the fulfilment of this clause.

By the early 1970s, the Commission had begun to question the value of large-scale, uncontrolled migration. Stress began to be laid on the ill effects for regions and countries losing manpower, the pressure on the urban social infrastructure, the slowing down of capital development in industry and the uncertain benefits for the sending countries (*EC Bulletin*, Supplement, 3/76, pp. 11–12). The moral strength which the EC derived from its policy of equality of treatment was rapidly diminished as it became obvious that most migrants could not benefit from it. The situation became further confused as unemployment grew, member nations began to ban recruitment of non-EC nationals, work permits expired and many third country migrants decided to stay in the EC illegally rather than join the queue for re-entry.

Despite an action programme, of which the Council 'took note' in February 1976, policy made uncertain progress. The improvements which were made to the rules covering EC workers were not automatically granted to non-Community migrants, whose rights and benefits are generally less favourable and derive from bilateral agreements. Migrants, irrespective of origin, became eligible for aid from the ESF for vocational training schemes and a directive of 1977 tried to improve the education of the children of migrants (Directive 77/486/EEC, *OJL*, 199/77). Believing that the unfavourable employment opportunities of young migrants could often be traced back to poor education, persistent language difficulties and erratic school attendance, the directive committed states to measures such as better reception facilities, language tuition, special training for teachers and it included the possibility of employing teachers from the children's own country. The emphasis was on the belief that the migrant would ultimately return home and, of course, the legal force only applied to the children of EC nationals.

Latterly, opinion has moved to the view that significant numbers of migrants will remain in the EC and that, as settlement matures, more attention will need to be paid to the needs of second and third generations, while new immigration from outside the EC will remain insignificant. Insofar as migrant groups become a permanent feature of EC society, so questions of integration into the wider community become ever more important; but this is just the area where the EC is itself weak. It is difficult, too, for it to insist upon the development of grassroots policies, although it is here that action is required. Recent guidelines for an EC policy on migration have been accepted by the Council (*OJC*, 186/85). These refer to the importance of concerting states' policies, of dealing more effectively with the social security needs of third country migrants and of ensuring greater participation in the life of the host country. The Commission is anxious to see more information and advice centres at local level, help provided to assist migrants obtain better housing and special services to help women who remain housebound through cultural and linguistic difficulties. A new type of help is becoming necessary as EC nationals return home after a working life spent abroad. Despite the Council resolution, member nations remain hostile to any effort to transfer powers to control immigration policies to the EC. However, similar rules on entry and residence, on the entry of political refugees and the right of asylum may come to be necessary.

With the growth of unemployment and the turbulence of the labour market, concern with the problem of illegal immigration became more vocal. Many migrants appeared willing to take the risk of over-staying; but they became the focus of public alarm and have often been exploited by employers and landlords. Some parents have been reluctant to send their children to school for fear of being detected. As work and residence permits dried up so, it was believed, increasing numbers were crossing frontiers illegally and this became part of a broader problem of frontier control in discussions on the introduction of an internal market. Internal security to control the passage of undesirables, with a corresponding strengthening of controls at the external boundaries of the EC has become an important area of cooperation; but a declaration attached to the SEA reaffirms the right of member states to take their own measures to control illegal immigration.

A belief that racial tensions in Western Europe were growing and that member nations did not always have strong anti-discrimination policies, or give a lead in establishing more reasoned attitudes, encouraged the European Parliament to ventilate the issue. This initiative was followed by a joint declaration between the Council, Commission and Parliament deploring the existence of racism and general xenophobia (*OJC*, 158/86).

The action programme of 1974 hoped to see migrants given civic and political rights and the fact that the Adonnino Report had to return to the same issue shows how reluctant member nations have been to welcome newcomers. Both documents have pointed out that it is inconsistent with the spirit of the free movement policy, and with the evolution of the EC, that Community nationals should be deprived of political rights unless they adopt a new nationality. They rarely have a voice in local politics, although much affected by local educational, housing and personal services. Suggestions that migrants should at least be able to vote in local elections and that EC nationals should be allowed to vote in elections for the European Parliament have made little, or no, progress. The introduction of a European passport has, at long last, become operative. The report on a people's Europe not only stressed again the need to extend voting rights but thought that border residents should be consulted when neighbouring countries wished to adopt policies which might affect them. It also suggested that holders of EC passports should be eligible for help from any EC embassy when abroad. It pointed out that the more effective implementation of existing EC law by all member nations would also benefit EC nationals. All in all, EC history shows that member states have been extremely reluctant to equate the rights of migrants, whatever their origin, with those of their own nationals and, although steps have been taken in relation to EC nationals, each one is hard fought, while member nations remain unwilling to contemplate a transfer to the EC of migration policy in respect of the outside world.

17.12 Equal treatment of men and women

One of the most fruitful areas of work for the EC in the social field has been that of the policy to promote the position of women. Starting from a limited legal base, the EC has been able to exploit the absence of effective national policies. Unusually in social affairs, it had a relatively clear field in which to make itself felt and to fulfil the leadership role for which its position makes it well suited.

An equal pay policy was written into the Treaty of Rome as one means of quietening French fears about its high industrial costs; but there remained a noticeable lack of enthusiasm concerning its application until the 1970s. Some publicity had been attracted to the problem by the case of a Sabena air hostess who had lodged a complaint in Belgium concerning the inequality in her conditions of service. The question of her pay, which was less than that of male stewards on the airline, led ultimately to a consideration by the European Court of Justice in the light of Article 119. The Court made clear its view that the article was intended to be taken seriously and properly applied. One result was to spur the Commission to produce a directive on equal pay in 1975 (Directive 75/117/EEC, *OJL*, 45/75). This included a definition of equal pay, to include both identical work and work of equal value, established certain controls, and insisted upon an effective appeals system. It therefore provided a much stricter framework within which member states were to apply the policy.

It soon became clear, however, that, by itself, this was a reform of limited value. Apart from the need to clarify the concept of equal pay, which is gradually being done through court judgements, men and women had very different social security cover and Directive 79/7/EEC, *OJL*, 6/79 required the progressive implementation of the principle of equal treatment over a six-year period. There were certain exclusions, notably over family and survivors' benefits and member nations had the right to continue some differences if they wished. The most important one was the right to use different ages for retirement pensions. In 1986, the principle was extended to cover occupational schemes and provision for the self-employed (Directive 86/378/EEC, *OJL*, 225/86, corrected *OJL*, 283/86). This should ensure equality of rights in the private sector by 1993 subject to a latitude allowed for actuarial differences of life expectancy. It is not necessary, at present, to use the same retirement age for men and women or to include survivors' pensions.

The Commission is now working on a new directive (COM(87)494 final). This aims to improve social security cover by including benefits previously outside the scope of EC directives. The effect will be to include groups such as the retired and dependents. It is also hoping to move the legal basis for entitlement to an individual right rather than deriving rights from the concept of dependency.

Underlying questions of pay and social security is the whole question of women's position in the labour force, which is still much more limited than that of men. Recognition of the lack of equal opportunities to obtain work and of equality of treatment at work has opened the way to the establishment of EC support programmes. These range from a consideration of the types of education provided at school to the importance of effective vocational training, support for the working mother and the need to encourage men to accept a fuller share of household and family responsibilities. Thus the twin paths of establishing a legal base for certain enforceable rights is supplemented by programmes to encourage a fuller social and working role for women. Equality of treatment for men and women in the labour market, and the need to pay more attention to the balance between employment and family responsibilities, received a modest priority in the first Social Action Programme (SAP) and resulted in a directive to establish equal opportunity with regard to employment, job recruitment, promotion and training (Directive 76/207/EEC, *OJL*, 39/76). A start, at least, has been made to apply the principle of equal treatment in self-employment, including agriculture (Directive 86/613/EE, *EC Bulletin*, 12/86, point 2.1.152 and *OJC*, 113/84). This should come into force in 1989. Although the attempts to strengthen, and equalise, the position of workers taking parental leave, or leave for family reasons, are currently blocked, they are closely related to the sharing of family responsibilities and they are a reminder that equal treatment may sometimes require more rights to be given to men.

For some years, training schemes to help women return to work after child rearing, to enter jobs normally reserved for men and to train for posts using new technologies have received grant aid from the ESF and these initiatives have probably helped considerably in raising the level of understanding about the problems faced by working women. Although the ESF now no longer allocates its grants by groups of worker, aid for women's training continues within the broader categories. It still remains the case, however, that the unemployment rate for women is generally higher than for men, that women are still under-represented in many jobs, and noticeably at higher levels of responsibility, and that the growth of part-time work, with its relative lack of protection, particularly affects women. New industries give the chance of a more even spread of work only if women are trained, and otherwise helped, to take on a full range of posts.

Member nations have shown themselves reluctant to ensure the application of the equal pay and related directives and a number of challenges have been made in the Court of Justice. As a result of early actions, the British government was forced to amend the Equal Pay Act of 1970 to ensure that work of equal value, as determined by effective comparison, was covered. The principle of equal treatment in social security was invoked to ensure that an invalid care allowance was paid to a married woman living in circumstances which would allow a married man to benefit. The equality in employment principle was used when the Court of Justice was asked to consider whether a public authority might insist that a woman retire at 60 years of age when a man might continue to work until 65 years (some cases involving the United Kingdom are Case 129/79, 1980, CMLR 2, p. 205; Case 96/80, 1981, CMLR 2, p. 24; Case 61/81, *ECJ* Reports 1982, p. 2,601; Case 150/85, 1986, CMLR 3, p. 43; Case 152/84, 1986, CMLR 1, p. 688). It must not be thought, however, that the successful outcome of a single case brings the need for vigilance to an end. Cases may be limited in their impact. Thus the Court of Justice declined to give the judgement on retirement age a 'horizontal effect' so that it could be assumed to apply in the private sector. Furthermore, there are many difficulties involved in ensuring the effective implementation of the rules in the member states. The initiative has to start with an individual and this is often prevented by ignorance, fear of reprisals or lack of expert advice on procedure, while national courts and tribunals are often ignorant of EC rulings. Recent comment (*The Times*, 17 September 1987) has referred to the lack of understanding shown by industrial tribunals in the United Kingdom and the confusion that exists between equal pay and equal treatment legislation. This, presumably, applies to both British and other EC nations' legislation.

One result of the growing interest in women's problems was the creation in 1976 of a small bureau for questions relating to women's employment. This office, now the Women's Employment and Equality Office, undertakes a promotional and informational role. Here, especially in relation to the training of girls and young women, it is helped by the work of CEDEFOP. A lively information service which develops contacts and networks and runs seminars is part of the Commission's Directorate for Information, Communications and Culture.

17.13 Problems of social disadvantage

The emphasis in the Treaty of Rome on the theme of economic integration makes it hard for the EC to come to grips with many of the more severe social problems of the day. This weakness was first highlighted during the 1960s when the darker side of affluence was revealed. The marginalisation of many groups, including the inhabitants of the inner cities, the migrants, the elderly, the disabled and the non-earners generally made clear that the EC lacks any direct responsibility to ameliorate the conditions of the most disadvantaged among the population. The increase in unemployment served to highlight the issue by increasing the number who were in difficulties and by exposing the inadequacies of national schemes of protection.

The strain felt by social security schemes was the result of several factors. A growing number of elderly persons were becoming eligible for pensions and the number was swollen further by schemes to encourage early retirement, by redundancy schemes which particularly affected older workers and by the reluctance of employers to take on older workers who were unemployed. Rapidly rising costs were also the result of the growth of health care expenditure. Unemployment itself had led both to the increased cost of benefit provision and to falling contributions. In these circumstances, most governments reacted by attempting to cut down on the expense of social security with the aim of, at least, achieving a slowing of the rate of growth of expenditure. The tendency was for the real value of benefits to fall (EC Commission, 1984d, para. 1).

The Commission has been interested, under these circumstances, in using its powers under Article 118 to promote collaboration and to undertake studies with the aim of considering the future functions of social security as the economy changes. Schemes are not well adapted to the needs of part-time and temporary workers, to the wish of many people to see a new balance between work and leisure, to a greater similarity between the social roles of men and women or to the reality of the female breadwinner. Health care systems, too, have to be re-examined in order to provide a better fit with modern lifestyles. It is in the analysis of these fundamental issues that the contribution of the EC lies, for it cannot directly control the scope and operation of social security schemes themselves or determine the 'right amount' that is required to support dependent population groups.

An anti-poverty programme was included in the first SAP as a result of an Irish initiative. Although small, it gave rise to interesting experiments and drew attention to the difficulties of cross-national social research. Grant aid for projects helping groups in poverty concentrated on small schemes with new, and sometimes unorthodox, procedures and thus formed some contrast to the grants from the ESF. The programme enabled the Commission to remain in direct, close contact with social reform movements and this was a significant gain for a body so often considered, however unfairly, as remote and bureaucratic.

In 1975, a two-year programme was adopted by the Council to allow financial aid for schemes which could be shown to be of value to the EC as a whole and which were, as far as possible, carried out with the participation of the recipients. A cross-national poverty study was also financed and the programme extended until 1980. The work was directed at traditional groups such as the unskilled, the migrants, the single parents, the elderly and handicapped; but it became clear that many of the new poor were excluded. Young people who could not get a job, workers in decaying areas and older workers who could not find re-employment often fell through the net of social security and many of the new employment opportunities came as low paid, temporary or part-time jobs leaving some employed people in poverty as well. A second anti-poverty programme, to run from 1985 until the end of 1988, was agreed by the Council in December 1984 with a budget of 29 million ECUs (this includes 4 million subsequently added to allow for the entry of Portugal and Spain (*OJL*, 199/75; *OJC*, 208/84; *OJL*, 2/85)).

17.14 New developments

New social concerns are bound to arise for the EC as society changes but also as the EC itself matures. Currently, interest is fixed on the implementation of the internal market and, therefore, those aspects of the Adonnino Report which relate particularly to it are to the fore on the social side. The rapid expansion of radio and television facilities makes possible the establishment of an EC interest but, in order for this to develop, problems relating to copyright, advertising and controls over programme content have to be overcome. A directive has been prepared to coordinate national provisions in broadcasting (*EC Bulletin*, 3/86, point 2.1.88). The Commission would like to see a greater use of programmes produced in other member states, the production of joint TV programmes and work to overcome the technical obstacles to transmission.

Consumer protection is not a new interest but, as services, goods and people flow more easily across the EC, it becomes of increasing importance. A formal policy for consumer protection dates back to 1975. This began to consider the implications of a free exchange of goods for the health and safety of the consumer, for rights of redress for faulty goods, for the need for much greater information about products and for the consumer interest to be better organised and represented. Ministers responsible for consumer affairs meet from time to time and a directive on liability for defective products was passed in 1985 (*OJL*, 210/86). An active programme of standard setting to cover, *inter alia*, safety, food additives and pharmaceutical standards is followed and developments planned to protect the consumer over matters such as credit card interest charges, after sales services, misleading advertising and door step selling (*OJC*, 167/86).

17.15 An overall view

The range of topics referred to in this chapter shows how diverse the social concerns of the EC now are. Its measures are perhaps better described as a miscellany rather than a coherent social policy informed by a few compelling themes. Nevertheless, the hard core remains. Great efforts have been expended on the creation of an active social policy, despite a rather uncertain treaty base, and here much depends upon the skill and enthusiasm of the Commission. A great deal of the work consists of minimum standard setting. However, while some of the health standards can be precisely set, those dealing with employment law and equal pay establish a general principle which can require further interpretation and are more difficult to make effective. Another feature is the support of investigatory activities, research and pilot schemes. In financial terms, this support is modest; but a wide range of projects is covered. Often they are cross-national in character and attempt fresh approaches to old problems – the anti-poverty programme and the pilot schemes under the ESF are both examples.

During the 1970s, it was agreed to set up three European institutes for study and research. In December 1977, CEDEFOP began work in Berlin. This was to give new impetus to the creation of a common policy through harmonising national systems of training and promoting new initiatives. In 1975, a Foundation for the Improvement of Living and Working Conditions was set up in Dublin. Finally, the Council agreed to support a project of the European Trades Union Confederation to set up a European Trades Union Institute for the study of union affairs. Such work merges into that of general promotion. Grant aid from the EC may be important, not so much because of its amount, but because it stimulates national governments to take action themselves, or to support action at home, which they might otherwise not have done.

Social policy has always to be seen in the wider context of other EC policies. It is now a long time since the Commission began to argue that, as the EC developed policies of its own in the economic field, so it would increasingly influence social conditions and, for this reason alone, required a more active social policy. Since the Paris summit it has been formally recognised that the goal of economic and monetary union cannot be pursued without adequate consideration of the social consequences. The SEA appears to mark a new stage where more specific action is wanted. While it recognises the need to improve health and safety standards, this is set in the context of minimum requirements, gradual implementation and of not over-straining small businesses. It is not clear how widely the goal of economic and social cohesion will be interpreted. The Adonnino Report is concerned with improvements to the free movement policy and with measures designed to make a popular appeal. Welcome, but limited, improvements are the likely outcome. It is true that there is enormous potential latent in the references in the preamble of the SEA to the fundamental rights enshrined in the Convention for the Protection of Human Rights and Fundamental Freedoms and the European Social Charter but there are no indications, at present, that the EC is moving towards accepting the goal of social justice as an operational rather than an aspirational policy. The history of social policy, whether in general or in particular fields, shows how strong is the grip of national states. The real brake on development is the lack of political will and not the uncertainties of the treaties. The EC is likely to edge forward slowly in the social field when member nations see it as opportune to allow a new initiative. Nevertheless, a glance back to 1951, or even to 1957, shows that there is now an EC dimension in matters of health, social security, pay and working conditions. Change occurs, albeit slowly. Broad social issues such as the migration of workers, pollution of the environment, industrial welfare and democracy and consumer protection are no longer questions for states to decide entirely for themselves.

Supranational social responsibilities are constantly clarified through the activities of the EC. Its institutions, after all, are in a better position than those of national governments to identify the broad processes of social and economic changes occurring in Western Europe. It is clear today that some of these issues require a social policy response to be taken in concert; but they only require a standardisation of policy in certain circumstances. Arguments are as lively as ever over the role of the EC in promoting social progress, the extent to which the internal market requires a social dimension and the necessity for EC social legislation. The Commission recently produced a draft Social Charter intended to bring together both declaratory principles and specific objectives. The latter relate to issues discussed in this chapter and could, later on, be given obligatory status. This document has evoked a strong, negative reaction from the British Prime Minister. She fears the legitimisation of the EC's right to establish social norms and that such rules would lead to a greater regulation of industry with harmful effects on its competitiveness. A particular objection concerns the question of worker participation in the decision making of firms. The episode supports the judgement that national sensitivities are extremely acute in the social field and it remains to be seen if the Charter leads to the adoption of any specific obligation which would not otherwise have existed.

18 Environmental policy

A. Marin

18.1 Background

For a long time it was not clear whether there was any legitimate basis at all for an EC policy on the environment. In the 1950s there was no influential generalised concern for the environment. Occasionally a specific particularly harmful episode of pollution would give rise to remedial action to deal with the specific problem, but no more. For example, in the winter of 1952–3 there was an even denser than usual smog[1] in London leading to a dramatic increase in mortality among the elderly and bronchitic. As a result, following an inquiry, new laws were introduced to allow the control of domestic coal fires. But the episode did not lead to a more widespread concern with air pollution generally. The same attitude was prevalent in other countries at that time. Hence the Treaty of Rome made no provision for any joint EC policy on controlling pollution, let alone more general environmental conservation.

By the end of the 1960s, however, a new attitude which led to demands for new policies had become widespread. Although, perhaps, not initially as strongly as in the United States, noticeable numbers of people in Western Europe had begun to express concern over degradation of the environment. There were serious strands, not always compatible, within the burgeoning 'environmentalist' movement, both in terms of the issues of concern and of the political outlooks of those most prominent.

One set of issues was sometimes described as 'the end of the world' or 'doomsday' concern. This focused on what was felt to be the inevitable, and fairly imminent, exhaustion of various natural resources if population growth and income growth continued. A series of influential studies predicting calamity was published in the early 1970s. Some of these were sponsored by an international group of business-men and others, known as 'The Club of Rome', with a prominent role in the group taken by a leading industrialist of the Fiat company. These studies contained little economic analysis, as usually understood (although some economists were involved), and were viewed sceptically by many economists.[2] The sceptics thought that too little care had been taken over the estimation of the individual relationships which were

373

then simulated into longer-run predictions showing *The Limits To Growth* (Meadows *et al.*, 1972). Solow (1973) caustically commented on a remark by Forrester, one of the leading modellers, implying that it did not matter if the details were correct provided the framework was right, by saying that 'I don't know what you call people who believe they can be wrong about everything in particular, but expect to be lucky enough somehow to get it right on the interactions. They may be descendants of the famous merchant Lapidus, who said that he lost money on every item he sold, but made it up on the volume.'

The point made by those economists who were sceptical of the arguments that economic growth was unsustainable because of the exhaustion of raw materials was that as any resource became scarcer relative to demand its price would increase. To quote Solow again, 'The most glaring defect of the . . . models is the absence of any sort of functioning price system.' The mechanical extrapolation from existing resource usage ignored the price mechanism. The increase in price of resources which were becoming physically scarce would encourage substitution by other inputs, induce resource-saving innovation and also lead to substitution in the demand for final products towards less-scarce-resource-intensive goods and services. The 'end of the worlders' replied that although the price mechanism might have worked in the past for particular inputs, it could not do so for all exhaustible resources together. Ultimately, it was almost a question of faith – some believed that just because something had worked in the past there was no reason for it to do so in the future; others believed that economic incentives via market forces would always lead to satisfactory solutions, even if by strict logic this could not be proved.[3]

Although fears of resource exhaustion played a role in arousing the consciousness which led to EC environmental policy, they did not have a longer-lasting effect on the forms of policy. To start with, real action would require global agreement, and not just within the member states of the Community; it would involve not only the United States but also the poorer countries which were trying to develop. Furthermore, the fears themselves became more of a minority concern.[4] They had struck a chord with a wider audience at a time when many raw material prices were rising rapidly, with the OPEC-inspired oil prices to the forefront; the public could take this as a sign that resource exhaustion was beginning to bite. Although the OPEC cartel kept oil prices high after 1973, and indeed managed further price rises in 1979–80, as the recession of the mid-1970s took hold (itself probably due to the oil price rises) the prices of other raw materials collapsed and stayed low – excess capacity in raw material production has been the rule rather than the exception in the 1980s. Even oil prices collapsed after 1984. Non-experts tended to lose interest in the possible shortage of raw materials. In addition, perhaps, there was something incongruous and unconvincing in the sight of groups headed by people who were among the most affluent in countries which were the most developed telling the world that incomes would have to stop rising and that the underdeveloped countries could not industrialise because of the insupportable strain it would put on our planet.[5]

There were other groups whose ideas partly coincided with the limits to growth approach, who had more effect on EC policy, especially where they injected a stronger crusading zeal into that aspect of environmental concern which had most influence on policy. These were the groups who stressed ecology and preservation. As well as the scientific ecologists themselves, there were the – primarily younger – groups which emerged from the 'counter-culture' of the late 1960s (the 'hippies') feeling that the political activism of the same period had failed (witness the lack of permanent results from the student-led movement of 1968) yet not approving of the terrorist route taken by some of those who despaired of changing society by other methods. It is not just that they have eventually succeeded in getting enough votes to have some Green Party members in the European Parliament, as well as some representatives at national and lower levels; some national governments have felt obliged to be seen to be responsive to public opinion on environmental issues, in order to try to keep the Greens from gaining enough seats to be a threat to the government majorities. These governments, initially primarily the German and Dutch, have an extra incentive to support EC environmental policies.

The areas which seem to be of general concern to the wider public (and where the Green movements have sometimes provided the impetus) are partly the preservation of natural amenity and wildlife, and, more importantly for EC policy, pollution. The change from 1957 is that pollution is seen to be a general, on-going, problem. Concern may be heightened by particularly harmful and/or well-publicised cases, for example the disposal of toxic waste from Seveso; but it is now considered that action should not be limited to reacting to such cases but should be introduced to control harm before blatantly dangerous situations occur.

As a result of the changes in attitudes just outlined, in October 1972 the heads of government (prompted by a report from the Commission earlier that year) called for an EC environmental programme, which led to approval in November 1973 of the 1st Environmental Programme 1973–78. This has been followed by subsequent consecutive programmes up to the current 4th Programme 1987–92.

Despite the agreement of the heads of government to an EC programme, and thus to a commitment to joint policies, for some years there was doubt as to whether there really was a legal basis for issuing directives in this area.[6] The doubts were particularly strongly expressed within the United Kingdom.[7] On several issues (as will be detailed later), up until the late 1980s the UK approach to pollution control differed sharply (or so it seemed in public statements) from the majority view among the other member states. There were some who proposed a challenge to the legality of the directives – although a recourse to the European Court of the Justice was never, in fact, pursued.

The official basis for actions that were clearly not foreseen in the Treaty of Rome was twofold. Firstly, a few of the types of pollution dealt with could result from the use of goods, for example noise and exhaust emissions from vehicles, or packaging and labelling of solvents. In these cases joint EC standards could clearly be justified as part of product harmonisation to prevent different national standards acting as a non-tariff barrier to inter-state trade.[8] However, many of the directives concerned types of pollution and environmental standards that could not constitute a hindrance to inter-state trade on any reasonable criterion, such as the quality of bathing (i.e. swimming) water or the hunting of wild birds.

The second basis claimed for EC environmental policies would justify joint policies on all types of environmental concern, even where trade is unaffected. Article 2 of the Treaty of Rome stated that 'The Community shall ... promote throughout the Community a harmonious development of economic activities, a continuous and balanced expansion, ... an accelerated raising of the standard of living'. It was claimed that measures to protect the environment could be considered to further a balanced expansion and raised standard of living, given the importance now attached to the environment by public opinion and the extent to which people's sense of well-being was threatened by pollution and environmental degradation.[9]

No legal challenge ever mounted to the Community's right to make decisions on the environment; the matter is now beyond dispute. In 1986, Articles 130R–130S were inserted into the Treaty by the Single European Act (SEA). These articles are explicitly devoted to the environment: see Chapter 17 for more on this and other developments. Furthermore, according to Article 100A, actions taken to further the 'completion of the internal market' (colloquially known as '1992') are supposed to take as their base a high level of environmental protection. In addition, allowance is made for individual member states to set higher environmental standards, provided these do not constitute barriers to trade – this allowance and the proviso may well require decisions by the Court of Justice to define the acceptable boundaries. Some conflicts may also arise over whether particular directives are to be treated as relating to product harmonisation (therefore falling under Article 100A concerning the internal market) and thus subject to majority votes or environmental protection (therefore falling under Article 130S) and requiring unanimous agreement.

Insofar as the SEA has increased the power of the European Parliament (which is the view of many, but not all, commentators) this may also lead to stronger EC policies on the environment, and the adoption of stricter standards. The European Parliament is generally considered to be more concerned about environmental issues than the Council. This is partly due to the Green MEPs, but seems to affect MEPs of other parties as well. At the time of writing (mid-1989) there has been one case where pressure from the Parliament has helped push the Council to take stronger action: Parliament's amendment in April 1989 of the Council's proposal on exhaust emissions resulted in more stringent limits which could be met only by using catalytic converters on all cars. Given the general movement towards environmental consciousness in the last year or two, the previous opponents of stringent limits (especially the United Kingdom) were not prepared to face the odium of no action at all as a result of rejecting the Parliament's amendment.

Whatever the legality according to the unamended Treaty of Rome of EC directives on issues affecting the environment, there still remains the question of why the governments of the member states wanted a *joint* environmental policy at all on those aspects where individual national policies would not be a barrier to trade and where transfrontier flows of pollution were not a problem. (As already indicated, the small group which could lead to barriers could be dealt with under the procedures on product harmonisation.) It is never possible to be completely sure what is in people's minds, but discussions at the time and subsequently suggest two primary motivations.

Firstly, statements by EC leaders often stressed that it was felt to be important that, if there were to be public support for the European ideal, the EC should be identified in the minds of the public with issues with which they were concerned. It should not be thought to be limited to 'boring' technical issues, whether product standard harmonisation or the minutiae of calculating transport costs between Rotterdam and Duisberg. Joint EC policies on an issue which had recently become the focus of much media discussion and campaigning would help to convince the public that the Community was relevant to them and responsive to their worries.

Secondly, it was clear to governments in member states that they would have to respond to public pressures over pollution and environmental preservation. This was especially true of the German and Dutch governments among the original six, but the others were not immune either. Many of the measures which would be required were likely to raise production costs. For example, firms would have to install new equipment rather than just pouring noxious waste into rivers or sewers, or would have to buy the more expensive low sulphur fuels to limit emissions of sulphur dioxide. If some countries were to have tighter standards than others, then their firms would face 'unfair competition' from firms which had lower production costs just because they were located in countries which had laxer requirements on pollution abatement.[10] Uniform emission standards (referred to as UES in the literature) would prevent this threat to competitiveness.[11] Hence the desire of governments for joint EC environmental policies which would affect all member states equally.

18.2 Economic (or economists') assessment of environmental policies

In order to judge the appropriateness of EC environmental policies it is necessary to have criteria. The criteria used elsewhere in this book are primarily (though not exclusively) those of standard neoclassical welfare economics.

For the policies examined in this chapter, equity – at least in terms of income distribution – has not been a major consideration.[12] However, it is worth noting that one difference between the approach of many environmentalists and that of many economists is related to the standard assumptions of welfare economics. Economists tend fundamentally to judge policies and institutions by their effects on the welfare of individuals.[13] Something which has no effect on any person will be ignored. Environmentalists, however, often feel that some things are worthwhile even if no humans are affected. They place a value on the diversity of natural habitats and the continuation of species, even where there is no benefit to man. By their training, many (though not all) economists are resistant to such a view.[14]

There have been few EC policies which deal with protection of species *per se*. One exception is the 1979 directive on the conservation of wild birds. Some have argued that the directives on water quality for river/estuaries containing fish or shellfish are not just to protect human health but also to protect the fish *per se*. Another, limited, exception is the 1985 directive requiring an environmental impact assessment before certain large development projects are undertaken. This exception is limited both because the types of project requiring the assessment are largely left to national governments and because, once the assessment has been made, there is no requirement for any weighting to be given to adverse environmental effects in deciding whether the project should proceed. There are also EC directives concerning other endangered species (seals and whales), but, although motivated by environmental concerns (and the repugnance at the methods of killing seal pups), these formally deal with trade in the products of the species.

Most of the EC environmental policies have concerned pollution in some form. For economists pollution is a problem which cannot be solved by the market mechanism – indeed it arises from a market mechanism – because it is an externality.[15] In fact, most textbooks on microeconomics use pollution as the classic example of an externality. One way of viewing externalities is that they are cases where the actions taken by one economic agent (individual or firm) affect others, but where there is no feedback mechanism leading the agent to correctly take account of the effects on others. It is not the existence of an effect on others that constitutes an externality, but the lack of incentive to take full account of it. Every economic action may affect others, but in a well-functioning system the price mechanism provides incentives to take account of the effects.

For example, when deciding whether to drive my car to the shops or walk, in reaching my decision I use my car only if the benefit is greater than the price I have to pay for the petrol. If the price equals the marginal cost (the usual criterion for Pareto optimality), then I will use my car only if the benefit is greater than the cost to society of the scarce resources used up in providing me with the petrol. Hence the price system provides me with the correct incentive to take account of the effects of my action (driving my car) on others (using up scarce resources, which are therefore not available to provide somebody else with that petrol). However, if the use of my car pollutes the air and causes annoyance, or more serious harm, to others there is no incentive for me to allow for this. I could be said to be using up another scarce resource (quiet and clean air), but I do not have to pay for it. Hence there will be times when I use my car even though the benefit to me is less than the true cost to society, i.e. the sum of the costs of which I take account (the petrol) plus those of which I do not (the pollution); the result is therefore not optimal. Thus another, exactly equivalent, way of expressing an externality is to define it as arising when the marginal private cost is not equal to the marginal social cost.[16]

There are two diagrams which are often used to analyse the problem of pollution and indicate possible policy solutions.[17] The older one concentrates on the divergence between social and private cost, usually in the context of a competitive industry which causes pollution during the production of some good. In Figure 18.1 the supply curve of the industry is, as always, equal to the sum of the marginal (private) costs of the firms. Given the demand curve, Q_0 is produced and sold at a price of P_0. This is not optimal. If the pollution emitted during production is allowed for, the true sum of marginal social costs for the firms is given by MSC, and the optimal output is where $P = MSC$, i.e. at Q_1 and P_1.

Figure 18.1 has the advantage of stressing that part of the result of pollution in

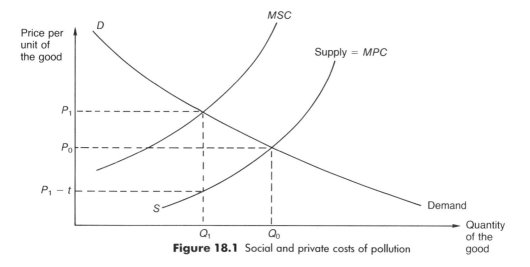

Figure 18.1 Social and private costs of pollution

production is that the price to consumers is too low and therefore consumption is too high. Conversely, any policy to achieve efficiency will involve a higher price and less output and consumption. It is therefore not surprising that both employers and trade unions in the industries affected are sometimes among those opposing particular EC policies to control pollution.[18] Nor is it surprising that in some countries of the EC (possibly in contrast to the United States), the importance attached to environmental policies declined in the second half of tl.e 1970s and early 1980s. The rise in unemployment led to more stress on the reduction in output that might result from pollution control measures – an example of the more general point that if displaced workers are not confident of finding alternative jobs easily, then employment becomes an aim in its own right and policies are not judged solely by the total consumption of goods (even allowing for the 'consumption' of 'bads' involved in pollution).[19]

As a means of analysing policies to control pollution, Figure 18.1 has the disadvantage of neither explicitly showing what happens to pollution nor showing whether pollution can be reduced by means other than a drop in production of the final output of the industry. For these reasons an alternative diagram is now often used, which draws attention to these aspects, although it has the disadvantage that the implications of Figure 18.1 to which we have drawn attention are left implicit and may therefore be inadvertently downplayed.

In Figure 18.2, pollution is measured explicitly. For convenience we have drawn the diagram with the abscissa measuring pollution abatement from the level that would occur with no policy controls. Some authors use pollution emissions instead. This is equivalent to Figure 18.2 working leftwards from the 100 per cent abatement (zero-remaining pollution) point. The diagram shows the abatement of some particular form of pollution for some particular industry. The marginal benefits (MB) of pollution abatement are the avoidance of the external costs placed on others – health,

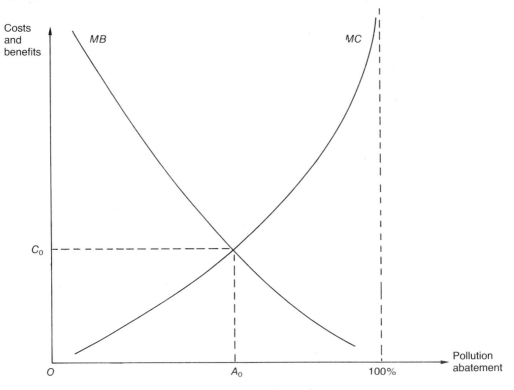

Figure 18.2 Costs of pollution abatement

annoyance at noise, loss of amenity, etc. The marginal costs (MC) of pollution abatement to the firms in the industry are the costs associated with various abatement techniques, such as the treatment plant for noxious effluents in our earlier example, as well as the loss of profits if emissions are reduced by cutting back on the level of output of the final product sold. The approach in Figure 18.2 draws explicit attention to the possibilities of using other resources (labour, capital) to reduce emissions (unlike Figure 18.1, which is usually drawn on the assumption that the externalities associated with each level of output are fixed).

The shapes of the marginal benefit and cost curves in Figure 18.2 follow from what is known for many types of pollution – some abatement is often easy but when 95 per cent of potential emissions have already been removed, removal of the remaining 5 per cent is usually much more expensive. On the benefit side the marginal curve is usually drawn downward sloping, although the justification is less well founded and there may be some forms of pollution (especially affecting amenity) where the downward slope is not correct. For example once a line of pylons has been put over a previously unspoiled mountain range any further developments do less marginal harm. However, most of the EC pollution policies deal with worries about effects of pollution on human health and for this the downward MB curve is usually reasonable

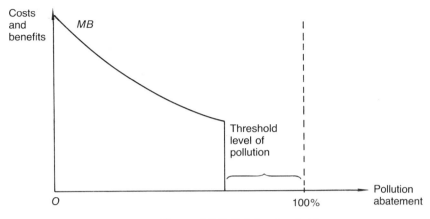

Figure 18.3 Pollution threshold

(as it is for the policies on sulphur dioxide and some car exhaust emissions where the motivation is partly human, partly the effects on forests).

In some cases it is suspected that there may be thresholds of pollution below which the body can cope but above which harm may start. In these cases the *MB* curve may have the shape in Figure 18.3.

Returning to the more general case of Figure 18.2, one important policy implication of this way of analysing pollution is that there is an optimum level of pollution. Except in very special cases, it is not optimal to aim for the complete elimination of pollution.[20] Less than 100 per cent abatement is desirable. The optimum level, which maximises welfare, is where the marginal costs of further abatement just equal the marginal benefits, level A_0 in Figure 18.2. This is an implication of the economists' approach which is uncongenial to some in the Green movement.

EC policies have followed the economists' approach on the whole. In the early years of EC action there were some clashes between member nations. The United Kingdom, in particular, advocated its traditional policies, summed up in such expressions as 'best *practicable* means' of pollution control. The notion of 'practicable' involves a weighing up of costs and benefits – although this balancing seems always to be implicit rather than explicit and to rely on the intuition of the relevant inspectorates. The United Kingdom feared that at times the other member states were proposing the approach of 'best *available* technology', i.e. pushing as far as technically feasible towards 100 per cent abatement irrespective of costs. Ultimately, although some directives still mentioned that best available technology should be adopted, there was no time limit set for adoption, or else the phrase was qualified by saying that the adoption should be provided if it did not entail 'excessive cost' – which reduces it to practicable – or else some other let out was included. It is actually doubtful that the other member states were completely unconcerned with costs. In reality, the apparent disagreements seem to have been rather over how much abatement was desirable, with the other countries saying in some cases that the United Kingdom tended to overestimate the costs of abatement and underestimate the benefits and urgency of reductions in pollution, and too often claim that more evidence was needed before action should be taken. One example is the UK position on sulphur dioxide, where for a long time the United Kingdom delayed partly because of claims that the evidence failed to show that UK emissions contributed significantly to forest damage elsewhere in West Europe. The new 'Environment' title inserted by the SEA specifically refers to the need to take account of 'the potential benefits and costs of action or lack of action' (Article 130R, 3(iii)).

If the problem is that of externality, the 'obvious' solution might seem to be to 'internalise the externality'. It is often suggested that an implication of the economists' analysis is that polluters should have to pay a tax equal to the external costs imposed on others. In terms of Figure 18.2, if a tax equal to C_0 were levied for each unit of pollution emitted, firms would abate up to level A_0. At abatement levels less than A_0 it is less costly for them to abate than to pay a tax of C_0. From A_0 onwards the marginal cost of further abatement is higher than the tax, hence it will be more profitable to continue to pollute and pay the tax. A tax will therefore achieve the optimum. The idea of controlling pollution by taxation rather than by quantitative regulations imposed on firms also seems to fit economists' predilection for relying on price (here the 'price' of using up clean air, etc.) rather than quantitative controls. The latter are supposed to require information that the central authorities rarely possess.

In the EC pollution taxes have hardly been used. Among the minor exceptions is the reduced tax in some countries on lead free petrol as compared to leaded petrol, during the period when both are available. In terms of Figure 18.1, a tax differential equal to t has been imposed on petrol containing lead.[21] Ironically, however, (in the year preceding the final Council agreement of 1989) the Commission – at the urging of the French and UK governments – had been threatening to take the Dutch to the Court of Justice for offering tax concessions to purchasers of cars fitted with catalytic converters which reduce exhaust pollution. This was said to be a distortion of trade – the British and French car makers not having moved as fast as the Germans and some others in adapting their production towards cars which can be easily fitted with converters.

Despite the common view that analyses like Figure 18.2 show the desirability of controlling pollution by taxes, and that all (respectable?) economists agree,[22] there is a serious flaw in the argument. To achieve the optimum level of pollution a government needs to know the size of the correct tax, C_0. But to know C_0 requires knowing the marginal costs and benefits of abatement and where the curves intersect. But this information is the same as required to know, and directly impose, A_0. Hence a government which can achieve optimality via taxes can achieve it via regulation as well.

Although it is easy to draw diagrams for hypothetical cases of unspecified pollutants and industries, to actually quantitatively estimate reliable MB and MC curves in real-life cases is much more difficult. Very often the MB curves are little more than guesses. There is a two-stage problem:

1. Working out the physical relationship between varying levels of the pollutant and the harm done (the dose-response relationship).
2. Putting a monetary valuation on the harm.

It is not just the economic problem of the latter stage – although that is often contentious enough – but that scientists usually have only sketchy and controversial evidence on the first stage, i.e. the way that the damage changes with different levels of the pollutant. The experts sometimes disagree over whether a substance is harmful at all, and often disagree over whether there is a safe threshold or whether even the minutest dose has some small chance of doing some harm to somebody; for example whether there are any safe levels of lead absorption or nuclear radiation.

As a result the level of pollution aimed at – often called the 'standard' in the EC literature – is often at best a very rough guess. However, perhaps surprisingly, once it is accepted that the aim is not an optimal level of pollution, there is then a strong argument for achieving the fairly arbitrary standard by the use of taxes, rather than by simply telling all firms contributing to the pollution to abate by some particular percentage, or telling all firms that they can each emit only some particular amount of pollution. The reason is that typically some polluters have lower abatement costs than others. To minimise the costs of achieving any given arbitrary level of aggregate abatement, more of the abatement should be done by firms who can abate more cheaply. Normally, the abatement should be spread between firms in such a way that the *marginal* cost of abatement is equal for each firm. But the argument given above as to how firms will react to a pollution tax shows that in response to a given tax, each firm will abate up to the point where the tax equals its marginal costs of abatement. Since each firm faces the same tax, they will all end up where they have equal marginal costs of abatement. Hence taxes will minimise the cost of abatement.

Despite this cost-minimisation argument, as stated, above, pollution taxes are rare in the EC.[23] Nevertheless the argument just outlined does have important implications for some controversies over EC environmental policies.

18.3 Further implications for EC policies

In the course of the above discussion of the standard economic analysis of pollution control, we have noted in passing a few of the implications for EC policies. There are other important aspects of the policies which can also be usefully examined in the light of the analysis.

18.3.1 Polluter pays principle (PPP)

The EC has followed the rest of the OECD in accepting this principle. At first many commentators mistakenly thought that the PPP was an acceptance of the taxation approach ascribed to economists, in which polluters pay taxes on unabated pollution.

However, this was not the meaning of the PPP. It was instead an agreement that governments should not subsidise firms for the costs imposed upon them by anti-pollution regulations. The PPP is satisfied if the polluters bear the cost of achieving the prescribed standards.

The PPP is thus a way of making firms 'internalise the externality'. If the standards they have to meet are correctly chosen, then, given the constraints placed on them, individual firms' own choices of abatement techniques and of output will be correct from a social standpoint.

It might also be noted that from the point of view of the first-order conditions for achieving efficiency, a subsidy per unit abated would achieve the same result as a tax per unit emitted (though in the long run the size of the industry might differ because of the different profitability). The opportunity cost to the firm of continuing to pollute would indicate subsidy forgone. Thus the rationale for PPP is not to enforce efficiency, but rather fears of 'unfair competition', as discussed above.

Within the EC, although PPP (as well as the general limits to state aids in Articles 92 and 93 of the Treaty of Rome – see Chapter 7) has meant that subsidies for pollution abatement are generally forbidden, this has been applied very strictly only for the higher running costs associated with operating equipment to reduce emissions. Transitional costs may be subsidised. At times the Commission has allowed some help with initial investment costs to install abatement equipment, or to speed the implementation of agreed standards prior to the final date for compliance.

18.3.2 Thresholds and standards

As stated above, it is very difficult to get convincing evidence about the dose–response relationships of pollutants. The problems of obtaining evidence make the techniques used much closer to those of econometricians rather than those of laboratory-based science testing. Where human health is concerned, it is simply unethical to laboratory test, by, for example, taking very young babies and giving them feeds containing different levels of nitrates to observe the level which causes serious damage. Most EC policies are concerned with potential health effects. But even where only amenity is at stake, the number of possible interactions and natural variations in them still make it difficult to gather conclusive evidence. The arguments over the cause of forest die back are a case in point. There are various possible pollutants which may interact in causing damage; damage may depend on soil and weather, and the route taken between emissions of sulphur dioxide and nitrogen oxide on the one hand and the precipitation of acid rain on the other is difficult to forecast.

One result of this is that it is important to try to obtain reliable data on a range of pollutants, over many years and at a sufficient number of locations, to enable statistical studies relating various aspects of health to pollution to be based on enough observations to be significant (in a statistical sense). One of the foci of EC Environmental Policy has been to require monitoring of pollutants.[24] The earliest requirements were for smoke and sulphur dioxide (from 1975 onwards), water pollution (from 1977 onwards) and more recently (from 1987) there has been an attempt to gather systematic data on damage to trees.

More fundamentally, the lack of definitive knowledge on the damage caused by different levels of pollution means that any standards adopted are done so largely by a political process disguised as a scientific one. Different groups put pressure on governments to be more or less lax, and the governments then take stands in the Council according to the balance of their feelings; often possibly the position they have previously taken domestically is then taken with respect to EC policy. Each government will claim scientific backing for its stand, usually refusing to admit the uncertainty. Those pushing for the laxest standard will tend to claim that there is no conclusive evidence of harm, while not admitting that there is no conclusive evidence of lack of harm either; the United Kingdom's position on sulphur dioxide mentioned above is one example. Others will mention the studies which suggest that there could well be serious damage caused by the current levels of pollution. As part of the process, there is the temptation to look for a threshold, as in Figure 18.3, even where there are no strong grounds for expecting its existence. If a threshold did exist, it would often make sense to adopt it as the standard – the *MC* curve would have to cut the *MB* curve to the left of the threshold to justify less abatement (higher pollution).

A large number of medical scientists are doubtful that overall thresholds exist for many pollutants. The levels of a pollutant, like smoke, that may be harmless to a healthy person may be deleterious to somebody already vulnerable, like a bronchitic old-age pensioner living in a damp flat. Thus a threshold which would be applicable to all might well be at so low a level of pollution as to be useless for policy.

Once a standard has been decided upon, by whatever process of bargaining based on whatever motives and justifications, it is then too often treated as though the agreed standard were really a well-defined threshold. On the one hand governments may use the fact that an EC standard exists to try to allay public anxiety over the potential harm from some pollutant and to claim that because levels are below the accepted standard there is nothing at all to worry about – even if new evidence has since emerged to suggest that low levels are more harmful than was thought before. On the other hand, environmentalist and other pressure groups may use the breach of a standard as an indication that the health of the public is being seriously damaged and argue that pollution must be immediately reduced down to the standard, whatever the cost.

In most cases, the EC has laid down that member states must notify the Commission if they cannot reach the agreed standard by the required date. The Commission then has to decide whether the failure can be condoned or not. At this stage the pressures mentioned in the previous paragraph come into play again: to what extent is the standard just a rough guess at the level at which marginal costs equal marginal benefits, so that less abatement is justified if a particular country can plausibly claim that its costs are especially high, or is it a well-defined threshold of pollution above which completely unacceptable harm is caused? The decision is complicated by the worry that if some member states are granted exemptions too readily, others will in future not comply because of fears of 'unfair competition' from those given exemptions.

18.3.3 Emission versus ambient standards

In the diagrams above we followed most of the literature in simply linking pollution to damage. However, on closer examination it becomes apparent that there are various stages of pollution. There is the initial emission at the point at which the pollution is produced such as the factory chimney or waste pipe outlet. The pollution may then flow through various media, for instance, it may be carried by wind through air, then deposited on plants, then eaten by animals which are then slaughtered. During the processes, the pollution from any one source is added to by pollution from other sources and simultaneously diluted by fresh air, water, etc., mixing with the carrying medium, and much of the substance is deposited where it does no harm. The ultimate stage to be considered is where the pollution finally directly affects man.

From the economist's, anthropocentric, viewpoint the pollution that matters is when it affects human beings. Typically, therefore, we are concerned with the ambient levels of pollution – i.e. the concentration – in the medium which affects health, such as micrograms per cubic metre of lead particles in the air or milligrams per litre of nitrates in drinking water.

In setting standards for pollution, a standard could be applied at any of the stages of the process. At the final stage, one could set standards of acceptable levels of absorption of pollution by people; for example there was at one time a Commission proposal to set a maximum limit for the level of lead in people's blood. Obviously one would hardly fine or imprison people with more lead in their blood than the standard. Instead, the idea was that if tests showed that anybody was above the limit, then the government of their country should take agreed action to reduce lead intake. In fact governments do use monitoring of human exposure or absorption as a trigger for action, and occasionally set standards in this form, such as radiation exposure limits for workers. In the EC case, partly as a result of UK pressure, the directive on blood lead levels was watered down somewhat and became one for an EC-wide screening programme, primarily for information gathering and with a member state required to take only such action as the government itself thought appropriate if too many people were above the specified values.[25]

The next stage back is that mentioned above, i.e. the concentration in the medium which directly affects people. In the EC, standards defined for this stage are sometimes called 'exposure standards' or 'primary protection standards'. Another example, in addition to those for drinking water or air, would be the bacteria content of bathing water.

Sometimes the standards are somewhat further back in the process, but still concern ambient levels. These are often called 'environmental quality standards'. The standards applying to water which could be taken for drinking but is still in rivers or lakes, or those for water with shellfish, are examples.

Standards may also be set at the initial emission stage. These are usually called 'emission standards'. A similar stage is when the pollution is caused by the use of products which are sold, such as car exhaust pollution or noise from lawnmowers. A somewhat similar stage is where the EC mandates labelling or other aspects of products to avoid *potential* danger from misuse, for example controls on the shipment of toxic waste.

As already stated, from an economist's viewpoint it would seem that the relevant standard should be as far down the chain as technically possible – exposure standards where possible or at least environmental quality standards. The only cases for EC standards on emissions would be either where they were also product standards (to allow unhindered trade) or where there was some reason why even environmental quality standards were infeasible. Otherwise it should be up to the relevant government inspectorate/agency to find the least cost way of achieving the environmental quality or exposure standard. If pollution taxes were not used, then the requirement for pollution abatement should be shared between the various sources of emissions in the most efficient way possible.[26] As explained earlier, the aim would be (subject to information/enforcement limitations) to require abatement by each polluter up to the point where the marginal cost of abatement was equal.

In the 1970s there was a heated controversy over whether the EC should define its policies by environmental quality standards (EQS) or uniform emission standards (UES), with the latter defined as maximum 'limit values' so that member states could have stricter emission limits if they wished. The issue arose over a linked series of directives on water quality aimed at rivers and estuaries: there was a framework directive, finally passed in 1976, on the approach to 'Dangerous substances discharged into the aquatic environment', followed by subsequent directives on specific pollutants/industries.[27] The contestants were the United Kingdom on the side of EQS and the other member states, plus the Commission, on the side of UES.

The reasons for the attachment of the Commission and the other member states to UES were partly explicable in terms of one of the motivations for having a joint EC policy at all: the fear of 'unfair competition' if different countries had different emission standards on a set of pollutants which were primarily industrial effluents. Countries, such as the United Kingdom, which had a long coastline with relatively fast flowing estuaries and rivers would be able to achieve any given EQS with much higher emissions than their trade partners (rivals?). In addition, countries which shared river systems (as along the Rhine) would find it difficult to allocate individual polluters' emission levels to achieve an EQS: upstream countries would have little incentive to impose severe cutbacks on their industries. The issue of transfrontier pollution is of less importance for the United Kingdom, which is not only primarily an island (ignoring Northern Ireland and its border) but has the fortune to be mainly upwind of its nearest neighbours. The other member states felt that the cooperation which should underlie the Community ought to lead to policies in a form which would help, not hinder, solution to joint problems, including transfrontier pollution.

On the other side of the debate, the United Kingdom put views which are close to part of the approach taken by most economists and outlined above. Since it is the damage to humans which is the problem, an EQS is what matters, not emissions *per se*. Emissions need only to be limited to the extent that they lead to unacceptable damage. In terms of a traditional British statement: 'There are no harmful substances, only harmful concentrations'. On the question of unfair competition, the UK government said that it was no more unfair that the United Kingdom should benefit from its coastline and estuaries than that Italy could benefit from its sunshine: it would be absurd to require the Italians to grow tomatoes in greenhouses just to stop them having an 'unfair' advantage over the Dutch. Although not stated in those terms, this was an application of the theory of comparative advantage applied to polluting industries.

In the end, a typical EC compromise was reached. Countries could choose *either* to accept UES in the form of limit values *or* to establish EQS, provided that they could show the Commission that the quality standard was being met. Only the United Kingdom chose the latter. The subsequent directives for particular dangerous and persistent pollutants followed the same compromise of a choice of either approach, though within the EQS approach it is odd that separate directives should be issued for separate industries.[28]

Despite the strong disagreements over UES or EQS, it could be argued that neither side was really consistent. The United Kingdom, despite the type of statement mentioned above, had in many cases applied uniform emission standards to whole industries (in some cases only to new plants; but the EC also made a similar distinction). For example, the old Alkali Inspectorate typically applied its notion of best practicable means to the whole of an industry it supervised. Conversely, other EC policies set EQS without any fuss from the member states, for example the air quality standards for nitrogen dioxide, sulphur dioxide and particulates. It could also be argued that the dispute forced the United Kingdom to be much more rigorous about the EQS that were needed.

18.3.4 Damage and designated areas

One last issue in EC environmental policy that we shall examine is also linked to the economic analysis. The stress on the costs and benefits of abatement implies that it is not merely the dumping itself of something into water, air or earth that matters, but the harm done relative to the benefits from the activity. The harm done will depend on the potential use by people (directly or indirectly) of the medium.

It therefore makes sense to vary the desired standard of pollution according to its use. Water used for drinking could well require stricter standards on its nitrate concentration than water used only for boating. The EC has followed such a policy.

In some cases the use of the medium is obvious, in other cases less so. In the latter cases there may be some decentralisation so that countries are allowed to designate particular areas for the application of particular standards. For example, the standards for bathing water apply to stretches of water where bathing is traditionally practised by large numbers of people. Similarly member states can designate areas where water standards need to be set to protect shellfish.

Although the approach seems sensible, the application has not always been so. In particular, insofar as governments have discretion over the areas designated, they can use this as a way of avoiding the effective implementation of EC policies that they feel are unnecessary. This has indeed happened. In the case of standards for water supporting different sorts of freshwater fish, and for the shellfish case already mentioned, some states simply did not designate any waters at all. Similarly, those readers who are familiar with English seaside resorts might be interested to know that the UK government originally used its discretion over how to assess where 'large numbers' traditionally bathed to exclude both Blackpool and Brighton. At that time the UK government was worried about public expenditure, and any improvement in water quality off beaches would require new sewerage works. Later on though, in 1987, in response to threats from the Commission over infringement, as well as strongly adverse comments from the Royal Commission on Environmental Pollution (and the beginning of a changed attitude by the UK government to its poor reputation on environmental issues), many more beaches were added to the list.

A final example is a 1975 directive on the sulphur contents of gas/diesel oil, which is a medium-grade oil used for heating of commercial, light industrial and domestic buildings as well as for diesel fuel for vehicles. The directive is interesting partly because it is a mixture of UES and EQS, although it is also concerned with product harmonisation. It set two limits on the sulphur content of the oil, and the higher sulphur type could be used only in areas designated by member states. The aim was that the higher sulphur oil should only be used where air pollution from sulphur dioxide was not a problem. In the event the UK government decided that the whole of the United Kingdom was to be designated for the use of the higher sulphur content oil *except for roads*. The road network would therefore be designated for the lower sulphur oil – since diesel for vehicles was already low sulphur compared to other gas/diesel oil – and the United Kingdom minus its roadway designated for higher sulphur.

18.4 Conclusions

In some ways the EC policies on the environment can be counted as a success story. Despite the fact that it may not be clear that common policies are required at all in many cases, nevertheless a set of policies has emerged. Furthermore, despite some of the problems mentioned above and despite the failure to move quickly on some other policies because of the conflicting interests of the member states, as compared to other common policies (such as for transport or agriculture) progress has been fairly steady and not too divisive, acrimonious or blatantly inefficient.

In the past few years there has been a revival of public interest in the environment, even in those member states where interest waned in the decade after 1974. Those in favour of stronger environmental policies may well feel divided about EC actions. Those who live in those member states where Green pressures are strong will feel that they are held back, as compared to what their governments could achieve (or be pressured into achieving) without the requirement to carry other member countries with them. Conversely, environmentalists who live in those countries whose governments tend only to move on these issues when really compelled can be grateful both for the more stringent standards set by EC policies and for the possibility that the Commission will enforce compliance.[29]

At the time of writing, the main anxieties affecting all member states are over the ozone layer and the greenhouse effect of carbon dioxide emissions. Both are global problems; but at least the tradition that has grown up within the EC as a result of its own policies means that the EC is unlikely to block further action on these serious threats to the future of us all.

Notes

1. In its original meaning of a fog in which smoke particles were trapped, as contrasted with its more recent usage of a fog in which any harmful substances are trapped.
2. There had been a few (very few) economists who had already cast doubt on the viability and/or desirability of continued economic growth well before the simulation studies of the 1970s provided a more systematic account. Among them were K. Boulding (1966) and Mishan (1967).
3. Induction is not a proof in logic – the fact that the sun has risen until now does not in itself prove that it must do so tomorrow.
4. Except insofar as the 'exhaustion' is due to pollution in some form, e.g. the exhaustion of stratospheric ozone. If worries about the greenhouse effect from the build up of carbon dioxide become taken seriously enough, the conclusion of this paragraph may need alteration.
5. I remember being struck by reading statements made by Ivan Illich, a guru figure of the time, as he travelled by jet plane from conference to conference at each of which he preached the necessity of everybody resorting to bicycles, giving up other modern modes of transport.
6. References to the *Official Journals* for the Environmental Programme and various directives can be found in the Economic and Social Committee (EC Commission, 1987c) outline or Haigh (1987).
7. Including reports during 1977–80 by the House of Lords Select Committee on the European Communities. Note that the Programme was adopted just before the oil price rises and the ensuing recession. The feeling that action on pollution which might lead to job losses in polluting industries and/or require government spending on cleaning up the environment was undesirable at a time of recession and cuts in government spending may have been stronger in the United Kingdom than in some of the more environmentally conscious states which had stronger Green movements.
8. Some of these directives predate the proposal for an EC Environmental Programme.
9. Once it was accepted that environmental policy could be fitted in as an objective of the Community, Article 235 then gave legal power for binding actions.
10. As in other applications of this notion of 'unfair competition', or 'distortion of competition' as it is often called in EC documents, it contains implicit assumptions about the fixity of wages, prices and exchange rates. These assumptions are often not realised and their validity may or may not be dubious.
11. Attempts to avoid the problem by subsidising firms would not only run counter to commitments under the OECD agreement on the polluter pays principle (to be discussed later) but might also be considered as state aids which would be illegal under Article 92 of the Treaty of Rome.
12. Although some of those opposed to action on the environment have alleged that concern

about environmental issues is a middle-class luxury, which is not shared by the working class or the poorer members of society.

13. Formally, the arguments in the social welfare function are the individual welfares or utilities, even if the functional form (weighting of individual welfares) may reflect egalitarianism or some other values.

14. Theoretically, in formal treatments there would be no obstacle to putting concern for endangered species into somebody's utility function, even where the person does not know of the existence of some of the species. Conversely, environmentalists sometimes appeal to the possible future uses to man of endangered species of plants, which would be forgone if the species were destroyed before the discovery of their uses.

15. This is not meant as an assertion that pollution occurs only in market systems. The severe pollution problems of Eastern Europe proved that it does not.

16. An externality also occurs when marginal private benefit is not equal to marginal social benefit. Pollution is a negative externality, i.e. private cost is less than social cost. Some older microeconomic textbooks sometimes use the term 'social cost' to refer only to the *excess* cost imposed on others, which is a different usage from that followed here.

17. For further detailed discussion there is now a wide range of textbooks on the economics of pollution control, e.g. Baumol and Oates (1988).

18. See note 12.

19. Another way of putting the same point is to say that the MPC curve in Figure 18.1 is too high because the true opportunity cost of labour is below the wage rate. Hence the *MSC*, which should measure the cost of resources by the value of their alternative use, includes some components which make it lower than the *MPC*: see Chapter 4. Note also that if the industry is not perfectly competitive, the output may be too low for the usual reasons, despite the externality – it depends on the balance between the strength of the externality (output too high) and the imperfection (output too low).

20. A possible exception is in the case of pollutants which are cumulative (non-degradable) and highly toxic: see Pearce (1976).

21. This case is suitable for Figure 18.1, as once the leaded petrol has been put into the fuel tank, the motorist has no realistic options for varying the total emissions of lead for each gallon bought.

22. A more detailed discussion of this and other problems of using pollution taxes is in Marin (1979). Also see Kelman (1981) for a study of some other reasons for the hostility of non-economists to the idea of pollution taxes.

23. See note 22.

24. The examples in this and the following paragraphs are taken from EC environmental policies.

25. The debates over this directive (77/312) illustrates not only the monitoring function of the EC mentioned above, but also the sensitivity to thresholds. Part of the objection to the original proposal was that it would suggest that the standard was a threshold which if exceeded by anybody would mean they were in danger.

26. Whether pollution taxes or quantitative regulations are used to apportion the necessary abatement between emitters, allowance should be made for the different contribution of emissions in different places to the pollution measured as environmental quality, e.g. because of prevailing wind or tide patterns.

27. An excellent detailed account of the controversies is given in Guruswamy, Papps and Storey (1983). As pointed out in that article, although originally the term 'environmental quality objective' meant something else, the EQS is now sometimes referred to as 'quality objective'.

28. Mercury from the chloralkali industry. The directive for the titanium dioxide industry had already been foreshadowed in the First Environmental Action Programme, together with controls for the pulp and paper industries (the latter has never been enacted).

29. At the time of writing, a politically important example in the United Kingdom is the Commission's threat to prosecute over the failure to meet the standards for nitrates in water (other countries besides the United Kingdom have also been threatened). In the absence of these threats, especially given UK official scepticism over the level of the EQS actually laid down in the directive, there would have been a lack of urgency over an issue which is so adverse for the privatisation process.

19 | Factor mobility

D. G. Mayes

Although the freedom of mobility of labour and capital were objectives enshrined in the Treaty of Rome itself, only fairly limited progress had been made by the early 1980s in turning this into a reality. Most countries had capital controls of one form or another and labour faced considerable constraints on movement through lack of recognition of qualifications and other problems over establishment. The slow progress stemmed from two sources. In the case of capital, member states were worried that having free movements would lead to destabilising flows which would disturb the running of the domestic economy. The main fear was a capital outflow which would depreciate the currency, driving up the rate of inflation and requiring monetary and fiscal contraction to offset it. Labour controls, on the other hand, were more concerned with inflows. Employees in the domestic economy feared that an inflow from other countries would lose them their jobs – countries would export their unemployment. Much of this was dressed up as a need to have certain skills, standards and local knowledge for the protection of consumers. A closer examination reveals that only some of this was necessary. However, much of the fear stemmed from ignorance of what others' qualifications meant and overcoming this required a long and tedious process of determination and negotiation.

The 1985 White Paper on completing the internal market and the 1986 Single European Act (SEA) have signalled the determination to break through this complex of restrictions and move to a much more open market, well before the end of 1992 in the case of capital. This reflects the increasing ease with which funds can be moved round the world but also the realisation that free capital movements in a relatively integrated area, particularly one with a commitment to try to limit mutual exchange-rate fluctuations, are to quite an extent a benefit rather than a threat. In the case of labour there are also two main factors involved. The first is simply that with the exception of Greece, Portugal and Spain there are not great pressures for major destabilising labour flows; hence their removal will not have major consequences. In the professions and more skilled jobs it is proving possible to move forward much more rapidly by countries accepting mutual recognition of each others' qualifications rather than attempting the extremely difficult task of agreeing a common standard. However, it remains to be seen in practice how such recognition will work. Even in highly internationalised professions such as the academic one employment of foreigners tends to be more on the basis of work they have published than the sheer qualification alone.

19.1 The historical perspective

Most of the emphasis and interest in negotiations and assessments concerning integration tends to concentrate on products rather than inputs. However, freedom of movement of products within the EC does not necessarily entail the absence of protection or completely free competition if there are still constraints on inputs; this is recognised by the 1992 programme. In the case of imported produced inputs, intermediate goods and services, the subject has been extensively explored with the measurement of effective protection. The differences between nominal rates and effective rates can be quite striking. If the EC's Common External Tariff (CET) were 5 per cent on a particular product, while the CET on the main produced inputs (which form 50 per cent of the production costs) were zero, then the effective rate of protection would be double the nominal rate (all other influences such as differential transport costs for the finished and intermediate products being ignored). Effective protection is thus the rate of protection of the value-added in the production of the final product – see El-Agraa (1989b).

Similar considerations apply to the non-produced inputs of labour and capital in the productive process. If there are restraints on the mobility of labour, then differences in the price of labour can exist between countries in the same way that differences between product prices can exist when the mobility of products is restricted. Thus, for products with a high labour content, considerable competitive advantages could accrue to the country with the lower wage levels even if trade in the products were completely free. This separation of labour markets is not, of course, just an international phenomenon. It occurs widely within individual countries and hence a range of wages is to be expected.

It might be possible to get round some of the problems of immobility of labour if capital were mobile. Thus, instead of labour moving to take up opportunities elsewhere, firms could set up new plants and hence remove much of the differential in wages. Where capital mobility is also restricted differences can persist across the EC.

It is important to recall that if a firm in one country wishes to sell a product to a consumer in a second country there are three ways in which it can go about it (assuming there is just one step in the productive process). It can export the finished product; it can set up a manufacturing plant in the second country; or it can set up a manufacturing plant in a third country. The first of these thus involves trade flows, the second capital flows and the third both. The development of trade patterns will be crucially affected by the degree of factor mobility. *Ceteris paribus* the greater factor mobility, the smaller trade needs to be for any particular pattern of consumption.

Although the single-market programme will remove many of the remaining restrictions on factor movements, it is unlikely that capital, let alone labour, will be as mobile as it is within individual member countries. Factors reducing mobility include differences in taste and customs and variations in risk. The 1992 programme enables integration; it does not compel it. Thus in the same way that the idealised total specialisation of trade in economic theory is rarely realised we would not expect total perfection in capital markets and nothing like it in labour markets where many other factors lead to continuing segmentation. To quite some extent this is affected by the nature and treatment of the services in which the labour is embodied which have national diversity in the same way as there is diversity in the demand for goods.

If factors and goods can move between countries freely then, neglecting any transport or transfer costs, the whole trading area can be treated as a single market with a uniform reward right across the area to each factor, and uniform product prices. However, such a system is not only very far from a description of the reality of the EC both now and after 1992 but is also indeterminate and does not tell us the extent to which the good rather than the factors move – a typical problem of under-identification.[1] The imperfections of the real world, however, are actually an aid in this case as they increase the chance of being able to identify the determinants of the various movements.

Although there are some differences in the way in which labour can move from one country to another, particularly when countries have common land frontiers, the movement of labour usually involves the person concerned moving to and living in the new country. However, in some cases it may be possible to commute across the border and work in a foreign country while continuing to be resident in the home country. Movements can be long term or only short term and the worker may or may not bring his or her family along too. Nevertheless, there is fairly straightforward behaviour involved in most movement of labour.

Capital, on the other hand, can be moved in a variety of ways. While the basic distinction lies between direct investment, which involves the setting up or acquisition of a 'subsidiary' in a foreign country, and portfolio investment, involving the purchase of shares and bonds or the making of other forms of loan to a company in a foreign country, other, more complicated, arrangements exist which involve the effective transfer of capital between countries even if this is not recorded as such in the statistics on capital movements. 'Back to back' loans are a simple example whereby exchange control can be evaded. In such a case although the parent company can use only domestic currency while wanting to invest in foreign currency in the foreign country it can make the domestic funds available to a foreign borrower who is essentially in the same position – his funds are in his own currency while he wishes to use foreign currency. The exact matching process may be much more complicated than this simple one-to-one swap. (The problem is more complicated if the investment abroad is financed solely by a loan raised abroad. In such a case there is not really any international movement of capital.) In a single capital market a firm can raise debt or equity anywhere in the market by having access to all financial services on the same basis as all other borrowers. In the same way of course providers of capital would have equal opportunity to offer services. Simple removal of exchange controls also does not necessarily achieve this.

In the case of labour movement, individuals physically move from one country to another and then provide their labour services in the second country. Capital, on the other hand, in the sense usually considered, involves the transfer of claims through a financial transaction and not the transfer of capital goods themselves in the form of plant, machinery and vehicles. However, if such physical capital is moved abroad it will not be treated as an export of goods if ownership does not change. (It is easy to see that there can be some confusion in the statistical record of capital transactions, for if the foreign subsidiary merely purchased the capital equipment direct from a UK supplier that would be recorded as an export – plus capital transfer – as opposed to domestic investment plus capital transfer in the case just outlined above.)

Some of the distinctions between types of capital movement may not be very important from the point of view of actual output and trade patterns. Portfolio investment resulting in control of the foreign enterprise may be largely indistinguishable from direct investment, for example. However, the major distinction normally lies in the type of investor.[2] Direct investment is undertaken by firms on their own behalf (or by governments). Portfolio investment, on the other hand, is more usually undertaken by financial companies of one form or another. Much of this latter investment may therefore not seem particularly relevant to the problem in hand as it relates to a change in the ownership of existing assets rather than the direct financing of the creation of new physical assets used for the production of goods and services. However, this is mistaken from two points of view: direct investment may also be purely a change in ownership, this time involving control; and secondly we need to inquire what subsequent use the funds released to the seller were put to. The ability to exchange domestic debt for foreign equity can affect the range of options open to a firm. Moreover, even if the purpose of capital inflows into a country is to 'enable' the foreign government to run a deficit which cannot be financed fully by its private domestic sector, such lending may permit a higher level of investment in physical capital in that country than would otherwise be the case.

Clearly, the latter form of capital flow is of more than passing interest in a group of countries which are attempting some coordination of their economic actions. When exchange rates are relatively fixed between member countries through the snake or the European Monetary System (EMS), balance of payments surpluses/deficits on current account may open up rather wider than would otherwise be the case. Insofar as these imbalances are not met by official movements (or reserves) they must be eliminated by countervailing capital movements, encouraged in the main by differences in covered interest rates.[3] With freely floating exchange rates, the exchange rate can take rather more of the burden of adjustment between countries and capital flows rather less. Coordination of fiscal or monetary policies between countries will also affect the ways in which capital flows have to balance the remaining transactions.[4]

These considerations raise many issues which lie outside the scope of this chapter; but it must be borne in mind that capital transfers take place between countries for reasons that are not necessarily related to the essentially microeconomic decisions of the individual firm. To invert the argument, wider issues influence the values of the macroeconomic variables which affect firms' decisions over their overseas investment and these wider issues themselves form part of the way in which the members of the EC choose to conduct the handling of economic policy, both jointly and independently. Since direct investment abroad and borrowing of foreign funds by enterprises in foreign countries may both involve not just the same size capital inflow but also the same increase in capital formation within the country, it is not possible to set aside either long-term or short-term portfolio investment as being irrelevant to the purpose in hand.

As is clear from Table 19.1, portfolio investment from abroad has usually been much less important for the United Kingdom than has direct investment.[5] Until the lifting of exchange controls in 1979 the same could have been said for the outflow of capital as well. The issue is complicated by the activities of oil companies which are separately covered in the table. Fortunately, the more detailed statistics (available in *Business Monitor MA4*) also distinguish non-oil investment, and in the discussion which follows we shall also try to omit oil investment as the movements of capital are largely unaffected by any considerations relating to the EC. The other EC countries do not exhibit these distortions to the pattern of capital flows in a manner which confuses their changes in response to the formation and development of the EC to the same extent as those of the United Kingdom.

19.2 Capital movements

Exchange controls were eliminated in the United Kingdom in October 1979, but the reasons for that move had little to do with membership of the EC. At that stage the remaining Community countries all had restrictions on capital flows, although these varied in their degree of tightness. Since the start of the 1992 programme these restrictions have been steadily removed and several of the other main countries now have effective freedom of capital movements and with the exception of the new members freedom throughout the Community should be in place well before the end of 1992. In most cases there has been a distinction between the controls applied to residents and non-residents, with the restrictions being lighter in the latter case. However, interestingly enough, such restrictions as do apply to non-residents usually apply equally to all such non-residents, regardless of whether they are residents of another EC country or of a third country. There is thus no counterpart to the preference system applied to trade through differential tariffs as far as capital movements are concerned, nor, it seems, is there any intention of taking the opportunity of introducing discrimination against third countries by making this freedom of movement only in respect of fellow members. To a large extent this is a practical matter because it is difficult to control some transactions when others do not have to be vetted. However, 'reciprocity' is an argument which is being used in other parts of the 1992 programme in order to obtain concessions for the EC in third country markets.

Table 19.1 Inward and outward investments in the United Kingdom 1972–82 (£ million)[a]

	1972	1974	1976	1978	1980	1982	1984	1985	1986	1987
Overseas investment in UK										
Direct investment	408	854	799	1,261	2,541	1,137	2,021	1,944	2,103	4,226
Investment by oil companies	78	924	819	666	1,714	1,770	-2,267	-2,179	1,923	1,437
Portfolio investment	290	323	438	-139	1,499	225	1,419	7,121	8,447	10,805
Miscellaneous investment	-4	103	35	35	100	120	65	90	150	290
Total	772	2,204	2,091	1,823	5,854	3,252	1,238	11,334	12,623	16,758
UK private investment overseas										
Direct investment	-737	-1,575	-2,145	-2,710	-3,371	-2,123	-5,813	-8,836	-11,547	-15,323
Investment by oil companies and miscellaneous investment[b]	-61	-298	-214	-810	-1,495	-1,968	-190	183	22	-49
Portfolio investment	-604	725	90	-1,073	-3,150	-7,563	-9,866	-19,440	-25,243	6,463
Total	-1,402	-1,148	-2,269	-4,593	-8,016	-11,654	-15,869	-28,093	-36,768	-8,909

Notes

[a] Assets and liabilities are shown from the point of view of the United Kingdom: increases (decreases) in assets + (−), increases (decreases) in liabilities − (+), both net of disinvestment.

[b] After 1983 oil is included in direct investment.

Source: UK Balance of Payments.

In one sense, therefore, this simplifies the analysis as one potential source of substitution and encouragement of capital flows does not in the main exist. However, the restrictions which matter are not in the capital movements themselves but in how those funds can be used to purchase physical assets. Thus constraints or indeed incentives apply to inward investment, to mergers and acquisitions and to the operation of multinational companies. Thus freedom of capital movements is to some extent a myth if there are further constraints on how the funds can be used. Nevertheless, it is clear that restrictions are being reduced.

Of the other EC countries, West Germany has probably had the most liberal capital controls. The controls in the Netherlands were also mainly intended to facilitate the inflow and outflow of capital (which was largely free) in the short run. There were, for example, restrictions on deposits from non-residents during the period 1972–5 to ease the pressure from high capital inflows. The Netherlands has been a net capital exporter in most recent years.

The situation in Belgium and Luxemburg, which can for the most part be treated as a single unit, has been complicated by a two-tier exchange-rate system. The two markets comprise a 'free' capital market and a controlled market for current transactions. The net effect, however, is not restrictive and the two categories are normally referred to as the 'financial franc' and the 'convertible franc'. It is in France and Italy that the greatest controls have been found, although in the French case direct investment is one of the two main exceptions to the tight controls on the export of capital. As is to be expected, inflows by non-residents were less controlled than outflows by residents. However, inwards direct investment has been subject to control by the French government when the foreign control of the companies entailed has been thought unsuitable. In Italy also restrictions relate to flows other than direct investment although, since import and export financing are exempted, it has been possible to get round many of the regulations.

The general direction of changes in controls on capital movements over the period has, of course, been for reduction. Thus, as for trade flows, we would expect to observe a more rapid increase in direct investment abroad than in GDP itself. However, the distribution of that investment by country of investor is unlikely to be affected by any changes relative to the EC as such because liberalisation has almost entirely been non-discriminatory. The influence of the EC on capital flows is as a result likely to be in changes in discrimination in the traded goods and services market. Increased trade flows are likely to involve changes in capital flows – to set up distribution networks and establish local production as market penetration increases – although the direction of the change is still problematic as we cannot tell *a priori* the extent to which trade and direct investment might be substitutes rather than complements.

19.3 The determinants of direct investment

Investment flows between countries cannot really be treated in the same manner as investment within the economy because, although total investment can be explained through well-known relationships, the split between home and foreign expenditure, on an economy-wide basis, is not so clear. In the first place, magnitudes are sufficiently small for a limited number of decisions by individual companies to have a noticeable effect on the final outcome. Secondly, we are concerned in this case not just with what resources firms are prepared to put into capital for future production, but where they are going to site it. Most consideration therefore has been devoted to the problem at the level of the firm itself rather than through modelling of the components of the capital account of the balance of payments. Even within the confines of aggregate explanation there has been a tendency to avoid modelling direct investment flows directly, modelling them indirectly through the determination of the exchange rate as a sort of reduced-form approach.[6]

Such an approach may be appropriate for the explanation of portfolio investment, particularly since much short-term portfolio investment is usually described as speculative in nature, but it is much less useful for direct investment because of the degree of permanence embodied in the existence of physical capital held abroad. Such capital will tend to generate profits, which themselves form direct investment if they are not remitted to the investing country. Furthermore, such productive facilities have costs of closure and require a continuing stream of new investment to remain profitable, thus reflecting rather different considerations from those that might be thought appropriate to portfolio investment decisions and allocations.

Perhaps the easiest route into the problem is to consider what the position of a supplier of a good on a worldwide scale would be. Other things being equal, sales to any particular foreign market would be affected by market size. Divergences from this simple position would occur as costs between the supplier and its competitors varied and according to the tastes in the particular market. Thus in the case of the EC one would expect greater trade between partner countries, first because of the discriminatory tariff and second because the countries tend to be near neighbours. Elaborating this to consider the problem from the point of view of the country rather than the firm, shares in markets will tend to be affected by the economic size of the supplying country as well. Such an approach leads to the sort of gravity models of trade put forward by Linnemann (1966) and Bluet and Systermanns (1968) and discussed in the context of the EC by Aitken (1973) and Mayes (1978). There the effects of the EC on trade flows can be measured as the *ex post* discrepancy between observed patterns in the EC and patterns in the rest of the world (allowing for distortions from other trading areas). The analysis would be more effective if the nature of the barriers to trade and the size of the distortion through preferential tariffs could actually be inserted in the equations as well.

The pattern of direct investment might be revealed by the other side of this same relation, namely, the trade model can show what desired trade is in a non-discriminatory world. The extent of the barriers and the degree to which actual trade diverges from this 'desired' level might then give an indication of the market which could be reached by production inside the trade barriers of the foreign country, hence giving the demand for direct investment abroad to set up the facilities to achieve the desired output. The distance between countries, since it contributes to transport costs, would also lead to direct investment rather than trade.

By this simple model, direct investment abroad among the EC countries would decrease as their tariffs on mutual trade fell, but that from (and in) third countries would increase: it would become increasingly difficult for these third countries to compete through trade as the costs of their partner competitors were reduced by the size of the tariff cut (although producers might choose to offset all or part of the gain). From this simple point of view, direct investment 'creation' and 'diversion' as a result of the lowering of tariff barriers on mutual trade by the EC would be of opposite sign to that of the corresponding trade creation and trade diversion. However, as with the two trading concepts, direct investment creation and diversion would be static effects lasting for a transitional period only.[7] There is, moreover, a major distinction between investment and trade which would blur the relation which has just been outlined even if it were correctly identified. Previous direct investment has resulted in the accumulation of capital in the form of a foreign subsidiary or associated company. Although, like all domestic companies in the foreign country, it will face increased competition for its products from companies in the other EC countries as tariffs are removed, the subsidiary may continue to make profits and to invest. Although no transfer of funds takes place with the parent company, any increase in assets of this form will be classified as direct investment according to the definition we have outlined. The foreign subsidiary is thus operating like any other domestic firm and it will participate in market growth like the other firms, thus continuing the upward path of direct foreign investment.

The behaviour of multinational companies is a reflection of variations in costs of inputs in various locations as well as the structure of markets it wishes to serve. The pressure for the European 'single market' came just as strongly from European multi-nationals as it did from political sources. Wisse Dekker, then head of Philips and the European Round Table of major companies put forward a plan in January 1985 to achieve a single market in five years, i.e. by 1990, thus anticipating the White Paper. This globalisation of markets reflects the nature of technology and the pace of change. New products have to be exploited quickly round the world rather than by tackling individual country markets one at a time.

These technical changes are complex, as with just-in-time manufacturing and other improvements to reduce inventory costs and improve quality, links between companies have to be closer and quicker to execute. One facet of this is to cut down on the number of suppliers. This may actually lead to a concentration of production, disturbing some of the simpler trends of direct investment.

However, the simple model disguises a further facet of investment abroad. The development of foreign sales will normally follow an evolutionary pattern which starts with trading (unless the barriers are insurmountable) and is only followed by direct investment once the potential market looks worthwhile. Initial investment is more likely to be in distribution rather than manufacturing, as an agency is replaced by a more direct arrangement. Once the market is adequately covered then production in the local market may follow.

Since there are economies of scale in production in many industries the number of overseas subsidiaries may be strictly limited on a regional basis. Thus US and Japanese firms may wish to invest in only one EC country and supply the rest of the

EC from that base. Similarly, for the multinational company, it may be advantageous to split various parts of the manufacturing operation to take advantage of particular resources which are available in different countries – raw materials, cheap hydro-electricity, etc.

While there were technical, customs and other barriers between the member states there was an incentive to invest in several member states rather than concentrate in a single location. This pressure is weakened in the single market and there is some incentive to reorganise. However, it appears that in practice countries not only want to get inward investment for themselves but they show reluctance to treat investment in others on an equal basis by demanding local content rules – as in the case of French resistance to Nissan Bluebird cars built in the United Kingdom.

This multinational structure of production and pressures to expand it have consequences for trade. The existence of subsidiaries rather than purely domestic firms tends to create trade between various parts of the multinational company. In 1980 30 per cent of exports covered by the Department of Trade enquiry across a sample of over 7,000 enterprises went to related enterprises abroad.[8] While this trade would not be zero if there were no related enterprises one would expect it to be much smaller. Unfortunately the statistics do not refer to related imports, so we cannot build up a symmetric picture. It is possible to break down the percentage by the main industrial categories and by whether they are United States controlled, controlled by other foreign companies, or are UK companies as shown in Table 19.2. But the number of firms in the sample is very small in some cases, so the results should be treated with care. Nevertheless, two figures stand out from the table. The first shows that almost two-thirds of motor vehicle exports go to related enterprises and the second that US-controlled UK enterprises have over half their exports going to related enterprises. On any basis, it is clear that the level of related exports is considerable when direct investment has taken place. The consequences for the structure of trade are therefore complex.

Most empirical work on direct investment flows in the EC has concentrated on inflows from the United States, partly because of the quality of data available. This is unfortunate in the context of 1992 as a lot of attention has turned towards Japan, whose direct investment has increased dramatically in the second half of the 1980s. In the United Kingdom, for example, there are approximately 100 Japanese subsidiaries; two-thirds of these have been set up since 1985. Japan has replaced the United States as an investment 'threat', with a heavier political overtone, as the US economy has always been fairly open to return investments and acquisitions. Indeed the level of recent direct investment in the United States has been so great that concern is being expressed, while Japan is a much more difficult economy to enter either through export or investment. Traditionally US investment in Europe has had a strong element of takeover of existing enterprises. Japanese investment, on the other hand, tends to be greenfield. Arrangements with existing European firms tend to be joint ventures without Japanese majority control. This generates worries about technology transfer, the greenfield sites often being assembly operations of established products while the joint ventures are sometimes accused of being more effective in transferring

Table 19.2 Percentage of direct exports from the United Kingdom going to related enterprises in 1980[a]

Industry	US-controlled UK enterprises	Other foreign-controlled UK enterprises	UK associates of foreign enterprises	UK enterprises with overseas affiliates	Total[b]
Food, drink and tobacco	45	19	—	28	26 (112)
Chemical and allied industries	40	49	10	45	41 (166)
Metal manufacture and engineering	53	46	20	23	32 (555)
Shipbuilding and vehicles N.E.S.	55	27	38	21	21 (32)
Motor vehicles	77	31	—	56	64 (32)
Other manufacturing industries	27	40	18	19	20 (609)
Other activities	35	21	20	25	16 (568)
Total	52 (375)	38 (378)	19 (59)	28 (622)	31 (2074)

Notes
[a] The number of enterprises is indicated by the figures in brackets.
[b] Includes UK enterprises with no overseas affiliates.

Source: Business Monitor MA4, 1980.

technology to Japan. Thus inferences from the experience of US investment will not necessarily be very instructive for predicting investment from other third countries. While external investment may be a response to expectations that third countries may find it difficult to gain full benefit from the single market as an exporter it is the use of investment to restructure industry on a European basis by European companies themselves which is of primary concern. Here traditions have varied and with the exception of the United Kingdom contested takeovers are a far less common means of imposing change. Thus while the availability of data compel us to look at US investment for models we shall examine such evidence as there is about the movements in response to 1992 at the end of this section.

An exchange between Scaperlanda and Balough (1983) and Lunn (1983) illustrates the use of the simple model based on the size of the market overseas and the barriers to trade and capital flows. Taking just market variables they find (see Table 19.3) that for manufacturing industry there is a clear simultaneous relationship between the change in sales and direct foreign investment, which is better determined when a more flexible lag structure is introduced. Thus a flexible accelerator form seems to work adequately for direct foreign investment by the United States in the EC over the period 1953–77. Introducing the variables relating to the effects of changes in barriers to trade and investment is not so satisfactory overall. Indeed, as is clear from equation

Table 19.3 US direct investment in manufacturing industry in EC 1953–77

Equation	Constant	S_{-1}	$\triangle S$	$\triangle S_{-1}$	$\triangle S_{-2}$	T	C	BS_{-1}	R^2	DW
(1)	245	0.00757	0.103							
	(2.42)	(1.21)	(2.60)						0.736	2.51
(2)	297	0.0212	−0.025	0.232	−0.195				0.832	2.01
	(3.17)	(1.76)	(0.49)	(3.29)	(2.12)					
(3)	475	0.138	0.166			1020	441	−0.688	0.824	2.36
	(2.04)	(2.26)	(3.13)			(2.40)	(1.43)	(2.20)		

Annual data

S = sales of manufactured goods by US foreign affiliates in EC
= $3956.9 - 33.987\,\triangle GNP + 120.00\,PC$ (data 1957, 1959, 1961–77)
    (8.23)   (3.61)   (50.41) $R^2 = 0.997$

T = proxy variable for tariff discrimination
= 1 − (tariff rate on intra-EC trade + 1953 tariff rate)
C = dummy variable for US capital controls
BS = book value of existing direct investment by US in EC manufacturing industry
GNP = EC GNP
PC = private credit outstanding in EC
T = values are shown in parentheses

Source: Scaperlanda and Balough, 1983.

(3), the preferred specification, even allowing for the existing stock of US investment in the EC, does not provide as close a representation of the data.

The information presented is insufficient to form a clear view. Despite the use of three lags on sales in equation (2) we are only told about the value of the Durbin–Watson statistic. Secondly, although equation (2) and equation (3) can be compared separately with equation (1) they cannot be compared with each other. Presumably the introduction of the barrier variables disturbs the lag structure. However, it is more unfortunate that the lagged stock of investment variable is introduced only in equation (3) as the inclusion of that variable changes the meaning of the model. Nevertheless, it appears that the effects of tariff discrimination against the United States by the EC in the form of reduction of intra-EC trade tariffs compared to the initial external tariff are significant and of the expected sign. However, this tariff discrimination dummy captures a combination of the effect of the fall of the EC external tariff from its 1953 level and the relative movement of extra- and intra-EC tariffs. We thus cannot conclude on the basis of this evidence that the overall pattern of direct investment flows is affected by tariff discrimination in the EC.

We can approach the problem more crudely simply by examining the development of direct investment flows into and out of the EC over the period of UK accession as this is the most recent example of a change in relative discrimination involving one of the main EC countries. These flows are shown in aggregate in Table 19.4 from which it is immediately clear that the patterns of outward and inward flows for the United Kingdom are very different. In the period before accession to the EC, around two-thirds of direct investment in the United Kingdom came from the United States;

Table 19.4 Direct outward and inward investment in the United Kingdom 1968–80 (£ million)

	1969	1970	1971	1972	1973	1974	1975	1976	1978	1980	1982	1984	1985
Outward													
Total	549	546	676	737	1,621	1,576	1,171	2,145	2,740	3,492	2,122	5,929	8,994
United States	54	134	129	105	377	401	244	378	969	1,784	1,414	2,767	3,187
% share	9.8	24.5	19.1	14.2	23.3	25.4	20.8	17.6	35.4	51.1	66.4	46.7	35.4
EC[a]	115	88	281	256	519	367	166	497	579	482	−173	−303	2,553
% share	20.9	16.1	41.6	34.7	32.0	23.3	14.2	23.2	21.1	13.8	−8.2	−5.1	28.4
Belgium and Luxemburg	23	13	58	31	64	49	32	85	37	19	−5	109	295
Denmark	1	2	4	9	10	25	9	5	15	23	3	28	15
France	18	27	35	62	119	74	68	79	69	109	45	191	248
W. Germany	41	20	103	64	149	109	53	176	113	376	47	11	290
Ireland	20	14	21	12	46	49	24	40	169	93	34	80	245
Italy	9	8	14	24	27	26	−20	39	47	32	23	153	120
Netherlands	14	10	53	42	105	35	1	73	130	−168	−321	−876	1,340
Inward													
Total	319	354	445	405	727	854	615	799	1,292	2,576	1,137	−246	4,331
United States	204	223	283	266	387	410	310	550	807	1,678	372	1,505	2,323
% share	64.0	63.0	63.6	65.7	53.2	48.0	50.4	68.8	62.5	65.1	32.7		53.6
EC[a]	35	51	35	38	110	76	96	177	310	153	167	−2,073	1,313
% share	11.0	14.4	7.9	9.6	15.1	8.9	15.6	22.2	24.0	5.9	14.7		30.3
Belgium and Luxemburg	1	6	20	3	25	6	19	22	42	15	13	132	81
Denmark	0	0	0	0	3	2	7	19	15	13	28	34	7
France	4	1	1	17	27	25	29	85	155	48	21	319	226
W. Germany	13	15	5	5	17	34	11	34	69	34	58	−219	44
Ireland	0	0	0	1	5	−7	1	37	23	24	20	0	6
Italy	6	4	−11	8	17	6	1	11	−4	−16	6	32	73
Netherlands	13	25	21	6	17	11	28	−31	9	35	20	−2,379	856

Note
[a] Includes all eight countries shown throughout, although Denmark and Ireland were not members until 1973.

but over the same period UK investment in the United States varied between only one-tenth and one-quarter of total outward investment. However, outward investment itself was more than twice as large as inward investment and thus simple proportionate comparisons give little idea of bilateral balances. The United Kingdom has invested widely abroad in both the developed and the developing world whereas, not surprisingly, it is mainly the developed world which has invested in the United Kingdom. (As countries gain increasing maturity they tend to move through a number of phases of direct investment flows. Initially they have difficulty in absorbing investment, then the ability to absorb inward investment increases while outward investment is negligible. Eventually, although the ability to absorb inward investment increases, outward investment also increases as the range of production widens. Finally outward investment exceeds inward investment as overseas locations of production offer increasing advantages and sales networks are expanded. See Chapter 3 of El-Agraa, 1988a, for a fuller explanation.)

As is clear from Tables 19.4 and 19.5 the United Kingdom is the largest direct investor overseas in the EC and is the second largest in the world after the United States. Only the Netherlands among other EC countries has been a net direct capital exporter over the last ten years, although West Germany has had substantial net exports since 1975. There was a clear surge in inward investment in the EC in 1973 and 1974, and more strikingly so in West Germany over the longer period of 1971–4. It was only in those four years that investment in Germany was greater than that in the United Kingdom. Investment in France, however, shows a strikingly different pattern, with France attracting the highest investment of all the EC countries in 1975 and 1981 and the second highest after the United Kingdom for the period 1977–80. At the other end of the scale is the very low level of direct investment in Italy. Thus, despite any attractiveness which may have existed from surplus and cheaper labour in Italy, this factor advantage has been met by labour outflow rather than capital inflow. Italy similarly has a low level of direct investment abroad, although it is still sufficiently large to show net capital exports over the last four years.

There is little of uniform pattern of investment flows among the EC countries. However, what is clear in general is that outward direct investment has been rising considerably faster than in the United States, while inward investment has risen more slowly. Thus, while in 1981 and 1982 the United States was a net capital importer, the EC was a substantial exporter. Much of EC direct investment must therefore be directed outside the EC rather than to other EC countries, as is clearly the case for the United Kingdom.

As in the case of the United Kingdom, the United States is the most important single source of inward direct investment and destination of outward investment for West Germany, as can be seen in Table 19.6. However, taking the other EC countries together, they are the destination of a third of all West German direct investment abroad and provide a rather larger share of inward investment, in both cases more than the United States. However, the importance of Switzerland illustrates how geographic proximity and economic development (coupled with a common language) can affect investment patterns.

Table 19.5 Direct investment flows of EC countries 1970–82 (million ECU)

	1970	1971	1972	1973	1974	1975	1976	1978	1980	1982	1984	1986	1987
Outward													
W. Germany	−854	−999	−1,394	−1,359	−1,608	−2,621	−2,191	−2,839	−2,940	−2,842	−4,208	−9,627	−7,956
France	−362	−328	−519	−761	−654	−1,154	−1,526	−1,407	−2,257	−2,869	−2,721	−5,324	−7,066
Italy	−108	−385	−191	−208	−168	−280	−142	−131	423	−1,048	−2,537	−2,719	−2,018
Netherlands	−539	−478	−654	−737	−1,439	−1,331	−1,004	−1,373	−2,340	−2,479	−3,405	−4,463	−6,787
Belgium and Luxemburg	−153	−173	−132	−140	−312	−122	−262	−284	−45	78	−359	−1,660	−2,326
United Kingdom	−1,282	−1,578	−1,637	−3,200	−3,091	−2,095	−3,467	−4,120	−5,687	−4,514	−5,069	−16,681	−21,898
Ireland	0	0	0	0	0	0	0	0	0	0	0	0	0
Denmark	−29	−50	−132	−79	0	−64	−57	−26	−140	−71	–	–	–
EC (9)	−3,326	−3,990	−4,659	−6,484	−7,272	−6,666	−8,649	−10,180	−12,986	−13,745		−40,474	−48,050
Inward													
W. Germany	582	1,078	1,721	1,643	1,786	556	942	1,223	172	842	1,409	1,026	1,669
France	583	463	519	916	1,550	1,170	926	1,926	2,393	1,599	3,232	2,792	3,779
Italy	593	499	556	511	507	509	83	402	−540	650	1,641	−41	3,522
Netherlands	525	565	539	689	813	788	317	524	1,411	715	796	2,418	2,034
Belgium and Luxemburg	311	429	359	575	901	744	710	1,018	1,048	1,420	458	644	2,028
United Kingdom	852	1,052	908	1,457	1,668	1,099	1,296	1,694	4,327	1,916	4,517	6,225	8,484
Ireland	32	24	28	43	43	127	155	295	206	247	152	−44	77
Denmark	104	120	146	172	−90	215	−170	70	76	102	–	–	–
EC (9)	3,582	4,229	4,775	6,007	7,177	5,209	4,258	7,423	9,093	7,491		13,021	21,594
Net													
W. Germany	−272	79	326	284	177	−1,065	−1,250	−1,616	−2,768	−2,000	−2,799	−8,600	−6,287
France	221	135	0	155	896	16	−599	520	136	−1,270	511	−2,532	−3,287
Italy	485	114	365	303	339	230	−59	270	−117	−398	−896	−2,760	1,504
Netherlands	−14	87	−116	−48	−626	−543	−687	−849	−929	−1,764	−2,809	−2,045	−4,753
Belgium and Luxemburg	158	256	227	435	588	622	448	734	1,003	1,498	99	−1,016	−297
United Kingdom	−430	−526	−730	−1,743	−1,423	−996	−2,171	−2,155	−1,360	−2,598	−552	−10,456	−13,414
Ireland	32	24	28	43	43	127	155	295	206	247	152	−44	77
Denmark	75	70	15	93	0	152	−227	44	−65	31	–	–	–
EC (9)	256	238	115	−478	−5	−1,457	−4,391	−2,757	−3,894	−6,254		−27,452	−26,456

Note

[a] Increases in assets are shown as negative and increases in liabilities as positive.

Source: Eurostat, Balance of Payments.

Table 19.6 Direct investment share, W. Germany 1980 (per cent)

Outward		Inward	
United States	21	United States	35
Belgium and Luxemburg	10	Switzerland	15
France	9	Netherlands	13
Switzerland	8	United Kingdom	12
Brazil	7	France	6
Canada	7	Belgium and Luxemburg	6
Netherlands	6	Japan	3
Spain	5	Iran	2
United Kingdom	4	Sweden	2
Italy	3	Italy	1
Other	20	Other	5
Total	100	Total	100

Direct investment abroad, like domestic investment, is substantially affected by trade cycles. Thus the peak in 1973–4 coincides with the peak of a cycle and the sharp fall in 1975 with the consequence of the first oil crisis. Of course, 1980 is an exception, for although there was a sharp downturn in UK activity (preceding that of the world in general) it coincided with the removal of exchange controls, whose effect we have already discussed. Accession to the EC may thus have its effects obscured by the trade cycle, as total direct investment could have been expected to increase at the same time as the transition period, purely because of the trade cycle. Looking at proportions may help to reduce this confusion. The most striking facets are, first, that there is no proportionate surge in investment by the other EC countries in the United Kingdom immediately following accession. There is some increase in 1976–8, but it is by no means clear that this represents any particular change in behaviour as wide year-to-year fluctuations have been observed earlier.

Outward investment by the United Kingdom in the EC, on the other hand, shows a very considerable surge *before* accession, in 1971–2, a process which is ended by 1974. Since the benefits from investment are usually not immediate, some anticipatory investment might have been expected to take full advantage of membership when it occurred. There is thus some change which could be viewed as evidence of an initial investment effect of membership in this one respect. Since we are dealing with proportions, changes in one area necessarily entail relative changes elsewhere. In the case of outward investment, the short-run decline was taken by the residual (non-EC, non-US) category – the same category that absorbed much of the surge in UK investment in the United States after 1977.

It is also not realistic to treat the EC as a largely homogeneous unit from the point of view of direct investment. For example, direct investment flows between the United Kingdom and the Netherlands were far larger than relative economic size would suggest both before and after accession to the EC. This presumably reflects, among other things, the number of Anglo-Dutch multinational companies. However, the nature of the relation is not clear as the major sectors of disinvestment in 1977,

1979 and 1980 were different (the disaggregate tables – 3.3 and 4.3 in *Business Monitor MA4*, 1980 – are rather difficult to interpret, as the sum of the parts is very different from the total, despite the existence of 'other' categories in both manufacturing and non-manufacturing industry).

Other differences between EC countries can readily be observed. Although West Germany is economically larger than France and the United Kingdom, outward investment has followed that relation and inward investment has followed a different pattern, with French investment tending to be the larger. However, in both cases UK investment has been larger than the reverse flow. Irish investment in the United Kingdom, which was negligible before accession to the EC, has picked up substantially since. This is perhaps more difficult to explain than geographical nearness might imply, as the easy movement of funds was possible prior to accession. The total picture is thus rather confused, but it suggests that there has been no dramatic switch in the nature of direct investment in the United Kingdom as a result of its accession to the EC.

As noted earlier, between one-half and three-quarters of net investment abroad by the United Kingdom is composed of profits by overseas subsidiaries and associated companies which are not remitted to the United Kingdom. Net acquisition of overseas companies' share and loan capital is, partly by consequence, around one-sixth to one-third of the total, except for the two years 1979 and 1980 when it was about half. Unfortunately, these same figures are only available for EC countries for the period 1975–80, so we cannot make any contrast of the position 'before' and 'after' accession to the EC. Nevertheless, for that period, taking the EC as a whole, unremitted profits were:

Unremitted profits as % of total net outward investment by United Kingdom

	1975	1977	1979	1980	1982	1984	1985
In EC	74	55	112	40	40	[a]	122
In all countries	40	63	71	33	80	82	55

[a] Net outward investment negative.

These figures do not seem to reflect the fact that on average a particularly larger share of investment in the EC was coming from what might be described as new funds.

The scale of net inward investment has meant that over the period 1973 to 1979 there has been a steady increase in foreign ownership of UK firms, from 15 per cent to 20 per cent of net output in manufacturing. Not surprisingly, direct investment tends to be concentrated on larger firms, for reasons of information if for no other and this 20 per cent of output was produced by 2.5 per cent of the total number of establishments in the United Kingdom. These firms also have a below average labour intensity (14 per cent of total employment) and about average investment flow (21.5 per cent of the total). This, however, gives us little indication about the nature of changes in investment flows which could be expected although it does suggest that foreign-owned firms make an important contribution to productivity and investment for future growth, thus emphasising the role that freedom of capital movement can play in increasing EC competitiveness.

It seems likely, therefore, that if we were to apply the same form of analysis as Scaperlanda and Balough (1983) to other flows of direct investment among the EC countries which involve the United Kingdom, we would not find any strong effect from changes in relative trade restrictions. Thus, while there may be some short-run effects, it does not appear likely that there are major changes in capital movements in the EC which involve the United Kingdom as there have been in trade patterns, as shown in Mayes (1983), for example.

As mentioned earlier, figures on US direct investment are rather more detailed and hence we can get some idea of whether the United States changed either the extent of its investment in the EC relative to other areas, after the expansion of the EC in 1973, or whether it changed the pattern of it among the member countries.

Prior to accession, the United Kingdom had a much larger proportion of US direct investment (Table 19.6) than its economic size alone would suggest. In the first few years after accession, although investment was still large in comparative terms, it was sufficiently lower to allow the United Kingdom's share of the existing stock of US investment in the EC to fall by nearly 4 per cent. However, since 1977 the share of investment has been running ahead of the stock share again: hence the stock share has recovered half its previous loss. The shares of other EC countries in the total stock have also changed little. This is partly because of the scale of the change in the flow

Table 19.7 US direct investment in the EC[a]

	1973	1977	1980	1984	1986	1987
Total stock ($ million)	18,501	27,747	41,476	69,500	95,410	118,614
% of total stock in individual countries						
United Kingdom	35.7	31.9	33.9	41.2	37.4	38.0
Belgium and Luxemburg	8.1	9.4	8.6	7.2	6.2	6.6
Denmark	0.4	0.5	0.5	1.7	1.2	0.9
France	15.9	14.9	14.3	9.3	9.3	9.8
W. Germany	24.0	25.3	23.3	21.4	21.8	20.8
Ireland	1.7	3.4	3.9	4.2	4.6	4.7
Italy	7.6	7.1	8.0	6.6	7.3	7.2
Netherlands	6.5	7.4	7.5	8.4	12.2	12.0
US investment in the EC as % of total US direct investment abroad	39.2	38.3	51.7	0.0	65.8	46.1
US investment in United Kingdom as % of US investment in the EC	29.7	39.2	58.5	[b]	40.6	17.6

Notes
[a] EC (9).
[b] Total investment in EC $8 million, investment in United Kingdom $891 million.

Source: US Department of Commerce, Survey of Current Business, Department of Industry, 1982.

(investment) required to make any substantial change in the capital stock over a period as short as seven years, but also because of limited shift in the investment flows themselves. Changes are nothing like as striking as for trade flows. Again, it must be remembered that this evidence is very limited in itself, but it contributes to the overall picture.

The question at issue now is whether this same pattern of investment flows will be extended by the responses to the 1992 programme. The evidence is mixed. It is clear on the one hand that the Japanese have followed the US path of preferring to invest in the United Kingdom relative to other EC countries, although Japanese industrial leaders have shown themselves sensitive to the need to have good economic relations throughout the Community by a spread of investment.[9] The United Kingdom (Table 19.7) also appears to be investing more than its EC partners although much of this investment continues to be in the United States. By contrast, there have been rapid increases in investment by the other European countries mainly focussed on Europe. Nevertheless the prime target of reorganisation still seems to be merger and acquisition within each member state rather than across them.

19.4 Labour movements

Although in the abstract economists tend to talk about the two main factors, capital and labour, in one breath, the differences in their behaviour from a practical point of view in the EC are enormous. At a simple level, it was noticeable that the total direct investment statistics for the United Kingdom in any one year were substantially affected by the behaviour of a single company. (For flows between any particular pair of countries a single company can dominate the total effect.) Labour flows, on the other hand, are the result of the decisions of a large number of independent households (although actions by companies and communities can have a strong influence on these decisions). With some limited exceptions involving transient staff and actions in border areas, movement of labour simply involves a person shifting his residence from one country to another to take up a job in the second country. There is not the same range of possible variations as in the case of capital movements. There is also the great simplification that there is no equivalent problem of the relation between the financial flows (or retained earnings) and the physical capital stock. The number of foreign nationals employed will be the sum of the net inflows, without any revaluation problems and only a relatively limited difficulty for retirements (through age, naturalisation, etc.).

A major incentive to move is an income differential in real terms. However, it is not merely that the same job will be better paid in the second country; it may mean that the person moving will be able to get a 'better' job in the second country (in the sense of a different job with higher pay). There are severe empirical problems in establishing what relative real incomes are, not just in the simple sense of purchasing-power parities, but in trying to assess how much one can change one's tastes to adapt to the new country's customs and price patterns and what extra costs would be involved if, for example, the household had to be divided, and so on. This is difficult to measure, not just in precise terms for the outside observer, but even in rough terms for the individual involved. This sort of uncertainty for the individual is typical of the large range of barriers which impede the movement of labour in addition to the wide range of official barriers that inhibit movement. Ignorance of job opportunities abroad, living conditions, costs, ease of overcoming language difficulties, how to deal with regulations, etc., is reduced as more people move from one country to another and are able to exchange experiences. Firms can reduce the level of misinformation by recruiting directly in foreign countries.

Even if it were possible to sort out what the official barriers are and establish the relative real incomes, there would still be a multitude of factors which could not be quantified but could perhaps be given some implicit costs. These other factors involve differences in language, differences in customs, problems of transferring assets (both physical and financial), disruptions to family life, changing of schooling, loss of friends, etc. Of course, some of these factors could work in a favourable direction: it might be easier to find accommodation abroad and setting up a new household and finding new friends might be an attractive prospect. All this suggests that margins in labour rewards between countries may be considerable in practice, even if free movement of labour is theoretically permitted. It should thus be no surprise to find that many differences in labour rewards exist among the EC countries. However, it would also be a mistake to think that there are no barriers in practice to employment in other EC countries. In the first edition of this book, El-Agraa and Goodrich (1980) set out the barriers which existed for one particular group: accountants. Skills and methods of working vary among the EC countries. There is a natural reluctance to accept those with different qualifications and experience and considerable effort has gone into trying to make movement easier between countries.

Bourguignon *et al.* (1977) identify two other main determinants of the ease of movement in addition to the income differential (which they interpret in narrow terms of the monetary difference), namely, age and the attitude to risk. Their model, however, relates to the nature of the people who move: younger people, with less responsibility, who are willing to take risks. This is not very useful in the current context, where we wish to deal with the flows among the EC countries and the flows from non-members in aggregate. In our case, we need to consider variables which are of a similar aggregate nature: average per capita income, distance between countries, language differences, common land boundaries, etc. These factors, like those influencing capital movements, can be classified into three general groups which we could label 'push' factors, 'pull' factors and impediments. 'Push' factors relate to the tendency to emigrate – from poor living conditions, etc. – without regard to the destination; 'pull' factors correspondingly relate to the features attracting immigrants – availability of jobs, etc. – without regard to origin. The impediments are both general – applying to all migrants (both to exit, as in the East European countries, and to entry) – and specific: lifting of restrictions on members of other EC countries, for example.

It is clearly much more difficult to set out a model of labour flows when many of the restraints are not on a price basis (like a tariff), nor on a simple quantitative basis (like a quota). If, as appears to be the case for many non-member countries, there is excess supply of willing migrants at the prevailing income differentials and associated social difficulties of movement, we merely need to examine what determines demand (assuming, that is, that 'workers' cannot move without a work permit and that work permits are issued only in respect of specific jobs). In most cases this will be a combination of the wishes of firms as employers and governments as regulators. The British experience of regulation of inflows from the new Commonwealth is one example of the operation of the quantitative restrictions. However, movements of nationals of member states are not so readily determined. It may very well be that there is still excess supply in that flows take place when there is a job to go to. (Returning home, however, does not necessarily occur immediately a job is lost as some unemployment benefits will probably have accrued.) However, excluding the new members, Greece, Portugal and Spain, with the possible exception of Italy, it is not likely that this is the case. If the market for within-EC migrants were demand constrained, then easing the restrictions could be expected to lead to rapid inflows from other member countries. Otherwise, the response would be more muted. Indeed, if the barriers did not result in any effective restriction, their removal would be without consequence.

19.5 Labour flows in the EC

The official position in the EC is straightforward. Freedom of movement of labour was part of the framework of the Treaty of Rome itself. However, the original six EC member nations had to start from a position of considerable restrictions of labour movement, and it was not until 1968 that work permits were abolished and preferences for home country workers no longer permitted. This situation applies to the member nations who joined in 1973 but it does not yet apply to Greece, Portugal and Spain, for which there are transitional arrangements. However, merely permitting labour mobility does not in itself either facilitate or encourage it. It is readily possible to make mobility difficult through measures relating to taxes and benefits which make a period of previous residence or contribution necessary for benefit. Although some of these anomalies have now been tackled some hindrances still remain.

The actual path of labour migration is heavily affected by overall circumstances. If an economy is growing and able to maintain 'full employment' it is likely to attract more labour from abroad for two reasons: firstly, because there are more job opportunities; and secondly because there is less domestic opposition to immigration. In the period after the first oil crisis, when unemployment rose sharply and the EC economies moved into recession, there was much more resistance to the flow of labour between countries and an encouragement to reverse the flow. Although the position has improved somewhat in the second half of the 1980s, unemployment is still a major problem and is likely to remain so for some time to come. The fall in the numbers of young people which has already begun and will continue for some time yet will ease the overall problem. Indeed that and any sustained increase in the growth of the EC economies, whether or not aided by the single market, will tend to lead to labour shortages in particular skills.

There are several examples – Finland and Sweden and Australia and New Zealand, for instance – where regular ebbs and flows in labour migration have been observed. Ebbs and flows in the EC seem to be less common to all countries with the possible exception of Ireland, where emigration has been common both to the United Kingdom and to the United States. While, as might be expected, the number of foreign workers fell after 1974 with the economic cycle in West Germany and the Netherlands, it rose in Belgium and Denmark. (There was little change in Italy and Luxemburg; suitable statistics on the same basis were not available from the Statistical Office of the EC for the remaining countries.)

The clearest feature of the development of the permitted mobility of labour among the EC countries was that restrictions were lifted on workers from other member countries rather than non-members. Nevertheless, as is clear from Table 19.8, only Belgium and Luxemburg have had a higher proportion of their foreign workers coming from within the EC than from outside it. Looking at from the point of view of country of origin, Table 19.9 shows that in all cases except the Irish Republic only a very small percentage of the labour force have moved to other countries. (Those who have moved and changed their nationality will be excluded, but that is unlikely to make more than a marginal difference to the total.) With the exception of Denmark and Italy it appears that size and percentage of working population abroad have an inverse relation. Looking at the same figures from a different point of view, with the exception of Luxemburg it is the EC countries with the lowest incomes which have the highest outward mobility. The three newest members of the Community, Greece, Spain and Portugal alter the picture fairly considerably. They all had above average numbers of people working elsewhere in the EC even before they joined, particularly Portugal. It is thus to be expected that as restrictions are removed there will be some expansion in movement.

Turning to inward flows the picture is a little more complex. Luxemburg stands out with around a third of the working population coming from foreign countries. France, Germany and Belgium form a second group with little less than 10 per cent of their workforce from abroad; and the remaining countries have smaller proportions, down to negligible numbers in the case of Italy. Since Italy is a major exporter of labour to West Germany, France and Belgium, it is not surprising to find that it is a negligible importer since these flows do not represent an exchange of *special* skills, but a movement of workers with *some* skills towards countries with greater manufacturing employment opportunities.

As only principal flows are shown in Table 19.8, it is difficult to make any generalisations across the whole range of behaviour. Some special relationships are apparent which relate to previous history rather than the EC as a determinant of the pattern of flows: former colonies in the case of France and the United Kingdom and, to a lesser extent, in the case of Belgium and the Netherlands; and the relationship between the United Kingdom and the Irish Republic. The West German policy of

Table 19.8 Foreign employees by nationality (thousand)

	W. Germany			France		Netherlands			Belgium			Luxemburg			UK		
	1974	1981[a]	1985	1975	1985	1974	1981	1985	1974	1979	1985	1974	1979	1985	1975	1981	1986
Total member countries	718	558	498	305	590	51	76	76	130	181	141	31	32	52	323	313	398
of which:																	
Belgium	na	na	7	na	12	22	26	22	—	—	—	na	na	9	na	na	3
W. Germany	—	—	—	na	15	na	na	16	na	na	6	na	na	6	na	na	8
Italy	341	292	188	230	85	na	na	7	83	na	61	11	11	8	na	na	57
Ireland	na	na	1	na	1	na	na	1	na	na	1	na	na	0	232	228	268
Total non-member countries	1,613	1,364	1,048	1,595	583	66	149	92	77	141	46	17	18	3	468	447	423
of which:																	
Algeria	na	na	2	440	190	na	na	0	na	na	2	na	na	0	na	na	0
Morocco	na	na	14	130	132	9	34	25	na	na	17	na	na	0	na	na	4
Portugal	82	56	35	475	351	3	5	3	3	6	4	13	13	0	3	8	2
Spain	159	83	65	265	111	11	12	7	16	31	15	2	2	1	21	15	15
Tunisia	na	na	8	70	47	na	na	1	18	35	2	na	na	0	na	na	1
Turkey	618	576	499	25	23	22	49	36	11	21	10	na	na	0	4	6	7
Yugoslavia	473	340	283	na	31	na	na	5	na	na	2	1	1	1	na	na	4
Total	2,331	1,922	1,547	1,900	1,173	117	226	169	207	322	141	48	50	55	791	760	821
As % of employees	9.0	7.5	6.9	9.2	6.4	2.5	4.6	3.6	5.4	8.6	6.2	31.2	31.6	37.4	3.2	3.2	3.8

Note

[a] At the end of January 1973 there were 268,000 Greeks employed in West Germany, 15,000 Moroccans and 11,000 Tunisians. By the end of June 1980 the number of Greeks had fallen to 133,000 but no comparable figures for Moroccans and Tunisians are available.

Source: Eurostat, OECD, *Labour Force Statistics*, 1970–81; for note a, Owen-Smith, 1983, p. 160.

encouraging foreign workers is clearly shown with the large numbers coming from Turkey and Yugoslavia. What is perhaps surprising is that despite the recruitment ban on countries outside the EC in 1973 the shares of member and non-member countries in number of foreign nationals employed in West Germany was approximately the same in 1974 and in 1981. The most recent data, for 1986, show a fall in foreign labour in most countries. However, the switch is much larger for those from non-member states than from the other members.

At first glance it appears that labour, in proportionate terms, is rather less mobile than capital, particularly if one takes the United Kingdom as an example. The balance of labour and capital flows tends to be in opposite directions according to the development of the various economies. However, there are many specific factors overriding this general relation. The wealthier countries have attracted labour and invested overseas at the same time, thus helping to equilibrate the system from both directions. However, there is little evidence inside the EC that there are large labour movements purely as a result of the existence of the EC. Some movement between contiguous countries is to be expected, especially where they are small, and also movements from

Table 19.9 Foreign employees in the EC 1976 (thousand)

	Nationals working in other member states 1	Domestic working population 2	(1) as a percentage of (2) 3
Belgium	68	3,713	1.8
Denmark	7	2,293	0.2
W. Germany	137	24,556	0.5
France	114	20,836	0.5
Ireland	455	1,021	44.6
Italy	694	18,930	3.6
Luxemburg	6	148	4.1
Netherlands	83	4,542	1.8
United Kingdom	61	24,425	0.2
Total EC	1,625	100,568	1.6
Spain	447	12,535	3.5
Greece	239	3,230	7.4
Portugal	569	3,279	17.4
Turkey	587	14,710	4.0
Yugoslavia	458		
Algeria	447		
Morocco	183		
Tunisia	85		
Others	1,392		
Total non-EC	4,407		
Total	6,032		

Source: Emerson, 1979.

those countries with considerable differences in income, primarily Italy and the Irish Republic. However, the major movements have been the inflow of workers from outside the EC, primarily into West Germany and France. Thus, despite discrimination in favour of nationals of member countries, the relative benefits to employers (the ability to offer worse conditions, readier dismissal, lower benefits, etc.) and to employees (the size of the income gain and the improvement in living standards for their families) makes flows from the lower income countries more attractive to both parties.

It should be no surprise that international mobility is limited when one sees the extent of reluctance to respond to economic stimuli for movement within countries. The existence of sharply different regional unemployment levels and regional wage differentials reveals the reluctance. In the United Kingdom the system of public sector housing is thought to aid labour rigidity. Possession of a council house in one district does not give any entitlement to one elsewhere. However, even for private sector house owners the transaction costs of sale and purchase are very considerable and hence act as a substantial restriction on mobility. Many of the social restraints also apply: disruption of the education of children, loss of friends, for example. The differentials in rewards or other incentives to move, therefore, have to be very considerable to induce international movement once a person has a family and a home. Mobility in the United States, on the other hand, is much greater, showing that the level of EC mobility is a facet of European society, not a necessary part of economic behaviour. Indeed if movement had been most common it is unlikely that the member states would have been willing to permit a free flow under 1992.

19.6 Capital and labour movements combined

As was noted at the outset, factor movements cannot legitimately be examined without looking at the behaviour of the markets for internationally traded goods and services at the same time. Nor are the two factor markets independent. While the capital market has little of the characteristics of discrimination in favour of fellow members of the EC that form the basis of trading relationships between the countries, the decision over whether to invest abroad or at home is related to decisions over whether or not to export from the domestic market. Other things being equal, investment at home will generate more domestic employment, indeed it may encourage an inflow of labour from abroad. Investment abroad, on the other hand, will tend to encourage employment in that country and a transfer of labour abroad as well.

The final outcome will depend very much upon whether there is full employment. When there is a shortage of skilled employees, or indeed a shortage of unskilled employees, at wages consistent with successful international competition, investment abroad, especially where costs are lower, may be a preferable substitute to labour-saving investment at home.

Clearly, within the EC there is less incentive to invest abroad where product prices are not subject to tariffs and hence no big gains in competitiveness can be made.

Indeed, one would expect investment from non-members to increase because of the increased size of the common market. Thus capital flows could be expected to change in the opposite direction to trade flows, with both an investment-reducing equivalent of trade creation and an investment-increasing switch from third countries as an equivalent to trade diversion. Controls on labour movements have been removed in a manner which favours inflows from EC members rather than non-members.

Running across these considerations are two other factors. Labour can be expected to move from where rewards are lower to where they are substantially higher (to cover the costs of moving), as is evidenced by the outflow from Italy. Secondly, capital investment could be expected to move to areas where labour costs are much lower, but this movement has been much less marked. Instead, capital movements have tended to follow sales opportunities and other locational advantages rather than just labour cost. Insofar as labour and capital movements do not take place, factor price differentials will continue to persist, assuming they are not eliminated by trade flows, and the allocation of resources among the EC countries, and indeed between them and non-members, will be inefficient.

Until the downturn in the European economy, this inefficiency would be expected to take the form of insufficiently capital-intensive investment, with a labour inflow being used to avoid restructuring. This would shift some more labour-intensive processes abroad to more labour-intensive EC members, or even outside the EC. Limits on labour mobility decrease this tendency, but with high levels of unemployment currently, and for much of the foreseeable future in the EC, it seems unlikely that any further encouragement to move will take place. Indeed, the pressures are the other way round. There is a danger that the new protectionism will apply not just to goods but to factor movements as well. Insofar as the EC continues its path towards increasing ease of factor mobility as set out in the 1992 programme, it may be able to maintain a competitive advantage over others who resort to this form of protection. It is not surprising therefore that third countries have been keen to operate inside the EC and are using just that freedom of capital movement to achieve it.

Notes

1. See Mayes (1988).
2. Indeed, it is the concept of control which distinguishes direct from portfolio investment. The technical definition adopted by the IMF (*Balance of Payments Manual*, fourth edition, 1977) is 'Direct Investment refers to investment that adds to, deducts from or acquires a lasting interest in an enterprise operating in an economy other than that of the investor, the investor's purpose being to have an effective voice in the management of the enterprise'. Clearly this distinction can be made only by asking companies themselves about their overseas investment – by the Department of Trade, the Bank of England and the British Insurance Association, in the case of the United Kingdom.
3. 'Covered' in the sense that the forward exchange rate premium or discount is taken into account in the computation of the difference in interest rates between countries.
4. As was pointed out by Padoa-Schioppa *et al.*, 1987, it is not possible to run a stable system with fixed exchange rates, free capital movements, free trade and independent fiscal policies.

One or other of these must be constrained (the last in the case of an integrated single market).

5. In each case the transactions shown are the *net* transactions of the particular category of investor. Thus outflows are net investments by UK firms abroad or by UK residents in foreign securities and inflows are net investments by foreign companies in UK companies, etc. A positive value for net portfolio investment overseas from the United Kingdom thus means that the portfolio of foreign assets has been run down (net disinvestment).

6. See Cuthbertson *et al.*, 1980, for a discussion of this work.

7. The analogy between trade diversion and creation and investment diversion and creation should not be pushed too far as the trade concepts are welfare changes, not just changes in trade patterns.

8. *Business Monitor MA4* (1980), Table 6.3 (oil and diamond companies are excluded). The equivalent figure in the 1976 survey was almost identical.

9. Several examples are shown in Dell and Mayes (1989).

20 External trade policy

D. McAleese[1]

The external trade policy of the EC impinges on fully one-fifth of world trade. Yet the Common Commercial Policy (CCP) remains a comparatively neglected field. It is notably under-researched relative to, say, US trade policy, even though the Community's level of trade activity exceeds that of the United States.

A number of reasons help to explain the limited research on the CCP. First, there is the lack of a tradition of thinking about economic issues at the EC level. Only six of the twelve member states can date their membership of the Community prior to 1973. To many European economists the implications of this or that aspect of the CCP for their own country are as important as the issue of what EC policy ought to be, taking the interests of the Community as a whole into account. Second, the CCP is inherently complex. It is multi-faceted and multi-dimensional, the outcome of numerous compromises at EC Council and Commission level. Some have gone so far as to conclude that the EC has not yet managed to develop a coherent policy in its external economic relations (Yannopoulos, 1985, p. 451). The Community's approach to trade matters can appear piecemeal and its untidy collection of regional and national trade agreements makes generalisation difficult. Third, documentation on trade policy issues is comparatively sparse. There is, for example, nothing published by the Commission or the European Parliament which describes the EC's approach to trade matters in comparable detail to the discussion of the US position in the Congressional Budget Office's *The GATT Negotiations and US Trade Policy* (1987). The Commission, of course, has to be cautious in its published statements on commercial policy. National susceptibilities must be taken into account. There is no EC government as such and consequently agreement on a programme of action on a CCP has to be achieved by a slow and painful process of consensus between national governments.

> A central theme of any study of EC external policy is inevitably the enormous difficulty of reconciling the different national and Community interests which assault the policy-maker in Brussels. It is hardly surprising that day-to-day understandings, the growth of habits of work, and sometimes sheer improvisation characterise much of EC activity in this area. (Farrands, 1983)

The above three factors may help to explain the sharp difference in perspective between the Commission and the outside world in their interpretation of the CCP. The EC has received a bad press and, more often than not, is cast in the role of an unreconstructed protectionist. This perception is reinforced by a tendency to see the EC from the better-documented perspective of the United States and Japan. Those charged with the task of framing the Community's policy, however, see things differently. They point to the hard struggle to win agreement for trade liberalisation measures affecting the developing countries (LDCs) and to the rapid increase in import penetration by the LDCs in the European market. Tremendous restructuring has taken place in the EC's steel, textile, clothing, footwear and shipbuilding industries. Serious efforts have been made, albeit not yet enough, to tackle the problem of the surpluses caused by the Common Agricultural Policy (CAP). The Community's official position on the on going Uruguay Round of GATT negotiations has, in its own estimation, been strongly positive.

In considering the EC's approach to external trade, the background and preoccupations of the Community policy maker must be kept in mind. Economic and political ties with former colonies go far to explaining the complex series of preferential arrangements with LDCs. The comparative newness of the EC is another factor. Unlike nation states, the Community is still in the process of defining its identity and forging solidarity among its members. The regional impact of trade policies assumes great importance and the historical tendency has been to hold the centre responsible for regional failings (Weiss, 1988). For example, from a US perspective, an employee who moves to San Francisco after losing his job in Dallas enters the national statistics as a happy example of internal mobility. An Italian citizen who moves to Munich after losing his job in Milan is seen in a different light. To the Italian government, emigration has overtones of domestic policy failure and, to the German government, immigrants are seen as a source of potential social disruption. EC countries may appreciate the economic advantages of factor mobility but this is tempered by concern over the regional distribution of these advantages and the need for economic and social cohesion. The point is that the existence of these strong regional and national loyalties, which are given expression through the Council, constitute a restraining force on trade policy. The constraints are further strengthened by the existence of persistently high unemployment in many parts of the EC. Efforts to liberalise the CCP have involved hard bargaining within the EC as well as between it and non-member states.

The background to EC trade policy, therefore, is different in many respects from that of the trade policy of other major trading groups. For this reason alone, it constitutes a worthwhile subject of study. The evolving nature of the EC itself makes such a study even more challenging and worthwhile. In recent years, the EC has undergone far reaching changes, each of which has had and will continue to have significant implications for the CCP.

This chapter is divided into five sections. The first presents an overview of the principles of the CCP. The second describes the pattern of trade between the EC and the outside world. The third considers EC trade policy with developed countries. The fourth is an analysis of trade policy issues with LDCs and state-trading countries. The concluding section considers the future development of the CCP in the context of the Mediterranean enlargement, the effects of the Single European Act (SEA), the new agreement with COMECON and the Uruguay Round.

20.1 Principles of the CCP

The EC is an association of states with a particular legal character. Its members are united more closely than in the traditional form of international cooperation between states. The EC is regarded as a community in international law, not as a nation, although it possesses many features of 'nationality'. Many EC laws and regulations are enforceable in member states without requiring ratification by national parliaments. These transferred sovereign powers include foreign trade and the right to conclude trade agreements with different countries (Pelkmans, 1984; and Chapters 1 and 2).

A common trade policy is *necessary* for the EC because in its absence internal trade will be impeded and the purpose of a common market frustrated. Much of the early discussion of this matter focused on the criteria for determining the common external tariff (CET) and on the consequences of this for individual member states. Nowadays attention has shifted to non-tariff trade barriers (NTBs). A common trade policy, moreover, is *desirable* in so far as it strengthens the bargaining power of the Community. Small member states in particular benefit from this: on their own they would be vulnerable to US and Japanese pressure.

The key provisions of the CCP are contained in Articles 110–16 inclusive. Article 110 contains the well-known aspiration:

> By establishing a customs union between themselves member states aim to contribute, in the common interest, to the harmonious development of world trade, the progressive abolition of restrictions on international trade and the lowering of customs barriers.

The really key article, the cornerstone of the CCP, is Article 113. It sets out the important rule that:

> the CCP shall be based on uniform principles, particularly in regard to changes in tariff rates, the conclusion of tariff and trade agreements, the achievement of uniformity in measures towards the liberalisation of export policy and in measures to protect trade such as those to be taken in the case of dumping or subsidies.

Article 113 is one of the few articles which have always (even prior to the adoption of the SEA) functioned on the basis of majority voting in the Council. This gives the Commission a strong political role since the Council can decide only on the basis of a Commission proposal and can overturn a Commission proposal only by unanimity – something which has become even more difficult to attain in the EC of twelve than was the case in the EC of six. Subject to the Council's approval, the Commission is empowered to conduct negotiations in consultation with a special committee appointed by the Council for this purpose and within the framework of such directives as the Council may issue to it. Trade agreements concluded by the Council are applicable to the entire EC. In the case of international commodity agreements, a common approach is developed prior to the settlement of individual country quotas. The EC has observer status at both FAO and the United Nations and negotiates on behalf of member states in GATT.

In order to avoid deflection of trade, Article 115 allows member states which have restrictions on direct imports from outside the Community to obtain Commission approval for restriction of imports of such products via other member states. It is the Commission's prerogative to act in such circumstances, not the individual member state's. With the advent of 1992, tighter criteria for Commission authorisation of Article 115 derogations have been put in place.[2]

The principles of the CCP are put into effect by means of certain trade policy *instruments*. One instrument has already been mentioned, namely the conclusion of regional trade and cooperation agreements. The EC has signed such agreements with EFTA, COMECON, ASEAN, ACP (see Chapter 20), the Gulf states and Mediterranean countries. Another instrument is the CET which applies to all imports entering the Community. A third instrument is the special tariff preferences provided to LDCs under the Generalised System of Preferences (GSP). Finally, NTBs are applied.

The EC subscribes to various codes of conduct in relation to subsidies, dumping and unfair trade practices, customs valuation and government procurement as laid down in successive GATT negotiations. Following the Tokyo Round, for example, the EC adopted the new Anti-Dumping Code, operational in Community law from 1980 onwards. Under this code, a protective response is permitted only when the dumping threatens to cause, or actually causes, 'material injury' to an industry. Normally damage suffered by a national segment of an EC industry will not provide sufficient grounds to launch an action. During the period 1980–6 there were 280 cases by and 214 against the Community (Finger and Olechowski, 1987). Anti-dumping actions are taken by the Commission: a member state may take action only on an emergency basis and that action can be revoked by the Commission.[3]

Three broad conclusions can be drawn about the principles of the CCP. First, the intention of the founding fathers of the EC was clearly towards a liberal trading order. Questions may be raised as to whether 'harmonious' trade relations imply some preconceived notions of bilateral balance but there is no ambiguity in Article 110's reference to 'the progressive abolition of restrictions on international trade'. Second, there is, however, some ambiguity as to what precise national powers have been transferred to the EC in relation to trade. Article 113(1) appears inconclusive in its insistence on uniform principles (references to specific forms of trade policy are clearly not intended to be exhaustive). The European Court of Justice has decided that wide interpretation of Article 113 is justified in order to allow the EC to control external trade (Steenbergen, 1980). Despite this, differences in external trade regimes in the form of NTBs continue to exist as between member states, some without the approval of the Commission. Third, even when, such as in relation to the Multi-Fibre

Agreements, individual member state quotas have been allocated by the Commission, this necessarily involves some disruption of the internal Community market.

With the passage of time, two trends are discernible. One concerns the continuing efforts by the Commission to centralise power over external relations policy in Brussels and, by so doing, to make the conduct of the CCP easier to adjust, quicker to implement and more efficient overall. The New Community Instrument adopted by the Council in 1984 was a case in point. It gave the Commission greater power to respond to prejudicial trade practices of non-member countries, including injury suffered by EC producers in third markets, and indicated a range of counter-measures which could be taken at the Commission's initiative (Pearce and Sutton, 1985). The Commission is fighting hard to restrict member states' powers with respect to safeguard clauses, voluntary export restraints (VERs) and similar measures.

Another important development has been the increasing interest being taken by the European Parliament in external relations. This interest was given a major fillip by the amendment of Article 238 in the SEA to the effect that majority approval by Parliament's 518 members is required for preferential trade and cooperation agreements proposed by the Community.[4] Parliament has not been shy about using its new powers. In 1988 it held up amendments to association agreements with both Israel and Turkey on grounds of dissatisfaction with the former's policies towards the West Bank and Gaza and the latter's progress in restoring civil rights.

20.2 EC trade patterns

The EC, comprising twelve industrialised countries and incorporating 360 million people within its borders, constitutes the largest trading bloc in the world. Excluding intra-EC trade, exports of the Community accounted for 20 per cent of world exports in 1987. The corresponding US and Japanese shares are 13 per cent and 12 per cent respectively (Table 20.1). Extra-Community exports were worth almost US$400 billion in 1987. Trade among member states was even greater, worth over US$550 billion in that year.

Over 60 per cent of extra-EC trade is directed towards developed (advanced) countries. Within the developed countries group, EFTA is the largest trading partner, followed by the United States and Japan (Table 20.2). If intra-EC trade is added to extra-EC trade with developed countries, we find that 84 per cent of the Community's trade is with industrialised countries. This explains why the EC has to give priority to the efficient conduct of intra-EC trade and to maintaining trade relations with the developed countries.

LDCs account for 13 per cent of total EC trade or about 30 per cent of extra-EC trade. The Middle East, Africa and Asia are of equal importance in terms of trade value, each absorbing over US$30 billion of EC products in 1987. Trade with the Lomé countries is a small fraction (only 2 per cent) of total EC trade.

Commercial links with the state-trading countries (which comprise the USSR, China and Eastern Europe) are not well developed, despite the geographical proximity

Table 20.1 The EC in world trade 1987

	US$ billion	%
Value of exports from		
EC (12)[a]	391	20.2
United States	244	12.6
Japan	229	11.9
Other developed countries	319	16.5
Developing countries	490	25.4
State-trading areas	258	13.3
Total[a]	1,931	100.0

Note
[a] Excludes intra-Community trade, estimated $559 million.

Source: GATT *International Trade 87–88*, Geneva, 1988.

Table 20.2 EC trade by area 1987

	Imports		Exports	
	$ billion	%	$ billion	%
World	950	100.0	951	100.0
Intra-EC (EC (12))	553	58.2	559	58.8
Extra-EC	397	41.8	392	41.2
Developed countries	232	24.4	241	25.3
of which:				
EFTA	94	9.9	104	10.9
United States	66	6.9	83	8.7
Japan	42	4.4	16	1.7
Other	30	3.2	38	4.0
Developing countries	126	13.3	117	12.3
State-trading areas	34	3.6	29	3.0
of which:				
China	6	0.6	6	0.6
Unspecified	5	0.5	5	0.5

Source: GATT *International Trade 87–88*, Geneva, 1988.

with the EC of many countries in this group. The area absorbed only 3 per cent of EC exports and accounted for just over 3 per cent of Community imports in 1987.

The commodity composition of EC trade changes markedly depending on the geographical area (Table 20.3). Thus, about three-quarters of the Community's trade with developed countries takes the form of trade in manufactured goods. Much of this trade consists of intra-industry trade, i.e. two-way exchange of products falling into the same industrial category. A contrasting pattern is evident in trade with LDCs. Over 80 per cent of EC exports to LDCs consists of manufactured goods but imports from LDCs are heavily concentrated in fuels (33 per cent) and food and other primary products (29 per cent). The precise share in each commodity group is likely to change from period to period – the influence of the fall in oil prices is evident in the fall in the

Table 20.3 Commodity composition of EC trade with major trading groups[a]

	Food and primary products (SITC, 0, 1, 2, 4)		Fuels (SITC 3)		Manufactured goods (SITC 5–8)	
% shares	Exports	Imports	Exports	Imports	Exports	Imports
Developed countries						
1973	9.6	36.1	3.3	1.8	87.1	62.1
1980	8.5	23.2	6.3	7.9	85.2	68.9
1985	8.7	17.5	7.4	10.1	83.9	72.4
1987	15.9	18.6	4.6	5.4	78.0	74.7
Developing countries						
1973	11.6	35.8	1.3	45.6	87.1	18.6
1980	12.2	20.0	3.4	61.8	84.5	18.2
1985	13.1	26.3	2.3	51.9	84.6	20.2
1987	13.1	28.8	1.5	33.2	82.7	37.3
State-trading areas						
1973	13.3	40.7	1.0	17.3	85.7	42.0
1980	16.6	17.7	2.0	44.9	81.4	37.4
1985	13.8	15.9	1.5	51.8	84.7	32.3
1987	11.6	21.0	0.6	37.1	85.9	40.8

Note
[a] Figures for 1987 do not add to 100 owing to rounding errors and unclassified items. Trade with developed countries includes intra-EC trade.

Source: Computed from Eurostat, *External Trade Statistical Yearbook* and GATT *International Trade 87–88*. Figures for 1987 refer to EC (12); all others to EC (10). The inclusion of the two new member states makes only a marginal difference to the data.

percentage share of fuel imports from 52 per cent in 1985 to 33 per cent in 1987. Manufactured goods form an increasingly important component of exports by the LDCs to the EC. Their share reached 37 per cent in 1987. Most of EC–LDCs trade in manufactures tends to be of the inter-industry type, with each side specialising in different industry groups. As we shall see later, this type of trade has created adjustment problems in the labour-intensive industries of the EC. With regard to manufactured goods, it is interesting to note that while the share of manufactured goods in EC exports has for many years been around 80 per cent, the share of manufactures in EC imports has been increasing over time – from 62 per cent to 75 per cent in the case of developed countries, and from 19 per cent to 37 per cent in the case of the LDCs.

A sustained rise has been evident over time in the importance of intra-EC trade (Table 20.4). This is the most dynamic element in total Community trade, having increased from 48 per cent in 1963 to 59 per cent in 1987. Trends in the composition of extra-EC trade are much distorted by the influence of oil prices. Thus the fall in oil prices in the 1980s was a major factor in explaining the decline in the developing areas' share of EC exports from 18 per cent to 12 per cent between 1980 and 1987.

Unlike the United States and Japan, the EC has no problem of imbalance in

Table 20.4 EC exports to main trading areas[a]

	Total value of exports $ billion	% distribution by area								
		Developed economies areas of which					Developing areas of which			State-trading areas
		Total	Intra-EC	EFTA (6)	North America	Japan	Total	Asia	Middle East	
1963	53.7	77.1	48.2	13.3	9.2	1.0	18.8	4.3	3.2	3.4
1973	218.9	81.6	55.9	11.3	8.7	1.32	13.1	2.4	2.7	1.1
1980	687.8	77.4	55.8	11.0	6.3	1.0	18.0	2.7	5.4	3.9
1987	950.0	84.1	58.8	10.9	9.8	1.6	12.3	3.5	3.2	3.0

Note
[a] Data refer to EC (12) in all years.

Source: Eurostat, *External Trade Statistical Yearbook* and GATT *International Trade 87–88*.

merchandise trade and balance of payments. Total merchandise exports in 1987 of US$951 billion were about equal to total imports. Extra-EC exports of $392 billion were about the same as extra-EC imports of US$397 billion. Exports and imports of each of the three major trading areas were also roughly equal. Looked at this way, one might have expected the EC to have enjoyed harmonious trade relationships with these countries. Certainly its overall trade balance in 1987 contrasts glaringly with the United States' trade deficit of US$180 billion and Japan's trade surplus of US$83 billion. Within this aggregate balance, however, there are pronounced imbalances at an individual country level and also within individual commodity categories and it is here that problems arise.

External trade has increased faster than Community GNP for most of the period since the 1960s and even during the era of slower growth in the 1980s trade has grown in tandem with GNP. The EC's trade partners have all benefited from this growth, some more than others. Import penetration, as measured by the ratio of imports to GNP, was 26 per cent in 1987, about the same level as a decade earlier but significantly higher than the 18 per cent level in 1963. This growth in trade has taken place against a background of a series of GATT rounds of tariff cuts, to which the EC has subscribed. The Community's average tariff has now fallen to 4.7 per cent, following a reduction of 29 per cent in its tariff levels in accordance with the Tokyo Round (Table 20.5). In terms of nominal protection, the EC has marginally higher rates than Japan and the United States, but there is a clear tendency to convergence. The main problem areas of EC trade policy concern NTBs which have become the major focus of attention in recent years.

One factor behind the use of NTBs has been penetration of the EC market by standardised labour-intensive LDC products. Another has been the increased competition for sales in the world agricultural market. A third factor relates to the Community's weakening position in high-technology industries. The share of the EC in OECD exports of these products has declined steeply during the past 25 years, from 35 per cent to 25 per cent (Table 20.6). This perceived deterioration in the EC's

Table 20.5 Tokyo Round tariff cuts by stage of processing for the EC, United States and Japan (per cent)

Country and period	Raw materials	Semi-manufactures	Finished manufactures	All industrial products
EC				
Rates before Tokyo	0.2	5.1	9.7	6.6
Rates after Tokyo	0.2	4.2	6.9	4.7
% cut	15.0	27.0	29.0	29.0
United States				
Rates before Tokyo	0.9	4.5	8.0	6.5
Rates after Tokyo	0.2	3.0	5.7	4.4
% cut	77.0	33.0	29.0	31.0
Japan				
Rates before Tokyo	1.5	6.6	12.5	5.5
Rates after Tokyo	0.5	4.6	6.0	2.8
% cut	67.0	30.0	52.0	49.0

Source: GATT figures as presented in Congressional Budget Office, 1987.

Table 20.6 Export market shares in high-technology manufactures

	Share in total exports of all OECD countries (including intra-EC trade)			
	1963	1973	1980	1985
High technology[a]				
EC (10)	35	28	27	25
United States	24	17	19	19
Japan	6	12	14	20
All industries				
EC (10)	32	27	27	26
United States	21	15	16	16
Japan	6	11	12	17

Note

[a] High technology = electrical equipment and electronics, office equipment, chemicals and pharmaceuticals.

Source: *European Economy*, no. 34, November 1987.

competitive position has caused widespread concern as being indicative of a weakness in strategic industries and long-run growth potential. It has led to a tough stance being taken towards imports of R&D goods, a readiness to subsidise where necessary and, above all, an appreciation of the urgent need to create a unified internal market as a basis for growth of high-technology industries.[5] A final factor in explaining the increased use of protection has been a sense of dissatisfaction with the GATT safeguards code.

20.3 Trade relations with developed countries

As we have seen, most of the Community's trade is transacted with three major industrial areas: EFTA, the United States and Japan. Canada and Australia are also significant trading partners but the issues affecting trade with them overlap those affecting trade with the larger countries. Although trade with industrial countries is in theory governed by the rules of GATT, this has not prevented controversy and disputes arising on many specific issues.

Trade relations between the EC and EFTA have been remarkably free of friction. Former EC Commissioner, Lord Cockfield, described this trade as presenting 'a marvellous example of economic cooperation to the benefit of both parties' (Cockfield, 1986). The EFTA–EC relationship was in origin a free trade agreement but the Luxemburg Declaration of 1984 extended cooperation into related areas such as technical legislation, simplification of documents, research and development and environmental questions. The aim was to create a 'homogeneous and dynamic European Economic Space'. With the advent of the single market, the main concern of EFTA nations has been to ensure that they do not lose out from the creation of a more integrated EC (Pintado *et al.*, 1988).

Three factors help to explain why EC–EFTA trade relations have been comparatively harmonious. First, trade has been concentrated in non-sensitive manufactured goods characterised by a large proportion of intra-industry trade. Secondly, agricultural trade, an inveterate generator of trade disputes, accounts for only 4 per cent of total trade between the two areas. Although EFTA countries protect their agricultural sectors, they have not become large net exporters of food in competition with EC producers. Third, the EC has had a consistent trade surplus with EFTA since 1973, while also being the indisputably more powerful party in the trade relations of the two groups.

In contrast with the comparatively unruffled nature of EFTA–EC trade, relations with the United States and Japan have been stormy and difficult, although in different ways and centring on different issues – see El-Agraa (1988a).

EC economic relations with the United States have been based on strong political and cultural ties as well as common economic interests. Yet the evolving pattern of United States–EC trade has been the subject of repeated disputes – see Baldwin *et al.* (1988). Indeed, at times it has appeared as if the two partners were locked into a state of perpetual crisis. Within the past few years, trade wars have threatened to erupt because of disputes over steel, pasta, citrus fruit, agricultural exports to Egypt, the Mediterranean enlargement and hormones in beef.

One major source of contention related to the balance of trade. For a long period up to 1984 the EC had a deficit on its trade balance with the United States. Since then the deficit has turned into a huge surplus. The scale of the change has been remarkable. In 1987 the surplus reached $17 billion compared with a $27 billion deficit in 1981, a total swing of $44 billion. The main force underlying this development has been the massive expansion of EC exports of manufactures to the United States. Exports of engineering products more than doubled in value between 1982 and 1987, rising from US$17 billion to US$44 billion. Exports of EC cars to the US market were also buoyant, having doubled to $14 billion in 1987 over a five-year period. Faster growth in the US economy and the opposite problem of slow growth in the EC explain this dramatic change. The buoyancy of the US economy has clearly had beneficial spillover effects in the EC via an increased export demand.

Trouble has also flared on a number of issues in relation to manufactured goods. In the case of steel, Airbus and some energy-intensive products, the arguments have focused on the existence of subsidies and on their trade-distorting effects. Technology exports to the USSR and the Middle East from US subsidiaries located in the EC have caused difficulties in that what to the United States is seen as a legitimate restriction on the exports of a US corporation is seen in the EC as an infringement of political sovereignty (the extra-territoriality issue). Trade in services has also led to tension with the Commission insisting on reciprocal access to the US market as a condition for relaxing the rules on establishment of US banks in the EC.

The third and most enduring cause of friction has been trade in agricultural products. The erosion of the US surplus in food trade with the EC has been ascribed to the domestic price support given by the CAP. The United States has further objected that the growing food surpluses of the EC are being sold at subsidised prices on third markets thereby creating difficulties for US exporters to these markets. The EC retorts, not without justification, that agricultural subsidies are applied on more than one side of the Atlantic. This underlines the problems that arise when all countries try to subsidise the same product.

A trade dispute of crisis proportions arose following the 1986 enlargement, with the United States claiming that their agricultural exports to the EC would suffer as a result of the extension of the CAP regime. During 1988, the main *casus belli* was the Community's threatened ban on US imports of beef containing hormones. The value of trade involved was only $100 million, an insignificant sum in the context of total EC imports from the United States of $66,000 million. But the issue was nevertheless highly charged, following as it did the US Omnibus Trade Act of 1987, which Europeans feared might presage an upsurge of US protectionism, and the prospect of 1992, which many Americans feared might lead to a protectionist Fortress Europe.

Although full-scale trade wars have threatened to break out on many occasions in the past, the strong mutuality of interests between the United States and the EC has, on each occasion so far, brought them back from the brink. Trade relations are characterised by constant levels of minor friction rather than deeply set divergence of interest. Certainly a tit-for-tat series of retaliation would leave both the EC and the United States much worse off, a fact which both sides appreciate.

Turning to Japan, the trade imbalance features prominently as a basis for contention but in this instance it is the EC which has a deficit to complain about. The rapidly growing deficit ($26 billion in 1987) is attributed to the combined effects of the strategic targeting by Japanese firms of specific markets and to Japan's unwillingness to open its market to EC exporters. Sore points include the construction of the Kansai airport where EC tenders were unsuccessful, alcoholic drinks' discreet protection because of Japan's distribution system, and asymmetric opportunities for entering the financial services sector in the two areas, Japanese firms' access to EC financial markets being compared unfavourably with movements the other way.

The persistent deficit in EC trade with Japan can be resolved by increased exports to Japan, by direct investment by Japanese business in the EC or by restrictions on Japanese products entering the Community. Action is in fact being taken on all three fronts. Thus, the EC has exerted strong pressure on Japan to liberalise access to its market.[6] Export-enhancing schemes such as assistance for marketing in Japan and special visit and study programmes have been initiated in order to ensure that EC business is in a position to make maximum use of improved access to the Japanese market. Japanese investment in the EC has also been increasing rapidly. Britain has been a major beneficiary of this trend and the less developed regions of the Community, which include Ireland and the Mediterranean countries, have a keen interest in raising their share. Policy towards such investment has, however, been ambivalent. Direct investment is, on the one hand, seen as an effective counter to the accusation that Japanese imports are 'destroying' jobs in the EC but, on the other hand, competition from Japanese subsidiaries is seen as a threat to established industry. (Never mind the fact that 'established' industry includes subsidiaries of non-EC firms such as Ford, whose only claim to preferment is that they got into the EC market first.) The French, for example, threatened to ban imports of British-made Nissan Bluebird cars in 1988 because less than 80 per cent of the value of the car was actually made in the EC. (The threat was subsequently withdrawn under pressure from the Commission.) An instance of restrictive action by the EC is the 1987 legislation directed against the so-called 'screwdriver factories' which assemble electronic typewriters, copiers and other items using few EC parts, on the grounds that they open the way for an indirect form of dumping.[7]

The attention focused on Japanese trade is scarcely proportionate to its relative significance for the EC. It accounts for only 7 per cent of total extra-EC trade. The main problem is Japanese pressure on specific sectors of EC industry such as electronic equipment (VTRs, photocopiers, etc.) and motor cars. Over 80 per cent of Japanese exports to the EC consist of engineering products (mostly SITC 7) compared with corresponding figures of 53 per cent and 32 per cent for US and EFTA exports. Expression of this problem is usually voiced via protestation as to the difficulty of surmounting Japanese NTBs and complaints about the trade deficit. Action taken usually involves negotiations with the Japanese authorities to exercise restraints on their exports (VERs) or the stringent imposition of anti-dumping duties which some argue are used improperly as a protectionist device.

Understandingly, the apparent bilateral emphasis of the Community's approach has attracted much criticism (Curzon and Curzon Price (1987), refer to the 'follies' of EC protectionism and to 'naive bilateralism' in this regard). Given the Community's healthy overall trade balance, the problem really is one of protection for key industries. Drawing not always convincing sustenance from modern strategic theories of protection (Krugman, 1986), the EC insists that its technological position must not be undermined and that reciprocity must be the key concern in industrial sectors characterised by small numbers of producers and extensive research and development externalities. Clearly, a strategy of increasing EC exports to Japan would be much superior to protectionism on economic grounds. The EC consumer has gained enormously from access to Japanese goods: one only has to think of the vast improvements in the quality of automobiles which has been pioneered by Japan and then imitated and developed in the EC. Expansion of EC exports would have the additional advantage of building up an EC interest group with a commitment to liberal trade relations with Japan and with power to moderate protectionist sentiment.

The Community's trade relations with developed countries are, therefore, by no means uniform. Overall trade balance exists, i.e. exports to extra-EC countries are roughly equivalent in value to imports from them. But this conceals many imbalances at sectoral and country level which has given rise to friction. In a strategic sense, the most serious problem relates to Japan because of the absence of a strong EC export lobby with an economic interest in selling to Japan, weak historical and cultural ties, concentration of pressure in high-technology industries and the huge trade imbalance. At a sectoral level, the most acute source of difficulty is agriculture and, as we have seen, disputes on food trade have caused intense frustration to both the United States and the EC. Clearly there is a need for progress in reducing agricultural protectionism.

20.4 Trade policy towards the LDCs

Trade relations with the LDCs are governed by a large number of separate agreements. Some indication of the range of these arrangements is given by Table 20.7, prepared for the World Bank by Christopher Stevens. Stevens refers to the pyramid of privilege: at the top of the pyramid, the small proportion of ACP trade receives the most favourable treatment while at the bottom the larger proportion has to make do with tariff preferences. In between are the beneficiaries of the Global Mediterranean policy, a series of independent association agreements with countries bordering the Mediterranean which enjoy special privileges with respect to agricultural goods and direct foreign investment (Pomfret, 1986), and other groups singled out for special treatment.

The most important regional agreement providing special and differential treatment is the Lomé Convention. Signed in 1975 and renewed in 1979 and 1984, it gives a group of 66 African, Caribbean and Pacific (ACP) countries preferential access to EC markets. The Lomé accord encompasses more than tariff reductions. It includes the relaxation of NTBs, less stringent enforcement of trade regulations, and exemptions from multilateral trade agreements such as the Multi-Fibre Agreement (MFA). Its trade provisions are supplemented by special aid and technical cooperation arrangements. ACP countries account for 17 per cent of EC imports from the LDCs but only 6 per cent of total EC imports: by contrast, the EC absorbs 38 per cent of total non-oil ACP exports. Due to the increasing significance of the ACP, the following chapter is devoted to its development.

For most LDCs GSP dictates the degree of preferential access for their exports to the EC. Initiated in 1971, the purpose of the GSP was to help LDCs to industrialise

Table 20.7 Major EC trade arrangements with developing countries

	Trade agreements[a]
ACP: African, Caribbean and Pacific countries	Lomé Convention
Least developed countries (LLDCs)	9 non-Lomé signatories in this category receive special concessions
Northern Mediterranean Cyprus, Malta, Turkey, Yugoslavia	Association agreements Trade and cooperation agreements
Southern Mediterranean Maghreb countries (Algeria, Morocco, Tunisia), Egypt, Jordan, Lebanon and Syria	Preferential trade and cooperation agreements involving free access for industrial exports, specific concessions for some agricultural output and financial aid and cooperation agreements
Asia India, Pakistan, Sri Lanka, China	Non-preferential commercial cooperation agreements with each country
Association of South-East Asian Nations (ASEAN): Indonesia, Malaysia, Philippines, Singapore, Thailand	Regional framework agreement
Latin America Argentina, Brazil, Mexico, Uruguay, Andean Pact countries	Non-preferential economic and trade cooperation agreements with each country
Central America	Regional framework agreement 1986
Near East Gulf states: Saudi Arabia, United Arab Emirates, Kuwait, Oman, Qatar, Bahrain	Gulf Cooperation Agreement
North Yemen	Non-preferential agreement covering trade and economic cooperation

Note
[a] Non-preferential' means receiving no preferences in addition to those available via GSP.

Source: Compiled from EC Commission, 1988.

through exports to the developed world. Most developed countries have by now adopted some version of the GSP, in the case of the United States and the United Kingdom not without some initial reluctance (MacBean and Snowden, 1981), and about 150 LDCs receive preferences. The EC was the first of the industrialised countries to introduce a GSP.

The GSP provides duty-free access for industrial products, subject to ceilings, in the case of 'sensitive' products, classified by country of origin and member state of destination. The Community's GSP involves something of the order of 40,000 different bilateral and EC-wide quotas and ceilings (Davenport, 1986). GSP also applies to nearly four hundred agricultural products, but preferences are limited and products which compete with CAP products are excluded. Coverage of manufactured goods is, therefore, the most relevant, although also very complicated because of the intricate methods of assigning tariff-free quotas. Products are divided into sensitive and non-sensitive categories and into further subdivisions within these categories. The GSP regimes for textiles and clothing are conditioned by the existence of the MFA, which has assigned quotas for these products. Another restrictive feature of the GSP is the exclusion or reduction of preference on exports of LDCs (on a country or product basis) which have acquired a certain percentage of EC imports. On the other hand, countries defined as least developed, such as Bangladesh, Haiti and Afghanistan, enjoy special advantages such as duty-free access for agricultural products (except tobacco) and remission of quotas.

In addition to GSP, different countries and groups of LDCs have negotiated special cooperative arrangements with the EC which cover issues such as financial aid, direct investment and technological assistance.

This multiplicity of agreements and special arrangements seems very favourable to LDCs' interests. Many critics, however, have argued that EC policy is not as supportive as appearances suggest. First, as tariffs have been reduced under the GATT rounds, the practical usefulness of tariff preferences has diminished. Nominal tariff averages on raw materials and fuels, commodities in which the LDCs have a large share of EC imports, are under 5 per cent (Table 20.8). But the same table shows that nominal tariffs are still high on other product groups of interest to the LDCs. Moreover, effective tariffs on these products, the best measure of the protective effect, are much higher than nominal tariffs. Second, NTBs to imports from the LDCs have been growing in importance, in the form of VERs, quotas or the use of

Table 20.8 Post-Tokyo tariff averages on Community imports from developing countries in Community trade 1987

Sector	Tariff average % (coefficient of variation)	Share of developing countries in total imports %
Food	13.8 (0.89)	55.4
Agricultural raw materials	3.3 (1.55)	30.5
Mineral fuels	3.4 (0.88)	65.1
Ores and metals	4.0 (0.67)	31.2
Manufacturing of which	7.0 (0.61)	20.3
Chemicals	4.2 (0.60)	14.1
Textiles and clothing	10.5 (0.39)	60.6
Machinery, transport and equipment	4.7 (0.69)	10.2
Other manufactures	5.2 (0.56)	19.0
All sectors	7.8 (0.92)	40.0

Source: MacBean, 1988.

Table 20.9 Ratio of labour content of manufactured imports to exports

	Trade with OECD countries	Trade with developing countries
Belgium	1.06	1.28
France	1.02	1.32
W. Germany	1.06	1.31
Italy	0.88	1.15
Netherlands	1.05	1.16
United Kingdom	0.94	1.41

Source: World Bank, 1988.

safeguard clauses, surveillance techniques and anti-dumping measures (World Bank, 1987). Instances of NTBs abound, particularly in the case of steel, TV sets, video-cassettes, cutlery and other manufactured exports from the newly industrialising economies (NIEs). Third, the Community's system of preferences has been criticised for being excessively complex and uncertain in its application. Successful exporters to the EC complain that their very success leads to the imposition of new rules and restrictions on their markets. Fourth, some argue that the Community's predilection for preferences weakens the GATT system of non-discrimination in trade and that in the long run the interests of the LDCs would be better served by multilateral agreements within GATT (Wolf, 1987; Pomfret, 1986).

A degree of resistance to manufactured imports from the LDCs could be expected in the EC, given the labour-intensive nature of such trade and the EC's high unemployment rate. The labour intensity of LDC exports, according to orthodox comparative advantage is, of course, the source of substantial gain to the EC consumer. Producers of competing imports in the EC, however, are vulnerable to redundancy and rationalisation as a result of import penetration. The contrast between the labour content of manufactured imports into member states from the LDCs and from the industrialised OECD countries is very marked (Table 20.9). In the case of trade with the LDCs, the labour content of imports is higher than exports by 41 per cent in the United Kingdom, 32 per cent in France and 31 per cent in Germany.

An important question is whether these protective measures have been effective in limiting import penetration and preserving jobs. Manufactured imports from the LDCs into the EC have been growing rapidly. Between 1984 and 1987, they increased by US$23 billion to a level of US$47 billion. Their share of total EC imports of manufactures rose, in the same period, from 6.7 per cent to 7.2 per cent. Imports from the LDCs increased significantly in real terms over the period 1976–84: the most notable increases were for chemical products, footwear, machinery, electrical products, precision and audio-visual instruments, furniture and toys (van Themaat and Stevens, 1987). Even more significantly, high levels of NTBs did not prevent a persistent rise in import penetration ratios of the six major NIEs in the EC market through the 1980s (Table 20.10). Between 1970 and 1985, import ratios for NIE

Table 20.10 Import penetration ratios[a]

	Total manufacturing (ISIC 3)		Textiles, clothing, leather and footwear (ISIC 32)		Electrical machines and appliances (ISIC 383-3832)		Radio, TV and communication equipment (ISIC 3832)	
	1970	1985	1970	1985	1970	1985	1970	1985
France	0.15	0.79	0.11	2.08	0.01	0.73	0.06	2.39
W. Germany	0.38	1.40	1.33	7.96	0.04	1.32	0.38	5.36
Italy	0.27	0.91	0.34	1.18	0.07	0.52	0.40	3.91
United Kingdom	0.41	1.42	2.10	7.74	0.14	1.15	0.37	4.11
United States	0.49	2.41	1.53	11.16	0.44	5.93	1.55	7.54
Japan	0.30	0.85	1.17	3.82	0.10	0.73	0.19	0.68

Note
[a] South Korea, Taiwan, Singapore, Mexico, Brazil, Hong Kong.

Source: OECD, 1988.

manufacturing imports rose more than threefold in the major EC countries. These figures vindicate Pelkmans's view that 'it would be inappropriate to misread the targeted increase in EC protection towards [NIEs] as a refusal to participate further in the world division of labour' (Pelkmans, 1987, p. 39). Moreover, despite criticism of protection, the EC's textile, clothing, iron and steel industries have been drastically rationalised, with the loss of over one million jobs in textiles and clothing alone during the past decade.

The Community's trade policy towards the LDCs contains trade-liberalising and trade-restricting tendencies. There has been enlargement of the product coverage and geographical scope of the EC's preferential arrangements and there is a genuine commitment at Commission level to the promotion of harmonious relations with the LDCs. Against this must be set the long list of special interventions against imports of individual LDCs in response to specific member country and industry pressures. Restrictions on imports of CAP-related products from the LDCs have also been a source of difficulty for many LDCs (Matthews, 1986). The balance between these opposing forces of liberalisation and restriction is hard to draw. The complexity and discretionary nature of the Community's trade policy makes such evaluation especially difficult. However, analysis of trends in trade indicates that, despite the barriers placed against them, the LDCs have made progress in selling in the EC market; and those most discriminated against have performed best of all.[8]

20.5 The development of the CCP

The external relations of the EC are likely to be affected both by internal changes in the EC itself and by developments outside it. Among internal developments the most important are the adjustment to the Mediterranean enlargement and the long-term consequences of the completion of the 'internal market' by 1992. The main external factor influencing the CCP is the Uruguay Round negotiations. The rapprochement between the CMEA (COMECON) and the EC also merits attention, despite the small share of state-trading countries in total trade. An important issue on the horizon is the Community's response to present and future applications for membership and closer association.

The first of these changes is the Mediterranean enlargement. The accession of Greece in 1981 was followed by Spain and Portugal in 1986. The expected economic impact of the enlargement has been extensively researched (Donges *et al.*, 1982; Tsoukalis, 1981). The economic impact relates not only to trade but also to the internal dynamics of adding three new and comparatively less well-off members to the EC of nine. As far as external relations are concerned, the main issues relate to:

1. The external trade creation effects following the alignment of the new entrants' protection to the common EC level.
2. Displacement effects in the case of manufactured goods exports from closely competing Mediterranean countries and NIEs.
3. Displacement/trade diversion effects on agricultural exports.

The strain on US–EC relations resulting from the reduction in US grain exports to Portugal and Spain has been noted earlier. Although the United States has gained from external trade creation, it is unfortunate that, as Yannopoulos (1988) observed:

> most of the trade diversion effects of the formation and extension of the EC were concentrated in agricultural trade – a section of trade inextricably linked with the critical issues of American domestic policy. (p. 112)

The effect of the enlargement on the CCP in the medium term has been another source of concern. While Latin American countries have benefited from stronger EC interest, partly owing to the historical ties between them and Spain and Portugal, there is some evidence of trade diversion from Latin America to ACP and EC suppliers (*IMF Survey*, 9 March 1989). Asian NIEs felt especially vulnerable and feared that the enlargement would result in a tougher CCP, more ready than before to apply restrictions on successful exporters and to invoke safeguard clauses. Although a plausible hypothesis, hard evidence to support it has not been forthcoming and the jury is still out.

The second major change was the SEA and the proposals in it for the completion of the internal market by 1992. The provisions of the SEA for a complete internal market will have direct and indirect consequences for trade policy. Thus, if intra-EC frontier controls are to be abolished by 1992, GSP national quotas will have to be eliminated as will those on imports from East Germany. National VERs will become unenforceable and intra-EC measures of protection will have to be amended. A key policy issue is whether the direction of the amendment will be towards higher protection as exponents of the Fortress Europe concept predict or whether, on the contrary, by stimulating internal growth, the SEA will strengthen the EC's commitment to a liberal trading order. Previous enlargements have led to more not less liberalisation. Clearly there is no logical inconsistency between pursuing internal reform and external liberalisation simultaneously. To the extent that completion of the internal market succeeds in reactivating the EC economy, adjustment to external competition becomes easier. But completion of the market will itself involve adjustment costs and member states may wish to minimise the further dislocation implicit in more liberal external trade policies (Henderson, 1989). EC producers will also be anxious to ensure that non-EC producers do not reap all the benefits of an integrated market. Calingaert (1988) expresses an American fear that efforts will be made to distinguish between 'local' and 'foreign' firms and to give preference to the 'local' companies. Commission President Delors in his January 1989 statement to the European Parliament asserted that 'the single market will be open but it will not be given away'. The first part of this sentence represents the conviction of the Commission: the second part is what gives ground for concern elsewhere. It is too soon to say for certain which view will be vindicated.

The Uruguay Round negotiations, which began in 1986 and are scheduled to end in 1990, will provide a testing ground for the ability of the EC to put principles into practice. The EC played a strong supporting role in getting the Round started. It recognised the need for trade liberalisation in goods and supported the inclusion of services on the agenda. The need to strengthen GATT structure and disciplines and to adapt them to new areas of application was also a theme of the Community's approach to the negotiations. The EC signalled its commitment to differential and more favourable treatment of the LDCs, while tempering this with the expectation that the more prosperous LDCs should be expected to make some reciprocal concessions in return. The Community's position on the details of the negotiations will be clarified only with the passage of time. There are many important areas of disagreement between the EC and both the developed as well as the developing countries. In agriculture, for example, the EC has opposed the United States and Cairns group proposal for complete liberalisation. Instead it proposed a phased reduction in subsidies and import barriers, beginning with emergency action in the most affected markets (cereals, dairy products and sugar).

On the important issue of GATT reform the EC adhered to its position that selective safeguard action should be permitted against individual country exports in case of damage to domestic industry, a position which has been opposed by many NIEs and Japan. In relation to manufactured goods, the phasing out of tariffs was supported by the EC but the removal of NTBs would have to be contingent on reciprocal action on the part of trading partners (except for the weaker LDCs) and agreed procedures for dealing with domestic difficulties arising from import penetration. A recurrent element in the Community's position is the stress on *balanced and genuine progress in liberalisation*. The same concern applies in the case of financial services where reciprocity in terms of market access is the central point at issue.

Trade in services is exceptionally important for the EC: in 1984 its balance of trade in services was in surplus by $9 billion. Talks on the liberalisation of trade in services have taken place as part of the global negotiations but, unlike goods trade, outside the framework of GATT. This procedural precaution should ease the introduction of rules for services which may be markedly different from those which normally apply within the GATT framework.

Relations between the CMEA and the EC have for many years been dogged by the former's refusal to afford the EC diplomatic status and the latter's insistence on its right to negotiate trade relations bilaterally. The EC justified its approach by arguing that the Commission had greater jurisdiction over trade relations than the CMEA. Another factor was the Community's reluctance to conclude an agreement which would strengthen Moscow's hold on Eastern Europe.

Following an approach by the CMEA to the EC in 1984, relations between the two blocs improved. In 1986, CMEA countries which included Moscow's six Warsaw Pact allies as well as Mongolia, Cuba and Vietnam, indicated their willingness to establish normal diplomatic relations with the EC and to deal with trade questions on a pragmatic basis. Two years later a formal joint declaration of mutual recognition was signed between the two parties.

To the East, the advantage sought was access to Europe's technological and financial resources as well as to foreign currency earnings from a prosperous market. The EC, for its part, saw economic advantages in trade with the CMEA in addition to the political benefit of gaining implicit recognition of West Berlin as part of the EC and strengthening ties with Eastern Europe (European Parliament, 1986). These considerations are specially pertinent for Germany which is the major participant in existing trade (accounting for 45 per cent of EC exports to the CMEA in 1986). East Germany, often called the 13th member of the Community, already has privileged access to the EC through the Federal Republic of Germany. Trade and cooperation agreements were concluded with Hungary and Czechoslovakia following the CMEA–EC declaration and more such agreements are likely to follow. Of the other non-CMEA members of the state-trading area, China has had diplomatic relations with the EC since 1975 and a trade and economic cooperation agreement entered into force in 1986. By then, China had become the Community's third most important source of imports among the LDCs.

As the process towards intra-EC integration intensifies, the question of membership of the EC has become increasingly important. Some non-member countries have been worried at the prospect of being excluded from the internal market. Turkey has applied for full membership and approaches have been made by Austria, Cyprus and Malta. There is a general uneasiness in EFTA countries about their exclusion from the decision-making process of an EC which is likely to have an increasingly important impact on their welfare.[9]

While the Treaty of Rome states that any European country may apply for membership, the Treaty also stipulates that a unanimous decision by Council is necessary for an application to be successful. At present, the vigorous campaign for full membership by Turkey is likely to founder on opposition from countries which fear the inclusion of this populous and low income state, as well as the more predictable opposition of Greece. Austria's position on neutrality is likely to be a source of difficulty in consideration of its application. Generally, there is a feeling in the EC that time is needed to absorb the latest enlargement and to adjust procedures and institutions before undertaking any new enlargement.

20.6 Conclusion

The EC is a large and powerful trading bloc. Its foreign trade policy affects other countries' welfare as much as if not more than its own. Through trade diplomacy and as a participant in GATT, the EC plays a key role in the evolution of the international trading system.

EC trade policy is based on liberal principles. Yet many aspects of the CCP have been a cause of concern to third countries. First, agricultural protection threatens third country producers with market disruption and has been a constant source of friction. Second, preferential agreements sit uneasily beside commitment to the GATT principle of non-discrimination. Besides, the EC is finding to its cost that, since preferences cannot by definition be afforded to all countries, the proliferation of preferential agreements leads to diminishing returns.[10] Third, NTBs are a source of friction in relations with both developed countries and LDCs. Fourth, the Community's position on selective application of quantitative restrictions (in the context of GATT Article XIX – the safeguard clause), its local content rules and approach to subsidies and dumping has been criticised as being mercantilist and contrary to its liberal rhetoric. Fifth, as services trade grows in importance the Community's emphasis on reciprocity in this area ('reciprocal and mutually advantageous arrangements'), although enshrined in GATT as a major principle, has also attracted censure and has fuelled support for the Fortress Europe view of the EC (Henderson, 1989).

This chapter has discussed what the Community's policy is and how it is likely to change. Clearly the policy is in a state of transition as the EC responds to new internal and external pressures. In responding to these pressures, the Commission will be conscious of past successes as well as potential dangers. Among the successes of the CCP can be included the establishment and gradual reduction of a CET, the stronger bargaining power of the Community, a positive approach to the LDCs and active participation in the GATT rounds. Its limitations as viewed by outsiders have been noted above. To member countries too there are special sources of concern. For one thing, the CCP is still not wholly uniform in its application. National quotas continue to exist (some of them sheltering under historical grandfather clauses; some permitted by the Commission as temporary restrictions under Article 115; others not approved by the Commission but enforced via national standards and certification procedures or industry-to-industry agreements).[11] Moreover, there is no common EC position relating to export subsidies: France, for example, offers extensive export credit on soft terms. Yet the logical corollary of a CET is a common approach to subsidies on exports. In addition to this, there is the constant problem of individual national interests pulling the EC in different directions and threatening paralysis in decision making on external policy.

In an effort to deal with these internal and external criticisms and at the same time to move towards a more liberal and ordered international trading environment, the EC has stressed the importance of reciprocity. Whether in the case of Japanese trade, a new services agreement or concessions to the better-off LDCs, a recurrent theme is the necessity for similar treatment of imports to prevail on both sides. This emphasis on reciprocity is helpful in securing agreement within the EC on trade-liberalising measures. The ethical attractions of a level playing field are obvious. The danger lies in defining it as one where each side scores an equal number of goals. The argument by EC automobile manufacturers that increased access to the Japanese market should be monitored in terms of target market shares is a case in point (Kelly *et al.*, 1988).

Alongside reciprocity, the EC has also emphasised the need for greater global exchange-rate stability and realistic exchange-rate policies in its trade partners. Exchange-rate volatility has not been helpful to the cause of a freer trade environment.

Protectionism will continue to exert an influence on the CCP. It has surfaced most strongly in response to large export expansions concentrated in a few products. The process has been described by Corden (1988) as one of 'conservative resistance'. With the advent of China into the international trading system, and resumption of export growth by Latin America countries, the problem of 'conservative resistance' is unlikely to go away.

Three forces will, however, tend to moderate protectionist pressures. First, faster growth in the EC and a decline in unemployment is expected as a result of market unification. If this is achieved, a more relaxed approach to import growth can be expected.

Second, the cost of protection to the EC consumer has begun to attract more attention. The CAP has raised EC food prices and has absorbed up to 75 per cent of the Community's budget. Industrial protection is also very costly. For example, the annual cost per job protected in the United Kingdom as a result of VERs was estimated to be £80,000 for videocassettes, £50,000 to £70,000 for automobiles and £13,000 for clothing in the early 1980s (Greenaway and Hindley, 1985; Digby, Smith and Venables, 1988). Research in other EC countries and for other industries shows costs of a similar order of magnitude for heavily protected sectors.

Third, more important than the cost of protection is the fear of the cost of an all out trade war which individual disputes might provoke. A spiral of retaliation and the break down of the international trading system would leave all countries poorer.

Notes

1. I am grateful to Alisdair MacBean, Alan Marin, Alan Matthews, David O'Sullivan (Directorate-General External Relations), Dermot Scott and Alan Winters for helpful comments. The author alone, however, is responsible for the views expressed in this chapter.
2. Other relevant articles include Article 36 which allows national import restrictions on grounds of 'public morality, public policy or public security'. Under Article 109, a member

state may, in response to a sudden crisis in its balance of payments, take action against imports.

3. In addition to anti-dumping rules the EC also applies countervailing duties to offset export subsidies. As Messerlin shows (1988), the two measures have tended to target the same industries (notably steel and industrial chemicals). Other important elements in the application of Community policy include rules of origin, safeguard clauses and voluntary export restraints (VERs).

4. Not all agreements are subject to this procedure. Trade and cooperation agreements in 1988–9 with Hungary and Czechoslovakia, for example, were concluded under Article 113 and were not subject to Parliament's assent. It is likely that the Parliament will press to have Article 228 used as a legal basis for future agreements.

5. Examples of policies guided by such concerns include Airbus, videocassettes and high density TVs. Failure to develop a European HDTV system could, it is feared, lead to all televisions being bought from Japan and all TV programmes being bought from the United States.

6. An example is the agreement by Japan following talks with EC officials in June 1987 to relax inspection procedures on EC imports of automobiles. The proposal is to test one out of every 100 imported cars rather than one out of every 50. It is significant that the member nations of the EC have already achieved a modest foothold in the Japanese market, with a 2 per cent share of the overall Japanese car market and a 30 per cent share of the expensive, luxury-car market.

7. The Council of Ministers adopted legislation in June 1987 which aimed at preventing the avoidance of anti-dumping duties by foreign-assembly-type operations – duties will, in such circumstances, attach to imported inputs as well as to the final output.

8. This conclusion seems to have wider applicability than to EC trade. A study of the effects of developed countries' protection found that increasing protection has had more effect on the commodity composition and geographical patterns of LDCs' exports than on the aggregate level of their export earnings (OECD, 1985, p. 183).

9. In terms of trading, EFTA countries are about as closely integrated with the Community as EC countries themselves (Krugman, 1988). Austria and Switzerland, for example, import more from the EC as a percentage of their total imports than most member states.

10. ACP countries, for example, issued a declaration objecting to cuts in tariffs offered by the EC on tropical products in late 1988 because these would erode their own preference margins in EC markets.

11. A list of Article 115 authorisations is provided in Kelly *et al.* (1988), Appendix I. Most of them relate to imports of textiles and clothing under MFA but automobiles, footwear and some agricultural products have also been included. Trade with state-trading countries is governed by special rules that permit the maintenance of national quotas.

21 The Lomé Agreement

A. Marin[1]

21.1 Background

The first Lomé Agreement was signed in Lomé, the capital of Togo, in 1975 between the EC and a group of 46 developing countries (LDCs) known as the ACP – the Afro–Caribbean–Pacific Group. The name ACP seems an odd way of describing a group of countries, but, as shown in Table 21.1, the countries in the group (which has now expanded by a steady accretion of new members to 66) have little in common except their underdeveloped status and all but two (Liberia and Ethiopia) are ex-colonies of EC states. However, the Asian ex-colonies of the EC states are excluded. The choice of the ungainly and unrevealing description Afro–Caribbean–Pacific was itself a reflection of the background to the signing of the agreement, the neutrality of the purely geographical terminology reflecting both an attempt to differentiate the agreement from its predecessors and officially a hope for an entirely new type of relationship between developed countries and the LDCs which would prove to be a desirable model for others to follow.

The initial predecessor of the Lomé Agreements was Part IV of the Treaty of Rome entitled 'Association of the Overseas Countries and Territories'. This part of the Treaty referred to the colonies of the original member states, of which the French were by far the most numerous.[2] Many commentators, in fact, viewed the association of the colonies as being in one respect like the Common Agricultural Policy (CAP) – part of the price (what economists now often call a 'side payment') paid to the French for agreeing to join a Community which was likely to be economically dominated by the Germans. In this case the payment took the form of enabling France to maintain its close economic relationship with its colonies, while obtaining EC help with its aid burden – see Chapters 2 and 7.

In addition to the securing of the aid, which was achieved by the establishment of a European Development Fund (EDF) as well as by some finance from the European Investment Bank (EIB), the Treaty laid down that the associated colonies should be able to export to all the EC states on the same free trade terms as the member states themselves. Although the colonies could keep tariffs where these were necessary for revenue raising (but, by implication, not for protection) they could not discriminate between member states, and this ruled out any preferential access for imports from the 'mother country' of a colony.[3] Nor could they discriminate against colonies of another member state.

In the 1957–62 period many colonies achieved independence. With one exception (Guinea) the ex-colonies wished to maintain the sort of relationship they had had with the EC under Part IV of the Treaty of Rome. As independent states, they were now able to negotiate on their own behalf and sign agreements for themselves, whereas they had not been involved either in the negotiations leading up to Part IV of the Rome Treaty or in acceptance of its application to them. Nevertheless the new agreement did not differ greatly from its predecessor. The agreement was reached in December 1962 and formally signed in 1963. It was known as the Yaoundé Convention, since it was signed in Yaoundé, Cameroon.

There were in fact two Yaoundé Conventions: 1963–8 and 1969–74.[4] Officially the signatories were to 'cooperate on a basis of complete equality', but the document recognised that the aim was 'to maintain their association'. The 18 ex-colonies even continued to use the word 'associate' in their name: Association of African and Malagasy States (AAMS).

Most of the apparent changes between Part IV of the Treaty of Rome and the Yaoundé Agreements were institutional changes arising from the independence of the associates; a Council of the Association and other joint bodies were formed. There were also some changes in the trade/aid provisions, though these were minor in practice. One such change was that although the associates were still allowed to levy tariffs on imports from the EC only when these were for revenue raising,[5] and although such tariffs could still not discriminate between EC states, the associates could levy protective tariffs against imports from each other. This provision aroused hostility from some other countries, especially the United States: unlike association under the Treaty of Rome, when the associated territories could be considered part of a wide free trade area together with the EC, the new provision meant the EC–AAMS was clearly not a single free trade area. Hence the United States and others claimed that there was no justification for EC exports to the (now-independent) associates to receive preferential access by facing lower tariffs than their own exports to the associates.

As well as the problem over the 'reverse preferences' granted by the AAMS to the EC, by the early 1970s there were other reasons why a simple extention to a Yaoundé III was no longer viewed as adequate. One change specific to the EC was the accession of the United Kingdom, which had its own ex-colonies, some of which had already signed agreements with the EC (the Lagos and Arusha Agreements).

Another change was a result of broader changes in world political/economic relationships. Parly inspired by the success of the OPEC countries in reversing their dependence on the West,[6] there was a general increase in assertiveness by the LDCs. They wanted a more equal relationship. This was often summarised in the call for a

NIEO – a New International Economic Order. On the whole, British ex-colonies were more sensitive to arrangements which maintained them in a blatantly dependent status than were the ex-French colonies.[7] Because of the general mood of the times, reinforced by the inclusion of the British ex-colonies, any new relationship with the EC would have to appear to be signed between equals. Hence the dropping of the word 'Associated' in the AAMS to the simple, unqualified, ACP as the designator of the new, broader group.

Another change in the early 1970s, as a result of the OPEC oil price rises, and the strategic embargo by its Arab members in 1973, was a fear by some in the West that the LDCs might successfully cartelise some other raw materials. This provided the EC with an extra motive for tightening links with a group of countries which included some major mineral and other raw material producers.[8]

As part of the background, the 1970s also saw the increasing importance of a particular group of LDCs – the newly industrialising economies (NIEs, see Chapter 20). The ACP countries excluded these 'success stories'. The non-oil African countries in particular, but the ACP countries as whole, were falling behind the NIEs both in their development and in their ability to sell manufactured goods to developed countries.

The exclusion of the NIEs has not just been a matter of chance. The Lomé Agreements follow the Yaoundé wording in limiting applications for new membership to countries 'whose economic structure and production are comparable with those of the ACP states' ('Associated states' in Yaoundé). The countries which are already signatories have to approve the new accessions. Furthermore, according to Matthews (1977) even in 1963, during the United Kingdom's first attempt to join the EC, it realised that association was unlikely to be extended to the non-African member nations of the Commonwealth. By the time the United Kingdom actually joined, a Protocol and Declaration of Intent to the 1972 Treaty of Accession explicitly distinguished the 'developing Commonwealth countries situated in Africa, the Indian Ocean, the Pacific Ocean and the Caribbean' (listed by name in an annex) from those 'in Asia (India, Pakistan, Singapore, Malaysia and Ceylon)'. The former, but not the latter, group were offered the choice of joining Yaoundé or arranging some other formal relationship with the EC. The reasons for the exclusions should be clear from the discussions below on aid (given the populations of India/Pakistan) and trade (NIEs, including Singapore).

The new agreement was signed in Lomé in February 1975. It became known as Lomé I (1975–9), and was followed by Lomé II (1980–4) and Lomé III (1985–9).[9] As shown in Table 21.1, there is a wide disparity in the population and income of the ACP. Even now, with twenty more members than in 1975, Nigeria on its own has about a quarter of the total population of the ACP, and for much of the time since 1974 (though not most recently) has contributed more than a third of all ACP–EC trade, both of ACP exports and imports.[10] The ACP includes many of the poorest LDCs and many of those with the least successful growth record, since it includes all the Sahel countries which were hit so badly by drought in the 1980s.

All of these factors, as well as others, are seen by some as relevant to the desire for

Table 21.1 The ACP countries: population and per capita income[a]

	Population 1986 (000s)	GNP per capita 1985 (US$)		Population 1986 (000s)	GNP per capita 1985 (US$)
Angola	8,980	690	Madagascar[b]	10,300	250
Antigue and	80	2,030	Malawi[b]	6,450	170
Barbuda			Mali[b]	8,440	140
Bahamas[b]	240	7,150	Mauritius[b]	990	1,070
Barbados[b]	250	4,680	Mauritania[b]	1,950	410
Belize	170	1,130	Mozambique	14,170	300
Benin[b]	4,040	270	Niger[b]	6,700	200
Botswana[b]	1,130	840	Nigeria[b]	98,520	760
Burkina Faso[b]	6,750	140	Papua New Guinea[b]	3,400	710
Burundi[b]	4,850	240	Rwanda[b]	6,270	290
Cameroon[b]	10,450	810	St Kitts and Nevis	50	1,520
Cape Verde	330	430	St Lucia	130	1,210
Central African	2,740	270	St Vincent and the	100	840
Republic[b]			Grenadines		
Chad[b]	5,140	80	Sao Tome and	110	310
Comores	480	280	Principe		
Congo[b]	1,790	1,020	Senegal[b]	6,610	370
Ivory Coast[b]	10,160	620	Seychelles	70	2,429
Djibouti	460	970	Sierra Leone[b]	3,670	370
Dominica	80	1,160	Solomon Isles	280	510
Ethiopia[b]	44,930	110	Somalia[b]	4,760	270
Fiji[b]	700	1,700	Sudan[b]	22,180	330
Gabon[b]	1,170	3,340	Surinam	380	2,570
Gambia[b]	660	230	Swaziland[b]	670	650
Ghana[b]	14,040	390	Tanzania[b]	22,460	270
Grenada[b]	110	970	Togo[b]	3,050	250
Guinea[b]	6,220	320	Tonga[b]	110	730
Guinea-Bissau[b]	910	170	Trinidad and	1,200	6,010
Equatorial Guinea[b]	400	341	Tobago[b]		
Guyana[b]	970	570	Uganda[b]	16,020	220
Jamaica[b]	2,370	940	Vanuatu	140	720
Kenya[b]	21,160	290	Western Samoa[b]	160	660
Kiribati and Tuvalu	60	450	Zaire[b]	30,850	170
Lesotho[b]	1,560	480	Zambia[b]	6,900	400
Liberia[b]	2,220	470	Zimbabwe	8,410	650

Notes
[a] In 1985 GNP per capita in the EC was US$8,270.
[b] Original signatory of Lomé I.

Source: *ACP Basic Statistics*, 1988.

a new agreement, and to its form and content. However, various assessments of the purposes and results of the Lomé Agreements are split by fundamental political disagreements. The preamble to the first Lomé Agreement stated that the contracting states:

> Anxious to establish, on the basis of complete equality between partners, close and continuing co-operation in a spirit of international solidarity ... resolved to establish a new model for relations between developed and developing States, compatible with the aspirations of the international community towards a more just and more balanced economic order.

The last phrase is probably to be taken as referring to the NIEO.

Some commentators have seen this preamble as a genuine expression of the true intentions of both sides: 'The EEC–ACP partnership represents a symbol of hope in a divided world'.[11]

From the beginning there have been others who took a diametrically opposed view and saw Lomé as a neo-colonialist successor to Part IV of the Treaty of Rome. That is, despite the apparent recognition of the ex-colonies as independent and equal partners in a joint agreement, the underlying motive of the EC states was to keep the ACP linked to them, yet still in a dependent position, at the least cost to themselves. It would always be the EC which made the decisions in its own interest and the ACP which had to go along with them.[12] A recent statement of this view is: 'The Lomé Convention was neo-colonial because it was a path chosen for the ACP by the European Community'.[13]

A third view is that of Moss and Ravenhill (1982) whose notion of 'collective clientism' views Lomé as an agreement between unequals, but where the dependent party (the ACP) was eager for the agreement. On this approach, the ACP countries knew that they were weak, even as compared to other LDCs, i.e. the NIEs. They attempted to construct an arrangement to preserve their position in the EC. This involved trying to place constraints on EC policy making in relevant areas, whereas the EC wanted to maintain its position in the ACP states at low cost (this part is not so far removed from the neo-colonialist position, although the first part is). To satisfy both sides there were ambiguities in Lomé: the ACP in 1975 thought that it had achieved a patronage relation whereby the EC would protect its interests even where Lomé was not specific. An alternative description of 'collective clientism' would be a kind of feudalism – the vassal pledged fealty in return for protection against outsiders and reassurance that the superior would not take untoward advantage of his power. Ravenhill sees the leaders of the ACP countries as feeling disappointed, even cheated, at the failure of the EC to fulfil what the ACP had expected its side of the bargain to be.

One way of classifying these views is in terms of what they see as the balance of the relative weight given to self-interest, altruism, frankness and consistency by the EC and by the ACP. The following sections will deal with the major provisions of the Lomé Agreements, in the two main areas, which are trade and aid. In these sections, I shall try to deal with the issues in a way that does not pre-judge where the truth lies.

21.2 General aid

The aid provisions of the Lomé Agreements fall into two groups. One is the traditional sort of aid, provided by the EDF and EIB under Part IV of the Rome Treaty,

Yaoundé and then under Lomé. In order to protect ACP sensitivities, (preserve the illusion of equality even where it is obviously inapplicable?), the relevant section of the Lomé Agreement is entitled 'Financial and technical co-operation'. As always, aid programmes are subject to differing opinions. On the one hand, since poverty and underdevelopment have continued in the ACP, and worsened in some of its members, aid has 'obviously' been insufficient and ineffective. On the other hand, any aid at all is 'obviously' better than nothing and could be said to represent generosity. Neither argument is necessarily convincing: to support the first argument one would need to know what would have happened otherwise. For the second argument not only are there the moralists who would say that the ex-colonial members of the EC have a moral debt to their ex-colonies, but there is also the neo-colonialist analysis which sees minimal aid as a way of tying the recipients to the donors – against the best long-run interests of the former. There are also some economists who see all aid as a harmful distraction from the true need of the LDCs.[14]

As well as the general problems associated with aid generally, there have been specific charges against EC aid programmes under Lomé. It is often alleged that delays in approving and then disbursing aid are excessive. Even by the bureaucratic standards of many EC institutions, the procedures for EDF aid seem particularly cumbersome. Although the ACP governments can submit proposals for aid projects, they are investigated by an EC 'delegate' accredited to the ACP country concerned. They then require approval by the EDF committee and by the EC Commission. The resulting delays can be considerable. For example, four years after the signing of Lomé II, only 18 per cent of Lomé II aid had been disbursed.[15] Nevertheless, it is only fair to mention that other multinational aid donor bodies can be as slow as the EDF.[16]

Those who criticise the Lomé agreements as merely having a façade of equality point to the requirement for appraisal and approval by the EC member states (the EDF committee) and the Commission.[17] The Lomé Treaty states: 'The Community shall be responsible for taking financing decisions on projects and programmes'. However, it could be argued that not only is the EC no worse than other donors in its unilateral right of decision, but that it has been criticised for being more willing to accept ACP proposals and less demanding in its assessments than other aid bodies, such as the World Bank. Within the EC, in 1982, the Development Commissioner, Pisani, criticised the EDF for agreeing to fund too many 'cathedrals in the desert', i.e. isolated grandiose projects pushed for prestige reasons by ACP governments.

Partly as a result of the last criticism, and partly as a result of changing ideas among all Western donor bodies generally, over the course of the three Lomé agreements there have been changes in the approach of the EC to aid projects. The sectoral allocation has always tended towards agriculture rather than industry, but under Lomé III there has been a switch to promoting more agricultural self-sufficiency and away from a stress on agricultural export goods for the world market.[18] There is a change in orientation to financing linked programmes and sectors, rather than discrete (and therefore, possibly, isolated) projects. Within this there is also an increased emphasis on 'micro-projects'.

Whether or not these changes are sensible, some of the ACP countries resented what they saw (whether correctly or not) as an attempt by the EC member nations to dictate to them what their developmental strategy and priorities should be, as if they could not be trusted to decide for themselves where the money they received should be spent. This resentment was even stronger over another change in the EC approach between Lomé I and Lomé III, which was the attempt to introduce a 'policy dialogue' into aid administration. In the account of the President of the Commission, Gaston Thorn:[19]

> the 'policy dialogue'. What passions were aroused, what anxiety and what mis-understandings caused by this idea, which the Community had put forward with the sole purpose of making aid more effective . . . some thought they could detect in it a move by the Community to make its aid conditional upon the adoption by its *partners* of policies decided elsewhere. (emphasis added)

In the end the ACP accepted 'cooperation' between the ACP recipient of aid and the EC in setting up programmes and in evaluating and checking how the money was being spent and its results. Qutie clearly, as the above quote shows, the fundamental divisions in views about Lomé apply here. On the one set of views, the EC was signalling its determination to keep total control, and/or showing that it did not trust the competence (and possibly the honesty) of the ACP governments. References to 'partners' and 'equal relationships' were just façades. On the other set of views, given the shortage of trained, often of even literate, manpower in most ACP countries, it was sensible to make use of EC expertise to help ensure the most effective use of scarce funds.

21.3 STABEX and SYSMIN

Many of the ACP countries are heavily dependent on the exports of a few raw materials – sometimes, as in the case of Ghana and cocoa, of a single product. Many of these commodities have aggregate market supplies which are inelastic in the short run, whereas demand in the industrialised countries may swing sharply with the state of the business cycle. Furthermore, as non-differentiated products with highly competitive markets, they are what is now often called 'flex price'. As a result, their prices tend to swing widely from year to year.[20] Exporters therefore suffer wide *variability* in their earnings. An extra source of instability in earnings occurs when the raw material is agricultural rather than mineral: weather conditions during the growing season can lead to wide fluctuations in yield in any one area. Since any one ACP country may not dominate the market, a drop in yield there is unlikely to lead to an offsetting rise in price: thus there are two independent causes of variability in earnings.

A major innovation of Lomé I[21] was a scheme to compensate ACP countries when their earnings from commodity exports fell. The system was called STABEX, and although formally not part of the aid package, is clearly aid rather than trade. Under Lomé I the scheme covered 29 products in twelve commodity groups; more products have been added to the list in the later Lomé Agreement. There are now 48 products;

Table 21.2 Products covered by STABEX[a]

1. Groundnuts, shelled or not	26. Vanilla
2. Groundnut oil	27. Cloves – whole fruit, cloves and stems
3. Cocoa beans	28. Sheep's or lambs' wool, not carded or
4. Cocoa paste	combed
5. Cocoa butter	29. Fine animal hair of Angora goats –
6. Raw or roasted coffee	mohair
7. Extracts, essences or concentrates of	30. Gum arabic
coffee	31. Pyrethrum – flowers, leaves, stems, peel
8. Cotton, not carded or combed	and roots; saps and extracts from
9. Cotton linters	pyrethum
10. Coconuts	32. Essential oils, not terpeneless, of cloves,
11. Copra	of niaouli and of ylang-ylang
12. Coconut oil	33. Sesame seed
13. Palm oil	34. Cashew nuts and kernels
14. Palm nut and kernel oil	35. Pepper
15. Palm nuts and kernels	36. Shrimps and prawns
16. Raw hides and skins	37. Squid
17. Bovine cattle leather	38. Cotton seeds
18. Sheep and lamb skin leather	39. Oilcake
19. Goat and kid skin leather	40. Rubber
20. Wood in the rough	41. Peas
21. Wood roughly squared or half-squared,	42. Beans
but not further manufactured	43. Lentils
22. Wood sawn lengthwise, but not further	44. Nutmeg
prepared	45. Shea nuts
23. Fresh bananas	46. Shea nut oil
24. Tea	47. Mangoes
25. Raw sisal	48. Dried bananas

Note
[a] Items 26–48 have been added since the signing of Lomé I.

all agriculture-based commodities (now including shrimps, prawns and squid as well), primarily tropical.[22] The current list is shown in Table 21.2.

The compensation is available to an ACP country where the product, or product group, is responsible for at least 6 per cent of the country's export earnings, and where the earnings from the product have fallen by 6 per cent.[23] The compensation is normally payable only on the country's exports to the EC. Because STABEX is supposed to be a *stabilisation* scheme, not just a minimum floor, in theory most ACP countries could have to repay their STABEX receipts when earnings recover, but the relevant criteria are both complex and vague in parts and have not generally been triggered.[24] The maximum funds available to the EDF for STABEX payments are laid down in advance by each Lomé Agreement. Particularly in 1981 and 1982 there was a serious shortfall of funds during a slump in commodity prices in the preceding years (payment is usually a year in arrears). In 1981 only 52.8 per cent and in 1982 only 40.4 per cent of legitimate ACP claims could be met. The 1987 meeting of ACP – EC ministers reported that:

The ACP States also continue to maintain that the Community is obliged to pay them the balance of the requests for the 1980 and 1981 years of applications, which were not met in full because of lack of resources. The Community disagrees.

At the time of writing this chapter, it looks as though there may be a STABEX shortfall for 1989 because of the large fall in coffee prices following the collapse of the International Coffee Agreement.

As the system has developed, a major source of conflict between the ACP and the EC has been over the use of receipts under STABEX.[25] The payments are given to the ACP government and, according to Lomé I (Article 20), 'the recipient ACP State shall decide how the resources will be used', and it merely had *ex post* to 'inform the Commission annually of the use to which it has put the resources transferred'. Despite this freedom given to the ACP – which in this way was treated as a responsible equal of the EC – many in the EC felt that the receipts should be used to help the producers adversely affected by the drop in their earnings. However, many ACP governments used much of the receipts from STABEX as part of their government revenue, using them to fund various of their general programmes, including development programmes, with at most the product covered by STABEX benefiting as part of the general gains expected from the projects.

Despite complaints by the EC at this 'diversion' of funds to the ACP governments, it can be argued that this is not an obviously inferior use of the STABEX receipts. For many of the ACP countries, given their low levels of literacy and thus the lack of formal accounting of domestic transactions, revenues from tariffs and from taxes on exports are necessarily a major part of government revenue.[26] Under such circumstances, a shortfall in the proceeds from export taxes and the revenues of the export marketing boards does represent a major problem in the orderly running of government-financed projects and services.

However, the argument has also been made that this justification is unconvincing. Firstly, the amounts received under STABEX are only very loosely related to shortfalls in government revenues – essentially because the implicit tax rate on exports of commodities covered by STABEX varies greatly between ACP countries.[27] In some it so low that STABEX receipts 'appropriated' by the government are greater than the tax revenue lost because of declines in the value of the exports. Secondly, the lag between the decline in export values and the actual payment of STABEX money means that the increase in government revenue because of the STABEX receipts may come just when revenues have recovered anyway. This is destabilising to government budgets and to the effects of their fiscal policies.[28]

Although, as just discussed, the issue is not clear cut, the EC has succeeded (against the initial wishes of the ACP, for the same reasons as with general aid 'cooperation') in altering Lomé III. STABEX transfers are now to be used either for 'maintaining financial flows in the sector affected' by export fluctuations or to promote diversification to other appropriate sectors – see the previous section on the switch in Lomé III to food self-sufficiency. Not only is the purpose of the use of the receipts now removed from the discretion of the ACP governments, but the actual request by an ACP government for a payment now has to include 'substantial information . . . on the programmes and operations to which the ACP State has allocated or *undertakes to allocate* the funds' (emphasis added).

As can be seen from Table 21.2, the commodities covered by STABEX do not include any mineral-based ones.[29] In the second Lomé Agreement, this omission was dealt with by a somewhat similar scheme known as SYSMIN which covered copper, phosphate, manganese, bauxite and alumina, tin and iron. There were, however, some differences between the two schemes.

Although the statement of aims for SYSMIN in the Lomé II Agreement mentioned export earnings, the context made it clear that the main aim was to enable the ACP states to maintain 'their capacity to export mining products to the Community'. The focus was to avoid the loss of mining capacity when income fell. In general, many mineral extraction facilities (especially underground) deteriorate if there is insufficient maintenance. The receipts from SYSMIN were to be used for maintaining the facilities.

Unlike STABEX, the trigger was 'a substantial fall in production or export *capacity*' (emphasis added). There is no figure given for the fall in export earnings, and the necessary fall is, in practice, assessed by the Commission.[30] Similarly the actual amount of SYSMIN aid needed was to be assessed by the Commission, and is not directly related to the drop in earnings. Less relevant for an analysis of the intentions and effects of SYSMIN, the substantial fall in capacity was taken to be 10 per cent, while the required proportion of export earnings from the commodity was generally 15 per cent.[31]

In the late 1970s the sharp fall in the real price of commodities and the excess capacity in mining industries was thought to be a temporary cyclical phenomenon, since the minerals involved were primarily industrial raw materials.[32] As the 'temporary' price depression and excess capacity stretched on into the 1980s, views changed and fears of an imminent shortage of raw materials receded. In Lomé III there was a loosening of the aims and conditions of SYSMIN payments to include other development projects which the ACP state had intended to finance from its mining revenue, even though the priority was still supposed to be that such aid was used for the rehabilitation and maintenance of the mineral production capacity.

Assessments of the STABEX and SYSMIN programmes vary widely, with differences in opinion often related to the fundamental differences in approaching Lomé that have been discussed above. On the one hand, these are schemes of a type that have often been strongly advocated by LDCs heavily dependant on primary product exports whose price fluctuates widely.[33] Thus the compensation when export earnings fall can be seen as an attempt by the EC to meet the worries, and demands, of the ACP.

The sceptical view sees these two programmes as an attempt to tie in the ACP states to the EC market. On this view, it is not coincidental that they were introduced when the West was worrying about the possibility of shortages of raw materials. Because STABEX and SYSMIN payments are usually linked to the recent exports to the EC, the ACP countries have an incentive to direct their exports of the commodities to the EC and not to other countries. Hence the EC was ensuring its share of the supplies of raw materials in the face of the worries just mentioned.[34] This view concentrates especially on the provisions of SYSMIN, under Lomé II, with its stress on 'maintaining capacity to export mining products to the *Community*' (Article 49, emphasis added). Only when the fears of not having sufficient access to the raw materials had disappeared was the EC prepared to consider diversification of output in the ACP.

Whatever one's assessment of the *aims* of the EC side in the Lomé Conventions, as a question of economic analysis, it should be noted that STABEX and SYSMIN do provide an incentive to produce the commodities covered by the scheme. The insurance (even if partial) against loss of income in 'bad years' is an economic gain if countries are risk averse and do not have access to perfect capital markets, and this gain is available only if the relevant commodities are produced.[35] Those economists who think that LDCs would do better in terms of their long-term standards of living if their resources were reallocated away from the production of primary products for export to other types of output (whether to manufactured output or to home food output) would consider the incentives inherent in STABEX/SYSMIN as undesirable. Economists who think that concentration on efficient production of primary products for export is a viable route of development for countries with a comparative advantage in those sectors will see the innovations under Lomé as beneficial.

21.4 Total aid

Because of the increase in the number of ACP countries, the increases in their population and the declines in the purchasing power of the European Currency Unit (ECU; EUA – European Unit of Account – for Lomé I/II) it is not easy to decide the level in real terms of total EC aid to the ACP. The problem is complicated by the existence of some payments which are not straightforward grants, and by the treatment of administrative costs.

The majority opinion is that there was a definite fall in the real per capita aid

Table 21.3 Comparisons of aid under Lomé I, II and III

	Lomé I	Lomé II	Lomé III
At current prices (millions EUA/ECU)	3,466	5,227	8,500
Percentage change from previous		+50.1%	+62.6%
Deflated for price change		+5%	+15.7%
Real per capita		−7%	−5%

Sources: Moss and Ravenhill, 1988, Table 8.11; Stevens, 1984, Table 2.

agreed at Lomé II. For Lomé III the aid was probably not quite as far below the Lomé II level. Table 21.3 gives an example of the sorts of results obtained.[36]

Although it is possible that the individual EC member nations would have given more aid to some (at least) of the ACP if they had not been contributing to the EDF, there is no evidence that this occurred. Ravenhill (Moss and Ravenhill, 1982), although generally sceptical about the benefits the ACP has received from the Lomé agreements, has analysed the various bilateral aid flows and concluded that probably no diversion occurred and that EDF donations were additional to the other aid grants of the EC member countries.

It might also be interesting to note, to put the figures into perspective, that during 1980–4 the EC countries which signed Lomé II gave total official aid of 60,500 million ECU (data from *World Bank Development Report*, 1988; Luxemburg omitted). Thus their contributions through Lomé were about 8.5 per cent of their total aid.

Even if there were falls in the real per capita value to the ACP of the aid they received as a result of the Lomé Agreements, the period 1980–5 was one in which the total real aid given by the West was relatively stagnant, and the real aid per capita is considered to have dropped sharply. The relatively minor falls in Lomé aid combined with its probable additionality suggest that, judged in terms of receipts, whatever the motives of the donors and the long-term implications of the procedures of implementation, the ACP countries gained from Lomé. This conclusion is reinforced by the fact that whatever their complaints, and whatever the views of commentators about the ultimate effects of Lomé on long-term patterns of development, no ACP countries have dropped out of the agreements (or even refused particular payments they were entitled to), and there has been a steady stream of new applicants.

21.5 Trade

Lomé I followed the Yaoundé Agreements in giving the developing countries involved tariff free access to the EC market. It went further, and did not require the ACP to provide tariff free access to EC exports – the only requirement was that each ACP state should provide the same terms of access to all EC exports, with no discrimination favouring any particular EC country.

Nevertheless the ACP has expressed strong dissatisfaction with the trade results of Lomé. In this section we first consider the actual export record of the ACP to the EC, and then consider why the record seems disappointing despite the apparent preferential access given to the ACP.

There are major difficulties in assessing how far, if at all, ACP exports have benefited. One difficulty is the high proportion that oil exports formed of the total (about 40 per cent in some years). The major swings of oil prices over the Lomé period can thus give misleading impressions of changes in the pattern of trade. Even if oil is considered separately, there are two major trends which could affect the data. On the one hand, over the period from 1975 to date, the EC has grown less fast than developed countries in general (particularly Japan and the United States). On the other, the African countries, which form the bulk of the ACP (see Table 21.1) have performed noticeably worse than many other LDCs.

Attempts to deal with these problems have been made. Probably the most thorough is a series of studies by Moss and Ravenhill. The first was published in 1982 and they have been updated, the most recent being 1987. They use two methods, each of which deals with one of the two problems mentioned above. The first is dealt with by looking at the proportion of ACP imports in total imports by the EC from the LDCs. This could still show a poor performance by the ACP due to the depressing effect of the second trend, even if the ACP were doing better in the EC than it would have done without the preferential access granted under Lomé. Conversely, the poor export performance of the ACP compared to other LDCs should not affect the second measure, which is the share of ACP exports which go to the EC as a proportion of their total exports. However, this measure would still be biased down, as a measure of the effects of Lomé, because of the relatively slow growth of the EC as a market. Taken together, however, the two measures might provide some indication of whether preferential access to the EC has helped ACP exports, even though if both biases were important one could still mistakenly reject the hypothesis of benefits to trade.

An example of the type of results is given in Table 21.4, where I have followed the approach of Moss and Ravenhill, though with slight differences on some details of the

Table 21.4 Shares of ACP countries in EC imports from developing countries

Year	EC imports from ACP (million ECU)	Imports from ACP as percentages of all EC imports from developing countries	Imports from non-oil ACP[a] as percentages of all EC imports from non-oil developing countries[b]
1960	2,826	23	27
1965	3,773	23	28
1970	5,472	23	32
1975	9,715	16	26
1977	13,515	16	25
1978	12,719	16	24
1979	15,746	16	21
1980	29,744	16	20
1981	18,802	13	16
1982	20,140	14	15
1983	21,903	16	18
1984	27,749	18	19
1985	30,310	19	17
1986	19,575	18	20
1987	16,374	15	16

Notes
[a] Non-oil ACP is ACP minus Nigeria, Gabon, Congo, Zaire, Bahamas and Trinidad and Tobago.
[b] Non-oil developing countries is all developing countries minus OPEC members and Congo, Zaire, Bahamas and Trinidad and Tobago (Nigeria and Gabon are in OPEC).

Source: EC *External Trade Statistics Yearbooks* 1987, 1988.

calculations. The table covers all 66 ACP and 12 EC countries over the whole period. Because of the expansion in both the ACP and EC membership over the period, if Lomé had any effect at all this should push the figures upwards. The downward trend actually found shows that at the very least Lomé failed to outweigh the other forces diminishing the ACP's share of EC imports. Moss and Ravenhill's findings on their other measures generally suggest a similar lack of impact of Lomé on ACP exports going to the EC.

However, there is some evidence for a diversification within the EC market. Although total ACP non-oil exports have not kept their share of the EC market, Moss and Ravenhill's findings show that there was a tendency for the British Commonwealth members of the ACP to send less of their exports to the United Kingdom and more to the other EC countries. Earlier analyses of the Yaoundé Agreements had shown a similar tendency: the AAMS countries tended to diversify their exports away from what had been their previous colonial 'parent country' towards the other EC States.[37] Finally, it might be noted that there is some evidence of slight improvement in exports to the EC of a few processed and manufactured products from a few ACP countries; but these are still a tiny proportion of ACP exports.[38]

There are a large number of possible reasons for these disappointing results (disappointing, at least, from the viewpoint of the ACP states). One point to notice is that because the ACP depends so heavily on exports of primary products, most of its exports would have been free of tariffs anyway since the EC does not impose any duties on these imports, whatever their origin. The exact proportions differ according to the period covered, but a recent EC estimate was that about two-thirds of ACP exports to the EC would have been zero rated regardless of origin (*The Courier*, May–June 1988).

Even if the ACP has no special advantage over other primary producers through Lomé, one might have thought that as a result of Lomé the countries involved would switch to higher value agricultural products, processed foods or manufactured goods, where their tariff free access would provide them with an advantage over competitors. However, this possibility is limited by several factors, some of which relate to provisos and exceptions in the Lomé Agreements.

One such limit on the usefulness of Lomé to the ACP is that a specific exception is made for products that are supported within the EC by the CAP. The EC has often pointed out that over 99 per cent of ACP exports enter the EC duty free: less than 1 per cent are CAP products. This, however, is irrelevant: what is relevant is what ACP exports of these products would be if they could enter the EC without any constraints or tariffs, not what they are if deterred. Even where some special arrangements have been made, for example for Botswana beef, critics have alleged that the concessions have been grudging, insufficient and trivial from the EC's point of view.[39]

This applies not only to the obvious CAP products but also to such items as Kenyan strawberries and cut flowers. As already mentioned, there are special, though limited, arrangements for a few products. For example, a quota of sugar is purchased at a guaranteed price, intended to compensate the ACP sugar producers for the trade diversion from their cane sugar to EC sugar beet when the United Kingdom entered

CAP as major problem

the EC. Nevertheless this does not compensate the ACP (and other) sugar-cane producers for the disastrous drop in world sugar prices, largely caused by the massive EC surplus of inefficient sugar-beet production induced by the CAP.[40]

One contentious set of limits on the ability of the ACP to export processed/manufactured products to the EC is due to the 'rules of origin' as to what constitutes an ACP product. It may be reasonable for the EC to avoid the entry of 'screwdriver' factory products, where an ACP country would be used to give a label entitling tariff free access to the EC for products nearly all of whose costs and profits of production accrue to a non-ACP, truly originating, country – as discussed in Chapter 20, the issue is applicable to a wider set of EC trade relationships. However the actual rules of origin in the Lomé Treaties are particularly complex. There are different rules of origin for different products. Some are by detailed description of the stages of production which must occur within an ACP country. Others are by percentage of value-added: for manufactured products generally 50 per cent of the value must accrue within the ACP, for some processed food the processing must add 70 per cent to be counted an originating product.

Although the idea of rules of origin might seem reasonable, the ACP countries have argued, bitterly at times, that the rules are too stringent. They, and those economists who support their view, say that for countries at their stage of development it is natural for industrialisation to occur in the form of using cheap labour to do the routine stages of assembly, etc., on products where the sophisticated higher-technology/capital-intensive stages take place in countries which are currently relatively scarce in unskilled labour but relatively abundant in capital (human and non-human). This is a sensible use of comparative advantage (compare the Hecksher–Ohlin theory). It is also the route apparently taken by some of NIEs, which have now moved on.[41]

The final reason we shall mention for the ACP failure to export non-raw materials to the EC is a mixture of Lomé itself and other factors. The latter are the system of EC preferential relationships with other groups discussed in Chapter 20, as well as the gradual reductions in tariffs agreed in the GATT rounds. Attention is most often drawn to the Generalised System of Preferences (GSP), as applying to the obvious competitors to the ACP but many of the other agreements listed in Table 20.7 cover countries producing some, at least, of the products the ACP might be expected to try to export to the EC. The ACP has protested against extension of the GSP, and also against other tariff cuts which erode its advantage. As mentioned in 20.6, a recent example is when the EC agreed to cuts in tariffs on tropical products as part of the GATT negotiations.

In response, the EC has often drawn attention to the various ceilings and complex non-tariff barriers limiting the value of the GSP and other agreements. The EC has said that the ACP receives preferential treatment because it is exempt from these ceilings and non-tariff barriers. However, the interaction with Lomé itself mentioned in the previous paragraph is that the ACP is also subject to the proviso that if ACP exports 'result in serious disturbance in a sector of the economy of the Community or of one or more of its Member States' the EC may take 'safeguard measures'.

Although the EC has never actually implemented the safeguard clause it has threatened to do so.[42] The issue arose in a 'sensitive' sector: textiles. General warnings were issued to the ACP in 1977 not to expand too far in this area and indicative quotas were set up on the ACP in areas covered by the Multi-Fibre Agreement. The crunch came with Mauritius. Under pressure from the French (who used a technique of delaying customs clearance that was later perfected on Japanese videocassette recorders), Mauritius agreed to a voluntary export restraint (VER) on its shipments to France. It then switched much of its textile exports to the United Kingdom and Ireland. Both complained to the Commission in 1979. The United Kingdom invoked the 'safeguard clause'. Under threat of imposition of the 'safeguard clause' Mauritius then agreed to a VER on its exports to the United Kingdom and Ireland.

Even if the safeguard clause has never actually been imposed, the possibility of its imposition, especially after the Mauritian case, is alleged to have created enough uncertainty to have inhibited investment in ACP production capacity directed at exports of manufactured goods which could fall foul of the safeguard. The nature of the EC sectors which face the most problems, and where the safeguard might be invoked, is that those are precisely the sectors where the LDCs are likely to have a comparatively advantage: EC problem sectors are those facing 'cheap' competition.

The assessment of the EC defence against ACP complaints of erosion of preferential advantage is thus uncertain. Probably the ACP has been subject to fewer VERs and other barriers than the LDCs relying on the GSP. The ACP itself, however, has not been unaffected either by actual barriers or by the threat of further barriers if they were to become more successful. Game theory would predict that threats which are credible can affect actions, without the threat having to be implemented.[43]

21.6 Conclusion

In this chapter we have discussed the outcome of the Lomé Agreements, and to some extent discussed the motivations of the two sides to the agreements. We have not dealt with the actual negotiations themselves and the relative cohesion and bargaining power of each side. The last sentence of the previous section suggests that an alternative method of approach would be to analyse the whole process in terms of the concepts from games theory – aims, threat points, possible strategies, degrees of information about the other players, learning, and likely pay-offs. Although such an analysis would be interesting and probably productive, as far as I know it has not been attempted so far.

Although I briefly outlined some of the different assessments of the motives of the two groups – the EC and the ACP – I have tried in analysing the mechanisms and outcomes of the Lomé Agreements to be as objective as possible and not to let my own views intrude too much. Complete objectivity on contentious issues is obviously impossible.

The conclusion of the discussions of effects of the trade and aid provisions of the Treaties would seem to be that the ACP has gained more, at least in terms of receipts, from the aid than from the trade concessions. However a comparison of the top rows of Tables 21.3 and 21.4 (remembering that Table 21.3 covers five-year periods) strongly suggests that trade results are quantitively far more important to the ACP than aid payments, and small percentage increases in trade receipts would outweigh much larger percentage increase in aid.[44] Indeed, ultimately, Lomé Agreements will be successful only if they effectively encourage the ACP to increase its possibility of producing, and of exporting (whether to the EC or elsewhere), enough to increase its standard of living and escape from the poverty summarised in Table 21.1.

Notes

1. I am grateful to D. McAleese for his helpful comments on a draft of this chapter. The usual disclaimer remains very necessary.
2. France distinguished between its colonies and its 'overseas departments', of which, in 1957, Algeria was the most important. The latter were dealt with separately in Article 227. Many of the subsequent developments, culminating in the Lomé Agreements, did not apply to them.
3. Although where the colony's protection was by quota, discrimination between EC member nations was still allowed. Some authors view this as a particular concession to French exporters to its colonies. There are several books which provide a detailed account of the pre-Lomé relationships of the EC and the associated territories. A recent example is Lister (1988).
4. For reasons connected with the first UK attempt to join the EC, the Yaoundé convention did not enter into force until July 1964.
5. Also, quantitative restrictions on imports from the EC were not allowed.
6. There is no single term which exactly covers the developed, non-Communist countries. For convenience we shall use the 'West', even though it includes Japan and even though the EC is to the east of the Caribbean members of the ACP.
7. See, for example, Lister (1988) for an account of the ideological underpinnings of the French approach to their colonies, and the resulting effects on the relationships.
8. This was linked to the more general limits to growth issue discussed in Chapter 19.
9. Although these dates are often given, Lomé I officially came into force in April 1976 and was due to expire in March 1980. Lomé II was signed in October 1979 but did not formally come into force until January 1981 and was due to expire February 1985. Lomé III was signed in December 1984, only formally came into force in May 1986 and is due to expire in February 1990. Some sources refer to Lomé I as 1975–80, and Lomé II as 1980–5.
10. Moss and Ravenhill (1988). Data on country-by-country trade can be found in the EC *External Trade Statistical Yearbooks*. As Ravenhill and Moss also point out, during 1979–83 71 per cent of ACP exports came from 10 of the 64 countries, while 70 per cent of EC exports went to 11 of the countries.
11. Cosgrove Twitchett (1978), p. xv. The title of the book is revealing.
12. The first leader of Ghana after independence wrote: 'The essence of neo-colonialism, is that the State which is subject to it is, in theory, independent and has all the trappings of international sovereignty. In reality its economic system and thus its political policy is directed from outside.' Nkrumah (1965), quoted in Lister (1988).
13. Lister (1988), p. 216.
14. The whole issue of whether any aid is appropriate and, if it is, in which form it should be given is one which has caused sharp debates among development economists. A sceptic might well claim that ideas on types of aid, as on suitable paths of development, have

changed simply to reflect the failure of each idea in turn to actually improve the position of the least developed countries.

15. Stevens (1984), who also gives a short summary of other aspects of the implementation of the Lomé funds.

16. See for example, Moss and Ravenhill (1988), Chapter 8 or Lister (1988), p. 139. She, like others, points out that since the funds are fixed in nominal terms, the delays mean a real loss when inflation reduces the purchasing power of the ECU.

17. For example Lister (1988) and Ravenhill's chapter in Boardman *et al.* (1985).

18. This particular switch may owe something to analyses of the Sahel famines, and possibly to Sen's analysis of famines generally, which stresses the risk of relying for purchasing power on sales to a (fluctuating) market rather than producing for own consumption. Note 14 is relevant for the change in sectoral emphasis and for the following points in the text. The emphasis on programmes and away from projects is paralleled by equivalent changes in the purely internal EC 'structural funds' such as the ERDF as well as the EIB.

19. *The Courier*, no. 89, January–February 1985.

20. Shorter fluctuations can be insured against by using futures markets.

21. Although before the formation of the EC France guaranteed to buy some raw materials from its colonies at prices above world levels, and there had been a partial precursor under Yaoundé.

22. Iron ore, which was the only exception and an anomaly, was shifted to SYSMIN. A few minor products (oil-cakes) have been removed as well.

23. In Lomé I both thresholds were 7.5 per cent, and were 6.5 per cent under Lomé II. These are lower thresholds for the poorest, landlocked or island ACP states (2.5 per cent under Lomé I, now 1.5 per cent) while sisal has a lower fluctuation threshold (5 per cent under Lomé I, now 4.5 per cent).

24. Though there have been cases where repayments have been offset against later STABEX payments due. The poorest ACP states are in any case exempt from repayments.

25. A detailed account is in Hewitt (1983).

26. Compare the situation in pre-industrial Britain. Not only does the whole genre of smugglers' tales reflect this reality, but disputes between King and Parliament over who was to have the right to the proceeds from the sale of the rights to international trading were one of the sources of conflict leading up to the Civil War.

27. See note 25.

28. This is similar to the familiar arguments in macroeconomics between monetarists and Keynesians over the possible destabilising effects of attempted stabilisation policies in the presence of lags. It is also possible for some 'advance payments' to be made under STABEX, but this provision has rarely been used.

29. See note 22.

30. According to Daniel (1984).

31. This was reduced to 10 per cent for the poorest ACP states.

32. The discussion of Chapter 18 on views on the 'limits to growth' is relevant here.

33. The third aim of the CAP (see Chapter 9) reflects the same pressure *within* the EC.

34. Daniel (1984), p. 66 summarises a 1976 submission by a group of EC mining companies to the Commission which is quite explicit on this point.

35. Insofar as repayments (see note 24) are rarely triggered and even if they are there is no interest rate applied in calculating repayment, STABEX/SYSMIN receipts are a gain to the ACP countries even if they had no risk aversion and (unrealistic for most ACP governments) could borrow unlimited amounts in perfect capital markets.

36. Stevens (1984) finds a much sharper fall in annual real per capita aid between Lomé I and II. In arriving at this conclusion he made an allowance for the late implementation of Lomé I, which meant that its aid was effectively spread over four years, not five.

37. The analysis can be found in the 1975 edition *ACP: Yearbook of Foreign Trade Statistics 1968–73* (published 1975) and is shown in graphs in Gandia (1981).

38. See Stevens and Watson (1984).
39. See Moss and Ravenhill (1982), Chapter 4 for further details. He quotes an EC spokesman during one set of arguments over access for CAP products as saying 'You must not ask us to scorn our own interest, that is not possible'.
40. See Roarty (1985) for details of the sugar problem, in the context of the CAP more generally.
41. Some, e.g. Moss and Ravenhill (1988), also point to the waiver of the rules for the part of the value added in an EC member nation as being a way of giving EC firms an advantage over those from other developed (or NIEs) countries.
42. The following account is based on Moss and Ravenhill (1988), Chapter 4.
43. The concluding paragraph of 20.6 suggests that the relationship between NTBs (including safeguards on 'sensitive' products) and success is not straightforward. The greater use against other LDCs may merely reflect their greater success, as compared to the ACP, in exporting manufactured goods to the EC.
44. The figures only 'strongly suggest', rather than prove, the advantage of percentage increases in 'trade over aid' because there will typically be some opportunity costs to increasing exports.

Part V

Conclusions

This final section of the book comprises three chapters devoted to the progress of the EC, the economics of 1992 and the future prospects for the EC. Since the creation of an internal market by 1992 is an objective of the EC, it is necessarily part of its present and future development; hence its inclusion in this section is perfectly justified.

22 The development of the EC

A. M. El-Agraa

The aim of this chapter is to provide a brief review of the progress made by the EC in terms of establishing a common market and moving towards an economic union. However, such a summary of events would not be complete without an adequate restatement of the most significant political developments that have taken place; indeed it could be argued that a list of EC accomplishments would be pointless without also explaining the political context within which they have been achieved. The first section of this chapter is therefore devoted to these developments while the remaining sections tackle the periods before and after the first enlargement of the EC, and the present. The future, being speculative and subject to many personal prejudices, is left to the final chapter. The intervening chapter is devoted to a brief summary of the economics of 1992.

22.1 Political developments

As stated in Chapter 2, the EC created a number of institutions to execute the tasks it had been entrusted with. These revolved around a legislative body (the Council of Ministers) and an initiator of policies (the Commission, which is also the administrator, mediator and police force of the EC), backed up by an advisory body (the European Parliament, with recently increased powers) and a guardian of the treaties (the Court of Justice). However, by the 1970s, it had become clear that the EC was entering a period of political change for which these institutions were less suitable than had initially been envisaged and for which they lacked adequate strength. However, rather than promoting a strengthening of the existing institutions, a method was found to bring national political leaders more closely into EC affairs by the introduction of summit meetings. As we have seen, these were formalised under the name of the European Council in 1974.

The first major summit was held in The Hague in December 1969. At that summit, the original six member nations of the EC effectively recognised that they

465

were so closely interdependent that they had no choice other than to continue as a united group. They were thus compelled to settle matters such as the Common Agricultural Policy (CAP) and changes in the general budget of the EC. A point of vital importance was the recognition that the EC possessed the political will to work for enlargement and hence had to confront the question of relations with the United Kingdom more positively.

The summit also recognised that the EC needed to reconsider its position in the world. The EC's responsibilities neither matched its economic weight nor allowed effective consideration of the political aspects of its external economic relations. Individual member nations still conducted external affairs themselves and could, therefore, undermine EC interests. The attraction of bringing foreign policy into the EC sphere was the greater effectiveness this might bring in international affairs; but the idea raised such sensitive issues as the relations with the United States and the USSR as well as defence matters.

In the end The Hague summit requested the foreign ministers to study the best way of achieving further political integration, within the context of commitment to EC enlargement, and to present a report. The later efforts made to achieve political cooperation, with emphasis upon international affairs, have been important in helping the EC identify its common aims and make the nature of the group coherent. Political cooperation has itself led to institutional innovation. This has occurred alongside the original institutions of the EC and not as part of them, although they are increasingly coming closer together.

In 1972 an important summit was held in Paris. This was attended by the three new members – Denmark, Ireland and the United Kingdom. The summit devoted considerable attention to the need to strengthen the social and regional aims of the EC. Furthermore, the deterioration in the international climate and the preoccupation of member governments with economic matters at home seemed to require frequent meetings of heads of government to ensure that the EC remained an effective economic unit.

The different philosophies and approaches of the governments of member countries to new problems made summit meetings essential for establishing the extent of common ground and for ensuring that this was used as the basis for action by the member nations. Initially, this seemed to strengthen the intergovernmental structure of the EC at the expense of the supranational element. However, it was also a reflection of the reality that the member nations had realised that their future aims were closely interdependent and required the formulation of joint goals and policies over a very wide field indeed. Informal discussion of general issues, whether economic or political, domestic or international, was a necessary preliminary to further, formal integration, and through the summit meetings and the political cooperation procedure the scope of the subject matter for the EC was steadily enlarged.

By the time of the Paris summit meeting in 1972 the member nations had laid down for themselves an ambitious programme of activity designed to lead to a European union. Much remained to be defined, but a number of external issues had been clearly identified. These included the need:

1. To maintain a constructive dialogue with the United States, Canada and Japan.
2. To act jointly in matters of external trade policy.
3. For member nations to make a concerted contribution to the 'Conference on Security and Cooperation in Europe'.

Foreign ministers were to meet more frequently in order to handle this last theme.

The global economic difficulties of the 1970s, triggered by the first oil shock, created a harsh environment within which the EC had to strive to establish its identity, future goals and executive responsibilities. It is easy to understand why progress was extremely slow during this period.

The Paris summit of 1974 formally agreed that the distinction between EC affairs and political cooperation was untenable, and in 1981 the foreign ministers agreed that political cooperation between the member nations had become central to their foreign policies. Proceedings became formalised and relations were established with the Commission.

The same summit asked the then Belgian prime minister (Leo Tindemans) to consult the governments of the member nations and write a report on the concept of European union. This brought out into the open the long-standing question of whether the member nations of the EC did, or could, constitute an effective economic whole or whether progress as a two-tier EC might be preferable.

The concept of a two-tier EC means that those member nations which have the will and ability to forge ahead towards such a union should do so. The others would lag behind, but would not be relieved from the need to achieve the ultimate goal. As Swann (1988) has argued, this could be interpreted pessimistically: the fact that the concept is discussed at all suggests lack of cohesion between the member nations. It could also be interpreted optimistically: in the absence of majority voting, some member nations could still forge ahead despite the disagreement of the rest of the member nations – the European Monetary System (EMS) was launched on such a basis since the United Kingdom refused to take part in the exchange-rate aspect of the scheme (see Chapter 15). So far, this question has been avoided in favour of special measures (financed by the structural funds) within the EC to help the weaker member nations (see Chapter 14).

A further proposition was that the EC should take steps towards making itself more of a citizens' Europe by including action in matters such as consumer rights, environmental protection and the safeguarding of fundamental rights – see Chapters 17 and 18.

Two further ideas were discussed:

1. A common stand in foreign policy, which could then be applied by the member states.
2. A tentative start on defence issues.

Institutional reform would be required in several directions. The interrelated issues of constitutional development and institutional reform continued to occupy the attention of those concerned with the EC, but for a number of years little progress was made. The EC appeared to be in danger of reaching a dead end:

1. The deepening of the integrative process required action which the member nations found controversial.
2. New member nations introduced their own problems and perspectives.
3. The recession meant that the attitudes of the member nations hardened towards the necessary compromise if cooperative solutions to problems were to be found.

A particular constraint was presented by the limits on EC finance (the size of the EC general budget) which prevented the development of EC policies and led to the bitter arguments about the resources devoted to the CAP (see Chapter 14).

Internal divisions were compounded by fears of a lack of dynamism in the EC economy which threatened a relative decline in international terms. Such worries suggested that a significant leap forward was needed to ensure a real 'common market' and to encourage new growth. However, to move the EC in this direction and to modernise EC institutions so that they worked more efficiently proved a laborious process. While member nations could agree upon the aims, in practice they fought hard to ensure that the reform incorporated measures favourable to themselves.

As the debate continued, a major division emerged between those who were primarily interested in the political ideal of European union and who wished to see institutional reform which would strengthen the EC's capacity to act, and those who had a more pragmatic approach which stressed the need for new policies, especially those directed to stimulating the EC economy. The idea of European union was developed further by an Italian–German proposal for a European Act (the Genscher–Colombo Plan) and by the European Parliament which adopted a 'Draft treaty on European union' in 1984.

In the mean time a series of summit meetings was keeping the momentum going at the level of heads of state or government. The Stuttgart summit meeting of 1983 agreed on an impressive work programme of issues which needed solution, and produced a 'Solemn declaration on European union'.

The vehement discussions of the following two years, often complicated by the need to solve more immediate problems, meant that it was not until the Luxemburg summit meeting of 1985 that the lines of the agreement could be settled. These were brought together in the Single European Act (SEA) which became operative on 1 July 1987.

22.2 The period from 1958 to 1969

Between 1958 and 1969, when the transition period came to an end, the original six member nations of the EC were preoccupied with the construction of the 'community' envisaged in the Treaty of Rome. Here, it is not necessary to describe all the measures that were undertaken during this period since these have been fully discussed earlier

Table 22.1 EC intra-area tariff reductions (per cent)

Acceleration of	Individual reductions made on the 1 January 1957 level	Cumulative reduction
1 January 1959	10	10
1 July 1960	10	20
1 January 1961	10	30
1 January 1962	10	40
1 July 1962	10	50
1 July 1963	10	60
1 January 1965	10	70
1 January 1966	10	80
1 July 1967	5	85
1 July 1968	15	100

Source: Commission of the European Communities, *First General Report on the Activities of the Communities* (EC Commission: Brussels), p. 34.

in this book. It is enough to state that the basic elements of the customs union (i.e. the removal of the internal tariffs, the elimination of import quota restrictions and the creation of the common external tariffs (CETs)) were established ahead of schedule – see Tables 22.1 and 22.2. Initial steps were undertaken and measures proposed to tackle the many non-tariff barriers to the free movement of goods, services and factors of production so that by 1969 a recognisably common market could be said to exist.

Progress was uneven in the area of common policies. Because of French demands, sometimes bordering on threats, the CAP was almost fully operational by 1969. However, as Gwilliam clearly shows in Chapter 11, the Common Transport Policy was slow to evolve. Moreover, Collins has demonstrated in Chapters 2 and 17 that the European Social Fund (ESF) and the European Investment Bank (EIB) were duly established and were fully operational at an early stage. Furthermore, as McAleese argued in Chapter 20, steps were taken to create a Common Commercial Policy

Table 22.2 The establishment of the CET (per cent)

Acceleration of	Industial products adjustment	Cumulative adjustment	Agricultural products' adjustment	Cumulative adjustment
1 January 1961	30	30		
1 January 1962			30	30
1 July 1963	30	60		
1 January 1966			30	60
1 July 1968	40	100	40	100

Source: Commission of the European Communities, *First General Report on the Activities of the Communities* (EC Commission: Brussels), p. 34.

(CCP), and, as Marin clearly shows in Chapter 21, the original six undertook appropriate trade and aid arrangements in respect of their colonial and increasingly ex-colonial dependencies. A rudimentary system of macroeconomic policy coordination was also devised (see Chapter 5).

Although during this period progress was evident and optimism about the success of the EC was much enhanced, there were some disappointments. From a 'federalist' point of view, perhaps the greatest was the French refusal to accept the supranational element in the Treaty decision-making system, hence the 'Luxemburg compromise'. When the member nations signed the Treaty of Rome, they opted for an EC Council of Ministers which could take decisions on the basis of a supranational majority voting system, but the Luxemburg compromise meant that any member state could insist that nothing should happen unless it agreed that it should happen, i.e. a veto system was adopted.

22.3 The period from 1969 to the early 1980s

When the transition period came to an end in 1969, it would have been possible for the original six to state that their mission had been accomplished. However, there were several reasons why it was neither possible nor appropriate for the EC to stop there. Firstly, the creation of common policies in such fields as agriculture and competition required an administration to operate them. This is because decisions regarding agricultural prices had to be taken on a seasonal or annual basis and markets had to be continuously manipulated in order that those prices should be received by farmers. The activities of businessmen and governments had to be continuously monitored in order that factors which would otherwise prevent, restrict or distort competitive trade should be eliminated. Secondly, although substantial progress had been made in achieving the aims listed in Article 3 of the Treaty, when the transition period was approaching its end it had to be admitted that substantial policy gaps still remained to be filled before it could be claimed that a truly common market existed.

Be that as it may, it would have been possible for the member nations to state that, subject to the need to operate existing policies and to fill obvious policy gaps, no further economic integration or institutional development should be attempted. In fact the EC decided quite the contrary: new areas of economic policy were opened up and old ones were substantially changed.

In 1969, during The Hague summit, the original six decided that the EC should progressively transform itself into an economic and monetary union (EMU). Although important measures were subsequently introduced in order to achieve the EMU, the goal of reaching this aim eventually failed. This was due to the global economic difficulties of the early 1970s and to the first enlargement of the EC. Nevertheless, the idea did not go away since in the late 1970s a more modest scheme was successfully introduced – EMS; and in 1989, the member nations endorsed the Delors Report, committing themselves to achieving an EMU in three stages, with the first to begin in December 1990 (see Chapter 5).

The EMU proposal was only one of a succession of new policy initiatives during 1969–72. Indeed, this period can be described as one of great activity. First, in 1970, the original six reached a common position on the development of a Common Fisheries Policy (CFP – see Chapter 10), although total agreement was not to be achieved until 1983. Second, at the Paris summit of 1973, agreement was reached on the development of new policies in relation to both industry and science and research. Third, the summit also envisaged a more active role for the EC in the area of regional policy, and decided that a European Regional Development Fund (ERDF) was to be established to channel EC resources into the development of the backward regions (see Chapter 16). Fourth, as we saw in Chapter 17, the summit also called for a new initiative in the field of social policy. Fifth, later in the 1970s, the relationship between the EC and its ex-colonial dependencies was significantly reshaped in the form of the 'Lomé Convention' (see Chapters 20 and 21). Finally, there was the series of institutional developments which we discussed briefly in the first section of this chapter (and, fully, in Chapter 2), especially the summit meetings and their formalisation into the European Council.

It is obvious from all these developments that the EC needed financial resources not only to pay for the day-to-day running of the EC but also to feed the various funds that were established: the ESF, ERDF and, most important of all, the European Agricultural Guidance and Guarantee Fund (EAGGF). As we have seen, in 1970 the EC took the important step of agreeing to introduce a system which would provide the EC, and specifically the EC General Budget, with its own resources, thus relieving it of the uncertainly of annual decisions regarding its finances as well as endorsing its political autonomy (see Chapter 14). Another step of great importance was the decision that the European Parliament should be elected directly by the people, not by the national parliaments. In addition, the EC decided to grant the European Parliament significant powers over the EC General Budget; as we saw in Chapter 2, this proved to be a very significant development. Finally, but by no means least, was the development of the political cooperation mechanism. It is important not to forget that the dedicated Europeans had always hoped that the habit of cooperation in the economic field would spill over into the political arena, i.e. into foreign policy matters. As we have seen, that has indeed happened: the political cooperation that we see today can be said to date from The Hague summit of 1969 and was formally inaugurated in 1970.

Although there have been a series of institutional developments, the relationship between the member nations has undergone a significant change. When the member nations signed the Treaty of Rome, they opted for an EC Council of Ministers which could take decisions on the basis of a supranational majority voting system. However, the insistence of the French led to the Luxemburg compromise. In addition, and especially after 1969, the centre of gravity of decision making within the EC became the European Council.

The method of operation of the European Council is cast in the traditional intergovernmental mould. As Swann (1988) argues, the development of intergovernmentalism might have been expected to slow down the pace of progress within the

EC: the unanimity principle would always force the EC to adopt the lowest common denominator and that might mean little or even no change whatever. However, that was certainly not the case in the early 1970s: as we have seen, a number of new initiatives were launched and in the main those initiatives were designed to further the process of integration.

Intergovernmentalism is still strong in the 1980s, but the performance of the intergovernmental EC of the early 1980s has been markedly less dynamic than that of the early 1970s. A good deal of activity within the EC then centred around quarrels over matters such as the reform of the CAP and the EC General Budget, especially the United Kingdom's contribution to it.

At this juncture it may be useful to stress two conclusions. The first is that, despite developments in foreign policy cooperation, the EC lacks two essential attributes of a state. These are responsibility for external affairs and defence. Thus, as Collins argues in Chapter 2, the EC has a great gap in its competences, but its weight makes it highly significant in world economics and thus in world politics. The second is that the significant achievements of the EC during the post-1969 period made it very attractive. This attraction is demonstrated by:

1. Its first round of enlargement to include Denmark, Ireland and the United Kingdom in 1973.
2. The adhesion of Greece in 1981.
3. Its second round of enlargement to include Portugal and Spain in 1986.
4. The recent applications for membership by Austria and Turkey.

Tables 22.3 and 22.4 give the timetable for the adjustments in the common external tariffs (CETs) and the dismantling of the internal tariffs for the three countries involved in the first enlargement: Denmark, Ireland and the United Kingdom. The tables do not cover all groups of commodities. For example, tariffs on coal imports were abolished from the day of accession, and tariffs on certain groups of commodities given in Annex III of the Treaty of Accession were abolished on 1 January 1974, etc. In the case of the CETs, those tariffs which differed by less than 15 per cent were adjusted on 1 January 1974. Import quota restrictions were also

Table 22.3 New members' intra-tariff reductions (per cent)

	Individual reductions made on 1 January 1972	Cumulative reduction
1 April 1973	20	20
1 January 1974	20	40
1 January 1975	20	60
1 January 1976	20	80
1 July 1977	20	100

Source: *Bulletin of the European Communities*, no. 8, 1978.

Table 22.4 Approaching the CET (per cent)[a]

	Individual adjustments made on 1 January 1972	Cumulative adjustment
1 January 1974	40	40
1 January 1975	20	60
1 January 1976	20	80
1 July 1977	20	100

Note
[a] For products which differ by more than 15 per cent from the CET.

Source: *Bulletin of the European Communities*, no. 8, 1978.

abolished from the date of accession. Measures having equivalent effects to the import quota restrictions were eliminated by the deadline of 1 January 1975. All three new member nations had no difficulties in achieving these changes.

In the case of Greece's membership of the EC, a five-year period was agreed for the progressive dismantling of residual customs duties on Greek imports of products originating in the EC and for the progressive alignment of Greek tariffs to the CET. Customs duties on Greek imports from the EC were to be reduced in six stages commencing on 1 January 1981, with a reduction of 10 percentage points followed by a further reduction of the same percentage points on 1 January 1982 and four annual reductions of 20 percentage points so that all customs duties on Greek intra-EC trade would be removed by 1 January 1986. Alignment of the CET was to follow the same timetable.

Quantitative restrictions between Greece and the EC were to be abolished on adhesion, with the exception of fourteen products for which Greece has been authorised to maintain transitional quotas. These quotas were to be progressively increased during the five-year transitional period and to be completely eliminated by 31 December 1985. As a general rule, the minimum rates of increase for such quotas was 25 per cent at the beginning of each year for quotas expressed in value terms and 20 per cent at the beginning of each year for quotas expressed in volume terms. Measures having equivalent effect to quantitative restrictions were to be eliminated upon adhesion, except for the Greek system of cash payments and import deposits which were to be phased out over three years (see *Bulletin of the European Communities*, no. 5, 1969 for these and further details.)

In the case of Portugal and Spain, a ten-year transitional period was agreed. For Portugal, this is divided into two equal (five-year) stages for the major products and a basic seven-year period for other products, although some measures will apply for the full ten years. For Spain, there are some variations, but the essentials are basically the same.

It can be stated that Greece has navigated its transition period successfully and it would seem that the Iberian member nations are having no difficulties accommodating their required changes either; but, of course, they still have a long way to go.

So far there has been one withdrawal. The position of Greenland was renegotiated in 1984 but it remains associated under the rules of 'Overseas countries and territories'. A special agreement regulates mutual fishing interests.

In contrast with this rosy picture one must register some reservations. Although efforts have been made to consolidate individual EC member nation rules into EC legislation, and although a number of nationally differentiated quantitative restrictions (QRs) have been formally incorporated into a CCP, a large number of the VERs (voluntary export restraints) and administrative restrictions remain outside this, and even the QRs which are officially (EC) recognised apply at a national level (France and Italy had 121 items in 1982, the United Kingdom 65 and Germany 31 – most of these are on cars, steel and textiles and clothing). Hence, with the EC level of external protection being punctured by national QRs, the EC is now effectively a free trade area rather than a customs union in this respect. 'It follows that if the level of external protection is different between members of a free trade area, only intra-area border controls can prevent trade deflection' (Holmes and Shepherd, 1983).

It may come as a surprise to learn that the EC is really a free trade area rather than a customs union as far as trade is concerned, i.e. goods on which import duties have been paid are not in free circulation within the EC. Holmes and Shepherd (1983) advance explanations for this surprising outcome.

> One reason for this arises out of the complex nature of customs regulations. In the UK it has been traditional for imported goods to be cleared at a port and thenceforward to be treated identically to domestic goods. Continental countries have evolved a different system; as a result of the many land frontiers an item may have to cross before it reaches a final destination, it is customary for goods to travel long distances in bond to their final destination where customs clearance takes place. Under the UK system any item physically in the country may be seen as innocent until proved guilty of being other than in free circulation. Elsewhere administrative procedures exist as a matter of routine which may be used to prevent any item from being sold freely unless it can be shown that it has been properly imported.
>
> The existence of such procedures and the frequent but not automatic invocation of Article 115 naturally leads policy makers to turn their minds not only to ways of combatting [sic] trade deflection but also of preventing trade diversion, where goods from another member of the integrated area replace external imports. Obstruction of imports from other members is of course largely illegal under the Treaty of Rome ..., but there is a logical inconsistency in differing degrees of external protection being combined with a totally free internal market. The fact that intra-EEC free trade is a fundamental legal requirement means that the devices to prevent it therefore lie in the nooks and crannies of administrative arrangements.

Holmes and Shepherd then proceed to consider a vast number of such hidden barriers to trade. However, before leaving this item, it should be emphasised that at a time of severe recession, with the EC external tariff being so small (see Chapter 20), it is understandable that a number of non-tariff barriers should come to the forefront. This does not mean that they should be condoned: indeed, every effort should be made to recognise them and eliminate them – see below.

22.4 The present

The present begins in the mid-1980s. Without a shadow of doubt, its star must be the Single European Act which now regulates all the activities of the EC. In the section on political developments, we examined the factors which led to its birth. As Collins has shown in Chapter 2, the SEA contains policy development which is based upon the intention of having a true single market in place by the end of 1992 with free movement of capital, labour, services and goods rather than the patchy arrangements of the past. The SEA also introduces, or strengthens, other policy fields. These include the following:

1. Responsibility towards the environment.
2. The encouragement of further action to promote health and safety at work.
3. Technological research and development (R&D).
4. Work to strengthen economic and social cohesion so that weaker members may participate fully in the freer market.
5. Cooperation in economic and monetary policy.

In addition, the SEA brings foreign policy cooperation into scope and provides it with a more effective support than it has had hitherto, including its own secretariat to be housed in the Council building in Brussels.

Institutionally, as we have seen, it was agreed that the European Council would take decisions on qualified majority vote in relation to the internal market, research, cohesion and improved working conditions and that, in such cases, the European Parliament should share in decision making. These developments were followed later by agreement regarding the control of expenditure on the CAP (which, as we have seen in Chapters 9 and 14, has been a source of heated argument for a number of years) and, most importantly, a fundamental change in the EC General Budget (see Chapter 14).

Moreover, one should add the recent agreement reached by the EC member nations for the creation of an EMU in three stages, with the first to commence in 1990, and its current pursuit of an EC Social Charter; but then one is crossing the borderline between the present and the future.

22.5 Conclusion

The main conclusion is that the EC has been successful not only in achieving *negative integration* (see Chapter 1), but also in adopting elements of *positive integration*. However, this conclusion cannot be pursued further without a full specification of the Commission's White Paper to which Chapter 23 is devoted. It is advisable to turn immediately to that chapter and its conclusion.

23 The economics of 1992

A. M. El-Agraa

In this book, the Single European Act (SEA), incorporating the package proposed by the Commission in its White Paper (Commission, 1985a) for the creation of an internal market by 1992, has been tackled as a natural but significant extension and development of the EC. Therefore, the reader who is interested in the details of the SEA and the internal market, and their implications for both the EC and the rest of the world, will have to go through virtually every chapter of the book for information; the implications of the single market are too wide and far reaching to be tackled in a vacuum. This approach may offend those who believe that the future should be highlighted and the past forgotten; but the emphasis in this book is on the evolution and dynamism of the EC. To follow the bandwagon by concentrating entirely on the economics of 1992 would be to negate the very foundations of our approach. However, at this juncture it may be in order to devote a chapter specifically to the internal market and to the benefits to be expected from its creation.

23.1 The aspirations of the White Paper

According to Lord Cockfield, then Commission Vice-President with a portfolio including the internal market, the completion of the single market was the first priority of the Commission to which he belonged. He went so far as to state that its accomplishment would be the greatest achievement of the Commission during its term of office. This was put more succinctly in the *Bulletin of the European Communities* (no. 6, 1985, p. 18):

> From the words of the Treaties themselves through successive declarations by the European Council since 1982, the need to complete the internal market has been confirmed at the highest level. What has been missing has been an agreed target date and a detailed programme for meeting it. The Commission has welcomed the challenge of providing the missing piece. It has interpreted the challenge in the most comprehensive way possible: the creation by 1992 of a genuine common market without internal frontiers.

According to the White Paper the completion of the internal market will become a reality when the EC has eliminated any physical, technical and fiscal barriers among its member nations. Before elaborating on these, it should be stressed that the Commission felt that the single market programme contained three main features:

> (i) there are to be no more attempts to harmonize or standardize at any price – a method originating in too rigid an interpretation of the Treaty; in most cases, an 'approximation' of the parameters is sufficient to reduce differences in rates or technical specifications to an acceptable level [see Chapter 13];
> (ii) the programme will propose no measures which, while supposedly facilitating trade or travel, in fact maintain checks at internal frontiers and therefore the frontiers themselves, the symbol of the Community's fragmentation; their disappearance will have immense psychological and practical importance; [and]
> (iii) a major factor for the success of the programme is its two-stage, binding timetable, with relatively short deadlines, relying as far as possible on built-on mechanisms; the programme is a comprehensive one, which means that it has the balance needed if general agreement is to be forthcoming. (*Bulletin of the European Communities*, no. 6, 1985, p. 18)

With regard to physical frontiers, the aim is to eliminate them altogether, not just to reduce them. The Commission argued that it is not sufficient to simply reduce the number of controls carried out at the borders because as long as persons and goods have to stop and be checked, the main aim will not be achieved: 'goods and citizens will not have been relieved of the costly delays and irritations of being held up at frontiers, and there will still be no real Community'.

In the White Paper the Commission provided a specification of all the functions carried out at border-crossing points. It pointed out those functions that could or should be unnecessary in a true common market. Moreover, where the function carried out at the frontier check point was still deemed to be necessary, the Commission recommended alternative ways of achieving it without border-crossing points. For example, with regard to health protection, the Commission suggested that checks on veterinary and plant health should be limited to destination points, the implication being that 'national standards be as far as possible aligned on common standards'. With regard to transport, quotas had to be progressively relaxed and eliminated, and common safety standards introduced for vehicles so that systematic controls could be dispensed with.

The Commission was quick to point out that it was quite aware of the implications of the elimination of border-crossing points for such sensitive issues as tax policy and the fight against drugs and terrorism. It stressed that it 'recognises frankly that these are difficult areas, which pose real problems', but maintained its belief that the objectives justify the effort that would be needed to solve them. Thus, it promised to put forward directives regarding the harmonisation of laws concerning arms and drugs.

As to the question of technical barriers, the Commission argued that the elimination of border-crossing points would be to no avail if both firms and persons inside the EC continued to be subjected to such hidden barriers. Therefore, the Commission carefully considered these technical barriers and suggested ways of eliminating them to a detailed timetable. The Commission proposals covered goods and services, freedom of movement for workers and professional persons, public procurement, capital movements and the creation of conditions for industrial cooperation.

In the case of goods, the Commission emphasised that, provided certain health and safety-related constraints and safeguards are met, goods which are 'lawfully' made and sold in one EC member nation should be able to move freely and go on sale *anywhere* within the EC. For this purpose, the EC's new approach to technical harmonisation and standards (see *Official Journal of the European Communities*, no. 136, 4 April 1985) was to be applied and extended.

With regard to the freedom to provide services, the Commission recognised that there had been much slower progress here than with the situation regarding goods. It claimed that the distinction between goods and services had never been a valid one and that the EC had undermined its own economic potential by retaining it. This was because the service sector was not only growing fast as a 'value-adding provider of employment in its own right', but it also gave vital support and back-up for the manufacturing sector. It stressed that this was already the case not just in such traditional services as banking, insurance and transport, but also in the new areas of information, marketing and audio-visual services. Thus the White Paper put forward proposals and a timetable for action covering all these services until 1992. The Commission concluded that, with the creation of a true common market for the services sector in mind, it should be possible to enable the exchange of 'financial products' such as 'insurance policies, home-ownership savings contracts and consumer credit, using a minimum coordination of rules as the basis of mutual recognition'. With regard to transport, proposals were to be sent to the Council for the 'phasing out of all quantitative restrictions (quotas) on road haulage and for the further liberalisation of road passenger services by 1989, of sea transport services by the end of 1986 and of competition in air transport services by 1987' (see Chapter 11).

In the case of audio-visual services, the aim should be to endeavour to create a single EC-wide broadcasting area. For this purpose, the Commission was to make specific proposals in 1985 based on its Green Paper of May 1984 on the establishment of a common market for broadcasting.

As to capital movements, the Commission stated that from 1992 onwards any residual currency control measures should be applied by means other than border controls (see Chapter 15).

The Commission stated that in the case of employees, freedom of movement was already almost entirely complete. Moreover, the rulings of the Court of Justice restricted the right of public authorities in the EC member nations to reserve jobs for their own nationals. However, the Commission was to bring forward the necessary proposals to dismantle any obstacles that still prevailed. It was also to take measures to eliminate the cumbersome administrative procedures relating to residence permits.

With regard to the right of establishment for the self-employed, the Commission conceded that little progress had been made. This was because of the complexities involved in trying to harmonise professional qualifications (see Chapter 19 of this edition of the book and Chapter 16 of the first edition on the accounting profession). However, such efforts had led to a substantial degree of freedom of movement for those in the health sector and in 1985 the Council adopted measures which extended such freedom to architects after '18 years of protectionist pressure and exaggerated defensive arguments' (*Bulletin of the European Communities*, no. 6, 1985, p. 20). The Commission concluded by stating that in an effort to remove obstacles to the right of establishment, it would lay before the Council (in 1985) a framework directive on a general system of recognition of degrees and diplomas, the main features of which would be:

> the principle of mutual trust between the [member nations]; the principle of comparability of university studies between the [member nations]; the mutual recognition of degrees and diplomas without prior harmonization of the conditions for access to and the exercise of professions.

Any difference between the member nations, especially with regard to training, would be compensated by professional experience.

In the field of fiscal frontiers, the Commission was of the opinion that taxation would be one of the principal areas in which the challenge of 1992 had to be faced. It argued that the rates of indirect taxation in the EC member nations were in some cases so divergent (see Chapter 13) that they would no doubt create trade distortions, leading to loss of revenue to the exchequers of the member states. It was convinced that frontier controls could not be eliminated if substantial differences in VAT and excise duties prevailed between the member nations. Its conclusion was that if frontiers and associated controls were to be eliminated, 'it will be necessary not only to set up a Community clearing system for VAT and a linkage system of bonded warehouses for excised products, but also to introduce a considerable measure of approximation of indirect taxes'. The first question that this raised was how close should the approximation be. As stated in Chapter 13, the 'Commission argued that the experience of countries like the United States indicated that controls could be eliminated without a complete equalisation of rates'. Variations would have to be narrowed, but 'differences of up to 5% may coexist without undue adverse effects. This would suggest a margin of 2.5% either side of whatever target rate or norm is chosen' (*Bulletin of the European Communities*, no. 6, 1985, p. 20). The Commission stated that a great deal of statistical and econometric work would have to be carried out before it could make specific proposals. However, it felt that it would be of great assistance if the Council agreed to exert extra effort to finalise work on the proposals it had already presented to it. At the same time, the Commission would propose a 'standstill clause' to guarantee that prevailing variations in the number and levels of VAT rates would not be widened, hoping that in 1986 it would propose target rates or norms and allowed ranges of variation. However, it stressed that the approximation of indirect taxation would result in a number of problems for some of the EC member nations, and hence it might be necessary to provide for derogations. Needless to add, the discussion in Chapter 13 clearly shows that the Commission has delivered these proposals as promised.

Finally, the Commission concluded by making it clear that the proposed measures to accomplish a single EC domestic market would not become a reality without some institutional changes. It argued that in many areas the possibility of reaching decisions by majority voting must be entertained and left this issue for a separate document.

23.2 Actions promised by the Commission

The details of the actual proposals put forward by the Commission to enable the creation of the single market are by now not only common knowledge (see *The Economist* of 9 July, 1988 and 8 July, 1989), but can be found in a number of academic books (see, *inter alia*, Emerson *et al.*, 1988; Pelkmans and Winters, 1988) as well as in the majority of the chapters in this book. They therefore need not detain us here. However, in the Commission's view, the achievement of the internal market meant the enactment of 300 directives, 21 of which have been quietly dropped since 1988. By the summer of 1989, about half of these directives have either been adopted by the

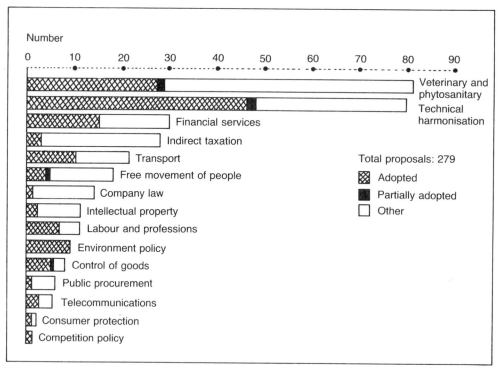

Figure 23.1 The number, type and status of White Paper Directives. (Some duplication occurs because of overlapping areas and some withdrawn proposals.)

European Council or have enjoyed the important common position within the Council (see Figure 23.1). Since there are still about two and a half years to go before the end of December 1992, it seems that the member nations are on target. However, if the discussion in Chapter 2 is recalled, it will be remembered that directives have to be incorporated into national law before they are put into practice, and some of the early directives had been in the pipeline long before the White Paper was published in 1985. Moreover, Butt Philip (1988) argues that although the *average* time taken for legislative proposals to pass through the Council is three years, many proposals have been in gestation in the Council for longer than this. He shows that in February 1987, 126 proposals from the Commission had been part of this 'logjam for over five years. Some thirty-eight proposals had been "under consideration" for over a decade'. His main explanation (p. 2) for such legislative delays at the EC level is that the negotiators for some of the member nations, 'in anticipation of implementation problems ahead, adopt a tough stance in order to ensure that the resulting decisions can be implemented by their own national administrations', and adds that other member nations such as Italy are 'less diligent in briefing their negotiators, and more frequently encounter administrative and other difficulties' when they come to apply the rules they have already endorsed. Furthermore, many of the directives have a contingent or voluntary outcome, especially those pertaining to the harmonisation of technical standards and the mutual recognition of rules. Only time can tell what the decisions will be and how the markets will respond to those decisions.

23.3 The expected benefits

According to the Cecchini Report, which summarises in 16 volumes the findings of a study carried out on behalf of the EC Commission (see EC Commission, 1988h; a popular version is to be found in Cecchini, 1988), the completion of the internal market will regenerate both the goods and services sectors of the EC. The study estimates the total potential gain for the EC as a whole to be in the region of 200 billion ECU, at constant 1988 prices. This would increase EC GDP by 5 per cent or more. The gains will come not only from the elimination of the costs of barriers to intra-EC trade, but also from the exploitation of economies of scale which are expected to lower costs by about 2 per cent of EC GDP. The medium-term impact of this on employment will be to increase it by about two million jobs. These estimates are considered to be minimal since the study points out that if the governments of the member nations of the EC pursue macroeconomic policies that recognise this potential for faster economic growth, the total gains could reach 7 per cent of EC GDP and increase employment by about five million jobs. If these predictions become a reality, the EC will gain a very substantial competitive edge over non-participating nations.

The summary of the Cecchini Report given in Cecchini (1988) is written for the general public. The definitive technical work is that by Emerson *et al.* (1988); Emerson is a leading economist who works for the Directorate-General for Economic and Financial Affairs, and in this capacity his (and his collaborators') work presents the official Commission analysis; hence the interested reader is advised to consult this work. Here it should be asked why the elimination of the various barriers mentioned above should lead to economic benefits for the EC. To answer this question meaningfully, one needs to specify the barriers, which are all of the non-tariff type, slightly differently, and in a more general context.

The barriers can be grouped into four major categories:

1. Differences in the technical regulations adopted in the various member nations which tend to increase the cost of intra-EC trade transactions.
2. Delays in the customs procedures at border-crossing points and related extra administrative tasks on both private firms and public organisations which further increase the costs of intra-EC trade transactions.
3. Public procurement procedures which effectively limit if not completely eliminate competition for public purchases to own member nation suppliers, a procedure often claimed to raise the price of such purchases.
4. Curtailment of one's ability either to transact freely in certain services, especially finance and transport, where barriers to entry are supposedly great, or to get established in them in another EC member nation.

No claim has been made to suggest that the cost of eliminating each of these barrier categories is substantial, but Emerson *et al.* (1988) have argued that the combination of these barriers, in an EC dominated by oligopolistic market structures, amounts to 'a considerable degree of non-competitive segmentation of the market', with the implication that the cost of eliminating all the barrier categories then becomes considerable. Since the emphasis is on costs (the Cecchini Report stresses them as the 'cost of non-Europe'), it follows that the elimination of these barriers will reduce the costs, i.e. increase the benefits; these are two sides of the same coin.

These benefits can also be expressed forthrightly. The elimination of the costs of non-Europe is tantamount to the removal of constraints which 'today prevent enterprises from being as efficient as they could be and from employing their resources to the full' (Emerson *et al.*, 1988, p. 2). They go on to argue that since these are constraints, their removal will 'establish a more competitive environment which will incite [the enterprises] to exploit new opportunities' (p. 2). They then claim that the combination of the elimination of the constraints and the creation of a more competitive situation will have four major types of effect:

1. A significant reduction in costs due to a better exploitation of several kinds of economies of scale associated with the size of production units and enterprises.
2. An improved efficiency in enterprises, a rationalisation of industrial structures and a setting of prices closer to costs of production, all resulting from more competitive markets.
3. Adjustments between industries on the basis of a fuller play of comparative advantages in an integrated market.
4. A flow of innovations, new processes and new products, stimulated by the dynamics of the internal market.

They were quick to add that these processes free resources for alternative productive uses, and when they are so utilised, the total sustainable level of consumption and investment in the EC economy will be increased. They stressed that this was their fundamental criterion of economic gain.

Given the definitive nature of the Emerson *et al.* (1988) book, it may be useful, at the risk of duplication, to quote the estimates of the gains as presented by them. To make sense of their calculations and, of course, of the overall results given above, it has to be recalled that all the calculations relate to 1985 when the total EC GDP was 3,300 billion ECU for the twelve member nations. However, the actual calculations were made for the seven largest EC member countries (accounting for 88 per cent of EC GDP for the twelve) with a total GDP of 2,900 billion ECU.

They claim that the overall estimates range from 70 billion ECU (2.5 per cent of EC GDP) for 'a rather narrow conception of the benefits' of eliminating the remaining barriers to the single market, to about 125 to 190 billion ECUs (4.5 per cent to 6.5 per cent of EC GDP) in the case of a more competitive and integrated market. Applying the same percentages to the 1988 GDP data, the gains were estimated to be between 175 and 255 billion ECUs. These gains are expected to increase the EC's annual growth rate by about 1 percentage point for the years until 1992. Also, 'there would be good prospects that longer-run dynamic effects could sustain a buoyant growth rate further into the 1990s' (p. 5).

These gains were obtained on the understanding that it might take five or more years for the upper limits to be achieved and that policies at both the microeconomic and macroeconomic level would ensure that the resources (basically labour) released by the savings in costs would be fully and effectively utilised elsewhere in the EC. These assumptions were made to simplify the analysis. However, in order to make the calculations look more professional, they used the estimates to generate macroeconomic simulations from macrodynamic models. For this purpose, the effects of the single market were classified into four groups according to their type of macroeconomic impact:

1. The elimination of customs delays and costs.
2. The exposing of public markets to competition.
3. The liberalisation and integration of financial markets.
4. Broader supply-side effects, 'reflecting changes in the strategic behaviour of enterprises in a new competitive environment' (p. 5).

The results of the simulations are then presented according to whether or not passive macroeconomic policies are pursued.

In the case of passive macroeconomic policies, the overall impact of the measures is felt most sharply in the earlier years in reduced prices and costs; but after a modest time lag output begins to increase. It is reported that the major impact is felt in the medium term (five to six years) when a cumulative impact of 4.5 per cent increase in GDP and a 6 per cent reduction in the price level may be expected. The effect on employment is slightly negative at the beginning, but increases by two million jobs (almost 2 per cent of the initial level of employment) by the medium term. Moreover, there is a marked improvement in the budget balance and a significant improvement in the current account.

In the case of more active macroeconomic policies, it is argued that since the main indicators of monetary and financial equilibrium would then be improved, it would be perfectly in order to 'consider adjusting medium-term macroeconomic strategy onto a somewhat more expansionary trajectory' (p. 6). Obviously, the extent of adjustment rests upon which constraint (inflation, budget or balance of payments deficit) is considered crucial. In the text, a number of variants is illustrated. For example, in the middle of the range there is a case in which the level of GDP is 2.5 per cent higher after the medium term. Since this is additional to the 4.5 per cent boost obtained with passive macroeconomic policies, the total effect is therefore 7 per cent. It is pointed out that in this instance, inflation would still be below its projected value in the absence of the single market, the budget balance would also be improved and the balance of payments might be worsened by a 'moderate but sustainable amount'.

Before going further, it is important to be explicit about certain assumptions behind these estimates:

> It is implicit, in order to attain the highest sustainable level of consumption and investment, that productivity and employment be also of a high order. In particular, where rationalisation efforts cause labour to be made redundant, this resource has to be successfully re-employed. Also implicit is a high rate of growth in the economy. The sustainability condition, moreover, requires that the major macroeconomic equilibrium constraints are respected, notably as regards price stability, balance of payments and budget balances. It further implies a positive performance in terms of world-wide competitivity. (Emerson *et al.*, 1988, p. 2)

Although these estimates depend largely on a number of crucial qualifications, Emerson *et al.* state that irrespective of these qualifications, the upper limits to the gains are unlikely to be overestimates of the potential benefits of a fully integrated EC market. This is because:

> the figures exclude some important categories of dynamic impact on economic performance. Three examples may be mentioned. Firstly, there is increasing evidence that the trend rate of technological innovation in the economy depends upon the presence of competition; only an integrated market can offer the benefits both of scale of operation and competition. Secondly, there is evidence in fast-growing high technology industries of dynamic or learning economies of scale, whereby costs decline as the total accumulated production of certain goods and services increase[s]; market segmentation greatly limits the scope of these benefits and damages performance in key high-growth industries of the future. Thirdly, the business strategies of European enterprises are likely to be greatly affected in the event of a rapid and extensive implementation of the internal market pro-gramme; a full integration of the internal market will foster the emergence of truly European companies, with structures and strategies that are better suited to securing a strong place in world market competition. (Emerson *et al.*, 1988, pp. 6–7)

23.4 Theoretical illustration

Before stating explicit reservations, it may be useful to provide some theoretical framework for some of the stated gains. Let us consider two cases. The first is one in which comparative advantage can be exploited by trade. The second concerns the case of enhanced competition where there is no comparative advantage between countries. The basic model behind the diagrams used below is fully set out in Chapter 4 and in standard trade theory books – see El-Agraa (1989b). No explanation will therefore be provided here.

The first case is illustrated by Figure 23.2. Due to the removal of certain market barriers and distortions, the relative price of a particular commodity is equalised throughout the entire EC market at the lower P_2 in the EC member country under consideration. As we have seen, this is because it is assumed that the presence of these barriers is costly, leading to the higher price level P_3 in that country. Since this country is a net importer from the rest of the EC, comparative advantage lies with the EC or, alternatively, this country has a comparative disadvantage.

In this member country, the removal of the barrier increases consumer surplus by areas A and B and reduces producer surplus by area A, giving a net benefit of area B. In the rest of the EC, there is an increase in producer surplus of areas C and D and a reduction in consumer surplus of area C, resulting in a net benefit of area D. Therefore, the total benefit to the EC as a whole is the sum of the two net benefits, i.e. areas B plus D. In short, the analysis in the case of the member country is the reverse of the one for tariffs considered in Chapter 9, while the analysis for the rest of the EC is exactly the same as that in the same chapter applied to agricultural surpluses.

The second case is illustrated by Figure 23.3. As barriers are removed, importers are able to reduce their prices from P_2 by the amount of direct costs saved. Domestic

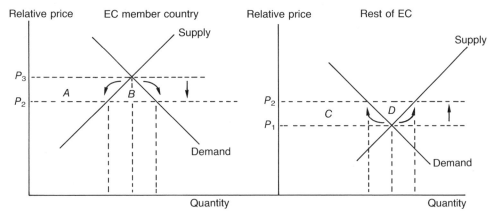

Figure 23.2 Effects of eliminating market barriers and distortions for a given commodity (the case in which comparative advantage can be exploited by trade). (Source: adapted from Emerson et al., 1988).

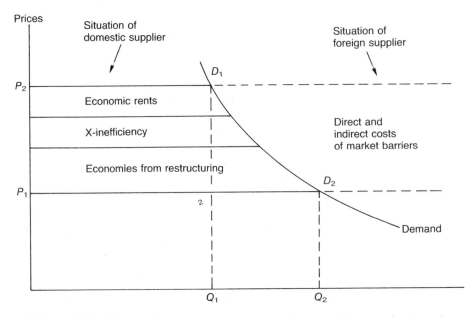

Figure 23.3 Effects of eliminating cost-increasing trade barriers (the case of enhanced competition where there are no comparative advantages between countries). Economic rents consist of the margins of excess profits or wage rates that result from market protection. X-inefficiency consists of, for example, the costs of overmanning, excess overhead costs and excess inventories (i.e. inefficiencies not related to the production technology of the firm's investments). Economies from restructuring include, for example, the greater economies of scale or scope obtained when inefficient production capacity is eliminated and new investments are made. Direct costs are those, such as delays at frontiers and the cost of differing technical regulations, that would immediately fall if the market barriers were eliminated. Indirect costs are those that would fall as foreign suppliers adjust to the more competitive situation with more efficient production and marketing. (Source: adapted from Emerson *et al.*, 1988).

producers respond by reducing their own prices through reductions in their excess profits and wages or by eliminating inefficiencies of various types (overhead costs, excess manning and inventories, etc.). As prices fall, demand increases beyond Q_1 and this induces investment in productive capacity in this industry which results in economies of scale and further price reductions. However, this is not the end of the story since this more competitive market environment is supposed to make industries reconsider their business strategies in a fundamental way, leading to restructuring (mergers and acquisitions, liquidations and investment) over a number of years until output increases to Q_2.

As can be seen from the diagram, there is an increase in consumer surplus equal to area $P_2D_1D_2P_1$, but what happens to producer surplus is not so clear. On the one hand, producers may be able to compensate for price cuts in terms of cost reductions; but they will lose some economic rent. On the other hand, since they have become more competitive, they may be able to sell outside the EC and so increase their output and profits. For the EC economy as a whole, it can be said that there is a net benefit since the gains to the EC consumer are in excess of the losses incurred by the EC producers. However, in the light of the discussion in Chapter 4, it must be emphasised that this analysis is extremely simple.

23.5 Reservations

There are two reservations to consider. The first is advanced by Pelkmans and Robson (1987). It is that the categorisation by the EC of these three types of barrier is somewhat arbitrary. Physical barriers are concerned with frontier controls on the movement of goods and persons. Fiscal barriers consist of all impediments and substantial distortions among member states that emanate from differences in the commodity base as well as in the rates of VAT and the duties on excises (see Chapter 13). All remaining impediments fall into the category of technical barriers. Therefore, this category comprises not only barriers arising from absence of technical harmonisation and public procurement procedures, but also institutional impediments on the free movement of people, capital and financial services, including transport and data transmission. It also comprises a miscellaneous collection of obstacles to the business environment which take the form of an inadequately harmonised company law, the lack of an EC patent and of an EC trade mark, together with issues of corporate taxation and several diverse problems concerned with the national application of EC law. However, even though this categorisation may make analysis more cumbersome, the approach adopted in this book shows that this is not a serious reservation.

The second reservation is more serious. It is that the estimates given in the Cecchini Report should not be taken at face value. First, in spite of the endorsement of the SEA by all the member nations, there does not seem to be a philosophy common to all of them to underpin the internal market. Second, these estimates do not take into consideration the costs to be incurred by firms, regions and governments in achieving them. Third, the internal market aims at the elimination of internal barriers to promote the efficient restructuring of supply, but it remains silent on the question of demand; thus the internal market seems to be directed mainly at the production side. Fourth, putting too much emphasis on economies of scale, when their very existence has to be proved, will encourage concentration rather than competition, and there is no evidence to support the proposition that there is a positive correlation between increased firm size and competitive success. Finally, the estimates are for the EC as a whole; thus it is likely that each member nation will strive to get the maximum gain for itself with detrimental consequences for all, i.e. this is like the classical oligopoly problem where the best solution for profit-maximisation purposes is for oligopolists to behave as joint monopolists, but if each oligopolist firm tries to maximise its own share of the joint profit, the outcome may be losses all round.

A rigorous specification of these reservations is fully set out in Chapters 4 and 5 of this book and in El-Agraa (1989a). Here it is sufficient to state that such potential benefits may prove rather elusive since the creation of the appropriate environment does not guarantee the expected outcomes. However, this does not mean that the EC should not be congratulated for its genuine attempts to create the necessary competitive atmosphere, only that one should not put too much emphasis on estimates which can easily be frustrated by the realities of every day EC economic life. However, some of the quotations given above clearly show that the experts are aware of these problems.

23.6 Conclusion

The conclusion is evident: the EC has been successful not only in achieving *negative integration* (see Chapter 1), but also in adopting elements of *positive integration*. Because in the latter progress has been slow, the EC has set itself an extensive programme, with deadlines, for accomplishing a true internal market and an EMU. Only history can tell whether or not the EC has been unduly optimistic, but in terms of the philosophy of the founding fathers it could be argued that the EC is at last on target. As to the future, only politics can help, which is why it is left to the final chapter.

24 The future of the EC

A. M. El-Agraa

Chapters 22 and 23 are devoted to a brief yet comprehensive assessment of the development of the EC. It is arguable whether those chapters should be located at the end or at the beginning of the book, but that is beside the point. What is important is that the whole book, including those chapters, is essential reading before reflecting on the future of the EC, which is the aim of this concluding chapter.

To answer meaningfully the question of what the future will bring to the EC, one needs a specification of what the future means. Is it the immediate future? Is it the immediate period after 1992, i.e. after the accomplishment of the internal market? Or is it the indefinite future?

24.1 The immediate and indefinite futures

If by the future one means the immediate term, then one must be thinking about whether or not the EC will be able to achieve its aim of creating a single market by 1992. In the light of the full discussion of almost all facets of the EC given in this book, it suffices to state that human ingenuity for creating non-tariff barriers to trade seems almost infinite. Thus one can rest almost assured that even if all the measures that are needed (requiring the enactment of the 279 directives) to create the internal market have been achieved by 1992, new distortions will have arisen by then. The history of the EC clearly demonstrates this: the EC treaties, as we have seen, have aimed to achieve a true common market before, yet this was never completely accomplished (the justifications advanced for this are not sufficient to negate this conclusion); so why should the internal market fare any better? Of course, if the concern is with whether or not the EC will be able to achieve the gains in economic growth predicted in the Cecchini Report, then, given the reservations expressed in the previous chapter, the answer is most certainly in the negative.

If by the future one is referring to an unlimited time period, then the answer is quite clear. As we have consistently indicated, not only the founding fathers of the EC but also more recently those who suggested a two-tier EC have had, and continue to have, a vision of a United States of Western Europe, i.e. the ultimate objective is the creation of a single nation. Until that aim is achieved, the efforts of those dedicated to this cause will still be devoted to finding ways of doing so.

24.2 The future immediately after 1992

However, if by the future one is concerned with what happens after 1992 (i.e. will the opening up of the EC internal market by 1992 be an end in itself or merely a staging post on the way to greater economic and political union?), then the answer requires a consideration of some recent interchanges, particularly between the British prime minister, Margaret Thatcher, and the incumbent President of the EC Commission, Jacques Delors.

During the middle of the summer of 1988, Mr Delors predicted that 'in ten years' time 80 per cent of economic, and perhaps social and tax, legislation will be of Community [EC] origin'. In early September of the same year, he followed this with a speech to the United Kingdom's Trade Union Congress (TUC) in which he spoke strongly of the 'social dimension' of the 'internal market', and called for a 'platform of guaranteed social rights', including the proposal that every worker should be covered by a collective agreement with his/her employer; a proposal which is close to the hearts of most, if not all, British trade unionists.

Later, during the same month (on 20 September), Mrs Thatcher, speaking in Bruges at the College of Europe, responded in very strong trems:

> We have not successfully rolled back the frontiers of the state in Britain only to see them re-imposed at a European level, with a European super-state exercising a new dominance from Brussels.

Since then, she has repeated the same emotive phrases regarding the 'nightmare of an EC government' on many occasions. She did this in Luxemburg and Madrid, along-side Lake Maggiore (in Italy) and before the Conservative Party Conference in Brighton (in the United Kingdom). Nor has she confined her attacks to broad policy issues. She has also done so with regard to every single practical measure by which her fellow EC leaders seek to achieve progress within the EC. She told a somewhat bemused Italian Prime Minister, (then) Ciriaco De Mita, at Lake Maggiore, 'I neither want nor expect to see a European central bank or a European currency in my lifetime or . . . for a long time afterwards'.

The first rebuttals of Mrs Thatcher's vehement utterances have not come from the 'socialist' leaders of the EC member nations, such as President Miterrand of France, Prime Minister Gonzalez of Spain or then Prime Minister Papandreou of Greece. They have sensibly kept their feelings to themselves, and have left it to the more right-wing prime ministers, Germany's Chancellor Helmut Kohl, Italy's Ciriaco

De Mita, Holland's Ruud Lubbers and Belgium's Wilfried Martens, to respond to her.

The most outspoken has been Chancellor Kohl, hitherto Mrs Thatcher's closest ally. He declared flatly in Brussels in November last year that:

1. All internal frontiers within the EC must disappear by 1992.
2. Tax harmonisation is indispensable.
3. A European police force is the answer to crime and terrorism.
4. By pooling sovereignty the EC states will gain and not lose.
5. The EC must have (in alliance with the United States) a common defence policy, leading to a European army.

He did not mention Mrs Thatcher by name, but every point he emphasised is one on which she is on record as taking the opposite view.

It should be stressed that Mrs Thatcher's stance on these matters suggests that she believes that the EC is predominantly a zero sum game: every increase in the EC's sovereignty is at the expense of the member nations', especially the United Kingdom's. However, most of the other EC leaders have fewer illusions about what the medium-sized member countries of the EC can achieve by themselves: they believe this is very little indeed. They believe that by 'pooling sovereignty' they increase the range of possibilities for the EC as a whole and thus indirectly for their own countries as well. Hence, Chancellor Kohl's carefully considered remarks on this subject should be much appreciated, particularly since Germany is not one of the smaller countries of the EC.

In short, it can be claimed that the other EC leaders see Mrs Thatcher following the example of Charles de Gaulle, whose anti-EC policies in the 1960s held back the development of the EC, including the admission of the United Kingdom – see the previous editions of this book. The comparison is almost certainly one which Mrs Thatcher herself may find flattering; but does she realise that de Gaulle's intransigence eventually did much to undermine French influence both within the EC and outside it?

Although Mrs Thatcher is in a minority of one within the EC, she has put herself in this position entirely by her own doing – her isolation is self-inflicted. She has been in this position before, when she fought her long and hard battle to reduce the UK contribution to the EC General Budget, but then she attracted much grudging admiration from the leaders of the other member nations. Although they objected to her tactics, they recognised that she was protecting a vital British interest and was seeking to remedy an evident injustice. Now their sympathy for her position is non-existent. She is seen as acting out of sheer perversity or, at best, out of nationalism of the narrowest kind.

However, what is intriguing is that the fact that she is in a minority of one does not offer much hope for the majority. Although the other eleven member states are reasonably united in their opposition to Mrs Thatcher, there is little they can do to get their way without asking the United Kingdom to forgo its membership of the EC. As we have seen, majority voting does not extend to such vital issues as tax harmonisation, the creation of a common central bank and one currency, and banking in general; these are still subject to unanimity. If Mrs Thatcher chooses to veto any proposed reforms in these fields, or any moves towards a political union, there is no way to prevent her from doing so. The fact that she surprised everyone by endorsing the Delors Report, subject to some provisos (see Chapter 5), is neither here nor there since she may still drag her feet over the second and final stages of the EMU and may even slow down the first stage by making a real issue of every problem encountered over those innocent provisos (see Chapter 5).

She may also be helped in slowing down the EC drive by a somewhat disgruntled European Parliament. In spite of the array of fairly significant powers conferred on the Parliament by the Single European Act (SEA), there still remains a substantial 'democratic deficit' (a term coined by Clinton Davis, who was UK Minister of Trade during 1974–9) in the operation of the EC institutions which leaves the Parliament in a less influential position relative to national parliaments. Given the Parliament's active past, it should be clear that it will endeavour to secure for itself additional powers in order to reduce this democratic deficit. Since extra powers cannot be granted to the Parliament without a further amendment of the treaties, it may act recklessly in its frustration at not achieving this. Thus, it may place its own determination to acquire additional powers over and above any other political considerations. This may make it more difficult for the Commission to secure agreements for its proposals in the Council, and in so doing it will indirectly assist Mrs Thatcher.

Moreover, the other EC leaders cannot wait until she retires from the political scene. She recently told *The Times* (London) that she would like to complete a fourth term of office, which could take her to 1997 or beyond. Given the divided state of Britain's opposition parties (the recent results of the elections for the European Parliament may cast only a shadow of doubt on this – see Chapter 2), this could be no idle boast. Few, if any, of the EC's other leaders have much hope of still being around then; two have already disappeared from the scene.

One may well ask who could change Mrs Thatcher's mind or coerce her into taking a different view? In theory, at least, her own political party could. The British Conservative Party led the United Kingdom into the EC and remained overwhelmingly committed when the Labour Party swung violently against. Moreover, the Conservative Party has a long tradition of being uncompromising in its choice of leader; therefore, if they agree that Mrs Thatcher is completely out of line, they are most likely to let her go. However, as discussed below, there is a recent twist to this argument.

The irony now is that the Labour Party is at last warming to the EC (the Labour Party's manifesto for the 1983 general election contained withdrawal from the EC as one of its four major issues), and President Jacques de Delors of the EC Commission was given a rapturous reception when he spoke to the TUC in September 1988. There is no reason to believe that the bulk of the Conservative Party has changed its mind about the EC, but there has been hardly a whisper of criticism of Mrs Thatcher's stance against the further development of the EC. Of course, it is still possible that the results of the recent (1989) elections for the European Parliament and one byelection in the United Kingdom may have a positive influence; indeed, it could be argued that Mrs Thatcher's endorsement of the EMU was entirely the result of this.

The reason for this state of affairs was cruelly exposed by a recent satirical television broadcast in the United Kingdom, which reported that a man had crawled on his hands and knees for 27 miles just to get into the *Guinness Book of Records*. The TV commentator suggested that 'if he had crawled another three miles, he might have got into the Cabinet'. That Mrs Thatcher has surrounded herself with yes-men is one of Britain's worst-kept secrets. These yes-men now dominate the Conservative Party, and that is why the party is less likely to sack Mrs Thatcher from her position over the question of the future of the EC, or indeed any other issue. However, one of the future contenders (Michael Heseltine) for the leadership of the party has recently published a book fully endorsing the future envisaged for the EC by the most demanding of its advocates; but he is out of the Cabinet at the moment.

As the years have gone by, there have become fewer and fewer people to whom she has been prepared to listen. One of them has certainly been ex-US President Ronald Reagan, but he is now gone. Will Mr Bush command her attention and persuade this superpatriotic leader that in diminishing the EC she is also diminishing her own country? If not, the EC faces the dim prospect of another decade of lost opportunities. However, Mr Bush is not likely to attempt to do so, given the present confrontation between the United States and the EC over agricultural and other matters, which is making progress very difficult indeed in the present round of GATT negotiations (see Baldwin *et al.*, 1988). Moreover, Mr Bush is more likely to be concerned with the Canada–US free trade area arrangement and the 'special relationship between the USA and Japan', i.e. he sees the centre of gravity to be increasingly moving towards the Pacific region, particularly with the USSR reducing its military forces in Europe and diverting them to the east.

Therefore, in spite of the endorsement of the EMU, all signs seem to suggest either that the achievement of the internal market in 1992 will be the eventual goal or that an EC without the United Kingdom will be the inevitable way forward. However, one cannot finish there since one has to address the serious issue of whether or not the EC can sack one of its members. This is a matter of vital importance, not only because it will have to be contemplated if Mrs Thatcher continues in office and insists on her declared position, but also because the EC has no precedent on this matter and its constitution is completely silent on it. The legal implications of this question have to be seriously investigated, but in the meantime let us hope that if this issue becomes a reality, the United Kingdom will do the honourable thing and simply withdraw from its membership of the EC.

Of course, one should also consider what would happen if Mrs Thatcher managed to persuade some of the other member nations of the EC to adopt her position. If this did happen, the outcome then would most certainly be a two-tier EC. However, all the signs indicate that the majority of the member nations will forge ahead with political integration, with the second of the two-tiers comprising no more than the United Kingdom. The result would be a United States of Western Europe minus the

United Kingdom. That might not be a bad thing because the British would then have to reconsider their position seriously, and such a reconsideration would inevitably result in the United Kingdom's applying to rejoin the EC, but then fully committed to a one-nation EC. Hence, in trying to prevent the further progress of the EC towards economic and political union, Mrs Thatcher may actually cause the EC to achieve this goal much sooner than its vehement supporters ever hoped for.

If the circumstances change so much as to enable the United Kingdom to secure the support of more EC member states, then the two-tier Europe would become a reality. Such an outcome would be most disappointing, given our discussion of the history of European unity. However, one cannot leave it there since as long as the European movement remains strong, the past suggests that a way out, and forward, will be found. Indeed, this may prove inevitable since the erosion of the illusionary sovereignty that Mrs Thatcher is worried about will certainly occur after the internal market has been achieved in 1992. By then:

1. The member nations of the EC will have to agree on a joint trade policy towards the rest of the world (see Chapters 20 and 23).
2. The ability of governments to set their own rates of VAT will become extremely limited (see Chapter 13).
3. The continued success of the EMS will ensure that the member states will move smoothly towards the second and final stages of the EMU (the complete fixity of exchange rates, the creation of an EC central Bank and the adoption of a single currency). Putting it differently, the success of the EMS will force them to align their monetary policies more closely if they are to keep their promise of allowing capital to move freely across the borders of member nations; this may prove impossible without a common central bank.

Thus, whichever way one looks at it, the inevitable conclusion is that Mrs Thatcher is bound to fail and the EC is set to achieve the cherished aims of its founding fathers. The sovereignty that Mrs Thatcher is so reluctant to compromise has already been subjected to that process. Those who think in terms of absolute sovereignty live in an imaginary world.

Bibliography

Throughout this book, reference is made to numerous Communications by the Commission of the European Communities to the Council. These are not given in full here because the EC system of referencing is quite clear. For example, COM(88)491 means Communication number 491, issued in 1988. Reference is also frequently made to the Treaties of the European Communities. Some of these are published by Her Majesty's Stationery Office (HMSO) in the United Kingdom, but the most comprehensive set is issued by Sweet & Maxwell, which is listed here.

Throughout the book, *EC Bulletin* is used to refer to the Commission of the European Communities' *Bulletin of the Economic Community* (various issues), and *OJC*, *OJL*, or *OJCL* (where L stands for legal) refer to the Commission's *Official Journal of the European Communities*. Again the EC's own system of referencing is clear.

Aho, C. M. and Bayard, T. O. (1982) 'The 1980s: twilight of the open trading system?', *The World Economy*, vol. 5, no. 4.

Agence Europe, (pamphlet) various dates.

Aitken, N. D. (1973) 'The effects of the EEC and EFTA on European trade: a temporal cross-section analysis', *American Economic Review*, vol. 68.

All Saints Day Manifesto (1975) *The Economist*.

Allais, M., Duquesne de la Vinelle, L., Oort, C. J., Seidenfuss, H. S. and del Viscoro, M. (1965) 'Options in transport policy', *EEC Studies, Transport Series*, no. 1.

Allen, G. H. (1972) *British Agriculture in the Common Market*, School of Agriculture, Aberdeen.

Allen, P. R. (1983) 'Cyclical imbalance in a monetary union', *Journal of Common Market Studies*, vol. 21, no. 2.

Allen, P. R. and Kenen, P. (1980) *Asset Markets, Exchange Rates and Economic Integration*, Cambridge University Press.

Alting von Geusau, F. A. (1975) 'In search of a policy', in M. Adelman and F. A. Alting von Geusau (eds.), *Energy in the European Communities*, Sijthoff.

Ardy, B. (1988) 'The national incidence of the European Community budget', *Journal of Common Market Studies*, vol. 26, no. 4.

Armington, P. S. (1969) 'A theory of demand for products distinguished by place of production', *IMF Staff Papers*, March.

Armstrong, H. (1978) 'Community regional policy: a survey and critique', *Regional Studies*, vol. 12, no. 5.

Armstrong, H. and Taylor, J. (1978) *Regional Economic Policy and Its Analysis*, Philip Allan.

Arndt, H. W. and Garnaut, R. (1979) 'ASEAN and the industrialisation of East Asia', *Journal of Common Market Studies*, vol. 17, no. 3.

Arndt, S. W. (1968) 'On discriminatory versus non-preferential tariff policies', *Economic Journal*, vol. 78.

Artis, M. J. (1981) 'From monetary to exchange rate targets', *Banca Nazionale del Lavoro Quarterly Bulletin*, September.

Artis, M. J. and Currie, D. A. (1981) 'Monetary targets and the exchange rate: a case for conditional targets', in W. A. Eltis and P. J. N. Sinclair, *The Money Supply and the Exchange Rate*, Oxford University Press.

Artus, J. R. and Crockett, A. D. (1978) 'Floating exchange rates and the need for surveillance', *Essays in International Trade*, Allen & Unwin.

Bacchetta, M. (1978) 'Oil refining in the European Community', *Journal of Common Market Studies*, vol. 11.

Bacon, R., Godley, W. and McFarquhar, A. (1978) 'The direct cost to Britain of belonging to the EEC', *Cambridge Economic Policy Review*, vol. 4.

Balassa, B. (1961) *The Theory of Economic Integration*, Allen & Unwin.

Balassa, B. (1967) 'Trade creation and trade diversion in the European Common Market', *Economic Journal*, vol. 77.

Balassa, B. (1975) *European Economic Integration*, North-Holland.

Baldwin, R. E. (1971) *Non-Tariff Distortions of International Trade*, Allen & Unwin.

Baldwin, R. E. *et al.* (eds.) (1988) *Issues in US–EC Trade Relations*, University of Chicago Press.

Ball, R. J., Burns, T. and Laury, J. S. E. (1977) 'The role of exchange rate changes in balance of payments adjustments – the UK case', *Economic Journal*, vol. 87.

Bank for International Settlements (1979) *Annual Report 1978*, Basle.

Bank for International Settlements (1989) *International Banking and Financial Market Developments*, February.

Bank of Canada (1983) 'The European Monetary System: the foreign exchange mechanism', *Bank of Canada Monthly Review*, August.

Bank of England (1979) 'Intervention arrangement in the European Monetary System', *Bank of England Quarterly Bulletin*, June.

Bank of England (1982) *Quarterly Bulletin*, March.

Barker, E. (1971) *Britain in a Divided Europe*, Weidenfeld & Nicolson.

Barten, A. P. *et al.* (1976) 'COMET: a medium-term macroeconomic model for the European Economic Community', *European Economic Review*, vol. 7.

Baumol, W. J. and Oates, J. E. (1988) *The Theory of Environmental Policy*, Cambridge University Press, second edition.

Bayliss, B. T. (1973) 'Licensing and entry to the market', *Journal of Transport Planning and Technology*, vol. 2, no. 1.

Bayliss, B. T. (1979) 'Transport in the European Communities', *Journal of Transport Economics and Policy*, vol. XIII, no. 1.

Begg, I. (1989) 'European integration and regional policy', *Oxford Review of Economic Policy*, vol. 5, no. 2.

Begg, I., Cripps, F. and Ward, T. (1981) 'The European Community problems and prospects', *Cambridge Economic Policy Review*, vol. 7, no. 2.

Bellis, J. F. (1976) 'Potential competition and concentration policy: relevance to EEC anti-trust', *Journal of World Trade Law*, vol. 10, no. 1, Jan/Feb.

Berglas, E. (1979) 'Preferential trading theory – the *n* commodity case', *Journal of Political Economy*, vol. 81.

Berglas, E. (1981) 'Harmonisation of commodity taxes', *Journal of Public Economics*, vol. 16.

Bergman, D. *et al.* (1970) *A Future for European Agriculture*, Atlantic Institute, Paris.

Berkhout, F., Boehmer Christiansen, S. and Skea, J. F. (1989) 'Deposit and repositories: electricity wastes in the UK and West Germany', *Energy Policy*, vol. 17.

Beveridge, W. (1940) *Peace by Federation?*, Federal Tract no. 1, Federal Union, London.

Bhagwati, J. N. (1965) 'On the equivalence of tariffs and quotas', in R. E. Baldwin *et al.* (eds.) *Trade, Growth and the Balance of Payments*, North-Holland.

Bhagwati, J. N. (1969) *Trade, Tariffs and Growth*, Weidenfeld & Nicolson.

Bhagwati, J. N. (1971) 'Customs unions and welfare improvement', *Economic Journal*, vol. 81.

Bieber, R. *et al.* (1988) *1992: One European Market? A critical analysis of the Commission's internal market strategy*, Nomos Verlagsgesellschaft.

Black, J. and Dunning, J. H. (eds.) (1982) *International Capital Movements*, Macmillan.

Black, R. A. (1977) 'Plus ça change, plus c'est la même chose: 9 governments in search of a common energy policy', in H. Wallace, W. Wallace and C. Webb (eds.), *Policy-Making in the European Communities*, Little Brown.

Blackoby, F. T. (1980) 'Exchange rate policy and economic strategy', *Three Banks Review*, June.

Blancus, P. (1978) 'The Common Agricultural Policy and the balance of payments of the EEC member countries', *Banca Nazionale del Lavoro Quarterly Review*, vol. 5, no. 3.

Bluet, J. C. and Systermanns, Y. (1968) 'Modèle gravitionel d'échanges internationaux de produits manufacturés', *Bulletin du CEPREMAP*, vol. 1, January (New Series).

Boardman, R. *et al.* (1985) *Europe, Africa and Lomé III*, University Press of America.

Bodenheimer, S. (1967) *Political Union, a Microcosm of European Politics*, Sijthoff.

Bootle, R. (1983) 'Foreign exchange intervention: a case of ill-founded neglect', *The Banker*, May.

Bos, M. and Nelson, H. (1988) 'Indirect taxation and the completion of the internal market of the EC', *Journal of Common Market Studies*, vol. 27, no. 1.

Boulding, K. E. (1966) 'The economics of the coming spaceship Earth', in H. Jarret (ed.), *Environmental Quality in a Growing Economy*, Johns Hopkins.

Bourguignon, F., Gallais-Hamonno, G. and Fernet, B. (1977) *International Labour Migrations and Economic Choices: the European case*, Development Centre of the OECD.

Bowers, J. K. (1972) 'Economic efficiency in agriculture', in Open University, *Decision Making in Britain III*, Parts 1–6.

Bowers, J. K. (ed.) (1979) *Inflation, Development and Integration: Essays in honour of A. J. Brown*, Leeds University Press.

Brada, J. C. and Mendez, J. A. (1985) 'Economic integration among developed, developing and centrally planned economies: a comparative analysis', *Review of Economics and Statistics*, vol. 67.

Brander, J. (1981) 'Intra-industry trade in identical commodities', *Journal of International Economics*, vol. 11.

Brander, J. and Spencer, B. (1984) 'Tariff protection and imperfect competition', in H. Kierzkowski (ed.), *Monopolistic Competition and International Trade*, Oxford University Press.

Breckling, J. *et al.* (1987) *Effects of EC Agricultural Policies: A general equilibrium approach*, Bureau of Agricultural Research, Canberra.

Breton, A. and Scott, A. (1978) 'The assignment problem in federal structures', in M. S. Feldstein and R. P. Inman (eds.), *The Economics of Public Services*, Macmillan.

Brewin, C. (1987) 'The European Community: A union of states without unity of government', *Journal of Common Market Studies*, vol. XXVI, no. 1, pp. 1–23.

Brown, A. J. (1961) 'Economic separatism versus a common market in developing countries', *Yorkshire Bulletin of Economic and Social Research*, vol. 13.

Brown, A. J. (1977) 'What is wrong with the British economy?', *The University of Leeds Review*, vol. 20.

Brown, A. J. (1979) 'Inflation and the British sickness', *Economic Journal*, vol. 89.

Brown, A. J. (1980a) 'The transfer of resources', in W. Wallace (ed.), *Britain in Europe*, Heinemann, Chapter 7.

Brüppacher, F. (1988) 'How European electricity trade is conducted', paper presented in the

Financial Times World Electricity Conference.

Bryant, R. C. (1980) *Money and Monetary Policy in Independent Nations*, The Brookings Institution, Washington.

Buck, T. (1975) 'Regional policy and economic integration', *Journal of Common Market Studies*, vol. 13.

Buckley, P. J. and Casson, M. (1976) *The Future of the Multinational Enterprise*, Macmillan.

Buckwell, A., Harvey, D. R., Thomson, K. J. and Parton, K. (1982) *The Costs of the Common Agricultural Policy*, Croom Helm.

Bundesbank (1979) *Monthly Review*, March.

Burrows, B., Denton, G. R. and Edwards, G. (1977) *Federal Solutions to European Issues*, Macmillan.

Butt Philip, A. (1981) 'The harmonisation of industrial policy and practices', in C. Cosgrove Twitchett (ed.), *Harmonisation in the EEC*, Macmillan.

Butt Philip, A. (1988) 'Implementing the European internal market: problems and prospects', *Discussion Paper*, no. 5, Royal Institute of International Affairs.

Button, K. J. and Gillingwater, D. (1976) *Case Studies in Regional Economics*, Heinemann.

Byé, M. (1950) 'Unions douanières et données nationales', *Economie Appliquée*, vol. 3. Reprinted (1953) in translation as 'Customs unions and national interests', *International Economic Papers*, no. 3.

Cairncross, Sir Alec *et al.* (1974) *Economic Policy for the European Community: The way forward*, Macmillan.

Calingaert, M. (1988) *The Challenge from Europe: Development of the European Community's internal market*, National Planning Association, Washington DC.

Cambridge Economic Policy Group (1981) *Cambridge Economic Policy Review*, vol. 7, no. 2, December.

Cameron, G. C. (1974) 'Regional economic policy in the United Kingdom', in N. M. Hansen (ed.), *Public Policy and Regional Economic Development*, Saxon House.

Camps, M. (1964) *Britain and the European Community 1955–63*, Oxford University Press.

Canenbley, C. (1972) 'Price discrimination and EEC cartel law: a review of the Kodak decision of the Commission of the European Communities', *The Antitrust Bulletin*, vol. 17, no. 1, Spring.

Carrier Licensing, Report of the Geddes Committee, HMSO.

Cecchini, P. (1988) *1992: The European challenge*, Gower.

Central Bank of Ireland (1979) 'A guide to the arithmetic of the EMS exchange rate mechanism', *Central Bank of Ireland Quarterly Bulletin*, Autumn.

Central Statistical Office (1981) *Britain in the European Community*, Reference Pamphlet 137, HMSO.

Choi, J.-Y. and Yu, E. S. H. (1984) 'Customs unions under increasing returns to scale', *Economica*, vol. 51.

Chard, J. S. and Macmillen, M. J. (1979) 'Sectoral aids and Community competition policy: the case of textiles', *Journal of World Trade Law*, vol. 13, no. 2, March/April.

Choufoer, J. H. (1982) 'Future of the European Energy Economy', address to the Conference of European Petroleum and Gas, Amsterdam.

Clark, C. (1962) *British Trade in the Common Market*, Stevens.

Clark, C., Wilson, F. and Bradley, J. (1969) 'Industrial location and economic potential in Western Europe', *Regional Studies*, vol. 3, no. 2.

Clavaux, F. J. (1969) 'The import elasticity as a yardstick for measuring trade creation', *Economia Internazionale*, November.

Cmnd. 8212 (1981) *Statement on the Defence Estimates*, vol. 1, HMSO.

Cnossen, S. (1986) 'Harmonisation of indirect taxes in the EEC', *British Tax Review*, vol. 4.

Cobham, D. (1982) 'Comments on Peeters and Emerson', in M. T. Sumner and G. Zis (eds.), *European Monetary Union: Progress and prospects*, Macmillan.

Cockfield, Lord (1986) Address to the International Management Institute, Geneva.

Coffey, P. (1976) *The External Relations of the EEC*, Macmillan.

Coffey, P. (1977), *Europe and Money*, Macmillan.

Coffey, P. (1979) *Economic Policies of the Common Market*, Macmillan.

Coffey, P. (1987) *The European Monetary System: Past, present and future*, Kluwer.

Coffey, P. and Presley, J. (1971) *European Monetary Integration*, Macmillan.

Cohen, B. J. (1981) 'The European Monetary System', *Essays in International Finance*, no. 142, Princeton University.

Cohen, C. D. (ed.) (1983) *The Common Market – Ten Years After*, Philip Allan.

Collier, P. (1979) 'The welfare effects of customs union: an anatomy', *Economic Journal*, vol. 89.

Collins, C. D. E. (1975) *The European Communities: the Social Policy of the first phase*, Martin Robertson.

Collins, C. D. E. (1980) 'Social Policy', in A. M. El-Agraa (ed.) *The Economics of the European Community*, Philip Allan, Chapter 15.

Comité intergouvernemental créé par la conférence de Messina (1956) *Rapport des chefs de délégation aux Ministres des Affaires Etrangères*, Brussels.

Commission of the European Communities (various issues) *Bulletin of the European Community*, or EC Bulletin.

Commission of the European Communities (various years) *Social Report*.

Commission of the European Communities (various issues and items) *Official Journal of the European Communities* (referred to throughout as OJC, OJL or OJCL, where L stands for Legal).

Commission of the European Communities (1953) *Report on Problems raised by the Different Turnover Tax Systems Applied within the Common Market* (The Tinbergen Report).

Commission of the European Communities (1960) *Community Energy Policy Objectives for 1985*, (COM(74)60).

Commission of the European Communities (1961) *Memorandum on the General Lines of a Common Transport Policy*.

Commission of the European Communities (1962) *Action Programme of the Community for the Second Stage*.

Commission of the European Communities (1963) *Report of the Fiscal and Financial Committee* (The Neumark Report).

Commission of the European Communities (1966) *Report on the Situation of the Fisheries Sector in the Member States and the Basic Principles for a Common Policy*.

Commission of the European Communities (1967) *Tenth Annual Report of the Activities of the Community*, Brussels.

Commission of the European Communities (1968) 'Premieres Orientations pour une politique energetique communautaire', *Communication de la Commission presente au Conseil le 18 December 1968*, Brussels.

Commission of the European Communities (1969) 'Memorandum on the Report of Agriculture in the European Economic Community', *Bulletin of the European Communities*, Supplement, January.

Commission of the European Communities (1970a) 'Report to the Council and the Commission on the realisation by stages of economic and monetary union in the Community', *Bulletin of the European Communities*, Supplement, no. 11 (The Werner Report).

Commission of the European Communities (1970b) *Industrial Policy in the Community: Memorandum from the Commission to the Council*.

Commission of the European Communities (1970c) *Corporation Tax and Income Tax in the European Communities* (The van den Tempel Report).

Commission of the European Communities (1971a) 'Preliminary guidelines for a social policy', *Bulletin of the European Communities*, Supplement 2/71.

Commission of the European Communities (1971b) 'General regional aid systems', *Official Journal, OJ* C111 of 4 November 1971.

Commission of the European Communities (1972a) *Competition Law in the European Economic Community and in the European Coal and Steel Community.*

Commission of the European Communities (1972b) *First Report on Competition Policy.*

Commission of the European Communities (1973a) 'Proposals for a Community regional policy', *Official Journal*, *OJ* C68 of 16 October 1973, and *OJ* C106 of 6 December 1973.

Commission of the European Communities (1973b) *Programme of Action in the Field of Technological and Industrial Policy*, SEC(73)3824 final, October.

Commission of the European Communities (1973c) *Communication from the Commission to the Council on the Development of the Common Transport Policy*, COM(73).

Commission of the European Communities (1974a) 'Social Action Programme', *Bulletin of the European Communities*, Supplement 2/74.

Commission of the European Communities (1974b) *Third Report on Competition Policy.*

Commission of the European Communities (1975a) 'Report and proposal decision on a programme of action for the European aeronautical sector', *Bulletin of the European Communities*, Supplement 11/75.

Commission of the European Communities (1975b) 'Council Regulation (EEC) 724/75 of 18 March 1975 establishing a European Regional Development Fund', *Official Journal*, *OJ* L73 of 21 March 1975.

Commission of the European Communities (1975c) *Report of the Study Group 'Economic and Monetary Union 1980'*, March (The Marjolin Report).

Commission of the European Communities (1976a) *Fifth Report on Competition – EEC.*

Commission of the European Communities (1976b) 'Action Programme in favour of migrant workers and their families', *Bulletin of the European Communities*, Supplement 3/76.

Commission of the European Communities (1977a) *Guidelines for Community Regional Policy*, COM(77)195 final.

Commission of the European Communities (1977b) 'Regional concentration in the countries of the European Community', *Regional Policy Series*, no. 4.

Commission of the European Communities (1977c) *Report of the Study Group on the Role of Public Finance in European Integration*, 2 vols. (The McDougall Report).

Commission of the European Communities (1977d) 'Community regional policy: new guidelines', *Bulletin of the European Communities*, Supplement, June.

Commission of the European Communities (1978a) 'Council Decision of 16 October 1978 empowering the Commission to contract loans for the purpose of promoting investment in the Community', *Official Journal*, *OJ* L298 of 25 October 1978.

Commission of the European Communities (1978b) *Twelfth General Report of the Activities of the European Communities in 1978.*

Commission of the European Communities (1978c) 'Regional aid systems', *Official Journal*, *OJ* C31 of 3 February 1979.

Commission of the European Communities (1978d) *Report on Some Structural Aspects of Growth.*

Commission of the European Communities (1979a) 'Regional incentives in the European Community', *Regional Policy Series*, no. 15.

Commission of the European Communities (1979b) 'The Regional Development Programmes', *Regional Policy Series*, no. 17.

Commission of the European Communities (1979c) 'Air Transport – a Community Approach', *Bulletin of the European Communities*, Supplement 5/79.

Commission of the European Communities (1979d) *Proposals for Reform of the Commission of the European Communities and its Services* (The Spierenburg Report).

Commission of the European Communities (1979e) *Eighth Report on Competition Policy.*

Commission of the European Communities (1980a) *La Suisse et la Communauté.*

Commission of the European Communities (1980b) *Official Journal of the European Communities*, Legislation, no. C149.

Commission of the European Communities (1980c) *Tenth Report on Competition Policy.*

Commission of the European Communities (1981a) *Communication to the Council on the Categories of Infrastructure to which the ERDF may Contribute in the Various Regions aided by the*

Fund, COM(81)38 final.

Commission of the European Communities (1981b) *Principal Regulations and Decisions of the Council of the European Communities on Regional Policy.*

Commission of the European communities (1981c) 'Proposal for a Council Regulation amending Regulation (EEC) 724/75 establishing a European Regional Development Fund', *Official Journal, OJ* C336 of 23 December 1981.

Commission of the European Communities (1981d) *New Regional Policy Guidelines and Priorities*, COM(81)152 final.

Commission of the European Communities (1981e) 'Deglomeration policies in the European Community – a comparative study', *Regional Policy*, no. 18.

Commission of the European Communities (1981f) 'Study of the regional impact of the Common Agricultural Policy', *Regional Policy Series*, no. 21.

Commission of the European Communities (1981g) 'Commission recommendation of 9.10.1981 on transfrontier coordination for regional development', *Official Journal, OJ* L321 of 10 November 1981.

Commission of the European Communities (1981h) *The Regions of Europe: First Periodic Report on the Social and Economic Situation in the Regions of the Community.*

Commission of the European Communities (1981i) 'The European Community's Transport Policy', Periodical 2/1981, EC Documentation.

Commission of the European Communities (1982a) *Fifteenth General Report of the Activities of the European Communities in 1981.*

Commission of the European Communities (1982b) *The Agricultural Situation in the Community – 1981 Report.*

Commission of the European Communities (1982c) *Ten Years in Europe.*

Commission of the European Communities (1983a) 'Memorandum of evidence to the House of Lords Select Committee on the European Communities', *House of Lords Report*, q.v.

Commission of the European Communities (1983b) *Twelfth Report on Competition Policy.*

Commission of the European Communities (1983c) *Seventeenth General Report on the Activities of the European Communities.*

Commission of the European Communities (1983d) *European Political Cooperation*, European File 13/83.

Commission of the European Communities (1984a) *Eighteenth General Report on the Activities of the European Communities.*

Commission of the European Communities (1984b) *Review of Member States' Energy Policies* (COM(84)88).

Commission of the European Communities (1984d) *Social Report.* Also, for other years.

Commission of the European Communities (1985a) *Completing the Internal Market (White Paper from the EC Commission to the EC Council) – (COM(85)310).*

Commission of the European Communities (1985b) *The European Community and its Regions.*

Commission of the European Communities (1985c) *14th Report on Competition Policy.*

Commission of the European Communities (1985d) *Community Energy Policy Objectives for 1985* (COM(74)1960).

Commission of the European Communities (1985e) *Fourteenth Report on Competition Policy.*

Commission of the European Communities (1985f) *Nineteenth General Report on the Activities of the European Communities.*

Commission of the European Communities (1986a) *Official Journal of the European Communities*, Legislation, no. C241.

Commission of the European Communities (1986b) *Communication on Natural Gas* (COM(86) 518).

Commission of the European Communities (1986c) *Twentieth General Report on the Activities of the European Communities.*

Commission of the European Communities (1987a) *Efficiency, Stability and Equity* (The Padoa-Schioppa Report).

Commission of the European Communities (1987b) *Completion of the Internal Market: Approxi-*

mation of indirect tax rates and harmonisation of indirect tax structure, Global Communication from the EC Commission (COM(87)320).

Commission of the European Communities (1987c) *European Environmental Policy*, Economic and Social Committee and Consultative Assembly.

Commission of the European Communities (1988a) *Bulletin of the European Communities*, Supplement 4/47.

Commission of the European Communities (1988b) *Review of Member States' Energy Policies – the 1995 Energy Objectives* (COM(88)174).

Commission of the European Communities (1988c) *Proposal for a Council Recommendation to the Member States to Promote Cooperation between Public Electricity Supply Companies and private Generators of Electricity* (COM(88)225).

Commission of the European Communities (1988d) *The Internal Energy Market* (COM(88)238).

Commission of the European Communities (1988e) *Review of the Community Oil Industry* (COM (88)491).

Commission of the European Communities (1988f) *Report on the Application of the Community Rules for State Aid to the Coal Industry in 1987* (COM(88)541).

Commission of the European Communities (1988g) *Completing the Internal Market: an area without internal frontiers* (COM(88)650).

Commission of the European Communities (1988h) *Research on the Cost of Non-Europe: Basic findings*, The Cecchini Report, 16 volumes.

Commission of the European Communities (1988i) *22nd General Report of the Activities of the European Communities*.

Commission of the European Communities (1988j) *Community R&TD Programmes*, special issue.

Commission of the European Communities (1989a) *Transparency in Energy Prices* (COM(89) 123).

Commission of the European Communities (1989b) *Energy in Europe*.

Commission of the European Communities (1989c) *ESPRIT Workprogramme*.

Commission of the European Communities (1989d) *A Framework for Community R&D Actions in the 90s*.

Congressional Budget Office (USA) (1987) *The GATT Negotiations and US Trade Policy*.

Coombes, D. (1970) *Politics and Bureaucracy in the European Community*, Allen & Unwin.

Cooper, C. A. and Massell, B. F. (1965a) 'A new look at customs union theory', *Economic Journal*, vol. 75.

Cooper, C. A. and Massell, B. F. (1965b) 'Towards a general theory of customs unions in developing countries', *Journal of Political Economy*, vol. 73.

Corbett, H. (1979) 'Tokyo Round: twilight of a liberal era or a new dawn?', *National Westminster Quarterly Review*, February.

Corden, W. M. (1965) 'Recent developments in the theory of international trade', *Special Papers in International Finance*, Princeton University Press.

Corden, W. M. (1972a) 'Economies of scale and customs union theory', *Journal of Political Economy*, vol. 80.

Corden, W. M. (1972b) 'Monetary integration', *Essays in International Finance*, no. 93, Princeton University.

Corden, W. M. (1973) 'The adjustment problem', in L. B. Krause and W. S. Salant (eds.), *European Monetary Unification and Its Meaning for the United States*, The Brookings Institution, Washington.

Corden, W. M. (1974) *Trade Policy and Economic Welfare*, Oxford University Press.

Corden, W. M. (1976) 'Monetary union', *Trade Policy Research Centre Paper on International Issues*, no. 2, December.

Corden, W. M. (1977) *Inflation, Exchange Rates and the World Economy*, Oxford University Press.

Corden, W. M. (1988) 'Trade policy and macroeconomic balance in the world economy', *IMF*

Working Paper.

Cosgrave, C. A. (1969) 'The EEC and developing countries', in G. R. Denton (ed.), *Economic Integration in Europe*, Weidenfeld & Nicolson.

Cosgrove Twitchett, C. (1978) *Europe and AFrica: From association to partnership*, Saxon House.

Cosgrove Twitchett, C. (ed.) (1981) *Harmonisation in the EEC*, Macmillan.

Council of the European Communities (various years) *Review of the Council's Work.*

Council of the European Communities (1986) *Report by the Chairman of the Fiscal Borders Abolition ad hoc Group.*

Cruickshank, A. and Walker, W. (1981) 'Energy research development and demonstration policy in the European Communities', *Journal of Common Market Studies*, vol. 20, no. 1.

Cunningham, S. and Young, J. A. (1983) 'The EEC Fisheries Policy: retrospect and prospect', *National Westminster Bank Quarterly Review*, May.

Curzon, G. and V. (1971) 'New-colonialism and the European Community', *Yearbook of World Affairs*, Institute of World Affairs, London.

Curzon, G. and Curzon Price, V. (1987) 'Follies in European trade relations with Japan', *World Economy*, June.

Curzon, G. and Curzon Price, V. (1989) 'The GATT, non-discrimination principles and the rise of "material reciprocity" in international trade', mimeo, Collège de Bruges.

Curzon Price, V. (1974) *The Essentials of Economic Integration*, Macmillan.

Curzon Price, V. (1982) 'The European Free Trade Association', in A. M. El-Agraa (ed.), *International Economic Integration*, Macmillan.

Curzon Price, V. (1988) '1992: Europe's last chance? From Common Market to single market', *Occasional Paper*, no. 81, Institute of Economic Affairs, London.

Cuthbertson, K. *et al.* (1980) 'Modelling and forecasting the capital account of the balance of payments: a critique of the "Reduced Form Approach"', *National Institute Discussion Paper*, no. 37.

Daintith, T. and Hancher, K. (eds.) (1986) *Energy Strategy in Europe: The legal framework*, de Gruyter.

Dam, K. W. (1970) *The GATT: Law and International Economic Organization*, Chicago University Press.

Daniel, P. (1984) 'Interpreting mutual interest: non-fuel minerals in EEC–ACP relations', C. Stevens (ed.) *EEC and the Third World: A Survey. 4: Regenerating Lomé*, London.

Dauphin, R. (1978) *The Impact of Free Trade in Canada*, Economic Council of Canada, Ottawa.

Davenport, M. (1986) *Trade Policy, Protectionism and the Third World*, Croom Helm.

Davies, G. (1982) 'The EMS: its achievements and failures', *Special Analysis*, Simon & Coates.

Dayal, R. and N. (1977) 'Trade creation and trade diversion: new concepts, new methods of measurement', *Weltwirtschaftliches Archiv*, vol. 113.

Deacon, D. (1982) 'Competition policy in the Common Market: its links with regional policy', *Regional Studies*, vol. 16, no. 1.

De Grauwe, P. (1973) *Monetary Interdependence and International Monetary Reform*, Saxon House.

De Grauwe, P. (1975) 'Conditions for monetary integration: a geometric interpretation', *Weltwirtschaftliches Archiv*, vol. 111.

De Grauwe, P. and Peeters, T. (1978) 'The European Monetary System after Bremen: technical and conceptual problems', paper delivered to the International Economics Study Group at the London School of Economics and Political Science.

De Grauwe, P. and Peeters, T. (1979) 'The EMS, Europe and the Dollar', *The Banker*, April.

Deaton, A. S. and Muellbauer, J. (1980a) 'An almost ideal demand system', *American Economic Review*, vol. 70.

Deaton, A. S. and Muellbauer, J. (1980b) *Economics and Consumer Behaviour*, Cambridge University Press.

Dell, E. and Mayes, D. G. (1989) *1992 and Environment for European Industry*, Centre for European Policy Studies.

Demekas, D. G. *et al.* (1988) 'The effects of the Common Agricultural Policy of the European Community: A survey of the literature', *Journal of Common Market Studies*, vol. 27, no. 2.

Denison, E. F. (1967) *Why Growth Rates Differ: Post-war experience in nine Western countries*, The Brookings Institution, Washington.

Dennis, G. E. J. (1979) 'German monetary policy and the EMS', mimeo, December.

Dennis, G. E. J. (1981) 'The United Kingdom's monetary interdependence and membership of the European Monetary System', in J. P. Abraham and M. Van den Abeele (eds.), *The European Monetary System and International Monetary Reform*, College of Europe, Brussels.

Denton, G. R. (ed.) (1969) *Economic Integration in Europe*, Weidenfeld & Nicolson.

Denton, G. R. (ed.) (1974) *Economic and Monetary Union in Europe*, Croom Helm.

Denton, G. R. (1981) 'How can the EEC help to solve the energy problem?', *The Three Banks Review*, March.

Department of Industry (1982) *Inward Investmewnt and the IIB 1977–82*.

Deutsche Bundesbank (1979) 'The European Monetary System', *Deutsche Bank Monthly Bulletin*, March.

De Vries, T. (1980) 'On the meaning and futures of the EMS', *Essays in International Finance*, no. 138, Princeton University.

Digby, C., Smith, M. A. M. and Venables, A. (1988) 'Counting the cost of voluntary export restrictions in the European car market', *Discussion Paper Series*, no. 249, Centre for Economic Policy Research.

Dixit, A. (1975) 'Welfare effects of tax and price changes', *Journal of Public Economics*, vol. 4.

Donges, J. B. *et al.* (1982) *The Second Enlargement of the Community: Adjustment requirements and challenges for policy reform*, Mohr.

Dosser, D. (1966) 'The economic analysis of tax harmonisation', in C. S. Shoup (ed.), *Fiscal Harmonisation in Common Markets*, vol. 2, Columbia University Press.

Dosser, D. (1971) 'Taxation', in J. Pinder (ed.), *The Economics of Europe*, Knight.

Dosser, D. (1973) *British Taxation and the Common Market*, Knight.

Dosser, D. (1975) 'A federal budget for the Community', in B. Burrows *et al.* (eds.), *Federal Solutions to European Issues*, Macmillan.

Dosser, D. and Hans, S. S. (1968) *Taxes in the EEC and Britain – the Problem of Harmonisation*, PEP/Institute of International Affairs.

Dunning, J. H. (1977) 'Trade, location of economic activity and the MNE: a search for an eclectic approach' in B. Ohlin *et al.* (eds.), *The International Allocation of Economic Activity*, Macmillan.

Dunning, J. H. (1982) 'Explaining the internal direct investment position of countries: towards a dynamic or developmental approach', in J. Black and J. H. Dunning (eds.), *International Capital Movements*, Macmillan.

Economic and Social Committee of the European Communities (1977) *EEC's Transport Problems with East European Countries*, EC Commission.

The Economist Intelligence Unit (1957) *Britain and Europe*, The Economist.

The Economist (1973) 'Europe and Britain's regions', *The Economist*, vol. 247, no. 6765, pp. 55–60.

Edwards, G. and Wallace, H. (1977) *The Council of Ministers of the European Community and the President-in-Office*, Federal Trust, London.

Eeckhout, J. C. (1975) 'Towards a common European industrial policy', *Irish Banking Review*, December.

EFTA Secretariat (1968) *The Effects on Prices of Tariff Dismanting in EFTA*.

EFTA Secretariat (1969) *The Effects of the EFTA on the Economies of Member States*.

EFTA Secretariat (1972) *The Trade Effects of the EFTA and the EEC 1959–1967*.

El-Agraa, A. M. (1978) 'On trade creation' and 'On trade diversion', *Leeds Discussion Papers*, nos 66 and 67, University of Leeds, School of Economic Studies.

El-Agraa, A. M. (1979a) 'Common markets in developing countries', in J. K. Bowers (ed.), *Inflation, Development and Integration: Essays in honour of A. J. Brown*, Leeds University Press.

El-Agraa, A. M. (1979b) 'On tariff bargaining', *Bulletin of Economic Research*, vol. 31.

El-Agraa, A. M. (1979c) 'On optimum tariffs, retaliation and international cooperation', *Bulletin of Economic Research*, vol. 31.

El-Agraa, A. M. (1981) 'Tariff bargaining: a correction', *Bulletin of Economic Research*, vol. 33.

El-Agraa, A. M. (1982a) 'Professor Godley's proposition: a theoretical appraisal', *Leeds Discussion Papers*, no. 105.

El-Agraa, A. M. (1982b) 'Professor Godley's proposition: a macroeconomic appraisal', *Leeds Discussion Papers*, no. 113.

El-Agraa, A. M. (ed.) (1982c) *International Economic Integration*, Macmillan.

El-Agraa, A. M. (1982d) 'Comments on Rybczynski', in M. T. Sumner, and G. Zis (eds.), *European Monetary Union*, Macmillan.

El-Agraa, A. M. (ed.) (1983a) *Britain within the European Community: The way forward*, Macmillan.

El-Agraa, A. M. (1983b) *The Theory of International Trade*, Croom Helm.

El-Agraa, A. M. (1984a) 'Is membership of the EEC a disaster for the UK?', *Applied Economics*, vol. 17, no. 1.

El-Agraa, A. M. (1984b) *Trade Theory and Policy: Some topical issues*, Macmillan.

El-Agraa, A. M. (ed.) (1987) *Conflict, Cooperation, Integration and Development: Essays in honour of Professor Hiroshi Kitamura*, Macmillan and St Martin's.

El-Agraa, A. M. (1988a) *Japan's Trade Frictions: Realities or Misconceptions?* Macmillan and St Martin's.

El-Agraa, A. M. (ed.) (1988b) *International Economic Integration*, Macmillan and St Martin's, second edition.

El-Agraa, A. M. (1989a) *The Theory and Measurement of International Economic Integration*, Macmillan and St Martin's.

El-Agraa, A. M. (1989b) *International Trade*, Macmillan and St Martin's.

El-Agraa, A. M. (1990) 'EC Budgetary politics: the rationality of the EC Commission being undermined by the irrationality of the member nations', forthcoming.

El-Agraa, A. M. and Goodrich, P. S. (1980) 'Factor mobility with specific reference to the accounting profession', in first edition of A. M. El-Agraa (ed.), *The Economics of the European Community*, Philip Allan, Chapter 16.

El-Agraa, A. M. and Jones, A. J. (1981) *The Theory of Customs Unions*, Philip Allan.

El-Agraa, A. M. and Majocchi, A. (1983) 'Devising a proper fiscal stance for the EC', *Revista Di Diritto Finanziario E Scienza Delle Finanze*, vol. 17, no. 3.

Ellis, F., Marsh, J. and Ritson, C. (1973) *Farmers and Foreigners – The Impact of the Common Agricultural Policy on the Associates and Associables*, Overseas Development Institute, London.

Emerson, M. (1979) 'The European Monetary System in the broader setting of the Community's economic and political development', in P. H. Trezise (ed.), *The European Monetary System: Its promise and prospects*, Brookings Institution, Washington.

Emerson, M. (1988) 'The Economics of 1992', *European Economy*, no. 35.

Emerson, M. *et al.* (1988) *The Economics of 1992: the EC Commission's assessment of the economic effects of completing the internal market*, Oxford University Press.

Emerson, M. and Dramais, A. (1988) *What Model for Europe?*, MIT Press.

Emmiger, O. (1979) 'The exchange rate as an instrument of policy', *Lloyds Bank Review*, July.

ESPRIT Review Board (1985) *The Mid-term Review of ESPRIT*, EC Commission.

Ethier, W. and Bloomfield, A. J. (1975) 'Managing the managed float', *Essays in International Finance*, no. 122, Princeton University.

European Economy (1982) 'Documents relating to the European Monetary System', no. 12, July.

European Investment Bank (1981) *Annual Report 1980*.

European Parliament (1980) *European Taxation 1980/81*, Energy Commission.

European Parliament (1986) 'Report on the relations between the European Community and the Council for Mutual Economic Assistance', DOC AZ187/86, 19 December.

Eurostat (annual) *Basic Statistics of the Community*.

Eurostat (annual) *Statistical Review*.

Eurostat (1980) *Review 1970–1979*, EC Commission.

Eurostat (1982) *Farm Accountancy Data Network*, microfiche.

Farrands, C. (1983) 'External relations: textile politics and the Multi-Fiber Arrangement', in H. Wallace *et al.*, *Policy Making in the European Community*, John Wiley, second edition.

Federal Reserve Bank of New York (1981) *Quarterly Review*, Summer.

Fennell, R. (1979) *The Common Agricultural Policy of the European Community*, Granada.

Finger, J. M. and Olechowski, A. (1987) *The Uruguay Round: a handbook on the multilateral trade negotiations*, World Bank.

Fitzmaurice, J. (1988) 'An analysis of the European Community's Co-operation Procedure', *Journal of Common Market Studies*, vol. 26, no. 4.

Fleming, J. M. (1971) 'On exchange rate unification', *Economic Journal*, vol. 81.

Flockton, C. (1970) *Community Regional Policy*, Chatham House.

Fogarty, M. (1975) *Work and Industrial Relations in the European Community*, Chatham House/PEP.

Foot, M. D. (1979) 'Monetary targets; nature and record in the major economies', in B. Griffiths and G. Wood, *Monetary Targets*, Macmillan.

Forsyth, M.(1980) *Reservicing Britain*, Adam Smith Institute, London.

Forte, F. (1977) 'Principles for the assignment of public economic functions in a setting of multi-layer government', in Commission of the European Communities, *Report of the Study Group on the Role of Public Finance in European Integration*, vol. II (The MacDougall Report).

Friedman, M. (1975) *Unemployment versus Inflation? an Evaluation of the Philips Curve*, Institute of International Affairs (London).

Gandia, D. M. (1981) *The EEC's Generalised System of Preferences and the Yaounde and Other Agreements*, Allenhead, Osmun & Co.

Gatsios, K. and Seabright, P. (1989) 'Regulation in the European Community', *Oxford Review of Economic Policy*, vol. 5, no. 2.

Gehrels, F. (1956–7) 'Customs unions from a single country viewpoint', *Review of Economic Studies*, vol. 24.

George, K. D. and Joll, C. (eds.) (1975) *Competition Policy in the United Kingdom and the European Economic Community*, Cambridge University Press.

Geroski, P. A. (1989) 'European industrial policy and industrial policy in Europe', *Oxford Review of Economic Policy*, vol. 5, no. 2.

Giavazzi, F. and Pagano, M. (1986) 'The advantage of tying one's hands: EMS discipline and central bank credibility', *European Economic Review*, vol. 28.

Giavazzi, F., Micossi, S. and Miller, M. (eds.) (1988) *The European Monetary System*, Cambridge University Press.

Giersch *et al.* (1975) 'A currency for Europe', *The Economist*, 1 November.

Godley, W. (1980a) 'Britain and Europe', *Cambridge Economic Policy Review*, vol. 6, no. 1.

Godley, W. (1980b) 'The United Kingdom and the Community Budget', in W. Wallace (ed.), *Britain in Europe*, Heinemann, Chapter 4.

Godley, W. and Bacon, R. (1979) 'Policies of the EEC', *Cambridge Economic Policy Review*, vol. 1, no. 5.

Graubard, S. (ed.) (1964) *A New Europe?*, Oldbourne Press.

Greenaway, D. and Hindley, B. (1985) 'What Britain pays for voluntary export restraints', *Thames Essays*, no. 43, Trade Policy Research Centre.

Guieu, P. and Bonnet, C. (1987) 'Completion of the internal market and indirect taxation', *Journal of Common Market Studies*, vol. 25, no. 3.

Guruswamy, I. D., Papps, I. and Storey, D. (1983) 'The development and impact of an EC directive: the control of discharges of mercury to the aquatic environment', *Journal of Common Market Studies*, vol. 22, no. 1.

Gwilliam, K. M. (1980) 'Realism and the common transport policy of the EEC', in J. B. Polak and J. B. van der Kemp (eds.), *Changes in the Field of Transport Studies*, Martinus Nijhoff, The Hague.

Gwilliam, K. M. (1985) 'The Transport Infrastructure Policy of the EEC', S. Klatt (ed.), *Perspektwm verkehrswissenschaftlicher Forschung: Festschrift für Fritz Voigt*, Berlin.

Gwilliam, K. M. and Allport, R. J. (1982) 'A medium term transport research strategy for the EEC – Part 1: context and issues', *Transport Review*, no. 3.

Gwilliam, K. M. and Mackie, P. J. (1975) *Economics of Transport Policy*, Allen & Unwin.

Gwilliam, K. M., Petriccione, S., Voigt, F. and Zighera, J. A. (1973) 'Criteria for the coordination of investments in transport infrastructure', *EEC Studies, Transport Series*, no. 3.

Haas, E. B. (1958 and 1968) *The Uniting of Europe*, Stevens.

Haas, E. B. (1967) 'The uniting of Europe and the uniting of Latin America', *Journal of Common Market Studies*, vol. 5.

Haberler, G. (1964) 'Integration and growth in the world economy in historical perspective', *American Economic Review*, vol. 54.

Haigh, N. (1987) *EEC Environmental Policy and Britain*, Longman, second edition.

Han, S. S. and Leisner, H. H. (1970) 'Britain and the Common Market', *Occasional Paper*, no. 27, Department of Applied Economics, University of Cambridge.

Hansard (1972), vol. 831, 15 February.

Hansen, N. M. (1977) 'Border regions: a critique of spatial theory and a European case study', *Annals of Regional Science*, vol. XI, no. 1.

Hayek, F. A. (1989) *The Fatal Conceit*, University of Chicago Press.

Hazlewood, A. (1967) *African Integration and Disintegration*, Oxford University Press.

Hazlewood, A. (1975) *Economic Integration: the East African Experience*, Heinemann.

Heidhues, T. *et al.* (1978) *Common Prices and Europe's Farm Policies*, Thames Essays, no. 14, Trade Policy Research Centre.

Hellman, R. (1977) *Gold, the Dollar and the European Currency System*, Praeger.

Helm, D. R., Kay, J. A. and Thompson, D. J. (eds.) (1989) *The Market for Energy*, Oxford University Press.

Helm, D. R. and McGowan, F. (1989) 'Electricity supply in Europe: lessons for the UK', in D. R. Helm, J. A. Kay and D. J. Thompson (eds.), *The Market for Energy*, Oxford University Press.

Helm, D. R. and Smith, S. (1989) 'The assessment: economic integration and the role of the European Community', *Oxford Review of Economic Policy*, vol. 5, no. 2.

Helpman, E. (1981) 'International trade in the presence of product differentiation, economies of scale and monopolistic competition', *Journal of International Economics*, vol. 11.

Henderson, D. (1989) *1992: the external dimension*, Group of Thirty, New York.

Hewitt, A. (1983) 'Stabex: analysing the effectiveness of an institution', in C. Stevens (ed.), *EEC and the Third World: a survey*, 3, *The Atlantic Rift*, Hodder & Stoughton.

Hill, C. and Wallace, W. (1979) 'Diplomatic trends in the European Community', *International Affairs*, January.

Hindley, B. (1974) *Theory of International Trade*, Weidenfeld & Nicolson.

Hine, R. C. (1985) *The Political Economy of European Trade*, Wheatsheaf.

HMSO (1967) *Treaty Setting up the European Economic Community*. The original was published in Rome in 1957 by the EC, and Sweet & Maxwell publish a regularly updated comprehensive set on the *European Community Treaties*.

HMSO (1985) *Employment: the Challenge to the Nation*, Cmnd. 9474.

Hocking, R. D. (1980) 'Trade in motor cars between the major European producers', *Economic Journal*, vol. 90.

Hodges, M. (ed.) (1972) *European Integration*, Penguin.

Hodges, M. (1977) 'Industrial policy: a directorate general in search of a role', in H. Wallace, W. Wallace and C. Webb (eds.), *Policy-Making in the European Communities*, John Wiley.

Holland, S. (1976a) *The Regional Problem*, Macmillan.

Holland, S. (1976b) *Capital versus the Regions*, Macmillan.

Holland, S. (1980) *Uncommon Market: Capital, class and power in the European Community*, Macmillan.

Holloway, J. (1981) *Social Policy Harmonisation in the European Community*, Gower.

Holmes, P. and Shepherd, G. (1983) 'Protectionist policies of the EEC', paper presented to the International Economics Study Group conference at Sussex University.

House of Commons (1985) *The European Monetary System*, Select Committee on the Treasury and Civil Service, report of a sub-committee.

House of Commons (1987) *Indirect Taxes: Harmonisation*, Select Committee on European Legislation, Eighth Report, HMSO.

House of Lords (1983) *European Monetary System*, report of the Select Committee on the European Communities, Fifth Report, 1983–4, HMSO.

House of Lords (1985–6) 'Single European Act and parliamentary scrutiny', in *12th Report of the House of Lords Select Committee on the European Communities*, no. 149.

Hu, Yao-Su (1979) 'German agricultural power: the impact on France and Britain', *The World Today*, vol. 35.

Hughes, M. (1982) 'The consequences of the removal of exchange controls on portfolios and the flow of funds in the UK', in D. C. Corner and D. G. Mayes (eds.), *Modern Portfolio Theory and Financial Institutions*, Macmillan, Chapter 9.

Hughes, T. P. (1983) *Networks of Power*, Johns Hopkins.

Hull, C. (1979) 'The implication of direct elections for European Community regional policy', *Journal of Common Market Studies*, vol. 17, no. 4.

Ingram, J. C. (1959) 'State and regional payments mechanisms', *Quarterly Journal of Economics*, vol. 73.

Ingram, J. C. (1962) 'A proposal for financial integration in the Atlantic Community', in *Factors Affecting the US Balance of Payments*, Joint Economic Committee Print, 87th Cong., 2nd Session, Washington.

Ingram, J. C. (1973) 'The case for European monetary integration', *Essays in International Finance*, no. 98, Princeton University.

International Energy Agency (1980) *Energy Policies and Programmes of IEA Countries, 1979 Review*, OECD.

International Energy Agency (1988a) *Coal Prospects and Policies in IEA Countries 1987*, IEA/OECD.

International Energy Agency (1988b) *Coal Information 1988*, IEA/OECD.

International Monetary Fund (various issues) *Balance of Payments Manual*.

International Monetary Fund (1974) *Guidelines for Floating Exchange Rates*, IMF, Washington.

International Monetary Fund (1979) 'The EMS', *IMF Survey*, Supplement.

International Monetary Fund (1989) *IMF Survey*.

Inukai, I. (1987) 'Regional integration and development in Eastern and Southern Africa', in A. M. El-Agraa (ed.), *Protection, Cooperation, Integration and Development: Essays in Honour of Professor Hiroshi Kitamura*, Macmillan and St Martin's.

Irving, R. W. and Fearne, H. A. (1975) *Green Money and the Common Agricultural Policy*, Centre for European Agricultural Studies, Wye College, Ashford, Kent.

Jacquemin, A. P. (1974) 'Application to foreign firms of European rules on competition', *The Antitrust Bulletin*, vol. 19, no. 1, Spring.

Jacquemin, A. P. (1988) 'Cooperative agreements in R&D and European antitrust policy', *European Economic Review*, vol. 32.

Jacquemin, A. P. and de Jong, H. W. (1977) *European Industrial Organisation*, Macmillan.

Janssen, L. H. (1961) *Free Trade, Protection and Customs Union*, Economisch Sociologisch Instituut, Leiden.

Jenkins, R. (1977) 'Europe's present challenge and future opportunity', *Bulletin of the European Communities*, vol. 10.

Jenkins, R. (1978) 'European Monetary Union', *Lloyds Bank Review*, January.

Jenkins, R. (ed.) (1983) *Britain and the EEC*, Macmillan.

Johnson, D. G. (1972) *World Agriculture in Disarray*, Macmillan, for the Trade Policy Research Centre.

Johnson, H. G. (1965a) 'Optimal trade intervention in the presence of domestic distortions', in R. E. Baldwin *et al.* (eds.), *Trade, Growth and the Balance of Payments*, North-Holland.

Johnson, H. G. (1965b) 'An economic theory of protectionism, tariff bargaining and the formation of customs unions', *Journal of Political Economy*, vol. 73.

Johnson, H. G. (1971) *Aspects of the Theory of Tariffs*, Allen & Unwin.

Johnson, H. G. (1973) 'Problems of European Monetary Union', in M. B. Krauss (ed.), *The Economics of Integration*, Allen & Unwin.

Johnson, H. G. (1974) 'Trade diverting customs unions: a comment', *Economic Journal*, vol. 81.

Johnson, H. G. and Krauss, M. B. (1973) 'Border taxes, border tax adjustments, comparative advantage and the balance of payments', in M. B. Krauss (ed.), *The Economics of Integration*, Allen & Unwin.

Joliet, R. (1971) 'Resale price maintenance under EEC antitrust law', *The Antitrust Bulletin*, vol. 16, no. 3, Fall.

Jones, A. J. (1979) 'The theory of economic integration', in J. K. Bowers (ed.), *Inflation Development and Integration: Essays in honour of A. J. Brown*, Leeds University Press.

Jones, A. J. (1980) 'Domestic distortions and customs union theory', *Bulletin of Economic Research*, vol. 32.

Jones, A. J. (1982) 'A macroeconomic framework for customs union theory', *Leeds Discussion Papers*, no. 112.

Jones, A. J. (1983) 'Withdrawal from a customs union: a macroeconomic analysis', in A. M. El-Agraa (ed.), *Britain within the European Community: The way forward*, Macmillan, Chapter 5.

Jones, R. T. (1976) 'The relevance to the EEC of American experience with industrial property rights', *Journal of World Trade Law*, vol. 10, no. 6.

Josling, T. (1969) 'The Common Agricultural Policy of the European Economic Community', *Journal of Agricultural Economics*, May.

Josling, T. *et al.* (1972) *Burdens and Benefits of Farm-Support Policies*, Trade Policy Centre, London.

Josling, T. (1979a) 'Agricultural policy', in P. Coffey (ed.), *Economic Policies of the Common Market*, Macmillan, Chapter 1.

Josling, T. (1979b) 'Agricultural protection and stabilisation policies: analysis of current and neomercantilist practices', in J. S. Hillman, and A. Schmitz (eds.), *International Trade and Agriculture: Theory and policy*, Westview Press.

Josling, T. and Harris, W. (1976) 'Europe's Green Money', *The Three Banks Review*, March.

Kaldor, N. (1966) *Causes of the Slow Rate of Economic Growth of the United Kingdom*, Cambridge University Press.

Kay, J. A. and Keen, M. (1987) 'Alcohol and tobacco taxes: criteria for harmonisation', in S. Cnossen (ed.), *Tax Coordination in the European Community*, Kluwer.

Kay, J. A. and King, M. A. (1983) *The British Tax System*, Oxford University Press.

Kelly, M. *et al.* (1988) 'Issues and developments in international trade policy', *Occasional Papers*, no. 63, IMF.

Kelman, S. (1981) *What Price Incentives?*, Auburn House.

Kenen, P. (1988) *Managing Exchange Rates*, Routledge.

Kern, D. (1978) 'An international comparison of major economic trends, 1953–76', *National Westminster Bank Quarterly Review*, May.

Kierzkowski, H. (1987) 'Recent advances in international trade theory', *Oxford Review of Economic Policy*, vol. 3, no. 1.

Klau, F. and Mittlestädt (1986) 'Labour market flexibility', *OECD Economic Studies*.

Knox, F. (1972) *The Common Market and World Agriculture*, Praeger, New York.

Koester, U. (1977) 'The redistributional effects of the Common Agricultural Financial System', *Economic Review of Agricultural Economics*, vol. 4, no. 4.

Kol, J. (1987) 'Exports from developing countries: some facts and scope', *European Economic Review*, vol. 29.

Krause, L. B. (1968) *European Economic Integration and the United States*, Brookings Institution, Washington.

Krause, L. B. and Salant, W. S. (eds.) (1973a) *European Economic Integration and the United States*, The Brookings Institution, Washington.

Krause, L. B. and Salant, W. S. (eds.) (1973b) *European Monetary Unification and Its Meaning for the United States*, The Brookings Institution, Washington.

Krauss, M. B. (1972) 'Recent developments in customs union theory: an interpretative survey', *Journal of Economic Literature*, vol. 10.

Krauss, M. B. (ed.) (1973) *The Economics of Integration*, Allen & Unwin.

Kreinin, M. E. (1961) 'The effects of tariff changes on the prices and volumes of imports', *American Economic Review*, vol. 51.

Kreinin, M. E. (1964) 'On the dynamic effects of a customs union', *Journal of Political Economy*, vol. 72.

Kreinin, M. E. (1969) 'Trade creation and diversion by the EEC and EFTA', *Economia Internazionale*, May.

Kreinin, M. E. (1972) 'Effects of the EEC on imports of manufactures', *Economic Journal*, vol. 82.

Kreinin, M. E. (1975) 'European integration and the developing countries', in B. Balassa (ed.) *European Economic Integration*, North-Holland.

Kreinin, M. E. (1979) *International Economics: a policy approach*, Harcourt Brace Jovanovich (also subsequent editions).

Kreuger, A. O. (1974) 'The political economy of the rent-seeking society', *American Economic Review*, vol. 64.

Krugman, P. R. (1979) 'Increasing returns, monopolistic competition and international trade', *Journal of International Economics*, vol. 9.

Krugman, P. R. (1983) New theories of trade among industrial countries', *AER Papers and Proceedings*, May.

Krugman, P. R. (1986) *Strategic Trade Policy and the New International Economics*, MIT Press.

Krugman, P. R. (1988) 'EFTA and 1992', *Occasional Papers*, no. 23, EFTA Secretariat.

Kruse, D. C. (1980) *Monetary Integration in Western Europe: EMU, EMS and beyond*, Butterworth.

Laidler, D. E. W. (1982) 'The case for flexible exchange rates in 1980', in M. T. Sumner and G. Zis (eds.), *European Monetary Union: Progress and prospects*, Macmillan.

Lamfalussy, A. (1963) 'Intra-European trade and the competitive position of the EEC', *Manchester Statistical Society Transactions*, March.

Lancaster, K. (1980) 'Intra-industry trade under monopolistic competition', *Journal of International Economics*, vol. 10.

Lantzke, U. (1976) 'International cooperation in energy', *The World Today*, March.

Laury, J. S. E., Lewis, G. R. and Ormerod, P. A. (1978) 'Properties of macroeconomic models of the UK economy: a comparative study', *National Institute Economic Review*, no. 83.

Layton, C. (1969) *European Advanced Technology*, Allen & Unwin.

Lenior, R. (1974) *Les Exclus: un Francais sur Dix*, Editions du Seuil.

Lévi-Sandri, L. (1968) 'Pour une politique sociale moderne dans la Communauté Européenne', reprint of speech to the European Parliament, March.

Lindberg, L. N. (1963) *The Political Dynamics of European Economic Integration*, Stanford University Press.

Lindberg, L. N. and Scheingold, S. A. (1970) *Europe's Would-Be Policy Patterns of Change in the European Community*, Prentice-Hall.

Linnemann, H. (1966) *An Econometric Study of International Trade Flows*, North-Holland.

Lipgens, W. (1968) *Europa-Föderationspläne der Widerstandsbewegungen 1940–45*, R. Oldenbourg Verlag for the Forschungsinstitut der Deutschen Gesellschaft für Auswärtige Politik.

Lipgens, W. (1982) *A History of European Integration*, vol. 1, *1945–47: The formation of the European Unity Movement*, Clarendon Press.

Lippert, A. (1987) 'Independent generators and the public utilities', paper presented to the *Financial Times* World Electricity Conference.

Lipsey, R. G. (1957) 'The theory of customs unions, trade diversion and welfare', *Economica*, vol. 24.

Lipsey, R. G. (1960) 'The theory of customs unions: a general survey', *Economic Journal*, vol. 70.

Lipsey, R. G. (1975) *An Introduction to Positive Economics*, Weidenfeld & Nicolson.

Lipsey, R. G. (1977) 'Comments', in F. Machlup (ed.), *Economic Integration, Worldwide, Regional, Sectoral*, Macmillan.

Lister, M. (1988) *The European Community and the Developing World*, Gower.

Llewellyn, D. T. (1980) *International Financial Integration: the limits of sovereignty*, Macmillan.

Llewellyn, D. T. (1982a) 'European monetary arrangements and the international monetary system', in M. T. Sumner and G. Zis (eds.), *European Monetary Union*, Macmillan.

Llewellyn, D. T. (1982b) in D. T. Llewellyn *et al.*, *The Framework of UK Monetary Policy*, Heinemann, Chapter 1.

Llewellyn, D. T. (1983) 'EC monetary arrangement: Britain's strategy', in A. M. El-Agraa (ed.), *Britain within the European Community: The way forward*, Macmillan.

Loewenheim, U. (1976) 'Trademarks and free competition within the European Community', *The Antitrust Bulletin*, vol. 21, no. 4, Winter.

Lucas, N. J. D. (1977) *Energy and the European Communities*, Europa Publications for the David Davies Memorial Institute of International Studies, London.

Ludlow, P. (1982) *The Making of the European Monetary System: a case study of the politics of the European Community*, Butterworth.

Lunn, J. L. (1983) 'Determinants of US direct investment in the EEC revisited again', *European Economic Review*, vol. 21.

MacBean, A. I. (1988) 'The Uruguay Round and the developing countries', paper presented to the annual conference of the International Economics Study Group, Sussex University.

MacBean, A. I. and Snowden, P. N. (1981) *International Institutions in Trade and Finance*, Allen & Unwin.

McDougall Report (1977), *see* Commission of the European Communities (1977c).

Machlup, F. (1977a) *A History of Thought on Economic Integration*, Macmillan.

Machlup, F. (1977b) *Economic Integration, Worldwide, Regional, Sectoral*, Macmillan.

Mackel, G. (1978) 'Green Money and the Common Agricultural Policy', *National Westminster Bank Review*, February.

MacLaren, D. (1981) 'Agricultural trade and the MCA's: a spatial equilibrium analysis', *Journal of Agricultural Economics*, vol. 32, no. 1.

MacLennan, M. C. (1979) 'Regional policy in a European framework', in D. MacLennan and J. B. Parr, *Regional Policy: Past experience and new directions*, Martin Robertson.

MacMahon, C. (1979) 'The long run implications of the EMS', in P. H. Trezise (ed.), *The European Monetary System: Its promise and prospects*, The Brookings Institution, Washington.

Magnifico, G. and Williamson, J. (1972) *European Monetary Integration*, Federal Trust, London.

Major, R. L. (1960) 'World trade in manufactures', *National Institute Economic Review*, July.

Major, R. L. (1962) 'The Common Market: production and trade', *National Institute Economic Review*, August.

Major, R. L. and Hays, S. (1963) 'Another look at the Common Market', in *The Market Economy in Western European Integration*, University of Louvain.

Malcor, R. (1970) 'Problèmes posés par l'application pratique d'une unification pour l'usage des infrastructures routières', *EEC Studies, Transport Series*, no. 2.

Manners, G. (1976) 'Reinterpreting the regional problem', *Three Banks Review*, no. 3.

Mansholt, S. (1969) *Le Plan Mansholt*, EC Commission.

Marer, P. and Montias, J. M. (1988) 'The Council for Mutual Economic Assistance', in A. M. El-Agraa (ed.), *International Economic Integration*, Macmillan and St Martin's.

Marin, A. (1979) 'Pollution control: economists' views', *Three Banks Review*, no. 121.

Marjolin Report (1975), *see* Commission of the European Communities (1975c).

Marquand, D. (1982) 'EMU: the political implications', in M. T. Sumner and G. Zis (eds.), *European Monetary Union: Progress and prospects*, Macmillan.

Marquand, J. (1980) 'Measuring the effects and costs of regional incentives', *Government Economic Service Working Paper*, no. 32, Department of Industry, London.

Marsh, J., and Ritson, C. (1971) *Agricultural Policy and the Common Market*, Chatham House, PEP European Series, no. 16.

Marsh, J. S. and Swanney, P. J. (1980) *Agriculture and the European Community*, Allen & Unwin. Second edition, 1985.

Masera, R. (1981) 'The first two years of the EMS: the exchange rate experience', *Banca Nazionale del Lavoro Review*, September.

Mathijsen, P. S. R. F. (1972) 'State aids, state monopolies, and public enterprises in the Common Market', *Law and Contemporary Problems*, vol. 37, no. 2, Spring.

Mathijsen, P. S. R. F. (1975) *A Guide to European Community Law*, Sweet & Maxwell/Matthew Bender.

Matthews, A. (1986) *The Common Agricultural Policy and the Less Developed Countries*, Gill & Macmillan.

Matthews, J. D. (1977) *Association System of the European Community*, Praeger.

Mayes, D. G. (1978) 'The effects of economic integration on trade', *Journal of Common Market Studies*, vol. 17, no. 1.

Mayes, D. G. (1981) *Applications of Econometrics*, Prentice-Hall.

Mayes, D. G. (1982) 'The problems of the quantitative estimation of integration effects', in A. M. El-Agraa (ed.), *International Economic Integration*, Macmillan.

Mayes, D. G. (1983a) 'EC trade effects and factor mobility', in A. M. El-Agraa (ed.), *Britain within the European Community: The way forward*, Macmillan, Chapter 6.

Mayes, D. G. (1983b) 'Memorandum of Evidence', in House of Lords Select Committee on the European Communities, *Trade Patterns: the United Kingdom's changing trade patterns subsequent to membership of the European Community*, HL(41), 7th Report, Session 1983–84 HMSO.

Mayes, D. G. (1988) 'Chapter three', in A. Bollard and M. A. Thompson (eds.), *Trans-Tasman Trade and Investment*, Institute for Policy Studies, Wellington, New Zealand.

Maynard, G. (1978) 'Monetary interdependence and floating exchange rates', in G. Maynard *et al.*, *Monetary Policies in Open Economics*, SUERF.

Mayne, R. (1970) *The Recovery of Europe*, Weidenfeld & Nicolson.

McCrone, G. (1969) *Regional Policy in Britain*, Allen & Unwin.

McCrone, G. (1971) 'Regional policy in the European Community', in G. R. Denton (ed.), *Economic Integration in Europe*, Weidenfeld & Nicolson.

McFarquhar, A., Godley, W. and Silvey, D. (1977) 'The cost of food and Britain's membership of the EEC', *Cambridge Economic Policy Review*, vol. 3.

McGowan, F. *et al.* (1989) 'A single European market for energy', *Chatham House Occasional Paper*, Royal Institute of International Affairs.

McKinnon, R. I. (1963) 'Optimum currency areas', *American Economic Review*, vol. 53.

McLachlan, D. L. and Swann, D. (1967) *Competition Policy in the European Community*, Oxford University Press.

McManus, J. G. (1972) 'The theory of the international firm', in G. Paquet (ed.), *The Multi-national Firm and the National State*, Collier Macmillan.

McMillan, J. and McCann, E. (1981) 'Welfare effects in customs unions', *Economic Journal*, vol. 91.

Meade, J. E. (1951) *The Balance of Payments*, Oxford University Press.

Meade, J. E. (1973) 'The balance-of-payments problems of a European free-trade area', in M. B. Krauss (ed.), *The Economics of Integration*, Allen & Unwin.

Meade, J. E., Liesner, H. H. and Wells, S. J. (1962) *Case Studies in European Economic Union: The mechanics of integration*, Oxford University Press.

Meadows, D. H. *et al.* (1972) *The Limits to Growth*, Earth Island.

Messerlin, P. (1988) 'The Uruguay negotiations on dumping and subsidies', World Bank mimeo.

Midland Bank (1970) 'The dollar: an end to benign neglect?' *Midland Bank Review*, Autumn.

Mikesell, R. F. and Goldstein, H. N. (1975) 'Rules for a floating rate regime', *Essays in International Finance*, no. 109, Princeton University.

Millward, R. (1981) 'The performance of public and private ownership', in E. Roll (ed.), *The Mixed Economy*, Macmillan.

Mingst, K. A. (1977/78) 'Regional sectoral economic integration: the case of OAPEC', *Journal of Common Market Studies*, vol. 16.

Mishan, E. J. (1967) *The Cost of Economic Growth*, Staples.

Molle, W. *et al.* (1980) *Regional Disparity and Economic Development in the European Community*, Saxon House.

Monnet, J. (1955) *Les Etats-Unis d'Europe ont Commencé*, Robert Laffont, Paris.

Moore, B. and Rhodes, J. (1975) 'The economic and Exchequer implications of British regional economic policy', in J. Vaizey (ed.), *Economic Sovereignty and Regional Policy*, Gill & Macmillan.

Morgan, A. D. (1980) 'The balance of payments and British membership of the European Community', in W. Wallace (ed.), *Britain in Europe*, Heinemann, Chapter 3.

Morgan, R. (1983) 'Political cooperation in Europe', in R. Jenkins (ed.), *Britain and the EEC*, Macmillan, Chapter 12.

Morris, C. N. (1980a) 'The Common Agricultural Policy', *Fiscal Studies*, vol. 1, no. 2.

Morris, C. N. (1980b) 'The Common Agricultural Policy: sources and methods', *Institute of Fiscal Studies Working Paper*, no. 6.

Morris, C. N. and Dilnot, A. W. (1981) 'The distributional effects of the Common Agricultural Policy', *Institute of Fiscal Studies Working Paper*, no. 28.

Morris, V. (1979) *Britain and the EEC – the Economic Issues*, Labour, Economic, Finance and Taxation Association, London.

Moss, J. and Ravenhill, J. (1982) 'Trade developments during the first Lomé Convention', *World Development*, vol. 10.

Moss, J. and Ravenhill, J. (1988) 'The evolution of trade under the Lomé Convention: the first ten years', in C. Stevens and J. V. van Themaat (eds.), *EEC and the Third World: a survey, 6, Europe and the International Division of Labour*, Hodder & Stoughton.

Mundell, R. A. (1961) 'A theory of optimum currency areas', *American Economic Review*, vol. 51.

Mundell, R. A. (1964) 'Tariff preferences and the terms of trade', *Manchester School*, vol. 32.

Munk, K. J. (1989) 'Price support to the EC agricultural sector: an optimal policy?', *Oxford Review of Economic Policy*, vol. 5, no. 2.

Musgrave, R. A. and P. B. (1976) *Public Finance in Theory and Practice*, McGraw-Hill.

National Institute of Economic and Social Research (1971) 'Entry into the EEC: a comment on some of the economic issues', *National Institute Economic Review*, no. 57, August.

National Institute of Economic and Social Research (1983) 'The European Monetary System', *National Institute Economic Review*, February.

Needleman, L. and Scott, B. (1964) 'Regional problems and the location of industry policy in Britain', *Urban Studies*, no. 12.

Neumark, F. (1963) *Report of the Fiscal and Financial Committee*, EC Commission.

Nevin, E. T. (1988) 'VAT and the European Budget', *The Royal Bank of Scotland Review*, no. 157.

Nkrumah, K. (1965) *Neo Colonialism: the last stage of imperialism*, Heinemann.

Noel, E. (1975) *Working Together*, EC Commission.

Oates, W. E. (1972) *Fiscal Federalism*, Harcourt Brace.

OECD (various years) *Economic Survey of Europe*.

OECD (1979) *The Case of Positive Adjustment Policies: A compendium of OECD documents 1978/79*, OECD.

OECD (1983) *The OECD Interlink Model*.

OECD (1985 and various years) *OECD Economic Outlook*, no. 38.

OECD (1985) *Costs and Benefits of Protection*.

OECD (1988) *The Newly Industrialising Countries: Challenges and opportunity for OECD industries*.

Oort, C. J. (1975) *Study of Possible Solutions for Allocating the Deficits which may occur in a System of charging for the Use of Infrastructures aiming at Budgetary Equilibrium*, EC Commission.

Open University (1973) *The European Economic Community: History and institutions, national and international impact*, Open University Press.

Oppenheimer, P. M. (1981) 'The economics of the EMS', in J. R. Sargent (ed.), *Europe and the Dollar in World-Wide Disequilibrium*, Sijthoff and Noordhoff.

Osborne, F. and Robinson, S. (1989) 'Oil', in F. McGowan *et al.*, *A Single European Market for Energy*, Chatham House Occasional Paper, Royal Institute of International Affairs.

Owens, S. and Hope, C. (1989) 'Energy and the environment – the challenge of integrating European policies', *Energy Policy*, vol. 17.

Owen-Smith, E. (1983) *The West German Economy*, Croom Helm.

Oxford Review of Economic Policy (1987), vol. 3, no. 1.

Padoa-Schioppa, T. (1983) 'What the EMS has achieved', *The Banker*, August.

Padoa-Schioppa, T. (1985) 'Policy cooperation in the EMS experience', in W. H. Buiter and R. C. Marston (eds.), *International Economic Policy Coordination*, Cambridge University Press.

Padoa-Schioppa, T. *et al.* (1987) *Efficiency, Stability and Equity* (Report of a study group appointed by the EC Commission).

Page, S. A. B. (1979) 'The management of international trade', *National Institute Discussion Papers*, no. 29.

Page, S. A. B. (1982) 'The development of the EMS', *National Institute Economic Review*, November.

Palmer, M. and Lambert, J. (1968) *European Unity*, Allen & Unwin.

Panić, M. (1982) 'Some longer term effects of short-run adjustments policies: behaviours of UK direct investment since the 1960s', in J. Black and J. H. Dunning (eds.), *International Capital Movements*, Macmillan.

Parkin, J. M. (1976) 'Monetary union and stabilisation policy in the European Community, *Banca Nazionale del Lavoro Review*, September.

Pauly, M. V. (1973) 'Income redistribution as a local public good', *Journal of Public Economics*, vol. 2.

Paxton, J. (1976) *The Developing Common Market*, Macmillan.

Peacock, A. T. (1972) *The Public Finance of Inter-Allied Defence Provision: Essays in honour of Antonio de Vito de Marco*, Cacucci Editore.

Peacock, A. T. and Wiseman, J. (1967) *The Growth of Public Expenditure in the UK*, Allen & Unwin.

Pearce, D. W. (1976) 'The limits of cost–benefit analysis as a guide to environmental policy', *Kyklos*, vol. 29.

Pearce, D. W. and Westoby, R. (1983) 'Energy and the EC', in A. M. El-Agraa (ed.), *Britain within the European Community: The way forward*, Macmillan, Chapter 10.

Pearce, J. and Sutton, J. (1985) *Protection and Industrial Policy in Europe*, Routledge & Kegan Paul.

Peeters, T. (1982) 'EMU: prospects and retrospect', in M. T. Sumner and G. Zis (eds.), *European Monetary Union: Progress and prospects*, Macmillan.

Pelkmans, J. (1984) *Market Integration in the European Community*, Martinus Nijhoff.

Pelkmans, J. (1987) 'The European Community's trade policy towards developing countries', in C. Stevens and J. V. van Themaat, *EEC and the Third World: a survey*, 6, *Europe and the International Division of Labour*, Hodder & Stoughton.

Pelkmans, J. and Robson, P. (1987) 'The aspirations of the White Paper', *Journal of Common Market Studies*, vol. 25, no. 3.

Pelkmans, J. and Winters, L. A. (1988) *Europe's Domestic Market*, Routledge.

Petith, H. C. (1977) 'European integration and the terms of trade', *Economic Journal*, vol. 87.

Phelps, E. S. (1968) 'Money-wage dynamics and labour market equilibrium', *Journal of Political Economy*, vol. 76.

Phillips, A. W. (1958) 'The relation between unemployment and the rate of change of money wages in the United Kingdom', *Economica*, vol. 25.

Pinder, J. (1968) 'Positive integration and negative integration', *The World Today*, March.

Pinder, J. (1969) 'Problems of European integration', in G. R. Denton (ed.), *Economic Integration in Europe*, Weidenfeld & Nicolson.

Pinder, J. (ed.) (1971) *The Economics of Europe*, Knight.

Pinder, J. (1982) 'Industrial policy in Britain and the European Community', *Policy Studies*, vol. 2, part 4, April.

Pintado, X. *et al.* (1988) 'Economic aspects of European economic space', *Occasional Papers*, no. 25, EFTA Secretariat.

Political and Economic Planning (PEP) (1962) *Atlantic Tariffs and Trade*, Allen & Unwin.

Political and Economic Planning (PEP) (1963) 'An energy policy for the EEC', *Planning*, vol. 29.

Pomfret, R. (1986) *Mediterranean Policy of the European Community: Study of Discrimination in Trade*, Macmillan.

Prais, S. J. (1982) *Productivity and Industrial Structure*, Cambridge University Press.

Presley, J. R. and Coffey, P. (1974) *European Monetary Integration*, Macmillan.

Prest, A. R. (1972) 'Government revenue, the national income and all that', in R. M. Bird and J. G. Read, *Modern Fiscal Issues*, Toronto University Press.

Prest, A. R. (1975) *Public Finance in Theory and Practice*, Weidenfeld & Nicholson.

Prest, A. R. (1979) 'Fiscal policy', Chapter 4 of P. Coffey (ed.), *Economic Policies of the Common Market*, Macmillan.

Prewo, W. E. (1974) 'Integration effects in the EEC', *European Economic Review*, vol. 5.

Pryce, R. (1962) *The Political Future of the European Community*, Marshbank.

Pryce, R. (1973) *The Politics of the European Community*, Butterworth.

Pryce, R. (ed.) (1987) *The Dynamics of European Union*, Croom Helm.

Raisman Report (1961) *East Africa: Report of the Economic and Fiscal Commission*, Cmnd 1279, Colonial Office.

Riezman, R. (1979) 'A 3 × 3 model of customs unions', *Journal of International Economics*, vol. 9.

Ritson, C. (1973) *The Common Agricultural Policy* in *The European Economic Community: Economics and agriculture*, Open University Press.

Ritson, C. (1980) 'Self sufficiency and food security centre for agricultural strategy', *Discussion Paper*, no. 8, University of Reading.

Ritson, C. and Tangermann, S. (1979) 'The economics and politics of Monetary Compensatory Amounts', *European Review of Agricultural Economics*, vol. 6.

Ritter, L. and Overburg, C. (1977) 'An attempt at a practical approach to joint ventures under the EEC rules on competition', *Common Market Law Review*, vol. 14, no. 4, November.

Roarty, M. J. (1985) 'The EEC's Common Agricultural Policy and its effects on less developed countries', *National Westminster Bank Quarterly Review*, February.

Robinson, P. W., Webb, T. R. and Townsend, M. A. (1979) 'The influence of exchange rate changes on prices: a study of 18 industrial countries', *Economica*, February.

Robson, P. (1980) *The Economics of International Integration*, Allen & Unwin, 2nd edn 1985.

Robson, P. (1983) *Integration, Development and Equity: Economic Integration in West Africa*, Allen & Unwin.

Robson, P. (1987) 'Variable geometry and automaticity: strategies for experience of regional integration in West Africa', in A. M. El-Agraa (ed.), *Conflict, Cooperation, Integration and Development: Essays in Honour of Professor Hiroshi Kitamura*, Macmillan and St Martin's.

Rogers, S. T. and Davey, B. H. (eds.) (1973) *The Common Agricultural Policy and Britain*, Saxon House.

Rollo, J. N. C. and Warwick, K. S. (1979) 'The CAP and resource flows among EEC member states', *Government Economic Service Working Paper*, no. 27, Ministry of Agriculture, Fisheries and Food, London.

Royal Institute of International Affairs (1953) *Documents on International Affairs, 1949–50*, RIIA.

Rybczynski, T. (1982) 'Fiscal Policy under EMU', in M. T. Sumner and G. Zis (eds.), *European Monetary Union*, Macmillan.

Sargent, T. J. and Wallace, N. (1976) 'Rational expectations and the theory of economic policy', *Journal of Monetary Economics*, April.

Sarna, A. J. (1985) 'The impact of a Canada–US free trade area', *Journal of Common Market Studies*, vol. 23, no. 4.

Sayigh, Y. (1982) *The Arab Economy*, Oxford University Press.

Scaperlanda, A. and Balough, R. S. (1983) 'Determinants of US direct investment in the EEC revisited', *European Economic Review*, vol. 21.

Scitovsky, T. (1958) *Economic Theory and Western European Integration*, Allen & Unwin.

Secretariat of the European Parliament (1983) *The European Parliament, Its Powers*.

Sellekaerts, W. (1973) 'How meaningful are empirical studies on trade creation and diversion?', *Weltwirtschaftliches Archiv*, vol. 109.

Shanks, M. (1977) *European Social Policy, Today and Tomorrow*, Pergamon Press.

Shlaim, A. and Yannopoulos, G. N. (eds.) (1976) *The EEC and the Mediterranean Countries*, Cambridge University Press.

Short, J. (1978) 'The regional distribution of public expenditure in Great Britain, 1969/70–1973/74', *Regional Studies*, vol. 12, no. 5.

Short, J. (1981) *Public Expenditure and Taxation in the UK Regions*, Gower.

Shoup, C. S. (ed.) (1966) *Fiscal Harmonisation in Common Markets*, 2 vols., Columbia University Press.

Shoup, C. S. (1972) 'Taxation aspects of international integration', in P. Robson (ed.), *International Economic Integration*, Penguin.

Shourd, M. (1980) *The Theft of the Countryside*, Temple Smith.

Smith, A. J. (1977) 'The Council of Mutual Economic Assistance in 1977: new economic power, new political perspectives and some old and new problems', in US Congress Joint Economic Committee's *East European Economics Post-Helsinki*.

Smith, S. (1988) 'Excise duties and the internal market', *Journal of Common Market Studies*, vol. 27, no. 2.

Solow, R. M. (1973) 'Is the end of the world at hand?', *Challenge*, March–April.

Spaak Report (1987) *The Single European Act: a New Frontier – Programme of the Commission for 1987*. Supplement 1/87 of the *Bulletin of the European Communities*.

Steenbergen, J. (1980) 'The Common Commercial Policy', *Common Market Law Review*, May.

Stern, J. (1989) 'Natural gas', in F. McGowan *et al.*, *A Single European Market for Energy*, Chatham House Occasional Paper, Royal Institute of International Affairs.

Stern, R., Francis, S. and Schumacker, B. (1976) *Price Elasticities in International Trade: an Annotated Bibliography*, Macmillan.

Stevens, C. (1984) 'The new Lomé Convention: imperfections for Europe's Third World policy', Paper No. 16, Centre for European Policy Studies.

Stevens, C. and Watson, A. (1984) 'Trade diversification: has Lomé helped?', in C. Stevens (ed.), *EEC and the Third World: a survey*, 4, *Renegotiating Lomé*, Hodder & Stoughton.

Stevens, C. and J. V. van Themaat (eds.) (1988) *EEC and the Third World: a survey*, 6, *Europe and the International Division of Labour*, Hodder & Stoughton.

Stewart, J. A. and Begg, H. M. (1976) 'Towards a European regional policy', *National Westminster Bank Quarterly Review*, May.

Stigler, G. J. (1971) 'The theory of economic regulation', *Bell Journal of Economics and management Science*, vol. 2.

Stoeckel, A. B. (1985) *Intersectoral Effects of the CAP: Growth, Trade and Unemployment*, Bureau of Agricultural Research (Canberra).

Strasser, D. (1981) 'The finances of Europe', *The European Perspectives Series*, EC Commission.

Sumner, M. T. and Zis, G. (eds.) (1982) *European Monetary Union: Progress and prospects*, Macmillan.

Sundelius, B. and Wiklund, C. (1979) 'The Nordic Community: the ugly duckling of regional cooperation', *Journal of Common Market Studies*, vol. 18, no. 1.

Swann, D. (1973) *The Economics of the Common Market*, Penguin, first edition.

Swann, D. (1978) *The Economics of the Common Market*, Penguin, second edition.

Swann, D. (1988) *The Economics of the Common Market*, Penguin, fourth edition.

Sweet & Maxwell (regularly updated) *European Community Treaties*, Sweet & Maxwell.

Swinbank, A. and Ritson, C. (1988) 'The Common Agricultural Policy, customs unions and the Mediterranean basin', *Journal of Common Market Studies*, vol. 27, no. 2.

Swoboda, A. K. (1983) 'Exchange rate regimes and European–US policy interdependence', *International Monetary Fund Staff Papers*, March.

Symons, E. and Walker, I. (1989) 'The revenue and welfare effects of fiscal harmonisation for the UK', *Oxford Review of Economic Policy*, vol. 5, no. 2.

Talbot, R. B. (1978) 'The European Community's regional fund', *Progress in Planning*, vol. 8, no. 3.

Thomas, S. D. (1984) *The Realities of Nuclear Power*, Cambridge University Press.

Thomas, S. D. (1988) 'Power plant life extension', *Energy the International Journal*.

Thomson, G. (1973) 'European regional policy in the 1970s', *CBI Review*, no. 10, Autumn.

Thomson, K. J. (1983) 'CAP budget projections to 1988', *Discussion Paper*, no. 4, Department of Agricultural Economics and Department of Agricultural Marketing, University of Newcastle.

Thorbecke, E. and Pagoulatos, E. (1975) 'The effects of European economic integration on agriculture', in B. Balassa (ed.), *European Economic Integration*, North-Holland.

Thurow, L. C. (1971) 'The income distribution as a public good', *Quarterly Journal of Economics*, vol. 85.

Thygesen, N. (1979) 'EMS: precursors, first steps and policy options', in R. Triffin (ed.), *The EMS: the emerging European Monetary System*, National Bank of Belgium.

Thygesen, N. (1981a) 'Are monetary policies and performance converging?', *Banca Nazionale del Lavoro Quarterly Review*, September.

Thygesen, N. (1981b) 'The EMS: an approximate implementation of the Crawling Peg?', in J. Williamson (ed.), *Exchange Rate Rules*, Macmillan.

Timberg, S. (1972) 'Antitrust in the Common Market: innovation and surprise', *Law and Contemporary Problems*, vol. 37, no. 2, Spring.

Tinbergen, J. (1952) *On the Theory of Economic Policy*, North-Holland.

Tinbergen, J. (1953) *Report on Problems Raised by the Different Turnover Tax Systems Applied within the Common Market* (The Tinbergen Report), European Coal and Steel Community.

Tinbergen, J. (1954) *International Economic Integration*, Elsevier.

Tindemans, L. (1976) 'European Union', *Bulletin of the European Communities*, Supplement.

Toulemon, R. (1972) 'Etat d'avancement des travaux en matière de politique industrielle dans la Communauté', paper presented to the conference organised by the European Communities on 'Industrie et société dans la Communauté Européenne', Venice.

Trezise, P. H. (ed.) (1979) *The European Monetary System: Promise and prospects*, The Brookings

Institution, Washington.

Truman, E. M. (1969) 'The European Economic Community: trade creation and trade diversion', *Yale Economic Essays*, Spring.

Truman, E. M. (1975) 'The effects of European economic integration on the production and trade of manufactured products', in B. Balassa (ed.), *European Economic Integration*, North-Holland.

Tsoukalis, L. (1981) *The European Community and its Mediterranean Enlargement*, Allen & Unwin.

Tsoukalis, L. (ed.) (1982) *The European Community Past, Present and Future*, Basil Blackwell.

Tullock, G. (1967) 'The welfare costs of tariffs, monopolies and theft', *Western Economic Journal*, vol. 5.

Ungerer, H., Evans, O. and Nyberg, P. (1983) 'The European Monetary System: the experience, 1979–82', *International Monetary Fund Occasional Papers*, no. 19, May.

Ungerer, H. *et al.* (1986) 'The European Monetary System – recent developments', *Occasional Papers*, no. 48, IMF.

United Nations (1982) 'Standardised input–output tables of EEC countries for years around 1975', *Statistical Standards and Studies*, no. 34.

United Nations Economic Commission for Africa (1984) *Proposals for Strengthening Economic Integration in West Africa*, UNECA (Addis Ababa).

University of Louvain (1963) *The Market Economy in West European Integration*, Editions Nauwelaerts.

Uribe, P., Theil, H. and De Leeuw, C. G. (1966) 'The information approach to the prediction of interregional trade flows', *Review of Economic Studies*, July.

van der Linde, J. G. and Lefeber, R. (1988) 'IEA captures the development of European Community energy law', *Journal of World Trade*, vol. 22.

van Doorn, J. (1975) 'European regional policy: an evaluation of recent developments', *Journal of Common Market Studies*, vol. 13, no. 3.

van Themaat, J. V. and Stevens, C. (1987) 'The division of labour between competition and the Third World', in C. Stevens and J. V. van Themaat, *EEC and the Third World: a survey*, 6, *Europe and the International Division of Labour*, Hodder & Stoughton.

Vanhove, N. and Klaassen, H. (1987) *Regional Policy: a European approach*, Gower, second edition.

Vaubel, R. (1978) *Strategies for Currency Unification*, J. C. B. Mohr/Paul Siebeck.

Verdoorn, P. J. (1954) 'A customs union for Western Europe: advantages and feasibility', *World Politics*, vol. 6.

Verdoorn, P. J. and Schwartz, A. N. R. (1972) 'Two alternative estimates of the effects of EEC and EFTA on the pattern of trade', *European Economic Review*, vol. 3.

Verdoorn, P. T. and Meyer zu Schlochtern, F. J. M. (1964) 'Trade creation and trade diversion in the Common Market', in *Integration européenne et réalité économique*, Collège d'Europe, Bruges.

Viner, J. (1950) *The Customs Union Issue*, Carnegie Endowment for International Peace, New York.

von Geusan, F.A. (1975) 'In search of a policy', in F.A. Geusan (ed.), *Energy Strategy in the European Communities*, Sijthoff.

Waelbroeck, J. (1977) 'Measuring the degree or progress of economic integration', in F. Machlup (ed.), *Economic Integration, Worldwide, Regional, Sectoral*, Macmillan.

Waelbroeck, M. (1976) 'The effect of the Rome Treaty on the exercise of national industrial property rights', *The Antitrust Bulletin*, vol. 21, no. 1, Spring.

Wallace, H. and Ridley, A. (1985) 'Europe: the challange of diversity', *Chatham House Papers*, no. 29, Routledge & Kegan Paul.

Wallace, H., Wallace, W. and Webb, C. (eds.) (1977) *Policy-Making in the European Communities*, John Wiley.

Wallace, W. (ed.) (1980) *Britain in Europe*, Heinemann.

Walter, I. (1967) *The European Common Market*, Praeger.

Walter, N. (1982) 'The EMS: performance and prospects', in M. T. Sumner and G. Zis (eds.), *European Economic Union: Progress and prospects*, Macmillan.

Walton, R. J. (1988) 'ECU financial activity', *Quarterly Bulletin*, Bank of England, November.

Webb, C. (1977) 'Variations on a theoretical theme', in H. Wallace, W. Wallace and C. Webb (eds.), *Policy-Making in the European Communities*, Wiley.

Weiss, F. D. (1988) 'A political economy of European trade policy against the less developed countries?', *European Economic Review*, vol. 30.

Wenban-Smith, G. C. (1981) 'A study of the movement of productivity in individual industries in the United Kingdom 1968–79', *National Institute Economic Review*, no. 3.

Werner Report (1970), *see* Commission of the European Communities (1970a).

West, E. G. (1973) ' "Pure" versus "Operational" economics in regional policy', in G. Hallet (ed.), *Regional Policy for Ever?*, London Institute of Economic Affairs.

Weyman Jones, T. (1986) *Energy in Europe*, Methuen.

Whalley, J. (1979) 'Uniform domestic tax rates, trade distortions and economic integration', *Journal of Public Economics*, vol. 11.

Whalley, J. (1985) *Trade Liberalisation among Major World Trading Areas*, MIT Press.

Williamson, J. and Bottrill, A. (1971) 'The impact of customs unions on trade in manufactures', *Oxford Economic Papers*, vol. 25, no. 3.

Winters, L. A. (1984a) 'British imports of manufactures and the Common Market', *Oxford Economic Papers*, vol. 36.

Winters, L. A. (1984b) 'Separability and the specification of foreign trade functions', *European Economic Review*, vol. 27.

Wise, M. (1984) *The Common Fisheries Policy of the European Community*, Methuen.

Wolf, M. (1983) 'The European Community's trade policy', in R. Jenkins (ed.), *Britain in the EEC*, Macmillan.

Wolf, M. (1987) 'An unholy alliance: the European Community and the developing countries in the international trading system', *Aussenwirtschaft*, vol. 1. Also in L. B. Mennes and J. Kol, *European Trade Policies and the Developing World*, Croom Helm.

Woodland, A. D. (1982) *International Trade and Resource Allocation*, North-Holland.

Woolley, P. K. (1975) 'The European Investment Bank', *Three Banks Review*, no. 105, March.

World Bank (1981) *World Development Report*, Oxford University Press.

World Bank (1988) *World Development Report 1987*.

Yannopoulos, G. N. (1985) 'EC external commercial policies and East–West trade in Europe', *Journal of Common Market Studies*, vol. 24, no. 1.

Yannopoulos, G. N. (1988) *Customs Unions and Trade Conflicts: the enlargement of the European Community*, Routledge.

Young, S. Z. (1973) *Terms of Entry: Britain's negotiations with the European Community, 1970–1972*, Heinemann.

Ypersele de Strihou, J. van. (1979) 'Operating principles and procedures of the European Monetary System', in P. H. Trezise (ed.), *The European Monetary System: Promise and prospects*, The Brookings Institution, Washington.

Yuill, D. and Allen, K. (1982) *European Regional Incentives – 1981*, Centre for the Study of Public Policy, University of Strathclyde Press.

Author Index

Subject Index